2001
GUIDE TO LITERARY AGENTS

570 AGENTS WHO SELL WHAT YOU WRITE

EDITED BY
DONYA DICKERSON

WRITER'S DIGEST BOOKS
CINCINNATI, OHIO

Managing Editor, Annuals Department: Doug Hubbuch
Editorial Director, Annuals Department: Barbara Kuroff
Supervisory Editor: Kirsten Holm
Production Editor: Rachel Vater

Writer's Digest Books website: www.writersdigest.com and www.writersmarket.com

2001 Guide to Literary Agents. Copyright © 2000 by Writer's Digest Books.
Published by F&W Publications, 1507 Dana Ave., Cincinnati, Ohio 45207. Printed and bound
in the United States of America. All rights reserved. No part of this book may be reproduced in
any form or by any electronic or mechanical means including information storage and retrieval
systems without written permission from the publisher, except by reviewers who may quote brief
passages to be printed in a magazine or newspaper.

International Standard Serial Number 1078-6945
International Standard Book Number 1-58297-011-4

Cover illustration by Jim Starr

Attention Booksellers: This is an annual directory of F&W Publications.
Return deadline for this edition is April 30, 2002.

contents at a glance

Contents

LITERARY AGENTS: NONFEE-CHARGING

Agents listed in this section generate 98 to 100 percent of their income from commission on sales. They do not charge for reading, critiquing, editing, marketing, or other editorial services.

⊿ *insider* reports

WRITERS' CONFERENCES

RESOURCES

INDEXES

From the Editor

Getting a book published is never a solitary endeavor. From the moment you send out your first manuscript, you'll encounter all types of publishing professionals. Instead of thinking of these people as roadblocks to your goal of publication, think of them as your teammates.

These teammates will guide you and your book through the publishing process. They are your agent, your editor, even your independent publicist. They show you the inside moves, navigate you through any opposition, and cheer for you during the ups and downs you encounter along the road to publication.

We like to think of ourselves as part of your team, too. Our job is to help you connect with the business people you will want on your publishing team. Through this book, we tell you who these people are, how to contact them, and how to win them over to your team. We also work hard to screen out any unscrupulous people who might prove detrimental to your team.

As someone who is on your side for the duration, an agent can be your most important player—orchestrating the business side of your career while at the same time encouraging your creative endeavors. Even if you have a great desire to work with an agent, sorting through the information in this book can be overwhelming. In order to make the *Guide to Literary Agents* as useful as possible, we've added new elements to help you build a strong team and new sections of listings to give you more access to potential team members.

- Look for the key icon (**O🔾**) in agency listings to quickly obtain fundamental information about an agency. Here agents list their specialties, including their areas of strength and other services they provide for their clients. You'll also be able to determine if your manuscript fits the current needs of the agency or if your subject is one the agent is not interested in reading.
- Other time-saving features are included to expedite your search. Openness icons (⬭ ⬭ ⬭ ⬭ ⬭) let you immediately assess how receptive an agent is to new clients. Bold-faced phrases like **Considers these nonfiction areas:** and **Considers these fiction areas:** can help you determine the agency's full range of interests. And numerous indexes lead you to the right agent for your specific needs.
- We've also included **Canadian and International** agencies to expose you to more opportunities for you and your work.
- Because we see our role as providing all the information writers need about the business side of publishing, we've added a very important new section—**Independent Publicists**. Using marketing expertise, a publicist will be the cheerleader who will enthuse your crowd of readers to purchase your book.

As you read through the articles in this book, pay particular attention to the ways writers, agents, editors, and publicists talk about their relationships with one another. Learn tips on forming a successful lineup of publishing professionals with business know-how. Then consider who you want as your players, and use the *Guide to Literary Agents* to build your winning team!

Donya Dickerson

literaryagents@fwpubs.com
www.writersmarket.com
www.writersdigest.com

Quick Start Guide to Using Your *Guide to Literary Agents*

Starting a search for a literary agent can seem overwhelming whether you've just finished your first book or you have several publishing credits on your résumé. You are more than likely eager to start pursuing agents—anxious to see your name on the spine of a book. But before you go directly to the listings of agencies in this book, take a few minutes to familiarize yourself with the way agents work and how you should approach agents. By doing so, you will be more prepared for your search, and ultimately save yourself time and unnecessary grief.

Read the articles

The book divides agents into three sections: nonfee-charging literary agents, fee-charging literary agents, and script agents. Each section begins with feature articles that give advice on the best strategies for contacting agents and provide perspectives on the author/agent relationship. The articles about literary agents are organized into four sections appropriate for each stage of the search process: **Before You Start, Narrowing Your List, Contacting Agents**, and **Before You Sign**. You may want to start by reading through each article, then refer back to relevant articles as you approach each new stage.

Because there are many ways to make that initial contact with an agent, we've provided Insider Reports throughout the book. These personalized interviews with agents and published authors offer both information and inspiration for any writer hoping to find representation.

Decide what type of agent you need

Chances are you already know if you need a literary or a script agent, or even a publicist, but whether you want a nonfee-charging agent or a fee-charging agent may not be as obvious. Reading the feature articles and the introduction to each section of agency listings will help you understand the difference between the two types of agents. In general, nonfee-charging agents earn income from commissions made on manuscript sales. Their focus is selling books, and they typically do not offer editing services. These agents tend to be more selective, often preferring to work with established writers and experts in specific fields.

Fee-charging agents, on the other hand, charge writers for various services (i.e., reading, critiquing, editing, evaluation, consultation, marketing, etc.) in addition to taking a commission on sales. These agents tend to be more receptive to handling the work of new writers. Some of them charge a reading or handling fee only to cover the additional costs of this openness. Those listings charging fees only to previously unpublished writers are preceded by a briefcase ($) symbol. Others offer services designed to improve your manuscript or script. But payment for any of these services rarely ensures representation. If you pay for a critique or edit, request references and sample critiques. If you do approach a fee-charging agent, know exactly what their fee will cover—what you'll be getting before any money changes hands.

Frequently asked questions about the Guide to Literary Agents

Why do you include agents who are not currently seeing clients?
We provide some information on well-known agents who have not answered our request for information. Because of these agents' reputations, we feel the book would be incomplete without an acknowledgement of their companies. Some agents even ask that their listings indicate they are currently closed to new clients.

Why do you include fee-charging agents, and how can I know if an agent who charges fees is legitimate?
There is a great debate in the publishing industry about whether literary agents should charge writers a reading or critiquing fee. There are fee-charging agents who make sales to prominent publishers. Therefore, we believe the decision to approach fee-charging agents should be made by the writer; and we include all the information writers need to make an educated choice. A legitimate agent makes sales, regardless of whether or not he charges a fee. Remember, you should never pay a fee if it makes you uncomfortable.

Why are some agents not listed in the *Guide to Literary Agents*?
Some agents may have not returned our request for information. We have taken others out of the book because we received very serious complaints about that agency. Refer to the index to see why an agency in last year's book isn't in this edition.

Do I need more than one agent if I write in different genres?
More than likely not. If you have written in one genre and want to switch to a new style of writing, ask your agent if he is willing to represent you for your new endeavor. Most agents will continue to represent clients no matter what genre they use. Occasionally an agent may feel he has no knowledge of a certain genre and will make recommendations to his client. Regardless, you should always talk to your agent about any potential career move.

Why don't you list foreign agents?
Most U.S. agents have relationships with agents in other countries, called "foreign co-agents." It is more common for a U.S. agent to work with a co-agent to sell a client's book abroad, than for a writer to work directly with a foreign agent. We do, however, list agents in England and Canada who sell to both U.S and foreign publishers.

Do agents ever contact a writer who is self-published?
Occasionally. If a self-published author attracts the attention of the press or if her book sells extremely well, an agent might approach the author in hopes of representing her.

Why won't the agent I queried return my material?
An agent may not return your query or manuscript for several reasons. Perhaps you did not include a self-addressed, stamped envelope (SASE). Many agents will throw away a submission without a SASE. Or, the agent may have moved. To avoid using expired addresses, use the most current edition of the *Guide to Literary Agents*. Another possibility is that the agent is simply swamped with submissions. Agents can be overwhelmed with queries, especially if the agent has recently spoken at a conference or has been featured in an article or book.

Reading the Listings in the *Guide to Literary Agents*

You could send a mass mailing to all the agencies listed in this book, but doing so will be apparent to agents and will likely turn them off. Instead, use the organizational tools in this book to help determine a core list of agents who are appropriate for you and your work.

First, determine whether you want a nonfee-charging or a fee-charging agent, or an independent publicist. The best way to make your decision is by reading the articles in this book. Then, depending on the type of material you write and whether you write fiction or nonfiction, start your search with the following indexes:

Agents specialties index

Striped for quick reference, this index immediately follows each section of listings and should help you compose a list of agents specializing in your areas. For literary agents, this index is divided by nonfiction and fiction subject categories. For script agents, this index is divided into various subject areas specific to scripts. Cross-referencing categories and concentrating on agents interested in two or more aspects of your manuscript might increase your chances of success. Some agencies are open to all topics and are grouped under the subject heading "open" in each section.

Agencies indexed by openness to submissions

This index lists agencies and independent publicists according to their receptivity to new clients.

Geographic index

For writers looking for an agent close to home, this index lists agents state-by-state and by country. Also included is a regional listing of independent publicists.

Agent index

Often you will read about an agent who is an employee of a larger agency and you may not be able to locate her business phone or address. We asked agencies to list the agents on staff, then we've listed the agents' names in alphabetical order along with the name of the agency they work for. Find the names of the persons you would like to contact and then check their listings.

Listing index

This index lists all agencies, conferences, and independent publicists appearing in this book.

HOW TO READ THE LISTINGS IN THIS BOOK

Once you have searched the various indexes and compiled a list of potential agents or independent publicists for your manuscript, you should read the listings for each agent on your list, eliminating those who seem inappropriate for your work or your individual needs. Before approaching any of the agents listed in this book, be sure to read the various articles in this book to fully understand the etiquette of contacting agents.

The following is a sample agency listing. Study it to understand what the information provided in it means. You also may want to refer to the brief introductions before each section of agency listings for other information specific to that particular section. For specific information on independent publicists, read the introduction to that section on page 322.

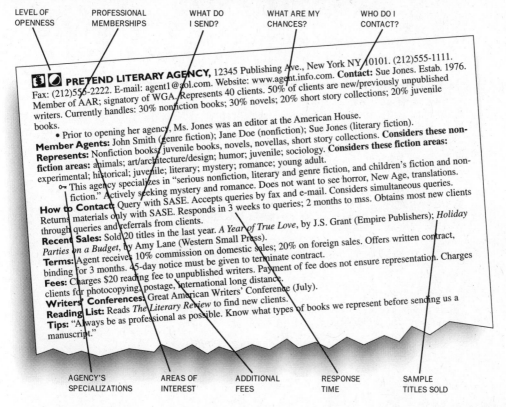

LEVEL OF OPENNESS · PROFESSIONAL MEMBERSHIPS · WHAT DO I SEND? · WHAT ARE MY CHANCES? · WHO DO I CONTACT?

$ ◎ PRETEND LITERARY AGENCY, 12345 Publishing Ave., New York NY 10101. (212)555-1111. Fax: (212)555-2222. E-mail: agent1@aol.com. Website: www.agent.info.com. **Contact:** Sue Jones. Estab. 1976. Member of AAR; signatory of WGA. Represents 40 clients. 50% of clients are new/previously unpublished writers. Currently handles: 30% nonfiction books; 30% novels; 20% short story collections; 20% juvenile books.

• Prior to opening her agency, Ms. Jones was an editor at the American House.

Member Agents: John Smith (genre fiction); Jane Doe (nonfiction); Sue Jones (literary fiction).

Represents: Nonfiction books, juvenile books, novels, novellas, short story collections. **Considers these non-fiction areas:** animals; art/architecture/design; humor; juvenile; sociology. **Considers these fiction areas:** experimental; historical; juvenile; literary; mystery; romance; young adult.

○━ This agency specializes in "serious nonfiction, literary and genre fiction, and children's fiction and non-fiction." Actively seeking mystery and romance. Does not want to see horror, New Age, translations.

How to Contact: Query with SASE. Accepts queries by fax and e-mail. Considers simultaneous queries. Returns materials only with SASE. Responds in 3 weeks to queries; 2 months to mss. Obtains most new clients through queries and referrals from clients.

Recent Sales: Sold 20 titles in the last year. *A Year of True Love,* by J.S. Grant (Empire Publishers); *Holiday Parties on a Budget,* by Amy Lane (Western Small Press).

Terms: Agent receives 10% commission on domestic sales; 20% on foreign sales. Offers written contract, binding for 3 months. 45-day notice must be given to terminate contract.

Fees: Charges $20 reading fee to unpublished writers. Payment of fee does not ensure representation. Charges clients for photocopying, postage, international long distance.

Writers' Conferences: Great American Writers' Conference (July).

Reading List: Reads *The Literary Review* to find new clients.

Tips: "Always be as professional as possible. Know what types of books we represent before sending us a manuscript."

AGENCY'S SPECIALIZATIONS · AREAS OF INTEREST · ADDITIONAL FEES · RESPONSE TIME · SAMPLE TITLES SOLD

SUBHEADS FOR QUICK ACCESS TO INFORMATION

Each listing is broken down into subheads to make locating specific information easier. The following are descriptions of the information found in each subhead and details indicating how you can use this information in your search for an agent.

Contact and basic information

In the first paragraph, you'll find the information you'll need to contact each agency, including where to send your query letter and who to send it to. You'll also learn if the agency belongs to any professional organization. If an agent is a member of the Association of Authors' Representatives (AAR), they are prohibited from charging reading or evaluating fees. If they are a member of the Writers Guild of America (WGA), they are not permitted to charge a reading fee to WGA members, but are allowed to do so to nonmembers. An explanation of all organizations' acronyms is available on page 366. An agent's willingness to work with new or previously unpublished writers is indicated by the percentages given here. The total number of clients an agency represents can also suggest what your status might be in the agency.

Member agents

Often different agents within an agency will have specific specialties. Listed here are agents and their individual specialties to help you know the best agent to query for your work.

Quick Reference Icons

At the beginning of some listings, you will find one or more of the following symbols for quick identification of features particular to that listing.

- [N] Listing new to this edition.
- [✓] Change in address, contact information, or phone number from last year's edition.
- [$] Agents who charge fees to previously unpublished writers only.
- [$] Fee-charging script agent.
- [□] Agents who make sales to electronic publishers.
- [✿] Canadian agency.
- [⊕] International agency.

Level of Openness

Each agency has an icon indicating its openness to submissions. Before contacting any agency, check the listing to make sure it is open to new clients.

- [○] Newer agency actively seeking clients.
- [◑] Agency seeking both new and established writers.
- [◐] Agency prefers to work with established writers, mostly obtains new clients through referrals.
- [◎] Agency handling only certain types of work or work by writers under certain circumstances.
- [∅] Agency not currently seeking new clients. We include these agencies to let you know they are currently not open to new clients. *Unless you have a strong recommendation from someone well respected in the field, our advice is to avoid approaching these agents.*

For quick reference, a chart of these icons and their meanings is printed on the inside covers of this book.

Represents

To expedite your search for an agent, only query agents who represent the type of material you write. Under this subhead, agents list what types of manuscripts they are interested in receiving. To help you find those agents more quickly, check the **Agents Specialties Index** immediately following each section of agency listings.

Look for the key icon (⚷) to quickly learn an agent's areas of specialization or specific strengths (i.e., editorial or marketing experience, sub-rights expertise, etc.). For agents open to a wide-range of subjects, we list the nonfiction and fiction areas they are actively seeking as well as subjects they do *not* wish to receive.

How to contact

Most agents open to submissions prefer initially to receive a query letter briefly describing your work. (For tips on and sample queries, read "Queries That Made It Happen" on page 31.) Some agents ask for an outline or sample chapters, but you should send these only if you are requested to do so. Agents indicate here if they are open to fax or e-mail queries, as well as if they consider simultaneous submissions. Always send a self-addressed, stamped envelope (SASE) or postcard for reply. If you have not heard back from an agent within the approximate reporting time given (allowing for holidays and summer vacations), a quick, polite phone call to ask when it will be reviewed would be in order. Also listed is the agent's preferred way of meeting new clients.

Recent sales

Another way to determine if an agent is appropriate for your manuscript is to look at other titles sold by that agent. Looking at the publisher of those titles can also tell you the caliber of publishing contacts the agent has developed. To give you an idea of how successful an agent has been, we also list the number of titles an agent sold last year. If an agency lists no sales information, we explain why.

Terms

Here you'll find the agent's commission, whether a contract is offered and for how long, and possible office expenses clients may have to pay (i.e., postage, photocopying, etc.). Most agents receive a 10 to 15 percent commission for domestic sales and a 15 to 20 percent commission for foreign or dramatic sales, with the difference going to the co-agent who places the work.

Fees

A separate subhead is included for agents who do charge fees in addition to their commissions. Often, payment of reading or critique fees does not ensure representation. To better understand the different issues surrounding fee-charging agents, read "Agents & Ethics: How to Get Published Without Losing Your Shirt" on page 13 and "Understanding Fees—What Writers Must Know" on page 17 *before* you pay for any services.

Writers' conferences

The conferences agents attend also give an idea of their professional interests and provide a way for writers to meet agents face-to-face. For more information about a specific conference, check the **Writers' Conference** section starting on page 333.

Reading list

Learn what magazines and journals agents read to discover potential clients.

Tips

This subhead contains direct quotes from agents revealing even more specifics about what the agent wants and giving you a better sense of the agent's personality.

OTHER RESOURCES AVAILABLE IN THIS BOOK

If you don't recognize a symbol or abbreviation, refer to the **Key to Symbols** on the front and back inside covers or the **Table of Acronyms** on page 366. For definitions of unfamiliar words or expressions, check the **Glossary** in the back of the book.

Starting on page 359 are additional resources available for writers including a list of **Professional Organizations** for writers, **Books & Publications of Interest** to further your knowledge about agents, and **Websites of Interest** to guide you to the best sites available for writers on the Internet.

Do I Need an Agent?

If you have a book ready to be published, you may be wondering if you need a literary agent. Making this decision can be tough; therefore, we've included this article with the information you need to make an educated choice about using an agent.

WHAT CAN AN AGENT DO FOR YOU?

An agent will believe in your writing and know an audience interested in your writing exists. As the representative for your work, your agent will tell editors your manuscript is the best thing to land on her desk this year. But beyond being enthusiastic about your book, there are a lot of benefits to using an agent.

For starters, today's competitive marketplace can be difficult to break into. Many larger publishing houses will only look at manuscripts from agents. In fact, approximately 80 percent of books published by the major houses are sold to them by agents.

But an agent's job isn't just getting your book through a publisher's door. In reality, that's only part of what an agent can do for you. The following describes the various jobs agents do for their clients, many of which would be difficult for a writer to do without outside help.

Agents know editors' tastes and needs

An agent possesses information on a complex web of publishing houses and a multitude of editors to make sure her clients' manuscripts are placed in the hands of the right editors. This knowledge is gathered through relationships she cultivates with acquisition editors—the people who decide which books to present to their publisher for possible publication. Through her industry connections, an agent becomes aware of the specializations of publishing houses and their imprints, knowing that one publisher only wants contemporary romances while another is interested solely in nonfiction books about the military. By networking with editors over lunch, an agent also learns more specialized information—which editor is looking for a crafty Agatha Christie-style mystery for the fall catalog, for example.

Agents track changes in publishing

Being attentive to constant market changes and vacillating trends is also a major requirement of an agent's job. He understands what it may mean for clients when publisher A merges with publisher B and when an editor from house C moves to house D. Or what it means when readers—and therefore editors—are no longer interested in westerns, but instead can't get their hands on enough Stephen King-style suspense novels.

Agents get your manuscript read faster

Although it may seem like an extra step to send your manuscript to an agent instead of directly to a publishing house, an agent can *prevent* writers from wasting months sending manuscripts to the wrong places or being buried in someone's slush pile. Editors rely on agents to save them time as well. With little time to sift through the hundreds of unsolicited submissions arriving weekly, an editor is naturally going to prefer a work that has already been approved by a qualified reader. For this reason, many of the larger publishers accept agented submissions only.

Agents understand contracts

When publishers write contracts, they are interested in their own bottom line over the best interests of the author. Writers unfamiliar with contractual language may find themselves bound to a publisher with whom they no longer want to work or unable to receive royalties on their first book until they have written several books. An agent uses her experience to negotiate a contract that benefits the writer while still respecting some of the publisher's needs.

Agents negotiate—and exploit—subsidiary rights

Beyond publication, a savvy agent keeps in mind other opportunities for your manuscript. If your agent believes your book will also be successful as an audio book, a Book-of-the-Month club selection, or even a blockbuster movie, he will take these options into consideration when shopping your manuscript. These additional mediums for your writing are called "subsidiary rights"; part of an agent's job is to keep track of the strengths and weaknesses of different publishers's subsidiary rights offices to determine the deposition of these rights to your work. After the contract is negotiated, the agent will seek additional money-making opportunities for the rights he kept for his client. For more information on specific subsidiary rights, see "Subsidiary Rights: Much More Than a Book" on page 45.

Agents get escalators

An escalator is a bonus agents can negotiate as part of the book contract. It is commonly given when a book appears on a bestseller list or if a client appears on a popular television show. For example, a publisher might give a writer a $50,000 bonus if she is picked for Oprah's Book Club™. Both the agent and the editor know such media attention will sell more books, and the agent negotiates an escalator to ensure the writer benefits from this increase in sales.

Agents track payments

Because an agent only receives payment when the publisher pays the writer, it is in her best interests to make sure the writer is paid on schedule. Some publishing houses are notorious for late payments. Having an agent distances you from any conflict over payment and allows you to spend your time writing instead of on the phone.

Agents are strong advocates

Besides standing up for your right to be paid on time, agents can ensure your book gets more attention from the publisher's marketing department, a better cover design, or other benefits you may not know to ask for during the publishing process. An agent can also provide advice during each step of this process as well as guidance about your long-term writing career.

WHEN MIGHT YOU NOT NEED AN AGENT?

Although there are many reasons to work with an agent, an author can benefit from submitting his own work. For example, if your writing focuses on a very specific field, you may want to work with a small or specialized publisher. These houses are usually open to receiving material directly from writers. Smaller houses can often give more attention to a writer than a large house, providing editorial help, marketing expertise, and other advice directly to the writer.

Some writers use a lawyer instead of an agent. If a lawyer specializes in intellectual property, he can help a writer with contract negotiations. Instead of giving the lawyer a commission, the lawyer is paid for his time only. If you know your book will only appeal to a small group of readers, working with a lawyer is an option to consider.

And, of course, some people prefer working independently instead of relying on others to do their work. If you are one of these people, it is probably better to shop your own work instead of constantly butting heads with an agent. And despite the benefits of working with an agent, it is possible to sell your work directly to a publisher—people do it all the time!

Three Editors Voice Their Opinions About Agents

A frequent concern of many writers considering working with an agent is the way agents are seen by editors. A writer may fear that as soon as she says, "I'll have to ask my agent," the editor's eyes will roll and the publishing opportunity will be lost forever. A common stereotype is that editors loathe agents, but this assumption is far from the truth. In fact, most editors *enjoy* working with agents and believe their writers greatly benefit by having representation.

We've asked three editors to share their views of agents. These editors—Michael Stearns of Harcourt Children's Books, Stacy Creamer of Penguin Putnam, Inc, and Fiona McCrae of Graywolf Press—discuss their experience with agents, reveal what happens when they interact with agents, and impart their advice for writers hoping to catch an agent's eye.

AN EDITOR'S ADVICE: GET AN AGENT
by Michael Stearns, senior editor, Harcourt Children's Books

"Do I *need* an agent?"

Whether the questioner is a beginning writer or one who is hip deep in publications, it's common to hear a by-my-bootstraps cockiness—an "I don't need *anybody*!" quality in the voice. It is always clear from the way the person asks the question—body language, intonation, an oily winking quality—that I'm supposed to say, "What? Agents? Are you *insane*?" and then slap my thigh and laugh heartily before moving on to the next question.

Or something like that.

Instead I say, "You don't *need* an agent, exactly, . . . but you probably *should* have an agent."

Some may think I'm merely toeing a line: I work for a publishing house that does not accept unsolicited manuscripts, and so my suggestion that writers should have agents is suspect. But my love of agents has nothing to do with the policy of the house I work for and everything to do with my trust in a process that has given me many great books—some of the best books on my lists at Harcourt, books of which I am unbearably proud.

Many beginning writers expect agents and editors to be in opposite trenches, hurling insults and the occasional manuscript at one another; or, nursed by bad Hollywood movies, they think all agents are bloodsucking weasels who thrive off the hard labor of their talent. "Fifteen percent!" these people wail; "That's practically theft!"

Nonsense. Truth is, an agent does a tremendous amount of labor for her 15 percent take of the writer's income. The agent's hard work makes the writer's job—and, most importantly for me, *my* job—considerably easier. And the work a good agent does isn't just work the writer doesn't have to do (the licking of stamps, say), but work the writer could never *hope* to do (the cultivation of relationships with editors and houses all over the world). Consider:

- **Agents know the big picture.** A good agent understands not only my tastes, but also how my tastes fit into the editorial makeup of my house, and how my house fits into the industry. She has a view of publishing that an author can't get without lots of study and hard work and schmoozing and lunches and phone calls—in short, without becoming an agent himself.
- **Agents keep the editorial relationship pure.** I've dealt with authors who in addition to being formidable writers are also fearsome contract negotiators, but that fearsomeness can

stain the editorial process. Nothing is worse than dealing with a writer who is bitter because an editor couldn't pay more for a project. An agent can soften such disappointments by setting the payment into a context that makes sense, or by that magic agents can work with their writers because agents are often a—how should I put this?

- **Agents are a project's first love.** Sounds cheesy, but I'm serious. I trust implicitly the taste of a handful of agents because the books they love have proven worthy of such devotion. What gets my attention, what first catches my fancy, is the articulate vision the agent conveys about the project. And that grows from a love, a belief, a *faith* in the project at hand.

An agent's faith will keep a manuscript on the market until it sells; an agent's faith will ensure that the right house publishes the manuscript; an agent's faith will ensure that the house publishes the book properly (because good agents don't stop working when the ink dries on the contract). And all of this happens while the writer does what the writer should be doing—writing new books.

Sounds like common sense when it's put that way, doesn't it?

THE AGENT/EDITOR RELATIONSHIP: FRIENDS, NOT FOES
by Stacy Creamer, vice president/senior editor, Penguin Putnam, Inc.

The relationship between agent and editor is sometimes mistaken for a contentious one because the initial interaction between them seems adversarial—the agent bargaining for top dollar; the editor trying to sign an author for the smallest amount needed to seal the deal. Usually, this situation is far from true. Both sides broker for the best price possible from their perspectives, but then they forget about that part of the deal; the advance—high or low—becomes water under the bridge. Once the contract is inked, agent and editor begin to collaborate—on the author's behalf.

The editor is the agent's best friend because the editor is the author's biggest in-house supporter. She has the passion to acquire the work and the vision to see the book successfully published.

The agent becomes the important liaison between the author and the editor because the agent knows the author and presumably has the author's trust. The agent can help educate the author about the publishing process. There is often a fairy-tale quality to having a novel accepted for publication, but signing the publishing contract doesn't guarantee living happily every after. When real life begins to diverge from the storybook ending, disgruntlement may result. A thoughtful agent can help head off disappointment by letting the author know what to expect.

There are also many tangible ways in which the agent and editor both continue to be the author's best friends. After I acquire a novel, I usually brainstorm with the agent. Does the agent represent any other authors whom I might pursue for dust jacket quotes? Do I work with any authors who might give a blurb? Does my house? Is this novel likely to hold any particular regional appeal? If so, should we concentrate our efforts on that area, or should we wage a national campaign?

The agent and editor gladly make time for this kind of collaborative thinking. Publicists are burdened with full rosters of authors to promote each season. At larger publishing houses, the sales force has several imprints' worth of books to pitch. The marketing people have every title in the catalog to consider for advertising. But the agent and editor are often as enthusiastic as new parents. They are proud of the book, and that pride erases the sense of burden that others may feel. They haven't been assigned this manuscript; they chose—and perhaps even fought for the right—to see it through to publication. They are the earliest believers in the book, and they genuinely want to see their belief confirmed by strong sales and great reviews.

Tom Clancy's and Patricia Cornwell's books enjoy megabuck marketing campaigns, but most first-time authors are not so blessed. A smart agent recognizes that no amount of bickering will yield a six-figure promotional campaign when the publishing house thinks a four-figure campaign is more than enough. But with judicious prodding, the agent and editor can double-team their way from no author tour to a three- or four-city schedule, or from modest advertising plans to a *New York Times* teaser-ad campaign. The editor can assess the in-house climate, and the agent can apply the pressure.

Formulating a specific request helps. It's easier to have a plan accepted than to try to get others to develop one. The editor and agent must work together to pick their shots. They may agree to push for the author tour but maybe not consumer advertising; or to reject those first four jacket designs but not insist on a spot matte lamination (which is very expensive) for the perfect fifth cover.

The bottom line is that the agent works for the author, and the editor works for the house. If the publisher is no longer interested in hearing the case for a bigger advertising budget or an author tour, the editor has to acquiesce. But the agent need never give up. The agent can continue to make the case—the very one that the editor is desperate to have advanced.

An agent's displeasure with a publishing plan can be conveyed by the editor to the publisher or directly by the agent himself. In many cases, the agent might have a long-standing relationship with the house through other authors he represents. He's a known quantity; his experience and his client list give him clout.

The editor occasionally suffers from Greek-messenger syndrome: in conveying disappointing news to the agent and author, she is mistaken for the source of the bad news when really she's just as disappointed. Remember, an editor's success is measured by the success of her books. Editors want bigger print runs, more advertising dollars, and more tour cities just as much as the agent and writer do. When an editor and agent combine forces creatively on behalf of an author, all three succeed.

A SMALL PRESS EDITOR'S TAKE ON AGENTS
by Fiona McCrae, publisher, Graywolf Press

Graywolf Press is one of the larger of the small literary presses. We are based in Saint Paul, Minnesota, and publish sixteen books a year. Our annual list comprises poetry, fiction, creative nonfiction, and literary or cultural essays. In general, we work directly (*sans* agent) with our poets. The fiction and nonfiction authors often do have agents, with whom we have had successful working relationships.

Some of our authors are just starting out, and the better agent can help explain the publishing process to the author. The agents' professionalism and experience can help navigate their writers through the often bewildering pre- and post-publication period. Agents can even serve as advocates for the publisher, in reassuring the author that things are proceeding smoothly. They can act as an important buffer between author and publisher if there are any difficulties. Many authors are diffident about discussing financial matters with their publishers because they fear that talking about this topic spoils the professional friendship they are developing with the house. The agent can de-personalize these discussions in a way that benefits both parties.

I have found that the New York agent (which is where most of them tend to be) can help spread the word about her author's book around Manhattan. She can "talk the book up" to paperback editors and other folks in the industry with whom she has contact during her regular day. Sometimes an agent can be helpful getting blurbs, too, by putting friendly pressure on their other clients to provide some words of endorsement for our author's book.

As a small press, our budgets for both royalty advances and marketing are modest. The author and the agent have to understand from the beginning what our limits are, and the agent can counsel her writers to have realistic expectations as to what a press of our size can provide. We have found that many of the literary agents with the strongest reputations are often eager to work with us in creative ways to help Graywolf find the audience for a given work. Agents understand the valuable role a small press can play in today's increasingly competitive market.

Agents & Ethics: Getting Published Without Losing Your Shirt

BY JEAN V. NAGGAR

Writing is usually a lonely occupation. When at last, after months, even years of wrestling with words and ideas, the writer types in "THE END," prints up the result of mighty labors, and feels the thrill of hefting a bulky pile of crisp pages, it would seem the Herculean task is over. Now, surely, it is merely a matter of locating the right agent, getting the right publisher interested, and the words and ideas, elegantly bound and jacketed, will appear on the shelves of bookstores everywhere.

Easy, right?

Wrong.

These days, the writer must not only create a fine work of the imagination. The aspiring writer must also learn a good deal about how the publishing business works, who the players are, and how to avoid falling into the clutches of a growing number of disreputable "agencies" and "editorial services" that survive on fees paid up front and not on commissions from a job well done. Throughout the years, hardworking, reputable literary agents have striven to distinguish their ways of doing business from the ways of the less particular.

A brief history of the Association of Authors' Representatives

Early in the 1970s, a small group of independent literary agents who had recently moved to agenting from editorial and other positions in publishing houses, began getting together informally to network and to exchange gossip, war-stories, and survival tips. The group quickly coalesced into something more formal and named itself the Independent Literary Agents Association (ILAA).

This energetic, proactive group of then relatively new agents operated alongside the venerable and respected Society of Authors Representatives (SAR) for some years, maintaining an independent-minded approach to reading fees as it did to other matters.

The SAR had long held its members to a code of appropriate behavior, and in time, a committee formed in the ILAA to discuss many questions of ethical behavior that came up in conversation and in practice. They discussed appropriate behaviors of member agents with each other, with their authors, and with the publishers and editors with whom they dealt. While not wishing in any way to impinge on the free and independent operation of its members, or to create a policing body, certain red-flag issues came up again and again, and the committee decided to develop a code of appropriate behavior for its members.

In 1990, the two associations joined forces and emerged as the Association of Authors' Representatives (AAR), an energized association of literary agents, committed to following high standards of behavior in their professional dealings, charging no reading fees, and avoiding any

JEAN V. NAGGAR *is the president of the Jean V. Naggar Literary Agency in New York, and has been working in publishing for thirty years. She was president of Association of Authors' Representatives from 1998 to 1999. A list of member-agents of the AAR, together with a brochure, can be obtained for $7 and a 99¢ SASE by writing to P.O. Box 237201, Ansonia Station, New York NY 10023. The AAR website is www.aar-online.org.*

situation that might introduce a conflict of interest, although it took time for some differences in philosophy to be resolved to the satisfaction of all.

The AAR currently numbers some 350 member agents nationwide. Member agents subscribe annually to a code of ethics that is fast becoming a standard in the publishing industry, and concern themselves with following the latest developments in contracts, royalties, and the optimal dispensation of all rights.

Creating an ethical standard

The Canon of Ethics that developed from this joining is signed yearly by every member of the AAR when dues are paid. It has produced high standards within an unregulated, unlicensed industry. It is notable that publishers have not developed a similar set of ethical guidelines for their behavior, nor are they likely to do so!

Briefly, the Canon of Ethics ensures the following:

- That members maintain two separate bank accounts so there is no commingling of clients' monies and the agency's operating expenses.
- That prompt disclosure and payment are made to clients regarding monies received from both domestic and foreign sales.
- That members are forbidden to charge reading fees to clients or potential clients, directly or indirectly, beyond the customary return postage charges. In an attempt to deflect potential abuses, the Ethics Committee recently extended this provision. Now, in addition, agents who belong to the AAR may not charge fees for reading manuscripts and proposals at writers' conferences.
- That members of the AAR may not receive a secret profit or enter into any arrangement regarding a client's work that might create a conflict of interest.

While providing this unique standard of ethical behavior authors can depend upon, the AAR still affirms the total independence of its members' individual operations, adoption or rejection of author-agent agreements, commission structures, and negotiations with publishers.

Sometimes, an author attempts to involve the cooperation of the Ethics Committee of the AAR in connection with a particular agent who is not an AAR member or for reasons outside the scope of the Canon of Ethics. Most of these matters, however, are not the purview of the Ethics Committee, which was never intended to be a policing body regarding general "agenting" complaints. Any complaints addressing a *member's* supposed violation of the Canon of Ethics are taken very seriously indeed, and no decision is made without a thorough exploration of all circumstances surrounding the complaint.

Cooperating to keep up with a changing industry

The AAR also works to inform and educate its agenting community on developments within the publishing industry. At present, the contractual and conceptual problems arising from new electronic technologies and the shrinking of publishing venues due to recent consolidations are taking much of the organization's attention. AAR members have formed task forces to work with publishers on these issues, and have organized forums for the discussion of cutting-edge technologies and their impact on all of us. The AAR makes sure its members are equipped with the information they need to make the decisions that best benefit their writers.

The association also appoints individual agents to act as liaisons with all the major writers' organizations. [See page 359 for a list of Professional Organizations.] They keep abreast of issues concerning these writers' communities and, in turn, inform them of AAR developments, maintaining a steady flow of information. It is more important than ever that authors and agents share information, insights, and move forward together into the changing world of today's publishing scene.

Making informed choices

Obviously, in choosing an agent, whether through the AAR list or otherwise, there are vast differences in temperament, sensibility, day-to-day practice, and personal style to take into account. To gain a sense of the personalities of several agents, read John Baker's *Literary Agents: A Writer's Introduction* (Macmillan). Every writer should choose the agent best suited for her own needs and disposition. By choosing an agent who is an AAR member, a writer can be sure the agent cares about ethical standards enough to sign on to them on a yearly basis, and because admission to membership requires several recommendations and sale of a specific number of books, it also ensures that the AAR agent you approach is respected by her peers and not a fly-by-night operation.

Your writing career is worth all the advance power you can find to fuel it, and although the temptations out there are many, be advised that reputable agents rarely if ever advertise—most reputable agents obtain new clients through referrals and word of mouth. Agents also cannot make promises about getting your work published. And if your book is going to be published, a reputable publisher will be paying you an advance, not the other way around.

There is no more precious a thing than the painstaking creation of a work of the imagination. Writers are the lifeblood of the publishing industry, the only indispensable element in a continuum that links writer to reader. But the publishing industry is becoming increasingly bound by corporate politics and policies, forcing writers to seek out other kinds of feedback. Publishers are also at the mercy of the media, whose enormous hyping of superlative advances and celebrity has created its own quicksand—into which many writers founder, lured by the pot of gold at the end of the rainbow.

Using freelance editors

Just when technology has provided aspiring writers with wonderful tools like "spellcheck" and the ability to restructure a manuscript several times without having to retype the entire work, the publishing industry itself has chosen to batten down the hatches, jettison imprints and editors in droves, and consolidate lists—all of which leave little room for the unpublished writer to slip a toe in the door.

Publishing has undergone seismic change. Mergers and consolidations have led to firings and departures of editors, and have caused a general sense of unease among those who are still employed. Departing editors are often not replaced, placing a greater burden on the shoulders of fewer editors, giving them neither the time nor the energy to take on projects that require a lot of editorial work. Unwilling to take risks that might land them among the unemployed, most people in publishing houses hold back on making decisions and choose the path of least resistance.

Consequently, many reputable and not-so-reputable individuals now offer "book-doctoring" services to evaluate material and pummel it into shape before it even reaches the critical eyes of agents and editors. Offering promises of magical editorial input, some of these self-styled "editorial services" exist solely to tease money from the hopeful and empty pockets of the uninformed. The pitfalls are many along the road to publication, and shape-shifting monsters lurk in the deep to seize the unwary and relieve them of their savings.

However, the happier side of this picture is that there *do* exist groups of seasoned professionals, working as individual freelance editors and exercising editorial skills honed from many years spent making decisions at publishing houses. Finding themselves out of a job because of new corporate groupings, they offer an important entrepreneurial opportunity within the changing landscape of the publishing industry. Some of them are beginning to coalesce into associations of their own. Others work alone. They usually do not advertise, and their services are expensive. But they are true publishing professionals and take genuine pleasure in using hard-won skills to help writers find their voices or to pull a publishable work out of chaos.

Finding Reputable Freelance Editors and Literary Agents

How can a writer tell which face of Janus is smiling in her direction? How do you sift the reputable from the disreputable when you live far from the centers of publishing activity and feed on hope to keep your dreams alive? When you have been rejected by an entire flotilla of agents, and someone out there offers you (for a "small" fee) the opportunity to have your manuscript read by a self-styled "professional" or better yet, offers you publication if you will come up with an "advance" toward it, could this be opportunity knocking at the door? Use the following guidelines to help you decide:

☑ Read *Publishers Weekly* for several months before you will need the services of either a book doctor or a literary agent, focusing on new agents who come out of substantial publishing (not necessarily agenting) experience.

☑ Attend writers' conferences, and ask around for names of freelance editors and agents with whom people have had positive experiences.

☑ From freelance editors, request an advance breakdown of fees before signing any contract including the cost of a reading and editorial letter and the cost of a subsequent in-depth editorial job. Beware of empty promises. A freelance editor cannot guarantee you publication.

☑ Ask freelance editors if they will provide samples of previous editing jobs, and discuss the level of editing you will receive for the fees you pay.

☑ Request a list of published writers who have worked with this editor, and try to check it out by looking at Acknowledgment pages, etc., unless you are fortunate enough to have access to one of these writers.

☑ Ask your librarian or local bookseller if the name of the editor you are considering is at all familiar. Librarians and booksellers read *Publishers Weekly* and attend book conventions, where they sometimes meet editors. They can also make inquiries for you and steer you toward a reputable editor.

☑ Familiarize yourself with what services a good agent can and should be able to provide.

Above all, bear in mind that a reputable publisher *will pay you* for the right to publish your book and will not require you to put up your own money.

The Authors Guild and other writers' organizations can provide information about editors and agents. The AAR has also moved consistently, over the years, to help prevent the abuse of authors within the ethical framework for its members. It has never been more important to be wary of golden promises. It has never been more important to enlist the help of a reputable professional.

Happily, writers are hard to discourage. I would only urge you to put as much energy and research into the "tools" with which you hope to achieve publication as you put into writing the work you hope to publish. In achieving a realistic understanding of the limitations and benefits of the publishing industry, and in gaining a sense of the names and roles of the players in that industry, you can avoid costly mistakes and make choices that lead to publication, rather than insolvency.

Understanding Fees—What Writers Must Know

Before you start searching for an agent, it is imperative that you have an understanding of the different types of fees some agents may charge. Most agents make their living from the commissions they receive after selling their clients' books, but some agents charge additional fees. This book separates the agency listings into two sections: nonfee-charging agents and fee-charging agents. The following explanations should help you decide which type of agent you want to approach.

Office expenses Many agents—both those who do and do not charge additional fees—ask the author to pay for photocopying, postage, long-distance phone calls, marketing, and other expenses. An agent should only ask for office expenses *after* agreeing to represent the writer. These expenses should be discussed upfront, and the writer should receive an accounting for them. This money is sometimes returned upon sale of the manuscript. Although a one-time office expense charge is fairly common, be wary of agents who request yearly, quarterly, or even monthly reimbursements without ever selling your manuscript.

Reading fees Agents who do not charge reading fees earn their money from commissions. Agencies that do charge reading fees often do so to cover the cost of additional readers or the time spent reading that could have been spent selling. This practice can save the agent time and open the agency to a larger number of submissions. Paying fees benefits writers because they know at least someone will look at their work. Whether such promises are kept depends upon the honesty of the agency. You may pay a fee and never receive a response from the agent, or you may pay someone who will not submit your manuscript to publishers. *In this book, only fee-charging agents who actively make sales are included.*

Reading fees vary from $25 to $500 or more. The fee is usually nonrefundable, but some agents refund the money if they take a writer on as a client or if they sell the writer's manuscript. Keep in mind, however, that payment of a reading fee does *not* ensure representation.

Officially, the Association of Authors' Representatives (AAR) in their Canon of Ethics prohibits members from directly or indirectly charging a reading fee, and the Writers Guild of America (WGA) does not allow WGA signatory agencies to charge a reading fee to WGA members, as stated in the WGA's Artists' Manager Basic Agreement. A signatory may charge you a fee if you are not a member, but most signatory agencies do not charge a reading fee as an across-the-board policy.

Critique fees Sometimes a manuscript will interest an agent, but he will point out areas still needing development. Some agencies offer criticism services for an additional fee. Like reading fees, payment of a critique fee does not ensure representation. When deciding if you will benefit from having someone critique your manuscript, keep in mind that the quality and quantity of comments vary widely. The critique's usefulness will depend on the agent's knowledge of the market. Also be aware that an agent who spends a significant portion of his time commenting on manuscripts will have less time to actively market your book.

Some agents refer writers to freelance editors or "book doctors." Make sure you research any critiquing service before sending your work, and don't be charmed by fancy brochures and compliments about your writing. Also be wary of agents who hurriedly refer you to editorial services. While it is not illegal to make a referral, some agents may abuse this practice.

The WGA has a rule preventing their signatories from making referrals to book doctors, and the AAR frowns on them as well if the agent is receiving financial compensation for making the referral. The WGA believes that, while an agent may have good intentions, differentiating agents trying to help writers from those who benefit financially from referrals is too difficult.

Three Truths About Agents

BY DENNIS PALUMBO

Nothing's more real in the world of a writer than dealing with agents. However, whenever I'm asked to say something about agents, I feel uneasy. Not because I don't have strong feelings about them, having had varied experiences, good and bad, with agents over a twenty-year span. What makes any discussion of agents so difficult is that, in my view, the most important aspects of a writer's relationship with his agent have almost nothing to do with the agent, and everything to do with the writer.

Let's face it. If there's a relationship that's as shrouded in mythology, half-truths, and just plain misconceptions as that between agent and client, I've never heard of one. Who's read A. Scott Berg's biography of Maxwell Perkins without thinking, "Jeez, I wish I had an agent like *him*." That is, until you read about some of the deals legendary agent Swifty Lazar got for *his* clients.

On the down side, we all know horror stories about agents abandoning clients, misrepresenting them, assailing their work, diminishing their esteem. Even the best agents blow hot and cold with their writers, or get distracted by the excitement of snagging a new, *wunderkind* client.

So before talking about what the writer needs to recognize as his own contribution to the sometimes puzzling, often painful relationship between writer and agent, let's list some sobering facts:

1) Your agent is not your parent. It's not the agent's job to encourage, support, or validate your creative ambitions, *insofar as they reflect your inner need to be loved and cherished.* Such needs were your birthright, and hopefully were given to you during your childhood. If, however, they were not, it's not an agent's job to pick up the slack.

2) Your agent is in business to make money. This is not a crime against humanity, an affront to the arts, or a personal repudiation of your aesthetic dreams. It is just a fact.

3) While your agent may indeed admire your talent, and share with you lofty creative and financial goals, he is not inclined or obligated to care about them as much as you do. In fact, *no one* cares about your career as much as you do. This means the burden of worrying about your artistic aspirations, income, reputation in the field, and level of personal and professional satisfaction rests entirely on your shoulders.

These three points aside, what every writer needs to understand is that the very nature of the artist's position in society contributes to the asymmetry of the relationship between writer and agent. The moment a writer offers his work for evaluation in the marketplace—whether to a book publisher, a magazine editor, a film producer, or a TV network—that writer is instantly placed in the vulnerable position analogous to that of child to caregiver. Since the marketplace holds the power to validate one's work, it retains the ability to mirror back to the writer either affirming or shaming messages about the writer's worth.

When dealing with an agent—a person equally embedded in the machinery of the market-place—the writer's vulnerabilities encourage him either to exaggerate or minimize the agent's

DENNIS PALUMBO, *formerly a Hollywood screenwriter* (My Favorite Year, Welcome Back, Kotter, *etc.*), *is now a psychotherapist in private pracice, specializing in creative issues. This piece is reprinted from* Writing from the Inside Out, *by Dennis Palumbo (© 2000, Palumbo). This piece is reprinted by permission of John Wiley & Sons, Inc.*

opinion; to place an unrealistic burden on the relationship with the agent, in terms of providing solace and support; and to use, as a child does, the agent's responses as a mechanism for emotional self-regulation.

The reality is, this primarily fiduciary arrangement can't tolerate such burdens. The writer expects too much in the way of esteem building, validation, and empathy. Like those who claim to be looking for a "soul mate" in their romantic relationships—which often betrays a desire for an exact mirror image of one's self so as to minimize conflicts—a writer who searches ardently for an agent who really "gets" him or her at a profound level is doomed to disappointment.

Which means that every unreturned phone call by the agent, every less-than-ecstatic response to a new piece of work, every real or imagined shift in vocal tonality during a conversation are experienced by the writer as concrete indicators of one's self-worth. The wise writer understands this, if only theoretically, and should at least strive to keep his relationship with an agent in context. Maybe it will lessen the blows, whatever they are and whenever they come. Then again, maybe it won't.

On the other hand, unlike one's parents, if you don't like your agent, you can always try another one. You'll probably discover that each new agent is just different from, not better than, the last. And that, when it comes to agents, soul mates are few and far between.

Which is good, because you can get back to your writing, the one true source of any success—financial or otherwise—you're likely to enjoy.

How to Find the Right Agent

BY DONYA DICKERSON

A writer's job is to write. A literary agent's job is to find publishers for her clients' books. Any writer who has endeavored to attract the attention of a publishing house knows this is no easy task. But beyond selling manuscripts, an agent must keep track of the ever-changing industry, writers' royalty statements, fluctuating reading habits, and the list continues.

Because publishing houses receive more unsolicited manuscripts each year, securing an agent is becoming more of a necessity. Nevertheless, finding an eager *and* reputable agent is a difficult task. Even the most patient of writers can become frustrated, even disillusioned. Therefore, as a writer seeking agent representation, you should prepare yourself before starting your search. By learning effective strategies for approaching agents, as well as what to expect from an author/agent relationship, you will save yourself time—and quite possibly, heartache. This article provides the basic information on literary agents and how to find one who will best benefit your writing career.

Make sure you are ready for an agent

With an agent's job in mind, you should ask yourself if you and your work are at a stage where you need an agent. Look at the "Ten Step Checklists for Fiction and Nonfiction Writers," and judge how prepared you are for contacting an agent. Have you spent enough time researching or polishing your manuscript? Sending an agent an incomplete project not only wastes your time but may turn him off in the process. Literary agents are not magicians. An agent cannot sell an unsalable property. He cannot solve your personal problems. He will not be your banker, CPA, social secretary, or therapist. Instead, he will endeavor to sell your book because that is how he earns his living.

Moreover, your material may not be appropriate for an agent. Most agents do not represent poetry, magazine articles, short stories, or material suitable for academic or small presses—the agents' commission earned does not justify spending time submitting these type of works. Those agents who do take on such material generally represent authors on larger projects first, and then represent these smaller items only as a favor for their clients.

If you strongly believe your work is ready to be placed with an agent, make sure you are personally ready to be represented. In other words, before you contact an agent, consider the direction in which your writing career is headed. Besides skillful writers, agencies want clients with the ability to produce more than one book. Most agents will say they represent careers, not books. So as you compose your query letter—your initial contact with an agent—briefly mention your potential. Let an agent know if you've already started drafting your second novel. Let him know that for you writing is more than a half-hearted hobby.

The importance of research

Nobody would buy a used car without at least checking the odometer, and the savvy shopper would consult the blue books, take a test drive, and even ask for a mechanic's opinion. Because you want to obtain the best possible agent for your writing, you should research the business of agents before sending out query letters. Understanding how agents operate will help you find an agent appropriate for your work, as well as alert you about the types of agents to avoid.

We often receive complaints from writers regarding agents *after* they have already lost money or their work is tied into a contract with an ineffective agent. If they'd put the same amount of

effort into researching agents as they did writing their manuscript, they would have saved themselves unnecessary grief.

The best way to educate yourself is to read all you can about agents and other authors. The
articles in this book will give you insight not only on how to contact an agent but also how the
author/agent relationship works. Organizations such as the Association of Authors' Representatives (AAR), the National Writers Union (NWU), American Society of Journalists and Authors
(ASJA), and Poets & Writers, Inc. all have informational material on agenting. (These, along
with other helpful organizations, are listed in the back of this book.) *Publishers Weekly* covers
publishing news affecting agents and others in the publishing industry in general; discusses
specific events in the "Hot Deals" and "Behind the Bestsellers" columns; and occasionally
lists individual author's agents in the "Forecasts" section.

Even the Internet has a wide range of sites devoted to agents. Through the different forums
provided on the Web, you can learn basic information about preparing for your initial contact
or more specific material about individual agents. Keep in mind, however, that not everything
printed on the Web is a solid fact; you may come across the site of a writer who is bitter because
an agent rejected his manuscript. Your best bet is to use the Internet to supplement your other
research. For particularly useful sites, refer to "Websites of Interest" in the back of this book.

Through your research, you will discover the need to be wary of some agents. Anybody can
go to the neighborhood copy center and order business cards which say she is a literary agent.
But that title does not mean she can sell your book. She may ask for a large sum of money, then
disappear from society. Becoming knowledgeable about the different types of fees agents may
charge is a *crucial* step to take before contacting any agent. Before paying any type of fee, read
"Understanding Fees—What Writers Must Know" on page 17 and the introduction to the Literary Agents: Fee-charging section on page 213.

An agent also may not have any connections with others in the publishing industry. An agent's
reputation with editors can be her major strength or weakness. While it's true that even top
agents are not able to sell every book they represent, an inexperienced agent who submits too
many inappropriate submissions will quickly lose her standing with any editor. It is acceptable
to ask an agent for recent sales before he agrees to represent you, but keep in mind that some
agents consider this information confidential. If an agent does give you a list of recent sales,
you can call the publishers' contracts department to ensure the sale was actually made by that
agent.

The pros and cons of location

For years, the major editors and agents were located in New York. If a writer wanted to be
published with a big-name house, he had to contact a New York agency. But this has changed
over time for many reasons. For starters, publishing companies are appearing all over the country—San Francisco, Seattle, Chicago, Minneapolis. And naturally, agents are locating closer to
these smaller publishing hubs.

The recent advances in technology have also had an impact on the importance of location.
Thanks to fax machines, the Internet, e-mail, express mail, and inexpensive long-distance telephone rates, an agent no longer needs to live in New York to work closely with a New York
publisher. Besides, if a manuscript is truly excellent, a smart editor will not care where the agent
lives.

Nevertheless, there are simply more opportunities for agents located in New York to network
with editors. They are able to meet face-to-face over lunch. The editor can share his specific
needs, and the agent can promote her newest talent. As long as New York remains the publishing
capital of the world, the majority of agents will be found there, too.

Before You Contact an Agent:
A Ten-step Checklist for Fiction Writers

☑ **Finish your novel** or short story collection. An agent can do nothing for fiction without a finished product.

☑ **Revise your novel.** Have other writers offer criticism to ensure your manuscript is as finished as you believe possible.

☑ **Proofread.** Don't let your hard work go to waste by turning off an agent with typos or poor grammar.

☑ **Publish** short stories or novel excerpts in literary journals, proving to potential agents that editors see quality in your writing.

☑ **Research** to find the agents of writers you admire or whose work is similar to your own.

☑ **Use the indexes** in this book to construct a list of agents open to new writers and looking for your type of fiction (i.e., literary, romance, mystery).

☑ **Rank your list.** Use the listings in this book to determine the agents most suitable for you and your work, and to eliminate inappropriate agencies.

☑ **Write your synopsis.** Completing this step early will help you write your query letter and save you time later when agents contact you.

☑ **Compose your query letter.** As an agent's first impression of you, this brief letter should be polished and to the point.

☑ **Read about the business** of agents so you are knowledgeable and prepared to act on any offer.

Contacting agents

Once your manuscript is prepared and you have a solid understanding of how literary agents work, the time is right to contact an agent. Your initial contact is the first impression you make on an agent; therefore, you want to be professional and brief.

Because approaching agents is an important topic, we've included several articles on contacting agents in this book: "The Basics of Contacting Literary Agents" on page 29; "Seven Insider Techniques for Targeting Agents" on page 25; "Queries That Made It Happen" on page 31; and "Commanding Book Proposals: The Rejection Slip's Greatest Enemy" on page 37.

Again, research plays an important role in getting an agent's attention. You'll want to show her you've done your homework. Read the listings in this book to learn her areas of interest, check out her website to learn more details about how she does business, and find out the names of some of her clients. If there is an author whose book is similar to yours, call the author's publisher. Someone in the "contracts" department can tell you the name of the agent who sold the title, provided an agent was used. Contact that agent, and impress her with your knowledge of her agency.

Evaluate any offer

Once you've received an offer of representation, you must determine if the agent is right for you. As flattering as any offer may be, you need to be confident that you are going to work well with this person and that this person is going to work hard to sell your manuscript.

You need to know what you should expect once you enter into a business relationship. You should know how much editorial input to expect from your agent; how often he gives updates about where your manuscript has been and who has seen it; and what subsidiary rights the agent represents.

Before You Contact an Agent:
A Ten-step Checklist for Nonfiction Writers

☑ **Formulate a concrete idea** for your book. Sketch a brief outline making sure you have enough material for an entire book-length manuscript.

☑ **Research** works on similar topics to understand the competition and determine how yours is unique.

☑ **Compose sample chapters.** This step should indicate how much time you will need to finish and if your writing needs editorial help.

☑ **Publish** completed chapters in journals. This validates your work to agents and provides writing samples for later in the process.

☑ **Polish your outline** to refer to while drafting a query letter and avoid wasting time when agents contact you.

☑ **Brainstorm** three to four subject categories that best describe your material.

☑ **Use the indexes in this book** to find agents interested in at least two of your subject areas and looking for new clients.

☑ **Rank your list.** Narrow your list further by reading the listings of agencies you found in the indexes; organize the list according to your preferences.

☑ **Write your query.** Describe your premise and your experience professionally and succinctly, to give an agent an excellent first impression of you.

☑ **Read about the business** of agents so you are knowledgeable and prepared to act on any offer.

More importantly, you should know when you will be paid. The publisher will send your advance and any subsequent royalty checks directly to the agent. After deducting his commission—usually 10 to 15 percent—your agent will send you the remaining balance. Most agents charge a higher commission of 20 to 25 percent when using a co-agent for foreign, dramatic, or other specialized rights. As you enter into a relationship with an agent, have him explain his specific commission rates and payment policy.

As your potential partner, you have the right to ask an agent for information that convinces you she knows what he's doing. Be reasonable about what you ask, however. Asking for recent sales is okay; asking for the average size of clients' advances is not. Remember, agents are very busy. Often asking general questions like, "How do you work?" or requesting a sample contract, can quickly answer your concerns. A list of suggested questions can be found on page 58. An agent's answers should help you make your decision. If you are polite and he responds with anger or contempt, that tells you something you need to know about what working together would be like.

Evaluate the agent's level of experience. Agents who have been in the business awhile have a larger number of contacts, but new agents may be hungrier, as well as more open to previously unpublished writers. Talk to other writers about their interactions with specific agents. Writers' organizations such as the National Writers Association (NWA), the American Society of Journalists and Authors (ASJA), and the National Writers Union (NWU) maintain files on agents their members have dealt with, and can share this information by written request or through their membership newsletters.

Understand any contract before you sign

Some agents offer written contracts, some do not. If your prospective agent does not, at least ask for a "memorandum of understanding" that details the basic relationship of expenses and commissions. If your agent does offer a contract, be sure to read it carefully, and keep a copy for yourself. Because contracts can be confusing, you may want to have a lawyer or knowledge-able writer friend check it out before you sign anything.

The National Writers Union (NWU) has drafted a Preferred Literary Agent Agreement and a pamphlet, *Understand the Author-Agent Relationship*, which is available to members. (Membership is $74 and open to all writers actively pursuing a writing career. See "Professional Organizations" in the back of the book for their address.) The union suggests clauses that delineate such issues as:

- the scope of representation (One work? One work with the right of refusal on the next? All work completed in the coming year? All work completed until the agreement is terminated?)
- the extension of authority to the agent to negotiate on behalf of the author
- compensation for the agent, and any co-agent, if used
- manner and time frame for forwarding monies received by the agent on behalf of the client
- termination clause, allowing client to give about thirty days to terminate the agreement
- the effect of termination on concluded agreements as well as ongoing negotiations
- arbitration in the event of a dispute between agent and client

If things don't work out

Because this is a business relationship, a time may come when it is beneficial for you and your agent to part ways. Unlike a marriage, you don't need to go through counseling to keep the relationship together. Instead, you end it professionally on terms upon which you both agree.

First check to see if your written agreement spells out any specific procedures. If not, write a brief, businesslike letter, stating that you no longer think the relationship is advantageous and you wish to terminate it. Instruct the agent not to make any new submissions and give her a thirty- to sixty-day limit to continue as representative on submissions already under consideration. You can ask for a list of all publishers who have rejected your unsold work, as well as a list of those who are currently considering it. If your agent charges for office expenses, you will have to reimburse him upon terminating the contract. For this reason, you may want to ask for a cap on expenses when you originally enter into an agency agreement. If your agent has made sales for you, he will continue to receive those monies from the publisher, deduct his commission and remit the balance to you. A statement and your share of the money should be sent to you within thirty days. You can also ask that all manuscripts in his possession be returned to you.

Final thoughts

Finding an agent is a challenge, but one may be necessary if you want a commercially successful book. Selecting an agent is a task which deserves a lot of time and careful consideration. Above all, it is important to find a person whom you trust and who believes in your work. Now that you know the steps to take to find a literary agent, get started on the right foot and select the right agent for you.

Seven Insider Techniques for Targeting Agents

I know many writers believe their submissions are routinely, even automatically, discarded by agents without being seriously considered. Based on my knowledge of the business, this isn't true. I am a busy literary agent with an active client list of more than fifty writers, yet I still consider everything that arrives in my office. In the first half of 2000, I had four important new sales from first-time writers we found in our slush pile—including our first e-mail query letter (See "Queries That Made It Happen" on page 31). Although it's true the overwhelming majority of submissions are returned with a form rejection, my agency is looking for books that excite us. When we find them, we pursue those authors vigorously.

How can you better your odds of finding an agent who will be excited about *your* book? By carefully targeting agents who are most likely to respond to your work and who have the special strengths to help your writing career realize it's full potential. Nothing is more important than the talent and accomplishment displayed in your book. Beyond that, however, you are trying to connect with one other human being, a professional who earns his living selling manuscripts. Since a lot of different choices are involved in finding an agent, I've written this article to show writers how to target agents.

PROVEN METHODS FOR FINDING REPRESENTATION

A fair amount of information is available on literary agents, including the listings in this book. By doing your homework—and you must do your homework—you improve your chances of finding a good agent. How can you best target an agent? Here are some recommendations:

1) Look for an agent who shares your interest

This step is obvious but fundamental. Target an agent who actively sells the kind of book you are writing. Read the listings in this book carefully. Don't send a novel to an agent who specializes in nonfiction. Don't send a memoir to an agent who never represents them. Thoughtfully consider the information you read. For example, an agent who has sold a children's book for a celebrity author is not necessarily a children's book agent. Instead, that agent may only represent celebrities. Sometimes there are subtleties to consider. If you've written a Civil War novel, does the agent of the top-selling Civil War novelist really make the best match for you? There's a good chance that agent won't be interested because he needs to concentrate on his top writer in this particular microniche. Nevertheless, finding an agent who represents the type of material you write is a crucial step in the querying process.

If you are querying one of the larger agencies which has multiple member agents, you may need to call first and ask "which agent represents such and such." Hopefully, you'll get a name in this fashion. If whoever answers the phone isn't willing to divulge any information, that may be a sign indicating the agency isn't interested in unsolicited work.

ETHAN ELLENBERG *has headed his own agency for sixteen years. His agency sells more than 100 new titles per year and has a special interest in commercial and literary fiction. Prior to founding his own agency, he was Contracts Manager of Berkley/Jove and Associate Contracts Manager at Bantam.*

If an agent doesn't list or even have a specialty, search for some of his actual sales to see if he is a match for your work. Besides the *Guide to Literary Agents*, there are a number of directories of literary agents you can consult, including the *Literary Market Place* (R.R. Bowker) or *Literary Agents: A Writer's Introduction*, by John Baker (MacMillian). Websites can also help you find more information about agents, and a lot of agents have their own websites. If other elements of the agent's profile suit you besides his specialties, try sending him a query letter. Read below to learn how to interpret the other elements to see if the agent is a good match for you.

2) Check the number of years the agent has been in publishing

An agent's business experience can be an important indicator of a number of things. You have to use your judgment here to decide what level of experience is best for you. A long-established agent may have great cachet but may be taking on few new clients, if any. Someone just entering the business may be hungry for clients but may lack contacts, experience, and knowledge. Our industry has been plagued with a number of fraudulent agents, so you have to be doubly careful of an agent's qualifications.

Get a feel for where this agent is in her career. Can you locate news of recent sales and new clients? Is the agency's listing welcoming? Are there new member agents who might be looking for new clients? Does the agent write articles for writing magazines or attend writers' conferences? Such attendance and article writing are also indicators that an agent is working full-time at building her agency and selling books. I think membership in writers' organizations (e.g., Mystery Writers of America, Romance Writers of America, Novelist, Inc., etc.) are important indicators of an agent's commitment to her job. Membership in the Association of Authors' Representatives, a trade association that has an ethics code, is also significant. (For more information about the AAR, see "Agents & Ethics: Getting Published Without Losing Your Shirt" on page 13.) All of these are small but important indicators of who you are really contacting.

3) Find out how the agent practices business

The ways an agent does business can indicate whether or not he is someone with whom you want to work. How does the agent handle some of the important fundamentals of the author/agent relationship? For example, are there any fees? How soon will your book be offered for sale and to how many houses? Often the answers to these two questions are related. As I said previously, our business has had a problem with fraudulent agents. These are agents who have no real intention of selling your books, and instead live on "reading," "marketing," or "editing" fees. I charge none of these fees; I never have. I don't believe they are legitimate. If you have to pay an agent, I take this as a bad sign—period. An agent who charges fees and refuses to share information about the editors who are reading your books is also someone to sidestep. I would avoid agents who request payment up front. They'll get paid—when they sell your book.

Find out if the agent offers a contract. I offer one to all clients—a simple agreement that spells out our mutual rights and obligations. I think it's wise to enter into an agency agreement with a written contract so you know where you stand legally. Written documents often reveal a person's sense of fair play. For instance, I offer contracts as short as six months. If I can't sell your book by then, you have the option of terminating the agreement and finding another agent. My contract also obligates me to pay all monies received promptly, no later than ten days after receipt. These are just examples of what I consider important indicators of fair play. All the good agencies follow these practices, and I've seen similar provisions in their agreements.

4) Research any additional strengths of the agency

Ascertain what a particular agency's strengths are, and decide whether their strengths fit your specific needs. For instance, some agents consider themselves editorial-oriented agents; they like to work with authors to improve their writing and direct their careers. Others see themselves as sales people—people who will find the deal. Such agents will maximize an opportunity for a writer but aren't particularly interested in starting someone out. I put a great deal of emphasis on my editorial skills; I like coaching storytellers and believe it's been a key to my success.

If you have started to establish your career or you believe you have a "big book," you may want to find an agency with a strong subsidiary rights department. By subsidiary rights, I mean the rights that are sold in addition to the book—e.g., movie rights, audio rights, and translations in foreign countries. (For more information, see "Subsidiary Rights: Much More Than a Book" on page 45.)

If you feel you need a lot of personal attention, you may want to target agents with small lists or agents who convey a desire to concentrate on only a few people. Perhaps you believe your book especially needs promotion. If so, you may want to try to locate an agent whose background is in sales or publicity.

5) Verify the agent's ability to make sales

Another fundamental indicator of an agent's experience is the actual sales the agent has made to publishers. When choosing agents to query, take a serious appraisal of the sales they list. Are the sales to major publishers? Agents who are only selling to e-publishers or to small, unknown publishers may not be actively selling books. Are all the sales for one or two clients or a range of clients? If a single client dominates all the sales information you have, the agent may not be selling work by a lot of new talent.

Look at the listings in this book to determine how many sales are for brand-new clients. This number can be an important indicator of whether or not an agent is interested in receiving query letters. Quantity is a factor as well. An agent who only lists one or two sales may not be active or successful. At my agency, we're making more than a hundred sales a year, including books, audio, movie, etc. It is not a challenge to list six or seven recent book sales for established or new clients. All of the good agencies I know could easily provide similar credits. Some agents will not list recent sales to protect the confidentiality of their clients. This practice is acceptable; however, an agent should share names of clients with you if she agrees to represent you.

6) Make sure the agent has a vision for your book

If the agent wants to represent your book, does she have a game plan? A lot of exact marketing plans will come later, but I rarely accept a book without considering which editors I can send it to and the number of truly viable submissions I can make. There's no reason why an agent should say, "Never mind about a plan, I like your book." This is your business—you don't want a fan; you want a business representative.

Another compelling factor is speed. Does the agent feel your book is ready to go? Is she ready to put it on sale? Is she willing to submit the book to multiple publishers or does she insist on sending it to one house at a time? We often hear from writers who claim their current agent has only made three submissions in two years. This behavior would not be acceptable to me.

7) Look for an agent who is responsive and committed to your work

This quality comes into play once you've begun to actively approach agents. Whatever an agent's reputation or credentials, you should be most concerned with how this agent is going to treat you. When you solicit an agent, how long does it take for him to get back to you? A quick response is usually a sign the agent is excited about your work. It also means this agent has hours available to work for you. How personal and intelligent is the response? Is the agent really focused on your work? Does he have a thorough understanding of your manuscript? Is the agent willing to answer your questions and spend a reasonable amount of time with you over the phone? The answers to these questions are also indicators of the agent's availability and commitment.

Publishing is a tough business, and an agent's personal commitment to you and your work is often the only thing you have going for you early on in your relationship. An agent must believe in the book and in you. If he doesn't, it's likely he'll lose heart after a few rejected submissions.

One thing that always strikes me is the huge gulf of knowledge between author and agent. This gulf is natural since one is a specialist, immersed in the business, and the other is a new-comer entering the business as "talent," not as a business person. Being a doctor, lawyer, or entrepreneur doesn't give you a knowledge of publishing. You need to ask questions, however "obvious." If your agent doesn't comfortably answer them, claims to be too busy, or says the question isn't important, that agent may not be willing to do the hard work necessary to maintain the relationship. You may want to consider finding an agent who is able to give you more time.

All of these small, important facts can help determine your search.

A PLAN FOR SENDING QUERY LETTERS

If you follow this basic course of action for targeting agents appropriate for your work, you will soon have a number of names of agents who fit these criteria in one way or another. Prior to the submission process, how should you proceed?

I recommend you organize your list by the standards listed above and start at the top with the agents you would most want to have regardless of the "odds." It's hard for a writer to know the value of his work, so there's no need to undersell yourself. Choose the top ten agents who you think have the skills, reputation, and track record to successfully market your book. Don't assume they are too busy for you or that your book isn't good enough. Approach these top ten following the protocols they ask for. If one or more of them is interested in you, and you're impressed with their willingness to work with you, you've found a great opportunity.

If your book is rejected by this first ten, analyze what might have gone wrong. Did you get any personal responses, or were the only responses form letters? If you did get a personal response, incorporate what you may have learned in your next batch of submissions. Reread your work, your introductory letter, and consider the whole package of material you are sending. If you are happy with it, it's simply time to try again.

Reconsider your list of targets. If you think you were rejected because you simply approached agents who were too busy, then construct your next list from people who have smaller client loads and fewer years in the business. Let's say your first list included only agents with fifty or more clients, who've been in business ten years or more. Now maybe it's time to consider agents who have twenty to thirty clients and who've been in the business three to seven years. You may also want to try an agent with a strong professional background, for example, someone who was a successful book editor and has just begun his agenting business. Continue this process until you've landed an agent or until you realize it may be premature to look for one.

Keep in mind, however, that a bad agent is worse than no agent at all. These are my thoughts on what makes a bad agent.

First, you should never pay a reading fee, marketing fee, or any other kind of fee to a literary agent. You should only pay the direct cost of office expenses or the expenses to market your book when you sign with an agent who will actively market it. You should never work with an agent who directs you to a vanity press or to an editor who charges to "fix" your book. It's true there are situations where this is a legitimate practice—some professional editors can make a huge difference, and these people do charge. Unfortunately, the potential for abuse in this situation has forced me to warn against this practice unless you are certain you know exactly what you're getting into. Finally, make certain you and the agent agree on exactly how many submissions and to whom they are going, and in what length of time. An agent who makes no submissions and performs no work is much worse than no agent at all.

At the beginning of this article, I sounded an optimistic note. Agents need good writers. Many agents are still growing their businesses, and many agents treasure the joy of discovering a new talent, as I do. Even though it's a long, arduous process, with the right targeting and the right manuscript, you can find the agent who will help you. Good luck in your search.

The Basics of Contacting Literary Agents

Once you and your manuscript are thoroughly prepared, the time is right to contact an agent. Finding an agent can often be as difficult as finding a publisher. Nevertheless, there are four ways to maximize your chances of finding the right agent: obtain a referral from someone who knows the agent; meet the agent in person at a writers' conference; submit a query letter or proposal; or attract the agent's attention with your own published writing.

Referrals

The best way to get your foot in an agent's door is to be referred by one of his clients, an editor, or another agent he has worked with in the past. Because an agent trusts his clients, he will usually read referred work before over-the-transom submissions. If you are friends with anyone in the publishing business who has connections with agents, ask politely for a referral. However, don't be offended if another writer will not share the name of his agent.

If you don't have a wide network of publishing professionals, use the resources you do have to get an agent's attention.

Writers' Conferences

Going to a conference is your best bet for meeting an agent in person. Many conferences invite agents to either give a speech or simply be available for meetings with authors. And agents view conferences as a way to find writers. Often agents set aside time for one-to-one discussions with writers, and occasionally they may even look at material writers bring to the conference. If an agent is impressed with you and your work, she may ask for writing samples after the conference. When you send her your query, be sure to mention the specific conference where you met and that she asked to see your work.

Because this is an effective way to connect with agents, we've asked agents to indicate in their listings which conferences they regularly attend. We've also included a section of **Writers' Conferences**, starting on page 330, where you can find out more information about a particular conference, as well as an agent's availability at a specific conference.

Submissions

The most common way to contact an agent is by a query letter or a proposal package. Most agents will accept unsolicited queries. Some will also look at outlines and sample chapters. Almost none want unsolicited complete manuscripts. Check the **How to Contact** subhead in each listing to learn exactly how an agent prefers to be solicited. Never call—let the writing in your query letter speak for itself.

Because a query letter is your first impression on an agent, it should be professional and to the point. As a brief introduction to your manuscript, a query letter should only be one page in length, or at maximum, two pages.

- The first paragraph should quickly state your purpose—you want representation.
- In the second paragraph, mention why you have specifically chosen to query him. Perhaps he specializes in your areas of interest or represents authors you admire. Show him you have done your homework.
- In the next paragraph or two, describe the project, the proposed audience, why your book will sell, etc. Be sure to mention the approximate length and any special features.

- Then, discuss why you are the perfect person to write this book, listing your professional credentials, speaking experience, or relevant expertise.
- Close your query with an offer to send either an outline, sample chapters, or the complete manuscript—depending on your type of book.

For examples of actual query letters that led authors straight to publication, see "Queries That Made It Happen" on page 31. For helpful hints on outlines and synopses, see "Commanding Book Proposals: The Rejection Slip's Greatest Enemy" on page 37.

Agents agree to be listed in directories such as the *Guide to Literary Agents* to indicate to writers what they want to see and how they wish to receive submissions. As you start to query agents, make sure you follow their individual submission directions. This, too, shows an agent you've done your research. Some agents ask for an outline or sample chapters, but you should send these only if you are requested to do so. Under the **How to Contact** subhead, agents also indicate if they are open to fax or e-mail query letters. Due to the volume of material agents receive, it may take a long time to receive a reply. You may want to query several agents at a time; agents also indicate in their listings if they consider simultaneous queries and submissions. If an agent requests a manuscript, make sure you provide sufficient postage for its return.

Like publishers, agencies have specialties. Some are only interested in novel-length works. Others are open to a wide variety of subjects and may actually have member agents within the agency who specialize in only a handful of the topics covered by the entire agency.

Before querying any agent, first consult the Agent Specialties Indexes in this book for your manuscript's subject, and identify those agents who handle what you write. Then, read the agents' listings to see if they are appropriate for you and for your work. For more information on targeting your submissions see "How to Find the Right Agent" on page 20 and "Seven Insider Techniques for Targeting Agents" on page 25.

Publishing credits

Some agents read magazines or journals to find writers to represent. If you have had an outstanding piece published in a periodical, you may be contacted by an agent wishing to represent you. In such cases, *make sure the agent has read your work*. Some agents send form letters to writers, and such agents often make their living entirely from charging reading fees, not from commissions on sales.

However, many reputable and respected agents do contact potential clients in this way. For them, you already posses attributes of a good client: you have publishing credits and an editor has validated your work. To receive a letter from a reputable agent who has read your material and wants to represent you is an honor.

Occasionally, writers who have self-published or who have had their work published electronically, may attract an agent's attention, especially if the self-published book has sold well or received a lot of positive reviews.

Recently, writers have been posting their work on the Internet in hope of attracting an agent's eye. With all the submissions most agents receive, they likely have little time to peruse writers' websites. Nevertheless, there are agents who do consider the Internet a resource for finding fresh voices. Only the future will show how often writers are discovered through this medium.

Queries That Made It Happen

BY TERRI SEE

Imagine you are on the subway—you and hundreds of others, jostling past each other in your usual routines. You pass through a sea of faces, varied but unremarkable. Then, a certain someone brushes by with just the right "excuse me" or "hello," and, inexplicably, your heart leaps. You're embarrassed to find yourself staring, craning your neck in order not to lose sight of this person. Something caught your attention, snapped you out of your lull, and you're not quite sure what happened. But it's of no matter right now. You're hooked, and you want to know more about that person.

If only your query letter could make such a stunning first impression! But catching an agent's attention is a matter of planning and calculation, rather than chemistry. And your letter has only one to two minutes to hook the agent's attention. Of the countless letters that cross an agent's desk, yours needs to enticingly say "Pick Me!" and not because of an interesting stamp on the envelope. In order to stand out above the competition, you need to know what agents want, what they crave. And you need to give it to them clearly and cleanly.

What agents want is actually quite simple: a succinct letter that tells who you are, what your book is about, and, briefly, why you are qualified to write it. Be specific, concise, and avoid being arrogant *or* self-effacing. Why you do or do not deserve to be published or how your book will make millions has no place in a query. An interesting letter will go far to showcase your writing talent. Style is important, but in this short space, clarity is key. Make your synopsis intriguing but rounded. You don't want to leave the agent thinking, *"What?"* Also, mention whether or not you have been published before. Contrary to common perception, publishing credits can work to your advantage either way. Some agents do prefer to work with previously published writers, but many others look specifically for first-time authors.

Overall, bear in mind that your query letter is a representation of you and, therefore, it needs to appear as professional as possible. Don't hand write your letter or use distracting, flashy stationery. Be certain you have the agent's name spelled properly (Terri or Terry? Mr. or Ms.?), and take extra care to ensure your punctuation and grammar are correct. These details matter as much as your letter's content and will illustrate how thorough and polished you are—or are not.

Following are the actual queries of two writers who found representation and whose agents have sold their books. The authors discuss how they selected their agents as well as the snags and surprises in their query processes, and they share some Do's and Don'ts they learned on the path to publication. Their agents, in turn, tell us what made the letters stand out and what they found appealing about these particular authors. Let the details of Rainelle Burton's or Marcus Wynne's experiences inspire you to write your own tempting query letter and soon you, too, may have an agent asking for more.

TERRI SEE *is an editor for Writer's Digest Books. She also edits and publishes* Greeting Card Writer *magazine online (www.GreetingCardWriter.com) and is Co-founder of CardReps.com, an agency representing freelance greeting card writers and artists.*

RAINELLE BURTON

Rainelle Burton took a somewhat winding path to get her book, *The Root Worker*, published. To begin with, her initial query was not to an agent, but instead she directly contacted an editor she met at an Oakland University writers' conference. She pitched her book to Bantam, and it resulted in a round of letters with a very encouraging editor. The editor made remarks, asked for changes, and Burton made the changes. They went back and forth for some time. But, at a point, life got in the way. In the middle of correspondence with Bantam, Burton suffered from a serious depression that lasted two years. During that time, she dropped all work on the book.

Burton eventually left her home and all its belongings to save her son from street gangs in Detroit. Finding a new home in a small town and a place to come back to other work, she eventually reacquainted herself with the desire to find a publisher for her book. "When I was trying to put my life back together, the editor was the first person I called. But she was gone," says Burton. "She had left Bantam, and they couldn't tell me where she went. I was back at square one." Determined to move forward, she looked up a friend who had contacts at Houghton Mifflin. He asked Burton what her agent had to say about her situation. "I said, 'I don't have an agent,' and he looked at me like I was crazy. He told me that having a publisher interested in taking on my book should get me my pick of an agent. 'Okay,' I thought, 'I didn't know that. I'll get an agent.' " Then, another turn in the road: "I picked up the book, after all this time had gone by, and said 'Whoa, this needs some work.' In some ways, my depression was clarifying."

Burton worked on revisions to the book for some time, then put it down for several months and picked it up again to see how it would read. Finally, when she felt the time was right, she looked for an agent. "I did a lot of reading in *Guide to Literary Agents, Writer's Market* and *Writer's Digest Magazine*, listened to agents at conferences—their Do's and Don'ts—and got all the information I could. I looked at listings of agents and made lists of the agents who took fiction, then I looked at the interests of those agents. I queried about thirty agents."

Burton received several letters requesting to see her manuscript. Amanda Materne with James Levine Communications, however, *called* her, and that more personal effort made a difference. Burton held off on responding to the other requests for her manuscript because it seemed the right thing to do. Even though James Levine Communications handles only two percent fiction, Burton says, "When I read the company's short biography and learned their interests, I thought my book was a possible fit." Upon request she sent Materne the other chapters. Burton was excited to hear from her again. "She said, 'Can you send the whole manuscript?' Then she asked if I would be interested in her representing me, and I said, 'Hell, yes!' " As a happy result, *The Root Worker* will be published in the spring of 2001 with The Overlook Press.

While Burton does not consider herself a highly organized person, she does believe strong organizational skills have played a helpful role in her career, first as a technical writer and freelance editor, and now as a published novelist. In the search for an agent, good record-keeping is vital. "List the agents you sent manuscripts to," advises Burton. "List when you sent them, including the dates and their responses. You need to log these things so that you do not appear confused when you're dealing with an agent."

Although Burton did not get her query format from a book, she knew through her research what the letter should include. "It has to be polite and to the point," she explains. "It should draw the agent's attention and express appreciation for the agent's consideration. Say what you need to say up front and never mind all that other stuff. Make your book sell without being overly pushy or tooting your own horn. Don't tell an agent, 'You'll regret it if you don't get this

Rainelle Burton
1702 Query Lane
Writers Town, MI 48111
(626) 555-1234

August 30, 1998

Amanda Materne
James Levine Communications
307 Seventh Avenue, Suite 1906
New York, NY 10001

The letter didn't have ridiculous mistakes such as spelling or grammatical errors, or being addressed to the wrong person.

Dear Amanda Materne:

Thank you in advance for taking the time to consider representing *The Root Worker*, my recently completed first novel.

The Root Worker, set in the 1960s, is based on the real life lower east side Detroit community that I grew up in, where root working—an urban African-American derivative of West African voodoo—is not only practiced, but controls the lives and relationships of its people. The story chronicles the tension and despair of a family and community that is bred, perpetuated, and exploited by one woman, the Root Worker. It explores the conflicts and similarities between the precepts of Catholicism and paganism, and their existence in a larger community that embraces traditional African-American religion.

This letter does not come off as pompous. Instead, the letter makes you want to read the actual novel.

The Root Worker also gives a view of the phenomena and effect of the urban flight of the 1960s, and the mass exodus of Catholic institutions in Detroit from the perspectives of those who remained behind.

Thank you again for your consideration. I look forward to hearing from you.

Sincerely,

Rainelle Burton

Writers need to have their query letters pretty spotless if they want an agent or publisher to consider their work. If you're careless with the query letter, it isn't the best "preview" of your writing ability. You want to have as much as you possibly can going your way when your piece is pulled from the stacks.

Comments provided by Amanda Materne

book!' And skip the fancy paper with all the squiggles. They'll be suspicious of your writing. A good synopsis will help, too."

When asked if she encountered any surprises in the process, Burton says, "The biggest surprise I had was finding that both the agent and the editor were approachable. From my reading, I thought they would be these people who sit up in the sky and pass judgment on you. And that you should not call an agent or an editor, and you must ask permission to speak. Not so! They are warm, genuine, and very human. I was able to ask questions."

Burton's advice in dealing with agents is to "be patient because the process takes time, and once your manuscript is out there, it's out there. You can't pull it back."

MARCUS WYNNE

Marcus Wynne has been a paratrooper, diplomatic bodyguard, close combat and counter-terrorism instructor, and emergency medical technician. He's traveled to more than fifty countries, many of them listed in *The World's Most Dangerous Places* (Harper Resource), coordinated embassy evacuations in Haiti during the 1991 coup, led a counter-terrorist Federal Air Marshall unit during the Gulf War, and was invited to South Africa to train Nelson Mandela's bodyguards. And if that were not dangerous enough, Wynne decided to dive into writing a novel.

Wynne has made a living as a freelance magazine journalist since 1983, writing articles on everything from psychology to military affairs, as well as crossing over to plays and industrial films. He credits this experience as a great leg up in getting his book out. "I was used to writing as a business, and I didn't bog myself down with the preciousness and naivete of the 'artistic' writer. I was used to writing for money and working as a writer in the business sense, and I'm one of the few freelancers who makes a decent living freelancing in journalism. I think anyone who expects to succeed at writing books has to separate the creative function from the business function, which includes marketing, public relations, and promotion. You need to learn to be your own best advocate because until you sell as many books as Tom Clancy, most publishers won't be." With this attitude in mind, Wynne was able to see the process of querying an agent purely as a business matter.

As was necessary in many of his other adventures, Wynne approached getting *Off the Reservation* published with careful, methodical preparation. Part of his caution was a result of a prior experience with an agent. As it happens, *Off the Reservation* is his second novel, and Ethan Ellenberg of the Ethan Ellenberg Literary Agency is his second agent. Wynne wrote a first novel, *Air Marshalls*, based on his experience in the Gulf War. His first agent had the book for a year and a half, and in that time only sent the book to three editors. Of those three editors, one wanted to publish it but held it for six months and eventually decided to pass on it. The second publisher did not want *Air Marshalls* but offered Wynne a nonfiction book contract, and the third publisher simply passed on it. "Knowing what I know now about the publishing industry, those are good signs," Wynne says. "But the agent told me that I should shelf it after just three rejections. I later discovered he sent out my manuscript without a cover letter. After that I decided it was best for us to part ways, and by then I was kind of discouraged with the book, so I shelved it. Then I immediately went to work on my second book, *Off the Reservation*."

Later, this seeming failure actually helped Wynne make a valuable connection. Before the offer of representation by his first agent, Wynne had done a mass query mailing. "Out of that huge mailing, I got a few responses, a whole lot of rejections, and a couple of nice letters," he says. One of the positive letters he received was from Ethan Ellenberg. Ellenberg, he says, looked at the book and said it needed more work than he was willing to put in to it. But he also indicated that when he had another manuscript, he would be interested in looking at it. This

Marcus Wynne
48 Published Way
Authorville, FL 54210
(989)555-4953

April 8, 1999

Mr. Ethan Ellenberg
549 Broadway
Suite 5E
New York, NY 10012

Dear Mr. Ellenberg:

My name is Marcus Wynne. I'm a novelist seeking representation for the enclosed psychological thriller. Last year you looked at my previous novel manuscript, *Air Marshalls*. While the book wasn't for you, you offered me some useful feedback and extended an invitation to send any new work to you. I've enclosed the first 100 pages of my new novel, *Off the Reservation*.

Marcus's letter is very focused—it has a lot of passion and self-awareness.

This book: The technical accuracy and thinly fictionalized real-world accounts of Richard Marcinko or Tom Clancy; the psychological insights of Thomas Harris; the narrative drive of John Sandford or Stephen Hunter. There's darkness, sex, and violence in it, interesting characters, and some great dialogue. There's also a lot of hidden truth in it—enough to worry some highly placed people in the special operations world.

He knew what he had written and felt strongly that it was a good book. That confidence appealed to me.

Me: Writer/consultant with a gun-toting past. Been publishing nonfiction nationally since 1983. This is my second novel. The first one (unpublished) is on the shelf where I won't trip over the training wheels.

I've enclosed an SASE for your reply. Return of the material is not necessary. Thanks for taking a look. I look forward to hearing from you soon.

Cheers,

I liked everything about the book. It is very well written and has a page-turning quality that will always be the hallmark of the thriller. It's fresh, it's different. There are appealing elements to the villain, similar to what Thomas Harris does with Hannibal Lechter. Discovering a great read and a great writer remains job number one for any agent serious about fiction, as I am.

Marcus Wynne

Comments provided by Ethan Ellenberg

brief note would make a difference later when Ellenberg's name again popped up in Wynne's agent search.

For *Off the Reservation*, Wynne began his precision campaign for an agent by closely reading *Guide to Literary Agents* and other sources. Next, he scanned bookstore shelves for books in genres similar to his and made note of the agents and editors mentioned in the authors' acknowledgements. Then he condensed this information into a short list and used Agent Research and Evaluation (www.agentresearch.com) to obtain a detailed breakdown of these agents and the names of their clients.

"Then I crafted individualized letters," Wynne explains. "I geared them toward each agent's particular area of interest. Out of my ten initial queries, I received seven requests to see the manuscript. Of those, I got solid offers for representation from three, including Ethan Ellenberg." Wynne called and interviewed all three agents, after first deciding what qualities he wanted in an agent. He recommends to writers, "Ask yourself if you are willing to trust your career to this person? If so, why? First impressions are important, but they're not always the answer. Ask hard questions, and be specific about what you expect. And listen carefully to how the agent treats you. If he is condescending or brusque, ask yourself if you are willing to put up with that behavior? Or ask if he treats you like a professional. Because that's what we all want to be, right?"

After interviewing the offers for representation, Wynne decided to go with Ellenberg because he owns a smaller but highly regarded agency, offering personal attention. "He took the time to explain how things worked and what to expect," Wynne says, "so I was quite comfortable and felt I could trust him." Wynne was surprised to find an agent willing to do business on a handshake. "He basically recognized my hesitation borne of inexperience in the publishing world and said we could enter a written agreement or go on a verbal agreement and see how it went. While I might not recommend that approach for everyone, I was comfortable with it. Also, he let me be an active participant when I needed to be." Wynne further compliments Ellenberg's professionalism, saying he tirelessly pushes a book until there is a buyer. "That's what an agent needs to do—find the one editor who believes in your book." And Ellenberg found that editor at Tor/Forge.

Looking back on his query letter, Wynne feels, "It was written to get Ellenberg's attention. It was a subject matter he knew, and it was short, sweet, sexy, and to the point." He feels his self-promotion in the letter was not only appropriate, but in this case, very helpful. "Having a marketable and promotable background that lends real authenticity to the work really helps, and anyone with a sense of publicity and promotion will sit up and notice. And I had to learn to push that aspect to the front, instead of being modest about it."

But, Wynne says, behind a good query letter needs to be a clear understanding of an agent's job. He explains, "Don't mistake the desire for an objective evaluation of your work with needing an agent. An agent's job is to sell your work. They may help you shape your manuscript and so on but only after they recognize they can sell it. You need to have your craft down, and you need to be writing up to your own personal best. Learning how to edit my own writing and really working at my fiction gave me confidence—as did a carefully chosen cadre of readers."

Commanding Book Proposals: The Rejection Slip's Greatest Enemy

BY DON PRUES

Many writers attempting to find an agent to represent their books perceive themselves to be a diminutive David staring down a monstrous Goliath. Even worse, they think no weapon exists to slay the giant and prove their book is worth publishing. Such folks are wrong. An effective weapon does exist: It's called a book proposal. The hitch, however, is that writers must build this weapon themselves.

And therein lies the problem: Most writers don't know which materials to use nor how to put the pieces together to stand a fighting chance. That's where this article comes in. We'll show you what you need to include in your proposal and how to assemble it, ultimately equipping you with the necessary weaponry to conquer even the most colossal rejection pile.

Before we get into the specifics about composing and organizing your proposal, we need to get one fact out of the way: The proposal you create depends upon what the agent wants. And the most nonintrusive way to know what she wants is to consult her listing in this book, and follow the submission specifications to a tee. Do nothing more, nothing less. Remember, you must play by each agent's rules if you want that agent to represent you.

THE NOVEL PROPOSAL

The golden rule in publishing fiction is your novel must be completed before you solicit an agent. Will you be permitted to send your entire novel upon initial contact? Probably not. Unsolicited manuscripts are ignored, returned, and sometimes even thrown away when sent to an agent who does not accept them. That's the catch with fiction: You need to have your novel finished before soliciting an agent, but rarely are you allowed to send the complete manuscript. Don't waste your time, energy, paper, and postage sending material to an agent who doesn't care about it.

Many agents prefer first to receive a one-page query letter, and only ask for the proposal or the manuscript after having their interests piqued by the query letter. Check the agent's listing to see what she accepts—rarely will it be a complete manuscript, but often it will be a novel proposal.

Novel proposals are easy to put together. You can anticipate sending a cover letter, a synopsis, three consecutive sample chapters (almost always your first three chapters) or the first fifty pages, possibly an author biography, and an endorsements page. These are by far the most important—and most requested—parts of your proposal. Some agents require only a cover letter and three sample chapters because, with fiction, the writing itself (your sample chapters) matters most. Again, what you send is determined by what the agent demands.

DON PRUES, *former editor of* Guide to Literary Agents, *now freelance writes and edits from home. He is managing editor for three websites (critics.com, kids-in-mind.com, and mediascreen.com). With Jack Neff, he co-authored* Formatting and Submitting Your Manuscript *(Writer's Digest Books).*

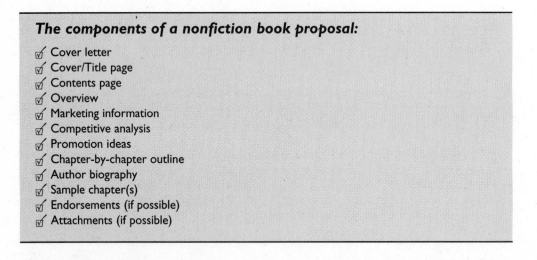

The components of a novel proposal:

- ☑ Cover letter
- ☑ Cover/Title page
- ☑ Contents page
- ☑ Synopsis
- ☑ Chapter-by-chapter outline (rarely requested, see below)
- ☑ Author biography
- ☑ First three sample chapters (or about fifty pages)
- ☑ Endorsements (if possible, see below)

THE NONFICTION BOOK PROPOSAL

Although you can still showcase your writing style with a nonfiction proposal, the *concept* of your book is much more important than the writing itself. Strong prose can only help your proposal, of course, but the agent's decision to represent you will rest with your book's commercial viability. Unlike fiction, you do not need to have your nonfiction book completed before soliciting an agent. But there's still a lot of work to be done when creating a nonfiction proposal.

Compared to novel proposals, nonfiction book proposals are complicated pitches that must contain a variety of elements—an overview, a marketing section, a competition section, a promotions section, a chapter-by-chapter outline, an author biography, and attachments. With your nonfiction proposal, you can expect to send a big package with lots of individual parts that hover around your unique and salable concept.

The components of a nonfiction book proposal:

- ☑ Cover letter
- ☑ Cover/Title page
- ☑ Contents page
- ☑ Overview
- ☑ Marketing information
- ☑ Competitive analysis
- ☑ Promotion ideas
- ☑ Chapter-by-chapter outline
- ☑ Author biography
- ☑ Sample chapter(s)
- ☑ Endorsements (if possible)
- ☑ Attachments (if possible)

THE COMPONENTS
Cover letters (for novel and nonfiction proposals)

The type of cover letter you compose depends on whether you're sending a blind ("unsolicited") proposal or a requested ("solicited") proposal.

If the agent accepts or even prefers a blind proposal upon initial contact (instead of a query letter), you'll need to tailor a sharp cover letter to hook the agent and encourage her to dive eagerly into the rest of your proposal. A cover letter accompanying a blind proposal submission is like a tightened version of a query letter (for more on queries, see "Queries That Made It

The basics of a cover letter

A good rule of thumb is to keep your cover letter to one page, containing three or four short paragraphs organized in the following order:

1. **The introductory paragraph.** State the book's title, and then spend two to five sentences hooking the agent with a brief description of your book and why it will sell.
2. **The biographical paragraph.** In one or two sentences explain a bit about yourself, including only information that's pertinent to the book, such as previous publishing credits or why you're sending it to this particular agency.
3. **The concluding paragraph.** Politely close the letter.

Happen" on page 31). Similar to the query letter, your cover letter lets the agent know who you are *and* what you have to offer. You don't need to spend much time arguing that your proposal is worthwhile because what you have to offer (the proposal) is actually enclosed.

If you've already sent the agent a query letter and she has requested a full proposal, keep the cover letter short—just a paragraph or two will do. Simply let the agent know what material you've enclosed, and mention whether any other agents are considering the same proposal.

Cover/Title page (for novel and nonfiction proposals)

Although the title is but a small part of a large book, a telling and catchy title can be so important. The difference between an adequate title and a superb title can mean the difference between mediocre book sales and gargantuan ones. Think about some of the successful titles you know—most are under five words (excluding the subtitle) and emit something unique about the book. Titles are particularly important with nonfiction; make them convey and convince.

For both nonfiction and fiction proposals, the cover page, or "title page," follows your cover letter. When formatting the cover page, be sure to put the book's title in all caps about a third of the way down the page. Include your contact information (name, address, phone number, fax, e-mail) with the date in the bottom right corner. Put the word count in the top right corner.

Table of contents (for novel and nonfiction proposals)

Your contents page lets the agent know precisely what's in your proposal package, and lends order and organization to all the disparate proposal elements. Be sure to list every item you're sending and the corresponding page numbers in the order they appear in your proposal. You obviously need to make your contents page neat and easy on the eyes. It should be double spaced and organized according to its sections. The contents pages should *not* be numbered.

The synopsis (for novel proposals)

A synopsis is a brief, general overview of your novel, sometimes referred to as a "short summary." The goal of your synopsis is to tell what your novel is about without making the agent read the novel in its entirety. You need to supply key information about the primary elements in your novel (plot, theme, characters, setting), then show how all these aspects work together to make your novel worthy of publication. The trick with the synopsis, however, is doing all of the above quickly.

How quickly? Well, that depends on the person you're soliciting. There are no hard and fast rules about the synopsis—some agents look at it as a one-page sales pitch, while others expect it to be a comprehensive summary of the entire novel. Not surprisingly, there's conflicting advice about the typical length of a synopsis. Over the years I've contacted numerous agents to get their take on just how long it should be, and nearly all agents prefer a short synopsis that runs from one to two single-spaced pages, or three to five double-spaced pages. Because every novel is different—with its own number of important characters, plot twists, subplots, etc.— there is obviously some disagreement among agents about the specific length of a typical synopsis. Nevertheless, every agent agrees there's one truism about a synopsis: "The shorter, the better." That's why one to five pages is generally the preferred length for a novel synopsis.

That said, some plot-heavy fiction, such as thrillers and mysteries, might need more space, and can run from ten to twenty-five double-spaced pages, depending on the length of the manuscript and the number of plot shifts. If you do opt to compose a longer synopsis, aim for a length of 1 synopsis page for every 25 manuscript pages (a 250-page manuscript should get a 10-page synopsis), but attempt to keep it as short as possible.

A few other important aspects of your synopsis:

- Write in third person (even if your novel is written in first person).
- Write in present tense (even if your novel is written in past tense).
- Only focus on the essential parts of your story, and try not to include sections of dialogue unless you think they are absolutely necessary.
- Make your story seem complete. Keep events in the same order as they occur in the novel (but don't break them down into individual chapters), and be sure your synopsis has a beginning, a middle, and an ending. And yes, you *must* tell how the novel ends.

Overview (for nonfiction proposals)

The overview should be the power punch of your nonfiction proposal. It is the quick pitch that tells an agent whether the rest of the proposal is worth reading. Make sure you immediately state what your book is about, why it should be published, and why you're the perfect person to author it. Start with a perfect lead sentence that both sums up your book and makes the agent eager to read on (ideally, such a sentence will be enticing and encouraging without being gimmicky). Although the overview typically runs only a few pages (even up to ten), it must be persuasive and should highlight the book's key concepts. It should also touch upon marketing, competition, and author information.

Marketing analysis (for nonfiction proposals)

Although the concept of your book is important, the marketing section is arguably the most crucial part of any nonfiction book proposal. The goal of this section is to convince the agent your book is worth her time and that she'll make money from it. Prove to her why, how, and where your book will sell. Show you know the audience for your book, and give compelling reasons why this audience will buy the book.

Unlike other parts of your proposal, your marketing section has no length limits; it's important to spend as much time as you need to prove your book will sell. Don't ramble, of course, but don't hold back either. Do as much research as possible, and provide as many facts as you can.

Your marketing analysis section should cover two things: your book and its readers. Provide the agent answers to the following questions when writing this section:

- Who will buy this book? Can you describe the audience? How big is your readership base, and will it increase? What organizations do potential buyers belong to? Where do they shop? How do they spend their money? Will they spend money on your book?

- Are there any trends that might help sell your book? For example, if you're writing a cookbook, can you prove more people are cooking at home these days?
- In what other venues could your book be sold? Any specialty outlets? Are there seasons of the year during which the book could sell particularly well?
- What ideas do you have for the book that will increase its appeal to readers? Will it have sidebars, callouts, interviews, pictures, charts, or other special features? Keep in mind, though, that publishers have final say over any book's visual elements.

To learn where you can find solid facts for your marketing analysis, see the following sidebar: "Market Research: Four Tips To Prove You Have an Audience."

Market Research: Four Tips To Prove You Have an Audience

So how do you know how to provide an agent with specifics about your book's audience? Here are four researching tips to help you determine the market numbers for your book.

Magazines

One way to estimate how many people might buy your book is to research magazines related to your book's subject. To find such information, go to *Writer's Market* (Writer's Digest Books) or *SRDS* (Condé Nast Publications). Check both consumer and trade magazines for comprehensive information on advertising in print publications. Keep track of every magazine—and its circulation—related to your subject.

You might want to call each magazine's advertising department (the phone numbers are provided in the *SRDS* listings) and ask for an advertising packet, or "media kit"; most magazines should provide one. Such packets include advertising rates, circulation figures, and market research/demographic reports (i.e., age, sex, profession, income, hobbies, etc.) about the magazine's readers. Add up all the information you acquire, and organize the facts to convince an editor that there's a sizeable readership for your book.

Websites

A second, current method of finding people who will buy your book is through websites devoted to your subject. If a site looks particularly relevant to your book's subject, find out the site's usage numbers (how many people visit the site). Such figures shouldn't be too difficult to obtain—many sites openly offer such information. Usually the usage numbers fall under site headings such as "FAQs" (Frequently Asked Questions), "Advertisers Click Here," "Usage Information," "Demographics," "Marketing," or "Our Users." Try to gather these statistics for every website geared toward your readership, and use those numbers to show agents and publishers how many users might be interested in your book.

Competitors

Another necessary approach for gauging how many potential people could buy your book is to find sales figures for your closest competitors (for more on competition, see "Competitive Analysis" on page 42). To obtain general information on how well books in your subject are selling, check *The Bowker Annual Library and Book Trade Almanac: Facts, Figures, and Reports* (Bowker), which lists statistics about the number of books sold in various subjects. You should also examine the publisher's catalog, which sometimes highlights the number of titles sold. Moreover, you might be able to find information on your competition by searching *Publishers*

Weekly's website (www.publishersweekly.com), which publishes specific print run and sales figures for some books. The more you can find out about how well your competition does, the better chance you'll have of knowing (and letting an agent know) how well your book might do. It's also a good idea to check the competition's copyright page to find the number of editions the book has gone through. If a book's gone through several printings, you can be pretty sure it sells well.

Organizations

One final but viable plan to estimate the numbers of people who might buy your book is to research all organizations associated with your subject. There's an organization for almost everything these days, and no doubt your book will sell well if there's already a group of folks interested in your topic. So identify all organizations likely to have an interest in your subject, and then find out how many people belong to those organizations. Your library can help you acquire most of this information. One helpful starting point is the *Encyclopedia of Associations* (Gale Group). Also, most organizations have a website these days, many of which provide membership statistics and links to related sites.

Once you use the above procedures to tap into the potential number of people interested in your subject, clearly organize all the information to prove there's a sizeable target audience for your book. Statistical support goes a long way with agents and publishers. Providing evidence of a solid market for your book means one less hoop you'll have to jump through in convincing an agent to represent your work.

—Don Prues

Competitive analysis (for nonfiction proposals)

Your competitive analysis outlines why your book is outstanding in its field and why it should be published. In this section, you should size up the competition and prove your book has what others lack. The best way to do this is to mention books similar to yours, how well they sell, and why your book is superior. While the temptation exists to say your book is the only one of its kind, a lack of competition can actually hurt your cause. Agents need to show publishers that similar books have sold well.

Begin your analysis with an overview of the genre or category into which your book fits. Show how those titles are doing in general, then specify what books are selling the best. Next pick the top four or five competitors, analyze why those books have done well, and prove why your book is still needed to fill a category void. Are some of the books poorly organized, terribly written, or even outdated? Good. Mention any flaws you can find among your bestselling competitors, and then delineate how your book's sales could capitalize on their shortcomings.

Three ways to find information on your competition:

- Go to a large, well-stocked bookstore, look for competing titles, and discuss how those books are selling with bookstore employees.
- Do some research with the industry standard *Books in Print* (Bowker). The electronic version is available through many libraries (www.booksinprint.com/bip/). Notice the number of titles in print compared to the number of titles on the bookstore shelves. How can you ensure your book will be one of the ones that gets a prized shelf space?
- Search the online booksellers (www.amazon.com and www.barnesandnoble.com) to find competing titles and to see how well they are selling. Although you can't get actual sales figures from these sites, you do get to see where the competing titles rank among all other titles. You also get to read comments from readers, and see which other books and authors

are popular with readers who might buy your book. Reviews of the books might also help you identify shortcomings in your competition.

Promotion ideas (for nonfiction proposals)

The promotions section of your proposal is the place where you tell the agent what you can do to help sell your book. This part of the proposal is often overlooked by authors, but it's a great place for tossing out ideas about what you have to offer the publisher in addition to what's contained in the pages of your book. Tell if you are a promotable author. What makes you so promotable? Do you already have a loyal following? Do you have a website? Are you an awesome public speaker? Why will your book benefit from a tour? Do you have any contacts who could prove useful when promoting your book? Do you know of any special events or venues that would benefit from your presence (and help sell hundreds or even thousands of copies of your book)? Do you look good on television? Have you done radio interviews before? Do you have an interesting slide presentation? What other promotion ideas can you come up with? Any promotion you do for your book is called your "platform." Most publishers only consider books from nonfiction writers who have already established a platform. For more information on the importance of self-promotion, see the section, "Independent Publicists," starting on page 314.

Make this section brief but to the point. Don't hold back on your suggestions, and don't hesitate to prove you are willing to be your book's strongest salesperson.

Chapter-by-chapter outline

An outline describes each chapter as its own entity; the descriptions range from a few paragraphs to two pages per chapter. In short, you're expanding and specifying what you've generally written in either the synopsis (for fiction) or the overview (nonfiction).

Few agents want chapter-by-chapter outlines with fiction (most just request a cover letter, a short synopsis, and a few sample chapters). Therefore, you should never submit an outline for your novel proposal unless an agent specifically asks for it. Chapter-by-chapter outlines will be requested occasionally with genre fiction, which often has numerous plot shifts. When possible, limit the novel outline to one paragraph per chapter.

With nonfiction proposals, a chapter-by-chapter outline is essential. Providing a very thorough one lets the agent know precisely what your book covers and in how much detail.

Author biography (for novel and nonfiction proposals)

If you think aspects of your life are important and relevant to the salability of your book, then include an author biography. The goal of your author bio is to sell yourself in ways that complement the proposal. Don't include information that doesn't directly help the pitch. Do tell about your profession, particularly if it's pertinent to your book, and always highlight noteworthy publishing credits, if you have any. Try to keep the author bio to one page.

Endorsements page (for novel and nonfiction proposals)

An endorsements page is not essential, but having one can improve the salability of your manuscript. Your endorsements must come from noteworthy people, typically prominent industry insiders (well-known authors, agents, experts on the topic) who've read your manuscript and commented favorably on it. Unless you have contacts, though, it is difficult to obtain a quote from someone noteworthy. But don't fret if your proposal doesn't have an endorsements page—few authors include one.

Attachments (for nonfiction proposal)

You might wish to send some attachments with your proposal. These include any radio, television, magazine, newspaper, or electronic mentions on your topic. Your goal with sending attachments is to show tangible proof that people are interested in your book's topic. Even feel free to supply copies of scholarly research articles conducted on your subject. In short, attach anything that helps prove your book matters. Be sensible, though, by making sure your attachments come from reputable sources and by supplying proper documentation for everything you send. Like endorsements, attachments aren't necessary; they simply help your cause—convincing the agent to represent you.

Sending a reply postcard (for novel and nonfiction proposals)

If you're a bit paranoid about whether or not your material actually makes it to the agent or publisher, you may send a reply postcard with your proposal package. Having it signed by the agent or someone on the staff and sent back to you will alleviate any worries that the package didn't make it to its destination. Two caveats: 1). Not all agents are gracious enough to send your reply postcards back—but most do. 2). Just because you receive a postcard reply, you cannot assume your proposal has been read or will be read in the next few weeks. Your reply postcard's only function is to let you know your package has been received.

Now you have all you need to know to craft a powerful proposal. Just be smart, target the right agent, honestly acknowledge the commercial viability of your proposal, and *send the agent what the agent wants to receive*. Sound doable? Good. Go do it—Goliath is waiting.

Subsidiary Rights:
Much More Than a Book

BY DONYA DICKERSON

Most writers who want to be published envision their book in storefronts and on their friends' coffee tables. They imagine book signings and maybe even an interview on *Oprah*. Usually the dream ends there—having a book published seems exciting enough. In actuality, a whole world of opportunities exists for published writers beyond seeing their books in print. These opportunities are called "subsidiary rights."

Subsidiary rights, or sub-rights, are the additional ways that a book—that your writing—can be presented. Any time a book is made into a movie or excerpted in a magazine, a subsidiary right has been sold. If these additional rights to your book are properly "exploited," you'll not only see your book in a variety of forms, but you'll also make a lot more money than you would derive from book sales alone.

Unfortunately, the terminology of subsidiary rights can be confusing. Phrases like "secondary rights," "traditional splits," or "advance against royalty" could perplex any writer. And the thought of negotiating the terms of these rights with a publisher is daunting.

Although there are many advantages to working with agents, the ability to negotiate sub-rights is one of their most beneficial attributes. Through her experience, an agent knows which publishing houses have great sub-rights departments. If she knows a house can make money with a right, she will grant that right to the publisher when the contract is negotiated. Otherwise, she'll keep, or "retain," certain rights for her clients, which she will try to exploit by selling them to her own connections. In an interview in the *2000 Guide to Literary Agents*, writer Octavia Butler said that working with an agent, "is certainly a good thing if you don't know the business. It's a good way to hang onto your foreign and subsidiary rights, and have somebody actively peddling those rights because there were years when I lived off subsidiary rights."

If you want to work with an agent, you should have a basic understanding of sub-rights for two reasons. First, you'll want to be able to discuss these rights with your agent intelligently (although you should feel comfortable asking your agent any question you have about sub-rights). Secondly, different agents have more expertise in some sub-right areas than others. If you think your book would make a great movie, you should research the agents who have strong film connections. A knowledge of sub-rights can help you find the agent best suited to help you achieve your dreams.

An agent negotiates sub-rights with the publishing house at the same time a book is sold. In fact, the sale of certain sub-rights can even determine how much money the publisher offers for the book. But the author doesn't get paid immediately for these rights. Instead, the author is paid an "advance against royalties." An advance is a loan to the author that is paid back when the book starts earning money. Once the advance is paid, the author starts earning royalties, which are a pre-determined percentage of the book's profit.

The agent always keeps certain rights, the publisher always buys certain rights, and the others are negotiated. When an agent keeps a right, she is then free to sell it at will. If she does sell it, the money she receives from the purchasing company goes immediately to the author, minus the agent's commission. Usually the companies who purchase rights pay royalties instead of a one-time payment.

If the publisher keeps a particular right, any money that is made from it goes toward paying off the advance more quickly. Because the publisher kept the right, they will keep part of the money it makes. For most rights, half the money goes to the publisher and half goes to the writer, although for some rights the percentages are different. This equal separation of payment is called a "traditional split" because it has become standard over the years. And, of course, the agent takes her commission from the author's half.

Most agents have dealt with certain publishers so many times that they have pre-set, or "boilerplate," contracts, which means they've already agreed to the terms of certain rights, leaving only a few rights to negotiate. The following describes the main sub-rights and discusses what factors an agent takes into account when deciding whether or not to keep a right. As you read through this piece, carefully consider the many opportunities for your book, and encourage your agent and publisher to exploit these rights every chance they get.

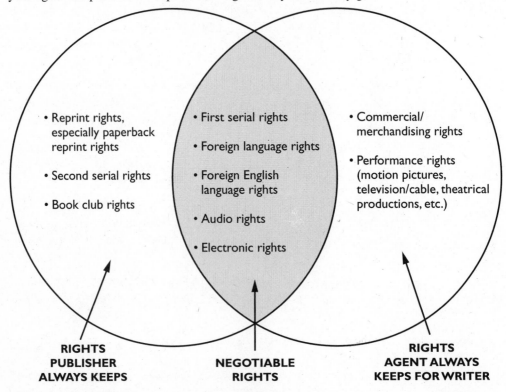

RIGHTS PUBLISHER ALWAYS KEEPS	NEGOTIABLE RIGHTS	RIGHTS AGENT ALWAYS KEEPS FOR WRITER
• Reprint rights, especially paperback reprint rights	• First serial rights	• Commercial/merchandising rights
• Second serial rights	• Foreign language rights	• Performance rights (motion pictures, television/cable, theatrical productions, etc.)
• Book club rights	• Foreign English language rights	
	• Audio rights	
	• Electronic rights	

RIGHTS THE PUBLISHER ALWAYS KEEPS

The following sub-rights are always kept by the publisher and are often called "non-negotiable rights." Money earned from these rights is split between the publisher and the author, and the author's share goes toward paying back the advance. Selling these rights helps the advance earn out faster which hopefully means the writer will receive royalty checks sooner.

Reprint rights

In publishing, a "reprint right" refers to the paperback edition of the book. When a hardcover book is reprinted in paperback, the reprint right has been used. According to agent Donald Maass, of the Donald Maass Literary Agency, "In deals with major trade publishers, it's a long-standing practice to grant them control of reprint rights. However, in some cases, a small press deal for instance, we withhold these rights." Traditionally, if a hardcover book sold really well, paperback houses bought the rights to reprint the book in a more affordable version. Any money earned from the paperback was then split fifty/fifty between the publisher and writer. Paperback houses often paid substantial amounts of money for these reprint rights.

But the recent consolidation of publishing houses has changed the value of reprint rights. "In the old days," explains Maass, "most books were hardcover, and paperbacks were cheap versions of the book. Today, so many paperback publishers have either merged with a hardcover publisher or begun their own hardcover publisher, that the business of selling reprint rights has diminished." Now, many publishers make what is called a "hard/soft deal" meaning the house will first print the book in hardcover, and, if the book sells well, they reprint the book in paperback. This type of deal can still benefit writers because they no longer have to split the money earned from reprint with the publisher. Instead, they earn royalties from both the hardcover and paperback versions.

Book club rights

These days it seems that a book club exists for every possible interest. There are the traditional book clubs, like Book-of-the-Month and its paperback counterpart, the Quality Paperback Book Club. But there are also mystery book clubs, New Age book clubs, book clubs for writers and artists, and even online book clubs. And many major publishers, like Scholastic or Doubleday, have their own book clubs. Most book clubs are very selective, and you should be flattered if your book is chosen for a book club. Like reprint rights, any money made from book club rights is split fifty/fifty between the publisher and the writer. If an agent believes a book will appeal to a certain book club's audience, she will target the manuscript to publishers who have good relationships with—or who own—that book club.

Serial rights

A serial is an excerpt of the book that appears in a magazine or in another book. To have your book serialized is wonderful because excerpts not only make additional money for you, but they also provide wonderful publicity for your book. There are actually two types of serial rights: first serial and second serial. First serial means the excerpt of the book is available *before* the book is printed. A second serial is an excerpt that appears *after* the book is already in bookstores. First serial rights are actually negotiable—sometimes the right to use them is kept by the agent. Usually an agent's decision is based upon her knowledge of the publications available in the book's subject. If she doesn't know the various magazines that focus on the book's topic, she will let the publisher have this right. Second serial rights, however, are almost always granted to the publisher.

Nonfiction books are more commonly excerpted than fiction. Nonfiction usually stands alone well, and magazines are always eager to use these excerpts because they usually cost less than hiring a freelancer to write original material. Recently, though, serialized fiction has regained popularity. In the past year, John Grisham's *A Painted House* made a giant splash by appearing, in six installments, in *The Oxford American*. According to Marc Smirnoff, editor of *The Oxford American*, response to Grisham's story has been "overwhelming. I've heard from several people who think it is the best writing John has done. John wanted to challenge himself and we're always looking for exciting work to publish." Grisham's success will certainly create opportunities for other writers who want to have their novels serialized.

RIGHTS NEGOTIATED BETWEEN THE AGENT AND PUBLISHER

The owner of these sub-rights is always determined when the book is sold. Often an agent and editor must compromise for these rights. In other words, an agent may agree to sell foreign rights if she can keep electronic rights. Or, an editor will offer more money if he can obtain the audio rights to a book.

Foreign language rights

If your book might appeal to audiences in a nonEnglish-speaking country, then you'll want an agent who has good connections with foreign co-agents. According to agent James Vines of The Vines Agency, Inc., a "foreign co-agent is someone who specializes in the sales of foreign publishing rights and who has good relationships with the heads of publishing houses throughout the world. These agents work on behalf of a New York City agency and approach the foreign publishers with manuscripts and proposals. They will typically have appointments booked at big trade shows like Frankfurt, London Book Fair, and BEA. That's where a lot of the big foreign deals happen." Usually an agent charges a 20 percent commission when a foreign co-agent is used, and the two split the earnings.

"All of my clients have benefited from the sale of foreign rights," continues Vines. For example, "*Kokology*, by Tadahiko Nagao and Isamu Saito started as a big phenomenon in Japan, selling over four million copies in Japan. A game you play about psychology, it's one of those ideas that crosses all languages and cultural boundaries because it's uniquely human—we all want to know more about ourselves." Vines sold the book to Simon & Schuster, then worked with a co-agent to sell it all over the world.

When agents are considering how a book will do abroad, they must be aware of trends in other countries. "Most agents try to stay on top of the foreign markets as much as possible and listen to what foreign co-agents have to say," says Vines. "Trends vary from territory to territory, and I try to keep those trends in mind. For example, in the United Kingdom the *Bridget Jones* phenomena is still in full swing. In Germany, historical novels are popular." Vines also points out that writers can benefit from different sub-rights over a period of time depending on how well a sub-right is selling. "Three or four years ago we were selling more film rights than we are now—studios are not as hungry as they were. Interestingly, as their interest tapered off, the foreign interest increased."

Many publishing houses have foreign counterparts, and often an agent will grant the publisher these rights if she knows the book can be printed by one of these foreign houses. If the publisher has foreign language rights, the author receives an average of 75 percent of any money made when the book is sold to a foreign publisher—minus the agent's commission, of course.

British rights

Like foreign language rights, the owner of a book's British rights can sell the book to publishers in England. Australia was once included in these rights, but Australian publishers are becoming more independent. If an agent keeps these rights, she will use a co-agent in England and the two will likely split a 20 percent commission. If a publisher has these rights, the traditional split is eighty/twenty with the author receiving the larger share.

Electronic rights

This year Stephen King caused a big commotion in the publishing world first by using an electronic publisher for his book, *Riding the Bullet*, and then by using the Internet to self-publish his serialized novel, *The Plant*. Many publishing professionals worried that King would start a trend drawing writers away from publishers, while others claimed only high-profile writers like King could ever compete successfully against the vast amounts of information on the Web. Regardless, King's achievement showed that readers are paying attention to the Internet.

Basically, electronic rights refer to the hand-held electronic, Internet, and print-on-demand versions of a book. This right is currently one of the hottest points of contention between agents and publishers because the potential for these rights is unknown—it is quite possible that electronic versions of a book will make a lot of money one day.

This area of publishing is changing so rapidly that both agents and editors struggle with how to handle electronic rights. Many publishers believe any version of a book is the same material as the printed book, and, therefore, they should own the rights. Agents worry, however, that if the publisher lets the book go out of print, the rights to the book will never be returned to the author. For more information on the pros and cons of electronic publishing, and an agent's changing role in this area, read "The Flight to Quantity: Will the Internet Ruin It for Everybody?" on page 51.

Audio rights

Before people feared that the Internet would cause the end of traditional book publishing, people worried that audio versions of books would erase the need to have printed books. In actuality, audio books have complimented their printed counterparts and have proven to be a fantastic source of additional income for the person who owns the rights to produce the book in audio form—whether through cassette tape or compact disc.

Many publishers own audio imprints and even audio book clubs, and if they are successful with these ventures, an agent will likely grant the audio rights to the publisher. The traditional split is fifty/fifty. Otherwise, the agent will try to save this right and sell it to a company that can turn it into a profit.

RIGHTS THE WRITER ALWAYS KEEPS

When a book is sold, an agent always reserves two rights for his authors: performance and merchandising. Some books are naturally more conducive to being made into films or products. And when those sub-rights are exploited, there is usually a lot of money to be made. And a smart agent can quickly identify when a book will be successful in these areas.

Performance rights

Many writers fantasize about seeing their books on the big screen. And a lot of times, agents share this dream—especially for best-selling titles. If your agent feels your book will work well as a movie, or even as a television show or video game, she will sell these rights to someone in the entertainment industry. This industry works fairly differently than the publishing industry. Usually a producer "options" the right to make your book into a movie. An option means the producer can only make the movie during a specific amount of time, like a year. If the movie isn't made during that time period, the rights revert back to you. You can actually option these rights over and over—making money for every option—without the book ever being made into a movie. Keep in mind, however, that once your book has been optioned, you'll likely lose any say over issues of creative control until the option expires.

As with foreign rights, agents usually work with another agent to sell performance rights. Usually these agents live in Los Angeles and have the connections to producers that agents outside California just don't have. A 20 percent commission is the norm for performance rights, and the money is split between the two agents who partnered to sell these rights.

Commercial/merchandising rights

Merchandising rights create products—like calendars, cards, action figures, stickers, dolls, and so on—that are based on characters or other elements of your book. Few books transfer well into such products, but they can be successful when they do. Keep in mind that if a producer options the performance rights to your book, the merchandising rights are usually included in the deal.

Agent Steven Malk, of Writers House, made wonderful use of these two rights for his client, Elise Primavera, and her book, *Auntie Claus* (Silver Whistle/Harcourt). According to Malk, "When I first read the manuscript of *Auntie Claus* and saw a couple of Primavera's sample illustrations, I immediately knew the book had a lot of possibilities in the sub-rights realm. First of all, the character of Auntie Claus is extremely memorable and unique, and, from a visual standpoint, she's stunning. Also, the basic concept of the book is completely fresh and original, which is very hard to accomplish with a Christmas book.

"The first thing I did was to approach Saks Fifth Avenue with the idea of featuring *Auntie Claus* in their Christmas windows. In addition to using the book as the theme for their window displays, they created some merchandise that was sold through Saks. It's a perfect project for them; the character of Auntie Claus is so sophisticated and refined, she seemed ideal for their windows.

"Shortly after that, the movie rights were optioned by Nickelodeon with Wendy Finerman attached as a producer—she produced *Forrest Gump* and *Stepmom*. Nickelodeon is currently developing the project, and, when it's released, more merchandise will likely follow."

Like Malk did for Primavera, many agents successfully exploit subsidiary rights every day. If you want the most for your book, look for an agent who has the know-how and connections to take your publishing dream beyond the book and to its fullest potential. And use the information in this article to help your agent make the most of your subsidiary rights.

The Flight to Quantity: Will the Internet Ruin It for Everybody?

BY RICHARD CURTIS

As recently as three years ago, critics of "Big Publishing" complained bitterly that it was impossible for the marketplace to absorb the 50,000 books published annually in the U.S. What will these critics say when the figure reaches 500,000? That's the number industry observer, M. L. Rose, projected in *wired.com news* as she eyed the river of self-published and e-published books rushing toward us.

Thanks to e-books, print-on-demand technology, and the Internet, the wherewithal to print, sell, and publicize a book is suddenly available to all. Under the auspices of dotcom companies like Xlibris, iUniverse, and fatbrain, and of countless self-styled publishers popping up daily, anyone can get a book published, and from the looks of it, everyone is doing just that.

Insiders' views are changing

Until now, writers who couldn't get their first novels, personal memoirs, and the like published any other way either self-published or paid subsidy publishers to do so. Subsidy houses customarily accept just about anything from anybody as long as the author pays for design and typesetting, printing and binding, advertising, and distribution. Unfortunately, few subsidy publishers have the ability to penetrate the marketplace, and their fees are often exorbitant. But writers who patronize them don't care as long as their dreams of publication are realized. Many an anxious author has succumbed to unscrupulous con artists promising them fame and fortune in the new world of Internet publishing, and the ease with which books can be produced and sold online has encouraged these predators to seduce unsuspecting authors into overpaying for services they could perform themselves for a few dollars.

Publishing professionals have traditionally looked down their noses at self- and subsidy publishing. They call it vanity publishing, emphasizing that real authors are supposed to be paid by publishers and not the other way around.

But now, major publishers like Random House, Simon & Schuster, and Time Warner are getting into the act. Random House has taken a position in Xlibris, a company involved in self-publishing on the Internet, and Time Warner has launched iPublish, which offers a program for writers with potential to break out of the unwashed masses of wannabes. The electronic revolution seems not only to be legitimizing self-publishing, but institutionalizing it.

To editorial patricians vested with the solemn duty of separating literary gold from dross, this new publishing model is appalling. Many decades ago someone coined the term "slush" for unsolicited manuscripts submitted to publishers. Although good books were occasionally pulled out of the slush pile and went on to become successful, most trade publishers discontinued

RICHARD CURTIS *is president of Richard Curtis Associates, Inc., a leading New York literary agency. He is also a well-known author advocate and author of numerous works of fiction and nonfiction including several books about the publishing industry. Late in 1998, Richard Curtis announced the formation of e-reads™, a publisher, retailer, and electronic rights clearinghouse. The company's mission is to assist authors, literary agents, and other content-providers to take advantage of fundamental changes in publishing and printing technology.*

the practice of sifting through the pile, which can amount to tens of thousands of submissions a year. These publishers now send a form rejection letter stating that their company will consider submissions only if solicited by literary agents—men and women of refined taste and commercial sensibilities who presumably have sifted the promising material from the junk. But now, suddenly, editors who have spent their careers shoveling "over the transom" submissions back over the transom are being asked to treat them as hot commodities. And this slush doesn't arrive in mail bags—it now comes in huge electronic files attached to e-mails.

Unlike the industry that the aging populace of publishing professionals grew up with, the fledgling e-book industry possesses no elite corps of editors, reviewers, and critics to filter out inferior product. In the dot-communistic world of self-publishing, no book is better or worse than any other. "Inferior" isn't even in the vocabulary of the young e-publishing entrepreneurs offering publication to anyone with a manuscript and a credit card.

Clearly, then, the number one challenge facing our industry in the coming era is "branding," separating good books from bad. However, like so many other values in these revolutionary times, the definitions of "good" and "bad" are now up for grabs. Today branding is performed by a society of professional arbiters—literary agents, editors, book store managers, reviewers, and critics. Will the process be performed by plebiscite or popularity contest tomorrow? For many shell-shocked refugees from the twentieth century publishing industry, it feels as if the inmates are taking over the asylum.

Three truths about the e-approach to publishing

Before we repudiate the proletarian approach to publishing, however, we would be wise to listen to the truths its advocates live by.

The first is that in matters of taste, the gatekeepers of traditional publishing have no right to cast stones at the newcomers. The ossifying system we generically call Big Publishing has arguably failed both writers and readers, all too often promoting scandalously overpaid superstars and tired formulas at the expense of fresh talent and original expression. Sure, the vast majority of self-published authors may be hopeless duffers, but among their ranks are many first-rate writers who are thrilled at last to have an alternative to the monolithic, indifferent establishment that dominated publishing throughout the twentieth century, when titles were picked based on the heartlessly cold sales figures generated by chain store computers.

The second truth is that the new industry happens to be very profitable. E-publishers have looked unsentimentally at publishing as a system and grasped that it essentially consists of an author, a reader, and a server. Low manufacturing and distribution costs enable e-publishers to turn a profit on the sale of a few hundred units of any given title. This may seem a laughable figure to old hands who are used to dealing in six- and seven-figure printings and bestseller lists that don't even show books on their radar screen until they have sold half a million copies. But who will have the last laugh ten years from now? Will it be the e-book press that consistently makes 40 percent profit uploading laundry lists and masters theses? Or the behemoth that takes a million dollar bath on a catastrophic overprinting of some tiresome celebrity biography?

The traditional publishing industry operates on a consignment basis. In anticipation of a good sale, publishers print more copies than they know they will sell. They distribute them and hope for the best. What does not get sold is returned for credit. The ratio of sold copies to the number of copies distributed is called the "sell-through." A successful sell-through percentage used to be something like 90 percent. Today publishers are happy if they report a 60 percent sell-through. What happens to the copies that aren't sold? The publishers must refund or credit the stores for the returned merchandise, and the author's hard work is then recycled or even pulped.

By contrast, an e-book publisher's sell-through percentage is 100 percent. Because of the print-on-demand feature of electronic publishing, no copy is printed or distributed until the customer has paid for it. Every copy sold stays sold and is purchased by a customer who really wants it. Which leads to the third significant truth about the new publishing model: it offers the potential for maximum exposure of one's writing to an audience that wants to buy and read it. Big Publishing simply cannot make that claim and because of its large brick-and-mortar overhead is not in a position to compete with virtual—purely electronic—delivery systems.

A downside of e-publishing

And yet there is one obstinate truth that the e-book industry has not come to grips with: we still need someone to tell us what to read. What has yet to be proved is whether John and Jane Doe's opinions are as good as any veteran editor's. Are we ready to trade our cherished elitism for egalitarian consensus?

Inevitably a new establishment of tastemakers will arise to guide our judgment and help us absorb the huge influx of new books. Does this simply mean e-versions of *Publishers Weekly, Kirkus*, or the *New York Times Book Review*? Not necessarily. Although dedicated review media for e-books are beginning to show up (*Publishers Weekly* devotes one page every few issues to e-book reviews, for instance), we still don't have the sort of review establishment that exists for the good old-fashioned book. However, with proletarian books come proletarian means of evaluating them. Zagat's initiated the successful technique of using ordinary people to review restaurants, and amazon.com followed suit with book reviewers. In Time Warner's iPublish model, writers critique and rate each other, and the highest rated ones move onto the publication track. New techniques have been developed that instantly gauge public responses to e-published texts and prompt authors to adjust their approach in order to give readers what they want to hear. Whether we like it or not, it is likely that the next generation of best-selling authors will come out of processes such as this.

The role of agents in this brave new world

Those processes will also create a profound displacement for literary agents, who may find themselves in the middle of relationships that no longer depend on middle men and women. If you can successfully deliver and sell your book directly to your readers, do you need a literary agent? Currently agents remain the primary forces in the sale of books to publishers, but as time goes by their relevance may become marginal.

I mention this because the overwhelming majority of new authors is focused on getting an agent. When I attend conferences, I see that the how-to-get-an-agent panels are crowded to capacity, whereas the how-to-get-happily-self-published ones are more sparsely attended.

A question I hear repeatedly is whether agents and editors are attracted to successfully self-published authors. I know of a number of cases where original books that sold well on a website were picked up by agents and even by publishers. But once again, the dynamic I have described here—the filtering of quality work from the slush pile—will ultimately make self-published books a turnoff for agents and publishers. Already, authors who spam the Internet with promotion for their books are being shunned because publishing professionals know all you need is a puffed-up press release and an e-mailing list to reach millions of would-be readers. If a literary agent receives ten such e-mails a day from self-promoting authors, all the puffery in the world is not going to move them even to read such e-mails let alone offer representation. What was once a novelty has become meaningless as growing numbers of desperate authors crowd onto the selling floor hawking their wares.

These are the truths we must look unflinchingly in the face. And perhaps the hardest one of all to accept is that in this fascinating new terrain, the biggest competitors of publishers are authors themselves. If publishers think the competition from their rivals is stiff, wait till authors start elbowing them for room in the marketplace!

As James Joyce put it, "Here comes everybody!"

Writers, Agents, and Creative Control: The Battle between Markets and Aesthetics

BY BRAD VICE

Whether you're an accomplished novelist with two decades of publishing behind you or a fledgling author still trying to sell your first book, chances are there is a certain amount of fear and trembling involved in approaching agents. Why the apprehension? What mystical powers do agents possess, and why are writers so intimidated by them? The answers to these questions often lie in the increasing commercial nature of the publishing industry and the special niche agents inhabit in that world. Your fear may stem from a concern that the agent will ask for further revisions to a manuscript you've already worked on for years. You may worry that the agent is more concerned with the demands of the marketplace than your own artistic integrity.

Because the writing life requires authors to spend most of their day typing away in isolation, writers are seen as living in a dream world, a pure realm of art with no concern for the needs of the marketplace. On the other hand, huge corporate publishers are immersed in the hard world of spreadsheets and bottom lines. As an intermediary in the battle between art and markets, an agent must be the perfect mixture of cutthroat entrepreneur and salon aesthete—a sort of illegitimate child of William Randolph Hearst and Virginia Woolf. So how can a writer determine if an agent's suggestions to improve her novel's marketability are justified when it means altering her creative vision?

A writer's need for creative freedom

According to established writer Allen Wier, "I love my agent, but no matter how successful you are as a writer, you never quite get over the feeling that you're coming to your agent with your hat in your hands." Wier's new novel, a western epic entitled *Tehano* (a Native American word meaning Texan), has just been accepted for publication by The Overlook Press despite its mammoth size. After almost eight years of meticulous research and thousands of hours banging away at the word processor, Wier produced a manuscript almost 1,500 pages long.

"The writing of *Tehano* was kind of a scary process," says Wier. "Most writers get upset if they don't hear from their agents every week. I'd just send a Christmas card to Ginger [Virginia Baker of The Writers Shop] once a year with a note saying, 'Still working on it,' and she'd send one back saying, 'Maybe this is the year.' She knew that with a project this large, there wasn't much advice she could give me. I was an experienced writer, and there was little she could do but let me write it out."

When it came time to deliver the manuscript, Wier found himself wondering if his artistic ambition to write an epic might cheat him of a chance at publication. "I sent the book to my agent and my friend Richard Bausch, and they read it at the same time. They both liked it and

---

BRAD VICE *is a freelance writer living in Cincinnati. His stories have appeared in* The Georgia Review, The Southern Review, Hayden's Ferry Review, The Greensboro Review, *and* New Stories from the South. *His nonfiction has appeared in* Novel & Short Story Writer's Market *and* Guide to Literary Agents.

gave me advice on revision. Ginger had a few misgivings about the ending, but went ahead and sent it out. It took the first editor almost four months to read it, so I began editing the book on my own and took the manuscript down to 1,200 pages. At that length my agent was able to find an editor who was interested in working with me, and we continued to cut more of the digressions. We all agreed the cuts had to be made in order to strengthen the narrative drive." Even with these cuts *Tehano* will be published at just under a thousand pages, but it *is* getting published.

Although Wier's novel was a difficult sale because of its epic length, his agent was probably able to make *Tehano* attractive to its editor because the novel will appeal to a cross-section of market niches: regional, literary, historical, and western. The conventions of the historical western easily accommodate Wier's epic ambition. Selling a long science fiction or mystery novel may have been more difficult to pull off. And appealing to a wide range of readers is increasingly important if you want your novel to succeed in today's marketplace.

Agents must consider the marketplace

According to agent Evan Marshall, of the Evan Marshall Agency and author of *The Marshall Plan for Novel Writing* (Writer's Digest Books), understanding market conventions is imperative to publishing a book. "In the old days it wasn't so important that the writing 'fit in,' but now the mid-list is dead. Horror, mystery, suspense, Southern, romance, literary fiction, women's fiction, gay fiction—I handle every kind of adult novel, and often I help writers make transitions from one market to another or help them expand toward a larger audience. Most of my writers are very accomplished, so if I give any advice at all it's usually about what readers expect from a certain genre. Be creative. Be original, but give the readers what they want." An important part of Marshall's job as an agent is giving creative suggestions that will make writers more interesting to one or more audience groups.

Such knowledge of the market can be important for a writer's career development. Because Marshall is keenly aware of reader expectations, he is something of an expert at helping authors make mid-career transformations. "I have a client I am very proud of, Erica Spindler, who used to write short category romance novels before she was with me. She has made a switch to writing novels with elements of both romance and mystery, and I have been helping her with the thriller aspects of the form. She ended up writing a murder mystery called *All Fall Down* (Mira Books) that appealed to both men and women, like a Sandra Brown or a James Patterson novel. *All Fall Down* was a big hit, and she already has another novel with similar elements, *Bone Cold*, which will be out in 2001."

Marshall warns that while he is willing to work with established writers to find larger audiences, he requires almost absolute perfection when taking on new writers. "A manuscript needs to be pretty close to publishable for me to take it on. I will be happy to fine-tune a book, but editors want books that are ready to go because, frankly, editors are not very interested in editing any more. You must be your own best editor. Some line editing can happen, but usually editors are concerned that macro elements of the novel make sense: conflict, plot, resolution. More and more I hear, 'I need a book that is ready to go.' "

Marshall's philosophy of agenting may seem to benefit the publisher at the expense of the writer's creative vision, but Marshall rightly points out that he is actually the writer's best friend. Not only does he help a client's book become more salable, but he can usually obtain something from the publisher few writers can get on their own—respect. "If a publisher doesn't pay a writer a significant sum of money for their work, they have no incentive to push the book. You can ask too much for a book, and then when it inevitably fails the publisher doesn't want to work with you again. I make sure writers get the amount they need to keep the publisher interested in the writer's career for a long time. Some of my biggest deals have been for books that haven't even been written yet because publishers have faith in my writers."

Does experience count?

Just because one is an accomplished writer or even has a successful book under his belt does not mean agents will not ask for revisions to increase a book's marketability. Take, for example, writer Avery Chenoweth, whose promising short story collection *Wingtips*, published in 1999, sold over four times the number of copies projected by its publisher, Johns Hopkins University Press, and was later nominated for the Library of Virginia Fiction Award. Bolstered by the local success of *Wingtips*, Chenoweth began an extensive search for an agent who could introduce his novels to a larger audience.

When Chenoweth was asked to moderate a panel discussion on agenting on C-Span 2, he jumped at the chance, hoping to discover the secrets of a successful agent/writer relationship. "I was interested in the issues of creative control between writers and agents, especially now since many editors have left the field. With the market forces playing such an important role in a publisher's decision to accept a book, my concern is that novels will no longer be midwifed into becoming what they ought to be, but will be streamlined into something standard—hip, dark, psycho, druggy, whatever the flavor of the season happens to be. You have to find an agent who is on your wavelength; otherwise you might spend a lot of time changing your book into something it's not—just to catch the next market craze turning fiction into cereal or running shoes."

Chenoweth weeded down his options of agents to a short list, and picked one that had impressed him with a concrete and detailed reading of the first fifty pages of his new book. But upon the novel's completion, Chenoweth was in for a nasty surprise. "I got dropped. The agent simply wasn't as interested in the rest of the book as he was the beginning. He said it was a matter of pacing. I write this languid, summery, Southern prose. He was used to representing something with more punch. He was not interested in revision because he admitted that although the book is a good book, 'Its greatest virtue is also the book's greatest weakness. To change it would be to ruin it.' It was an amiable parting, between me and the agent. I originally chose to work with him because I liked him, and I still like him. The search simply continues."

How revision can benefit the writer

Although Chenoweth's story seems to confirm Marshall's opinion that writers must pay close attention to readers' and publishers' demands if they hope to publish, there are notable exceptions to this rule.

Take the case of the novella *Poachers*, by Tom Franklin, which became a hit among readers of mystery and literary fiction alike. While it may have been slightly difficult to sell Allen Wier's epic-length *Tehano*, it is a standing rule in the world of publishing that shorter novellas are the least marketable literary form. But this did not stop agent Nat Sobel of Sobel Weber Associates from taking on Franklin as a client after discovering *Poachers* in a small literary journal. Sobel, who also represents mystery writers like James Ellroy and literary writers like Richard Russo, saw traces of both of those authors' voices shining through in Franklin's novella. Sobel asked Franklin if he had any more stories the agent could peruse.

After quite a bit of revision Sobel put a collection of Franklin's stories up for sale. "Taking on a collection of stories is real act of faith for an agent these days," says Sobel. "While there are more collections being published by trade houses than a few years ago, it's still a tough sell. I approach a collection as I would a novel. It has to engage me early on. The order of stories is important as well. I like a strong opening and a strong finish. For this reason, the collection starts with 'Grit' and ends with 'Poachers.' "

According to Franklin, Sobel's suggestion to unify the entire collection thematically like a novel paid off. "Nat asked me to take out a surreal story about golf courses with thousands of holes that he thought was a little goofy and didn't fit in with the rest of the book. Then he asked me to write a couple more stories. He wanted to get rid of another story in the collection,

"Alaska," but I asked to keep it in. The problem was not enough happens in the beginning of the story; eight pages go by before anything really gets going. So I cut that down to four, and we decided to keep it. Then Nat asked me to revise an essay I'd written about hunting, to serve as an introduction—a sort of explanation as to why the book is so violent. I'd never heard of doing such a thing, but the result was great," and the book was sold to HarperPerennial.

Despite the marginalized status that novellas and short stories have in the publishing industry, *Poachers* sold more books than some novelists dream of selling in a lifetime. And *Poachers* the novella was selected for inclusion in *New Stories From the South* (Algonquin Books of Chapel Hill), *Best American Mystery Stories* (Houghton Mifflin Company), and the *Best American Mystery Stories of the Century* anthology (Houghton Mifflin Company).

When agents and authors work together

When it comes to creative control, both writers and agents must give serious thought to the personal aspect of their relationship which goes beyond markets and revision. Even though agents must have a tough business exterior part of the time, that veneer will end up damaging a writer's work if it intimidates the author as well. A writer should feel confident calling his agent to chat about markets, revision, or just for moral support, even though one should do it gingerly or, as Wier describes, "with hat in hand."

Short story writer and novelist Michael Knight and his agent Warren Frazier of John Hawkins & Associates, Inc. are a good example of a friendly writer/agent partnership, which resulted in a two-book deal with Dutton Plume for the author. Knight says, "When I was close to finishing my short story collection, *Dogfight*, I sent a few packets around. Warren was interested. At the time he didn't have any known clients, but I didn't care because he talked to me in a way that showed he really understood my fiction. He is a really good reader, and we're from the same part of the country, south Alabama and north Florida. We have become friends. He got Dutton interested in my collection and in a book idea I had, which became my novel *Divining Rod*."

According to the down-to-earth Frazier, having a cordial relationship with a client is the only way to take care of business. "Ninety-nine percent of my writers are successful because I can be frank with them when something doesn't work. For the most part, I let my clients write; I don't want to control them. I will give them advice on New York trends if they really want to know, but I don't think chasing trends is such a good idea. By the time the book gets out, the fad could be old news." Frazier's method of agenting privileges the author's creative potential. He spends less time coaching a certain kind of revision, and more time hunting down editors who are willing to work on the material at hand. "Some people say editors are not interested in editing anymore. I'm pretty new to the business, so I don't know what editors were like twenty years ago. But I can tell you there are plenty of editors who still edit. I try to get my writers those editors because they make the best advocates. Editors want to build relationships with writers, too. We all love books. That's why we do this job."

What to Ask—and Not Ask—an Agent

If an agent is interested in representing your work, congratulations! Nevertheless, you may have some concerns about whether this agent is the best person for you. The following is a list of appropriate questions to ask an agent who offers you a contract. Because an agent is busy, you'll want to pick only five or six of the questions most important to you to ask.

These are questions you ask only *after* the agent agrees to take you on as a client. In other words, don't take up the agent's time with these questions if you are only considering sending the agent a query letter. Also listed below are questions that you'll want to avoid asking—doing so may cause an agent to doubt your professionalism.

Do ask:

1) What about my work interests you?
2) What can I do to be a good client?
3) Who are some other authors you represent and what are examples of recent sales you've made for those authors?
4) How much career guidance do you give clients?
5) Are you interested in representing me for this one title or throughout my writing career?
6) What is your commission? Does your commission change if you use a foreign or film co-agent?
7) Do you charge clients for office expenses? If so, what is your policy? Do you have a ceiling amount for such expenses?
8) Do you charge any other fees (i.e., reading fee, critiquing fee)?
9) What are your agency's strengths?
10) How often should I expect to be in contact with you?
11) Will you show me rejections from publishers if I request them?
12) Will you consult with me before accepting any offer?
13) Do you work with independent publicists?
14) What are your policies if, for whatever reason, we decided to part company?
15) Do you offer a written contract? If not, what legal provisions can be made to avoid any misunderstandings between us?

For a list of further questions recommended by the Association of Authors' Representatives, go to www.aar-online.org.

Don't ask:

1) What are some recent advances you've negotiated for your clients?
2) Can I have the phone numbers for some of your clients to use as references?
3) Can you call me at this specific time?
4) How much money are you going to get for my book?
5) Who do I need to talk to in order to get my book made into a movie?

Listing Policy and Complaint Procedure

Listings in *Guide to Literary Agents* are compiled from detailed questionnaires, phone interviews, and information provided by agents. The industry is volatile, and agencies change frequently. We rely on our readers for information on their dealings with agents and changes in policies or fees that differ from what has been reported to the editor of this book. Write to us if you have new information, questions, or problems dealing with the agencies listed.

Listings are published free of charge and are not advertisements. Although the information is as accurate as possible, the listings are *not* endorsed or guaranteed by the editor or publisher of *Guide to Literary Agents*. If you feel you have not been treated fairly by an agent or representative listed in *Guide to Literary Agents*, we advise you to take the following steps:

☑ First try to contact the agency. Sometimes one phone call or a letter can clear up the matter.

☑ Document all your correspondence with the agency. When you write to us with a complaint, provide the name of your manuscript, the date of your first contact with the agency and the nature of your subsequent correspondence.

☑ We will enter your letter into our files and attempt to contact the agency.

☑ The number, frequency, and severity of complaints will be considered in our decision whether or not to delete the listing from the next edition.

Guide to Literary Agents reserves the right to exclude any agency for any reason.

Contributors to the Insider Reports

IAN BESSLER

Ian Bessler is the editor of *Songwriter's Market*, and is a fiction writer and musician.

NANCY BREEN

Nancy Breen is production editor for *Poet's Market* and *Novel & Short Story Writer's Market*, and is also a poet and fiction writer.

SHEREE BYKOFSKY

Sheree Bykofsky is a literary agent in New York and the author of over a dozen books, including *The Complete Idiot's Guide to Getting Published* (Alpha Books) and *The Complete Idiot's Guide to Publishing Magazine Articles* (Alpha Books). If you wish to query Bykofsky, send a one-page snail mail letter and SASE to her at Sheree Bykofsky Associates, Inc., 16 W. 36th Street, 13th Floor, New York, NY 10018. Website: www.shereebee.com.

CINDY DUESING

Cindy Duesing is production editor for *Artist's & Graphic Designer's Market* and *Children's Writer's & Illustrator's Market*. Previously, she worked as a greeting card writer and editor for Gibson Greetings, Inc. She is also an award-winning poet and a published composer of liturgical music.

KELLY MILNER HALLS

Kelly Milner Halls is a full-time freelance writer based in Spokane, Washington. Her work regularly appears in Writer's Digest Books' publications as well as the *Denver Post*, *The Chicago Tribune*, *Spokesman Review*, *New Jersey Monthly*, *Highlights for Children*, *Boy's Life*, *Guidepost for Teens*, *Freezone*, and dozens of other publications. Her latest children's book is *Bought a Baby Chicken* (Boyds Mills Press, 2000).

JEFF HILLARD

Jeff Hillard is a poet, journalist, novelist, and screenwriter who has written three books of poetry. Additionally, he is editor for *Writer Online* and is an associate professor of English at the College of Mount St. Joseph in Cincinnati, Ohio.

ALICE POPE

Alice Pope is editor of *Children's Writer's & Illustrator's Market*. She's a frequent contributor to Writer's Digest Books' publications.

Literary Agents:
Nonfee-charging

Agents listed in this section generate 98 to 100 percent of their income from commission on sales. They do not charge for reading, critiquing, or editing. Sending a query to a nonfee-charging agent means you pay only the cost of postage to have your work considered by an agent with an imperative to find salable manuscripts: Her income depends on finding the best publisher for your manuscript.

Because her time is more profitably spent meeting with editors, she will have little or no time to critique your writing. Agents who don't charge fees must be selective and often prefer to work with established authors, celebrities, or those with credentials in a particular field.

Some agents in this section may charge clients for office expenses such as photocopying, foreign postage, long distance phone calls, or express mail services. Make sure you have a clear understanding of what these expenses are before signing any agency agreement. While most agents deduct expenses from the advance or royalties before passing them on to the author, a few agents included in this section charge their clients a one-time "marketing" or "handling" fee up front. These agents have a ($) preceding their listing.

For the first time, we've included the section, Canadian/International Nonfee-charging Literary Agents. To learn more about the pros and cons of using an agent outside the United States, read the introduction to this section on page 180.

When reading through the listings of nonfee-charging literary agents, use the following key to help you fully understand the information provided:

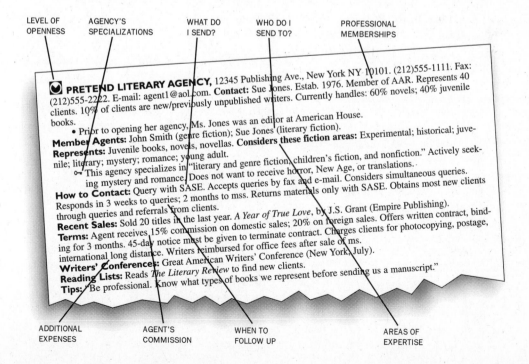

LEVEL OF OPENNESS   AGENCY'S SPECIALIZATIONS   WHAT DO I SEND?   WHO DO I SEND TO?   PROFESSIONAL MEMBERSHIPS

ADDITIONAL EXPENSES   AGENT'S COMMISSION   WHEN TO FOLLOW UP   AREAS OF EXPERTISE

Quick Reference Icons

At the beginning of each listing, you will find one or more of the following symbols to help you quickly identify features particular to that listing.

N.   Agency new to this edition.

☑   Change in address, contact information or phone number from last year's edition.

$ Agents who charge fees to previously unpublished writers only.

■   Agents who make sales to electronic publishers. For more information on this topic, read "The Flight to Quantity: Will the Internet Ruin It for Everybody" on page 51.

✠   Canadian agency.

⊕   International agency.

Level of Openness

Each agency has an icon indicating its openness to submissions. Before contacting any agency, check the listing to make sure it is open to new clients.

◯   Newer agency actively seeking clients.

◑   Agency seeking both new and established writers.

◐   Agency prefers to work with established writers, mostly obtains new clients through referrals.

◎   Agency handling only certain types of work or work by writers under certain circumstances.

⊘   Agency not currently seeking new clients. We include these agencies to let you know they are currently not open to new clients. *Unless you have a strong recommendation from someone well respected in the field, our advice is to avoid approaching these agents.*

For quick reference, a chart of these icons and their meanings is printed on the inside covers of this book.

SUBHEADS FOR QUICK ACCESS TO INFORMATION

Each listing is broken down into subheads to make locating specific information easier. In the first section, you'll find contact information for each agency. You'll also learn if the agency belongs to any professional organizations, which can tell you a lot about an agency. For example, members of the Association of Authors' Representatives (AAR) are prohibited from charging reading or evaluating fees. (An explanation of all organizations' acronyms is available on page 366.) Further information is provided which indicates an agency's size, its willingness to work with a new or previously unpublished writer, and its general areas of interest.

Member Agents: Agencies comprised of more than one agent list member agents and their individual specialties to help you determine the most appropriate person for your query letter.

Represents: Here agencies specify what nonfiction and fiction subjects they consider. Make sure you query only agents who represent the type of material you write. To help narrow your search, check the **Agents Specialties Index** immediately following the Canadian/International nonfee-charging listings.

○⇒   Look for the key icon to quickly learn an agent's areas of specialization or specific strengths (i.e., editorial or marketing experience, sub-rights expertise, etc.). Agents also mention here what specific areas they are currently seeking as well as subjects they do *not* wish to receive.

How to Contact: Most agents open to submissions prefer initially to receive a query letter briefly describing your work. (See "Queries That Made It Happen" on page 31.) Some agents ask for an outline and a number of sample chapters, but you should send these only if requested to do so. Here agents also mention if they accept queries by fax or e-mail, if they consider simultaneous submissions, and their preferred way of meeting new clients.

Recent Sales: To give a sense of the types of material they represent, agents provide specific titles they've sold as well as a sampling of clients' names. Some agents consider their client list confidential and may only share names once they agree to represent you.

Terms: Provided here are details of an agent's commission, whether a contract is offered and for how long, and what additional office expenses you might have to pay if the agent agrees to represent you. Standard commissions range from 10 to 15 percent for domestic sales, and 15 to 20 percent for foreign or dramatic sales with the difference going to the co-agent who places the work.

Writers' Conferences: A great way to meet an agent is at a writers' conference. Here agents list the ones they attend. For more information about a specific conference, check the **Writers' Conferences** section starting on page 330.

Reading List: Learn what magazines and journals agents read to discover potential clients.

Tips: Agents offer advice and additional instructions for writers looking for representation.

SPECIAL INDEXES TO HELP YOUR SEARCH

Additional Nonfee-charging Agents: Many literary agents are also interested in scripts; many script agents will also consider book manuscripts. Nonfee-charging script agents who primarily sell scripts but also handle at least 10 to 15 percent book manuscripts appear among the listings in this section, with the contact information, breakdown of work currently handled, and a note to check the full listing in the script section. Those nonfee-charging script agencies that sell scripts and less than 10 to 15 percent book manuscripts appear at the end of this section on page 179. Complete listings for these agents appear in the Script Agents section.

Agents Specialties Index: Immediately following the section of Canadian/International Nonfee-charging Agents is an index which organizes agencies according to the subjects they are interested in receiving. This index should help you compose a list of agents specializing in your areas. Cross-referencing categories and concentrating on agents interested in two or more aspects of your manuscript might increase your chances of success. Agencies open to all nonfiction or fiction topics are grouped under the subject heading "open."

Agencies Indexed by Openness to Submissions: This index lists agencies according to their receptivity to new clients.

Geographic Index: For writers looking for an agent close to home, this index lists agents state-by-state.

Agents Index: Often you will read about an agent who is an employee of a larger agency and you may not be able to locate her business phone or address. Starting on page 379 is a list of agents' names in alphabetical order along with the name of the agency they work for. Find the name of the person you would like to contact, then check the agency listing.

Listing Index: This index lists all agencies, independent publicists, and writers' conferences listed in the book.

For More Information

For a detailed explanation of the agency listings and for more information on approaching agents, read "Reading the Listings in the *Guide to Literary Agents*" and "How to Find the Right Agent." Be sure to read the several informative articles at the beginning of this book to fully understand the process a writer should go through when finding a literary agent.

NONFEE-CHARGING AGENTS

⊘ **CAROLE ABEL LITERARY AGENT**, 160 W. 87th St., New York NY 10024. Member of AAR. This agency did not respond to our request for information. Query before submitting.

[N] ⊘ **AGENCY WEST ENTERTAINMENT**, 6255 W. Sunset Blvd., #908, Hollywood CA 90028. (323)468-9470. Fax: (323)468-0867. **Contact:** Dackeyia Q. Simmons. Estab. 1995. Signatory of WGA. Represents 10 clients. 25% of clients are new/previously unpublished writers. Currently handles: 10% nonfiction books; 5% juvenile books; 5% novels; 40% movie scripts; 40% TV scripts.
   • See the expanded listing for this agency in Script Agents.

◖ **AGENTS INC. FOR MEDICAL AND MENTAL HEALTH PROFESSIONALS**, P.O. Box 4956, Fresno CA 93744. (559)438-8289. Fax: (559)438-1883. **Contact:** Sydney H. Harriet, Ph.D., Psy.D., director. Estab. 1987. Member of APA. Represents 49 clients. 70% of clients are new/previously unpublished writers. Currently handles: 80% nonfiction books; 20% novels.
   • Prior to becoming an agent and author, Dr. Harriet was a professor of English, psychologist, and radio and television reporter.
Represents: Nonfiction books, novels, multimedia projects. **Considers these nonfiction areas:** law; health/medicine; cooking/food/nutrition; psychology; reference; science/technology; self-help/personal improvement; sociology; sports medicine/psychology; mind-body healing. **Considers these fiction areas:** mystery/suspense; psychological thrillers and commercial fiction. *Currently representing previously published novelists only.*
   ○━ This agency specializes in "writers who have education and experience in the business, legal and health professions. It is helpful if the writer is licensed but not necessary. Prior nonfiction book publication not necessary. For fiction, previously published fiction is prerequisite for representation." Does not want memoirs, autobiographies, stories about overcoming an illness, science fiction, fantasy, religious materials and children's books.
How to Contact: Query with vita and SASE. Accepts query letters only. Considers simultaneous queries and submissions. Responds in 1 month to queries; 1 month to mss "we request to read. Craft must be outstanding since 99% of fiction mss are rejected. We do not respond to book pitches over the phone. Always submit a carefully prepared query or proposal with a SASE."
Recent Sales: Sold 5 titles in the last year. *Infantry Soldier*, by George Neil (University of Oklahoma Press); *SAMe, The European Arthritis and Depression Breakthrough*, by Sol Grazi, M.D. and Marie Costa (Prima); *What to Eat if You Have Diabetes*, by Danielle Chase M.S. (Contemporary); *The Red Yeast Diet Breakthrough*, by Maureen Keane, M.S. (Adams Media Corporation); *The Senior Golfer's Answer Book*, by Sol Grazi, M.D. and Syd Harriet, Ph.D., Psy.D. (Batsford-Brassey's).
Terms: Agent receives 15% commission on domestic sales; 20% on foreign sales. Offers written contract, binding for 6-12 months (negotiable).
Writers' Conferences: Scheduled as a speaker at a number of conferences across the country in 2001-2002. "Contact agency to book authors and agents for conferences."
Tips: "Remember, query first. *Do not call to pitch an idea.* The only way we can judge the quality of your idea is to see how you write. Please, unsolicited manuscripts will not be read if they arrive without a SASE. Currently we are receiving more than 200 query letters and proposals each month. Send complete proposal/manuscript only if requested. Please, please, ask yourself why someone would be compelled to buy your book. If you think the idea is unique, spend the time to create a query and then a proposal where every word counts. Fiction writers need to understand that the craft is just as important as the idea. 99% of the fiction is rejected because of sloppy overwritten dialogue, wooden characters, predictable plotting and lifeless narrative. Once you finish your novel, put it away and let it percolate, then take it out and work on fine-tuning it some more. A novel is never finished until you stop working on it. Would love to represent more fiction writers and probably will when we read a manuscript that has gone through a dozen or more drafts. Because of rising costs, we no longer can respond to queries, proposals, and/or complete manuscripts without receiving a return envelope and sufficient postage."

[N] ◖ ◎ **JOSEPH AJLOUNY LITERARY AGENCY, (Specialized: humor, popular culture and reference)**, Federal Bureau of Entertainment 29205 Greening Blvd., Farmington Hills MI 48334-2945. (248)932-0090. Fax: (248)932-8763. E-mail: jsapub@aol.com. Website: www.the-feds.com. **Contact:** Joseph Ajlouny, director. Estab. 1988. Signatory of WGA; member of Mid-America Publishers Association, Michigan Publishers Association. Represents 80 clients. 20% of clients are new/previously unpublished writers. Currently handles: 60% nonfiction books; 20% stage plays; 5% syndicated material; 15% licensing.
   • Prior to becoming an agent, Mr. Ajlouny was an editor of art books and Ms. Foss was a journalist.
Member Agents: Gwen Foss (humor, popular reference, science); Joseph S. Ajlouny (theatricals, licensing, history).
Represents: Nonfiction books, scholarly books, musical theater, science and technical books. **Considers these nonfiction areas:** art/architecture/design; biography/autobiography; crafts/hobbies; current affairs; history; how-to; humor; language/literature/criticism; music/dance/theater/film; popular culture; science/technology; sports.

O⭲ This agency specializes in humorists and satirists; popular reference and cultural titles on film, TV, sports, art and music. Does not want to receive relationship or employment humor; self-improvement; memoirs by recovering addicts; religious narratives or novels.

Also Handles: Playscripts only. **Considers these script subject areas:** comedy; erotica; experimental; musical theater; interactive theater. Actively seeking interactive (participatory theatrical scripts).

How to Contact: Query with SASE. Accepts queries by e-mail. Considers simultaneous queries. Responds in 1 month to queries; 2 months to mss. Returns material only with SASE. Obtains most new clients through queries/solicitations.

Recent Sales: Sold 16 titles and 6 script projects in the last year. *Techno Rebels*, by Dan Sicko (Billboard Books); *How to Live Forever*, by Joey West (Gramercy); *The Avant Garde Prima Donna*, by A. Booten (Random House); *Pass the Pepper*, by Annette Wong (Bantam).

Terms: Agent receives 15% commission on domestic sales; 20% on foreign sales. Offers written contract. 60-day notice must be given to terminate contract. Charges clients for annual administration fee of $50/title payable from earned royalties only.

Writers' Conferences: Oakland Writers Cnference (Rochester Hills, MI, October 2001).

☑ ◐ **ALIVE COMMUNICATIONS, INC.**, 7680 Goddard St., Suite 200, Colorado Springs CO 80920. (719)260-7080. Fax: (719)260-8223. Website: www.alivecom.com. **Contact:** Submissions Dept. Estab. 1989. Member of AAR, CBA. Represents 175 clients. 5% of clients are new/previously unpublished writers. Currently handles: 40% nonfiction books; 10% juvenile books; 4% short story collections; 40% novels; 1% syndicated material; 5% novellas.

Member Agents: Rick Christian, president (blockbusters, bestsellers); Greg Johnson (popular/commercial nonfiction and fiction); Kathy Yanni (literary nonfiction and fiction); Jerry "Chip" MacGregor (popular/commercial nonfiction and fiction, new authors with breakout potential).

Represents: Nonfiction books, juvenile books, novels, novellas, short story collections. **Considers these nonfiction areas:** biography/autobiography; business; child guidance/ parenting; how-to; religious/inspirational; self-help/personal improvement; sports; women's issues/women's studies. **Considers these fiction areas:** action/adventure; contemporary issues; detective/police/crime; family saga; historical; humor/satire; juvenile; literary; mainstream; mystery/suspense; religious/inspirational; thriller/espionage; westerns/frontier; young adult.

O⭲ This agency specializes in humor, American popular culture, popular reference and commercial nonfiction. Actively seeking inspirational/literary/mainstream fiction and work from authors with established track record and platforms. Does not want to receive poetry, young adult paperback, scripts, dark themes.

How to Contact: Send outline/synopsis and 3 sample chapters. Include bio/résumé, publishing history and SASE. Does not accept queries by e-mail or fax. Considers simultaneous submissions, "if clearly noted in cover letter." Responds in 2 weeks to queries; 1 month to mss. Returns materials only with SASE. Obtains most new clients through recommendations from clients and publishers.

Recent Sales: Sold 300 titles in the last year. *Left Behind* series, by Tim LaHaye and Jerry B. Jenkins (Tyndale); *Jerusalem Vigil*, by Bodie and Brock Thoene (Viking).

Terms: Agent receives 15% commission on domestic sales; 15-20% on foreign sales. Offers written contract. 60-day written notice must be given to terminate contract.

Reading List: Reads literary, religious, and mainstream journals to find new clients. "Our goal is always the same—to find writers whose use of language is riveting and powerful."

Tips: "Rewrite and polish until the words on the page shine. Provide us with as much personal and publishing history information as possible. Endorsements and great connections may help, provided you can write with power and passion. Alive Communications, Inc. has established itself as a premiere literary agency and speakers bureau. Based in Colorado Springs, we serve an elite group of authors and speakers who are critically acclaimed and commercially successful in both Christian and general markets."

☑ ◐ **LINDA ALLEN LITERARY AGENCY**, 1949 Green St., Suite 5, San Francisco CA 94123-4829. (415)921-6437. **Contact:** Linda Allen. Estab. 1982. Member of AAR. Represents 35-40 clients.

Represents: Nonfiction, novels (adult). **Considers these nonfiction areas:** anthropology/archaeology; art/architecture/design; biography; business; child guidance/parenting; computers/electronics; ethnic/cultural interests; gay/lesbian issues; government/politics/law; history; music/dance/theater/film; nature/environment; popular culture; psychology; sociology; women's issues/women's studies. **Considers these fiction areas:** action/adventure; contemporary issues; detective/police/crime; ethnic; feminist; gay; glitz; horror; lesbian; literary; mainstream; mystery/suspense; psychic/supernatural; regional; thriller/espionage.

O⭲ This agency specializes in "good books and nice people."

How to Contact: Query with SASE. Considers simultaneous queries. Responds in 3 weeks to queries. Returns materials only with SASE. Obtains new clients "by referral mostly."

Recent Sales: This agency prefers not to share information on specific sales.

Terms: Agent receives 15% commission. Charges clients for photocopying.

◒ **JAMES ALLEN, LITERARY AGENT**, P.O. Box 278, Milford PA 18337-0278. **Contact:** James Allen. Estab. 1974. Represents 40 clients. 10% of clients are new/previously unpublished writers. Currently handles: 2% nonfiction books; 8% juvenile books; 90% novels.

insider report

Christian agents:
a leap of faith pays off

Until the almost miraculous ascension of Jerry Jenkins's and Tim LaHaye's best-selling *Left Behind* book series (Tyndale House Publishers, Inc.), Christian literature suffered a somewhat cloistered existence.

"There have always been success stories within the religious ranks," says Lynn Garrett, religion editor at *Publishers Weekly*. "And Frank Peretti is probably the granddaddy of the genre." The combined sale of two of Peretti's most popular titles, *This Present Darkness* and *Piercing the Darkness* (both published by Crossway Books), could top five million in 2001.

"Janette Oke is another powerhouse in her own right," Garrett continues. Oke writes historical romances about the Canadian prairie and received the Christian Booksellers Association's

Rick Christian

lifetime achievement tribute in 1999 for selling more than nineteen million books. But outside of the fifty-year-old CBA, no one was talking about it.

Why? "The Christian book industry has traditionally functioned within a world of its own," says Garrett. "But the *Left Behind* series is the perfect example of what can happen when people come together within that niche."

Jenkins's exceptional writing skills may have upped the ante in the Christian market, but it was super agent Rick Christian who made the leap of faith by signing Jenkins in 1991 and his scriptural collaborator Dr. Tim LaHaye in 1990—the year after his literary agency, Alive Communications, Inc. (www.alivecom.com) opened for business.

"One of our first deals was pairing Jenkins and LaHaye for the *Left Behind* series," Christian says. "But it was delayed because the opportunity arose for Jerry to work with Billy Graham on his memoir, *Just As I Am* (HarperCollins Publishers)."

"I offered to pull out of *Left Behind* and let them go with someone else," Jenkins says. But instinct told Christian to wait out the one-year delay. Considering the series had sold better than twenty-two million copies as of June of 2000, those instincts were dead on. But where did Rick Christian come from? And where will he and Christian literature go from here?

"I always thought I'd pen the Great American Novel," Christian says, reflecting on his academic career at Stanford University. "But after graduation I had a new bride and an aversion to starvation," he says, so he took a job as a newspaper reporter. Stints with magazines (including an executive editor spot at the *The Saturday Evening Post*) and a small press followed, as did a number of nonfiction book contracts.

"I found myself pathetically unable to negotiate a decent contract for myself," he admits. "I couldn't find an agent willing to handle Christian content." A little investigation told him he wasn't alone. "There was an entire market niche of writers," Christian says.

Everything changed when Christian was asked "to mediate a messy situation between a publisher and a National Book Award-winning author." To his surprise, his background as both a working writer and a publisher helped him successfully negotiate someone else's contract. And that negotiation allowed him to discover his own destiny. "I came out of it knowing what I would do with the rest of my life."

Christian quit his secure publishing job and spent the equity in his family home in California to launch his agenting enterprise, with his wife's blessing. "We both felt that the venture would either be hugely successful or that we'd end up without two nickels to rub together." With a staff of ten, including five full-time agents and a spacious new office building in Colorado Springs, Colorado, the gamble obviously paid off.

Why Colorado? "We checked out several sites," Christian says. "We looked at Seattle. We looked at Oregon. But my wife and I knew Colorado from vacations, so it was an easy choice—mountains, outdoor lifestyle, clean air, no mosquitoes. We're living on a twenty-five acre ranch. After negotiating with publishers all day, I come home and shovel you-know-what. The smell of hay and horses keeps my head clear."

Despite his undeniable success, Christian remains a maverick not only geographically, but in the realm of literary representation as well. "I don't know of any agents who specialize in Christian literature," says Laura Langlie of New York's Kidde, Hoyt & Picard agency. Christian confirms only a handful of agents mirror his spiritual inclinations.

Focus on the Family entertainment executive Mike Trout believes this lack of agents specializing in the Christian market could soon change. "There is a wider and wider gulf developing between our society's secular side and its religious side," he says. "On the one side, we are moving toward societal taboos. On the other, the popularity of books like the *Left Behind* series is on the rise." With an increased economic incentive, there will be a rise in religious representation, he says.

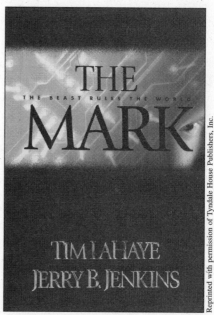

The Mark is the eighth in the *Left Behind* series (Tyndale House Publisher, Inc.) which has broken new ground for Christian fiction. The seventh book, *The Indwelling*, spent four weeks in the number one spot on *The New York Times* hardcover bestseller list. Four other books have appeared on *The New York Times* list as well. By working with agent Rick Christian, authors Tim LaHaye and Jerry B. Jenkins have definitely brought Christian books into the mainstream.

Others suggest the success of *Left Behind* was part of a millennial fluke. "The first books didn't expressly say the end of the world was coming with the end of the century," says *Publishers Weekly*'s Garrett, "but the timing was no accident."

Jenkins says Garrett is misinformed. "No one was thinking of the end of the millennium in 1995 when we started working together," he says. "The books are set in the future—that could be tomorrow or a thousand years from now." The year 2000, he says, would have been "way too predictable."

One aspect of the series's success that experts like Garrett might not have anticipated was the Christian networking—word of mouth among the devout. "People are talking," Christian says. "They're telling their friends; they're buying copies for family members. I was with Jerry at a midnight book signing in Phoenix for the release of *Assassins*, and a thousand people showed up and bought five or six books each. They wanted each copy signed to a different person. That's buzz."

The measure of success, according to Jenkins, is incredibly humbling. "I had hoped we might have a Christian bestseller," he says, "maybe sell 100,000 or 200,000 copies. But the books are selling at an average of 1.1 million copies a month. The *Left Behind* website (www.leftbehind. com) gets 80,000 hits a day.

"I'd love to say it's the great writing that has inspired this success," Jenkins jokes, "but it's so big, I know it isn't me. You'd have to say this is a God thing. I just feel blessed to be a part of the team."

Christian's assessment is essentially the same. "I still like waking up at four in the morning with a 'Yeow!'" he says. "But I try to take things a day at a time."

Rick Christian's tips on working with an agent

For ten years, agent Rick Christian has been guiding spirit-filled authors towards successful publication. These tips, straight from Christian himself, offer focus to writers not yet personally acquainted with Christian or his Colorado literary agency, Alive Communications, Inc.

What should a Christian writer look for in a good agent?

First and foremost, professional competence—an experienced and accurate knowledge of the Christian market, including how it differs from the general market. What often makes the qualitative difference, however, is that the agent is like minded and shares core values. Some agents' operative motto is, "Sell it, don't smell it." Because of this attitude, we've gotten top authors on the rebound from a strained relationship with other agencies in New York and Los Angeles. A frequent complaint: "My agent just didn't get what I'm all about."

Religious and spiritual sensitivity is important not just for understanding the market, but also for identifying with the writer's passion and personal calling. Also, the agent needs to have an intimate knowledge of what's hot and what's not; a gut instinct for spotting holes in the market; a passion for words and big ideas; an ability to move people outside of in-the-box thinking; and a salesman's knack for closing a deal. You want to know your agent understands the pathos of your trade and can also decipher pesky pro formas (the publisher's profit and loss estimation that projects a book's potential success).

What type of agent should a Christian writer avoid?

All agents have different strengths, but beware of those who simply close a deal and move on.

Steer clear of disingenuous agents who are all happy talk at the front end but won't return your calls after inking a deal. And bail out if you sense a major disconnection at the human level or if there's any question about integrity or character. Your son or daughter, your spouse or mother should all be comfortable in your agent's presence. Bedside manners count.

What kind of talent are you looking for at Alive Communications, Inc.?

Each year we receive truckloads of submissions, most of which we can't take on. It's not enough to have a good idea; you must have a thorough, tight proposal, matching credentials, and killer talent. When those three elements come together, you should hear the hooting and hollering in our office! Finding that rare talent is one of the greatest natural highs.

Is there a market for Christian children's books? Do you represent them?

There's a market, but we're very selective. Most of our children's books are with existing clients, but you never know what tomorrow's FedEx delivery will bring.

What's in demand in the Christian book market?

The big, edge-of-the-seat thrillers and adventure novels that appeal to both men and women are few and far between, as are those written by professionals in medicine, law, entertainment, government defense, and the like. And we're always on the lookout for well-researched historicals and gripping contemporaries. With nonfiction, author platform is critical. We handle our share of celebrity books, but we're most intrigued by authors with an authoritative voice whose words will reverberate in readers' minds and hearts.

Do you approach only Christian publishers with your clients?

It depends on the author and content. Certain books would be inappropriate for Christian publishers; others are specifically targeted to them. Our top books are pitched to all comers, and some of our splashiest sales and biggest long-term successes have been with secular New York houses. We spent a lot of time through the years helping various editors understand the multibillion dollar size of the Christian market. We talked demographics and buying patterns. Once it was understood that churchgoers shopped where everybody else did, the next step was obvious. Editors began competing on key titles, and we had some spectacular successes. Remember, John Grisham and Jan Karon were first published by small Christian houses, and only hit *The New York Times* list after switching to a New York house. On the other hand, Tyndale House Publishers, Inc., Thomas Nelson Publishers, and Zondervan Publishing House authors are hitting the major lists on a regular basis. But it takes a great book, a top agent, and an aggressive publishing plan to make that happen.

Final tips for beginning writers?

Keep your day job, and don't go into writing to improve your self-esteem. But don't be afraid to dream—and keep feeding your passion. It has to start with you. When it spreads to others, hold on for the ride! And learn a few good jokes along the way. Selling books and forging significant careers is serious business, but agents appreciate authors who are good for an occasional laugh.
—*Kelly Milner Halls*

Represents: Nonfiction books, novels. **Considers these nonfiction areas:** history; true crime/investigative. **Considers these fiction areas:** action/adventure; detective/police/crime; family saga; fantasy; glitz; historical; horror; mainstream; mystery/suspense; romance (contemporary, historical); science fiction; young adult.

    O— "I handle all kinds of genre fiction (except westerns) and specialize in science fiction and fantasy." Actively seeking "well-written work by people who at least have their foot in the door and are looking for someone to take them to the next (and subsequent) levels." Does not want to receive "petitions for representation from people who do not yet have even one booklength credit."

How to Contact: Query with SASE. Responds in 1 week to queries; 2 months to mss. "I prefer first contact to be a query letter with two- to three-page plot synopsis and SASE with a response time of one week. If my interest is piqued, I then ask for the first four chapters, response time within a month. If I'm impressed by the writing, I then ask for the balance of the manuscript, response time about two months."

Recent Sales: Sold about 35 titles in the last year. *China Sea*, by David Poyer (St. Martin's Press), *Aranur's Tale*, by Tara K. Harper (Del Rey), *The Devil in Ol' Rosie*, by Louise Moeri (Atheneum/S&S). Other clients include Doug Allyn, Judi Lind, Robert Trout, Juanita Coulson, Jan Clark.

Terms: Agent receives 10% commission on domestic print sales; 20% on film sales; 20% on foreign sales. Offers written contract, binding for 3 years "automatically renewed. No reading fees or other up-front charges. I reserve the right to charge clients for extraordinary expenses (in practice, only the cost of book purchases when I need copies to market a title abroad). I do not bill the author but deduct the charges from incoming earnings."

Tips: *"First time at book length need NOT apply*—only taking on authors who have the foundations of their writing careers in place and can use help in building the rest. A cogent, to-the-point query letter is necessary, laying out the author's track record, and giving a brief blurb for the book. The response to a mere 'I have written a novel, will you look at it?' is universally, 'NO!' "

◪ ALLRED AND ALLRED LITERARY AGENTS, 7834 Alabama Ave., Canoga Park CA 91304-4905. (818)346-4313. **Contact:** Robert Allred. Estab. 1991. Represents 5 clients. 100% of clients are new/previously unpublished writers. Currently handles: books, movie scripts, TV scripts.

    ● Prior to opening his agency, Mr. Allred was a writer, assistant producer, associate director and editorial assistant.

Member Agents: Robert Allred (all); Kim Allred (all).

Represents: Nonfiction books, scholarly books, textbooks, juvenile books, novels, short story collections, syndicated material. **Considers these nonfiction areas:** anthropology/archaeology; art/architecture/design; biography/autobiography; cooking/food/nutrition; crafts/hobbies; current affairs; education; ethnic/cultural interests; health/medicine; history; how-to; humor; interior design/decorating; juvenile nonfiction; language/literature/criticism; military/war; music/dance/theater/film; New Age/metaphysics; photography; popular culture; psychology; religious/inspirational; science/technology; self-help/personal improvement; sociology; sports; true crime/investigative; women's issues/women's studies. **Considers these fiction areas:** action/adventure; confessional; contemporary issues; detective/police/crime; erotica; ethnic; family saga; fantasy; feminist; gay; glitz; historical; horror; humor/satire; juvenile; lesbian; literary; mainstream; mystery/suspense; psychic/supernatural; regional; religious/inspirational; romance (contemporary, gothic, historical, regency); science fiction; sports; thriller/espionage; westerns/frontier; young adult.

Also Handles: Feature film, TV MOW, episodic drama, sitcom, soap opera, theatrical stage play, animation, documentary, variety show. **Considers all script subject areas.**

How to Contact: Query with SASE. Book: send first 25 pages. Script: send entire script. For both, include 1-2 page synopsis, cover letter and SASE. "The synopsis must cover the entire length of the project from beginning to end." Does not accept queries by e-mail or fax. Considers simultaneous queries and submissions. Responds in 3 weeks to queries; 2 months to mss. Returns materials only with SASE. Obtains most new clients through recommendations and solicitation.

Recent Sales: This agency prefers not to share information on specific sales.

Terms: Agent receives 10% commission on domestic sales; 10% on foreign sales with foreign agent receiving additional 10%. Offers written contract, binding for 1 year. 100% of business derived from commissions on ms.

Tips: "A professional appearance in script format, dark and large type, and simple binding go a long way to create good first impressions in this business, as does a professional business manner. We must be able to at least estimate the potential of the whole project before we can expend the time reading it in its entirety. Writers who try to sell us with overblown hyperbole or titillate our curiosity by vaguely hinting at a possible outcome do themselves a disservice; agents don't have time for reading sales copy—just tell us what it's about, and let us make the decision about whether we want to see the entire project."

◪ ALTAIR LITERARY AGENCY, 141 Fifth Ave., Suite 8N, New York NY 10010. (212)505-3320. **Contact:** Nicholas Smith, partner. Estab. 1996. Member of AAR. Represents 75 clients. Currently handles: 95% nonfiction books; 2% juvenile books; 1% multimedia; 2% novels.

Member Agents: Andrea Pedolsky, partner (nonfiction); Nicholas Smith, partner.

Represents: Nonfiction books. **Considers these nonfiction areas:** anthropology/archaeology; art/architecture/design; biography/autobiography; business; ethnic/cultural interests; gay/lesbian issues; government/politics/law; health/medicine; history; how-to; illustrated books; money/finance/economics; music/dance/theater/film; nature/environment; photography; popular culture; popular reference; psychology; religious/inspirational; science/technology; self-help/personal improvement; sociology; sports; women's issues/women's studies. **Considers these fiction areas:** historical; literary. Also interested in book to CD conversion and book to museum exhibition.

☛ This agency specializes in nonfiction with an emphasis on authors who have a direct connection to their topic, and at least a moderate level of public exposure. Actively seeking solid, well-informed authors who have or are developing a public platform for the subject specialty. Does not want to receive true crime, memoirs, romance novels.

How to Contact: Query with SASE. Considers simultaneous queries and submissions. Responds in 3 weeks to queries; 1 month to mss. Obtains most new clients through recommendations, solicitations, author queries.

Recent Sales: *Women of Discovery*, by Milbry Polk and Mary Tiegreen (Crown/Clarkson Potter); *Building a Business the Zen Way*, by Geri Larkin (Ten Speed/Celestial Arts); *Date Smart!*, by David Coleman and Rick Doyle (Prima); *Extreme Science*, by Peter Taylor (McGraw-Hill).

Terms: Agent receives 15% commission on domestic sales; 20% on foreign sales. Offers written contract, exclusive for 1 year. 60-day notice must be given to terminate contract. Charges clients for photocopying (edits of the proposal/chapters/ms to author, copies of proposal for submissions), postage (correspondence to author, proposals for submission, and marketing book for translation rights. May refer writers to outside editor but receives no compensation for referral.

Tips: "Beyond being able to write a compelling book, have an understanding of the market issues that are driving publishing today."

◖ **MIRIAM ALTSHULER LITERARY AGENCY**, 53 Old Post Rd. N., Red Hook NY 12571. (845)758-9408. Fax: (845)758-3118. E-mail: malalit@ulster.net. **Contact:** Miriam Altshuler. Estab. 1994. Member of AAR. Represents 40 clients. Currently handles: 45% nonfiction books; 45% novels; 5% short story collections; 5% juvenile books.

● Ms. Altshuler has been an agent since 1982.

Represents: Nonfiction, novels, short story collections, juvenile books. **Considers these nonfiction areas:** biography/autobiography; ethnic/cultural interests; history; language/literature/criticism; memoirs; multicultural; music/dance/theater/film; nature/environment; popular culture; psychology; sociology; women's issues/women's studies. **Considers these fiction areas:** contemporary issues; literary; mainstream; multicultural; thriller/espionage.

How to Contact: Query with SASE. Does not accept queries by e-mail or fax. Considers simultaneous queries; prefers to read full mss exclusively. Responds in 2 weeks on queries; 3 weeks on mss. Returns materials only with SASE. Obtains most new clients through recommendations from others.

Recent Sales: This agency prefers not to share information on specific sales.

Terms: Agent receives 15% commission on domestic sales; 20% on foreign sales. Does not offer written contract. Charges clients for overseas mailing, photocopies.

Writers' Conferences: Bread Loaf Writers' Conference (Middlebury, VT, August).

✔ ◖ **AMG/RENAISSANCE**, (formerly Renaissance Literary Agency), 9465 Wilshire Blvd., 6th Floor, Beverly Hills CA 90212. (310)860-8249. **Contact:** Joel Gotler. Represents 350 clients. 10% of clients are new/previously unpublished writers. Currently handles: 90% novels; 10% movie and TV scripts.

Member Agents: Judy Fark (film rights); Joel Gotler, partner (film rights); Lisa Hamilton (book publishing); Allan Nevins, partner (book publishing); Michael Prevett (film rights); Irv Schwartz, partner (TV writers).

Represents: Nonfiction books, novels. **Considers these nonfiction areas:** biography/autobiography; history; film; true crime/investigative. **Considers these fiction areas:** action/adventure; contemporary issue; detective/police/crime; ethnic; family saga; fantasy; historical; humor/satire; literary; mainstream; mystery/suspense; science fiction; thriller/espionage.

☛ This management company specializes in selling movies and TV rights from books.

Also Handles: Feature film. **Considers these script subject areas:** action/adventure; cartoon/animation; comedy; contemporary issues; detective/police/crime; erotica; ethnic; experimental; family saga; fantasy; feminist; gay; historical; horror; juvenile; lesbian; mainstream; mystery/suspense; psychic/supernatural; regional; romantic comedy and drama; science fiction; sports; teen; thriller/espionage; westerns;frontier.

How to Contact: Query via recommendation. Obtains most news clients through recommendations from others.

Recent Sales: *The Fall of the Soviet Union*, by Anthony Cave-Brown (Harcourt-Brace); *Film/TV rights optioned/sold: Fake Liar Cheat*, by Tod Goldberg (Miramax); *The Discrete Charm of Charlie Monk*, by David Ambrose (StudioCanal); *Big Tears Fall*, by Harlan Coben (Artists Production Group); *Natasha: A Biography of Natalie Wood*, by Suzanne Finstad (ABC); *Sector Seven*, by David Wiesner (Nickelodeon/Good Machine); *Scripting assignments: Flamingo Rising*, based on a novel by Larry Baker, adapted by Richard Russo (Hallmark); *Merlin* and *Jackie Ethel Joan—The Women of Camelot*, both by David Stevens.

Terms: Manager receives 15% commission on domestic books; 15% on film sales.

⬤ BETSY AMSTER LITERARY ENTERPRISES, P.O. Box 27788, Los Angeles CA 90027-0788. **Contact:** Betsy Amster. Estab. 1992. Member of AAR. Represents over 50 clients. 40% of clients are new/previously unpublished writers. Currently handles: 65% nonfiction books; 35% novels.

• Prior to opening her agency, Ms. Amster was an editor at Pantheon and Vintage for 10 years, and served as editorial director for the Globe Pequot Press for 2 years. "This experience gives me a wider perspective on the business and the ability to give focused editorial feedback to my clients."

Represents: Nonfiction books, novels. **Considers these nonfiction areas:** biography/autobiography; business; child guidance/parenting; cyberculture; ethnic/cultural interests; gardening; health/medicine; history; how-to; money/finance/economics; popular culture; psychology; self-help/personal improvement; sociology; women's issues/women's studies. **Considers these fiction areas:** ethnic; literary.

O—¬ Actively seeking "outstanding literary fiction (the next Jane Smiley, Wally Lamb or Jhumpa Lahiri) and high profile self-help/psychology." Does not want to receive poetry, children's books, romances, westerns, science fiction.

How to Contact: For fiction, send query, first 3 pages and SASE. For nonfiction, send query with SASE. For both, "include SASE or no response." Does not accept queries by e-mail or fax. Considers simultaneous queries and submissions. Responds in 1 month to queries; 2 months to mss. Obtains most new clients through recommendations from others, solicitation, conferences.

Recent Sales: *The Green Suit*, by Dwight Allen (Algonquin); *Esperanza's Box of Saints*, by María Amparo Escandón (Scribner); *The Backbone of the World: A Season Along the Continental Divide*, by Frank Clifford (Broadway); *The Flag of Yoshio Shimizu: A Daughter Discovers Her Father's War*, by Louise Steinman (Algonquin); *Dogtionary*, by Sharon Montrose (Viking Studio); *Twenty $ecrets to Money & Independence: The DollarDiva's Guide to Life*, by Joline Godfrey (St. Martin's Press); *Storybook Travels*, by Colleen Dunn Bates and Susan LaTempa (Crown).

Terms: Agent receives 15% commission on domestic sales. Offers written contract, binding for 1-2 years. 60-day notice must be given to terminate contract. Charges clients for photocopying, postage, long distance phone calls, messengers, galleys, and books used in submissions to foreign and film agents and to magazines for first serial rights.

Writers' Conferences: Squaw Valley, Maui Writers Conference; Pacific Northwest Conference; San Diego Writers Conference; UCLA Writers Conference; Book Passage Travel Writers Conference.

⬤ MARCIA AMSTERDAM AGENCY, 41 W. 82nd St., New York NY 10024-5613. (212)873-4945. **Contact:** Marcia Amsterdam. Estab. 1970. Signatory of WGA. Currently handles: 15% nonfiction books; 70% novels; 10% movie scripts; 5% TV scripts.

• Prior to opening her agency, Ms. Amsterdam was an editor.

Represents: Nonfiction, novels. **Considers these nonfiction areas:** child guidance/parenting, humor, popular culture, self-help/personal improvement. **Considers these fiction areas:** action/adventure; detective; horror; humor; mainstream; mystery/suspense; romance (contemporary, historical); science fiction; thriller/espionage; westerns/frontier; young adult.

Also Handles: Feature film, TV MOW, sitcom. **Considers these script subject areas:** comedy, mainstream, mystery/suspense, romance (comedy, drama).

How to Contact: Send outline plus first 3 sample chapters and SASE. Responds in 1 month to queries.

Recent Sales: *Rosey In the Present Tense*, by Louise Hawes (Walker); *Flash Factor*, by William H. Lovejoy (Kensington). *TV scripts optioned/sold:* *Mad About You*, by Jenna Bruce (Columbia Tristar TV).

Terms: Agent receives 15% commission on domestic sales; 20% on foreign sales, 10% on scripts. Offers written contract, binding for 1 year, "renewable." Charges clients for extra office expenses, foreign postage, copying, legal fees (when agreed upon).

Tips: "We are always looking for interesting literary voices."

⬤ ⬤ BART ANDREWS & ASSOCIATES INC., **(Specialized: entertainment)**, 7510 Sunset Blvd., Suite 100, Los Angeles CA 90046. (213)851-8158. **Contact:** Bart Andrews. Estab. 1982. Represents 25 clients. 25% of clients are new/previously unpublished authors. Currently handles: 100% nonfiction books.

Represents: Nonfiction books. **Considers these nonfiction areas:** biography/autobiography; music/dance/theater/film; TV.

O—¬ This agency specializes in nonfiction only, and in the general category of entertainment (movies, TV, biographies, autobiographies).

How to Contact: Query with SASE. Responds in 1 week to queries; 1 month to mss. Does not accept queries by e-mail or fax. Considers simultaneous submissions.

Recent Sales: Sold 50 titles in the last year. *Roseanne*, by J. Randy Taraborrelli (G.P. Putnam's Sons); *Out of the Madness*, by Rose Books packaging firm (HarperCollins).

Terms: Agent receives 15% commission on domestic sales; 15% on foreign sales (after subagent takes his 10%). Offers written contract, "binding on a project-by-project basis." Charges clients for all photocopying, mailing, phone calls, postage, etc. Writers reimbursed for office fees after the sale of ms.

Writers' Conferences: Frequently lectures at UCLA in Los Angeles.

Tips: "Recommendations from existing clients or professionals are best, although I find a lot of new clients by seeking them out myself. I rarely find a new client through the mail. Spend time writing a query letter. Sell yourself like a product. The bottom line is writing ability, and then the idea itself. It takes a lot to convince me. I've seen it all! I hear from too many first-time authors who don't do their homework. They're trying to get a book published and they haven't the faintest idea what is required of them. There are plenty of good books on the subject and, in my opinion, it's their responsibility—not mine—to educate themselves before they try to find an agent to represent their work. When I ask an author to see a manuscript or even a partial manuscript, I really must be convinced I want to read it—based on a strong query letter—because I have no intention of wasting my time reading just for the fun of it."

APPLESEEDS MANAGEMENT, 200 E. 30th St., Suite 302, San Bernardino CA 92404. (909)882-1667. For screenplays and teleplays only, send to 1870 N. Vermont, Suite 560, Hollywood CA 90027. **Contact:** S. James Foiles. Estab. 1988. 40% of clients are new/previously unpublished writers. Currently handles: 15% nonfiction books; 75% novels; 5% movie scripts; 5% teleplays (MOW).
• This agency reports that it is not accepting unsolicited screenplays and teleplays at this time.
Represents: Nonfiction books, novels. **Considers these nonfiction areas:** film; true crime/investigative. **Considers these fiction areas:** detective/police/crime; fantasy; horror; mystery/suspense; psychic/supernatural; science fiction; true crime/investigative.
Also Handles: Movie scripts. TV MOW, no episodic. This agency specializes in materials that could be adapted from book to screen; and in screenplays and teleplays.
How to Contact: Query with SASE. Responds in 2 weeks to queries; 2 months to mss.
Recent Sales: This agency prefers not to share in information on specific sales.
Terms: Agent receives 10-15% commission on domestic sales; 20% on foreign sales. Offers written contract, binding for 1-7 years.
Tips: "In your query, please describe your intended target audience and distinguish your book/script from similar works."

AUTHENTIC CREATIONS LITERARY AGENCY, 875 Lawrenceville-Suwanee Rd., Suite 310-306, Lawrenceville GA 30043. (770)339-3774. Fax: (770)995-7126. E-mail: ron@authenticcreations.com. Website: www.authenticcreations.com. **Contact:** Mary Lee Laitsch. Estab. 1993. Member of Sisters in Crime. Represents 70 clients. 60% of clients are new/previously unpublished writers. Currently handles: 50% nonfiction books; 50% novels.
• Prior to becoming agents, Ms. Laitsch was a librarian and elementary school teacher; Mr. Laitsch was an attorney and a writer.
Member Agents: Mary Lee Laitsch; Ronald E. Laitsch.
Represents: Nonfiction books, scholarly books, novels. **Considers these nonfiction areas:** anthropology/archaeology; biography/autobiography; child guidance/parenting; crafts/hobbies; current affairs; history; how-to; science/technology; self-help/personal improvement; sports; true crime/investigative; women's issues/women's studies. **Considers these fiction areas:** action/adventure; contemporary issues; detective/police/crime; family saga; literary; mainstream; mystery/suspense; romance; sports; thriller/espionage.
How to Contact: Query with SASE. Responds in 2 weeks to queries; 2 months to mss. "We prefer not to receive queries by e-mail." Considers simultaneous queries and submissions.
Recent Sales: Sold 15 titles in the last year. This agency prefers not to share information on specific sales.
Terms: Agent receives 15% commission on domestic sales; 15% on foreign sales. Charges clients for photocopying and postage.
Tips: "Service to our authors is the key to our success. We work with authors to produce a fine product for prospective publishers."

AUTHORS ALLIANCE INC., 25 Claremont Ave., Suite 3C, New York NY 10027. Phone/Fax: (212)662-9788. E-mail: camp544@aol.com. **Contact:** Chris Crane. Represents 25 clients. 10% of clients are new/previously unpublished writers. Currently handles: 40% nonfiction books, 30% movie scripts, 30% novels.
• Prior to opening the agency, Chris Crane worked for Bantam Doubleday Dell Publishing and Warner Books.
Represents: Nonfiction books, movie scripts, novels. **Considers these nonfiction areas:** biography/autobiography; business; child guidance/parenting; computers/electronics; cooking/food/nutrition; crafts/hobbies; current affairs; government/politics/law; health/medicine; history; how-to; language/literature/criticism; memoirs; military/war; money/finance/economics; music/dance/theater/film; nature/environment; New Age/metaphysics; psychology; religious/inspirational; self-help/personal improvement; sports; true crime/investigative. **Considers these fiction areas:** contemporary issues; detective/police/crime; glitz; historical; literary; mainstream; mystery/suspense; thriller/espionage.
O→ This agency specializes in "biographies, especially of historical figures and big name celebrities and business books." Actively seeking mainstream and literary fiction/nonfiction. Does not want to receive children's books or poetry.
How to Contact: Published authors should send query by e-mail. Responds in 2 weeks to queries; 1 month to mss. *No unsolicited mss will be accepted.* Obtains most clients through recommendations and queries.
Recent Sales: *License to Steal*, by Scott Gilman (HarperCollins); *Moscow Madness*, by Tim Harper (McGraw-Hill).
Terms: Agent receives 15% commission on domestic sales; 10% on foreign sales. Offers written contract. Charges clients for postage, photocopying.

THE AXELROD AGENCY, 49 Main St., P.O. Box 357, Chatham, NY 12037. (518)392-2100. Fax: (518)392-2944. E-mail: steve@axelrodagency.com. **Contact:** Steven Axelrod. Estab. 1983. Member of AAR. Represents 20-30 clients; 1% of clients are new/previously unpublished writers. Currently handles: 5% nonfiction books; 95% novels.
• Prior to becoming an agent, Mr. Axelrod was a book club editor.

Represents: Nonfiction, novels. **Considers these fiction areas**: mystery/suspense; romance; women's fiction.
How to Contact: Query with SASE. Prefers to read materials exclusively. Responds in 3 weeks on queries; 6 weeks on mss. Returns materials only with SASE. Obtains most new clients through recommendations from others.
Recent Sales: This agency prefers not to share information on specific sales.
Terms: Agent receives 15% commission on domestic sales; 20% on foreign sales. Does not offer written contract.
Writers' Conferences: Romance Writers of America (July).

⊘ JULIAN BACH LITERARY AGENCY, 22 E. 71st St., New York NY 10021. Member of AAR. This agency did not respond to our request for information. Query before submitting.

✓ ⊘ MALAGA BALDI LITERARY AGENCY, 204 W. 84th St., Suite 3C, New York NY 10024. (212)579-5075. **Contact:** Malaga Baldi. Estab. 1985. Represents 40-50 clients. 80% of clients are new/previously unpublished writers. Currently handles: 60% nonfiction books; 40% fiction.
• Prior to opening the agency, Malaga Baldi worked in a bookstore.
Represents: Nonfiction books, novels. **Considers these nonfiction areas:** agriculture/horticulture; animals; anthropology/archaeology; art/architecture/design; biography/autobiography; business; cooking/food; current affairs; ethnic/cultural interests; gay/lesbian issues; government/politics; health/medicine; history; interior design/decorating; language/literature/criticism; memoirs; money/finance/economics; music/dance/theater/film; nature/environment; photography; psychology; science/technology; sociology; travel; true crime/investigative; women's issues/women's studies. **Considers these fiction areas:** action/adventure; contemporary issues; detective; erotica; ethnic; experimental; feminist; gay; historical; lesbian; literary; mainstream; mystery/suspense; regional; thriller.
　　O→ This agency specializes in quality literary fiction and nonfiction. Actively seeking well-written fiction and nonfiction. Does not want to receive child guidance, crafts, juvenile nonfiction, New Age/metaphysics, sports, family saga, fantasy, glitz, juvenile fiction, picture book, psychic/supernatural, religious/inspirational, romance, science fiction, western or young adult.
How to Contact: Query first with SASE. Responds after a minimum of 10 weeks. "Please enclose self-addressed stamped jiffy bag or padded envelope with submission. For acknowledgement of manuscript receipt send via certified mail or UPS."
Recent Sales: Sold 13 titles in the last year. This agency prefers not to share information on specific sales.
Terms: Agent receives 15% commission on domestic sales; 20% on foreign sales. Offers written contract. Charges clients "initial $50 fee to cover photocopying expenses. If the manuscript is lengthy, I prefer the author to cover expense of photocopying."

⊘ BALKIN AGENCY, INC., P.O. Box 222, Amherst MA 01004. (413)548-9835. Fax: (413)548-9836. **Contact:** Rick Balkin, president. Estab. 1972. Member of AAR. Represents 50 clients. 10% of clients are new/previously unpublished writers. Currently handles: 85% nonfiction books; 5% scholarly books; 5% reference books; 5% textbooks.
• Prior to opening his agency, Mr. Balkin served as executive editor with Bobbs-Merrill Company.
Represents: Nonfiction books, textbooks, reference, scholarly books. **Considers these nonfiction areas:** animals; anthropology/archaeology; biography; current affairs; health/medicine; history; how-to; language/literature/criticism; music/dance/theater/film; nature/environment; popular culture; science/technology; social science; translations; travel; true crime/investigative.
　　O→ This agency specializes in adult nonfiction. Does not want to receive fiction, poetry, screenplays, computer books.
How to Contact: Query with outline/proposal and SASE. Responds in 1 week to queries; 2 weeks to mss. Returns materials only with SASE. Obtains most new clients through referrals.
Recent Sales: *A Natural History of Falsehood*, W.W. Norton Co., 2001 *Adolescent Depression* (Henry Holt), 2001 *Eliz. Van Lew: A Union Spy in the Heart of the Confederacy* (biography, Oxford U.P.).
Terms: Agent receives 15% commission on domestic sales; 20% on foreign sales. Sometimes offers written contract, binding for 1 year. Charges clients for photocopying and express or foreign mail.
Tips: "I do not take on books described as bestsellers or potential bestsellers. Any nonfiction work that is either unique, paradigmatic, a contribution, truly witty or a labor of love is grist for my mill."

Ⓝ ◯ BARBARA'S LITERARY AGENCY, 145 E. Sierra Madre, Sierra Madre CA 91024. **Contact:** Barbara Cocores. Estab. 2000. Represents 1 client. Currently handles: children's books; stage plays.
• Prior to becoming an agent, Ms. Cocores wrote a recipe book, *Home-Baked Scones*.
Represents: Nonfiction, children's books. **Considers these nonfiction areas:** animals, women's issues/women's studies. **Considers these fiction areas:** fantasy, juvenile.
　　O→ Actively seeking children's books, women's issues, fantasy.
How to Contact: Query with proposal and SASE. Responds in 1 month. Returns materials only with SASE.
Recent Sales: This is a new agency with no recorded sales.
Terms: Agent receives 25% commission on domestic sales; 25% on foreign sales. Offers written contract. Charges clients for photocopies, phone calls.
Tips: "I'm interested in children's books and fantasy. Send SASE."

✓ ◎ **LORETTA BARRETT BOOKS INC.**, 101 Fifth Ave., New York NY 10003. (212)242-3420. Fax: (212)807-9579. **Contact:** Loretta A. Barrett, president, or Nick Mullendor. Estab. 1990. Member of AAR. Represents 70 clients. Currently handles: 35% fiction; 65% nonfiction.

• Prior to opening her agency, Ms. Barrett was vice president and executive editor at Doubleday for 25 years.

Represents: Nonfiction, fiction. **Considers all areas of nonfiction:** history, biography, sociology, science, spirituality, self-help, psychology, parenting, memoir, narrative nonfiction, adventure/outdoors, cultural studies, religion. Considers these fiction areas: action/adventure; confessional; contemporary issues; detective/police/crime; ethnic; experimental; family saga; feminist; gay; glitz; historical; humor/satire; lesbian; literary; mainstream; mystery/suspense; psychic/supernatural; religious/inspirational; romance; sports; thriller/espionage. "No children's or juvenile."

○━ This agency specializes in general interest books. Does not want to receive children's or juvenile.

How to Contact: Query first with SASE. Considers simultaneous queries and submissions. Responds in 6 weeks to queries. Returns materials only with SASE.

Recent Sales: *Inviting God to Your Wedding*, by Martha Williamson (Harmony); *Line of Sight*, by Jack Kelly (Hyperion); *Lip Service*, by M.J. Rose (Pocket); *If You Can't be Free, be a Mystery: Myths & Meanings of Billie Holiday*, by Farah Griffin (Free Press); *Were You Always an Italian?*, by Maria Laurino (W.W. Norton).

Terms: Agent receives 15% commission on domestic sales; 20% on foreign sales. Offers written contract. Charges clients for shipping and photocopying.

Writers' Conferences: San Diego State University Writer's Conference; Maui Writer's Conference.

✓ ◎ **THE BEDFORD BOOK WORKS, INC.**, 7-11 Legion Dr., Valhalla NY 10595. (914)328-4999. Fax: (914)328-5432. **Contact:** Joel E. Fishman, president. Estab. 1993. Represents 50 clients. 50% of clients are new/previously unpublished writers. Currently handles: 80% nonfiction books, 20% novels.

• Prior to becoming agents, Mr. Fishman served as senior editor at Doubleday; Mr. Lang worked as Doubleday's foreign rights director; Mr. Reichert is a former consumer products and health-care marketer and entreprenuer and coauthor of four books.

Member Agents: Kevin Lang (commercial fiction, humor, nonfiction, category nonfiction); James Reichert (business, sports, outdoors).

Represents: Nonfiction books, novels. **Considers these nonfiction areas:** biography/autobiography; business; current affairs; health/medicine; history; how-to; humor; money/finance/economics; popular culture; psychology; science/technology; sports. **Considers these fiction areas:** contemporary issues; detective/police/crime; mainstream; mystery/suspense; thriller/espionage.

How to Contact: Query with SASE. Accepts queries by e-mail and fax. Prefers to read materials exclusively. Responds in 2 weeks to queries; 2 months to mss. Obtains most new clients through recommendations and solicitation.

Recent Sales: *Business as a Calling*, by Commander Robert Watson of the Salvation Army (Crown); *Back to Bedlam*, by Robert Whitaker (Perseus); *Breathwalk*, by Gurucharan Singh Khalsa and Yogi Bhajan (Broadway); *The Corporate Athlete*, by Jack Groppel with Bob Andelman (John Wiley & Sons); *The Global Me*, by G. Pascal Zachary (Public Affairs); *Beyond Pleasure and Pain*, by Steven Reiss (Tarcher-Putnam).

Terms: Agent receives 15% commission on domestic sales; 20% on foreign sales. Offers written contract, binding for 1 year with 60-day cancellation clause. Charges clients for postage and photocopying.

Tips: "Grab my attention right away with your query—not with gimmicks, but with excellent writing."

◎ **PAM BERNSTEIN & ASSOCIATES, INC.**, 790 Madison Ave., Suite 310, New York NY 10021. Member of AAR. This agency did not respond to our request for information. Query before submiting.

◎ **MEREDITH BERNSTEIN LITERARY AGENCY**, 2112 Broadway, Suite 503 A, New York NY 10023. (212)799-1007. Fax: (212)799-1145. Estab. 1981. Member of AAR. Represents approximately 100 clients. 20% of clients are new/previously unpublished writers. Currently handles: 50% nonfiction books; 50% fiction.

• Prior to opening her agency, Ms. Bernstein served in another agency for 5 years.

Member Agents: Meredith Bernstein; Elizabeth Cavanaugh.

Represents: Fiction and nonfiction books. **Considers these nonfiction areas:** business, e-commerce, politics, health/fitness, science, psychology, relationships, parenting, pets, narrative nonfiction, spirituality. **Considers these fiction areas:** romance, mystery, literary, women's fiction.

○━ This agency does not specialize, "very eclectic."

How to Contact: Query first with SASE. Obtains most new clients through recommendations from others, queries and at conferences; also develops and packages own ideas.

Recent Sales: *Bone Density Diet Book*, by Dr. George Kessler (Ballantine); *Natural Healing for Dogs and Cats*, by Amy Shujai (Rodale); *Interview with An Angel*, by Linda Nathanson and Stephen Thayer (Dell).

Terms: Agent receives 15% commission on domestic sales; 20% on foreign sales. Charges clients $75 disbursement fee per year.

Writers' Conferences: Southwest Writers Conference (Albuquerque, August); Rocky Mountain Writers Conference (Denver, September); Beaumont (TX, October); Pacific Northwest Writers Conference; Austin League Writers Conference; Willamette Writers Conference (Portland, OR); Lafayette Writers Conference (Lafayette, LA); Surrey Writers Conference (Surrey, BC.); San Diego State University Writers Conference (San Diego, CA).

DANIEL BIAL AGENCY, 41 W. 83rd St., Suite 5-C, New York NY 10024-5246. (212)721-1786. E-mail: dbialagency@juno.com. **Contact:** Daniel Bial. Estab. 1992. Represents under 50 clients. 15% of clients are new/previously unpublished writers. Currently handles: 95% nonfiction books; 5% novels.

• Prior to opening his agency, Mr. Bial was an editor for 15 years.

Represents: Nonfiction books, novels. **Considers these nonfiction areas:** animals; anthropology/archaeology; biography/autobiography; business; child guidance/parenting; cooking/food/nutrition; current affairs; ethnic/cultural interests; gay/lesbian issues; government/politics/law; history; how-to; humor; language/literature/criticism; memoirs; military/war; money/finance/economics; music/dance/theater/film; nature/environment; New Age/metaphysics; popular culture; psychology; religious/inspirational; science/technology; self-help/personal improvement; sociology; sports; travel; true crime/investigative; women's issues/women's studies. **Considers these fiction areas:** action/adventure; comic; contemporary issues; detective/police/crime; erotica; ethnic; feminist; gay; humor/satire; literary.

How to Contact: Send outline/proposal with SASE. Accepts queries by e-mail. Considers simultaneous queries. Responds in 2 weeks to queries. Returns materials only with SASE. Obtains most new clients through recommendations, solicitation, "good rolodex, over the transom."

Recent Sales: This agency prefers not to share information on specific sales.

Terms: Agent receives 15% commission on domestic sales; 20% on foreign sales. Offers written contract, binding for 1 year with cancellation clause. Charges clients for overseas calls, overnight mailing, photocopying, messenger expenses.

Tips: "Good marketing is a key to success at all stages of publishing—successful authors know how to market themselves as well as their writing."

BIGSCORE PRODUCTIONS INC., P.O. Box 4575, Lancaster PA 17604. (717)293-0247. Fax: (717)293-1945. E-mail: bigscore@starburstpublishers.com. Website: www.starburstpublishers.com. **Contact:** David A. Robie. Estab. 1995. Represents 5-10 clients. 50% of clients are new/previously unpublished writers.

• Mr. Robie is also the president of Starburst Publishers, an inspirational publisher that publishes books for both the ABA and CBA markets.

Represents: Nonfiction, fiction.

○── This agency specializes in inspirational and self-help nonfiction and fiction.

How to Contact: Query over e-mail. Responds in 1 month to proposals. "Queries *only* accepted at bigscore@starburstpublishers.com. Do not send file attachments!" Does not accept queries by fax. Considers simultaneous queries and submissions.

Recent Sales: *The Chile Pepper Diet*, by Heidi Allison (HCI); *Leggett's Antique Atlas 2001*, by David and Kim Leggett (Crown); *My Name Isn't Martha, but I Can Renovate My Home* series, by Sharon Hanby-Robie (Pocket Books).

Terms: Agent receives 15% on domestic sales. Offers a written contract, binding for 6 months. Charges clients for shipping, ms photocopying and preparation, and books for subsidiary rights submissions.

Tips: "Very open to taking on new clients. Submit a well-prepared proposal that will take minimal fine-tuning for presentation to publishers. Nonfiction writers must be highly marketable and media savvy—the more established in speaking or in your profession, the better."

VICKY BIJUR, 333 West End Ave., Apt. 513, New York NY 10023. Member of AAR. This agency did not respond to our request for information. Query before submitting.

DAVID BLACK LITERARY AGENCY, INC., 156 Fifth Ave., New York NY 10001. (212)242-5080. Fax: (212)924-6609. **Contact:** David Black, owner. Estab. 1990. Member of AAR. Represents 150 clients. Currently handles: 90% nonfiction; 10% novels.

Member Agents: Susan Raihofer (general nonfiction to literary fiction); Gary Morris (commercial fiction to psychology); Joy E. Tutela (general nonfiction to literary fiction); Laureen Rowland (business, health).

Represents: Nonfiction books, fiction. **Considers these nonfiction areas:** biography/autobiography; business; history; memoirs; military/war; money/finance/economics; multicultural; politics; sports. **Considers these fiction areas:** literary; mainstream; multicultural; commercial.

○── This agency specializes in business, sports, politics, novels.

How to Contact: Query with outline and SASE. Does not accept queries by e-mail or fax. Considers simultaneous queries. Responds in 2 months to queries. Returns unwanted materials only with SASE.

Recent Sales: *Body For Life*, by Bill Phillips with Mike D'Orso (HarperCollins); *Walking with the Wind*, by John Lewis with Mike D'Orso (Simon & Schuster).

Terms: Agent receives 15% commission. Charges clients for photocopying and books purchased for sale of foreign rights.

BLEECKER STREET ASSOCIATES, INC., 532 LaGuardia Place, New York NY 10012. (212)677-4492. Fax: (212)388-0001. **Contact:** Agnes Birnbaum. Estab. 1984. Member of AAR, RWA, MWA. Represents 60 clients. 20% of clients of new/previously unpublished writers. Currently handles: 65% nonfiction books; 25% novels; 10% syndicated material.

• Prior to becoming an agent, Ms. Birnbaum was an editor at Simon & Schuster, Dutton/Signet and other publishing houses.

Represents: Nonfiction books, novels. **Considers these nonfiction areas:** animals; anthropology/archaeology; biography/autobiography; business; child guidance/parenting; computers/electronics; cooking/food/nutrition; current affairs;

ethnic/cultural interests; gay/lesbian issues; government/politics/law; health/medicine; history; how-to; humor; juvenile nonfiction; memoirs; military/war; money/finance/economics; nature/environment; New Age/metaphysics; popular culture; psychology; religious/inspirational; science/technology; self-help/personal improvement; sociology; sports; true crime/investigative; women's issues/women's studies. **Considers these fiction areas:** detective/police/crime; erotica; ethnic; family saga; feminist; gay/lesbian; historical; literary; mystery; psychic/supernatural; romance; thriller/espionage.

O→ "We're very hands-on and accessible. We try to be truly creative in our submission approaches. We've had especially good luck with first-time authors." Does not want to receive science fiction, westerns, poetry, children's books, academic/scholarly/professional books, plays, scripts.

How to Contact: Query with SASE. Does not accept queries by fax or e-mail. Considers simultaneous queries. Responds in 1 week to queries "if interested"; 1 month on mss. Returns materials only with SASE. Obtains most new clients through recommendations from others, queries, conferences. "Plus, I will approach someone with a letter if his/her work impresses me."

Recent Sales: Sold 35 titles in the last year. *Star Spangled Banner*, by Irvin Molotsky (Dutton); *Dicey Deere Mysteries*, by Harriet La Barre (St. Martin's Press); *Ophelia's Mom*, by Nina Shandler, Ph.D (Crown); *Business Planning*, by Marlene Jensen (Adams Media).

Terms: Agent receives 15% commission on domestic sales; 25% on foreign sales if co-agent is used, if not, 15% on foreign sales. Offers written contract, exclusive on all work. 30-day notice must be given to terminate contract. Charges clients for postage, long distance, fax, messengers, photocopies, not to exceed $150.

Tips: "Keep query letters short and to the point; include only information pertaining to book or background as writer. Try to avoid superlatives in description. Work needs to stand on its own, so how much editing it may have received has no place in a query letter."

REID BOATES LITERARY AGENCY, 69 Cooks Crossroad, Pittstown NJ 08867. (908)730-8523. Fax: (908)730-8931. E-mail: rboatesla@aol.com. **Contact:** Reid Boates. Estab. 1985. Represents 45 clients. 5% of clients are new/previously unpublished writers. Currently handles: 85% nonfiction books; 15% novels; "very rarely accept short story collections."

Represents: Nonfiction books, novels. **Considers these nonfiction areas;** animals; anthropology/archaeology; art/architecture/design; biography/autobiography; business; child guidance/parenting; current affairs; ethnic/cultural interests; government/politics/law; health/medicine; history; language/literature/criticism; nature/environment; psychology; science/technology; self-help/personal improvement; sports; true crime/investigative; women's issues/women's studies. **Considers these fiction areas:** contemporary issues; family saga; mainstream; thriller/espionage.

O→ This agency specializes in general fiction and nonfiction, investigative journalism/current affairs; bios and celebrity autobiographies; serious self-help; literary humor; issue-oriented business; popular science. Does not want to receive category fiction.

How to Contact: Query with SASE. Responds in 2 weeks to queries; 6 weeks to mss. Obtains most new clients through recommendations from others.

Recent Sales: Sold 20 titles in the last year. This agency prefers not to share information on specific sales.

Terms: Agent receives 15% commission on domestic sales; 20% on foreign sales. Offers written contract, binding "until terminated by either party." Charges clients for photocopying costs above $50.

BOOK DEALS, INC., 417 N. Sangamon St., Chicago IL 60622. (312)491-0030. Fax: (312)491-8091. E-mail: bookdeals@aol.com. Website: www.bookdealsinc.com. **Contact:** Caroline Francis Carney. Estab. 1996. Member of AAR. Represents 50 clients. 25% of clients are new/previously unpublished writers. Currently handles: 75% nonfiction books, 25% fiction.

● Prior to opening her agency, Ms. Carney was editorial director for a consumer book imprint within Times Mirror and held senior editorial positions in McGraw-Hill and Simon & Schuster.

Represents: Narrative nonfiction, novels. **Considers these nonfiction areas:** business; nutrition; ethnic/cultural interests; health/medicine; history; how-to; money/finance/economics; popular culture; science/technology; inspirational; parenting; popular psychology; self-help. **Considers these fiction areas:** contemporary women's fiction; ethnic; literary; mainstream; white collar crime stories; financial and medical thrillers; urban literature.

O→ This agency specializes in highly commercial nonfiction and well-crafted action. Actively seeking well-crafted fiction and nonfiction from authors with engaging voices and impeccable credentials.

How to Contact: Fiction by referral only. For nonfiction, send synopsis, outline/proposal with SASE. Accepts queries by e-mail. Considers simultaneous queries and submissions. Responds in 1 month to queries.

Recent Sales: Sold 15 titles in the last year. *Out of the Dark*, by Maurice Possley and Rick Kogan (Putnam and film rights to Warner Bros.); *The Most Important Thing I Know . . .* , by Lorne Adrain (Andrews McMeel); *Silver Spoons: How to Raise a Child in an Age of Affluence*, by Jon and Eileen Gallo (Contemporary Books); *Coloring Outside the*

CHECK THE AGENT SPECIALTIES INDEX to find agents who are interested in your specific nonfiction or fiction subject area.

Lines: How to Raise a Smarter Kid by Breaking all the Rules, by Dr. Roger Schank (HarperCollins); *Yet a Stranger: Why Black Americans Still Don't Feel at Home*, by Deborah Mathis (Warner); *A is for Attitude: An Alphabet for Living*, by Pat Russell-McCloud (HarperCollins); *Intuitive Astrology*, by Elizabeth Rose Campbell (Ballantine).
Terms: Agent receives 15% commission on domestic sales; 20% on foreign sales. Offers a written contract. Charges clients for photocopying and postage.

THE BOOK PEDDLERS, 18326 Minnetonka Blvd., Deephaven MN 55391. Member of AAR. This agency did not respond to our request for information. Query before submitting.

BOOKS & SUCH, (Specialized: Christian market), 3093 Maiden Ln., Altadena CA 91001. (626)797-1716. Fax: (626)398-0246. E-mail: jkgbooks@aol.com. **Contact:** Janet Kobobel Grant. Estab. 1996. Associate member of CBA. Represents 27 clients. 22% of clients are new/previously unpublished writers. Currently handles: 58% nonfiction books, 18% juvenile books, 10% novels, 14% children's picture books.
● Before becoming an agent, Ms. Grant was an editor for Zondervan and managing editor for Focus on the Family.
Represents: Nonfiction books, juvenile books, novels. **Considers these nonfiction areas:** child guidance/parenting; humor; juvenile nonfiction; religious/inspirational; self-help/personal improvement; women's issues/women's studies. **Considers these fiction areas:** contemporary issues; family saga; historical; juvenile; mainstream; picture book; romance; religious/inspirational; young adult.
○┅ This agency specializes in "general and inspirational fiction, romance, and in the Christian booksellers market." Actively seeking "material appropriate to the Christian market."
How to Contact: Query with SASE. Accepts queries by e-mail. Considers simultaneous queries. Responds in 3 weeks to queries; 6 weeks to mss. Returns materials only with SASE. Obtains most new clients through recommendations, conferences.
Recent Sales: Sold 29 titles in the last year. *Hidden Diary Series*, by Sandra Byrd (Bethany House); *Winter Passing*, by Cindy Marthusen (Tyndale); *Girlfriend Gatherings*, by Janet McHenry (Harvest House); *The White Pony*, by Sandra Byrd (WaterBrook Press); *Brenda's Gift*, by Cynthia Yates (Broadman & Holman); *What My Dog Taught Me About Life*, by Gary Stanley (Honor Books); *Departures*, by Robin Jones Gunn and Wendy Nentwig (Bethany House). Other clients include Joanna Weaver, Jane Orcutt, Jim Watkins.
Terms: Agent receives 15% commission on domestic and foreign sales. Offers written contract. 2 months notice must be given to terminate contract. Charges clients for postage, photocopying, telephone calls, fax and express mail.
Writers' Conferences: Romance Writers of America; Mt. Hermon Writers Conference (Mt. Hermon, CA, April 14-18); Glorieta Writers Conference (Glorieta NM, October 17-21).
Tips: "The heart of my motivation is to develop relationships with the authors I serve, to do what I can to shine the light of success on them, and to help be a caretaker of their gifts and time."

GEORGES BORCHARDT INC., 136 E. 57th St., New York NY 10022. (212)753-5785. Fax: (212)838-6518. Estab. 1967. Member of AAR. Represents 200 clients. 10% of clients are new/previously unpublished writers. Currently handles: 60% nonfiction books; 1% juvenile books; 37% novels; 1% novellas; 1% poetry books.
Member Agents: Anne Borchardt; Georges Borchardt; DeAnna Heindel; Lourdes Lopez; Valerie Borchardt.
Represents: Nonfiction books, novels. **Considers these nonfiction areas:** anthropology/archaeology; biography/autobiography; current affairs; history; memoirs; travel; women's issues/women's studies. **Considers literary fiction.** "Must be recommended by someone we know."
○┅ This agency specializes in literary fiction and outstanding nonfiction.
How to Contact: Responds in 1 week to queries; 1 month to mss. Obtains most new clients through recommendations from others.
Recent Sales: Sold 100 titles in the last year. *A Friend of the Earth*, by T.C. Boyle (Viking/Penguin); *Aiding and Abetting*, by Muriel Spark (Doubleday); *Grammars of Creation*, by George Steiner (Yale UP); *Embracing Defeat*, by John W. Dower (Winner of Bancroft & Pulitzer Prize). Also new books by Adam Hoohschile, Robert Fagles, Diane Middlebrook, Francine du Plessix Gray, and first novels by Akhil Sharma and Martin Pousson.
Terms: Agent receives 15% commission on domestic and British sales; 20% on foreign sales (translation). Offers written contract. "We charge clients cost of outside photocopying and shipping mss or books overseas."

THE BOSTON LITERARY GROUP, 156 Mount Auburn St., Cambridge MA 02138-4875. (617)547-0800. Fax: (617)876-8474. E-mail: agent@bostonliterary.com. **Contact:** Elizabeth Mack. Estab. 1994. Member of PEN New England. Represents 30 clients. 25% of clients are new/previously unpublished writers. Currently handles: 95% nonfiction books, 5% fiction books.
Member Agents: Kristen Wainwright (psychology, biography, health, current events, memoir, business); Heather Moehn (science, history, fiction).
Represents: Nonfiction books. **Considers these nonfiction areas:** animals; anthropology/archaeology; art/architecture/design; biography/autobiography; business; child guidance/parenting; current affairs; ethnic/cultural interests; government/politics/law; health/medicine; history; military/war; money/finance/economics; nature/environment; photography; psychology; science/technology; sociology; true crime/investigative; women's issues/women's studies.
○┅ Actively seeking "nonfiction manuscripts that have something new and fascinating to say. Good writing skills are essential." Does not want to receive poetry, cookbooks, children's literature.

How to Contact: Query with SASE. Accepts queries by e-mail. Accepts queries by fax. Prefers to read materials exclusively. Responds in 6 weeks to queries. Returns materials only with SASE. Obtains most new clients through referrals and journal articles.

Recent Sales: Sold 10 titles in the last year. *Zero: The Biography of a Dangerous Idea*, by Charles Seife (Viking Penguin); *The Skin We're In: Teaching Our Children to be Emotionally Strong*, by Janie Ward (Free Press); *Managing Creativity: The Science of Enterprise-Wide Innovation*, by Jeff Mauzy and Richard Harriman (Harvard Business School Press); *The Resurrection Gene, The Story of the Incredible Race to Clone the Woolly Mammoth*, by Richard Stowe (Perseus).

Terms: Agent receives 15% commission on domestic sales; 10% on foreign sales. Offers written contract, binding for 1 year. 60-day notice must be given to terminate contract. Charges clients for expenses associated with manuscript submissions (postage, photocopy). Makes referrals to editing service. "We match-make with development editors on promising projects."

✓ ◖ THE BARBARA BOVA LITERARY AGENCY, 3951 Gulfshore Blvd., PH1-B, Naples FL 34103. (941)649-7237. Fax: (941)649-0757. E-mail: Bova64@aol.com. **Contact:** Barbara Bova. Estab. 1974. Represents 30 clients. Currently handles: 35% nonfiction books; 65% novels.

Represents: Nonfiction, novels. **Considers these nonfiction areas:** biography; business; cooking/food/nutrition; how-to; money/finance/economics; self-help/personal improvement; social sciences; true crimes/investigative; women's issues/women's studies. **Considers these fiction areas:** action/adventure; contemporary issues; detective/police/crime; family saga; glitz; mainstream; mystery/suspense; regional; romance (contemporary); science fiction; thrillers/espionage.

　　O→ This agency specializes in fiction and nonfiction, hard and soft science.

How to Contact: Query with SASE. "Published authors only." Prefers to read materials exclusively. Obtains new clients only through recommendations from others.

Recent Sales: Sold 6 titles in the last year. *Ender Hegemon*, by Orson Scott Card (TOR); *Jupiter*, by Ben Bova (TOR); *Chameleon*, by Shirley Kennett (Kensington); *Ice Covers the Hole*, by Rick Wilber (TOR/Forge); *Following Through*, by Steve Levinson and Pete C. Greider (Kensington).

Terms: Agent receives 15% commission on domestic sales; handles foreign rights, movies, television, CDs. Charges clients for overseas postage, overseas calls, photocopying, shipping.

[N] ◖ BRANDENBURGH & ASSOCIATES LITERARY AGENCY, 24555 Corte Jaramillo, Murrieta CA 92562. (909)698-5200. E-mail: donbrand@murrieta.net. **Contact:** Don Brandenburgh. Estab. 1986. Represents 5 clients. Works with a small number of new/previously unpublished authors. Currently handles: 70% nonfiction books; 20% novels.

　　● Prior to opening his agency, Mr. Brandenburgh served as executive director of the Evangelical Christian Publishers Association.

Represents: Nonfiction books, novels. Not accepting new fiction clients at this time.

　　O→ This agency specializes in adult nonfiction for the religious market; limited fiction for religious market.

How to Contact: Query with outline and SASE. Accepts queries by e-mail. Considers simultaneous queries. Responds in 2 weeks to queries. No response without SASE. "We prefer previously published authors, but will evaluate submissions on their own merits."

Recent Sales: *Timelines of the Western Church*, by Susan Lynn Peterson (Zondervan); *Dinah*, by Evelyn Minshull (Guideposts).

Terms: Agent receives 15% commission on domestic sales; 20% on dramatic sales; 20% on foreign sales. Charges clients $35 mailing/materials fee with signed agency agreement.

[N] ◖ THE JOAN BRANDT AGENCY, 788 Wesley Dr., Atlanta GA 30305-3933. (404)351-8877. **Contact:** Joan Brandt. Estab. 1980. Represents 30 clients. 50% of clients are new/previously unpublished writers. Currently handles: 45% nonfiction books; 45% novels; 10% juvenile books.

Represents: Nonfiction books, novels, short story collections, juvenile books. **Considers these fiction areas:** contemporary issues; detective/police/crime; family saga; literary; mainstream; mystery/suspense; thriller/espionage.

How to Contact: Query with SASE. Does not accept queries by e-mail or fax. Considers simultaneous queries. Returns materials only with SASE. Obtains most new clients through queries/solicitations.

Recent Sales: This agency prefers not to share information on specific sales.

Terms: Agent receives 15% commission on domestic sales; 20% on foreign sales. No written contract.

◖ BRANDT & BRANDT LITERARY AGENTS INC., 1501 Broadway, New York NY 10036. (212)840-5760. Fax: (212)840-5776. **Contact:** Carl Brandt, Gail Hochman, Marianne Merola, Charles Schlessiger. Estab. 1913. Member of AAR. Represents 200 clients.

Represents: Nonfiction books, scholarly books, juvenile books, novels, novellas, short story collections. **Considers these nonfiction areas**: agriculture/horticulture; animals; anthropology/archaeology; art/architecture/design; biography/autobiography; business; child guidance/parenting; cooking/food/nutrition; crafts/hobbies; current affairs; ethnic/cultural interests; gay/lesbian issues; government/politics/law; health/medicine; history; interior design/decorating; juvenile nonfiction; language/literature/criticism; military/war; money/finance/economics; music/dance/theater/film; nature/environment; psychology; science/technology; self-help/personal improvement; sociology; sports; true crime/investigative; women's issues/women's studies. **Considers these fiction areas**: action/adventure; contemporary issues; detective/

police/crime; erotica; ethnic; experimental; family saga; feminist; gay; historical; humor/satire; lesbian; literary; mainstream; mystery/suspense; psychic/supernatural; regional; romance; science fiction; sports; thriller/espionage; westerns/frontier; young adult.

How to Contact: Query with SASE. Prefers to be read materials exclusively. Responds in 1 month to queries. Returns materials only with SASE. Obtains most new clients through recommendations from others or "upon occasion, a really good letter."

Recent Sales: Sold 50 titles in the last year. This agency prefers not to share information on specific sales. Clients include Scott Turow, Carlos Fuentes, Ursula Hegi.

Terms: Agent receives 15% commission on domestic sales; 20% on foreign sales. Charges clients for "manuscript duplication or other special expenses agreed to in advance."

Tips: "Write a letter which will give the agent a sense of you as a professional writer, your long-term interests as well as a short description of the work at hand."

⊘ **THE HELEN BRANN AGENCY, INC.**, 94 Curtis Rd., Bridgewater CT 06752. Member of AAR. This agency did not respond to our request for information. Query before submitting.

Ⓝ Ⓜ **M. COURTNEY BRIGGS**, 100 N. Broadway Ave., 20th Floor, Oklahoma City, OK 73102-8806. **Contact:** M. Courtney Briggs. Estab. 1994. Represents 30 clients; 25% of clients are new/previously unpublished writers. Currently handles: 5% nonfiction books; 10% novels; 80% juvenile books; 5% multimedia.

  • Prior to becoming an agent, Ms. Briggs was in subsidiary rights at Random House for 3 years; an associate agent and film rights associate with Curtis Brown, Ltd.; and a attorney for 9 years.

Represents: Nonfiction, novels, juvenile books. **Considers these nonfiction areas:** animals; biography/autobiography; heatlh/medicine; juvenile nonfiction; self-help/personal improvements; young adult. **Considers these fiction areas:** juvenile; mainstream; picture book; young adult.

  ⚬━ M. Courtney Briggs is an agent and an attorney. "I work primarily, but not exclusively, with children's book authors and illustrators. I will also consult or review a contract on an hourly basis." Actively seeking children's fiction, children's picture books (illustrations and text), young adult novels, fiction, nonfiction.

How to Contact: Query with SASE. Does not accept queries by e-mail or fax. Prefers to read materials exclusively. Responds in 2 weeks on queries; 6 weeks on mss. Returns materials only with SASE. Obtains most new clients through recommendations from others.

Recent Sales: This agency prefers not to share information on specific sales.

Terms: Agent receives 15% commission on domestic sales; 25% on foreign sales. Offers written contract, can be terminated at will. 60-day notice must be given to terminate contract.

Writers' Conferences: National Conference on Writing & Illustrating for Children (August).

⊘ **BROADWAY PLAY PUBLISHING**, 56 E. 81st St., New York NY 10028-0202. Member of AAR. This agency did not respond to our request for information. Query before submitting.

✔ ⊘ **MARIE BROWN ASSOCIATES INC.**, 412 W. 154th St., New York NY 10032. (212)939-9725. Fax: (212)939-9728. E-mail: mbrownlit@aol.com. **Contact:** Marie Brown. Estab. 1984. Represents 60 clients. Currently handles: 75% nonfiction books; 10% juvenile books; 15% other.

Member Agents: Janell Walden Agyeman; Lisa Davis; Dorathy Branch.

Represents: Nonfiction, juvenile books. **Considers these nonfiction areas:** art; biography; business; ethnic/cultural interests; history; juvenile nonfiction; music/dance/theater/film; religious/inspirational; self-help/personal improvement; women's issues/women's studies. **Considers these fiction areas:** contemporary issues; ethnic; juvenile; literary; mainstream.

  ⚬━ This agency specializes in multicultural and African-American writers.

How to Contact: Query with SASE. Does not accept queries by e-mail or fax. Prefers to read materials exclusively. Responds in 6 weeks to queries. Obtains most new clients through recommendations from others.

Recent Sales: *Lookin for Luv*, by Carl Weker (Kensington); *Brown Sugar*, by Carol Taylor (Dutton); *Waiting in Vain*, by Colin Channer (Ballantine/One World); *Defending the Spirit* and *The Debt*, by Randall Robinson (Dutton); *Gender Talk*, by Johnnetta Cole and Beverly Guy Sheftall (Farrar, Straus & Giroux).

Terms: Agent receives 15% commission on domestic sales; 20% on foreign sales. Offers written contract.

Ⓒ **CURTIS BROWN LTD.**, 10 Astor Place, New York NY 10003-6935. (212)473-5400. Member of AAR; signatory of WGA. **Contact:** Perry Knowlton, chairman emeritus; Timothy Knowlton, CEO. Also: 1750 Montgomery St., San Fancisco CA 94111. (415)954-8566. **Contact:** Peter Ginsberg, president.

Member Agents: Laura Blake Peterson; Ellen Geiger; Emilie Jacobson, vice president; Maureen Walters, vice president; Virginia Knowlton; Timothy Knowlton (film, screenplays, plays); Marilyn Marlow, executive vice president; Ed Wintle (film, screenplays, plays); Andrew Pope; Clyde Taylor; Mitchell Waters; Dave Barbor (translation rights); Elizabeth Harding; Douglas Stewart.

Represents: Nonfiction books, juvenile books, novels, novellas, short story collections, poetry books. **Considers all categories of nonfiction and fiction.**

Also Handles: Movie scripts, feature film, TV scripts, TV MOW, stage plays. **Considers these script subject areas:** action/adventure; comedy; detective/police/crime; ethnic; feminist; gay; historical; horror; lesbian; mainstream; mystery/suspense; psychic/supernatural; romantic comedy and drama; thriller; westerns/frontier.

How to Contact: *No unsolicited mss.* Query first with SASE. Does not accept queries by e-mail or fax. Prefers to read materials exclusively. Responds in 3 weeks to queries; 5 weeks to mss (only if requested). Obtains most new clients through recommendations from others, solicitation, at conferences, query letters.

Recent Sales: This agency prefers not to share information on specific sales.

Terms: Offers written contract. Charges clients for photocopying, some postage. "There are no office fees until we sell a ms."

ANDREA BROWN LITERARY AGENCY, INC., (Specialized: juvenile), P.O. Box 371027, Montara CA 94037-1027. (650)728-1783. E-mail: ablit@home.com. **Contact:** Andrea Brown, president. Estab. 1981. Member of AAR, WNBA, SCBWI and Authors Guild. 10% of clients are new/previously unpublished writers. This agency specializes in "all kinds of children's books—illustrators and authors." Currently handles: 98% juvenile books; 2% novels.

• Prior to opening her agency, Ms. Brown served as an editorial assistant at Random House and Dell Publishing and as an editor with Alfred A. Knopf.

Member Agents: Andrea Brown; Laura Rennert.

Represents: Juvenile books. **Considers these juvenile nonfiction areas:** animals; anthropology/archaeology; art/architecture/design; biography/autobiography; current affairs; ethnic/cultural interests; history; how-to; juvenile nonfiction; nature/environment; photography; popular culture; science/technology; sociology; sports. **Considers all juvenile fiction areas; all genres of fiction.**

How to Contact: Query with SASE. Responds in 1 month to queries; 3 months to mss. Accepts queries by e-mail. "Do not call, or fax queries of manuscripts." Considers simultaneous queries and submissions. Obtains most new clients through recommendations, from editors, clients and agents.

Recent Sales: Sold 50 titles in the last year. *Music Teacher From the Black Lagoon*, by Mike Thaler (Scholastic); *Split Image*, by Mel Glenn (HarperCollins); *I Saw Him Standing There, Paul McCartney on Tour*, by Jorie Cracen (Watson-Creptill).

Terms: Agent receives 15% commission on domestic sales; 20% on foreign sales. Offers written contract. Charges clients for shipping costs.

Writers' Conferences: Austin Writers League; SCBWI, Orange County Conferences; Mills College Childrens Literature Conference (Oakland CA); Asilomar (Pacific Grove CA); Maui Writers Conference, Southwest Writers Conference; San Diego State University Writer's Conference; Big Sur Children's Writing Workshop (Director).

Tips: "Query first. Taking on very few picture books. Must be unique—no rhyme, no anthropomorphism."

PEMA BROWNE LTD., HCR Box 104B, Pine Rd., Neversink NY 12765-9603. (914)985-2936. Website: www.geocities.com/~pemabrowneltd. **Contact:** Perry Browne or Pema Browne ("Pema rhymes with Emma"). Estab. 1966. Member of SCBWI, RWA. Signatory of WGA. Represents 50 clients. Currently handles: 50% nonfiction books; 35% juvenile books; 10% novels; 5% movie scripts.

• Prior to opening their agency, Mr. Browne was a radio and TV performer; Ms. Browne was a fine artist and art buyer.

Member Agents: Pema Browne (children's fiction and nonfiction, adult nonfiction); Perry Browne (adult fiction, nonfiction).

Represents: Nonfiction books, reference books, juvenile books, novels. **Considers these nonfiction areas:** business; child guidance/parenting; cooking/food/nutrition; ethnic/cultural interests; gay/lesbian issues; health/medicine; how-to; juvenile nonfiction; military/war; money/finance/economics; nature/environment; New Age/metaphysics; popular culture; psychology; religious/inspirational; reference; self-help/personal improvement; sports; true crime/investigative; women's issues/women's studies. **Considers these fiction areas:** action/adventure, contemporary issues; detective/police/crime; ethnic; feminist; gay; glitz; historical; humor/satire; juvenile; lesbian; literary; mainstream commercial; mystery/suspense; picture book; psychic/supernatural; religious/inspirational; romance (contemporary, gothic, historical, regency); science fiction; thriller/espionage; young adult.

O— Actively seeking nonfiction, juvenile, middle grade, some young adult, picture books.

How to Contact: Query with SASE. No fax queries. No e-mail queries. Responds in 3 weeks to queries; within 6 weeks to mss. Prefers to read materials exclusively. "We do not review manuscripts that have been sent out to publishers." Returns materials only with SASE. Obtains most new clients through "editors, authors, *LMP, Guide to Literary Agents* and as a result of longevity!"

IF YOU'RE LOOKING for a particular agent, check the Agents Index to find the specific agency where the agent works. Then check the listing for that agency in the appropriate section.

Recent Sales: Sold 25 titles in the last year. *Career Reexplosion: Reinvent Yourself in 30 Days*, by Gary J. Grappo (Berkley); *Healing the Trauma From Past Lives*, by Thelma Freedman, Ph.D. (Carol Publ); *Echoes*, by Linda Cargill (Cora Verlag); *Dead & Breakfast*, by Susan Scott (Cora Verlag); *Athena's Conquest*, by Noelle Gracy (Kensington); *Laura Ingalls Wilder—"Fairy Poems,"* compiled by Stephen Hines, illustrated by Richard Hull (Doubleday).
Terms: Agent receives 15% commission on domestic sales; 20% on foreign sales.
Tips: "If writing romance, be sure to receive guidelines from various romance publishers. In nonfiction, one must have credentials to lend credence to a proposal. Make sure of margins, double-space and use clean, dark type."

⊘ KNOX BURGER ASSOCIATES, LTD., 39½ Washington Square South, New York NY 10012. Member of AAR. This agency did not respond to our request for information. Query before submitting.

◐ SHEREE BYKOFSKY ASSOCIATES, INC., 16 W. 36th St., 13th Floor, New York NY 10018. Website: www.shereebee.com. **Contact:** Sheree Bykofsky. Estab. 1984. Incorporated 1991. Member of AAR, ASJA, WNBA. Represents "a limited number" of clients. Currently handles: 80% nonfiction; 20% fiction.
  • Prior to opening her agency, Ms. Bykofsky served as executive editor of The Stonesong Press and managing editor of Chiron Press. She is also the author or co-author of more than 10 books, including *The Complete Idiot's Guide to Getting Published.*
Represents: Nonfiction, fiction. **Considers all nonfiction areas,** especially biography/autobiography; business; child guidance/parenting; cooking/foods/nutrition; current affairs; ethnic/cultural interests; gay/lesbian issues; health/medicine; history; how-to; humor; music/dance/theater/film; popular culture; psychology; inspirational; self-help/personal improvement; true crime/investigative; women's issues/women's studies. **Considers these fiction areas:** commercial; literary.
  ○┐ This agency specializes in popular reference nonfiction. Does not want to receive poetry, children's, screenplays.
How to Contact: Query with SASE. No unsolicited mss or phone calls. Considers simultaneous queries. Responds in 1 week to short queries; 1 month on solicited mss. Returns materials only with SASE. Obtains most new clients through recommendations from others.
Recent Sales: Sold 100 titles in the last year. *How to Make People Like You in 90 Seconds or Less*, by Nicholas Boothman (Workman); *Dealers, Healers, Brutes and Saviors*, by Gerald and Susan Meyers (Wiley); *Heavenly Miracles*, by Jamie Miller, Jennifer Basye Sander and Laura Lewis (Morrow).
Terms: Agent receives 15% commission on domestic sales; 15% on foreign sales. Offers written contract, binding for 1 year "usually." Charges clients for postage, photocopying and fax.   •
Writers' Conferences: ASJA (NYC); Asilomar (Pacific Grove CA); Kent State; Southwestern Writers; Willamette (Portland); Dorothy Canfield Fisher (San Diego); Writers Union (Maui); Pacific NW; IWWG; and many others.
Tips: "Read the agent listing carefully, and comply with guidelines. I have wide-ranging interests, but it really depends on quality of writing, originality, and how a particular project appeals to me (or not). I take on very little fiction unless I completely love it—it doesn't matter what area or genre."

N: CARLISLE & COMPANY, 24 E. 64th St., New York NY 10021. (212)813-1881. Fax: (212)813-9567. E-mail: mvc@carlisleco.com. **Contact:** Michael Carlisle. Member of AAR. Estab. 1998. Represents 70 clients. "Few" clients are new/previously unpublished writers. Currently handles: 70% nonfiction books; 30% novels.
  • Prior to opening his agency, Mr. Carlisle was the Vice President of William Morris for 18 years. Ms. Fletcher was an agent and rights manager at the Carol Mann Agency.
Member Agents: Michael Carlisle; Christy Fletcher (literary fiction, biography, narrative nonfiction, pop culture, business, science); Emma Parry (literary fiction, general nonfiction); Lary Chilnick (health, cookbook, psychology, self-help).
Represents: Nonfiction books, novels, short story collections. **Considers these fiction areas:** literary; mainstream; mystery; suspense.
  ○┐ This agency has "expertise in nonfiction. We have a strong focus on editorial input on fiction before submission." Does not want to receive science fiction, fantasy or romance.
How to Contact: Query with SASE. E-mail queries OK. Responds in 10 days to queries, 3 weeks for mss. Obtains most new clients through referrals.
Recent Sales: Sold 15 titles in the last year. *Galileo's Daughter*, by Dava Sobel (Walker & Co.); *Faster*, by James Gleick (Viking); *Nearer Than the Sky*, by T. Greenwood (St. Martin's Press); *Your Body: A Girl's Guide*, by Janis Brody, Ph.D. (St. Martin's Press); *Be Quick, Don't Hurry*, by Andy Hill with John Wooden (Simon & Schuster); *The Rehearsal*, by Sarah Willis (FSG).
Terms: Agent receives 15% commission on domestic sales; 20% on foreign sales. Offers written contract; binding "for one book only."
Writers' Conferences: Squaw Valley Community Conference (California).
Tips: "Be sure to write as original a story as possible. Remember, you're asking the public to pay $25 for your book."

✓ ◐ MARIA CARVAINIS AGENCY, INC., 1350 Avenue of the Americas, Suite 2905, New York NY 10019. (212)245-6365. Fax: (212)245-7196. E-mail: mca@mariacarvainisagency.com. **Contact:** Maria Carvainis. Estab. 1977. Member of AAR, Authors Guild, ABA, MWA, RWA, signatory of WGA. Represents 35 clients. 10% of clients are new/previously unpublished writers. Currently handles: 34% nonfiction books; 65% novels; 1% poetry books.

insider report

Luck or strategy: one agent's view of publishing

I've been playing Scrabble® since I was five. When I got addicted to cryptograms at seven, my penchant for word games became clear. Twenty-four years later, I actually found a use for my talent on *Wheel of Fortune*, the television game show that rewards people for solving hangman-type puzzles. Since I was often able to solve the puzzles with zero, one or two letters filled in, I figured I'd mosey on to the show and waltz home with some cash. No problem, I thought.

Sheree Bykofsky

First, however, I had to get through the *Wheel of Fortune* gatekeepers. And who were those fire-breathing creatures? Producers. People who spend their days in dark studios selecting bubbly contestants from hundreds of hopefuls, then escorting them to makeup mavens and wheel-spinning school.

What does all this have to do with writing? Everything. Think about your own efforts to get published. As you'll see, the situations are similar.

After many unsuccessful telephone attempts to talk with someone at *Wheel of Fortune*, I wrote a letter. *Wheel* sent me a postcard, promising to notify me when they came to New York for auditions. After *several* months, I received a letter telling me where to go for tryouts. I bought a VCR and studied every show. My goal was to figure out what qualities the producers were looking for in a contestant so that when the tryouts came, I would be that person.

I noticed the women on the show never dressed in all black or all white. Their dresses had high necklines—not because they were conservative, I later learned, but to prevent impropriety when they bent over to spin the wheel. I noticed how contestants spoke about themselves, how show host, Pat Sajak, spoke to them. I studied how they played the game, how they clapped and yelled.

I decided the ideal contestant was someone anyone's grandmother would love: someone who was confident but not harsh, who would have fun, win or lose, and who liked games but not gambling.

I wrote a brief speech and instructed my friends to pick random moments to say, "And here we have Sheree Bykofsky: tell me about yourself, Sheree." I would jump right into, "I am a literary agent and book producer; I create and develop books for publishers. In my spare time, I love to play racquetball." Big smile.

When tryout day finally came, I was one of two hundred would-be contestants, of whom perhaps five would be chosen. I passed the written test. One hundred fifty people failed and were sent home. Next came several levels of interviews and mock games. I got to use my speech, and it worked. I clapped, bubbled, and paid no attention to how much money I was "winning." I concentrated on smiling, being calm, and having a good time. Voila! I was chosen.

Publishing has gatekeepers, too. And to get through those gatekeepers, you must think like someone who works in publishing. When I tried out to be a *Wheel of Fortune* contestant, I was one of two hundred wannabes of whom five would be chosen. Were my chances 2½ percent? I don't think so. I think my chances were better than 50/50. And your chances of becoming a published author are at least as high—if you're willing to do the work.

For writers, publishers and agents are what a *Wheel* producer is to a potential contestant. As an agent, I only represent about five out of every two hundred proposals and manuscripts I request. But the good news for you is that whereas there is only one *Wheel of Fortune*, there are hundreds of other agents and many, many publishers—big and small. If one is not perfect for you, the next one might be.

First, realize that different publishers look for different types of books. A typical Alfred A. Knopf book might have an esoteric or literary quality whereas St. Martin's Press might publish a book about knitting with dog hair. Both publishers know their readers, and they're good at recognizing writers who cater to their readers. They develop relationships with agents who know how to satisfy their tastes with the least hassle. That's why agents specialize, too.

When I tried out for *Wheel of Fortune*, I thought like the producers, remembering to be all they were looking for. I was able to tell—almost flawlessly—who would be eliminated and who would continue. I recall one strikingly beautiful woman. I could see that the producers were as mesmerized by her as I was, but when she gave her speech, she added that she liked to . . . *gamble*! She forgot to think of the grandmother in Iowa who would not approve and blew her chances in one sentence. Similarly, you can hurt your chances of finding an agent or a publisher by not doing your research, or by not thinking like an agent or publisher.

You have a greater chance of being represented if you target the most receptive agent. Approach that agent using a tried and true procedure, namely a snail mail query with SASE. Knowing that you need to send a query with SASE to the most appropriate agent is only part of the process. Just like the woman who said she likes to gamble, you can sabotage an otherwise slam dunk deal with a simple typo. Nobody was about to tell her what she could and couldn't say when she got on the air. If she didn't know, that was her problem.

Matching your specific interests and strengths with an agent's interests and strengths is also vital. When writers research my interests, they'll learn, for example, that I don't represent children's books, poetry, or gory thrillers. If I'm afraid to turn the page of your novel, how could I be a good agent for you? Even the next Stephen King would be wasting a stamp writing to me. The information you need to know about different agents is available—if you're willing to work at finding it. The important thing is to find out all you need to know *before* you go to the tryouts.

Before you begin submitting to agents, read at least one book about getting published, and do your best to follow its advice. Read books on your subject, and familiarize yourself with publishers' lists. Many publishers and agents have helpful websites, catalogs, and guidelines they will mail upon request. Try to make your submission count the first time because, usually, you'll only have one chance.

And to agents, publishers are the *Wheel of Fortune* producers. We need to interest them in the way they expect to be interested. It's simple and it works—often. Contestants get chosen. Authors get published. Or there is no book and no show! As a client, you can help your agent by having a good, timely, original idea and by writing the best book you can. Although it's exciting finding an agent and publisher, just as it was exciting getting on the show, the feeling would be diminished by playing poorly and leaving with just a ceramic Dalmatian. *Wheel of Fortune* producers don't really breathe fire and neither do agents. They'll help you once you prove to them you've got what it takes. I think you can do it. I won $25,000 by solving the phrase: "Words Per Minute." Show me that you can be a winning contestant, too.

—*Sheree Bykofsky*

● Prior to opening her agency, Ms. Carvainis spent more than 10 years in the publishing industry as a senior editor with Macmillan Publishing, Basic Books, Avon Books, where she worked closely with Peter Mayer and Crown Publishers. Ms. Carvainis has served as a member of the AAR Board of Directors and AAR Treasurer, as well as serving as chair of the AAR Contracts Committee. She presently serves on the AAR Royalty Committee.

Member Agents: Dana Levin (liaterary associate); Margaret Mary (literary assistant).

Represents: Nonfiction books, novels. **Considers these nonfiction areas:** biography; business; health/medicine; personal memoirs; popular science; women's issues. **Considers these fiction areas:** fantasy; historical; literary; mainstream; mystery/suspense; romance; thriller; young adult.

○➤ Does not want to receive science fiction or children's.

How to Contact: Query first with SASE. Responds within 3 weeks to queries; within 3 months to solicited mss. "60% of new clients derived from recommendations or conferences. 40% of new clients derived from letters of query."

Recent Sales: *The Alibi* and *Standoff*, by Sandra Brown (Warner Books); *The Guru Guide to the New Economy*, by Joseph H. Boyett and Jimmie T. Boyett (John Wiley and Sons); *Bearing Witness*, by Michael Kahn (TOR/Forge); *Dead of Winter*, by P.J. Parrish (Kensington); *Heroin*, by Charlie Smith (W.W. Norton). Other clients include Mary Balogh, David Bottoms, Pam Conrad, Cindy Gerard, Sarah Isidore, Samantha James, Kristine Rolofson, William Sessions, Jose Yglesias.

Terms: Agent receives 15% commission on domestic sales; 20% on foreign sales. Offers written contract, binding for 2 years "on a book-by-book basis." Charges clients for foreign postage, bulk copying.

Writers' Conferences: BEA; Frankfurt Book Fair.

◍ ◎ **MARTHA CASSELMAN LITERARY AGENCY, (Specialized: cookbooks)**, P.O. Box 342, Calistoga CA 94515-0342. (707)942-4341. Fax: (707)942-4358. **Contact:** Martha Casselman. Estab. 1978. Member of AAR, IACP. Represents 30 clients.

Represents: Nonfiction proposals only, food-related proposals and cookbooks. **Considers these nonfiction areas:** agriculture/horticulture; anthropology/archaeology; biography/autobiography; cooking/food/nutrition; health/medicine; women's issues/women's studies.

○➤ This agency specializes in "nonfiction, especially food books." Does not want to receive children's book material.

How to Contact: Send proposal with outline, SASE, plus 3 sample chapters. Do not send any submission without query. "Don't send mss!" Responds in 3 weeks to queries. Obtains most new clients through referrals.

Recent Sales: This agency prefers not to share information on specific sales.

Terms: Agent receives 15% commission on domestic sales; 20% on foreign sales (if using subagent). Offers contract review for hourly fee, on consultation with author. Charges clients for photocopying, overnight and overseas mailings.

Writers' Conferences: IACP, other food-writers' conferences.

Tips: "No tricky letters; no gimmicks; *always* include SASE or mailer, or we can't contact you."

◍ **CASTIGLIA LITERARY AGENCY**, 1155 Camino Del Mar, Suite 510, Del Mar CA 92014. (858)755-8761. Fax: (858)755-7063. **Contact:** Julie Castiglia. Estab. 1993. Member of AAR, PEN. Represents 50 clients. Currently handles: 55% nonfiction books; 45% fiction.

Member Agents: Winifred Golden; Julie Castiglia.

Represents: Fiction, nonfiction. **Considers these nonfiction areas:** animals; anthropology/archaeology; biography/autobiography; business; child guidance/parenting; cooking/food/nutrition; current affairs; ethnic/cultural interests; finance; health/medicine; history; language/literature/criticism; nature/environment; New Age/metaphysics; psychology; religious/inspirational; science/technology; self-help/personal improvement; sociology; women's issues/women's studies. **Considers these fiction areas:** contemporary issues; ethnic; glitz; literary; mainstream; mystery/suspense; women's fiction especially.

○➤ Does not want to receive horror, science fiction, screenplays or academic nonfiction.

How to Contact: Send query letters only. Does not accept queries by fax. Considers simultaneous queries. Responds in 2 months to mss. Returns materials only with SASE. Obtains most new clients through solicitations, conferences, referrals.

Recent Sales: Sold 24 titles in the last year. *Mothers Work*, by Rebecca Matthias (Doubleday); *Squeeze the Moment*, by Karen O'Connor (Watebrook/Doubleday); *Outside the Bungalow*, by Doug Keister and Paul Duscherer (Penguin); *The Miracle of Silence*, by Ron Rathbun (Berkley); *150 Ways to Boost Your Child's Self-Esteem*, by Karin Ireland (Berkley); *The Marketing Game*, by Eric Sculz (Adams Media).
Terms: Agent receives 15% commission on domestic sales; 20% on foreign sales. Offers written contract. 6-week notice must be given to terminate contract. Charges clients for excessive postage and copying.
Writers' Conferences: Southwestern Writers Conference (Albuquerque NM August); National Writers Conference; Willamette Writers Conference (OR); San Diego State University (CA); Writers At Work (Utah).
Tips: "Be professional with submissions. Attend workshops and conferences before you approach an agent."

✔ ◖ ◎ **CHARISMA COMMUNICATIONS, LTD., (Specialized: organizations)**, 250 W. 54th St., Suite 807, New York NY 10019. (212)832-3020. Fax: (646)227-0828. E-mail: chariscomm@aol.com. **Contact:** James W. Grau. Estab. 1972. Represents 10 clients. 20% of clients are new/previously unpublished writers. Currently handles: 50% nonfiction books; 20% movie scripts; 20% TV scripts; 10% other.
Member Agents: Phil Howart; Rena Delduca (reader).
Represents: Nonfiction books, novels. **Considers these nonfiction areas:** biography/autobiography; current affairs; government/politics/law; military/war; true crime/investigative. **Considers these fiction areas:** contemporary issues; detective/police/crime; mystery/suspense; religious/inspirational; sports; cult issues.
  ⊶ This agency specializes in organized crime, Indian casinos, FBI, CIA, secret service, NSA, corporate and private security, casino gaming, KGB.
Also Handles: Movie scripts, TV scripts. **Considers these script areas:** feature film, documentary, TV MOW, miniseries.
How to Contact: Send outline/proposal. Prefers to read materials exclusively. Responds in 1 month to queries; 2 months to mss. "New clients are established writers."
Recent Sales: Untitled documentary (Scripps Howard).
Terms: Agent receives 10% commission on domestic sales; variable commission on foreign sales. Offers variable written contract. 100% of business is derived from commissions on sales.

⊞ ◖ **JAMES CHARLTON ASSOCIATES**, 680 Washington St., #2A, New York NY 10014. (212)691-4951. Fax: (212)691-4952. **Contact:** Lisa Friedman. Estab. 1983. Currently handles: 100% nonfiction books.
Represents: Nonfiction books. **Considers these nonfiction areas:** child guidance/parenting; nutrition; health/medicine; how-to; humor; military/war; popular culture; sports.
  ⊶ This agency specializes in military history, sports.
How to Contact: Query with SASE for response. Responds in 2 weeks to queries. Obtains most new clients through recommendations from others.
Recent Sales: Sold about 24 titles in the last year. *The Violence Handbook*, by Dr. George Gellert (West View); *Wisdom of the Popes*, by Tom Craughwell (St. Martin's Press).
Terms: Agent receives 15% commission on domestic sales. Offers written contract, with 60-day cancellation clause.
Writers' Conferences: Oregon Writers' Conference (Portland); Oklahoma Writer's Conference.

⊘ **JANE CHELIUS LITERARY AGENCY**, 548 Second St., Brooklyn NY 11215. Member of AAR. This agency did not respond to our request for information. Query before submitting.

⊘ **FAITH CHILDS LITERARY AGENCY, INC.**, 915 Broadway, Suite 1009, New York NY 10010. Member of AAR. This agency did not respond to our request for information. Query before submitting.

⊞ ⊘ **CINE/LIT REPRESENTATION**, 7415 181st Place SW, St. Edmonds WA 98026. Member of AAR. This agency did not respond to our request for information. Query before submitting.

✔ ⊘ **CIRCLE OF CONFUSION LTD.**, 575 Lexington Ave., 4th Floor, New York NY 10022. (212)527-7579. Fax: (212)572-8304. E-mail: circleltd@aol.com. **Contact:** Lawrence Mattis, Tricia Smith, Jessica G. Estab. 1990. Signatory of WGA. Represents 25 clients. 30% of clients are new/previously unpublished writers. Currently handles: 5% novels; 90% movie scripts; 5% other.
  • See the expanded listing for this agency in Script Agents.

⊞ ◖ **WM CLARK ASSOCIATES**, 325 W. 13th St., New York NY 10014-1219. (212)675-2659. Fax: (212)675-8394. E-mail: wcquery@wmclark.com. Website: www.wmclark.com. **Contact:** William Clark. Estab. 1999. Member of AAR. 4.25% of clients are new/previously unpublished writers. Currently handles: 50% nonfiction books; 50% novels.
  • Prior to opening WCA, Mr. Clark was an agent at the Virginia Barber Literary Agency and William Morris Agency.
Represents: Nonfiction books, novels, short story collections. **Considers these nonfiction areas:** art/architecture/design; biography/autobiography; current affairs; ethnic/cultural interests; history; memoirs; music/dance/theater/film;

popular culture; religious/inspirational (Eastern religion philosophy only); science/technology; sociology; translations. **Considers these fiction areas:** action/adventure; contemporary issues; ethnic; historical; literary; mainstream; thriller/espionage; Southern fiction.

O➥ As one of the new breed of media agents recognizing their expanded roles in today's ever-changing media landscape, William Clark represents a diverse range of commercial and literary fiction and quality nonfiction to the book publishing, motion picture, television, and new media fields.

How to Contact: E-mail queries only. Prefers to read materials exclusively. Reponds in 2 weeks to queries. *No unsolicited mss.* Obtains most new clients through recommendations from others.

Recent Sales: Sold 25 titles in the last year. *The VOGUE Photographic Archive* (Viking Studio); *Boogie Woogie*, by Danny Moynihan (St. Martin's Press); *Housebroken*, by David Eddie (Riverhead); *Stardust Melodies*, by Will Friedwald (Alfred A. Knopf); *Mark Hampton: The Art of Friendship*, by Duane Hampton (HarperCollins). Other clients include Molly Jong-Fast, William Monahan, Cornelia Bailey, Sarah Schulman, James St. James, Jonathan Stone, Dr. Doreen Virtue, Mian Mian.

Terms: Agent receives 15% commission on domestic sales; 20% on foreign sales. Offers written contract.

Tips: "E-mail queries should include a general description of the work, a synopsis/outline if available, biographical information, and publishing history, if any."

☑ ◐ **CLAUSEN, MAYS & TAHAN, LLC**, 249 W. 34th St., Suite 605, New York NY 10001-2815. (212)239-4343. Fax: (212)239-5248. E-mail: cmtassist@aol.com. **Contact:** Stedman Mays, Mary M. Tahan. Estab. 1976. 10% of clients are new/previously unpublished writers. Handles mostly nonfiction.

Member Agents: Stedman Mays; Mary M. Tahan. Associates: Michael Mezzo; Kristy Sottalano.

Represents: Nonfiction. **Considers these nonfiction areas:** women's issues, relationships, psychology, memoirs, biography/autobiography, history, true stories, health/medicine, nutrition, how-to, money/finance/economics, spirituality, religious, fashion/beauty/style, humor. Rights for books optioned for TV movies and feature films.

O➥ This agency specializes in nonfiction with a strong backlist.

How to Contact: Send queries or outline/proposal with sufficient postage for return for materials. Does not accept queries by e-mail or fax. Considers simultaneous queries and submissions. Responds in 3 weeks to queries; 1 month or less after receiving requested proposals and sample chapters.

Recent Sales: *Everlasting Health—The Okinawa Way*, by Bradley Willcox, M.D., Craig Willcox, Ph.D. and Makoto Suzuki, M.D. (Clarkson Potter); *The Stranger in the Mirror: Dissociation, The Hidden Epidemic*, Marlene Steinberg, M.D. and Maxine Schnall (HarperCollins); *The War Journal of Major Damon "Rocky" Gause*, by Major Damon "Rocky" Gause (Hyperion); *The Official Rent-a-Husband Guide to a Safe, Problem-Free Home*, by Kaile Warren and Jane Maclean Craig (Doubleday); *What the IRS Doesn't Want You to Know*, Marty Kaplan, CPA and Naomi Weiss (Villard).

Terms: Agent receives 15% commission on domestic sales; 20% of foreign sales. Charges clients for postage, shipping and photocopying.

Tips: "Research proposal writing and the publishing process. Always study your book's competition. Send a proposal and outline instead of complete manuscript for faster response. Always pitch books in writing, not over the phone."

◖ **CLIENT FIRST—A/K/A LEO P. HAFFEY AGENCY**, P.O. Box 128049, Nashville TN 37212-8049. (615)463-2388. E-mail: c1@nashville.net. Website: www.c-1st.com or www.nashville.net/~c1. **Contact:** Robin Swensen. Estab. 1990. Signatory of WGA. Represents 21 clients. 25% of clients are new/previously unpublished writers. Currently handles: 40% novels; 60% movie scripts.

● See the expanded listing for this agency in Script Agents.

◙ **THE COHEN AGENCY**, 331 W. 57th St. #176, New York NY 10019. Member of AAR, signatory of WGA. This agency did not respond to our request for information. Query before submitting.

◙ **RUTH COHEN, INC. LITERARY AGENCY**, P.O. Box 7626, Menlo Park CA 94025. Member of AAR. This agency did not respond to our request for information. Query before submitting.

◙ **JOANNA LEWIS COLE, LITERARY AGENT**, 404 Riverside Dr., New York NY 10025. Member of AAR. This agency did not respond to our request for information. Query before submitting.

◖ **FRANCES COLLIN LITERARY AGENT**, P.O. Box 33, Wayne PA 19087-0033. (610)254-0555. **Contact:** Marsha S. Kear. Estab. 1948. Member of AAR. Represents 90 clients. 1% of clients are new/previously unpublished writers. Currently handles: 50% nonfiction books; 1% textbooks; 48% novels; 1% poetry books.

TO FIND AN AGENT near you, check the Geographic Index.

Represents: Nonfiction books, novels. **Considers these nonfiction areas:** anthropology/archaeology; biography/auto-biography; health/medicine; history; nature/environment; true crime/investigative. **Considers these fiction areas:** detective/police/crime; ethnic; family saga; fantasy; historical; literary; mainstream; mystery/suspense; psychic/supernatural; regional; romance (historical); science fiction.

How to Contact: Query with SASE. Responds in 1 week to queries; 2 months to mss. Obtains most new clients through recommendations from others.

Recent Sales: This agency prefers not to share information on specific sales.

Terms: Agent charges 15% commission on domestic sales; 20% on foreign sales. Offers written contract. Charges clients for overseas postage for books mailed to foreign agents; photocopying of mss, books, proposals; copyright registration fees; registered mail fees; passes along cost of any books purchased.

⊘ COLUMBIA LITERARY ASSOCIATES, INC., 7902 Nottingham Way, Ellikolt City MD 21043-6721. Member of AAR. This agency is currently not taking on new clients.

✓ ◎ COMMUNICATIONS AND ENTERTAINMENT, INC., 2851 S. Ocean Blvd., #5K, Boca Raton FL 33432-8407. (561)391-9575. Fax: (561)391-7922. E-mail: jlbearde@bellsouth.net. **Contact:** James L. Bearden. Estab. 1989. Represents 10 clients. 50% of clients are new/previously unpublished writers. Currently handles: 5% juvenile books; 40% movie scripts; 10% novel; 40% TV scripts.
   • See the expanded listing for this agency in Script Agents.

✓ ◎ DON CONGDON ASSOCIATES INC., 156 Fifth Ave., Suite 625, New York NY 10010-7002. (212)645-1229. Fax: (212)727-2688. E-mail: congdon@veriomail.com. **Contact:** Don Congdon, Michael Congdon, Susan Ramer, Cristina Concepcion. Estab. 1983. Member of AAR. Represents approximately 100 clients. Currently handles: 50% fiction; 50% nonfiction books.

Represents: Nonfiction books, novels. **Considers all nonfiction and fiction areas, especially literary fiction.**

How to Contact: Query with SASE. "If interested, we ask for sample chapters and outline." Responds in 1 week to queries; 1 month to mss. Obtains most new clients through referrals from other authors.

Recent Sales: *Me Talk Pretty One Day*, by David Sedaris (Little, Brown); *The Gravity of Sunlight*, by Rosa Shand (Soho); *You Only Die Twice*, by Edna Buchanan (HarperCollins).

Terms: Agent receives 15% commission on domestic sales. Charges clients for postage, photocopying, copyright fees and book purchases.

Tips: "Writing a query letter with a self-addressed stamped envelope is a must."

✓ ◎ CONNOR LITERARY AGENCY, 2911 West 71st St., Minneapolis MN 55423. (612)866-1426. Fax: (612)869-4074. E-mail: coolmkc@aol.com. **Contact:** Marlene Connor Lynch. Estab. 1985. Represents 50 clients. 30% of clients are new/previously unpublished writers. Currently handles: 50% nonfiction books; 50% novels.
   • Prior to opening her agency, Ms. Connor served at the Literary Guild of America, Simon and Schuster and Random House. She is author of *What is Cool: Understanding Black Manhood in America* (Crown).

Member Agents: Deborah Coker (children's books); John Lynch (assistant).

Represents: Nonfiction books, novels, children's books (especially with a minority slant). **Considers these nonfiction areas:** business; child guidance/parenting; cooking/food/nutrition; crafts/hobbies; current affairs; ethnic/cultural interests; government/politics/law; health/medicine; how-to; humor; interior decorating; language/literature/criticism; money/finance/economics; photography; popular culture; self-help/personal improvement; sports; true crime/investigative; women's issues/women's studies. **Considers these fiction areas:** contemporary issues; detective/police/crime; ethnic; experimental; family saga; horror; literary; mystery/suspense.
   ⊶ This agency specializes in popular fiction and nonfiction.

How to Contact: Query with outline/proposal and SASE. Considers simultaneous queries. Responds in 1 month to queries; 6 weeks to mss. Obtains most new clients through "queries, recommendations, conferences, grapevine, etc."

Recent Sales: *Simplicity's Simply the Best Sewing Book*, Revised Edition (Doubleday); *Black Sun Signs*, by Thelma Baljour (Simon and Schuster); *How to Love a Black Man*, by Ronn Elmore (Warner Books); *Essence, 25 Years of Celebrating Black Women*, by the Editors of *Essence Magazine* (Abrams); *Grandmother's Gift of Memories*, by Danita Green (Broadway Books).

Terms: Agent receives 15% commission on domestic sales; 25% on foreign sales. Offers a written contract, binding for 1 year.

Writers' Conferences: Howard University Publishing Institute; BEA; Detroit Writer's Conference; Mid-West Romance Writer's Conference.

Tips: "Seeking previously published writers with good sales records and new writers with real talent."

◎ THE DOE COOVER AGENCY, P.O. Box 668, Winchester MA 01890. (781)721-6000. Fax: (781)721-6727. **Contact:** Doe Coover, president. Estab. 1985. Represents 75 clients. Currently handles: 80% nonfiction; 20% fiction.
   • Prior to becoming agents, Ms. Coover and Ms. Mohyde were editors for over a decade.

Member Agents: Doe Coover (cooking, general nonfiction); Colleen Mohyde (literary and commercial fiction, general nonfiction and journalism).

Represents: Nonfiction books, fiction. **Considers these nonfiction areas:** anthropology; biography/autobiography; business; child guidance/parenting; cooking/food; ethnic/cultural interests; finance/economics; health/medicine; history; language/literature/criticism; memoirs; nature/environment; psychology; sociology; travel; true crime; women's issues/women's studies. **Considers these fiction areas:** literary, commercial.

    ○➔ This agency specializes in cookbooks, serious nonfiction—particularly books on social issues—as well as fiction (literary and commercial), journalism and general nonfiction. Does not want to receive children's books.

How to Contact: Query with outline and SASE. Considers simultaneous queries and submissions. "All queries and submissions must include SASE." Respose time varies on queries. Returns materials only with SASE. Obtains most new clients through recommendations from others and solicitation.

Recent Sales: Sold 25-30 titles in the last year. *This Far by Faith*, by Blackside, Inc. (Wm Morrow & Company); *Love Among the Ruins*, by Robert Clark (W.W. Norton); *Bombay Time*, Thrity Umrigar (Picador USA). *Movie optioned: Mr. White's Confession*, by Robert Clark (James B. Harris Productions). Other clients include Peter Lynch, Suzanne Berne, Deborah Madison, Sandra Shea, Rick Bayless, Marion Cunningham.

Terms: Agent receives 15% commission on domestic sales; 15% on foreign sales.

Writers' Conferences: BEA (Chicago).

Ⓓ CORE CREATIONS, INC., 9024 S. Sanderling Way, Littleton CO 80126. (303)683-6792. E-mail: agent@eoncity .com. Website: www.eoncity.com/agent. **Contact:** Calvin Rex. Estab. 1994. Represents 10 clients. 70% of clients are new/previously unpublished writers. Currently handles: 30% nonfiction books; 60% novels; 5% novellas; 5% games.

    • Prior to becoming an agent, Mr. Rex managed a small publishing house.

Member Agents: Calvin Rex.

Represents: Nonfiction books, novels, novellas. **Considers these nonfiction areas:** gay/lesbian issues; how-to; humor; psychology; true crime/investigative. **Considers these fiction areas:** detective/police/crime; horror; science fiction.

    ○➔ This agency specializes in "bold, daring literature." Agency has strong "experience with royalty contracts and licensing agreements."

How to Contact: Query with outline/proposal and SASE. Responds in 3 weeks to queries; 3 months to mss. Obtains most new clients through recommendations from others, through the Internet and from query letters.

Recent Sales: This agency prefers not to share information on specific sales.

Terms: Agent receives 15% commission on domestic sales; 20% on foreign sales. Offers written contract. "Either party may terminate contract at any time." Charges clients for postage (applicable mailing costs).

Writers' Conferences: Steamboat Springs Writers Group (Colorado, July); Rocky Mountain Fiction Writers Colorado Gold Conference.

Tips: "Have all material proofread. Visit our webpage before sending anything. We want books that dare to be different. Give us a unique angle, a new style of writing, something that stands out from the crowd!"

Ⓓ ROBERT CORNFIELD LITERARY AGENCY, 145 W. 79th St., New York NY 10024-6468. Member of AAR. This agency did not respond to our request for information. Query before submitting.

Ⓓ CRAWFORD LITERARY AGENCY, 94 Evans Rd., Barnstead NH 03218. (603)269-5851. Fax: (603)269-2533. **Contact:** Susan Crawford. Estab. 1988. Represents 40 clients. 10% of clients are new/previously unpublished writers. Currently handles: 50% nonfiction books; 50% novels.

Member Agents: Susan Crawford; Lorne Crawford (commercial fiction); Scott Neister (scientific/techno thrillers); Kristen Hales (parenting, psychology, New Age, self help).

Represents: Commercial fiction and nonfiction books.

    ○➔ This agency specializes in celebrity and/or media-based books and authors. Actively seeking action/adventure stories, medical thrillers, suspense thrillers, celebrity projects, self-help, inspirational, how-to and women's issues. Does not want to receive short stories, poetry.

How to Contact: Query with SASE. Doesn't accept queries by e-mail or fax. Considers simultaneous queries; no simultaneous ms submissions. Responds in 3 weeks to queries. Returns materials only with SASE. Obtains most new clients through recommendations, conferences, queries.

Recent Sales: *Stan Lee*, memoir by creator of Spiderman, The 'X Men (Simon & Schuster); *All that Glitters is Not Gold*, by Marla Maples (Regan Books); *Housebroken*, by Richard Karn and George Mair (HarperCollins); *With Ossie & Ruby*, by Ruby Dee and Ossie Davis (William Morrow); *Psi/Net*, by Billy Dee Williams and Rob MacGregor (TOR/Forge). Other clients include John Travolta, Billy Dee Williams, Producer Jonathan Krane.

Terms: Agent receives 15% commission on domestic sales; 20% on foreign sales. Offers written contract, binding for 90 days. 100% of business is derived from commissions on sales.

Writers' Conferences: International Film & Writers Workshop (Rockport ME); Maui Writers Conference.

Ⓝ Ⓓ THE CREATIVE CULTURE, 853 Broadway, Suite 1715, New York NY 10003. Member of AAR. This agency did not respond to our request for information. Query before submitting.

☑ Ⓜ RICHARD CURTIS ASSOCIATES, INC., 171 E. 74th St., Suite 2, New York NY 10021. (212)772-7363. Fax: (212)772-7393. E-mail: jhackworth@curtisagency.com. Website: www.curtisagency.com. **Contact:** Pam Valvera. Estab. 1969. Member of AAR, RWA, MWA, WWA, SFWA, signatory of WGA. Represents 100 clients. 5% of clients are new/previously unpublished writers. Currently handles: 50% nonfiction books; 50% novels.

• Prior to opening his agency, Mr. Curtis was an agent with the Scott Meredith Literary Agency for 7 years and has authored over 50 published books.

Member Agents: Amy Victoria Meo; Jennifer Hackworth; Richard Curtis.

Represents: Nonfiction books, scholarly books, novels. **Considers all nonfiction and fiction areas.**

○→ This agency specializes in general and literary fiction and nonfiction, as well as genre fiction such as science fiction, women's romance, horror, fantasy, action-adventure.

How to Contact: "We do not accept fax or e-mail queries, conventional queries (outline and 3 sample chapters) must be accompanied by SASE." Responds in 1 month to queries; 1 month to mss. Obtains most new clients through recommendations from others, solicitations, conferences.

Recent Sales: Sold 100 titles in the last year. *Hardcase,* by Dan Simmons (St. Martin's Press); *Darwin's Radio,* by Greg Bear (Del Rey/Random House); *Ascending,* by James Gardner (Avon). Other clients include Dan Simmons, Jennifer Blake, Leonard Maltin, Earl Mindell, Barbara Parker.

Terms: Agent receives 15% commission on domestic sales; 20% on foreign sales. Offers written contract, binding on a "book by book basis." Charges clients for photocopying, express, international postage, book orders.

Writers' Conferences: Romance Writers of America; Nebula Science Fiction Conference.

☑ ⊘ **JAMES R. CYPHER, THE CYPHER AGENCY**, 816 Wolcott Ave., Beacon NY 12508-4247. Phone/fax: (845)831-5677. E-mail: jimcypher@prodigy.net. Website: pages.prodigy.net/jimcypher/. **Contact:** James R. Cypher. Estab. 1993. Member of HWA, MWA and Authors Guild. Represents 47 clients. 52% of clients are new/previously unpublished writers. Currently handles: 67% nonfiction book; 33% novels.

• Mr. Cypher is a special contributor to Prodigy Service Books and Writing Bulletin Board. Prior to opening his agency, Mr. Cypher worked as a corporate public relations manager for a Fortune 500 multi-national computer company for 28 years.

Represents: Nonfiction books, novels. **Considers these nonfiction areas:** biography/autobiography; current affairs; ethnic/cultural interests; gay/lesbian issues; government/politics/law; health/medicine; history; how-to; language/literature/criticism; money/finance/economics; music/dance/theater/film; nature/environment; popular culture; psychology; science/technology; self-help/personal improvement; sociology; sports; true crime/investigative; women's issues/women's studies; travel memoirs. **Considers these fiction areas:** literary; mainstream; crime fiction; horror.

○→ Actively seeking a wide variety of topical nonfiction. Does not want to receive humor; pets; gardening; cookbooks; crafts; spiritual; religious or New Age topics.

How to Contact: For nonfiction: send outline proposal, 2 sample chapters and SASE. For fiction: send synopsis, 3 sample chapters and SASE. Accepts queries by e-mail or fax. Considers simultaneous queries and submissions. Responds in 2 weeks to queries; 6 weeks to mss. Obtains most new clients through referrals from others, networking on online computer services, and attending writers' conferences.

Recent Sales: Sold 6 titles in the last year. *At Speed: Up Close and Personal with the People, Places and Fans of NASCAR,* by Monte Dutton (Brassey's, Inc.); *The Brain Disorders Sourcebooks,* by Roger S. Cicala, M.D. (Lowell House); *Estate Planning: Plan Now or Pay Later,* by Jane B. Lucal (BLoomberg press); *Hoare and the Headless Captains* (historical mystery), by Wilder Perkins (St. Martin's Press).

Terms: Agent receives 15% commission on domestic sales; 20% on foreign sales. Offers written contract, with 30 day cancellation clause. Charges clients for postage, photocopying, overseas phone calls and faxes. 100% of business is derived from commissions on sales.

Tips: " 'Debut fiction' is very difficult to place in today's tight market, so a novel has to be truly outstanding to make the cut. Because I have strong line-editing skills, I work closely with all clients to ensure manuscripts submitted to acquisitions editors are as nearly 'perfect' as possible. I also help nonfiction book writers develop sound book proposals which will make their proposed works more attractive to editors. I render these value-added services at no additional charge because I feel strongly that well-presented submissions increase the likelihood of eventual placement."

N ⊘ LAURA DAIL LITERARY AGENCY, INC., 250 W. 57th St., Suite 1314, New York NY 10107. Member of AAR. This agency did not respond to our request for information. Query before submitting.

⊘ **DARHANSOFF & VERRILL LITERARY AGENTS**, 179 Franklin St., 4th Floor, New York NY 10013. Member of AAR. This agency did not respond to our request for information. Query before submitting.

◐ **JOAN DAVES AGENCY**, 21 W. 26th St., New York NY 10010. (212)685-2663. Fax: (212)685-1781. **Contact:** Jennifer Lyons, director; Heather Currier, assistant. Estab. 1960. Member of AAR. Represents 100 clients. 10% of clients are new/previously unpublished writers.

Represents: Nonfiction books, novels. **Considers these nonfiction areas:** biography/autobiography; gay/lesbian issues; popular culture; translations; women's issues/women's studies. **Considers these fiction areas:** ethnic; family saga; gay; literary; mainstream.

○→ This agency specializes in literary fiction and nonfiction, also commercial fiction.

How to Contact: Query with SASE. Considers simultaneous submissions. Responds in 3 weeks to queries; 6 weeks to mss. Returns materials only with SASE. Obtains most new clients through editors' and author clients' recommendations. "A few queries translate into representation."

Recent Sales: Sold 70 titles in the last year. *Strange Fire,* by Melvin Jules Bukiet (W.W. Norton); *SLUT! Growing Up Female with a Bad Reputation,* by Leora Tannenbaum; *Candor and Perversion,* by Roger Shattuck (W.W. Norton).

Terms: Agent receives 15% commission on domestic sales; 20% on foreign sales. Offers written contract, binding on a per book basis. Charges clients for office expenses. 100% of business is derived from commissions on sales.

Reading List: Reads *The Paris Review*, *Missouri Review*, and *Voice Literary Supplement* to find new clients.

◐ LIZA DAWSON ASSOCIATES, 240 W. 35th St., Suite 500, New York NY 10001. **Contact:** Liza Dawson at (212)465-9071 or Rebecca Kurson at (212)629-9212. Member of AAR, MWA, Women's Media Group. Represents 30 clients. 10% of clients are new/previously unpublished writers. Currently handles: 60% nonfiction books; 40% novels.
- Prior to becoming an agent, Ms. Dawson was an editor for 20 years, spending 11 years at William Morrow as vice president and 2 at Putnam as executive editor.

Member Agents: Liza Dawson, Rebecca Kurson (science, women's issues, narrative nonfiction, literary fiction).

Represents: Nonfiction books, scholarly books, novels. **Considers these nonfiction areas:** biography/autobiography; business; health/medicine; history; how-to; memoirs; psychology; self-help/personal improvement; sociology; women's issues/women's studies. **Considers these fiction areas:** ethnic; family saga; historical; literary; regional; suspense; thriller.

    O— This agency specializes in readable literary fiction, thrillers, mainstream historicals and women's fiction, academics, historians, doctors, journalists, self-help and psychology. "My specialty is shaping books and ideas so that a publisher will respond quickly." Actively seeking talented professionals. Does not want to receive westerns, science fiction, sports, computers, juvenile.

How to Contact: Query with SASE. Responds in 3 weeks to queries; 6 weeks to mss. Obtains most new clients through recommendations, writers' conferences.

Recent Sales: Sold over 35 titles in the last 2 years. *Back Roads*, by Tawni O'Dell (Viking); *Organize Yourself*, by Ronnie Isenburg and Kate Kelly (Hyperion); *The Inscription*, by Pamela Binder (Pocket Books); *Memoir*, by Olympis Dukakis (HarperCollins); **Books sold by Rebecca Kurson:** *Loser, A History of Noble Failures*, by Paul Collins; (St. Martin's Press); *Grace*, by Jane Roberts-Wood (Dutton); *Untitled book about Poker*, by Andy Bellin (HarperCollins).

Terms: Agent receives 15% commission on domestic sales; 20% on foreign sales. Offers written contract. Charges clients for photocopying and overseas postage.

Writers' Conferences: Pacific Northwest Book Conference (Seattle area, July).

Reading Lists: Reads *The Sun*, *New York Review of Books*, *The New York Observer*, *Utne Reader*, and *The Wall Street Journal* to find new clients.

Tips: "Please include a detailed bio with any query letter, let me know somehow that you've done a little research, that you're not just interested in any agent but someone who is right for you."

⧉N ◐ DeFIORE AND COMPANY, 853 Broadway, Suite 1715, New York NY 10003. (212)505-7979. Fax: (212)505-7779. E-mail: info@defioreandco.com. Website: www.defioreandco.com. **Contact:** Brian DeFiore. Estab. 1999. Represents 25 clients. 50% of clients are new/previously unpublished writers. Currently handles: 70% nonfiction books; 30% novels.
- Prior to becoming an agent, Mr. DeFiore was Publisher of Villard Books 1997-1998; Editor-in-Chief of Hyperion 1992-1997; Editorial Director Delacorte Press 1988-92.

Member Agents: Brian DeFiore (popular nonfiction, business, pop culture, parenting, commercial fiction); Mark S. Roy (literary fiction, spirituality, gay & lesbian).

Represents: Nonfiction books, novels. **Considers these nonfiction areas:** biography/autobiography; business; child guidance/parenting; cooking/food/nutrition; gay/lesbian issues; health/medicine; money/finance/economics; multicultural; popular culture; psychology; religious/inspirational; self-help/personal improvement; sports. **Considers these fiction areas:** ethnic; gay/lesbian; literary; mainstream; mystery/suspense; thriller/espionage.

How to Contact: Query with SASE. Accepts queries by e-mail. Considers simultaneous queries. Reponds in 2 weeks to queries; 6 weeks to mss. Returns materials only with SASE. Obtains most new clients through recommendations from others.

Recent Sales: Sold 10 titles in the last year. *The Fourth Mega-Market*, by Ralph Acompora (Hyperion); *Life is More Than Just a Stress Rehearsal*, by Loretta La Roche (Broadway); *The Mailroom*, by David Rensin (Ballantine); *Parenting the Extreme Teenager*, by Scott Sells, PhD. (St. Martin's Press). Other clients include Jeff Arch, Jerome Brasset, Corey Donaldson, Lori Fairweather, Norman Green, Joel Engel, Christopher Keane, Robin McMillan, Jessica Teich, Michael Webb, Brian D'Amato.

Terms: Agent receives 15% commission on domestic sales; 20% on foreign sales. Offers written contract. 30-day notice must be given to terminate contract.

Writers' Conferences: Maui Writers Conference (Maui, HI, September.)

☑ ◐ DH LITERARY, INC., P.O. Box 990, Nyack NY 10960-0990. (845)358-7364. E-mail: dhendin@aol.com. **Contact:** David Hendin. Estab. 1992. Member of AAR. Represents 30 clients. Currently handles: 50% nonfiction books; 10% textbooks; 10% scholarly books; 10% fiction; 20% syndicated material.
- Prior to opening his agency, Mr. Hendin served as president and publisher for Pharos Books/World Almanac as well as senior vp and COO at sister company United Feature Syndicate.

Represents: Nonfiction books, novels, scholarly books, syndicated material. **Considers these nonfiction areas:** animals; anthropology/archaeology; biography/autobiography; child guidance/parenting; current affairs; ethnic/cultural interests; government/politics/law; health/medicine; history; how-to; language/literature/criticism; money/finance/economics; nature/environment; popular culture; psychology; science/technology; self-help/personal improvement; true crime/investigative; women's issues/women's studies. "**Fiction by referral only.**"

O→ This agency specializes in trade fiction, nonfiction, and newspaper syndication of columns or comic strips.

How to Contact: Query with SASE. Accepts queries by e-mail, "but no downloads." Does not accept queries by fax. Prefers to read materials exclusively. Responds in 6 weeks to queries. Returns materials only with SASE. Obtains most new clients through referrals from others (clients, writers, publishers).

Recent Sales: Sold 15 titles in the last year. *Stormchasers*, by David Toomey (Norton); *Eve's Seed*, Robert McElvaine (McGraw Hill); *Pink Flamingo Murders*, by Elaine Viets (Dell); *Age of Anxious Anxiety*, by Tom Tiede (Grove Atlantic); *History of American Etiquette*, by Judith Martin (Norton); *To See You Again*, by Betty Schimmel (Dutton).

Terms: Agent receives 15% commission on domestic sales; 20% on foreign sales. Offers written contract, binding for 6 months. Charges clients for out of pocket expenses for postage, photocopying manuscript, and overseas phone calls specifically related to a book.

Tips: "Have your project in mind and on paper before you submit. Too many writers/cartoonists say 'I'm good . . . get me a project.' Publishers want writers with their own great ideas and their own unique voice."

☑ ◖ **DHS LITERARY, INC.**, 6060 N. Central Expwy., Suite 624, Dallas TX 75206-5209. (214)363-4422. E-mail: submissions@dhsliterary.com. Website: www.dhsliterary.com. **Contact:** David Hale Smith, president. Estab. 1994. Represents 40 clients. 25% of clients are new/previously unpublished writers. Currently handles: 60% nonfiction books; 40% novels.

• Prior to opening his agency, Mr. Smith was an editor at a newswire service.

Represents: Nonfiction books, novels. **Considers these nonfiction areas:** biography/autobiography; business; child guidance/parenting; computers/electronics; cooking/food/nutrition; current affairs; ethnic/cultural interests; gay/lesbian issues; popular culture; sports; true crime/investigative. **Considers these fiction areas:** detective/police/crime; erotica; ethnic; feminist; gay; historical; literary; mainstream; mystery/suspense; sports; thriller/espionage; westerns/frontier.

O→ This agency specializes in commercial fiction and nonfiction for adult trade market. Actively seeking thrillers, mysteries, suspense, etc., and narrative nonfiction. Does not want to receive poetry, short fiction, children's books.

How to Contact: One-page query via e-mail only. No paper queries accepted unless requested by agency. Will request more material if appropriate. Considers simultaneous queries. Responds in 1 month to queries. Obtains most new clients through referrals from other clients, editors and agents.

Recent Sales: Sold 35 titles in the last year. *Critical Space*, by Greg Rucka (Bantam); *The Origins Diet*, by Elizabeth Somer (Holt); *Life Makeovers*, by Cheryl Richardson (Broadway).

Terms: Agent receives 15% commission on domestic sales; 25% on foreign sales. Offers written contract, with 10-day cancellation clause or upon mutual consent. Charges clients for expenses, i.e., postage, photocopying. 100% of business is derived from commissions on sales.

Reading List: Reads *Outside Magazine*, STORY, *Texas Monthly*, *Kenyon Review*, *Missouri Review* and *Mississippi Mud* to find new clients. "I like to see good writing in many formats. I'll often call a writer who has written a good short story, for example, to see if she has a novel."

Tips: "Remember to be courteous and professional, and to treat marketing your work and approaching an agent as you would any formal business matter. When in doubt, always query first via e-mail. Visit our website for more information."

 CLOSE UP with David Hendin, DH Literary, Inc.

On writers interested in newspaper syndication . . .

"I spent twenty-three years in the newspaper syndicate business, all with the same company. When I left United Feature Syndicate in 1993, I was Senior Vice President/Editorial Director/COO. I was senior executive when 'Garfield' was in only around twenty newspapers and then started to take off. I'm also proud to say that on my watch we signed up comic strips such as 'Dilbert,' 'Rose is Rose,' and 'Robotman.'

"I am only interested in the *most professional* submissions of comic strips. I am *not* interested in people with ideas who cannot draw. And I am not interested in people who can draw but have no ideas.

"If you would like to submit a cartoon to me, please query me by e-mail first, and tell me a bit about yourself and your comic strip. Be warned: I take on perhaps one or two strips for representation every year. That makes the odds very long."

THE DICKENS GROUP, 3024 Madelle Ave., Louisville KY 40206. (502)897-6740. Fax: (502)894-9815. E-mail: sami@thedickens.win.net. Website: www.dickensliteraryagency.com. **Contact:** Ann Bloch. Estab. 1991. Currently handles: 50% nonfiction books; 50% novels.

• Prior to becoming agents, Dr. Solinger (president of Dickens) was a professor of pediatric cardiology; Ms. Hughes (vice president) was a professional screenwriter and editor.

Member Agents: Bob Solinger (literary and contemporary American fiction; (Ms.) Sam Hughes (top-list nonfiction, commercial and literary fiction); Ted Solinger (computer/electronic, fiction and nonfiction, sports, physical fitness).

Represents: Nonfiction books, novels. **Considers these nonfiction areas:** biography/autobiography; business; computers/electronics; cooking/food/nutrition; current affairs; government/politics/law; health/medicine; history; popular culture; science/technology; true crime/investigative. **Considers these fiction areas:** ethnic; literary; mainstream; mystery/suspense; thriller/espionage.

O─┐ Actively seeking biographers, journalists, investigative reporters—"professionals writing fiction and nonfiction in their specialties." Does not want to receive poetry, essays, short stories, juvenile.

How to Contact: Query with SASE. *No unsolicited material.*

Recent Sales: *The Ten Thousand,* by Michael C. Ford (St. Martin's Press); *Secrets & Shadows: Colonel Tom Parker,* by Alanna Nash (Simon & Schuster); *Printer's Ink: Publishers Blood,* by Leise Staman (St. Martin's Press).

Terms: Agent receives 15% commission on domestic sales; 20% on foreign sales. Offers written contract "only if requested by author."

Tips: "Write a good concise, nonhyped query letter; include a paragraph about yourself."

SANDRA DIJKSTRA LITERARY AGENCY, PMB 515, 1155 Camino del Mar, Del Mar CA 92014-2605. (858)755-3115. **Contact:** Sandra Zane. Estab. 1981. Member of AAR, Authors Guild, PEN West, Poets and Editors, MWA. Represents 100 clients. 30% of clients are new/previously unpublished writers. Currently handles: 60% nonfiction books; 5% juvenile books; 35% novels.

Member Agents: Sandra Dijkstra.

Represents: Nonfiction books, novels. **Considers these nonfiction areas:** anthropology; biography/autobiography; business; child guidance/parenting; nutrition; current affairs; ethnic/cultural interests; government/politics; health/medicine; history; literary studies (trade only); military/war (trade only); money/finance/economics; nature/environment; psychology; science/technology; self-help/personal improvement; sociology; sports; true crime/investigative; women's issues/women's studies. **Considers these fiction areas:** contemporary issues; detective/police/crime; ethnic; family saga; feminist; literary; mainstream; mystery/suspense; thriller/espionage.

O─┐ "We specialize in a number of fields."

How to Contact: Send "outline/proposal with sample chapters for nonfiction, synopsis and first 50 pages for fiction and SASE. Please no e-mail submissions." Responds in 6 weeks. Obtains most new clients primarily through referrals/recommendations, but also through queries and conferences and often by solicitation.

Recent Sales: *The Mistress of Spices*, by Chitra Divakaruni (Anchor Books); *The Flower Net*, by Lisa See (HarperCollins); *Outsmarting the Menopausal Fat Cell*, by Debra Waterhouse (Hyperion); *Stiffed: The Betrayal of the American Man*, by Susan Faludi (William Marrow).

Terms: Agent receives 15% commission on domestic sales; 20% on foreign sales. Offers written contract, binding for 1 year. Charges clients for expenses "from years we are *active* on author's behalf to cover domestic costs so that we can spend time selling books instead of accounting expenses. We also charge for the photocopying of the full manuscript or nonfiction proposal and for foreign postage."

Writers' Conferences: Squaw Valley (Santa Barbara, Asilomar); Southern California Writers Conference; Rocky Mountain Fiction Writers. "We also speak regularly for writers groups such as PEN West and the Independent Writers Association."

Tips: "Be professional, and learn the standard procedures for submitting your work. Give full biographical information on yourself, especially for a nonfiction project. Always include SASE with correct return postage for your own protection of your work. Query with a 1 or 2 page letter first and always include postage. Nine page letters telling us your life story, or your book's, are unprofessional and usually not read. Tell us about your book and write your query well. It's our first introduction to who you are and what you can do! Call if you don't hear within a reasonable period of time. Be a regular patron of bookstores and study what kind of books are being published. READ. Check out your local library and bookstores—you'll find lots of books on writing and the publishing industry that will help you! At conferences, ask published writers about their agents. Don't believe the myth that an agent has to be in New York to be successful—we've already disproved it!"

THE JONATHAN DOLGER AGENCY, 49 E. 96th St., Suite 9B, New York NY 10128. (212)427-1853. President: Jonathan Dolger. **Contact:** Herbert Erinmore. Estab. 1980. Member of AAR. Represents 70 clients. 25% of clients are new/previously unpublished writers. Writer must have been previously published if submitting fiction. Prefers to work with published/established authors; works with a small number of new/previously unpublished writers.

• Prior to opening his agency, Mr. Dolger was vice president and managing editor for Simon & Schuster Trade Books.

Represents: Nonfiction books, novels, illustrated books.

O─┐ This agency specializes in adult trade fiction and nonfiction, and illustrated books.

How to Contact: Query with outline and SASE. Does not accept queries by e-mail.

Recent Sales: Sold 15-20 titles in the last year. This agency prefers not to share information on specific sales.
Terms: Agent receives 15% commission on domestic and dramatic sales; 25% on foreign sales. Charges clients for "standard expenses."

Ø DONADIO AND OLSON, INC., 121 W. 27th St., Suite 704, New York NY 10001. Member of AAR. This agency did not respond to our request for information. Query before submitting.

[N] Ø JANIS A. DONNAUD & ASSOCIATES, INC., 525 Broadway, 2nd Floor, New York NY 10012. (212)431-2664. Fax: (212)431-2667. E-mail: jdonnaud@aol.com. **Contact:** Janis A. Donnaud. Member of AAR. Signatory of WGA. Represents 50 clients. 10% of clients are new/previously unpublished writers. Currently handles: 90% nonfiction books; 10% novels.
   • Prior to opening her agency, Ms. Donnaud was Vice President, Associate Publisher, Random House Adult Trade Group.
Represents: Nonfiction, novels.
   O→ This agency specializes in health, medical, cooking, humor, pop psychology, narrative nonfiction, photography, art, literary fiction, biography, parenting, current affairs. "We give a lot of service and attention to clients." Actively seeking serious narrative nonfiction; literary fiction; commercial fiction; cookbooks; health and medical. Does not want to receive poetry, mysteries, juvenile books, romances, science fiction, young adult, religious, fantasy.
How to Contact: Query with description of book and 2-3 pages of sample material with SASE. Accepts queries by fax and e-mail "but we will *not* download attached files." Prefers to read materials exclusively. Responds in 2 weeks to queries; 1 month to mss. Obtains most new clients through recommendations from other clients.
Recent Sales: Sold 40 titles in the last year. *Nancy Silverton's Mornings at the La Brea Bakery*, by Nancy Silverton (Random House); *A Year of Weddings*, by Maria McBride-Mellinger (HarperCollins); *The Fosters Markets Cookbook*, by Sara Foster (R.H.); *Heart Program for Women*, by Dr. Nieca Golbergs (Ball).
Terms: Agent receives 15% commission on domestic sales; 20% on foreign sales. Offers written contract. 30-day notice must be given to terminate contract. Charges clients for messengers, photocopying, purchase of books.

Ø JIM DONOVAN LITERARY, 4515 Prentice St., Suite 109, Dallas TX 75206. **Contact:** Jim Donovan, president; Kathryn McKay. Estab. 1993. Represents 25 clients. 25% of clients are new/previously unpublished writers. Currently handles: 75% nonfiction; 25% novels.
Member Agents: Jim Donovan (president); Kathryn McKay.
Represents: Nonfiction books; novels. **Considers these nonfiction areas:** biography/autobiography; business; child guidance/parenting; current affairs; health/medicine; history; military/war; money/finance/economics; music/dance/theater/film; nature/environment; popular culture; sports; true crime/investigative. **Considers these fiction areas:** action/adventure; detective/police/crime; historical; horror; literary; mainstream; mystery/suspense; sports; thriller/espionage; westerns/frontier.
   O→ This agency specializes in commercial fiction and nonfiction. Does not want to receive poetry, humor, short stories, juvenile, romance or religious work.
How to Contact: For nonfiction, send query letter. For fiction, send 2- to 5-page outline and 3 sample chapters with SASE. Does not accept queries by e-mail or fax. Considers simultaneous queries and submissions. Responds in 1 month to queries and mss. Obtains most new clients through recommendations from others and solicitation.
Recent Sales: Sold 22 titles in the last year. *The Burning: The Massacre and Destruction of a Place Called Greenwood*, by Tim Madigan (St. Martin's Press); *Secrets of Sunset Boulevard*, by Sam Staggs (St. Martin's Press); *I Watched a Wild Hog Eat My Baby (and Vice Versa)*, by Bill Sloan (Prometheus Books).
Terms: Agent receives 15% commission on domestic sales; 20% on foreign sales. Offers written contract, binding for 1 year. Written letter must be received to terminate a contract. Charges clients for "some" postage and photocopying— "author is notified first." Writers reimbursed for office fees after the sale of ms.
Tips: "The vast majority of material I receive, particularly fiction, is not ready for publication. Do everything you can to get your fiction work in top shape before you try to find an agent. I've been in the book business since 1981, in retail (as a chain buyer), as an editor, and as a published author. I'm open to working with new writers if they're serious about their writing and are prepared to put in the work necessary—the rewriting—to become publishable."

Ø DOYEN LITERARY SERVICES, INC., 1931 660th St., Newell IA 50568-7613. (712)272-3300. President: (Ms.) B.J. Doyen. Estab. 1988. Represents 20 clients. 20% of clients are new/previously unpublished writers. Currently handles: 88% nonfiction books; 2% juvenile books; 10% novels.
   • Prior to opening her agency, Ms. Doyen worked as a published author, teacher, guest speaker and wrote and appeared in her own weekly TV show airing in 7 states.
Represents: Nonfiction books, novels. **Considers most nonfiction areas. Considers these fiction areas:** contemporary issues; family saga; historical; literary; mainstream; psychic/supernatural.
   O→ This agency specializes in nonfiction and occasionally handles genre and mainstream fiction for adults. Actively seeking business, health, how-to, psychology; all kinds of adult nonfiction suitable for the major trade publishers. Does not want to receive pornography, children's, poetry.
How to Contact: Query first with SASE. Considers simultaneous queries. Responds immediately to queries; 3 weeks to mss. Returns materials only with SASE. Prefers fiction from published novelists only.

Recent Sales: *Homemade Money*, by Barbara Brabec (Betterway); *Gardening by Heart*, by McGreevy (Sierra/Random); *The Family Guide to Financial Aid for Higher Education*, by Black (Putnam/Perigee).

Terms: Agent receives 15% commission on domestic sales; 20% commission on foreign sales. Offers written contract, binding for 1 year.

Tips: "Our authors receive personalized attention. We market aggressively, undeterred by rejection. We get the best possible publishing contracts. We are very interested in nonfiction book ideas at this time; will consider most topics. Many writers come to us from referrals, but we also get quite a few who initially approach us with query letters. Do *not* use phone queries unless you are successfully published or a celebrity. It is best if you do not collect editorial rejections prior to seeking an agent, but if you do, be up-front and honest about it. Do not submit your manuscript to more than one agent at a time—querying first can save you (and us) much time. We're open to established or beginning writers—just send us a terrific letter with SASE!"

✅ ◎ **ROBERT DUCAS**, The Barn House, 244 Westside Rd., Norfolk CT 06058. (860)542-5733. Fax: (860)542-5469. E-mail: robertducas@aol.com. **Contact:** R. Ducas. Estab. 1981. Represents 55 clients. 15% of clients are new/previously unpublished writers. Currently handles: 70% nonfiction books; 2% scholarly books; 28% novels.

● Prior to opening his agency, Mr. Ducas ran the *London Times* and the *Sunday Times* in the U.S. from 1966 to 1981.

Represents: Nonfiction books, novels, novellas. **Considers these nonfiction areas:** animals; biography/autobiography; business; current affairs; gay/lesbian issues; government/politics/law; health/medicine; history; memoirs; military/war; money/finance/economics; nature/environment; science/technology; sports; travel; true crime/investigative. **Considers these fiction areas:** action/adventure; contemporary issues; detective/police/crime; family saga; literary; mainstream; mystery/suspense; sports; thriller/espionage.

○━ This agency specializes in nonfiction, journalistic exposé, biography, history. Does not want to receive women's fiction.

How to Contact: Responds in 2 weeks to queries; 2 months to mss. Obtains most new clients through recommendations.

Recent Sales: Sold 10 titles in the last year. This agency prefers not to share information on specific sales.

Terms: Agent receives 15% commission on domestic sales; 20% on foreign sales. Charges clients for photocopying, postage, messengers, overseas couriers to subagents.

◎ **HENRY DUNOW LITERARY AGENCY**, 22 W. 23rd St., 5th Floor, New York NY 10010. Member AAR. This agency did not respond to our request for information. Query before submitting.

Ⓝ ◎ **DUPREE/MILLER AND ASSOCIATES INC. LITERARY**, 100 Highland Park Village, Suite 350, Dallas TX 75205. (214)559-BOOK. Fax: (214)559-PAGE. E-mail: dmabook@aol.com. President: Jan Miller. **Contact:** Submissions Department. Estab. 1984. Member of ABA. Represents 200 clients. 20% of clients are new/previously unpublished writers. Currently handles: 75% nonfiction books; 25% novels.

Member Agents: Jan Miller; Michael Broussard; Shannon Miser-Marven (business affairs).

Represents: Nonfiction books, scholarly books, novels, syndicated material. Considers all nonfiction areas. Considers these fiction areas: action/adventure; contemporary issues; detective/police/crime; ethnic; experimental; family saga; feminist; gay; glitz; historical; humor/satire; lesbian; literary; mainstream; mystery/suspense; picture book; psychic/supernatural; religious/inspirational; sports; thriller/espionage.

○━ This agency specializes in commercial fiction, nonfiction.

How to Contact: Send query letter and outline. Responds in 4 months. Obtains most new clients through conferences, lectures, other clients and "very frequently through publisher's referrals."

Recent Sales: *Ten Things I Wish I'd Known*, by Maria Shriver; *Play Like a Man, Win Like a Woman*, Gail Evan; *What Matters Most*, by Hyrom Smith.

Terms: Agent receives 15% commission on domestic sales. Offers written contract, binding for "no set amount of time. The contract can be cancelled by either agent or client, effective 30 days after cancellation." Charges clients $20 processing fee and express mail charges.

Writers' Conferences: Southwest Writers (Albuquerque NM); Brazos Writers (College Station TX).

Tips: If interested in agency representation, "it is vital to have the material in the proper working format. As agents' policies differ, it is important to follow their guidelines. The best advice I can give is to work on establishing a strong proposal that provides sample chapters, an overall synopsis (fairly detailed) and some bio information on yourself. Do not send your proposal in pieces; it should be complete upon submission. Remember you are trying to sell your work and it should be in its best condition."

◎ ◎ **DWYER & O'GRADY, INC., (Specialized: children's books)**, P.O. Box 239, Lempster NH 03605-0239. (603)863-9347. Fax: (603)863-9346. E-mail: dosouth@mindspring.com. **Contact:** Elizabeth O'Grady. Estab. 1990. Member of SCBWI. Represents 20 clients. 20% of clients are new/previously unpublished writers. Currently handles: 100% juvenile books.

● Prior to opening their agency, Mr. Dwyer and Ms. Grady were booksellers and publishers.

Member Agents: Elizabeth O'Grady (children's books); Jeff Dwyer (children's books).

Represents: Juvenile books. **Considers these nonfiction areas:** juvenile nonfiction. **Considers these fiction areas:** juvenile; picture book; young adult.

O━ This agency represents only writers and illustrators of children's books. Does not want to receive nonjuvenile submissions.

How to Contact: *Not accepting new clients*. No unsolicited mss. Obtains most new clients through referrals or direct approach by agent to writer whose work they've read.

Recent Sales: Sold 13 titles in the last year. *A Gardener's Alphabet*, by Mary Azarian (Houghton Mifflin); *Many Many Moons*, by Mary Azarian (Little Brown); *Hinkley Fire*, by Ted Rose (Houghton Mifflin); *Talkin 'Bout Bess*, by Earl B. Lewis (Orchard Books). Other clients include Kim Ablon, Mary Azarian, Tom Bodett, Odds Bodkin, Donna Clair, Pat Lowery Collins, Leonard Jenkins, E.B. Lewis, Ted Rose, Rebecca Rule, Steve Schuch, Virginia Stroud, Natasha Tarpley, Zong-Zhou Wang, Rashida Watson.

Terms: Agent receives 15% commission on domestic sales; 20% on foreign sales. Offers written contract. 30-day notice must be given to terminate contract. Charges clients for "photocopying of longer manuscripts or mutually agreed upon marketing expenses."

Writers' Conferences: Book Expo; American Library Association; Society of Children's Book Writers & Illustrators.

🖉**JANE DYSTEL LITERARY MANAGEMENT**, One Union Square West, Suite 904, New York NY 10003. (212)627-9100. Fax: (212)627-9313. Website: www.dystel.com. **Contact:** Miriam Goderich, Todd Keithley. Estab. 1994. Member of AAR. Presently represents 200 clients. 50% of clients are new/previously unpublished writers. Currently handles: 65% nonfiction books; 25% novels; 10% cookbooks.

Member Agents: Stacey Glick; Todd Keithley; Eric Sommers (foreign rights); Jane Dystel; Miriam Goderich; Jo Fagan; Tracey Gardner.

Represents: Nonfiction books, novels, cookbooks. **Considers these nonfiction areas:** animals; anthropology/archaeology; biography/autobiography; business; child guidance/parenting; cooking/food/nutrition; current affairs; education; ethnic/cultural interests; gay/lesbian issues; government/politics/law; health/medicine; history; humor; military/war; money/finance/economics; New Age/metaphysics; popular cultures; psychology; religious/inspirational; science/technology; true crime/investigative; women's issues/women's studies. **Considers these fiction areas:** action/adventure; contemporary issues; detective/police/crime; ethnic; family saga; gay; lesbian; literary; mainstream; thriller/espionage.

O━ This agency specializes in commercial and literary fiction and nonfiction plus cookbooks.

How to Contact: Query with SASE. Responds in 3 weeks to queries; 6 weeks to mss. Obtains most new clients through recommendations from others, solicitation, at conferences.

Recent Sales: *The Sparrow* and *Children of God*, by Mary Russell; *Water Carry Me*, by Thomas Moran; *Syrup*, by Maxx Barry; *Keep It Simple, Stupid*, by Judge Judy Sheindlin; *Chasing Hepburn*, by Gus Lee.

Terms: Agent receives 15% commission on domestic sales; 19% of foreign sales. Offers written contract on a book to book basis. Charges clients for photocopying. Galley charges and book charges from the publisher are passed on to the author.

Writers' Conferences: West Coast Writers Conference (Whidbey Island WA, Columbus Day weekend); University of Iowa Writer's Conference; Pacific Northwest Writer's Conference; Pike's Peak Writer's Conference; Santa Barbara Writer's Conference.

🖉 **ANNE EDELSTEIN LITERARY AGENCY**, 404 Riverside Dr., New York NY 10025. Member of AAR. This agency did not respond to our request for information. Query before submitting.

🖉 🖉 **EDUCATIONAL DESIGN SERVICES, INC., (Specialized: education)**, P.O. Box 253, Wantagh NY 11793-0253. (718)539-4107 or (516)221-0995. **Contact:** Bertram L. Linder, president; Edwin Selzer, vice president. Estab. 1979. Represents 17 clients. 70% of clients are new/previously unpublished writers. Currently handles: 100% textbooks.

Represents: Textbooks, scholarly books. **Considers these nonfiction areas:** anthropology/archaeology; business; child guidance/parenting; current affairs; ethnic/cultural interests; government/politics/law; history; juvenile nonfiction; language/literature/criticism; military/war; money/finance/economics; science/technology; sociology; women's issues/women's studies; K-12 market.

O━ This agency specializes in textual material for educational market.

How to Contact: Query with outline/proposal or outline plus 1-2 sample chapters. "SASE essential." Considers simultaneous queries and submissions. Responds in 1 month to queries; 6 weeks to mss. Obtains most new clients through recommendations, at conferences and through queries.

Recent Sales: Sold 4 titles in the last year. *How to Solve Word Problems in Arithmetic Grades 6-8*, by P. Pullman McGraw-Hill (Schaum); *How to Solve Word Problems in Mathematics*, by D. Wayne McGraw-Hill (Schaum); *First Principles of Cosmology*, by E.V. Linder (Addison-Wesley Longman).

Terms: Agent receives 15% commission on domestic sales; 25% on foreign sales. Offers written contract. Charges clients for photocopying, actual postage/shipping costs.

🖉 **PETER ELEK ASSOCIATES**, Box 223, Canal Street Station, New York NY 10013-2610. (212)431-9368. Fax: (212)966-5768. E-mail: info@theliteraryagency.com. **Contact:** Lauren Mactas. Estab. 1979. Represents 20 clients. Currently handles: 30% juvenile books.

Member Agents: Gerardo Greco (director of project development/multimedia).

Represents: Juvenile books (nonfiction, picture books); adult nonfiction. **Considers these nonfiction areas:** anthropology; parenting; juvenile nonfiction; nature/environment; popular culture; science; true crime/investigative.

○━ This agency specializes in children's picture books, adult nonfiction.

How to Contact: Query with outline/proposal and SASE. Responds in 3 weeks to queries; 5 weeks to mss. Obtains most new clients through recommendations and studying bylines in consumer and trade magazines and in regional and local newspapers.

Recent Sales: *Legendary Brides*, by Letitia Baldridge (HarperCollins); *Today I Feel Silly*, by Laura Cornell (HarperCollins); *When Animals Speak*, by Barbara Hehner (Barron's); *Secrets in Stone*, by Laurie Coulter (Little, Brown).

Terms: Agent receives 15% commission on domestic sales; 20% on foreign sales. If required, charges clients for wholesale photocopying, typing, courier charges.

Writers' Conferences: Frankfurt Book Fair (Frankfurt Germany, October); LIBF (England); Bologna Children's Book Fair (Italy); APBA (Sidney, Australia).

Tips: "Do your research thoroughly before submitting proposal. Only fresh and original material considered."

N 🖳 ○ ◎ ELITE ONLINE, (Specialized: online publishing), P.O. Box 145, Highspire PA 17034-0145. (717)948-0666. Fax: (717)948-4131. E-mail: eliteonlinedmkisssu.edu. **Contact:** Daniel M. Kane. Estab. 2000. Represents 7 clients; 29% of clients are new/previously unpublished writers. Currently handles: 33% novels; 34% short story collections; 33% novellas.

Member Agents: Daniel M. Kane; Alma Maria Garcia (science fiction).

Represents: Novels, short story collections, novellas. **Considers these fiction areas:** feminist; gay/lesbian; horror; humor/satire; psychic/supernatural; science fiction.

○━ This agency specializes in the placement of e-books. "We offer quick response time and the author never pays reading fees or for editorial assistance. We make an investment of time in each of our authors." Actively seeking horror, science fiction: both novels and short stories. Does not want to receive religious.

How to Contact: Send entire manuscript and diskette in MS Word. Does not return material. Prefers to read material exclusively. Responds in 2 weeks on mss. Obtains most new clients through recommendations from others, queries/solicitations.

Recent Sales: Sold 1 title in the last year. *The Other Side of Life* (4GoodBooks.com).

Terms: Agent receives 18% commission on electronic sales. "We represent no one exclusively (unless requested), but rather on a per project basis." Offers written contract, renewable after 14 months. 90-day notice must be given to terminate contract. Charges clients for photocopying, postage, diskettes.

Tips: "To paraphrase Clive Barker, no matter how dark or bizarre your imagination, there's probably a market for your work. When in doubt, submit. Include your e-mail address, where most of our correspondence takes place. Our pet peeve is problems with basic grammar/spelling."

◑ ETHAN ELLENBERG LITERARY AGENCY, 548 Broadway, #5-E, New York NY 10012. (212)431-4554. Fax: (212)941-4652. E-mail: ellenbergagent@aol.com. Website: www.ethanellenberg.com. **Contact:** Ethan Ellenberg, Michael Psaltis. Estab. 1983. Represents 70 clients. 10% of clients are new/previously unpublished writers. Currently handles: 25% nonfiction books; 75% novels.

• Prior to opening his agency, Mr. Ellenberg was contracts manager of Berkley/Jove and associate contracts manager for Bantam.

Member Agents: Michael Psaltis (commercial fiction, literary fiction, mysteries, cookbooks, women's fiction, popular science and other unique nonfiction); Ethan Ellenberg.

Represents: Nonfiction books, novels. **Considers these nonfiction areas:** biography/autobiography; business; child guidance/parenting; cooking/food/nutrition; current affairs; health/medicine; history; humor; juvenile nonfiction; New Age/metaphysics; popular culture; psychology; religious/inspirational; science/technology; self-help/personal improvement; true crime/investigative. **Considers these fiction areas:** detective/police/crime; family saga; fantasy; historical; juvenile; literary; mainstream; mystery/suspense; picture book; romance; science fiction; thriller/espionage; young adult.

○━ This agency specializes in commercial fiction, especially thrillers and romance/women's fiction. "We also do a lot of children's books." Actively seeking commercial and literary fiction, children's books, break-through nonfiction. Does not want to receive poetry, westerns, autobiographies.

How to Contact: For fiction: Send introductory letter (with credits, if any), outline, first 3 chapters, SASE. For nonfiction: Send query letter and/or proposal, 1 sample chapter if written, SASE. For children's books: Send introductory letter (with credits, if any), up to 3 picture book mss, outline and first 3 chapters for longer projects, SASE. Accepts queries by e-mail but no attachments; does not accept fax queries. Considers simultaneous queries and submissions. Responds in 10 days to queries; 1 month to mss. Returns materials only with SASE.

Recent Sales: Sold over 100 titles in the last year. *Legacy Trilogy*, by Bill Keith (Avon); *Diabetes*, by Kris Napier (Prentice-Hall); *Edemons*, by Louis Pinault (Harper Business); *Seriously Simple*, by Diane Worthington (Chronicle Books); two contemporary romances, by Kathleen Kane (St. Martin's Press); two historical romances, by Beatrice Small (Kensington Books).

Terms: Agent receives 15% on domestic sales; 10% on foreign sales. Offers written contract, "flexible." Charges clients for "direct expenses only: photocopying, postage." Writers reimbursed for office fees after the sale of ms.

Writers' Conferences: Attends RWA National and Novelists, Inc.

Tips: "We do consider new material from unsolicited authors. Write a good clear letter with a succinct description of your book. We prefer the first three chapters when we consider fiction. For all submissions you must include SASE for return or the material is discarded. It's always hard to break in, but talent will find a home. We continue to see natural storytellers and nonfiction writers with important books."

✔ ◑ **NICHOLAS ELLISON, INC.,** 55 Fifth Ave., 15th Floor, New York NY 10003. (212)206-6050. Fax: (212)463-8718. Affiliated with Sanford J. Greenburger Associates. **Contact:** Alička Pistek. Estab. 1983. Represents 70 clients. Currently handles: 25% nonfiction books; 75% novels.
   • Prior to becoming an agent, Mr. Ellison was an editor at Minerva Editions, Harper & Row and editor-in-chief at Delacorte.
Member Agents: Alička Pistek.
Represents: Nonfiction, novels. **Considers most nonfiction areas. Considers literary and mainstream fiction.**
   O➤ Does not want to receive biography or self-help.
How to Contact: Query with SASE. Responds in 6 weeks.
Recent Sales: *The Lion's Game*, by Nelson DeMille (Warner); *Equivocal Death*; by Amy Gutman (Little, Brown). Other clients include Olivia Goldsmith, P.T. Deutermann, James Webb, Nancy Geary.
Terms: Agent receives 15% commission on domestic sales; 20% commission on foreign sales.

◐ **ANN ELMO AGENCY INC.,** 60 E. 42nd St., New York NY 10165. (212)661-2880, 2881. Fax: (212)661-2883. **Contact:** Lettie Lee. Estab. 1961. Member of AAR, MWA, Authors Guild.
Member Agents: Lettie Lee; Mari Cronin (plays); A.L. Abecassis (nonfiction).
Represents: Nonfiction, novels. **Considers these nonfiction areas:** anthropology/archaeology; art/architecture/design; biography/autobiography; business; child guidance/parenting; computers/electronics; cooking/food/nutrition; crafts/hobbies; current affairs; education; health/medicine; history; how-to; juvenile nonfiction; money/finance/economics; music/dance/theater/film; photography; popular culture; psychology; self-help/personal improvement; true crime/investigative; women's issues. **Considers these fiction areas:** action/adventure; contemporary issues; detective/police/crime; ethnic; family saga; feminist; glitz; historical; juvenile; literary; mainstream; mystery/suspense; psychic/supernatural; regional; romance (contemporary, gothic, historical, regency); thriller/espionage; young adult.
How to Contact: "Letter queries *only* with SASE." No queries by fax. Responds in 3 months "average" to queries. Obtains most new clients through referrals.
Recent Sales: This agency prefers not to share information on specific sales.
Terms: Agent receives 15% commission on domestic sales; 20% on foreign sales. Offers written contract (standard AAR contract). Charges clients for "special mailings or shipping considerations or multiple international calls. No charge for usual cost of doing business."
Tips: "Query first, and when *asked* only please send properly prepared manuscript. A double-spaced, readable manuscript is the best recommendation. Include SASE, of course."

Ⓝ ◑ **FELICIA ETH LITERARY REPRESENTATION,** 555 Bryant St., Suite 350, Palo Alto CA 94301-1700. (650)375-1276. Fax: (650)375-1277. E-mail: feliciaeth@aol.com. **Contact:** Felicia Eth. Estab. 1988. Member of AAR. Represents 25-35 clients. Works with established and new writers. Currently handles: 85% nonfiction; 15% adult novels.
Represents: Nonfiction books, novels. **Considers these nonfiction areas:** animals; anthropology; biography; business; child guidance/parenting; current affairs; ethnic/cultural interests; gay/lesbian issues; government/politics/law; health/medicine; history; nature/environment; popular culture; psychology; science/technology; sociology; true crime/investigative; women's issues/women's studies. **Considers these fiction areas:** ethnic; feminist; gay; lesbian; literary; mainstream; thriller/espionage.
   O➤ This agency specializes in "provocative, intelligent, thoughtful nonfiction on a wide array of subjects which are commercial and high-quality fiction; preferably mainstream and contemporary."
How to Contact: Query with outline and SASE. Accepts queries by e-mail. Considers simultaneous queries. Responds in 3 weeks to queries; 1 month to proposals and sample pages.
Recent Sales: Sold 7-10 titles in the last year. *Recovering the Power of the Ancestral Mind*, by Dr. Gregg Jacobs (Viking); *The Ulster Path*, by Will Ferguson (Grove/Atlantic); *Socrates Cafe*, by Chris Phillips (W.W. Norton); *An Unburdened Heart*, by Mariah Nelson (HarperCollins); *Hand Me Down Dreams*, by Mary Jacobsen (Crown Publishers); *Java Joe & the March of Civilization*, by Stewart Allen (Soho Press); *The Charged Border*, by Jim Nolman (Henry Holt & Co.).
Terms: Agent receives 15% commission on domestic sales; 20% on dramatic sales; 20% on foreign sales. Charges clients for photocopying, express mail service—extraordinary expenses.
Writers' Conferences: Independent Writers of (LA); Conference of National Coalition of Independent Scholars (Berkeley CA); Writers Guild.
Tips: "For nonfiction, established expertise is certainly a plus, as is magazine publication—though not a prerequisite. I am highly selective but also highly dedicated to those projects I represent."

THE PUBLISHING FIELD is constantly changing! Agents often change addresses, phone numbers, or even companies. If you're still using this book and it is 2002 or later, buy the newest edition of *Guide to Literary Agents* at your favorite bookstore or order directly from Writer's Digest Books at (800)289-0963.

☑ ☺ **MARY EVANS INC.**, 242 E. Fifth St., New York NY 10003. (212)979-0880. Fax: (212)979-5344. E-mail: merrylit@aol.com. **Contact:** Carlotta Vance. Member of AAR. Represents 45 clients. Currently handles: 45% nonfiction books; 5% story collections; 50% novels.
Member Agents: Mary Evans, Tanya McKinnon.
Represents: Nonfiction books, novels. **Considers these nonfiction areas:** biography/autobiography; computers/electronics; current affairs; gay/lesbian issues; government/politics/law; history; nature/environment; popular culture; science/technology. **Considers these fiction areas:** contemporary issues; ethnic; literary; upmarket.
　　O→ This agency specializes in literary fiction and serious nonfiction. Actively seeking "professional well-researched nonfiction proposals; literary novels." Does not want to receive children's books.
How to Contact: Query with SASE. Accepts queries by e-mail, but no attachments. Prefers to read materials exclusively. Obtains most new clients through recommendations from others.
Recent Sales: Sold 15 titles in the last year. *The Amazing Adventures of Kavalier & Clay*, by Michael Chalon (Random House); *Mitten Strings for God*, by Katrina Kenison (Warner Books); *Amazing Grace*, by 3 Dog Bakery (Workman).
Terms: Agent receives 15% commission on domestic sales; 20% on foreign sales.

Ø **FALLON LITERARY AGENCY**, 15 E. 26th St., Suite 1609, New York NY 10010. Member of AAR. This agency did not respond to our request for information. Query before submitting.

☑ ☺ **FARBER LITERARY AGENCY INC.**, 14 E. 75th St., #2E, New York NY 10021. (212)861-7075. Fax: (212)861-7076. E-mail: farberlit@aol.com. Website: www.donaldfarber.com. **Contact:** Ann Farber, Dr. Seth Farber. Estab. 1989. Represents 40 clients. 50% of clients are new/previously unpublished writers. Currently handles: 40% fiction; 15% scholarly books; 45% stage plays.
Member Agents: Ann Farber (novels); Seth Farber (plays, scholarly books, novels).
Represents: Nonfiction books, textbooks, juvenile books, novels, stage plays. **Considers these nonfiction areas:** child guidance/parenting; cooking/food/nutrition; music/dance/theater/film; psychology. **Considers these fiction areas:** action/adventure; contemporary issues; humor/satire; juvenile; literary; mainstream; mystery/suspense; thriller/espionage; young adult.
How to Contact: Send outline/proposal, 3 sample chapters and SASE. Accepts queries by e-mail or fax. Prefers to read materials exclusively. Responds in 1 month to queries; 2 months to mss. Obtains most new clients through recommendations from others.
Recent Sales: Sold 6 titles in the last year. *Live a Little*, by Colin Neenan (Harcourt Brace & Co.); *Saving Grandma*, by Frank Schaeffer (The Putnam Berkley Publishing Group, Inc.); *Step on a Crack*, by M.T. Coffin (Avon/Camelot Publishing Co.); *Bright Freedom Song*, by Gloria Houston (Harcourt Brace & Co.).
Terms: Agent receives 15% commission on domestic sales; 20% on foreign sales. Offers written contract, binding for 1 year. Client must furnish copies of ms, treatments and any other items for submission.
Tips: "Our attorney, Donald C. Farber, is the author of many books. His services are available to the agency's clients as part of the agency service at no additional charge."

☑ Ø **FEIGEN/PARRENT LITERARY MANAGEMENT**, 10158 Hollow Glen Circle, Bel Air CA 90077-2112. (310)271-4722. Fax: (310)274-0503. E-mail: reellifewomen@compuserve.com. **Contact:** Brenda Feigen, Joanne Parrent. Estab. 1995. Member of PEN USA West, Authors Guild, and LA County Bar Association. Represents 35-40 clients. 20-30% of clients are new/previously unpublished writers. Currently handles: 40% nonfiction books; 25% movie scripts; 30% novels; 5% TV scripts.
　　● Ms. Feigen is also an attorney and producer; Ms. Parrent is also a screenwriter and author.
Member Agents: Brenda Feigen (books, books-to-film); Joanne Parrent (screenplays).
Represents: Nonfiction books, novels. **Considers these nonfiction areas:** biography/autobiography; business; current affairs; gay/lesbian issues; government/politics/law; health/medicine; how-to; money/finance/economics; memoirs; theater/film; psychology; self-help/personal improvement; women's issues/women's studies. **Considers these fiction areas:** contemporary issues; family saga; feminist; gay; lesbian; literary. "Manuscripts must be less than 75,000 words for a new author."
　　O→ This agency is actively seeking "material about women, including strong, positive individuals. The material can be fiction, memoir or biographical." Does not want to receive horror, science fiction, religion, pornography; "poetry or short stories unless author has been published by a major house."
Also Handles: Feature film, TV MOW. **Considers these script areas:** action/adventure; comedy; contemporary issues; family saga; feminist; lesbian; thriller. "Must be professionally formatted and under 130 pages."
How to Contact: Query only with 2-page synopsis and author bio with SASE. Does not accept queries by fax. "Prefers regular mail." Considers simultaneous queries. Prefers to read ms exclusively. Responds in 3 weeks to queries; 6 weeks to mss. Returns materials only with SASE. Obtains most new clients through recommendations from other clients and publishers, through the Internet, and listings in *Literary Market Place*.
Recent Sales: Sold 6 book titles and 1 script project in the last year. *How They Achieved*, by Lucinda Watson (Wiley); *An Independent Woman*, by Anne Allen (Praeger); *Rape of Nanking*, by Iris Chang (Basic Books); *The Women's Movement*, by Joanne Parrent (Random House). **Movie/TV MOW script(s) optioned/sold:** *The Cowboys of Haddington Moor*, by David Martin Anderson (James Coburn, producer).
Terms: Agent receives 15% commission on domestic sales; 20% on foreign sales. Offers written contract, binding for 1 year. Charges clients for postage, long distance calls, photocopying.

Tips: "If we like a book or screenplay we will either, at the writer's choice, represent it as agents or offer to produce it ourselves if the material is of real interest to us, personally."

■ ◐ **JUSTIN E. FERNANDEZ, AGENT/ATTORNEY,** P.O. Box 20038, Cincinnati OH 45220. E-mail: lit4@ao l.com. **Contact:** Justin E. Fernandez. Estab. 1996. Represents 10-15 clients. 20% of clients are new/previously unpublished writers. Currently handles: 40% nonfiction; 50% fiction; 5% Internet, 5% other.
  • Prior to opening his agency, Mr. Fernandez, a 1992 graduate of the University of Cincinnati College of Law, served as a law clerk with the Ohio Court of Appeals, Second Appellate District (1992-94), and as a literary agent for Paraview, Inc., New York (1995-96).
Member Agents: Paul A. Franc (associate agent); Justin E. Fernandez.
Represents: Nonfiction, fiction, screen/teleplays and digital "art," (software, multimedia/Internet-related products). **Considers most nonfiction and fiction genres.**
How to Contact: Query first. "E-mail queries are preferred and free; postal queries require a $10 handling fee—send a check made payable to 'Agency For The Digital & Literary Arts, Inc.' Do NOT send a letter-sized SASE with a query. Never send loose postage—or metered postage on a return package." Considers simultaneous queries and submissions. Obtains most new clients through referrals or queries from listings.
Recent Sales: *No Risk Used Car Buying*, by Robert F. Stamps (Usedcars.com).
Terms: Agent receives 10% commission on domestic sales; 15% on foreign sales; 20% with foreign co-agent. Offers written contract.
Tips: "Query letters are business letters. The tone should be measured, reasonably formal and matter-of-fact. Include facts such as book length (word count), genre, intended audience, favorable comparisons to other successful books of its type, and information about the book's niche (how much competition is there and what is it?) Ultimately, you should try to explain why your book will succeed in its niche. Keep personal data to a minimum unless it relates to publication credit or notoriety. Manuscripts should be very carefully edited for typos, grammar, sense, word-choice, brevity, clarity, and 'flow' of the narrative."

✓ ◐ **FIRST BOOKS,** 3000 Market St., NE, #527, Salem OR 97301. (503)588-2224. E-mail: firstbooks@aol.com. Website: www.firstbooks.com. **Contact:** Jeremy Solomon. Estab. 1988. Represents 80 clients. 25% of clients are new/previously unpublished writers.
Member Agents: Jeremy Solomon; Bernadette Duperron.
Represents: Fiction and nonfiction for the adult and juvenile market.
  ☞ This agency specializes in book-length fiction and nonfiction for the adult and juvenile markets. Does not want to receive category fiction (romance, western, horror), short stories or poetry, religious or spiritual titles, textbooks. Looking for fiction and nonfiction that tells a good tale.
How to Contact: Query with SASE. No e-mail queries. Prefers to read materials exclusively. Responds in 3 weeks to queries. Returns materials only with SASE. Obtains most new clients through recommendations from others and website, as well as unsolicited submissions.
Recent Sales: Sold 40 titles in the last year. *Mastering the Markets*, by Ari Kiev (John Wiley & Sons); *So Many Strange Things*, by Charise Mericle (Little, Brown & Co.); *Turning Lead Into Gold*, by Robin Pinkley (St. Martin's Press); *How Murray Saved Christmas*, by Mike Reiss (Price Stern Sloan/Penguin-Putnam); *The Same Phrase Describes My Marriage and My Breasts: Before the Kids They Used to Be Such a Cute Couple*, by Amy Krouse Rosenthal (Andrews McMeel Universal).
Terms: Agent receives 15% commission on domestic sales; 20% on foreign sales. Offers written contract, with cancellation on demand by either party.

◐ **FITZGERALD LITERARY MANAGEMENT,** 84 Monte Alto Rd., Santa Fe NM 87505. Phone/fax: (505)466-1186. **Contact:** Lisa FitzGerald. Estab. 1994. Represents 12 clients. 75% of clients are new/previously unpublished writers. Currently represents: 75% movie scripts; 15% film rights to novels; 5% TV scripts; 5% films rights to stage plays.
  • See expanded listing for this agency in Script Agents.

◐ **JOYCE A. FLAHERTY, LITERARY AGENT,** 816 Lynda Court, St. Louis MO 63122-5531. (314)966-3057. **Contact:** Joyce Flaherty. Estab. 1980. Member of AAR, RWA, MWA, Authors Guild. Represents 40 clients. Currently handles: 15% nonfiction books; 85% novels.
  • Prior to opening her agency, Ms. Flaherty was a journalist, public relations consultant, and executive director of a large suburban Chamber of Commerce.
Member Agents: Joyce A. Flaherty.
Represents: Nonfiction books, novels. **Considers these nonfiction areas:** Americana; animals; child guidance/parenting; cookbooks; health/medicine; how-to; memoirs; nature; popular culture; psychology; self-help/personal improvement; sociology; travel; true adventure sagas; women's issues. **Considers these fiction areas:** contemporary issues; family saga; feminist; historical; mainstream; military; mystery/suspense; thrillers; women's genre fiction.
  ☞ Actively seeking "high concept fiction, very commercial; quality works of both fiction and nonfiction; gripping nonfiction adventure." Does not want to receive "poetry, novellas, short stories, juvenile, syndicated material, film scripts, essay collections, science fiction, traditional westerns."

How to Contact: Send outline plus 1 sample chapter and SASE. *No unsolicited mss.* Does not accept queries by e-mail or fax. Prefers to read materials exclusively. Responds in 1 month to queries; 2 months to mss unless otherwise agreed on. Returns materials only with SASE. "At this time we are adding only currently published authors." Obtains most new clients through recommendations from editors and clients, writers' conferences, and from queries. Preference given to published book authors.

Recent Sales: Sold 51 titles in the last year. *Murder of a Small Town Honey*, by Denise Swanwon (Signet/NAL); *The Irish Rogue*, by Judith E. French (Ballantine); *Primary Target*, by Joe Weber (Putnam-Berkley); *Princess*, by Gaelen Foley (Ballantine).

Terms: Agent receives 15% commission on domestic sales.

Writers' Conferences: Often attends Romance Writers of America.

Tips: "Be concise and well focused in a letter or by phone. Always include a SASE as well as your phone number. Know something about the agent beforehand so you're not wasting each other's time. Be specific about word length of project and when it will be completed if not completed at the time of contact. Be brief!"

N ◑ FLAMING STAR LITERARY ENTERPRISES, 320 Riverside Dr., New York NY 10025. **Contact:** Joseph B. Vallely or Janis C. Vallely. Estab. 1985. Represents 100 clients. 25% of clients are new/previously unpublished writers. Currently handles: 100% nonfiction books.
  • Prior to opening the agency, Joseph Vallely served as national sales manager for Dell; Janis Valley was associate publisher of Doubleday.

Represents: Nonfiction books. **Considers these nonfiction areas:** current affairs; government/politics/law; health/medicine; nature/environment; New Age/metaphysics; science/technology; self-help/personal improvement; sports.
  ⊶ This agency specializes in upscale commercial nonfiction.

How to Contact: Query with SASE. Responds in 1 week to queries. Obtains most new clients over the transom and through referrals.

Recent Sales: This agency prefers not to share information on specific sales.

Terms: Agent receives 15% commission on domestic sales; 20% on foreign sales. Offers written contract. Charges clients for photocopying, postage only.

◑ ◎ FLANNERY LITERARY, (Specialized: juvenile books), 1140 Wickfield Court, Naperville IL 60563-3300. (630)428-2682. Fax: (630)428-2683. **Contact:** Jennifer Flannery. Estab. 1992. Represents 33 clients. 90% of clients are new/previously unpublished writers. Currently handles: 100% juvenile books.
  • Prior to opening her agency, Ms. Flannery was an editorial assistant.

Represents: Juvenile books. **Considers all juvenile nonfiction areas. Considers these fiction areas:** humor/satire; juvenile; literary; mainstream; mystery/suspense; picture book; young adult.
  ⊶ This agency specializes in children's and young adult, juvenile fiction and nonfiction.

Also Handles: Feature film, animation, TV MOW, miniseries, animation. **Considers these script subject areas:** action/adventure; cartoon/animation; comedy; contemporary issues; ethnic; family saga; historical; humor; juvenile; mainstream; mystery/suspense; sports; teen; western/frontier.

How to Contact: Query with SASE. Responds in 3 weeks to queries; 1 month to mss; 1 month to scripts. Obtains most new clients through referrals and queries.

Recent Sales: Sold over 20 titles in the last year. This agency prefers not to share information on specific sales.

Terms: Agent receives 15% commission on domestic sales; 20% on foreign sales. Offers written contract, binding for life of book in print, with 30 day cancellation clause. 100% of business is derived from commissions on sales.

Writers' Conferences: SCBWI Fall Conference.

Tips: "Write an engrossing, succinct query describing your work."

◑ PETER FLEMING AGENCY, P.O. Box 458, Pacific Palisades CA 90272. (310)454-1373. **Contact:** Peter Fleming. Estab. 1962. Currently handles: 100% nonfiction books.
  • Prior to becoming an agent, Mr. Fleming worked his way through the University of Southern California at CBS TV City.

Represents: Nonfiction books. **Considers "any nonfiction area** with a positive, innovative, helpful, professional, successful approach to improving the world (and abandoning special interests, corruption and patronage)."
  ⊶ This agency specializes in "nonfiction books: innovative, helpful, contrarian, individualistic, pro-free market . . . with bestseller big market potential."

How to Contact: Query with SASE. Obtains most new clients "through a *sensational*, different, one of a kind idea for a book usually backed by the writer's experience in that area of expertise."

Recent Sales: *Launching Your Child in Show Biz*, by Dick Van Patten (General Publishing); *Sexual Compulsion*, by Dr. Paul Fick (Judith Regan-HarperCollins).

Terms: Agent receives 15% commission on domestic sales; 25% on foreign sales. Offers written contract, binding for 1 year. Charges clients "only those fees agreed to *in writing*, i.e., NY-ABA expenses shared. We may ask for a TV contract, too."

Tips: "If you give seminars, you can begin by self-publishing, test marketing with direct sales. One of my clients sold 100,000 copies through his speeches and travels, and another writing duo sold over 30,000 copies of their self-published book before we offered it to trade bookstore publishers."

☑ ☑ **B.R. FLEURY AGENCY**, P.O. Box 149352, Orlando FL 32814-9352. (407)895-8494. Fax: (407)898-3923. E-mail: brfleuryagency@juno.com. **Contact:** Blanche or Margaret Fleury. Estab. 1994. Signatory of WGA. Currently handles: 70% books; 30% scripts.

Represents: Nonfiction books, novels. **Considers these nonfiction areas:** health/medicine; how-to; humor; money/finance/economics; New Age/metaphysics; self-help/personal improvement; investigative. **Considers these fiction areas:** fantasy; horror; humor/satire; literary; psychic/supernatural; science fiction; thriller/espionage.

Also Handles: Feature film, TV MOW. Will only "consider scripts based on books by authors we represent."

How to Contact: Query with SASE or call for information. Accepts queries by fax and e-mail, "2 pages maximum." Prefers to be the only reader. Responds immediately to queries; 3 months to mss. Obtains most new clients through referrals and listings.

Recent Sales: This agency prefers not to share information on specific sales.

Terms: Receives commission according to WGA guidelines. Agent receives 15% commission on domestic sales. Offers written contract, binding as per contract. Charges clients for business expenses directly related to work represented.

Tips: "Read your work aloud before you send it to us."

☑ **THE FOGELMAN LITERARY AGENCY**, 7515 Greenville, Suite 712, Dallas TX 75231. (214)361-9956. Fax: (214)361-9553. Also: 599 Lexington Ave., Suite 2300, New York NY 10022. (212)836-4803. E-mail: foglit@aol.com. Website: www.fogelman.com. **Contact:** Evan Fogelman. Estab. 1990. Member of AAR. Represents 100 clients. 2% of clients are new/previously unpublished writers. Currently handles: 40% nonfiction books; 10% scholarly books; 40% novels; 10% TV scripts.

● Prior to opening his agency, Mr. Fogelman was an entertainment lawyer.

Member Agents: Evan Fogelman (nonfiction, women's fiction); Linda Kruger (women's fiction, nonfiction).

Represents: Nonfiction, novels. **Considers these nonfiction areas:** biography/autobiography; business; child guidance/parenting; current affairs; education; ethnic/cultural interests; government/politics/law; health/medicine; popular culture; psychology; sports; true crime/investigative; women's issues/women's studies. **Considers these fiction areas:** historical; literary; mainstream; and all sub-genres of romance.

    O➡ This agency specializes in women's fiction and nonfiction. "Zealous author advocacy" makes this agency stand apart from others. Actively seeking "nonfiction of all types; romance fiction." Does not want to receive children's/juvenile.

How to Contact: Query with SASE. Accepts queries by e-mail. Considers simultaneous queries and submissions. Responds "next business day" to queries; 3 months to mss. Returns materials only with SASE. Obtains most new clients through recommendations from others.

Recent Sales: Sold over 60 titles in the last year. This agency prefers not to share information on specific sales.

Terms: Agent receives 15% commission on domestic sales; 10% on foreign sales. Offers written contract, binding on a project-by-project basis.

Writers' Conferences: Romance Writers of America; Novelists, Inc.

Tips: "Finish your manuscript, and see our website."

☑ **THE FOLEY LITERARY AGENCY**, 34 E. 38th St., New York NY 10016-2508. (212)686-6930. **Contact:** Joan or Joseph Foley. Estab. 1956. Represents 10 clients. Currently handles: 75% nonfiction books; 25% novels.

Represents: Nonfiction books, novels.

How to Contact: Query with letter, brief outline and SASE. Responds promptly to queries. Rarely takes on new clients. Obtains most new clients through recommendations from others.

Recent Sales: This agency prefers not to share information on specific sales.

Terms: Agent receives 10% commission on domestic sales; 15% on foreign sales. 100% of business is derived from commissions on sales.

Tips: Desires *brevity* in querying.

☑ ☑ **FORT ROSS INC. RUSSIAN-AMERICAN PUBLISHING PROJECTS**, 26 Arthur Place, Yonkers NY 10701-1703. (914)375-6448. Fax: (914)375-6439. E-mail: ftross@ix.netcom.com. Website: www.fortross.net. **Contact:** Dr. Vladimir P. Kartsev. Estab. 1992. Represents about 100 clients. 2% of clients are new/previously unpublished writers. Currently handles: 50% nonfiction books; 10% juvenile books; 40% novels.

Member Agents: Ms. Olga Borodyanskaya, St. Petersburg, Russia, phone: 7-812-1738607 (fiction, nonfiction); Mr. Konstantin Paltchikov, Moscow, Russia, phone: 7-095-2035280 (romance, science fiction, fantasy, thriller).

Represents: Nonfiction books, juvenile books, novels. **Considers these nonfiction areas:** biography/autobiography; history; memoirs; music/dance; psychology; self-help/personal improvement; true crime/investigative. **Considers these fiction areas:** action/adventure; detective/police/crime; fantasy; horror; mystery/suspense; romance (contemporary, gothic, historical, regency); science fiction; thriller/espionage; young adult; juvenile.

    O➡ This agency specializes in selling rights for Russian books and illustrations (covers) to American publishers and vice versa; also Russian-English and English-Russian translations. Actively seeking adventure, fiction, mystery, romance, science fiction, thriller from established authors and illustrators for Russian and East European markets.

How to Contact: Send published book or galleys. Accepts queries by fax or e-mail. Considers simultaneous queries and submissions. Returns materials only with SASE.

Recent Sales: Sold 8 titles in the last year. *Russian Titanic*, by David Chapkis (Byron Dreiss, NY); *Lolita's Diaries*, by Pia Pera (AST, Russia); *Sex, Boys and You*, by Joni Arredia (Premiere, Russia).

Terms: Agent receives 10% commission on domestic sales; 20% on foreign sales. Offers written contract, binding for 2 years with 2-month cancellation clause.

Tips: "Authors and book illustrators (especially cover art) are welcome for the following genres: romance, fantasy, science fiction, mystery and adventure."

◯ FORTHWRITE LITERARY AGENCY, 23852 W. Pacific Coast Hwy., Suite 701, Malibu CA 90265. (310)456-5698. Fax: (310)456-6589. E-mail: literaryag@aol.com. Website: www.Kellermedia.com. **Contact:** Wendy Keller. Estab. 1989. Member of Women's National Book Assn., National Speakers Association, Publisher's Marketing Association, National Association for Female Executives, Society of Speakers, Authors & Consultants. Represents 20 clients. 10% of clients are new/previously unpublished writers. Currently handles: 80% nonfiction books; 20% foreign and other secondary rights.

• Prior to opening her agency, Ms. Keller was the associate publisher of Los Angeles' second largest Spanish-language newspaper.

Represents: "We handle business books (sales, finance, marketing and management especially); self-help and how-to books on many subjects." **Considers these commercial nonfiction areas:** business; self-help; how-to; pop psychology; health; alternative health; child care/parenting; inspirational; spirituality; home maintenance and management; cooking; crafts; interior design; art; biography; writing; film; consumer reference; ecology; current affairs; women's studies; economics and history. "Particularly books by speakers and seminar leaders."

    0→ This agency specializes in "serving authors who are or plan to also be speakers. Our sister company is a speaker's bureau." Actively seeking "professional manuscripts by highly qualified authors." Does not want to receive "fiction, get-rich-quick or first person narrative on health topics."

Also Handles: Foreign, ancillary, upselling (selling a previously published book to a larger publisher) & other secondary & subsidiary rights.

How to Contact: "Prefer 1 page e-mail query (no attachments)." *No unsolicited mss!* Considers simultaneous queries and submissions. Responds in 2 weeks to queries if interested; 6 weeks to ms. Returns materials only with SASE or recycles. Obtains most new clients through referrals, recommendations by editors, queries, satisfied authors, conferences.

Recent Sales: Sold approximately 16 titles in the last year. *Questions from Earth Answers from Heaven*, by Cher Margolis (St. Martin's Press); *Spirit in Action*, by Dr. Irene Lamberti (Random/Ballantine); *Super Smoothies*, by Cherie Calbom (Warner); *L'Onda Perfetta*, by Sergio Bambaren (Sperling & Kupfer—Italy); *Ein Strand für meine Träume*, by Sergio Bambaren (Kabel—Germany); *The Cult of the Born Again Virgin: How Single Women Are Reclaiming Their Sexual Power*, by Wendy Keller (HEALTH Communications, Inc.).

Writers' Conferences: BEA; Frankfurt Booksellers' Convention; Maui Writer's Conference; some regional conferences and regularly talks on finding an agent, how to write nonfiction proposals, query writing, creativity enhancement, persevering for creatives.

Tips: "Write only on a subject you know well, and be prepared to show a need in the market for your book. We prefer to represent authors who are already presenting their material publicly through seminars or other media."

✓ ◯ FOX CHASE AGENCY, INC., Public Ledget Bldg. 930, Philadelphia PA 19106. Member of AAR. This agency did not respond to our request for information. Query before submitting.

✓ ◯ LYNN C. FRANKLIN ASSOCIATES, LTD., 1350 Broadway, Suite 2015, New York NY 10018. (212)868-6311. Fax: (212)868-6312. E-mail: agency@fsainc.com. **Contact:** Lynn Franklin and Claudia Nys. Estab. 1987. Member of PEN America. Represents 30-35 clients. 50% of clients are new/previously unpublished writers. Currently handles: 90% nonfiction books; 10% novels.

Represents: Nonfiction books, novels. **Considers these nonfiction areas:** biography/autobiography; current affairs; health/medicine; history; memoirs; New Age/metaphysics; psychology; religious/inspirational; self-help/personal improvement. **Considers literary and mainstream commercial fiction.**

    0→ This agency specializes in general nonfiction with a special interest in health, biography, international affairs and spirituality.

How to Contact: Query with SASE. Accepts queries by fax. Considers simultaneous queries and submissions. No unsolicited mss. Responds in 2 weeks to queries; 6 weeks to mss. Obtains most new clients through recommendations from others and solicitations.

Recent Sales: *The Rich Part of Life*, by Jim Kokorus (St. Martin's Press/film rights secured by Columbia Pictures).

Terms: Agent receives 15% commission on domestic sales; 20% on foreign sales. Offers written contract, with 60-day cancellation clause. Charges clients for postage, photocopying, long distance telephone if significant. 100% of business is derived from commissions on sales.

✓ ◯ JEANNE FREDERICKS LITERARY AGENCY, INC., 221 Benedict Hill Rd., New Canaan CT 06840. Phone/fax: (203)972-3011. E-mail: jfredrks@optonline.net. **Contact:** Jeanne Fredericks. Estab. 1997. Member of AAR. Represents 80 clients. 10% of clients are new/previously unpublished writers. Currently handles: 98% nonfiction books; 2% novels.

• Prior to opening her agency, Ms. Fredericks was an agent and acting director with the Susan P. Urstadt Inc. Agency.

Represents: Nonfiction books. **Considers these nonfiction areas:** animals; anthropology/archeaology; art/architecture; biography/autobiography; business; child guidance/parenting; cooking/food/nutrition; crafts/hobbies; current affairs; health/medicine/alternative health; history; horticulture; how-to; interior design/decorating; money/finance; nature/environment; photography; psychology; science; self-help/personal improvement; sports; women's issues. **Considers these fiction areas:** family saga; historical; literary.

O─╖ This agency specializes in quality adult nonfiction by authorities in their fields.

How to Contact: Query first with SASE, then send outline/proposal or outline and 1-2 sample chapters with SASE. No fax queries. Accepts queries by e-mail. "If short—no attachments." Considers simultaneous queries and submissions. Responds in 3 weeks to queries; 6 weeks to mss. Returns material only with SASE. Obtains most new clients through referrals, submissions to agency, conferences.

Recent Sales: Sold 21 titles in the last year. *Waterworks,* by Maureen Gilmer and Michael Glassman (NTC/Contemporary); *Lasting Impressions,* by Laura Martin (AVC Books); *CIG to Antique,* by Enyl Jenkii.

Terms: Agent receives 15% commission on domestic sales; 20% on foreign sales; 25% with foreign co-agent. Offers written contract, binding for 9 months. 2-month notice must be given to terminate contract. Charges clients for photocopying of whole proposals and mss, overseas postage, priority mail and Federal Express.

Writers' Conferences: PEN Women Conference (Williamsburg VA, February); Connecticut Press Club Biennial Writers' Conference (Stamford CT, April); ASJA Annual Writers' Conference East (New York NY, May); BEA (New York, June).

Tips: "Be sure to research the competition for your work and be able to justify why there's a need for it. I enjoy building an author's career, particularly if s(he) is professional, hardworking, and courteous. Aside from ten years of agenting experience, I've had ten years of editorial experience in adult trade book publishing that enables me to help an author polish a proposal so that it's more appealing to prospective editors. My MBA in marketing also distinguishes me from other agents."

N◘ ◙JAMES FRENKEL & ASSOCIATES, 414 S. Randall Ave., Madison WI 53715. (608)255-7977. Fax: (608)255-5852. E-mail: jamesfrenkelandassociates@compuserve.com. **Contact:** James Frenkel. Estab. 1987. Represents 35 clients. 40% of clients are new/previously unpublished writers. Currently handles: 5% nonfiction books; 7% juvenile books; 2% movie scripts; 7% story collections; 1% scholarly books; 65% novels; 1% syndicated material; 2% novellas; 6% anthologies; 4% media tie-ins.

● Mr. Frenkel has been involved in the publishing industry for 25 years, in positions ranging from editor to publisher.

Member Agents: James Frenkel; Tracy Berg; Kristopher O'Higgins.

Represents: Nonfiction books, novels. **Considers these nonfiction areas:** biography/autobiography; true crime/investigative. **Considers these fiction areas:** contemporary issues; detective/police/crime; ethnic; fantasy; feminist; historical; mainstream; mystery/suspense; science fiction; thriller/espionage; westerns/frontier; young adult.

O─╖ "We welcome and represent a wide variety of material."

How to Contact: Query with outline, 4 sample chapters and SASE. Does not accept queries by fax or e-mail. "I only read materials exclusively." Responds in 2 months to queries; 6 months to mss. Obtains most new clients through recommendations from others and conferences.

Recent Sales: Sold 9 titles in the last year. *The Wayfarer Redemption,* by Sara Douglass (TOR Books, 7-book deal); *Dancing on the Head of a Pin,* by Lyda Morehouse (Roc).

Terms: Agent receives 15% commission on domestic sales; 25% on foreign sales. Offers written contract, binding until terminated in writing. Charges clients for office expenses. "Amounts vary from title to title, but photocopying and submission costs are deducted after (and only after) a property sells."

Tips: "If there are markets for short fiction or nonfiction in your field, use them to help establish a name that agents will recognize. Too many times we receive poorly written letters and manuscripts rife with simple spelling errors. This is your work—take the time and effort to put together the best presentation you can."

◙ CANDICE FUHRMAN LITERARY AGENCY, 2440C Bush St., San Francisco CA 94115. (415)674-7654. Fax: (415)674-4004. Member of AAR. This agency did not respond to our request for information. Query before submitting.

◙ SHERYL B. FULLERTON ASSOCIATES, 1095 Amito Ave., Berkeley CA 94705. (510)841-9898. Fax: (510)841-9909. E-Mail: sfullerton@aol.com. Website: www.YouCanWrite.com. **Contact:** Sheryl Fullerton. Estab. 1994. Represents 20 clients. 70% of clients are new/previously unpublished writers. Currently handles: 96% nonfiction books; 3% scholarly books; 1% textbooks.

● Prior to opening her agency, Ms. Fullerton was an editor, then editor-in-chief of a college textbook publisher.

ALWAYS INCLUDE a self-addressed, stamped envelope (SASE) for reply or return of your query or manuscript.

Represents: Nonfiction books. **Considers these nonfiction areas:** anthropology/archaeology; business/management; health; gay/lesbian issues; ethnic/cultural interests; how-to; grounded spirituality; popular culture; psychology; self-help/personal improvement; women's issues/women's studies.

O→ This agency specializes in nonfiction subject areas. Actively seeking psychology, business/management, popular culture and health nonfiction. Does not want to receive inspirational, parenting, fiction, poetry or screenplays.

How to Contact: Query with description, bio and SASE. Accepts queries by e-mail but do not send attachments. Considers simultaneous queries. Responds in 2 weeks to queries; 1 month to mss. Returns materials only with SASE. Obtains most new clients through recommendations, referrals, and through previous contacts.

Recent Sales: Sold 10 titles in the last year. *Bring Your Soul to Work: A Practicle Guide*, by Alan Briskin and Cheryl Peppers (Berrett-Koehler Publishers); *Ask Your Pharmacist: Answers to the 250 Most Commonly Asked Questions*, by Lisa Chavis (St. Martin's Press); *Watches Tell More Than Time: Product Design, Information, and the Quest for Harmony and Elegance*, by Del Coates (McGraw-Hill); *The Time Management Workshop*, by Patricia Haddock (AMACOM).

Terms: Agent receives 15% commission on domestic sales; 20% on foreign sales. Offers written contract, binding for 1 year, then renewable. 60-day notice must be given to terminate contract. Charges clients for reimbursement of phone calls, postage, photocopies.

Tips: Visit our website, YouCanWrite.com, the online reality check for aspiring nonfiction writers with just the information writers need to avoid rejection and get published.

☑ ◉ **MAX GARTENBERG, LITERARY AGENT**, 521 Fifth Ave., Suite 1700, New York NY 10175-0038. (212)292-4354. Fax: (973)535-5033. E-mail: grebnetrag@msn.com. **Contact:** Max Gartenberg. Estab. 1954. Represents 30 clients. 5% of clients are new writers. Currently handles: 90% nonfiction books; 10% novels.

Represents: Nonfiction books. **Considers these nonfiction areas:** agriculture/horticulture; animals; art/architecture/design; biography/autobiography; child guidance/parenting; current affairs; health/medicine; history; military/war; money/finance/economics; music/dance/theater/film; nature/environment; psychology; science/technology; self-help/personal improvement; sports; true crime/investigative; women's issues/women's studies.

How to Contact: Query with SASE. Does not accept queries by e-mail or fax. Considers simultaneous queries. Responds in 2 weeks to queries; 6 weeks to mss. Obtains most new clients "primarily by recommendations from others, but occasionally by following up on good query letters."

Recent Sales: *Biography of Charles Adams*, by Linda Davis (Random House); *Great Exploration Hoaxes*, by David Roberts (Modern Library).

Terms: Agent receives 15% commission on first domestic sale, 10% commission on subsequent domestic sales; 15-20% on foreign sales.

Tips: "This is a small agency serving established writers and new writers whose work it is able to handle are few and far between. Nonfiction is more likely to be of interest here than fiction, and category fiction not at all."

☑ ◉ **GELFMAN SCHNEIDER LITERARY AGENTS, INC.**, 250 W. 57th St., New York NY 10107. (212)245-1993. Fax:(212)245-8678. **Contact:** Jane Gelfman, Deborah Schneider. Estab. 1981. Member of AAR. Represents 150 clients. 10% of clients are new/previously unpublished writers.

Represents: "We represent adult, general, hardcover fiction and nonfiction, literary and commercial, and some mysteries."

O→ Does not want to receive romances, science fiction, westerns or children's books.

How to Contact: Query with SASE. Responds in 1 month to queries; 2 months to mss. Obtains most new clients through recommendations and referrals.

Recent Sales: This agency prefers not to share information on specific sales.

Terms: 15% commission on domestic sales; 20% on foreign sales. Offers written contract. Charges clients for photocopying, messengers and couriers.

☑ ◉ **GHOSTS & COLLABORATORS INTERNATIONAL, (Specialized: ghost writing)**, Division of James Peter Associates, Inc., P.O. Box 670, Tenafly NJ 07670. (201)568-0760. Fax: (201)568-2959. E-mail: bertholtje@compuserve.com. **Contact:** Bert Holtje. Parent agency established 1971. Parent agency is a member of AAR. Represents 54 clients. Currently handles: 100% nonfiction books.

● Prior to opening his agency, Mr. Holtje was a book packager.

Represents: Nonfiction collaborations and ghost writing assignments.

O→ This agency specializes in representing only published ghost writers and collaborators, nonfiction only.

Recent Sales: This agency prefers not to share information on specific sales. Clients include Alan Axelrod, Carol Turkington, George Mair, Brandon Toropov, Alvin Moscow, Richard Marek, Susan Shelly.

Terms: Agent receives 15% commission on domestic sales; 20% on foreign sales. Offers written contract.

Tips: "We would like to hear from professional writers who are looking for ghosting and collaboration projects. We invite inquiries from book publishers who are seeking writers to develop house-generated ideas and to work with their authors who need professional assistance."

☑ **THE GISLASON AGENCY**, 219 Main St. SE, Suite 506, Minneapolis MN 55414-2160. This agency did not respond to our request for information. Query before submitting.

◐ GOLDFARB & ASSOCIATES, 1501 M St. NW, Washington DC 20005-2902. (202)466-3030. Fax: (202)293-318. E-mail: rglawlit@aol.com. **Contact:** Ronald Goldfarb. Estab. 1966. Represents "hundreds" of clients. "Minority" of clients are new/previously unpublished writers. Currently handles: 75% nonfiction books; 25% fiction. Increasing TV and movie deals.

    ● Ron Goldfarb's book (his ninth), *Perfect Villains, Imperfect Heroes*, was published by Random House. Other books include *TV or not TV: Courts, Television, and Justice* (NYU Press), 1998.

Member Agents: Ronald Goldfarb, Esq. (nonfiction); Robbie Anna Hare; Kristin Auclair.

Represents: Nonfiction, fiction. **Considers all nonfiction areas. Considers these adult fiction areas:** action/adventure; contemporary issues; detective/police/crime; ethnic; feminist; glitz; literary; mainstream; mystery/suspense; thriller/espionage; and "considerable holocaust literature on behalf of museums and individual authors."

    ○━ This agency specializes primarily in nonfiction but has a growing interest in well-written fiction. "Given our D.C. location, we represent many journalists, politicians and former federal officials. We arrange collaborations. We also represent a broad range of nonfiction writers and novelists." Actively seeking "fiction with literary overtones; strong nonfiction ideas." Does very little children's fiction or poetry.

How to Contact: Send outline or synopsis plus 1-2 sample chapters (include SASE if return requested). Does not accept queries by fax. Responds in 1 month to queries; 2 months to mss. Obtains most new clients mostly through recommendations from others.

Recent Sales: Sold approximately 35 titles in the last year. *Crimes of War*, by Roy Gutman, David Rieff (Norton); *Plato or Prozac*, by Lou Marinoff (HarperCollins); *Agent of Destiny*, by John S.D. Eisenhower (Free Press); *In the Forest of Harm*, by Sallie Bissell (Bantam Books). Other clients include Congressman John Kasich, Diane Rehm, Susan Eisenhower, Dan Moldea, Roy Gutman, Leonard Garment, Sargent Shriver.

Terms: Charges clients for photocopying, long distance phone calls, postage.

Writers' Conferences: Washington Independent Writers Conference; Medical Writers Conference; VCCA; participate in many ad hoc writers' and publishers' groups and events each year.

Tips: "We are a law firm which can help writers with related legal problems, Freedom of Information Act requests, libel, copyright, contracts, etc. As published authors ourselves, we understand the creative process."

⊘ FRANCES GOLDIN, 57 E. 11th St., New York NY 10003. Member of AAR. This agency did not respond to our request for information. Query with SASE before submitting.

◐ GOODMAN ASSOCIATES, 500 West End Ave., New York NY 10024-4317. (212)873-4806. **Contact:** Elise Simon Goodman. Estab. 1976. Member of AAR. Represents 100 clients. "Presently accepting new clients on a very selective basis."

    ● Arnold Goodman is current chair of the AAR Ethics Committee.

Member Agents: Elise Simon Goodman; Arnold P. Goodman.

Represents: Nonfiction, novels. **Considers most adult nonfiction and fiction areas.**

    ○━ Does not wish to receive "poetry, articles, individual stories, children's or YA material."

How to Contact: Query with SASE. Responds in 10 days to queries; 1 month to mss.

Recent Sales: This agency prefers not to share information on specific sales.

Terms: Agent receives 15% commission on domestic sales; 20% on foreign sales. Charges clients for certain expenses: faxes, toll calls, overseas postage, photocopying, book purchases.

Ⓝ ⊘ IRENE GOODMAN LITERARY AGENCY, 521 Fifth Ave., 17th Floor, New York NY 10017. Member of AAR. This agency did not respond to our request for information. Query before submitting.

Ⓒ CARROLL GRACE LITERARY AGENCY, P.O. Box 10938, St. Petersburg FL 33733. (727)865-2099. **Contacts:** Pat Jozwiakowski, Sunny Mays. Estab. 1999. Represents 50 clients. 95% of clients are new/previously unpublished writers. Currently handles: 20% nonfiction books; 80% novels.

Member Agents: Ms. Sunny Mays (acquisitions director); Ms. Pat Jozwiakowski (agent).

Represents: Nonfiction books, novels. **Considers these nonfiction areas:** art; biography/autobiography; cooking/food/nutrition; crafts/hobbies; education; health/medicine; history; how-to; interior design/decorating; photography; true crime/investigative; women's issues/women's studies. **Considers these fiction areas:** action/adventure; detective/police/crime; family saga; fantasy; historical; horror; literary; mainstream; mystery/suspense (amateur sleuth, cozy, culinary); psychic/supernatural; romance (contemporary, gothic, historical, regency); thriller/espionage; westerns/frontier.

    ○━ "We understand how difficult it is for a new writer to obtain an agent or a publisher. We want to guide careers and encourage our clients to their top potential by offering our experience and knowledge." Actively seeking romance, fantasy, mystery/suspense, psychic supernatural, timeswept (romance w/time travel).

How to Contact: Query with SASE and send synopsis and first 5 sample chapters. Does not accept queries by e-mail or fax. Considers simultaneous queries. Responds in 6 weeks to queries, 2 months to mss.

Recent Sales: This is a new agency with no recorded sales.

Terms: Agent receives 15% commission on domestic sales; 20% on foreign sales. Offers written contract, on book-by-book basis. 90-day notice must be given to terminate contract. Charges clients for photocopying, international and express postage, faxes, postage.

Tips: "Make sure your manuscript is as near to finished as possible—be neat and orderly. Study manuscript formatting, check your manuscript for spelling, grammar and punctuation errors."

Ghostwriter finds success with her own novel

Although Sallie Bissell has been published seven times as a ghost-writer for the Bonnie Bryant Saddle Club series (Skylark), she has waited a long time to find success with her own creative vision. But now, with the publication of her first wilderness sus-pense novel, *In the Forest of Harm* (Bantam Books), and Robbie Anna Hare of Goldfarb & Associates on board as her agent, Bis-sell's literary aspirations are coming true.

Photo by William Landing

Sallie Bissell

 Bissell had a taste of success with a short story written during college which she eventually sold to a romance fiction magazine. However, a long time would pass before she experienced the same sort of success again. "I received $238 and five copies of the magazine. I was thrilled and thought I had this writing thing licked. It was the last thing I was to sell for twenty years."

Following this initial success—and after establishing a family of three children—she wrote a novel and eagerly began submitting her manuscript to agents. "When my youngest son went to kindergarten, I enrolled in a writing class, joined a writers' group, and wrote a novel my friends and I thought was great. I submitted it with the same high hopes that I had with my romance story, but lightning was not to strike twice. After about ten encouraging rejections, I put it in a box and shoved it under my bed."

A few years later, she moved with her family to Asheville, North Carolina, a place she describes as "a very literary-attuned town. I quit writing for a couple of years, but then I realized how much I missed it. I started writing again, this time determined not to give up so easily. I joined a new writers' group, wrote another novel, and again received about a dozen rejections, most of which said, 'Loved the characters, but nothing happened.' I decided to write a novel where a lot of stuff happens, and that's how *In the Forest of Harm* was started."

In the Forest of Harm is the story of Mary Crow, a half-Cherokee lawyer with a dark past. While visiting a sacred site with friends during a camping trip in the southern Appalachian Mountains, she must survive confrontations with this past, other humans, and the rugged landscape itself. Bissell feels the novel reflects some of her own fascinations as well as her desire to write something a little different from more typical suspense novels. "I'm really drawn to adventure stories and, being a Southerner, to books where the past haunts the present. I'm fascinated by the ways people deal with their histories. Mostly you see books of this nature with men as the protagonists. I wondered how women would react in situations of real physical threat and harm, beyond just being victims."

Bissell submitted the manuscript to an agent who suggested adding another 30,000 words. She decided to set the manuscript aside so she could come back to it with a fresh eye and, in the meantime, began ghostwriting for Bonnie Bryant after a recommendation from a friend in her writers' group. "Bonnie sent me a 'test' of sorts. The trick was not only writing well, but writing like Bonnie, in the distinct Saddle Club style. I would receive a 30-page outline from Bonnie and flesh it out into a 130-page novel. By writing on deadline, I learned not to let anything get in the way of me and a certain number of pages a day. I learned a lot about plotting and action while writing the Saddle Club books."

Bissell feels the time spent ghostwriting between drafts of *In the Forest of Harm* was beneficial to staying sharp as a writer. "It was great to take a break from my own stuff and write something else. It kept the wheels greased, so to speak. I think maintaining the physical habit of writing is much like practicing an instrument or working on your tennis serve. You've got to be ready when the Muse visits."

After about a year, Bissell was ready to look at her own manuscript again. She began a lengthy process of polishing and testing its effectiveness on volunteer readers. "For six months, I totally devoted myself to adding the words and sharpening the dialog. I made a couple of writer friends read it in one sitting, then I asked a couple of nonwriter pals to do the same. When my nonwriter pals said they couldn't put it down, I knew I had something."

In addition to the time spent rewriting her manuscript, Bissell also spent time reading books from the suspense novel genre to get a better idea of where her novel fit in to the marketplace. "To educate myself about the market I read all the suspense fiction I could before my second rewrite. I knew I had something a little unusual, so I felt I had a good chance at publication."

When she was sure her manuscript was the best it could possibly be, Bissell looked to her next crucial step in her long-range plan to land an agent—writing a query letter. She knew a strong query was how to entice an agent into reading her full manuscript, so she set aside time to give it her full attention. "I don't think I've worked harder on any piece of writing in my life," she says. "I knew I had a one-page shot to grab their attention, so I spent two solid weeks making my query work. I think a writer's time is well spent making her query as compelling as possible."

After polishing her query letter, she picked up *Guide to Literary Agents* and systematically selected a list of ten agents she thought would be a good match for her manuscript. "I'd heard the only way you could get an agent was to chat one up at a cocktail party at a writers' conference. Since I'm not a born schmoozer, I bought a copy of the *Guide to Literary Agents* and poured over it. I looked for two things—agents who represented authors who wrote suspense fiction and agents who were amenable to working with minimally published writers. I made an initial list of fifty, then divided them into five sets of ten. Robbie Anna was among those first ten, so there were many agents I never queried at all. I started with letters to the top ten agents I wanted. I think I got a pretty good response, too. Within two weeks, five wanted to see the manuscript, three turned me down with form rejections, and two never responded at all."

When the time came to send her full manuscript to the interested agents, Bissell took pains to make sure the manuscript was clean, clearly printed, and physically prepared in a pleasing manner. "I'd written enough Saddle Clubs to know that 20-lb. bond paper and Courier 12, double spaced was the standard format. I found a bright white paper, bought a new ink cartridge for my printer, and spell-checked and proofread until the wee small hours. I found a box just the right size for manuscripts at my local UPS drop and did all the labels on the computer. It took time to make sure the pages were crisp and clear, but I wanted to show the agents and editors I respected their time and eyesight. Robbie Anna complimented the professionalism of my manuscript and told me it was the least amount of work she'd had to spend on a submission in a long time."

Bissell carefully considered what sort of personal and professional dynamic she wanted from the agent/author relationship before making her choice. She knew a harmonious relationship between an agent and an author would be reflected in the handling of her work. A month into her search for an agent, Bissell chose Hare. "I loved her quick response and her unreserved enthusiasm for the book. There was an immediate simpatico between us. I had spoken several times with another agent who was interested in the project, but she had this really critical, you-can't-write-like-that-if-you-want-to-work-with-me attitude. She was a well-respected, knowledgeable agent, but I found myself cringing every time I received an e-mail from her, so I knew she wasn't going to be the one. Agents are simply too important not to have one with whom you feel comfortable. Ron Goldfarb has also been terrific. He's a writer, as well as an attorney, and he made some excellent suggestions for the manuscript, too."

Within one month, Hare sold the book to Kate Miciak at Bantam Books as part of a two-book contract. Several months later, publishers in Germany and the Netherlands acquired overseas publishing rights. When asked to analyze her own path to publication for the benefit of other writers, Bissell stresses hard work, planning, and preparation as the most important elements of her own success.

"I would say it's a dream come true, except the writing of a book is not a dream but a lot of very hard work. It's more like the satisfaction you feel from accomplishing something you've struggled toward for a long time. Don't believe people when they say you can't get anything published unless you know somebody. I didn't know anybody, but I did my research. I'm very proud to be a writer published from one of the 'over the transom' submissions. I think it reinforces the idea that who you know is not as important as the quality of your work, and publishing success can come to anyone."

—Ian Bessler

⊘ **ASHLEY GRAYSON LITERARY AGENCY**, 1342 18th St., San Pedro CA 90732. Member of AAR. This agency did not respond to our request for information. Query before submitting.

◑ **SANFORD J. GREENBURGER ASSOCIATES, INC.**, 55 Fifth Ave., New York NY 10003. (212)206-5600. Fax: (212)463-8718. **Contact:** Heide Lange. Estab. 1945. Member of AAR. Represents 500 clients.
Member Agents: Heide Lange; Faith Hamlin; Beth Vesel; Theresa Park; Elyse Cheney; Daniel Mandel; Nancy Slender.
Represents: Nonfiction books, novels. **Considers all nonfiction areas. Considers these fiction areas:** action/adventure; contemporary issues, detective/police/crime; ethnic; family saga; feminist; gay; glitz; historical; humor/satire; lesbian; literary; mainstream; mystery/suspense; psychic/supernatural; regional; sports; thriller/espionage.
  ○⊓ Does not want to receive westerns or romances.
How to Contact: Query first. Responds in 2 weeks to queries; 2 months to mss.
Recent Sales: Sold 200 titles in the last year. This agency prefers not to share information on specific sales. Clients include Andrew Ross, Margaret Cuthbert, Nicholas Sparks, Mary Kurcinka, Linda Nichols, Edy Clarke, Peggy Claude Pierre.
Terms: Agent receives 15% commission on domestic sales; 20% on foreign sales. Charges clients for photocopying, books for foreign and subsidiary rights submissions.

◐ **ARTHUR B. GREENE**, 101 Park Ave., 26th Floor, New York NY 10178. (212)661-8200. Fax: (212)370-7884.
Contact: Arthur Greene. Estab. 1980. Represents 20 clients. 10% of clients are new/previously unpublished writers. Currently handles: 25% novels; 10% novellas; 10% short story collections; 25% movie scripts; 10% TV scripts; 10% stage plays; 10% other.
  ● See the expanded listing for this agency in Script Agents.

N: ◐ **BLANCHE C. GREGORY, INC.**, 2 Tudor City Place, New York NY 10017. (212)989-2076. Fax: (212)918-2076. Website: www.bcgliteraryagency.com. **Contact:** Gertrude Breman. Member of AAR. Represents nonfiction and fiction books, some juvenile books.
Represents: Nonfiction, fiction, juvenile books.
  ○⊓ This agency is especially strong in international subrights sales.

How to Contact: Query with SASE.
Recent Sales: Clients include Lilian Jackson Braun, Peter Miller, Thomas Savage.
Terms: Agent receives 15% commission on domestic sales; 20% on foreign sales.

⊘ MAXINE GROFFSKY LITERARY AGENCY, 2 Fifth Ave., New York NY 10011. Member of AAR. This agency did not respond to our request for information. Query before submitting.

:Ⓝ: ○ JILL GROSJEAN LITERARY AGENCY, 1390 Millstone Rd., Sag Harbor NY 11963-2214. (631)725-7419. Fax: (631)725-8632. E-mail: JILL6981@aol.com. Website: www.hometown.aol.com/JILL6981/myhomepage/index.ht ml. **Contact:** Jill Grosjean. Estab. 1999. Represents 9 clients. 100% of clients are new/previously unpublished writers. Currently handles 1% nonfiction books; 99% novels.
   • Prior to becoming an agent, Ms. Grosjean was manager of an independent bookstore. She also worked in publishing and advertising.
Represents: Mostly novels, some nonfiction books. **Considers these nonfiction areas:** art/architecture/design; humor; interior design/decorating; nature/environment; travel; women's issues/women's studies; gardening. **Considers these fiction areas:** contemporary issues; historical; humor/satire; literary; mainstream; mystery/suspense; regional; romance; thriller/espionage.
   O─π This agency offers some editorial assistance (i.e., line-by-line edits). Actively seeking mysteries, thrillers, suspense novels. Does not want to receive any nonfiction subjects not indicated above.
How to Contact: Query with SASE. Accepts queries by e-mail. Considers simultaneous queries. Responds in 1 week to queries; 1 month to mss. Returns materials only with SASE. Obtains most new clients through recommendations from others, queries/solicitations.
Recent Sales: Sold 2 titles in the last year. This agency prefers not to share information on specific sales.
Terms: Agent receives 15% commission on domestic sales; 20% on foreign sales. No written contract. Charges clients for photocopying, mailing expenses. Writers reimbursed for office fees after the sale of ms.
Writers' Conferences: Romance Writers of America (Washington D.C. July).

☑ ◉ THE GROSVENOR LITERARY AGENCY, 5510 Grosvenor Lane, Bethesda MD 20814. (301)564-6231. Fax: (301)581-9401. E-mail: 2cgrosveno@aol.com. **Contact:** Deborah C. Grosvenor. Estab. 1995. Member of Nat'l Press Club. Represents 30 clients. 10% of clients are new/previously unpublished writers. Currently handles: 80% nonfiction books; 20% novels.
   • Prior to opening her agency, Ms. Grosvenor was a book editor for 18 years.
Represents: Nonfiction books, novels. **Considers these nonfiction areas:** animals; anthropology/archaeology; art/architecture/design; biography/autobiography; business; child guidance/parenting; current affairs; government/politics/law; health/medicine; history; how-to; language/literature/criticism; military/war; money/finance/economics; music/dance/theater/film; nature/environment; New Age/metaphysics; photography; popular culture; psychology; religious/inspirational; science/technology; self-help/personal improvement; sociology; translations; true crime/investigative; women's issues/women's studies. **Considers these fiction areas:** contemporary issues; detective/police/crime; family saga; gay; historical; lesbian; literary; mainstream; mystery/suspense; romance (contemporary, gothic, historical); thriller/espionage.
How to Contact: Send outline/proposal for nonfiction; send outline and 3 sample chapters for fiction. Does not accept queries by e-mail or fax. Responds in 1 month to queries; 2 months to mss. Returns materials only with SASE. Obtains new clients almost exclusively through recommendations from others.
Recent Sales: *What it Felt Like: Living in the American Century*, by Henry Allen (Pantheon); *Elvis and Nixon* (fiction), by Jonathan Lowy (Crown Publishing).
Terms: Agent receives 15% commission on domestic sales; 20% on foreign sales. Offers a written contract with a 10-day cancellation clause.

☑ ⊘ H.W.A. TALENT REPRESENTATIVE, (formerly Preferred Artists Talent Agency), 3500 W. Olive Ave., Suite 1400, Burbank CA 91505. (818)972-4310. Fax: (818)972-4313. **Contact:** Kimber Wheeler. Estab. 1985. Signatory of WGA. 90% of clients are new/previously unpublished writers. Currently handles: 90% movie scripts, 10% novels.
   • See the expanded listing for this agency in Script Agents.

:Ⓝ: ◉ REECE HALSEY AGENCY, 8733 Sunset Blvd., Suite 101, Los Angeles CA 90069. (310)652-2409. Fax: (310)652-7595. E-mail: gulyas911@aol.com. **Contact:** Dorris Halsey. Also: Reece Halsey North, 98 Main St., #704,

---

Tiburon CA 94920. (415)789-9191. Fax: (415)789-9177. **Contact:** Kimberley Cameron. Estab. 1957. Member of AAR. Represents 40 clients. 30% of clients are new/previously unpublished writers. Currently handles: 30% nonfiction books; 60% novels; 10% movie scripts.

● The Reece Halsey Agency has an illustrious client list largely of established writers, including the estate of Aldous Huxley and has represented Upton Sinclair, William Faulkner and Henry Miller. Ms. Cameron has recently opened a Northern California office and all queries should be addressed to her at the Tiburon office.

Member Agents: Dorris Halsey; Kimberley Cameron.

Represents: Nonfiction books, novels. Considers these nonfiction areas: biography/autobiography; current affairs; history; language/literature/criticism; popular culture; true crime/investigative; women's issues/women's studies. Considers these fiction areas: action/adventure; contemporary issues; detective/police/crime; ethnic; family saga; historical; literary; mainstream; mystery/suspense; science fiction; thriller/espionage; women's fiction.

O— This agency specializes mostly in books/excellent writing.

How to Contact: Query with SASE. Does not accept queries by e-mail or fax. Prefers to read materials exclusively. Responds in 3 weeks to queries; 3 months to mss.

Also Handles: *Movie scripts to Los Angeles office only.*

Terms: Agent receives 15% commission on domestic sales of books, 10% commission on script sales. Offers written contract, binding for 1 year. Requests 6 copies of ms if representing an author.

Writers' Conferences: ABA and various writer conferences, Maui Writers Conference.

Tips: Obtains most new clients through recommendations from others and solicitation. "Always send a well-written query and include a SASE with it!"

REECE HALSEY NORTH, 98 Main St., PMB 704, Tiburon CA 94920. (415)789-9191. Fax: (415)789-9177. E-mail: bookgirl@worldnet.att.net. Website: www.reecehalseynorth.com or kimberlycameron.com. **Contact:** Kimberley Cameron. Estab. 1957. Member of AAR, signatory of WGA. Represents 40 clients. 30% of clients are new/previously unpublished writers. Currently handles: 30% nonfiction books; 70% fiction.

● The Reece Halsey Agency has an illustrious client list largely of established writers, including the estate of Aldous Huxley and has represented Upton Sinclair, William Faulkner and Henry Miller. Ms. Cameron has recently opened a Northern California office and all queries should be addressed to her at the Tiburon office.

Member Agents: Doris Halsey (by referral only, LA office); Kimberley Cameron (Reese Halsey North).

Represents: Fiction and nonfiction. **Considers these nonfiction areas:** biography/autobiography; current affairs; history; language/literature/criticism; memoirs; popular culture; spiritualism; true crime/investigative; women's issues/ women's studies. **Considers these fiction areas:** action/adventure; contemporary issues; detective/police/crime; ethnic; family saga; historical; literary; mainstream; mystery/suspense; science fiction; thriller/espionage; women's fiction.

O— This agency specializes in mystery, literary and mainstream fiction, excellent writing.

How to Contact: Query with SASE. Does not accept queries by e-mail or fax. Considers simultaneous queries and submissions. Responds in 3 weeks to queries; 3 months to mss. Obtains most new clients through recommendations from others, solicitation.

Recent Sales: This agency prefers not to share information on specific sales.

Terms: Agent receives 15% commission on domestic sales of books. Offers written contract, binding for 1 year. Requests 6 copies of ms if representing an author.

Writers' Conferences: BEA; Maui Writers Conference and various writer conferences.

Reading List: Reads *Glimmer Train*, *The Sun* and *The New Yorker* to find new clients. Looks for "writing that touches the heart."

Tips: "Please send a polite, well-written query and include a SASE with it!"

THE MITCHELL J. HAMILBURG AGENCY, 8671 Wilshire Blvd., Suite 500, Beverly Hills CA 90211-2913. (310)657-1501. **Contact:** Michael Hamilburg. Estab. 1937. Signatory of WGA. Represents 70 clients. Currently handles: 70% nonfiction books; 30% novels.

Represents: Nonfiction, novels. **Considers all nonfiction areas and most fiction areas.**

O— Does not want to receive romance.

How to Contact: Send outline, 2 sample chapters and SASE. Responds in 1 month to mss. Obtains most new clients through recommendations from others, at conferences or personal search.

Recent Sales: *A Biography of the Leakey Family*, by Virginia Morrell (Simon & Schuster); *A Biography of Agnes De Mille*, by Carol Easton (Little, Brown).

Terms: Agent receives 10-15% commission on domestic sales.

Tips: "Good luck! Keep writing!"

JEANNE K. HANSON LITERARY AGENCY, 5441 Woodcrest Dr., Edina MN 55424-1649. Member of AAR. This agency did not respond to our request for information. Query before submitting.

HARDEN CURTIS ASSOCIATES, 850 Seventh Ave., Suite 405, New York NY 10019. Member of AAR. This agency did not respond to our request for information. Query before submitting.

HARRIS LITERARY AGENCY, P.O. Box 6023, San Diego CA 92166. (619)697-0600. Fax: (619)697-0610. E-mail: hlit@adnc.com. Website: www.HarrisLiterary.com. **Contact:** Barbara J. Harris. Estab. 1998. Represents 60 clients. 65% of clients are new/previously unpublished writers. Currently handles: 40% nonfiction books; 60% novels.
Member Agents: Barbara J. Harris (nonfiction, fiction); Norman J. Rudenberg (fiction, science-fiction, thrillers).
Represents: Nonfiction books, novels. **Considers these nonfiction areas:** biography/autobiography; health/medicine; how-to; humor; psychology; science/technology; self-help. **Considers these fiction areas:** action/adventure; contemporary young adult; detective/police/crime; humor/satire; juvenile; mainstream; mystery/suspense; science fiction; techno-thriller; thriller/espionage.
    ◯— This agency specializes in mainstream fiction.
How to Contact: Query with SASE. "The initial query should contain a one- to two-page description plus the author's pertinent biography, neatly typed in 12 point font with accurate spelling and proper punctuation. Make sure it is clear and succinct. Tell what the work is about and do not add hype. Include the ending and tell us how many words and pages are in your work." Accepts queries by e-mail. "Do not query by sending long e-mail messages. Tell about your work in 200-300 words." Considers simultaneous queries. Responds in 2 weeks to queries; 1 month to mss. Returns materials only with SASE. Obtains most new clients through directories, recommendations, internet listings.
Recent Sales: Sold 8 titles in the last year. *The Sweep of the Second Hand*, by Dean Monti (Academy Chicago Publishers); *Caught in the Web*, by Ron Joseph (Beijia Publishing House); *Meltdown*, by Rick Slater (Beijia Publishing House); *The Protocol*, by Keith Barton (Beijia Publishing House); *Trojan Horse*, by Nigel Mitchell (Beijia Publishing House); *A Cure by Death*, by Brain Dorner (Beijia Publishing House).
Terms: Agent receives 15% commission on domestic sales; 20% on foreign sales. Offers written contract. 30 days notice must be given to terminate contract. Charges clients for photocopying, postage. No reading or agency fees.
Writers' Conferences: BEA.
Tips: "Professional guidance is imperative in bringing along new writers. In the highly competitive publishing arena, strict guidelines must be adhered to." See website for agency guidelines.

☑ ◯ THE JOY HARRIS LITERARY AGENCY, INC., 156 Fifth Ave., Suite 617, New York NY 10010. (212)924-6269. Fax: (212)924-6609. E-mail: gen.office@jhlitagent.com. **Contact:** Joy Harris. Member of AAR. Represents 150 clients. Currently handles: 50% nonfiction books; 50% novels.
Member Agents: Leslie Daniels.
Represents: Nonfiction, novels. **Considers "adult-type books, not juvenile." Considers all fiction areas** except fantasy; juvenile; science fiction; westerns/frontier.
    ◯— Does not want to receive screenplays.
How to Contact: Query with outline/proposal and SASE. Responds in 2 months to queries. "No unsolicited manuscripts, just query letters." Obtains most new clients through recommendations from clients and editors.
Recent Sales: Sold 15 titles in the last year. This agency prefers not to share information on specific sales.
Terms: Agent receives 15% commission on domestic sales; 20% on foreign sales. Charges clients for some office expenses.

◯ JOHN HAWKINS & ASSOCIATES, INC., 71 W. 23rd St., Suite 1600, New York NY 10010. (212)807-7040. Fax: (212)807-9555. E-mail: jhawkasc@aol.com. **Contact:** John Hawkins, William Reiss. Estab. 1893. Member of AAR. Represents over 100 clients. 5-10% of clients are new/previously unpublished writers. Currently handles: 40% nonfiction books; 20% juvenile books; 40% novels.
Member Agents: Warren Frazier; Anne Hawkins; Moses Cardona; Elly Sidel; John Hawkins; William Reiss.
Represents: Nonfiction books, juvenile books, novels. **Considers all nonfiction areas** except computers/electronics; religion/inspirational; translations. **Considers all fiction areas** except confessional; erotica; romance.
How to Contact: Query with outline/proposal. Accepts queries by e-mail. Responds in 1 month to queries. Returns materials only with SASE. Obtains most new clients through recommendations from others.
Recent Sales: *Blonde*, by Joyce Carol Oates (HarperCollins); *House of Leaves*, by Mark Danielewski (Pantheon); *The Living Blood*, by Tananarive Due (Pocket Books).
Terms: Agent receives 15% commission on domestic sales; 20% on foreign sales. Charges clients for photocopying.

☑ ◯ HEACOCK LITERARY AGENCY, INC., P.O. Box 927, Main Branch, Malibu CA 90265-0927. (310)589-1775. Fax: (310)589-2825. E-mail: gracebooks@aol.com. **Contact:** Rosalie Grace Heacock. Estab. 1978. Member of AAR, Authors Guild, SCBWI. Represents 60 clients. 10% of clients are new/previously unpublished writers. Currently handles: 100% nonfiction books.
Represents: Adult nonfiction books, children's picture books. **Considers these nonfiction areas:** art/architecture/design; biography; hiking; how-to; music; nature/environment; psychology; science/technology; self-help/personal improvement; spirituality; women's issues/women's studies. **Considers limited selection of top children's book authors; no beginners, please.**
    ◯— Does not want to receive scripts.
How to Contact: Query with SASE. "No multiple queries, please." Prefers to read materials exclusively. Responds in 3 weeks to queries; 2 months to mss. Returns materials only with SASE. Obtains most new clients through "referrals from present clients and industry sources as well as mail queries."
Recent Sales: Sold 22 titles in the last year. This agency prefers not to share information on specific sales.

Terms: Agent receives 15% commission on domestic sales; 25% on foreign sales, "if foreign agent used; if sold directly, 15%." Offers written contract, binding for 1 year. Charges clients for actual expense for telephone, postage, packing, photocopying. "We provide copies of each publisher submission letter and the publisher's response." 95% of business is derived from commission on ms sales.

Writers' Conferences: Maui Writers Conference; Santa Barbara City College Annual Writer's Workshop; Pasadena City College Writer's Forum; UCLA Symposiums on Writing Nonfiction Books; Society of Children's Book Writers and Illustrators, Southwest Writers Conference (Albuquerque), SCBWI Los Altos.

Reading List: Reads "all trade journals, also literary magazines and environmental periodicals" to find new clients. Looks for "new ways to solve old problems."

Tips: "Take time to write an informative query letter expressing your book idea, the market for it, your qualifications to write the book, the 'hook' that would make a potential reader buy the book. Always enclose SASE; we cannot respond to queries without return postage. Our primary focus is upon books which make a contribution."

☑ ◎ **RICHARD HENSHAW GROUP**, 132 W. 22nd St., 4th Floor, New York NY 10011. (212)414-1172. Fax: (212)727-3279. E-mail: rhgagents@aol.com. Website: www.rich.henshaw.com. **Contact:** Rich Henshaw. Estab. 1995. Member of AAR, SinC, MWA, HWA, SFWA. Represents 35 clients. 20% of clients are new/previously unpublished writers. Currently handles: 30% nonfiction books; 70% novels.
   • Prior to opening his agency, Mr. Henshaw served as an agent with Richard Curtis Associates, Inc.

Represents: Nonfiction books, juvenile books, novels. **Considers these nonfiction areas:** animals; biography/autobiography; business; child guidance/parenting; computers/electronics; cooking/food/nutrition; current affairs; gay/lesbian issues; government/politics/law; health/medicine; how-to; humor; juvenile nonfiction; military/war; money/finance/economics; music/dance/theater/film; nature/enrironment; New Age/metaphysics; popular culture; psychology; science/technology; self-help/personal improvement; sociology; sports; true crime/investigative; women's issues/women's studies. **Considers these fiction areas:** action/adventure; detective/police/crime; ethnic; family saga; fantasy; glitz; historical; horror; humor/satire; juvenile; literary; mainstream; psychic/supernatural; romance; science fiction; sports; thriller/espionage; young adult.
   ○┓ This agency specializes in thrillers, mysteries, science fiction, fantasy and horror.

How to Contact: Query with SASE. Responds in 3 weeks to queries; 6 weeks to mss. Obtains most new clients through recommendations from others, solicitations, at conferences and query letters.

Recent Sales: Sold 17 titles in the last year. *Midnight Comes Again*, by Dana Stabenow (St. Martin's Press); *Deadstick*, by Megan Mallory Rust (Berkley); *Bad Lawyer*, by Stephen Solomita (Carroll & Graf); *The Well Trained Mind*, by Susan Wise Bauer and Jessie Wise (W.W. Norton); *Silk and Song*, by Dana Stabenow (Warner).

Terms: Agent receives 15% commission on domestic sales; 20% on foreign sales. No written contract. Charges clients for photocopying manuscripts and book orders. 100% of business is derived from commission on sales.

Tips: "Always include SASE with correct return postage. Please visit our website for more information and current interests."

◎ **THE JEFF HERMAN AGENCY LLC**, 332 Bleecker St., New York NY 10014. (212)941-0540. E-mail: jeff@jeff herman.com. Website: www.jeffherman.com. **Contact:** Jeffrey H. Herman. Estab. 1985. Member of AAR. Represents 100 clients. 10% of clients are new/previously unpublished writers. Currently handles: 85% nonfiction books; 5% scholarly books; 5% textbooks; 5% novels.
   • Prior to opening his agency, Mr. Herman served as a public relations executive.

Member Agents: Deborah Levine (vice president, nonfiction book doctor); Jeff Herman; Amanda White.

Represents: Nonfiction. **Considers these nonfiction areas:** business, computers; health; history; how-to; politics; popular psychology; popular reference; recovery; self-help; spirituality.
   ○┓ This agency specializes in adult nonfiction.

How to Contact: Query with SASE.

Recent Sales: *Joe Montana on the Magic of Making Quarterback*, by Joe Montana (Henry Holt); *A Man Named Dave*, by Dave Peizer (Dutton).

Terms: Agent receives 15% commission on domestic sales. Offers written contract.

◎ **SUSAN HERNER RIGHTS AGENCY**, P.O. Box 303, Scarsdale NY 10583-0303. (914)725-8967. Fax: (914)725-8969. **Contact:** Susan Herner or Sue Yuen. Estab. 1987. Represents 100 clients. 30% of clients are new/previously unpublished writers. Currently handles: 60% nonfiction books; 40% novels.

Member Agents: Susan Herner, president (nonfiction, thriller, mystery, strong women's fiction); Sue Yuen, vice president (adult commercial fiction); Betty Anne Crawford, director of subrights (nonfiction, limited children and young adult fiction, science fiction/fantasy).

Represents: Adult nonfiction books, novels. **Consider these nonfiction areas:** anthropology/archaeology; biography/autobiography; business; child guidance/parenting; cooking/food/nutrition; current affairs; ethnic/cultural interests; gay/lesbian issues; government/politics/law; health/medicine; history; how-to; language/literature/criticism; nature/environment; New Age/metaphysics; popular culture; psychology; religious/inspirational; science/technology; self-help/personal improvement; sociology; true crime/investigative; women's issues/women's studies. "I'm particularly interested in women's issues, popular science, and feminist spirituality." **Considers these fiction areas:** action/adventure; contemporary issues; detective/police/crime; ethnic; family/saga; fantasy; feminist; glitz; historical; horror; literary; mainstream; mystery; romance (contemporary, gothic, historical, regency); science fiction; thriller.

O→ This agency is eager to work with new/previously unpublished writers. "I'm particularly looking for strong women's fiction."

How to Contact: Query with outline, sample chapters and SASE. Considers simultaneous queries. Responds in 1 month to queries. Returns materials only with SASE.

Recent Sales: *Feng Shui For Lovers*, by Raphael Simons (Crown); *Catch A Dream*, by Mary Jane Meier (Signet).

Terms: Agent receives 15% commission on domestic sales; 20% on dramatic sales; 20% on foreign sales. Charges clients for extraordinary postage, handling and photocopying. "Agency has two divisions: one represents writers on a commission-only basis; the other represents the rights for small publishers and packagers who do not have in-house subsidiary rights representation. Percentage of income derived from each division is currently 80-20."

Writers' Conferences: Vermont League of Writers (Burlington, VT); Gulf States Authors League (Mobile, AL).

FREDERICK HILL ASSOCIATES, 1842 Union St., San Francisco CA 94123. (415)921-2910. Fax: (415)921-2802. **Contact:** Irene Moore. Estab. 1979. Represents 100 clients. 50% of clients are new/previously unpublished writers.

Member Agents: Fred Hill (president); Bonnie Nadell (vice president); Irene Moore (associate).

Represents: Nonfiction books, novels. **Considers these nonfiction areas:** biography/autobiography; cookbooks; current affairs; government/politics/law; literature; women's issues/women's studies. **Considers literary and mainstream fiction.**

O→ This agency specializes in general nonfiction, fiction.

How to Contact: Query with SASE. Does not accept queries by e-mail or fax. Considers simultaneous queries. Returns materials only with SASE.

Recent Sales: *Dark Lady*, by Richard North Patterson; *Brief Interviews with Hideous Men*, by David Foster Wallace (Little, Brown); *Living to Tell*, by Antonya Nelson (Scribner).

Terms: Agent receives 15% commission on domestic sales; 15% on dramatic sales; 20% on foreign sales. Charges clients for photocopying.

JOHN L. HOCHMANN BOOKS, 320 E. 58th St., New York NY 10022-2220. (212)319-0505. Director: John L. Hochmann. **Contact:** Theodora Eagle. Estab. 1976. Represents 23 clients. Member of PEN. Prefers to work with published/established authors. Currently handles: 80% nonfiction; 20% textbooks.

Member Agents: Theodora Eagle (popular medical and nutrition books).

Represents: Nonfiction trade books, college textbooks. **Considers these nonfiction areas:** anthropology/archaeology; art/architecture/design; biography/autobiography; cooking/food/nutrition; current affairs; gay/lesbian issues; government/politics/law; health/medicine; history; military/war; music/dance/theater/film; sociology.

O→ This agency specializes in nonfiction books. "Writers must have demonstrable eminence in field or previous publications."

How to Contact: Query first with detailed chapter outline, titles and sample reviews of previously published books and SASE. Responds in 1 week to queries; 1 month to solicited mss. Obtains most new clients through recommendations from authors and editors.

Recent Sales: *Granite and Rainbow: The Life of Virginia Woolf*, by Mitchell Leaska (Farrar, Straus & Giroux); *Manuel Tuig and the Spider Woman*, by Suzanne Jill Levine (Farrar, Staus & Giroux); *Feeding Your Baby the Healthiest Foods*, by Louise Lambert-Lagasse (Stodart).

Terms: Agent receives 15% commission on domestic sales; 25% on foreign sales.

Tips: "Detailed outlines are read carefully; letters and proposals written like flap copy get chucked. We make multiple submissions to editors, but we do not accept multiple submissions from authors. Why? Editors are on salary, but we work for commission, and do not have time to read manuscripts on spec."

BERENICE HOFFMAN LITERARY AGENCY, 215 W. 75th St., New York NY 10023. (212)580-0951. Fax: (212)721-8916. **Contact:** Berenice Hoffman. Estab. 1978. Member of AAR. Represents 55 clients.

Represents: Nonfiction, novels. **Considers all nonfiction areas and most fiction areas.**

O→ Does not want to receive romance.

How to Contact: Query with SASE and 2 sample chapters. Responds in 1 month to queries. "No fax queries." Obtains most new clients through referrals from industry contacts.

Recent Sales: This agency prefers not to share information on specific sales.

Terms: Agent receives 15% on domestic sales. Sometimes offers written contract. Charges clients for out of the ordinary postage, photocopying.

BARBARA HOGENSON AGENCY, 165 West End Ave., Suite 19-C, New York NY 10023. (212)874-8084. Fax: (212)362-3011. **Contact:** Barbara Hogenson or Sarah Feider. Estab. 1994. Member of AAR; signatory of WGA. Represents 60 clients. 5% of clients are new/previously unpublished writers. Currently handles: 35% nonfiction books; 15% novels; 15% movie scripts; 35% stage plays.

• See the expanded listing for this agency in Script Agents.

HOPKINS LITERARY ASSOCIATES, (Specialized: romance/women's fiction), 2117 Buffalo Rd., Suite 327, Rochester NY 14624-1507. (716)429-6559. E-mail: pamhopkins@aol.com. **Contact:** Pam Hopkins. Estab. 1996. Member of AAR, RWA. Represents 30 clients. 5% of clients are new/previously unpublished writers. Currently handles: 100% novels.

Represents: Novels. **Considers these fiction areas:** historical; mainstream; romance.

    O⁻ᴙ This agency specializes in women's fiction particularly historical, contemporary and category romance as well as mainstream work.

How to Contact: Send outline and 3 sample chapters. Does not accept queries by e-mail or fax. Considers simultaneous queries and submissions. Responds in 2 weeks to queries; 1 month to mss. Returns material only with SASE. Obtains most new clients through recommendations from others, solicitations and conferences.

Recent Sales: Sold 50 titles in the last year. *The Horse Soldier*, by Merline Lovelace (MIRA); *By Possession*, by Madeline Hunter (Bantam); *The Doctor's Wife*, by Cheryl St. John (Harlequin); *Fortunes Bride*, by Victoria Malvey (Pocket); *Mother of the Year*, by Lori Handeland (Harlequin); *The Cat's Fancy*, by Julie Kenner (Dorchester).

Terms: Agent receives 15% commission on domestic sales; 20% on foreign sales. No written contract. 30-day written notice must be given to terminate verbal contract.

Writers' Conferences: Romance Writers of America.

Ø INTERNATIONAL CREATIVE MANAGEMENT, 40 W. 57th St., New York NY 10019. (212)556-5600. Fax: (212)556-5665. West Coast office: 8942 Wilshire Blvd., Beverly Hills CA 90211. (310)550-4000. Fax: (310)550-4100. **Contact:** Literary Department. Member of AAR, signatory of WGA.

Member Agents: Esther Newberg and Amanda Urban, department heads; Lisa Bankoff; Kristine Dahl; Mitch Douglas; Suzanne Gluck; Sloan Harris; Heather Schroder; Denise Shannon; Richard Abate; Sam Cohn.

Terms: Agent receives 10% commission on domestic sales; 15% on UK sales; 20% on translations.

◖ J DE S ASSOCIATES INC., 9 Shagbark Rd., Wilson Point, South Norwalk CT 06854. (203)838-7571. **Contact:** Jacques de Spoelberch. Estab. 1975. Represents 50 clients. Currently handles: 50% nonfiction books; 50% novels.

    ● Prior to opening his agency, Mr. de Spoelberch was a publishing editor at Houghton Mifflin.

Represents: Nonfiction books, novels. **Considers these nonfiction areas:** biography/autobiography; business; current affairs; ethnic/cultural interests; government/politics/law; health/medicine; history; military/war; New Age; self-help/personal improvement; sociology; sports; translations. **Considers these fiction areas:** detective/police/crime; historical; juvenile; literary; mainstream; mystery/suspense; New Age; westerns/frontier; young adult.

How to Contact: Query with SASE. Responds in 2 months to queries. Obtains most new clients through recommendations from authors and other clients.

Recent Sales: This agency prefers not to share information on specific sales.

Terms: Agent receives 15% commission on domestic sales; 20% on foreign sales. Charges clients for foreign postage and photocopying.

◖ JABBERWOCKY LITERARY AGENCY, P.O. Box 4558, Sunnyside NY 11104-0558. (718)392-5985. **Contact:** Joshua Bilmes. Estab. 1994. Member of SFWA. Represents 40 clients. 25% of clients are new/previously unpublished writers. Currently handles: 25% nonfiction books; 5% scholarly books; 65% novel; 5% other.

Represents: Nonfiction books, scholarly books, novels. **Considers these nonfiction areas:** biography/autobiography; business; cooking/food/nutrition; current affairs; gay/lesbian issues; government/politics/law; health/medicine; history; humor; language/literature/criticism; military/war; money/finance/economics; music/dance/theater/film; nature/environment; popular culture; science/technology; sociology; sports; true crime/investigative; women's issues/women's studies. **Considers these fiction areas:** action/adventure; cartoon/comic; contemporary issues; detective/police/crime; ethnic; family saga; fantasy; gay; glitz; historical; horror; humor/satire; lesbian; literary; mainstream; psychic/supernatural; regional; science fiction; sports; thriller/espionage.

    O⁻ᴙ This agency represents quite a lot of genre fiction and is actively seeking to increase amount of nonfiction projects.

How to Contact: Query letters only with SASE; *no ms material unless requested*. Does not accept queries by e-mail or fax. Considers simultaneous queries and submissions. Responds in 2 weeks to queries. Returns materials only with SASE. Obtains most new clients through recommendation by current clients, solicitation, "and through intriguing queries by new authors."

Recent Sales: Sold 20 titles in the last year. *Shakespeare's Trollop*, by Charlaine Harris (Dell); *Beyond the Blue Moon*, by Simon Green (Roc); *Against the Odds*, by Elizabeth Moon (Baen); *Lupus: Alternate Therapies*, by Sharon Moore (Inner Traditions). Other clients include Tanya Huff, Kristine Smith, Edo van Belkom.

Terms: Agent receives 12.5% commission on domestic sales; 20% on foreign sales. Offers written contract, binding for 1 year. Charges clients for book purchases, photocopying, international book/ms mailing, international long distance.

Writers' Conferences: Malice Domestic (Washington DC, May); World SF Convention (Philadelphia, August); Icon (Stony Brook NY, April).

Reading list: Reads *New Republic, Analog* and various newspapers to find new clients.

TO HELP YOU UNDERSTAND and use the information in these listings, see "Reading the Listings in the *Guide to Literary Agents*" in the front of this book.

Tips: "In approaching with a query, the most important things to me are your credits and your biographical background to the extent it's relevant to your work. I (and most agents I believe) will ignore the adjectives you may choose to describe your own work."

⊘ MELANIE JACKSON AGENCY, 250 W. 57th St., Suite 1119, New York NY 10107. This agency did not respond to our request for information. Query before submitting.

⊘ JAMES PETER ASSOCIATES, INC., P.O. Box 772, Tenafly NJ 07670-0751. (201)568-0760. Fax: (201)568-2959. E-mail: bertholtje@compuserve.com. **Contact:** Bert Holtje. Estab. 1971. Member of AAR. Represents 54 individual authors and 5 corporate clients (book producers). 15% of clients are new/previously unpublished writers. Currently handles: 100% nonfiction books.
• Prior to opening his agency, Mr. Holtje was a book packager, and before that, president of an advertising agency with book publishing clients.
Represents: Nonfiction books. **Considers these nonfiction areas:** anthropology/archaeology; art/architecture/design; biography/autobiography; business; child guidance/parenting; current affairs; ethnic/cultural interests; gay/lesbian issues; government/politics/law; health/medicine; history; language/literature/criticism; memoirs (political or business); military/war; money/finance/economics; music/dance/theater/film; popular culture; psychology; self-help/personal improvement; travel; women's issues/women's studies.
   O→ This agency specializes in nonfiction, all categories. "We are especially interested in general, trade and reference." Actively seeking "good ideas in all areas of adult nonfiction." Does not want to receive "children's and young adult books, poetry, fiction."
How to Contact: Send outline/proposal and SASE. Does not accept queries by e-mail or fax. Prefers to read materials exclusively. Responds in 1 month to queries. Returns materials only with SASE. Obtains most new clients through recommendations from other clients and editors, contact with people who are doing interesting things, and over-the-transom queries.
Recent Sales: Sold 37 titles in the last year. *Elizabeth I: C.E.O.*, by Dr. Alan Axelrod (Prentice-Hall); *Out of the Ordinary: A Biographical Dictionary of Women Explorers*, by Sarah Purcell and Edward Purcell (Routledge); *Ace Your Mid Terms and Finals—A 5-book series*, by The Ian Samuel Group (McGraw-Hill); *How to Save Your Heart*, by Carol Turkington and Dr. K. Kensey (Contemporary).
Terms: Agent receives 15% commission on domestic sales; 20% on foreign sales. Offers written contract on a per book basis.

⊘ JANKLOW & NESBIT ASSOCIATES, 598 Madison Ave., New York NY 10022. Member of AAR. This agency did not respond to our request for information. Query before submitting.

⊘ JCA LITERARY AGENCY, 27 W. 20th St., Suite 1103, New York NY 10011. (212)807-0888. Fax: (212)807-0461. **Contact:** Jeff Gerecke, Tony Outhwaite. Estab. 1978. Member of AAR. Represents 100 clients. 20% of clients are new/previously unpublished writers. Currently handles: 20% nonfiction books; 5% scholarly books; 75% novels.
Member Agents: Jeff Gerecke; Tony Outhwaite.
Represents: Nonfiction books, scholarly books, novels. **Considers these nonfiction areas:** anthropology/archaeology; biography/autobiography; business; current affairs; government/politics/law; health/medicine; history; language/literature/criticism; memoirs; military/war; money/finance/economics; music/dance/theater/film; nature/environment; popular culture; science/technology; sociology; sports; translations; true crime/investigative; women's issues/women's studies. **Considers these fiction areas:** action/adventure; contemporary issues; detective/police/crime; family saga; historical; literary; mainstream; mystery; sports; thriller/espionage.
   O→ Does not want to receive screenplays, poetry, children's books, science fiction/fantasy, genre romance.
How to Contact: Query with SASE. Does not accept queries by fax or e-mail. Considers simultaneous queries and submissions. "We occasionally may ask for an exclusive look." Responds in 2 weeks to queries; 10 weeks to mss. Returns materials only with SASE. Obtains most new clients through recommendations, solicitations, conferences.
Recent Sales: *The Lost Glass Plates of Wilfred Eng*, by Thomas Orton (Counterpoint); *Sharp Shooter*, by David Healey (The Berkley Publishing Group/Jove); *A Healthy Place to Die*, by Peter King (St. Martin's Press). Other clients include Ernest J. Gaines, W.E.B. Griffin, Polly Whitney, David J. Garrow.
Terms: Agent receives 15% commission on domestic sales; 20% on foreign sales. No written contract. "We work with our clients on a handshake basis." Charges clients for postage on overseas submissions, photocopying, mss for submission, books purchased for subrights submission, and bank charges, where applicable. "We deduct the cost from payments received from publishers."
Tips: "We do not ourselves provide legal, accounting, or public relations services for our clients, although some of the advice we give falls somewhat into these realms. In cases where it seems necessary we will recommend obtaining outside advice or assistance in these areas from professionals who are not in any way connected to the agency."

N ⊘ JELLINEK & MURRAY LITERARY AGENCY, 3623 Kumu St., Honolulu HI 96822. (808)988-8461. Fax: (808)988-8462. E-mail: jellinek@lava.net. **Contact:** Roger Jellinek. Estab. 1995. Represents 65 clients. 90% of clients are new/previously unpublished writers. Currently handles: 60% nonfiction books; 40% novels.
• Prior to becoming an agent, Mr. Jellinek was editor, New York Times Book Review (1966-74); Editor-in-Chief, New York Times Book Company (1975-1981); editor/packager book/TV projects (1981-1995).

Member Agents: Roger Jellinek (general fiction, nonfiction); Eden-Lee Murray (general fiction, nonfiction).
Represents: Nonfiction books, textbooks, novels, movie/TV scripts from book clients. **Considers these nonfiction areas:** animals; anthropology/archaeology; art/architecture/design; biography/autobiography; business; child guidance/parenting; computers/electronics; cooking/food/nutrition; current affairs; ethnic/cultural interests; gay/lesbian issues; government/politics/law; health/medicine; history; how-to; memoirs; military/war; money/finance/economics; nature/environment; New Age/metaphysics; popular culture; psychology; religious/inspirational; science/technology; self-help/personal improvement; travel; true crime/investigative; women's issues/women's studies. **Considers these fiction areas:** action/adventure; confessional; contemporary issues; detective/police/crime; erotica; ethnic; family saga; feminist; gay/lesbian; glitz; historical; horror; humor/satire; literary; mainstream; multicultural; mystery/suspense; New Age/metaphysical; picture book; psychic/supernatural; regional; thriller/espionage; westerns/frontier.

    O⊸ This agency is one of only a few literary agencies in Hawaii. "Half our clients are based in Hawaii, half all over the world. We accept submissions (after a query) via e-mail attachment; we only send out fully-edited proposals and manuscripts." Actively seeking first-rate writing.

How to Contact: Query with SASE. Send outline and 2 sample chapters, if requested. Accepts queries by e-mail and fax. Considers simultaneous queries and submissions. Responds in 2 weeks to queries; 2 months to mss. Returns materials only with SASE. Obtains most new clients through recommendations from others, queries/solicitations, conferences.
Recent Sales: Sold 10 titles, 1 script project in the last year. *God's Photo Album*, by Shelly Mecum (HarperSanFrancisco); *The Cookie Never Crumbles*, by Wally Adams (St. Martin's Press).
Terms: Agent receives 15% commission on domestic sales; 25% on foreign sales. Offers written contract, binding indefinitely with 30-day walkaway clause. Charges clients for photocopies and postage. May refer to editing services occasionally, if author asks for recommendation. "We have no income deriving from our referrals. Referrals to editors do not imply representation."
Tips: "Would-be authors should be well read and knowledgeable about their field and genre."

☑ ⊘ **CAROLYN JENKS AGENCY**, 24 Concord Ave., Suite 412, Cambridge MA 02138. (617)354-5099. E-mail: cbjenks@worldnet.att.net. Website: www.carolynjenksagency.com. **Contact:** Carolyn Jenks. Re-estab. 1990. Signatory of WGA. 40% of clients are new/previously unpublished writers. Currently handles: 15% nonfiction books; 75% novels; 5% movie scripts; 5% plays. Co-agents for TV in Los Angeles.
    ● Prior to opening her agency, Ms. Jenks was a managing editor, actor and producer.
Represents: Nonfiction and fiction. **Considers these nonfiction areas:** animals; biography/autobiography; ethnic/cultural interests; gay/lesbian issues; history; language/literature/criticism; theater/film; nature/environment; science/technology; sociology; translations; women's issues/women's studies. **Considers these fiction areas:** contemporary issues; ethnic; feminist; gay; historical; lesbian; literary; mainstream; mystery/suspense; romance (contemporary, historical); thriller/espionage; westerns.

    O⊸ This agency specializes in "development of promising authors." Actively seeking "exceptionally talented writers committed to work that makes a contribution." Does not want to receive gratuitous violence; drugs scenes that are a cliché; war stories unless they transcend; sagas, or clichéd coming of age stories."

Also Handles: Feature film, TV MOW. **Considers these script subject areas:** contemporary issues; historical; mainstream; mystery; romantic comedy and drama; thriller.
How to Contact: Query with bio and SASE. Accepts queries by e-mail; does not accept faxed queries. Considers simultaneous queries and submissions. Responds in 2 weeks to queries; 6 weeks to mss. Returns materials only with SASE. "No cold calls."
Recent Sales: Sold 2 book titles in the last year. *The Red Tent*, now a bestseller by Anita Diamant (St. Martin's Press); *This Way to Heaven*, by Tom Foley (Forge); *Hunger*, by Jane Ward (Forge).
Terms: Agent receives 15% commission on domestic sales; 10% on film and TV. Offers written contract.
Tips: "Query first in writing with SASE or to cbjenks@worldnet.att.net. Do not send samples of writing by e-mail."

🄽 ⊘ **JLM LITERARY AGENTS**, 5901 Warner Ave., #61, Huntington Beach CA 92649. (714)547-4870. Fax: (714)840-5660. **Contact:** Judy Semler. Estab. 1985. Represents 25 clients. 5% of clients are new/previously unpublished writers. Currently handles: 90% nonfiction books; 10% novels.
Represents: Nonfiction books, novels. **Considers these nonfiction areas:** biography/autobiography; business (popular); current affairs; music/dance/theater/film; nature/environment; popular culture; psychology; religious/inspirational; self-help/personal improvement; sociology; true crime/investigative; women's issues/women's studies. **Considers these fiction areas:** glitz; mystery/suspense; psychic/supernatural; contemporary romance.

    O⊸ This agency is "generalist with an affinity for high-quality, spiritual self-help psychology and mystery/suspense."

How to Contact: For nonfiction, send outline with 2 sample chapters. For fiction, query with 3 chapters—except for mystery/suspense, send entire ms. "Accepting very few manuscripts in fiction." Does not accept queries by e-mail or fax. Considers simultaneous queries. Responds in 1 month to queries; 10 weeks to mss. "Most of my clients are referred to me by other clients or editors."
Recent Sales: Sold 15 titles in the last year. *The Blue Angel: The First 50 Years* (Motor Book); *The Breast Cancer Companion*, by Kathy LaTour (Morrow/Avon).
Terms: Agent receives 15% commission on domestic sales; 10% on foreign sales plus 15% to subagent. Offers written contract, binding for 1 year, with 30-day escape clause. Charges clients for routine office expenses associated with marketing. 100% of business is derived from commissions on ms sales.

Tips: "If you want to be successful, learn all you can about proper submission and invest in the equipment or service to make your project *look* dazzling. Computers are available to everyone and the competition looks good. You must at least match that to even get noticed."

⦿ **JOY LITERARY AGENCY**, PO Box 957-856, Hoffman Estates IL 60195-7856. (847)310-0003. Fax: (847)310-0893. E-mail: joyco2@juno.com. **Contact:** Carol Joy. Represents 15 clients. 95% of clients are new/previously unpublished writers. Currently handles: 30% nonfiction books; 10% juvenile books; 10% scholarly books; 50% novels.
- Prior to becoming an agent, Ms. Joy was a bookstore owner for eight years.

Represents: Nonfiction books, juvenile books, scholarly books, novels. **Considers these nonfiction areas:** biography/autobiography; cooking/food/nutrition; education; health/medicine; how-to; juvenile nonfiction; nature/environment; religious/inspirational; self-help/personal improvement; sociology; women's issues/women's studies. **Considers these fiction areas:** action/adventure; contemporary issues; literary; mainstream; religious/inspirational.

How to Contact: Query with outline/proposal and SASE. Does not accept queries by e-mail or fax. Considers simultaneous queries and submissions. Responds in 2 weeks to queries; 1 month to mss. Obtains new clients through queries by mail only.

Recent Sales: This agency prefers not to share information on specific sales.

Terms: Agent receives 15% commission on domestic sales. Offers written contract, binding for 2 years. 30 days notice must be given to terminate contract. Charges clients for postage and photocopying. "Limit established prior to contract." Writers reimbursed for office fees after the sale of ms.

Writers' Conferences: Write-to-Publish (Wheaton IL, June); Christian Writers (Chicago IL, July); Bloomingdale Writers (Bloomingdale IL, September).

Tips: "Proofread carefully. Always include SASE. We are willing to look at a new writer's material and often give personal brief critiques for no extra change. Extensive critiques available for fee."

🔲⦿ **THE KARPFINGER AGENCY, INC.**, 357 W. 20th St., Americas, New York NY 10011. Member of AAR. This agency did not respond to our request for information. Query before submitting.

☑🔲☻ **THE KELLOCK COMPANY INC.**, 20423 State Rd. 7 #508, Boca Raton FL 33498. (561)558-8603. E-mail: kellock@aol.com. **Contact:** Alan C. Kellock. Estab. 1990. Represents 60 clients. 15% of clients are new/previously unpublished writers. Currently handles: 100% nonfiction books.
- Prior to opening his agency, Mr. Kellock served as Director of Sales & Marketing with Harcourt Brace, Vice President Marketing with Waldenbooks and President and Publisher for Viking Penguin.

Member Agents: Loren Kellock (licensing).

Represents: Nonfiction books. **Considers these nonfiction areas:** anthropology/archaeology; art/architecture/design; biography/autobiography; business; child guidance/parenting; crafts/hobbies; current affairs; education; ethnic/cultural interests; government/politics/law; health/medicine; history; how-to; humor; interior design/decorating; military/war; money/finance/economics; music/dance/theater/film; nature/environment; popular culture; psychology; self-help/personal improvement; sociology; sports; women's issues/women's studies.

> ○➔ This agency specializes in a broad range of practical and informational nonfiction, including illustrated works. Represents authors, packagers, and smaller publishers to larger print and electronic publishers and third party sponsors. "Many of our clients are not career writers but people who are highly successful in other walks of life."

How to Contact: Query with SASE. Accepts queries by e-mail. Considers simultaneous queries. Responds in 1 week to queries. Obtains most new clients through referrals, but all queries are carefully considered.

Recent Sales: *Learn By Doing* books (Macmillan Computer Publishing); *Nice Job!* (Ten Speed); *You've Got E-Mail Business!* (Maximum Press).

Terms: Agent receives 15% commission on domestic sales; 25% on foreign and multimedia sales. Offers written contract. Charges clients for postage, photocopying.

⦿ **NATASHA KERN LITERARY AGENCY**, P.O. Box 2908, Portland OR 97208-2908. (503)297-6190. Website: www.natashakern.com. **Contact:** Natasha Kern. Estab. 1986. Member of RWA, MWA, SinC.
- "This agency has sold over 500 books." Prior to opening her agency, Ms. Kern worked as an editor and publicist for New York publishers (Simon & Schuster, Bantam, Ballentine).

Represents: Adult commercial nonfiction books and novels. **Considers these nonfiction areas:** animals; anthropology/archaeology; biography/autobiography; business; child guidance/parenting; current affairs; education; ethnic/cultural interests; health/medicine; nature/environment; New Age/metaphysics; popular culture; psychology; science/technology; self-help/personal improvement; women's issues/women's studies; spirituality; gardening; personal finance; investigative journalism. **Considers these fiction areas:** detective/police/crime; ethnic; feminist; historical; mainstream; mystery/suspense; romance (contemporary, historical); medical, technical and historical thrillers; magical realism; inspirational fiction and romance; novels of the West.

> ○➔ This agency specializes in commercial fiction and nonfiction for adults. "A full service agency." Does not represent sports, true crime, scholarly works, coffee table books, war memoirs, software, scripts, literary fiction, photography, poetry, short stories, children's, horror, fantasy, genre science fiction, stage plays or traditional Westerns.

How to Contact: "Send a detailed, one-page query with a SASE, including the submission history, writing credits and information about how complete the project is. For fiction send a two- to three-page synopsis. For nonfiction, submit a proposal consisting of an outline, two chapters, SASE, and a note describing market and how project is different or better than similar works. Also send a blurb about the author and information about the length of the manuscript." Does not accept queries by e-mail or fax. Accepts online queries on website. Considers simultaneous queries and submissions. Responds in 3 weeks to queries.

Recent Sales: Sold 46 titles in the last year. *The Shepherd's Voice*, by Robin Lee Hatcher (HarperCollins); *The Skull Mantra*, by Eliot Pattison (St. Martin's Press); *Biological Exuberance*, by Bruce Bagemihl (St. Martin's Press).

Terms: Agent receives 15% commission on domestic sales; splits 20% on foreign sales; splits 15% on film rights.

Writers' Conference: RWA National Conference and many regional conferences.

Tips: "Our idea of a Dream Client is someone who participates in a mutually respectful business relationship, is clear about needs and goals, and communicates about career planning. If we know what you need and want, we can help you achieve it. A dream client has a storytelling gift, a commitment to a writing career, a desire to learn and grow, and a passion for excellence. We want clients who are expressing their own unique voice and truly have something of their own to communicate. This client understands that many people have to work together for a book to succeed and that everything in publishing takes far longer than one imagines. Trust and communication are truly essential."

LOUISE B. KETZ AGENCY, 1485 First Ave., Suite 4B, New York NY 10021-1363. (212)535-9259. Fax: (212)249-3103. E-mail: ketzagency@aol.com. **Contact:** Louise B. Ketz. Estab. 1983. Represents 25 clients. 15% of clients are new/previously unpublished writers. Currently handles: 100% nonfiction books.

Represents: Nonfiction books only. **Considers these nonfiction areas:** biography; business; current affairs; history; military/war; money/finance/economics; science/technology; sports.

O→ This agency specializes in science, business, sports, history and reference.

How to Contact: Send outline and 2 sample chapters plus author bio with qualifications for authorship of work. Responds in 6 weeks. Obtains most new clients through recommendations and idea development.

Recent Sales: This agency prefers not to share information on specific sales.

Terms: Agent receives 15% commission on all sales.

VIRGINIA KIDD AGENCY, INC., (Specialized: science fiction/fantasy), 538 E. Harford St., P.O. Box 278, Milford PA 18337-0728. (717)296-6205. Fax: (717)296-7266. **Contact:** James Allen. Estab. 1965. Member of SFWA, SFRA, SFTA. Represents 80 clients.

- Prior to opening her agency, Ms. Kidd was a ghost writer, pulp writer and poet.

Member Agents: Virginia Kidd; James Allen; Christine Cohen (historical fiction); Nanci McCloskey (women's fiction).

Represents: Fiction. **Considers these fiction areas:** speculative fiction, science fiction, fantasy (special interest in non-traditional fantasy), mystery, literary, mainstream, feminist, glitz, suspense, historical, young adult.

O→ This agency specializes in "science fiction but we do not limit ourselves to it."

How to Contact: Query with SASE. Does not accept queries by e-mail or fax. Prefers to read materials exclusively. Responds in 1 week to queries; 6 weeks to mss. Obtains most new clients through recommendations from others.

Recent Sales: Sold 60 titles in the last year. *Tales from Earthsea*, by Ursula K. Le Guin (Harcourt Brace); *Pern*, by Anne McCaffrey (Del Rey); *18th Annual Year's Best in Science Fiction and Fantasy*, edited by Gardner Dozois; *Kingdoms of Light*, by Alan Dean Foster (Penguin Putnam); also film rights to *The Orphan*, by Robert Stallman to a German production company. Other clients include Gene Wolfe, R.A. Lafferty, Joe L. Hensley, William Tenn, Al Coppel.

Terms: Agent receives 10% commission on domestic sales; 20% on foreign sales. Offers written contract, binding until canceled by either party. 30-day notice must be given to terminate contract. Charges clients for photocopying and copies of books used to market subsidiary rights.

Tips: "If you have a novel of speculative fiction, romance, or mainstream that is *really extraordinary*, please query me, including a synopsis, a cv and a SASE."

KIDDE, HOYT & PICARD, 335 E. 51st St., New York NY 10022. (212)755-9461. Fax: (212)223-2501. **Contact:** Katharine Kidde, Laura Langlie. Estab. 1980. Member of AAR. Represents 80 clients. Currently handles: 15% nonfiction books; 5% juvenile books; 80% novels.

- Prior to becoming agents, Ms. Kidde was an editor/senior editor at Harcourt Brace, New American Library and Putnam; Ms. Langlie worked in production and editorial at Kensington and Carroll & Graf.

Member Agents: Kay Kidde (mainstream fiction, general nonfiction, mysteries, romances, literary fiction); Laura Langlie (romances, mysteries, literary fiction, general nonfiction).

Represents: Nonfiction books, novels. **Considers these nonfiction areas:** the arts; biography; current events; ethnic/cultural interests; gay/lesbian issues; history; language/literature/criticism; memoirs; popular culture; psychology; self-help/personal improvement; sociology; women's issues. **Considers these fiction areas:** contemporary; detective/police/crime; feminist; gay; glitz; historical; humor; lesbian; literary; mainstream; mystery/suspense; romance (contemporary, historical, regency); thriller.

O→ This agency specializes in mainstream fiction and nonfiction. Actively seeking "strong mainstream fiction." Does not want to receive "male adventure, science fiction, juvenile, porn, plays or poetry."

How to Contact: Query with SASE. Considers simultaneous queries and submissions. Responds in a few weeks to queries; 1 month to mss. Returns materials only with SASE. Obtains most new clients through query letters, recommendations from others, "former authors from when I was an editor at NAL, Harcourt, etc.; listings in *LMP*, writers' guides."

Recent Sales: *The Book of the Lion*, by Michael Cadnum (Viking); *Whose Little Girl Are You?*, by Bethany Campbell (Bantam); *Night Bus*, by Janice Law (Forge/TOR); *False Witness*, by Lelia Kelly (Kensington). Other clients include Michael Cadnum, Jim Oliver, Julia Whitty, Bethany Campbell, Corinne Browne, Heather Remoff, Mark Miano.

Terms: Agent receives 15% commission on domestic sales; 20% on foreign sales. Charges clients for photocopying.

Reading List: Reads literary journals and magazines, *Harper's*, *DoubleTake*, etc. to find new clients.

Tips: "We look for beautiful stylistic writing, and that elusive treasure, a good book (mostly fiction). As former editors, we can help launch authors."

◪ ◎ KIRCHOFF/WOHLBERG, INC., AUTHORS' REPRESENTATION DIVISION, (Specialized: children's books), 866 United Nations Plaza, #525, New York NY 10017. (212)644-2020. Fax: (212)223-4387. Director of Operations: John R. Whitman. **Contact:** Liza Pulitzer-Voges. Estab. 1930s. Member of AAR, AAP, Society of Illustrators, SPAR, Bookbuilders of Boston, New York Bookbinders' Guild, AIGA. Represents over 50 authors. 10% of clients are new/previously unpublished writers. Currently handles: 5% nonfiction books; 80% juvenile books; 10% novels; 5% young adult.

• Kirchoff/Wohlberg has been in business for over 60 years.

Member Agents: Liza Pulitzer-Voges (juvenile and young adult authors).

Represents: "We are interested in any original projects of quality that are appropriate to the juvenile and young adult trade book markets. *But, we take on very few new clients as our roster is full.*"

O→ This agency specializes in juvenile through young adult trade books.

How to Contact: "Send a query that includes an outline and a sample for a novel; for picture book submissions, please send ms in its entirety. SASE required." Does not accept queries by e-mail or fax. Considers simultaneous queries and submissions. Responds in 1 month to queries; 2 months to mss. Please send to the attention of Liza Pulitzer-Voges. Obtains most new clients through recommendations from authors, illustrators and editors.

Recent Sales: Sold over 50 titles in the last year. This agency prefers not to share information on specific sales.

Terms: Agent receives standard commission "depending upon whether it is an author only, illustrator only, or an author/illustrator book." Offers written contract, binding for not less than 1 year.

◪ JEFFREY M. KLEINMAN, ESQ., OF GRAYBILL & ENGLISH L.L.C., 1920 N. St., NW, #620, Washington DC 20036. (202)861-0106. Fax: (202)457-0662. E-mail: jmkagent@aol.com. Website: www.expertbiz.com/jmk/. **Contact:** Jeff Kleinman. Estab. 1998. 50% of clients are new/previously unpublished writers.

• Prior to becoming an agent, Mr. Kleinman was an attorney.

Represents: Nonfiction books, scholarly books, novels. **Considers these nonfiction areas:** agriculture/horticulture; animals; anthropology/archaeology; art/architecture/design; biography/autobiography; business; child guidance/parenting; computers/electronics; cooking/food/nutrition; crafts/hobbies; current affairs; current affairs; education; ethnic/cultural interests; gay/lesbian issues; government/politics/law; health/medicine; history; how-to; humor; interior design/decorating; language/literature/criticism; money/finance/economics; music/dance/theater/film; nature/environment; photography; popular culture; psychology; science/technology; self-help/personal improvement; sociology; translations; true crime/investigative; women's issues/women's studies. **Considers these fiction areas:** action/adventure; cartoon/comic; contemporary issues; erotica; ethnic; family saga; fantasy; feminist; gay/lesbian; glitz; historical; horror; humor/satire; literary; mainstream; mystery; psychic/supernatural; regional; romance; science fiction; thriller/espionage; young adult. Also considers multimedia tie-ins with literary projects.

O→ This agency specializes in narrative nonfiction; nonfiction; fiction. Does not want to receive military, romance, sports, children's literature or poetry.

How to Contact: Query with SASE, outline/proposal, or send outline and 3 sample chapters. Accepts queries by e-mail (no attachments) and fax. Considers simultaneous queries and submissions. Responds in 2 weeks to queries; 1 month to mss. Returns materials only with SASE. Obtains most new clients through recommendations and solicitations.

Recent Sales: Sold 6 titles in the last year. *The Last President*, by William R. Coason and Joseph J. Taento (The Free Press); *Girders*, by Bruce Watson (Viking/Penguin); *Walrus on My Table*, by Guglielmo and Lynn (St. Martin's Press); *Chaos to Calm*, by Heininger and Weiss (Perigee/Putnam).

Terms: Agent receives 15% commission on domestic sales; 20% on foreign sales. Offers written contract. 30-day notice must be given to terminate contract. Charges clients for postage, long distance, photocopying.

Writers' Conferences: Baltimore Writers (Baltimore MD, September); Mid-Atlantic Creative Nonfiction Summer Writer's Conference (Baltimore MD, August); Chesterfield Writer's Workshop (Chesterfield VA, March).

Reading List: Reads *Smithsonian Magazine*, *Zoetrope* and *Salon.com* to find new clients. Looks for "great ideas and solid writing."

☑ ◓ HARVEY KLINGER, INC., 301 W. 53rd St., New York NY 10019. (212)581-7068. E-mail: klingerinc@aol.com. **Contact:** Harvey Klinger. Estab. 1977. Member of AAR. Represents 100 clients. 25% of clients are new/previously unpublished writers. Currently handles: 50% nonfiction books; 50% novels.

Member Agents: David Dunton (popular culture, parenting, home improvement, thrillers/crime); Laurie Liss (literary fiction, human interest, politics, women's issues); Jenny Bent (fiction, nonfiction).

Represents: Nonfiction books, novels. **Considers these nonfiction areas:** biography/autobiography; cooking/food/ nutrition; health/medicine; psychology; science/technology; self-help/personal improvement; spirituality; sports; true crime/investigative; women's issues/women's studies. **Considers these fiction areas:** action/adventure; detective/police/ crime; family saga; glitz; literary; mainstream; thriller/espionage.

O➡ This agency specializes in "big, mainstream contemporary fiction and nonfiction."

How to Contact: Query with SASE. Accepts queries by e-mail. "We do not accept queries by fax." Prefers to read materials exclusively. Responds in 1 month to queries; 2 months to mss. Obtains most new clients through recommendations from others.

Recent Sales: Sold over 25 titles in the last year. *The Carousel*, by Richard Paul Evans (S&S); *Sacred Ground*, by Barbara Wood (St. Martin's Press); *Secrets About Life Every Woman Should Know*, by Barbara De Angelis (Hyperion); *Torn Jeans: Levi Strauss and the Denim Dynasty*, by Ellen Hawkes (Lisa Drew Books/Scribner); *The Looking Glass*, by Richard Paul Evans (Simon & Schuster); *The Women of Troy Hill*, by Clare Ansberry (Harcourt Brace); *Exit Music: The Radiohead Story*, by Mac Randall (Dell).

Terms: Agent receives 15% commission on domestic sales; 25% on foreign sales. Offers written contract. Charges clients for photocopying manuscripts, overseas postage for mss.

✅ 🄲 **THE KNIGHT AGENCY**, P.O. Box 550648, Atlanta GA 30355. Also: 2407 Matthews St., Atlanta GA 30319. (404)816-9620. Fax: (404)237-3439. E-mail: deidremk@aol.com. Website: www.knightagency.net. **Contact:** Deidre Knight. Estab. 1996. Member of AAR, RWA, Authors Guild. Represents 30 clients. 40% of clients are new/ previously unpublished writers. Currently handles: 50% nonfiction books; 50% novels.

Represents: Nonfiction books, novels. **Considers these nonfiction areas:** biography/autobiography; business; child guidance/parenting; computers/electronics; cooking/food/nutrition; current affairs; ethnic/cultural interests; health/medicine; history; how-to; money/finance/economics; music/dance/theater/film; popular culture; psychology; religious/inspirational; self-help/personal improvement; sports. **Considers these fiction areas:** ethnic; literary; mainstream; romance (contemporary, historical, inspirational); women's fiction; commercial fiction.

O➡ "We are looking for a wide variety of fiction and nonfiction. In the nonfiction area, we're particularly eager to find personal finance, business investment, pop culture, self-help/motivational and popular reference books. In fiction, we're always looking for romance, women's fiction, ethnic and commercial fiction."

How to Contact: Query with SASE. Accepts queries by e-mail. Considers simultaneous queries and submissions. Responds in 2 weeks to queries; 2 months to mss.

Recent Sales: Sold 40 titles in the last year. *This Joint is Jumpin: The Complete History of Swing*, by Tanja Crouch (TV Books); *The Highlander's Touch*, by Karen Marie Moning (Bantam Dell).

Terms: Agent receives 15% commission on domestic sales; 20-25% on foreign sales. Offers written contract, terminates upon 30-day notice. Charges clients for postage/overnight shipping and copies. "These are deducted from the sale of the work, not billed up front."

Tips: "At the Knight Agency, a client usually ends up becoming a friend."

🄲 **LINDA KONNER LITERARY AGENCY**, 10 W. 15th St., Suite 1918, New York NY 10011-6829. (212)691-3419. E-mail: ldkonner@cs.com. **Contact:** Linda Konner. Estab. 1996. Member of AAR, ASJA; signatory of WGA. Represents 50 clients. 5-10% of clients are new/previously unpublished writers. Currently handles: 100% nonfiction books.

Represents: Nonfiction books (adult only). **Considers these nonfiction areas:** business; child care/parenting; diet/ nutrition; gay/lesbian issues; health/medicine; how-to; personal finance; popular culture; psychology; relationships; self-help/personal improvement; women's issues.

 CLOSE UP with Linda Konner, Linda Konner Literary Agency

On having a marketing platform . . .

"Having a platform before you write your book—or even your proposal—has become more and more critical. Publishers demand it, with rare exception. New authors ask me, 'But isn't it my publisher's job to get me media to help promote my book?' The answer is: 'Yes . . . and no.' So you might as well help the cause.

"I will ask potential clients if they have experience with national TV shows, radio shows like NPR, major print publications, popular websites, or major seminar/lecturing work in anticipation of an editor asking *me* about it. Often, when an author has excellent credentials in a field and a terrific book idea but no media platform, I'll say wait six to twelve months until you get more exposure to enhance the chances of the book being accepted by a publisher. It's time and effort well spent."

O—¬ This agency specializes in health, self-help, how-to.
How to Contact: Query with SASE. Send outline or proposal with sufficient return postage. Responds in 1 month. Obtains most new clients through recommendations from others and occasional solicitation among established authors/ journalists.
Recent Sales: Sold 16 titles in the last year. *Village Shape-Up Program*, by Jonny Bowden (Perseus); *Love Lessons from Bad Breakups*, by Sherry Amatenstein (Perigee).
Terms: Agent receives 15% commission on domestic sales; 25% on foreign sales. Offers written contract. Charges clients $75 one-time fee for domestic expenses; additional expenses may be incurred for foreign sales.
Writers' Conferences: American Society of Journalists and Authors (New York City, May).
Reading List: Reads *New York Times Magazine* and women's magazines to find new clients.

◍ **ELAINE KOSTER LITERARY AGENCY, LLC**, 55 Central Park West, Suite 6, New York NY 10023. (212)362-9488. Fax: (212)712-0164. **Contact:** Elaine Koster. Member of AAR, MWA. Represents 30 clients. 25% of clients are new/previously unpublished writers. Currently handles: 30% nonfiction books; 70% novels.
● Prior to opening her agency, Ms. Koster was president and publisher of Dutton NAL.
Represents: Nonfiction books, novels. **Considers these nonfiction areas:** biography/autobiography; business; child guidance/parenting; cooking/food/nutrition; current affairs; ethnic/cultural interests; gay/lesbian issues; health/medicine; history; how-to; money/finance/economics; nature/environment; New Age/metaphysics; popular culture; psychology; self-help/personal improvement; women's issues/women's studies. **Considers these fiction areas:** action/adventure; confessional; contemporary issues; detective/police/crime; ethnic; family saga; feminist; gay/lesbian; glitz; historical; literary; mainstream; mystery (amateur sleuth, cozy, culinary, malice domestic); regional; suspense; thriller/espionage.
O—¬ This agency specializes in quality fiction and nonfiction. Does not want to receive juvenile, screenplays.
How to Contact: Query with outline, 3 sample chapters and SASE. Does not accept queries by e-mail or fax. Prefers to read materials exclusively. Responds in 3 weeks to queries; 1 month to mss. Returns materials only with SASE. Obtains most new clients through recommendations from others.
Recent Sales: Sold 23 titles in the last year. *Special Agent*, by Candice DeLong (Hyperion); *Sounds of the River*, by Da Chen (HarperCollins); *Tilting at Windmills*, by Joseph Pittman (Pocket Books).
Terms: Agent receives 15% commission on domestic sales; 20% on foreign sales. Offers written contract, 60-day notice must be given to terminate contract. Charges clients for photocopying, messengers, express mail, books and book galley, ordered from publisher to exploit other rights, overseas shipment of mss and books.
Tips: "We prefer exclusive submissions."

☑ ◍ **BARBARA S. KOUTS, LITERARY AGENT**, P.O. Box 560, Bellport NY 11713. (631)286-1278. **Contact:** Barbara Kouts. Estab. 1980. Member of AAR. Represent 50 clients. 10% of clients are new/previously unpublished writers. Currently handles: 20% nonfiction books; 60% juvenile books; 20% novels.
Represents: Nonfiction books, juvenile books, novels. **Considers these nonfiction areas:** biography/autobiography; child guidance/parenting; current affairs; ethnic/cultural interests; health/medicine; history; juvenile nonfiction; music/ dance/theater/film; nature/environment; psychology; self-help/personal improvement; women's issues/women's studies. **Considers these fiction areas:** contemporary issues; family saga; feminist; historical; juvenile; literary; mainstream; mystery/suspense; picture book; young adult.
O—¬ This agency specializes in adult fiction and nonfiction and children's books.
How to Contact: Query with SASE. Responds in 3 days to queries; 6 weeks to mss. Obtains most new clients through recommendations from others, solicitation, at conferences.
Recent Sales: *Dancing on the Edge*, by Han Nolan (Harcourt Brace); *Cendrillon*, by Robert San Souci (Simon & Schuster).
Terms: Agent receives 10% commission on domestic sales; 20% on foreign sales. Charges clients for photocopying.
Tips: "Write, do not call. Be professional in your writing."

◐ **IRENE KRAAS AGENCY**, 220 Copper Trail, Santa Fe NM 87505. (505)474-6212. Fax: (505)474-6216. Estab. 1990. Represents 30 clients. 75% of clients are new/previously unpublished writers. Currently handles: 30% juvenile books; 70% novels.
Represents: Adult fiction. **Considers these fiction areas:** action/adventure; detective/police/crime; mystery/suspense; science fiction.
O—¬ This agency specializes in fiction only, middle grade through adult. Actively seeking "books that are well written with commercial potential." Does not want to receive romance, short stories, plays or poetry
How to Contact: Send cover letter and first 30 pages. Must include return postage and/or SASE. Does not accept e-mail queries. Considers simultaneous submissions. Returns materials only with SASE.
Recent Sales: *St. Germain in India*, by Chelsea Quino Yarbro (Forge); *Cold Heart*, by Chandler McGraw (Bantam); *A Matter of Profit*, by Hilari Bell (Harper/Avon); *Any Kind of Luck*, by Bill Sibley (Kensington); *Edge of the Sword*, by Rebecca Tingle (Putnam); *The Bean Kings Daughter*, by Jennifer Stewart (Holiday House); *Wenny Has Wings*, by Janet Lee Carey (Atheneum); Other clients include Denise Vitola, Duncan Long, Shirley-Raye Redmond, Torry England.
Terms: Agent receives 15% commission on domestic sales. Offers written contract, binding for 1 year "but can be terminated at any time for any reason with written notice." Charges clients for photocopying and postage.
Writers' Conferences: Southwest Writers Conference (Albuquerque); Pacific Northwest Conference (Seattle); Vancouver Writers Conference (Vancouver BC); Austin Writers Workshop; Wilamette Writers' Group.

⊘ **STUART KRICHEVSKY LITERARY AGENCY, INC.**, One Bridge St., Suite 26, Irvington NY 10533. Member of AAR. This agency did not respond to our request for information. Query before submitting.

Ⓝ ⊘ **EDDIE KRITZER PRODUCTIONS**, 8484 Wilshire Blvd., Suite 205, Beverly Hills CA 90211. (323)655-5696. Fax: (323)655-5173. E-mail: producedby@aol.com. Website: www.eddiekritzer.com. **Contact:** Clair Wee, executive story editor. Estab. 1995. Represents 20 clients. 50% of clients are new/previously unpublished writers. Currently handles 25% nonfiction books; 5% novels; 10% movie scripts; 15% TV scripts; 1% stage plays; 1% syndicated material. **Member Agents:** Eddie Kritzer (nonfiction); Claire Wee (nonfiction, fiction).
Represents: Nonfiction books, novels. **Considers these nonfiction areas:** animals; biography/autobiography; business; computers/electronics; cooking/food/nutrition; current affairs; health/medicine; how-to; humor; self-help/personal improvement; true crime/investigative. **Considers these fiction areas:** action/adventure; confessional; contemporary issues; detective/police/crime.
  ○┐ This agency specializes in TV and movies. Actively seeking compelling material.
Also Handles: Movie scripts, TV scripts, feature film, TV movie of the week, sitcom, documentary, syndicated. **Considers these script subject areas:** action/adventure; biography/autobiography; contemporary issues; detective/police/crime; family saga; fantasy; horror; romantic comedy.
How to Contact: Query with SASE. Accepts queries by e-mail and fax. Prefers to read materials exclusively. Responds in 3 days to queries; 3 weeks to mss. Discards unwanted queries and mss. Obtains most new clients through recommendations from others, queries/solicitations.
Recent Sales: Sold 2 titles and 2 script projects in the last year. *Kids Say the Darndest Things*, by Art Linkletter (Workman). **Movie/TV MOW script optioned:** *Chat*, by Russ Thartwig (Renee Valente). Other clients include Dr. Alfred Jones, Dr. Bob Murphy, Arthur Satterfield.
Terms: Agent receives 15% commission on domestic sales; 20% on foreign sales. Offers written contract.
Writers' Conferences: Michale Levine (Santa Monica, May).
Tips: "Be succinct."

Ⓝ ⊘ **EDITE KROLL LITERARY AGENCY INC.**, 12 Grayhurst Park, Portland ME 04102. (207)773-4922. Fax: (207)773-3936. **Contact:** Edite Kroll. Estab. 1981. Represents 40 clients. Currently handles: 60% adult books; 40% juvenile books.
  • Prior to opening his agency, Edite Kroll served as a book editor and translator.
Represents: Nonfiction books, juvenile books, humor. **Considers these nonfiction areas:** social and political issues (especially feminist). **Considers these fiction areas:** juvenile; picture books by author/artists; humor books by author/artists.
  ○┐ Does not want to receive fantasy or genre.
How to Contact: Query in writing only with SASE. Does not accept queries by phone or fax. For nonfiction: send outline and proposal. For fiction: send outline and 1 sample chapter. For picture books and humor, send dummy. Responds in 1 month to queries; 2 months to mss.
Terms: Agent receives 15% commission on domestic sales; 20% on foreign sales. Charges clients for photocopying and legal fees with prior approval from writer.

✓ ⊘ **THE CANDACE LAKE AGENCY**, 9200 Sunset Blvd., Suite 820, Los Angeles CA 90069. (310)247-2115. Fax: (310)247-2116. E-mail: clagency@earthlink.net. **Contact:** Candace Lake. Estab. 1977. Signatory of WGA, member of DGA. 50% of clients are new/previously unpublished writers. Currently handles: 20% novels; 40% movie scripts; 40% TV scripts.
  • See the expanded listing for this agency in Script Agents.

◉ **PETER LAMPACK AGENCY, INC.**, 551 Fifth Ave., Suite 1613, New York NY 10176-0187. (212)687-9106. Fax: (212)687-9109. E-mail: renbopla@aol.com. **Contact:** Loren G. Soeiro. Estab. 1977. Represents 50 clients. 10% of clients are new/previously unpublished writers. Currently handles: 20% nonfiction books; 80% novels. **Member Agents:** Peter Lampack (psychological suspense, action/adventure, literary fiction, nonfiction, contemporary relationships); Sandra Blanton (foreign rights); Loren G. Soeiro (literary and commercial fiction, mystery, suspense, nonfiction, narrative nonfiction, high-concept thrillers).
Represents: Nonfiction books, novels. **Considers these nonfiction areas:** anthropology/archaeology; art/architecture/design; biography/autobiography; business; current affairs; government/politics/law; health/medicine; history; money/finance/economics; music/dance/theater/film; popular culture; high profile true crime/investigative; women's issues. **Considers these fiction areas:** action/adventure; contemporary relationships; detective/police/crime; family saga; historical; literary; mainstream; mystery/suspense; thriller/espionage.
  ○┐ This agency specializes in commercial fiction, male-oriented action/adventure, thrillers/suspense, contemporary relationships, distinguished literary fiction, nonfiction by a recognized expert in a given field. Actively seeking literary and commercial fiction, thrillers, mysteries, suspense, psychological thrillers, high-concept. Does not want to receive romance, science fiction, western, academic material.
How to Contact: Query with SASE. *No unsolicited mss.* Does not accept queries by fax. Accepts queries by e-mail. Considers simultaneous queries and submissions. Responds in 3 weeks to queries; 2 months to mss. Obtains most new clients from referrals made by clients.

Recent Sales: *Summer of Storms*, by Judith Kelman (Berkley); *In Her Defense*, by Stephen Horn (HarperCollins); *Atlantis Found*, by Clive Cussler (Putnam).
Terms: Agent receives 15% commission on domestic sales; 20% on foreign sales.
Writers' Conferences: BEA (Chicago, June).
Tips: "Submit only your best work for consideration. Have a very specific agenda of goals you wish your prospective agent to accomplish for you. Provide the agent with a comprehensive statement of your credentials: educational and professional."

◪ SABRA ELLIOTT LARKIN, Bly Hollow Rd., Cherry Plain NY 12040-0055. Phone/fax: (518)658-3065. E-mail: becontree@taconic.net. **Contact:** Sabra Larkin. Estab. 1996. Represents 10 clients. 90% of clients are new/previously unpublished writers. Currently handles: 80% nonfiction books; 20% novels.
   ● Prior to opening her agency, Ms. Larkin worked for over 30 years in publishing: 5 years in editorial at Dutton; 7 years at Ballantine Books in publicity and advertising; 10 years at Avon Books; and 10 years at Putnam Berkley as Vice President of Publicity, Promotion, Advertising and Public Relations
Represents: Nonfiction books, scholarly books, novels, illustrated books/(adult) art and photography. **Considers these nonfiction areas:** agriculture/horticulture; animals; anthropology/archeaology; art/architecture/design; biography/autobiography; business; cooking/food/nutrition; current affairs; education; ethnic/cultural interests; government/politics/law; health/medicine; history; how-to; language/literature/criticism; money/finance/economics; music/dance/theater/film; nature/environment; photography; popular culture; psychology; science/technology; true crime/investigative; women's issues/women's studies. **Considers these fiction areas:** action/adventure; contemporary issues; detective/police/crime; ethnic; experimental; family saga; glitz; historical; humor/satire; literary; mainstream; mystery/suspense; regional; thriller/espionage.
How to Contact: Query with SASE. Send outline and 2-3 sample chapters with return postage. Accepts queries by e-mail. Considers simultaneous queries; prefers to read ms submissions exclusively. Responds in 1 month to queries; 2 months to mss. Returns materials only with SASE. Obtains most new clients through recommendations from others and queries.
Recent Sales: Sold 1 title in the last year. Clients include James Chlovechok, Steve Stargen, Eric Evans.
Terms: Agent receives 15% commission on domestic sales; 20% on foreign sales. Offers written contract, binding for 5 years. 60-day notice must be given to terminate contract. Charges clients for postage and photocopying of mss. "Copies of receipts for dollar amounts are supplied to clients. Not applicable to contracted clients."

◪ MICHAEL LARSEN/ELIZABETH POMADA LITERARY AGENTS, 1029 Jones St., San Francisco CA 94109-5023. (415)673-0939. E-mail: larsenpoma@aol.com. Website: www.Larsen-Pomada.com. **Contact:** Mike Larsen or Elizabeth Pomada. Estab. 1972. Members of AAR, Authors Guild, ASJA, NWA, PEN, WNBA, California Writers Club. Represents 100 clients. 40-45% of clients are new/previously unpublished writers. Currently handles: 70% nonfiction books; 30% novels.
   ● Prior to opening their agency, both Mr. Larsen and Ms. Pomada were promotion executives for major publishing houses. Mr. Larsen worked for Morrow, Bantam, and Pyramid (now part of Berkley), Ms. Pomada worked at Holt, David McKay, and The Dial Press. Larsen is also co-author of *Guerilla Marketing for Writers* (Writers Digest Books).
Member Agents: Michael Larsen (nonfiction), Elizabeth Pomada (fiction, books of interest to women).
Represents: Adult nonfiction books, novels. **Considers these nonfiction areas:** anthropology/archaeology; art/architecture/design; biography/autobiography; business; cooking/food; current affairs; ethnic/cultural interests; futurism; gay/lesbian issues; government/politics; health/medicine; history; how-to; humor; interior design/decorating; language/literature/criticism; memoirs; money/finance/economics; music/dance/theater/film; nature/environment; New Age; parenting; photography; popular culture; psychology; inspirational; science/technology; self-help/personal improvement; sociology; sports; travel; investigative; women's issues/women's studies. **Considers these fiction areas:** action/adventure; contemporary issues; detective/police/crime; ethnic; experimental; family saga; fantasy; feminist; gay; glitz; historical; humor/satire; lesbian; literary; mainstream; mystery/suspense; psychic/supernatural; religious/inspirational; romance (contemporary, gothic, historical).
   ⊶ This agency is eager to work with new/previously unpublished writers. Actively seeking commercial and literary fiction, and "fresh voices with new ideas of interest to major publishers." Does not want to receive children's books, plays, short stories, screenplays, pornography.
How to Contact: Query with synopsis and first 10 pages of completed novel. Responds in 2 months weeks to queries. For nonfiction, "please read Michael's book *How to Write a Book Proposal* (Writer's Digest Books) and then mail or e-mail the title of your book and a promotion plan." Does not accept queries by fax or e-mail. Considers simultaneous queries. Always include SASE. Send SASE for brochure and title list.
Recent Sales: Sold over 30 titles in the last year. *Fire Dragon* (11th book in the Deverry Series), by Katharine Kerr (Bantam/Spectra); *Raphael & His Noble Task*, by Catherine Salton (HarperCollins); *Day of Deceit*, by Robert Stinnett (Free Press); *The Dream of Space Flight*, by Wyn Wachhorst (Basic Books).
Terms: Agent receives 15% commission on domestic sales; 15% on dramatic sales; 20-30% on foreign sales. May charge writer for printing, postage for multiple submissions, foreign mail, foreign phone calls, galleys, books, and legal fees.
Writers' Conferences: BEA; Santa Barbara Writers Conference (Santa Barbara); Maui Writers Conference (Maui); ASJA.

Tips: "We have very diverse tastes. We look for fresh voices and new ideas. We handle literary, commercial and genre fiction, and the full range of nonfiction books."

◐ THE MAUREEN LASHER AGENCY, P.O. Box 888, Pacific Palisades CA 90272-0888. (310)459-8415. **Contact:** Ann Cashman. Estab. 1980.
• Prior to becoming an agent, Ms. Lasher worked in publishing in New York.
Represents: Nonfiction books, novels. **Considers these nonfiction areas:** animals; anthropology/archaeology; art/architecture/design; biography/autobiography; business; child guidance/parenting; cooking/food/nutrition; current affairs; ethnic/cultural interests; government/politics/law; health/medicine; history; how-to; nature/environment; popular culture; psychology; science/technology; self-help/personal improvement; sociology; sports; true crime/investigative; women's issues/women's studies. **Considers these fiction areas:** action/adventure; contemporary issues; detective/police/crime; family saga; feminist; historical; literary; mainstream; sports; thriller/espionage.
How to Contact: Send outline/proposal and 1 sample chapter with SASE.
Recent Sales: *My Life as a Dog*, by Moose (aka Eddie from Frasier) (HarperCollins); *Never Too Late: A Prosecutor's Story*, by Bobby DeLaughter (Scribner); *Untitled companion book to PBS series*, by Regina Campbell (Morrow); *Relax, This Won't Hurt*, by Judith Reichman (Morrow); *Now This*, by Judy Muller (Putnam).
Terms: No information provided. Does not charge a reading fee or offer criticism service.

☑ ◐ LAWYER'S LITERARY AGENCY, INC., One America Plaza, 600 W. Broadway, Suite 175, San Diego CA 92101. (619)696-3300. Fax: (619)696-3808. E-mail: allenetling@spherion.com. **Contact:** H. Allen Etling. Estab. 1994. Represents 10 clients. 50% of clients are new/previously unpublished writers. Currently handles: 90% nonfiction books; 10% fiction.
Represents: Fiction, nonfiction books, movie scripts, TV scripts. **Considers these nonfiction areas:** biography/autobiography (of lawyers); law; true crime/investigative. **Considers these fiction areas:** thriller (political, science fiction).
O— This agency specializes in true crime, including trial aspect written by attorneys, and lawyer biographies and autobiographies.
How to Contact: Query with outline, 3 sample chapters and SASE. Responds in 30 days. Obtains most new clients through recommendations from others.
Recent Sales: *Undying Love: A Key West Love Story*, by Ben Harrison (New Horizon Press).
Terms: Agent receives 15% commission on domestic sales; does not handle foreign rights. Offers written contract for 1 year, with 30-day cancellation clause.
Tips: "Many of the best real stories are true crime stories—including depiction of the crime, background of the participants, official investigation by authorities, defense/prosecution preparation and the trial. There are hundreds of intriguing cases that occur annually in the US and not all of them are handled by attorneys who are household names. We are looking for the most compelling of these stories where there is also a good chance of selling TV movie/feature movie rights. Manuscripts can entail one case or multiple cases. Those involving multiple cases would probably resemble an attorney's biography. The story or stories can be told by defense and prosecution attorneys alike."

☑ ◐ LAZEAR AGENCY INCORPORATED, 800 Washington Ave. N, Suite 660, Minneapolis MN 55401. (612)332-8640. Fax: (612)332-4648. **Contact:** Editorial Board. Estab. 1984. Represents 250 clients. Currently handles: 60% nonfiction books; 10% juvenile books; 30% novels; 2.5% movie and TV scripts; 2.5% syndicated material.
• The Lazear Agency opened a New York office in September 1997.
Member Agents: Jonathon Lazear; Wendy Lazear; Christi Cardenas; Anne Blackstone; John P. Larson; Tanya Cromey.

 CLOSE UP with **Michael Larsen, Michael Larsen/Elizabeth Pomada Literary Agency**

On publishing in journals before approaching agents . . .

"Use an article to attract agents and editors. The right article in the right newspaper or magazine at the right time will sell a book. If your idea and your article about it are impressive enough:

• editors and agents will find you. If you have a novel in progress, your short story may enable you to sell it with only a partial manuscript and a synopsis.

• you may be able to use the article as a sample chapter in a nonfiction proposal. Your idea and your ability as a writer will have greater credibility if a magazine pays you to write about it."

Taken from *Guerrilla Marketing for Writers* (Writer's Digest Books).

Represents: Nonfiction books, novels, juvenile books, syndicated material, new media with connection to book project. **Considers all nonfiction areas. Considers all fiction areas.**

Also Handles: Feature film, television programming, licensing.

How to Contact: Query with outline/proposal and SASE. Does not accept queries by e-mail or fax. Prefers to read materials exclusively. Responds in 3 weeks to queries; 1 month to ms; 1 month to scripts. Highly selective. No phone calls or faxes. Returns materials only with SASE. Obtains most new clients through recommendations from others, "through the bestseller lists, word-of-mouth."

Recent Sales: Sold over 50 titles in the last year. *Reason for Hope*, by Jane Goodall with Phillip Berman (Warner); *The Old Neighborhood*, by Ray Suarez (FreePress/Simon & Schuster); *Smart Money*, by Chris Farrell (Random House); *Home & Away*, by Scott Simon (Hyperion).

Terms: Agent receives 15% commission on domestic sales; 20% on foreign sales. Offers written contract, binding "for term of copyright." Charges clients for "photocopying, international express mail, bound galleys and finished books used for subsidiary rights sales. No fees charged if book is not sold."

Reading List: Reads *The New Yorker*, *Harper's* and various newspapers and other magazines to find new clients. Looks for "originality, broad interest."

Tips: "The writer should first view himself as a salesperson in order to obtain an agent. Sell yourself, your idea, your concept. Do your homework. Notice what is in the marketplace. Be sophisticated about the arena in which you are writing."

Ø SARAH LAZIN, 126 Fifth Ave., Suite 300, New York NY 10011. Member of AAR. This agency did not respond to our request for information. Query before submitting.

Ø THE NED LEAVITT AGENCY, 70 Wooster St., New York NY 10012. Member of AAR. This agency did not respond to our request for information. Query before submitting.

◐ LESCHER & LESCHER LTD., 47 E. 19th St., New York NY 10003. (212)529-1790. Fax: (212)529-2716. **Contact:** Robert or Susan Lescher, Michael Choate. Estab. 1966. Member of AAR. Represents 150 clients. Currently handles: 80% nonfiction books; 20% fiction.

Represents: Nonfiction books, fiction. **Considers mysteries and cookbooks.**

   ⊶ Does not want to receive screenplays or science fiction.

How to Contact: Query with SASE. Obtains most new clients through recommendations from others.

Recent Sales: This agency prefers not to share information on specific sales. Clients include Neil Sheehan, Madeleine L'Engle, Calvin Trillin, Judith Viorst, Thomas Perry, Anne Fadiman, Frances Fitzgerald.

Terms: Agent receives 15% commission on domestic sales; 20-25% on foreign sales.

☑ ◐ JAMES LEVINE COMMUNICATIONS, INC., 307 Seventh Ave., 19th Floor, New York NY 10001. (212)337-0934. Fax: (212)337-0948. E-mail: levine@jameslevine.com. Website: www.jameslevine.com. Estab. 1989. Member of AAR. Represents 150 clients. 33⅓% of clients are new/previously unpublished writers. Currently handles: 90% nonfiction books; 10% fiction.

Member Agents: James Levine; Daniel Greenberg; Arielle Eckstut.

   ● Prior to opening his agency, Mr. Levine served as Vice President of the Bank Street College of Education.

Represents: Nonfiction books, novels. **Considers these nonfiction areas:** animals; art/architecture/design; biography/ autobiography; business; child guidance/parenting; computers/electronicsInternet; cooking/food/nutrition; gardening; gay/lesbian issues; health/medicine; money/finance/economics; nature/environment; New Age/metaphysics; psychology; religious/inspirational; science/technology; self-help/personal improvement; sociology; sports; women's issues/women's studies. **Considers these fiction areas:** contemporary issues; literary; mainstream.

   ⊶ This agency specializes in business, psychology, parenting, health/medicine, narrative nonfiction, psychology, spirituality, religion, women's issues.

How to Contact: See www.jameslevine.com for full submission procedure. Obtains most new clients through client referrals.

Recent Sales: *Our Dumb Century*, by The Onion (Crown); *Lipshtick*, by Gwen Macsai (HarperCollins); *CNBC five book series* (Wiley).

Terms: Agent receives 15% commission on domestic sales; 20% on foreign sales. Offers written contract; length of time varies per project. Does not charge reading fee. Charges clients for out-of-pocket expenses—telephone, fax, postage and photocopying—directly connected to the project.

Writers' Conferences: ASJA Annual Conference (New York City, May).

Tips: "We work closely with clients on editorial development and promotion. We work to place our clients as magazine columnists and have created columnists for *McCall's* and *Child*. We work with clients to develop their projects across various media—video, software, and audio."

◗ PAUL S. LEVINE LITERARY AGENCY, 1054 Superba Ave., Venice CA 90291-3940. (310)450-6711. Fax: (310)450-0181. E-mail: pslevine@ix.netcom.com. Website: www.netcom.com/~pslevine/lawliterary.html. **Contact:** Paul S. Levine. Estab. 1996. Member of the Attorney-State Bar of California. Represents over 100 clients. 75% of clients are new/previously unpublished writers. Currently handles: 30% nonfiction books; 30% novels; 10% movie scripts; 30% TV scripts.

● Prior to becoming an agent, Mr. Levine was an entertainment law attorney for almost 20 years and has represented both authors and publishers. "I know the book business from both sides of the table."

Represents: Nonfiction books, novels. **Considers these nonfiction areas:** art/architecture/design; biography/autobiography; business; child guidance/parenting; computers/electronics; cooking/food/nutrition; crafts/hobbies; current affairs; education; ethnic/cultural interests; gay/lesbian issues; government/politics; health/medicine; history; how-to; humor; interior design/decorating; language/literature/criticism; memoirs; military/war; money/finance/economics; music/dance/theater/film; nature/environment; New Age/metaphysics; photography; popular culture; psychology; religious/inspirational; science/technology; self-help/personal improvement; sociology; sports; true crime/investigative; women's issues/women's studies. **Considers these fiction areas:** action/adventure; cartoon/comic; confessional; contemporary issues; detective/police/crime; erotica; ethnic; experimental; family saga; fantasy; feminist; gay/lesbian; glitz; historical; horror; humor/satire; literary; mainstream; mystery; picture book; psychic/supernatural; regional; romance; religious/inspirational; sports; thriller/espionage; westerns/frontier; young adult.

○➤ Actively seeking commercial fiction and nonfiction. Does not want to receive science fiction or children's material.

Writers' Conferences: California Lawyers for the Arts (Los Angeles CA); "Colorado Gold Conference" (Rocky Mountain Fiction Writers (Lakewood CO); "Hollywood Pitch Workshop" (Los Angeles CA); National Writers Club (Los Angeles CA); "Selling to Hollywood" Writer's Connection (Glendale CA); "Spotlight on Craft" Willamette Writers Conference (Portland OR); Women in Animation (Los Angeles CA); and many others.

Also Handles: Movie scripts, feature film, episodic drama, TV scripts, TV MOW, sitcom, documentary, syndicated material, miniseries, animation. **Considers these script subject areas:** action/adventure; biography/autobiography; cartoon/animation; comedy; contemporary issues; detective/police/crime; erotica; ethnic; experimental; family saga; fantasy; feminist; gay/lesbian; glitz; historical; horror; juvenile; mainstream; multimedia; mystery/suspense; psychic/supernatural; religious/inspirational; romantic comedy; romantic drama; science fiction; sports; teen; thriller/espionage; western/frontier.

How to Contact: Query with SASE. Accepts queries by fax and e-mail. Considers simultaneous queries and submissions. Responds in 1 day to queries; 2 months to mss. Returns materials only with SASE. Obtains most new clients through writers conferences, referrals, listings on various websites and through listings in directories.

Recent Sales: Sold 25 titles in the last year. This agency prefers not to share information on specific sales.

Terms: Agent receives 15% commission on domestic sales; 20% on foreign sales. Offers written contract. Charges clients for messengers, long distance, postage. "Only when incurred. No advance payment necessary."

◖ **ELLEN LEVINE LITERARY AGENCY, INC.**, 15 E. 26th St., Suite 1801, New York NY 10010. (212)889-0620. Fax: (212)725-4501. **Contact:** Ellen Levine, Elizabeth Kaplan, Diana Finch, Louise Quayle. Estab. 1980. Member of AAR. Represents over 100 clients. 20% of clients are new/previously unpublished writers. Currently handles: 55% nonfiction books; 5% juvenile books; 40% fiction.

Member Agents: Ellen Levine; Elizabeth Kaplan; Diana Finch; Louise Quayle.

Represents: Nonfiction books, juvenile books, novels, short story collections. **Considers these nonfiction areas:** anthropology; biography; current affairs; health; history; memoirs; popular culture; psychology; science; women's issues/women's studies; books by journalists. **Considers these fiction areas:** literary; mystery; women's fiction, thrillers.

How to Contact: Query with SASE. Responds in 3 weeks to queries, if SASE provided; 6 weeks on mss, if submission requested. Obtains most new clients through recommendations from others.

Recent Sales: *The Day John Died*, by Christopher Andersen (William Morrow); *Anil's Ghost*, by Michael Ondaati; *The Frailty Myth*, by Colette Dowling (Little, Brown). Other clients include Russell Banks, Cristina Garcia, Garrison Keillor.

Terms: Agent receives 15% commission on domestic sales; 20% on foreign sales. Charges clients for overseas postage, photocopying, messenger fees, overseas telephone and fax, books ordered for use in rights submissions.

Tips: "My three younger colleagues at the agency (Louise Quayle, Diana Finch, and Elizabeth Kaplan) are seeking both new and established writers. I prefer to work with established writers, mostly through referrals."

◖ **KAREN LEWIS & COMPANY**, P.O. Box 741623, Dallas TX 75374-1623. (972)772-5260. Fax: (972)772-5276. E-mail: bashaoo@aol.com. **Contact:** Karen Lewis. Estab. 1995. Represents 27 clients. 25% of clients are new/previously unpublished writers. Currently handles: 60% nonfiction books; 40% novels.

● Prior to opening her agency, Ms. Lewis served as a creative writing instructor.

Member Agents: Karen Lewis; Tracy Bisere.

Represents: Nonfiction books, juvenile books, novels. **Considers these nonfiction areas:** ethnic/cultural interests; gay/lesbian issues; juvenile nonfiction; New Age/metaphysics; self-help/personal improvement; women's issues/women's studies. **Considers these fiction areas:** action/adventure; detective/police/crime; erotica; ethnic; literary; mainstream; mystery/suspense; science fiction; thriller/espionage.

How to Contact: Query with SASE. Accepts queries by fax and e-mail. Considers simultaneous queries and submissions. Responds in 1 month to queries; 2 months to mss. Returns materials only with SASE. Obtains most new clients through "conferences and referrals from people I know."

Recent Sales: Sold 16 titles in the last year. *Tunnel Runner*, by Richard Sand (Durban House Publishing); *Roadhouse Blues*, by Baron Birtcher (Durban House Publishing).

Terms: Agent receives 15% commission on domestic sales; 20% on foreign sales. Offers written contract, binding for 1 year, with 30-day cancellation clause. Sometimes makes referrals to editing services. 100% of business is derived from commissions on sales.

Writers' Conferences: Southwest Writers (Albuquerque NM); Romance Writer's of America; Austin Writers' League; Faulkner Writer's Conference.

Reading List: "Sometimes we check Internet sites for new clients. We look for a fresh new voice with something unique to say."

Tips: "Write a clear letter succinctly describing your book. Be sure to include a SASE. If you receive rejection notices, don't despair. Keep writing! A good book will always find a home."

N ◎ **LICHTMAN, TRISTER, SINGER & ROSS**, 1666 Connecticut Ave., Suite 501, Washington D.C. 20009. Member of AAR. This agency did not respond to our request for information. Query before submitting.

✓ ◎ **ROBERT LIEBERMAN ASSOCIATES**, 400 Nelson Rd., Ithaca NY 14850-9440. (607)273-8801. E-mail: RHL10@cornell.edu. Website: www.people.cornell.edu/pages/RHL10/. **Contact:** Robert Lieberman. Estab. 1993. Represents 30 clients. 50% of clients are new/previously unpublished writers. Currently handles: 20% nonfiction books; 80% textbooks.

Represents: Scholarly books, textbooks. **Considers these nonfiction areas:** agriculture/horticulture; anthropology/archaeology; art/architecture/design; business; computers/electronics; education; health/medicine; memoirs (by authors with high public recognition); money/finance/economics; music/dance/theater/film; nature/environment; psychology; science/technology; sociology; college, high school and middle school level textbooks.

   ○— This agency specializes in university/college level textbooks, CD-ROM/software and popular tradebooks in science, math, engineering, economics and others. Does not want to receive fiction, self-help or screenplays.

How to Contact: Send initial inquiries by mail with SASE or e-mail. E-mail preferred. Prefers to read materials exclusively. Responds in 2 weeks to queries; 1 month to mss. Will not respond to mail queries without SASE. Obtains most new clients through referrals.

Recent Sales: Sold 20 titles in the last year. This agency prefers not to share information on specific sales.

Terms: Agent receives 15% commission on domestic sales; 20% on foreign sales. Offers written contract, binding for open-ended length of time, with 30-day cancellation clause. "Fees are charged to clients only when special reviewers are required." 100% of business is derived from commissions on sales.

Tips: "The trade books we handle are by authors who are highly recognized in their fields of expertise. Client list includes Nobel prize winners and others with high name recognition, either by the public or within a given area of expertise."

◎ **RAY LINCOLN LITERARY AGENCY**, Elkins Park House, Suite 107-B, 7900 Old York Rd., Elkins Park PA 19027. Phone/fax: (215)635-0827. **Contact:** Mrs. Ray Lincoln. Estab. 1974. Represents 30 clients. 35% of clients are new/previously unpublished writers. Currently handles: 30% nonfiction books; 20% juvenile books; 50% novels.

Member Agents: Jerome A. Lincoln; Mrs. Ray Lincoln.

Represents: Nonfiction books, scholarly books, juvenile books, novels. **Considers these nonfiction areas:** animals; anthropology/archaeology; art/architecture/design; biography/autobiography; business; child guidance/parenting; cooking/food/nutrition; crafts/hobbies; current affairs; ethnic/cultural interests; gay/lesbian issues; government/politics/law; health/medicine; history; horticulture; interior design/decorating; juvenile nonfiction; language/literature/criticism; money/finance/economics; music/dance/theater/film; nature/environment; psychology; science/technology; self-help/personal improvement; sociology; sports; women's issues/women's studies. **Considers these fiction areas:** action/adventure; contemporary issues; detective/police/crime; ethnic; family saga; fantasy; feminist; gay/lesbian; historical; humor/satire; juvenile; lesbian; literary; mainstream; mystery/suspense; psychic/supernatural; regional; romance (contemporary, gothic, historical); sports; thriller/espionage; young adult.

   ○— This agency specializes in biography, nature, the sciences, fiction in both adult and children's categories.

How to Contact: Query first with SASE, then on request send outline, 2 sample chapters and SASE. "I send for balance of manuscript if it is a likely project." Responds in 2 weeks to queries; 1 month to mss. Obtains most new clients from recommendations.

Recent Sales: *The Blanders*, by Barbara Robinson (HarperCollins); *Stargirl*, by Jerry Spinelli (Knopf); *To Wanda and Me*, by Susan Katz (Simon & Schuster); *Rise the Moon*, by Eileen Spinelli (Dial/Penguin Putnam).

Terms: Agent receives 15% commission on domestic sales; 20% on foreign sales. Offers written contract, binding "but with notice, may be cancelled." Charges clients for overseas telephone calls; upfront postage fee for unpublished authors only. "I request authors to do manuscript photocopying themselves."

Tips: "I always look for polished writing style, fresh points of view and professional attitudes."

◎ **WENDY LIPKIND AGENCY**, 165 E. 66th St., New York NY 10021. (212)628-9653. Fax: (212)628-2693. **Contact:** Wendy Lipkind. Estab. 1977. Member of AAR. Represents 60 clients. Currently handles: 80% nonfiction books; 20% novels.

Represents: Nonfiction, novels. **Considers these nonfiction areas:** biography; current affairs; health/medicine; history; science; social history; women's issues/women's studies. **Considers mainstream and psychological/suspense fiction.**

   ○— This agency specializes in adult nonfiction. Does not want to receive mass market originals.

How to Contact: For nonfiction, query with outline/proposal. For fiction, query with SASE only. Prefers to read materials exclusively. Responds in 1 month to queries. Returns materials only with SASE. Obtains most new clients through recommendations from others.

Recent Sales: Sold over 10 titles in the last year. *Wired Style*, by Hale/Scanlon (Broadway Books); *Maybe You Know My Adolescent*, by Mary Fowler (Broadway Books).

Terms: Agent receives 15% commission on domestic sales; 20% on foreign sales. Sometimes offers written contract. Charges clients for foreign postage, messenger service, photocopying, transatlantic calls, faxes.

Tips: "Send intelligent query letter first. Let me know if you sent to other agents."

◗ LITERARY AND CREATIVE ARTISTS, INC., 3543 Albemarle St. NW, Washington DC 20008-4213. (202)362-4688. Fax: (202)362-8875. **Contact:** Muriel Nellis, Jane Roberts. Estab. 1982. Member of AAR, Authors Guild, associate member of American Bar Association. Represents over 75 clients. Currently handles: 70% nonfiction books; 15% novels; 10% audio/video; 5% film/TV.

Member Agents: Muriel Nellis, Jane Roberts, Stephen Rowe, Jessica Lee.

Represents: Nonfiction, novels, audio, film/TV rights. **Considers these nonfiction areas:** biography; business; cooking; health; how-to; human drama; lifestyle; medical; memoir; philosophy; politics.

How to Contact: Query with outline, bio and SASE. *No unsolicited mss.* Responds in 3 weeks to queries. "While we prefer published writers, it is not required if the proposed work has great merit." Requires exclusive review of requested material; no simultaneous submissions.

Recent Sales: *Odds*, by Patty Friedman (Counterpoint); *How to Know God*, by Deepak Chopra (Harmony Books); *How to Think Like Leonardo Da Vinci*, by Michael Gelb (Delacorte); *The Emerging Mind*, by Karen Shanor (Renaissance Books); *Peak Performance Fitness*, by Jennifer Rhodes (Hunter House); *Growing Up in a Korean Kitchen*, by Hi Soo Hepinstall (Ten Speed).

Terms: Agent receives 15% commission on domestic sales; 20% on dramatic sales; 25% on foreign sales. Charges clients for long-distance phone and fax, photocopying, shipping.

☑ ◖ THE LITERARY GROUP, 270 Lafayette St., #1505, New York NY 10012. (212)274-1616. Fax: (212)274-9876. E-mail: litgrpfw@aol.com. Website: www.theliterarygroup.com. **Contact:** Frank Weimann. Estab. 1985. Represents 150 clients. 75% of clients are new/previously unpublished writers. Currently handles: 60% nonfiction books; 40% novels.

Member Agents: Frank Weimann (fiction, biography); Jim Hornfischer (serious nonfiction); Jessica Wainwright (women's issues, romance, how-to); Brian Rago (how-to's, cookbooks).

Represents: Nonfiction books, novels. **Considers these nonfiction areas:** animals; anthropology/archaeology; biography/autobiography; business; child guidance/parenting; cookbooks; crafts/hobbies; current affairs; education; ethnic/cultural interests; gay/lesbian issues; government/politics/law; health/medicine; history; how-to; humor; juvenile nonfiction; language/literature/criticism; memoirs; military/war; money/finance/economics; music/dance/theater/film; nature/environment; New Age/metaphysics; popular culture; psychology; religious/inspirational; science/technology; self-help/personal improvement; sociology; sports; true crime/investigative; women's issues/women's studies. **Considers these fiction areas:** action/adventure; cartoon/comic; contemporary issues; detective/police/crime; ethnic; family saga; fantasy; feminist; gay/lesbian; horror; humor/satire; mystery/suspense; psychic/supernatural; romance (contemporary, gothic, historical, regency); sports; thriller/espionage; westerns/frontier; young adult.

    ⊶ This agency specializes in nonfiction (true crime; biography; sports; how-to).

How to Contact: Query with outline plus 3 sample chapters and SASE. Accepts queries by e-mail. Prefers to read materials exclusively. Responds in 1 week to queries; 1 month to mss. Returns materials only with SASE. Obtains most new clients through referrals, writers' conferences, query letters.

Recent Sales: Sold 80 titles in the last year. *Flags of Our Fathers*, by James Bradley (Bantam); *The Last Dive*, by Bernie Chowdury (HarperCollins); *Britney Spears' Heart to Heart*, by Britney Spears/Lynne Spears (Three Rivers Press). Other clients include Ed McMahon, Sam Giancana.

Terms: Agent receives 15% commission on domestic sales; 20% on foreign sales. Offers written contract, which can be cancelled after 30 days.

Writers' Conferences: Detroit Women's Writers (MI); Kent State University (OH); San Diego Writers Conference (CA); Maui Writers Conference; Austin Writers' Conference.

◗ STERLING LORD LITERISTIC, INC., 65 Bleecker St., New York NY 10012. (212)780-6050. Fax: (212)780-6095. **Contact:** Peter Matson. Estab. 1952. Signatory of WGA. Represents over 600 clients. Currently handles: 50% nonfiction books; 50% novels.

Member Agents: Peter Matson; Sterling Lord; Jody Hotchkiss (film scripts); Philippa Brophy; Chris Calhoun; Jennifer Hengen; Charlotte Sheedy; George Nicholson; Neeti Madan.

Represents: Nonfiction books, novels. "Literary value considered first."

How to Contact: Query with SASE. Responds in 1 month to mss. Obtains most new clients through recommendations from others.

Recent Sales: This agency prefers not to share information on specific sales. Clients include Kent Haruf, Dick Francis, Mary Gordon, Sen. John McCain.

Terms: Agent receives 15% commission on domestic sales; 20% on foreign sales. Offers written contract. Charges clients for photocopying.

✓ ◯ **NANCY LOVE LITERARY AGENCY**, 250 E. 65th St., New York NY 10021-6614. (212)980-3499. Fax: (212)308-6405. **Contact:** Nancy Love or Daniel Genis. Estab. 1984. Member of AAR. Represents 60-80 clients. Currently handles: 90% nonfiction books; 10% mysteries and thrillers.
Member Agents: Nancy Love.
Represents: Nonfiction books, fiction ("mysteries and thrillers only!"). **Considers these nonfiction areas:** animals; biography/autobiography; child guidance/parenting; cooking/food/nutrition; current affairs; ethnic/cultural interests; government/politics/law; health/medicine; history; how-to; memoirs; nature/environment; New Age/metaphysics; popular culture; psychology; science/technology; self-help/personal improvement; sociology; travel (armchair only, no how-to travel); true crime/investigative; women's issues/women's studies. **Considers these fiction areas:** mystery/suspense; thriller/espionage.

    O→ This agency specializes in adult nonfiction and mysteries. Actively seeking health and medicine (including alternative medicine); parenting; spiritual and inspirational. Does not want to receive novels other than mysteries and thrillers.

How to Contact: "For nonfiction, send a proposal, chapter summary and sample chapter. For fiction, query first. Does not accept queries by e-mail or fax. Considers simultaneous queries and submissions. Prefers to read fiction materials exclusively. Responds in 3 weeks to queries; 6 weeks to mss. Returns materials only with SASE. Obtains most new clients through recommendations and solicitations.
Recent Sales: Sold 18 titles in the last year. *The One-Minute Mediator*, by David Nichols, M.D. and William Circhard (Perseus); *Brotherman Rising: Raising Black Boys*, by Warren Spielberg, Ph.D. and Kirkland Vaughans, Ph.D. (HarperCollins); *Deadly Nightshade*, by Cynthia Riggs (St. Martin's Press).
Terms: Agent receives 15% commission on domestic sales; 20% on foreign sales. Offers written contract. Charges clients for photocopying, "if it runs over $20."
Tips: Needs an exclusive on fiction. "Nonfiction author and/or collaborator must be an authority in subject area and have a platform."

◉ **LOWENSTEIN ASSOCIATES, INC.**, 121 W. 27th St., Suite 601, New York NY 10001. (212)206-1630. Fax: (212)727-0280. **Contact:** Barbara Lowenstein, president. Estab. 1976. Member of AAR. Represents 150 clients. 20% of clients are new/previously unpublished writers. Currently handles: 60% nonfiction books; 40% novels.
Member Agents: Barbara Lowenstein (president); Nancy Yost (agent); Eileen Cope (agent); Dorian Karchmar (agent); Norman Kurz (business affairs).
Represents: Nonfiction books, novels. **Considers these nonfiction areas:** animals; anthropology/archaeology; biography/autobiography; business; child guidance/parenting; craft/hobbies; current affairs; education; ethnic/cultural interests; gay/lesbian issues; government/politics/law; health/medicine; history; how-to; humor; language/literature/criticism/; memoirs; money/finance/economics; music/dance/theater/film; nature/environment; New Age/metaphysics, popular culture; psychology; religious/inspirational; science/technology; self-help/personal improvement; sociology; sports; travel; true crime/investigative; women's issues/women's studies. **Considers these fiction areas:** contemporary issues; detective/police/crime; erotica; ethnic; feminist; gay; historical; lesbian; literary mainstream; mystery/suspense; romance (contemporary, historical, regency); medical thrillers.

    O→ This agency specializes in health, business, spirituality, creative nonfiction, commercial fiction, especially suspense, crime and women's issues. "We are a full-service agency, handling domestic and foreign rights, film rights, and audio rights to all of our books."

How to Contact: Send query with SASE, "otherwise will not respond." For fiction, send outline and 1st chapter. *"Please do not send manuscripts."* Does not accept queries by e-mail or fax. Prefers to read materials exclusively. Responds in 6 weeks to queries. Returns materials only with SASE. Obtains most new clients through "referrals, journals and magazines, media, solicitations and a few conferences."
Recent Sales: Sold approximately 75 titles in the last year. *Move to Strike*, by Perri O'Shaughnessy (Delacorte/Dell); *Jon Benet: Inside the Ramsey Murder Investigation*, by Steve Thomas and Don Davis (St. Martin's Press); *Emotional Alchemy: Using the Mind to Heal the Heart*, by Tara Bennett-Goleman (Harmony Books). Other clients include Gina Barkhordar Nahai, Ishmael Reed, Michael Waldholz, Myrlie Evers Williams, Barry Yourgrau, Deborah Crombie, Jan Burke, Leslie Glass.
Terms: Agent receives 15% commission on domestic sales; 20% on foreign sales; 20% on dramatic sales. Offers written contract on a book-by-book basis. Charges clients for large photocopy batches and international postage.
Writers' Conference: Malice Domestic; Bouchercon.
Tips: "Know the genre you are working in and READ!"

◉ **DONALD MAASS LITERARY AGENCY**, 157 W. 57th St., Suite 703, New York NY 10019. (212)757-7755. **Contact:** Donald Maass, Jennifer Jackson or Michelle Brummer. Estab. 1980. Member of AAR, SFWA, MWA, RWA. Represents over 100 clients. 5% of clients are new/previously unpublished writers. Currently handles: 100% novels.

    ● Prior to opening his agency, Mr. Maass served as an editor at Dell Publishing (NY) and as a reader at Gollancz (London). Maass is the current president of AAR.

Member Agents: Donald Maass (mainstream, literary, mystery/suspense, science fiction); Jennifer Jackson (commercial fiction: especially romance, science fiction, fantasy, mystery/suspense); Michelle Brummer (fiction: literary, contemporary, feminist, science fiction, fantasy).

Represents: Novels. **Considers these fiction areas:** detective/police/crime; fantasy; historical; horror; literary; mainstream; mystery/suspense; psychic/supernatural; romance (historical, paranormal, time travel); science fiction; thriller/espionage.

O— This agency specializes in commercial fiction, especially science fiction, fantasy, mystery, romance, suspense. Actively seeking "to expand the literary portion of our list and expand in romance and women's fiction." Does not want to receive nonfiction, children's or poetry.

How to Contact: Query with SASE. Considers simultaneous queries and submissions. Returns materials only with SASE. Responds in 2 weeks to queries, 3 months to mss (if requested following query).

Recent Sales: Sold over 100 titles in the last year. *Slaves of Obsession*, by Anne Perry (Ballantine); *The Lightstone*, by David Zindell (Warner Aspect); *Midnight Robber*, by Nalo Hopkinson (Warner Aspect); *The Avalanche Soldier*, by Susan Matthews (Avon Eos); *Confluence II: Ancient of Days*, by Paul McAuley (Avon Eos).

Terms: Agent receives 15% commission on domestic sales; 20% on foreign sales. Charges clients for large photocopying orders and book samples, "after consultation with author."

Writers' Conferences: Donald Maass: World Science Fiction Convention; Frankfurt Book Fair; Pacific Northwest Writers Conference; Bouchercon; and others. Jennifer Jackson: World Science Fiction and Fantasy Convention; RWA National; and others. Michelle Brummer: ReaderCon; World Science Fiction Convention; Luna Con.

Tips: "We are fiction specialists, also noted for our innovative approach to career planning. Few new clients are accepted, but interested authors should query with SASE. Subagents in all principle foreign countries and Hollywood. No nonfiction or juvenile works considered."

◐ **GINA MACCOBY LITERARY AGENCY**, P.O. Box 60, Chappaqua NY 10514. (914)238-5630. **Contact:** Gina Maccoby. Estab. 1986. Represents 35 clients. Currently handles: 33% nonfiction books; 33% juvenile books; 33% novels. Represents illustrators of children's books.

Represents: Nonfiction, juvenile books, novels. **Considers these nonfiction areas:** biography; current affairs; ethnic/cultural interests; history; juvenile nonfiction; pop culture; women's issues/women's studies. **Considers these fiction areas:** juvenile; literary; mainstream; mystery/suspense; thriller/espionage; young adult.

How to Contact: Query with SASE. *"Please, no unsolicited mss."* Considers simultaneous queries and submisssions. Responds in 2 months. Returns materials only with SASE. Obtains most new clients through recommendations from own clients.

Recent Sales: Sold 18 titles in the last year. *Untitled Suspense Novel*, by Rick Riodan (Bantam); *It's Simple Said Simon*, by Mary Ann Hoberman (Crown).

Terms: Agent receives 15% commission on domestic sales; 25% on foreign sales. Charges clients for photocopying. May recover certain costs such as airmail postage to Europe or Japan or legal fees.

✔ ◐ **ROBERT MADSEN AGENCY**, 1331 E. 34th St., Suite #1, Oakland CA 94602-1032. (510)223-2090. **Contact:** Robert Madsen. Senior Editor: Liz Madsen. Estab. 1992. Represents 5 clients. 100% of clients are new/previously unpublished writers. Currently handles: 25% nonfiction books; 25% fiction books; 25% movie scripts; 25% TV scripts.

● Prior to opening his agency, Mr. Madsen was a writing tutor and worked in sales.

Represents: Nonfiction books, fiction. **Considers all nonfiction and fiction areas.**

O— This agency is "willing to look at subject matter that is specialized, controversial, even unpopular, esoteric and outright bizarre. However, it is strongly suggested that authors query first, to save themselves and this agency time, trouble and expense."

Also Handles: Feature film, TV scripts, radio scripts, video, stage plays. **Considers all script subject areas.**

How to Contact: Query with SASE. Does not accept queries by fax on e-mail. Considers simultaneous queries and submissions. Responds in 1 month. Returns materials only with SASE. Obtains most new clients through recommendations or by query.

Recent Sales: Sold 1 book title in the last year. *The Art of War*, by Wei Li (International). Clients include Theresa Ohmit.

Terms: Agent receives 10% commission on domestic sales; 20% on foreign sales. Offers written contract, binding for 3 years.

Tips: "Be certain to take care of business basics in appearance, ease of reading and understanding proper presentation and focus. Be sure to include sufficient postage and SASE with all submissions."

◐ **CAROL MANN AGENCY**, 55 Fifth Ave., New York NY 10003. (212)206-5635. Fax: (212)675-4809. E-mail: cmlass@aol.com. **Contact:** Carol Mann. Estab. 1977. Member of AAR. Represents over 100 clients. 25% of clients are new/previously unpublished writers. Currently handles: 70% nonfiction books; 30% novels.

Member Agents: Ms. Gareth Esersky (contemporary nonfiction); Jim Fitzgerald (literary, cinematic, Internet projects).

Represents: Nonfiction books, novels. **Considers these nonfiction areas:** anthropology/archaeology; art/architecture/design; biography/autobiography; business; child guidance/parenting; current affairs; ethnic/cultural interests; government/politics/law; health/medicine; history; money/finance/economics; psychology; self-help/personal improvement; sociology; women's issues/women's studies. **Considers literary fiction.**

O— This agency specializes in current affairs; self-help; psychology; parenting; history. Actively seeking "nonfiction: pop culture, business and health; fiction: literary fiction." Does not want to receive "genre fiction (romance, mystery, etc.)."

How to Contact: Query with outline/proposal and SASE. Responds in 3 weeks to queries.

Recent Sales: *Radical Healing*, by Rudolph Ballentine, M.D. (Harmony); *Timbuktu*, by Paul Auster (Holt); *Stopping Cancer Before It Starts*, by American Institute for Cancer Research (Golden). Other clients include Dr. William Julius Wilson, Barry Sears (*Mastering The Zone*), Dr. Judith Wallerstein (*The Good Marriage, The Unexpected Legacy of Divorce*), Lorraine Johnson-Coleman (*Just Plain Folks*), Pulitzer Prize Winner Fox Butterfield, David Bodanis (*E-MC²*), Sonny Barger (*Hell's Angels*) and James Tobin, NBCC Award Winner for *Ernie Pyle* (Free Press).

Terms: Agent receives 15% commission on domestic sales; 20% on foreign sales. Offers written contract.

Tips: "No phone queries. Must include SASE for reply."

⬤ MANUS & ASSOCIATES LITERARY AGENCY, INC., 375 Forest Ave., Palo Alto CA 94301. (650)470-5151. Fax: (650)470-5159. E-mail: manuslit@manuslit.com. Website: www.manuslit.com. **Contact:** Jillian Manus. Also: 417 E. 57th St., Suite 5D, New York NY 10022. (212)644-8020. Fax: (212)644-3374. **Contact:** Janet Manus. Estab. 1985. Member of AAR. Represents 75 clients. 30% of clients are new/previously unpublished writers. Currently handles: 55% nonfiction books; 5% juvenile books; 40% novels.

● Prior to becoming agents, Jillian Manus was associate publisher of two national magazines and director of development at Warner Bros. and Universal Studios; Janet Manus has been a literary agent for 20 years.

Member Agents: Jandy Nelson (self-help, health, memoirs, narrative nonfiction, literary fiction, multicultural fiction, thrillers); Jill Maverick (self-help, health, memoirs, dramatic nonfiction, women's fiction, commercial literary fiction, Southern writing, thrillers); Stephanie Lee (self-help, memoirs, dramatic nonfiction, commercial literary fiction, multicultural fiction, quirky/edgy fiction).

Represents: Nonfiction books, novels. **Considers these nonfiction areas**: biography/autobiography; business; child guidance/parenting; computers/electronics; current affairs; ethnic/cultural interests; health/medicine; how-to; memoirs; money/finance/economics; nature/environment; popular culture; psychology; science/technology; self-help/personal improvement; women's issues/women's studies; dramatic/narrative nonfiction; Gen X and Gen Y issues. **Considers these fiction areas**: literary; thriller/espionage; women's fiction; commercial literary fiction; multicultural fiction; Southern fiction; quirky/edgy fiction.

○━ This agency specializes in commercial literary fiction, narrative nonfiction, thrillers, health, pop psychology, women's empowerment. "Our agency is unique in the way that we not only sell the material, but we edit and develop concepts and participate in the marketing effort. We specialize in large, conceptual fiction and nonfiction, and always value a project that can be sold in the TV/feature film market." Actively seeking high-concept thrillers, commercial literary fiction, women's fiction, celebrity biographies, memoirs, multicultural fiction, popular health, women's empowerment. Does not want to receive horror, science fiction/fantasy, romance, westerns, young adult, children's, poetry, cookbooks, magazine articles.

How to Contact: Query with SASE. If requested, send outline and 2-3 sample chapters. Accepts queries by fax and e-mail. Considers simultaneous queries and submissions. Responds in 2 months to queries; 6 weeks to mss. Returns materials only with SASE. Obtains most new clients through recommendations from editors, clients and others; conferences; and unsolicited materials.

Recent Sales: *Catfish & Mandala*, by Andrew X. Pham (Farrar, Straus & Giroux); *Jake & Mimi*, by Frank Baldwin (Little, Brown); *Crane River*, by Lalita Tademy (Warner Books); *Forgive for Good*, by Dr. Frederick Luskin (HarperCollins). Other clients include Marcus Allen, Carlton Stowers, Alan Jacobson, Ann Brandt, Dr. Richard Marrs, Mary Loverde, Lisa Huang Fleishman, Judy Carter, Daryl Ott Underhill, Glen Klein.

Terms: Agent receives 15% commission on domestic sales; 20-25% on foreign sales. Offers written contract, binding for 2 years. 60-day notice must be given to terminate contract. Charges clients for copying and postage; "we reimburse ourselves out of the client's advance."

Writers' Conferences: Maui Writers Conference (Maui HI, Labor Day); San Diego Writer's Conference (San Diego CA, January); Willamette Writers Conference (Willamette OR, July).

Tips: "Research agents using a variety of sources, including *LMP*, guides, *Publishers Weekly*, conferences and even acknowledgements in books similar in tone to yours."

◖ MARCH TENTH, INC., 4 Myrtle St., Haworth NJ 07641-1740. (201)387-6551. Fax: (201)387-6552. E-mail: schoron@aol.com. **Contact:** Harry Choron, vice president. Estab. 1982. Represents 40 clients. 30% of clients are new/previously unpublished writers. Currently handles: 75% nonfiction books; 25% fiction.

Represents: Nonfiction books, fiction. **Considers these nonfiction areas:** biography/autobiography; current affairs; health/medicine; history; humor; language/literature/criticism; music/dance/theater/film; popular culture. **Considers these fiction areas:** confessional; ethnic; family saga; historical; humor/satire; literary; mainstream.

THE PUBLISHING FIELD is constantly changing! Agents often change addresses, phone numbers, or even companies. If you're still using this book and it is 2002 or later, buy the newest edition of *Guide to Literary Agents* at your favorite bookstore or order directly from Writer's Digest Books at (800)289-0963.

O—¬ "Writers must have professional expertise in their field."

How to Contact: Query with SASE. Accepts queries by e-mail. Considers simultaneous queries; prefers to read mss exclusively. Does not read unsolicited mss. Responds in 1 month. Returns materials only with SASE. Prefers to work with published/established writers.

Recent Sales: Sold 12 titles in the last year. *Lynyrd Skynyrd*, by Lee Ballinger (Avon); *Moon: The Story of Keith Moon*, by Tony Fletcher (Avon); *Songs*, by Bruce Springsteen (Avon); *Dilemma*, by James Saywell and Ann-Marie Rotti (Villard); *Everything You Need to Know About Mercury Retrograde*, by Chrissie Blaze (Warner).

Terms: Agent receives 15% commission on domestic sales; 20% on dramatic sales; 20% on foreign sales. Charges clients for postage, photocopying, overseas phone expenses. "Does not require expense money upfront."

⊠ ◖ BARBARA MARKOWITZ LITERARY AGENCY, 117 N. Mansfield Ave., Los Angeles CA 90036-3020. (323)939-5927. **Contact:** Barbara Markowitz, president. Estab. 1980. Represents 14 clients. Works with a small number of new/previously unpublished authors. Currently handles: 25% nonfiction books; 25% novels; 50% juvenile books.

• Prior to opening her agency, Ms. Markowitz owned the well-known independent bookseller, Barbara's Bookstores, in Chicago.

Member Agents: Judith Rosenthal (psychology, current affairs, women's issues, biography); Barbara Markowitz.

Represents: Nonfiction books, novels, juvenile books. **Considers these nonfiction areas:** biography/autobiography; current affairs; juvenile nonfiction; music/dance/theater/film; nature/environment; popular culture; sports; women's issues/women's studies. **Considers these fiction areas:** contemporary issues; detective/police/crime; ethnic; historical; humor/satire; juvenile; mainstream; mystery/suspense; sports; thriller/espionage; young adult.

O—¬ This agency specializes in mid-level and YA; contemporary fiction; adult trade fiction and nonfiction. Actively seeking mid-level historical and contemporary fiction for 8- to 11-year-olds, 125-150 pages in length; adult mysteries/thrillers/suspense. Does not want to receive illustrated books, science fiction/futuristic, poetry.

How to Contact: Query with SASE and first 2-3 chapters. Does not accept queries by e-mail or fax. Considers simultaneous queries. Responds in 3 weeks.

Recent Sales: Sold 6 titles in the last year. *Moon Pie and Ivy*, by Barbara O'Conner (FSG/Frances Foster); *Tartabulls Throw*, by Henry Garfield (Atheneum/Richard Jackson). Other clients include Mary Batten, Cynthia Lawrence.

Terms: Agent receives 15% commission on domestic sales; 20% on dramatic sales; 20% on foreign sales. Charges clients for mailing, postage.

Tips: "We do *not* agent pre-school or early reader books. Only mid-level and YA contemporary fiction and historical fiction. We receive an abundance of pre-school and early reader mss, which our agency returns if accompanied by SASE. No illustrated books. No sci-fi/fable/fantasy or fairy tales."

◖ ELAINE MARKSON LITERARY AGENCY, 44 Greenwich Ave., New York NY 10011. (212)243-8480. Fax: (212)691-9014. Estab. 1972. Member of AAR and WGA. Represents 200 clients. 10% of clients are new/previously unpublished writers. Currently handles: 35% nonfiction books; 55% novels; 10% juvenile books.

Member Agents: Geri Thoma, Sally Wofford-Girand, Elizabeth Sheinkman, Elaine Markson.

Represents: Quality fiction and nonfiction.

O—¬ This agency specializes in literary fiction, commercial fiction, trade nonfiction.

How to Contact: Obtains new clients by recommendation only.

Recent Sales: *The River King*, by Alice Hoffman (Putnam); *Where the Heart Is*, by Billie Letts (Warner); *The Heartsong of Charging Elk*, by James Welch (Doubleday); *Goldman Sachs: The Culture of Success*, by Lisa Endlich (Knopf).

Terms: Agent receives 15% commission on domestic sales; 20% on foreign sales. Charges clients for postage, photocopying, foreign mailing, faxing, and other special expenses.

◖ THE EVAN MARSHALL AGENCY, 6 Tristam Place, Pine Brook NJ 07058-9445. Member of AAR. This agency did not respond to our request for information. Query before submitting.

◖ ELISABETH MARTON AGENCY, One Union Square Room 612, New York NY 10003-3303. Member of AAR. This agency did not respond to our request for information. Query before submitting.

◖ HAROLD MATSON CO. INC., 276 Fifth Ave., New York NY 10001. Member of AAR. This agency did not respond to our request for information. Query before submitting.

◖ JED MATTES, INC., 2095 Broadway, Suite 302, New York NY 10023-2895. Member of AAR. This agency did not respond to our request for information. Query before submitting.

✓ ◖ MARGRET McBRIDE LITERARY AGENCY, 7744 Fay Ave., Suite 201, La Jolla CA 92037. (858)454-1550. Fax: (858)454-2156. E-mail: staff@mcbrideliterary.com. Website: www.mcbrideliterary.com. Estab. 1980. Member of AAR, Authors Guild. Represents 50 clients. 15% of clients are new/previously unpublished writers.

• Prior to opening her agency, Ms. McBride served in the marketing departments of Random House and Ballantine Books and the publicity departments of Warner Books and Pinnacle Books.

Represents: Nonfiction books, novels, audio, video film rights. **Considers these nonfiction areas:** biography/autobiography; business; child guidance/parenting; cooking/food/nutrition; current affairs; ethnic/cultural interests; gay/lesbian issues; government/politics/law; health/medicine; history; how-to; money/finance/economics; music/dance/theater/film;

popular culture; psychology; religious/inspirational; science/technology; self-help/personal improvement; sociology; sports; true crime/investigative; women's issues/women's studies. **Considers these fiction areas:** action/adventure; detective/police/crime; ethnic; historical; humor; literary; mainstream; mystery/suspense; thriller/espionage; westerns/frontier.

O— This agency specializes in mainstream fiction and nonfiction. Does not want to receive screenplays.
How to Contact: Query with synopsis or outline and SASE. Considers simultaneous queries and submissions. *No unsolicited mss.* Responds in 6 weeks to queries. Returns materials only with SASE.
Recent Sales: Sold 4 titles in the last year. *Special Circumstances*, by Sheldon Siegel (Bantam); *Instant Emotional Healing*, by George Pratt Ph.D. and Peter Lambrou Ph.D. (Broadway); *Big Bucks*, by Ken Blanchard and Sheldon Bowles (William Morrow).
Terms: Agent receives 15% commission on domestic sales; 15% on dramatic sales; 25% on foreign sales. Charges clients for overnight delivery, photocopying.

◎ GERARD McCAULEY, P.O. Box 844, Katonah NY 10536. (914)232-5700. Fax: (914)232-1506. Estab. 1970. Member of AAR. Represents 60 clients. 5% of clients are new/previously unpublished writers. Currently handles: 65% nonfiction books; 15% scholarly books; 20% college level textbooks.
Represents: *Currently not accepting new clients.*
O— This agency specializes in history, biography and general nonfiction.
How to Contact: Query with SASE. Responds in 1 month to queries; 2 months to mss. Prefers to read materials exclusively. Obtains most new clients through recommendations.
Recent Sales: Sold 40 titles in the last year. *Jazz*, by Ken Burns; *Founding Brothers*, by Joseph Ellis; *Approaching Fury*, by Stephen Oates.
Terms: Agent receives 15% commission on domestic sales; 20% on foreign sales.
Tips: "Always send a personal letter—not a form letter with recommendations from published writers. Will not read manuscripts and proposals sent simultaneously to several agencies and publishers."

◎ ANITA D. McCLELLAN ASSOCIATES, 50 Stearns St., Cambridge MA 02138. Member of AAR. This agency did not respond to our request for information. Query before submitting.

◎ RICHARD P. McDONOUGH, LITERARY AGENT, 34 Pinewood, Irvine CA 92604-3274. (949)654-5480. Fax: (949)654-5481. E-mail: cestmoi@msn.com. **Contact:** Richard P. McDonough. Estab. 1986. Represents over 30 clients. Currently handles: 80% nonfiction books; 20% fiction.
Represents: Nonfiction books, novels.
O— This agency specializes in nonfiction for general market and literary fiction. Does not want to receive genre material.
How to Contact: Query with outline and SASE. Does not accept queries by fax or e-mail. Considers simultaneous queries; no simultaneous submissions. Responds in 2 weeks to queries; 2 months to mss. Returns materials only with SASE.
Recent Sales: Sold 10 titles in the last year. *Muddy Waters* (biography), by Robert Gordon (Little, Brown & Co.); Untitled book of essays, by Thomas Lynch.
Terms: Agent receives 15% commission on domestic sales; 15% on dramatic sales; 15% on foreign sales. Charges clients for photocopying; postage for sold work only.

◎ McHUGH LITERARY AGENCY, 1033 Lyon Rd., Moscow ID 83843-9167. (208)882-0107. Fax: (847)628-0146. E-mail: elisabetmch@turbonet.com. **Contact:** Elisabet McHugh. Estab. 1994. Represents 81 clients. 40% of clients are new/previously unpublished writers. Currently handles: 80% nonfiction books, 20% novels.
● Prior to opening her agency, Ms. McHugh was a full-time writer for 14 years.
Represents: Nonfiction books; novels. **Considers these nonfiction areas:** animals; anthropology/archaeology; biography/autobiography; business; child guidance/parenting; cooking/food/nutrition; current affairs; health/medicine; history; how-to; military/war; nature/environment; science/technology; self-help/personal improvement; true crime/investigative; investing; alternative medicine. **Considers these fiction areas:** historical, mainstream, mystery, romance, thriller/espionage.
O— Does not want to receive children's books, poetry, science fiction, fantasy.
How to Contact: Query by e-mail. Considers simultaneous queries and submissions. Returns materials only with SASE.
Recent Sales: Sold 31 titles in the last year. *The Palestinian Solution*, by Charles Crone (Fictionworks); *The Life of Clark Gable*, by Christopher Spicer (McFarland & Co.); *Crimson Sky: The Air Battle for Korea*, by John Bruning (Brassey's, Inc.); *The Ten Commandments of Small-Business Success*, by Marguerite Kirk (Bookhome Publishing).
Terms: Agent receives 15% commission on domestic sales; 20% on foreign sales. Offers written contract. "Client must provide all copies of manuscripts needed for submissions."
Tips: "Be professional."

🅽 ◎ McINTOSH AND OTIS, INC., 310 Madson Ave., New York NY 10017. Member of AAR. This agency did not respond to our request for information. Query before submitting.

☑ **CLAUDIA MENZA LITERARY AGENCY**, 1170 Broadway, Suite 807, New York NY 10001. (212)889-6850. **Contact:** Claudia Menza. Estab. 1983. Member of AAR. Represents 111 clients. 50% of clients are new/previously unpublished writers. Currently handles 50% nonfiction books; 30% novles; 1% story collections; 2% juvenile books; 3% scholarly books; 1% poetry; 2% movie scripts; 2% TV scripts; 2% stage plays; 2% photographic books; 5% memoir.
  • Prior to becoming an agent, Ms. Menza was an editor/managing editor at a publishing company.
Represents: Nonfiction books, novels, story collections, juvenile books, scholarly books, poetry, photographic books, memoir, especially interested in African-American material. **Considers these nonfiction areas:** business; current affairs; education; ethnic/cultural interests; health/medicine; history; how-to; multicultural; music/dance/theater/film; photography; psychology; self-help/personal improvement.
  ⚬━ This agency specializes in African-American fiction and nonfiction, and editorial assistance.
Also Handles: Movie scripts, TV scripts, stage plays.
How to Contact: Send outline and 1 sample chapter. Prefers to read materials exclusively. Reponds in 2 weeks to queries; 4 months to mss. Returns materials only with SASE. Obtains most new clients through recommendations from others, queries/solicitations.
Recent Sales: This agency prefers not to share information on specific sales.
Terms: Agent receives 15% commission on domestic sales; 20% on foreign sales. Offers written contract.

☑ **HELEN MERRILL, LTD.**, 425 W. 23 St., 1F, New York NY 10011. Member of AAR. This agency did not respond to our request for information. Query before submitting.

☑ ☑ **DORIS S. MICHAELS LITERARY AGENCY, INC.**, 1841 Broadway, Suite #903, New York NY 10023. (212)265-9474. E-mail: mail@dsmagency.com. Website: www.dsmagency.com. **Contact:** Doris S. Michaels. Estab. 1994. Member of AAR, WNBA. Represents 30 clients. 50% of clients are new/previously unpublished writers. Currently handles: 40% nonfiction books; 60% novels.
  • Prior to opening her agency, Ms. Michaels was an editor for Prentice-Hall, consultant for Prudential-Bache, and an international consultant for the Union Bank of Switzerland.
Member Agents: Faye Bender.
Represents: Nonfiction books, novels. **Considers these nonfiction areas:** biography/autobiography; business; current affairs; ethnic/cultural interests; health; history; how-to; money/finance/economics; music/dance/theater/film; nature/environment; self-help/personal improvement; sports; women's issues/women's studies. **Considers these fiction areas:** action/adventure; contemporary issues; family saga; feminist; historical; literary; mainstream.
How to Contact: Query by e-mail. Considers simultaneous queries. *No phone calls or unsolicited mss.* Returns requested materials only with SASE. Obtains most new clients through recommendations from others and at conferences.
Recent Sales: Sold over 30 titles in the last year. *E-Writing*, by Dianna Booher (Pocket Books/Simon & Schuster); *All Roads to October*, by Maury Allen (St. Martin's Press); *How To Be A Rainmaker*, by Jeffrey J. Fox (Hyperion); *The Neatest Little Guide to Making Money Online*, by Jason Kelly (Plume). Other clients include Jeffrey J. Fox, Jason Kelly.
Terms: Agent receives 15% commission on domestic sales; 20% on foreign sales. Offers written contract, binding for 1 year, with 30-day cancellation clause. Charges clients for office expenses including deliveries, postage, photocopying and fax, not to exceed $150 for postage, photocopying, etc. without written permission. 100% of business is derived from commissions on sales.
Writers' Conferences: BEA (Chicago, June); Frankfurt Book Fair (Germany, October); London Book Fair; Society of Southwestern Authors; San Diego State University Writers' Conference; Willamette Writers' Conference; International Women's Writing Guild; American Society of Journalists and Authors; Maui Writers Conference.

☑ **MARTHA MILLARD LITERARY AGENCY**, 293 Greenwood Ave., Florham Park NJ 07932. Member of AAR. This agency did not respond to our request for information. Query before submitting.

☒ ☑ **THE MILLER AGENCY**, 1650 Broadway, New York NY 10019. (212)957-1933. Fax: (212)957-1953. E-mail: milleragency@compuserve.com. **Contact:** Angela Miller, Joan Ward. Estab. 1990. Represents 100 clients. 5% of clients are new/previously unpublished writers. Currently handles: 99% nonfiction books.
Represents: Nonfiction books. **Considers these nonfiction areas:** anthropology/archaeology; art/architecture/design; biography/autobiography; business; child guidance/parenting; cooking/food/nutrition; current affairs; ethnic/cultural interests; gay/lesbian issues; health/medicine; language/literature/criticism; New Age/metaphysics; psychology; self-help/personal improvement; sports; women's issues/women's studies.
  ⚬━ This agency specializes in nonfiction, multicultural arts, psychology, self-help, cookbooks, biography, travel, memoir, sports.
How to Contact: Send outline and sample chapters. Responds in 1 week to queries. Obtains most new clients through referrals.
Recent Sales: *The Circadian Connection*, by Sidney Baker, M.D. and Karen Baer; *Baby Minds*, by Linda Acredolo, Ph.D. and Susan Goodwyn, Ph.D.; *Simple to Complex*, by Jean-Georges Vongerichten and Mark Bittman (Broadway Books).
Terms: Agent receives 15% commission on domestic sales; 20-25% on foreign sales. Offers written contract, binding for 2-3 years, with 60-day cancellation clause. Charges clients for postage (express mail or messenger services) and photocopying. 100% of business is derived from commissions on sales.

MAUREEN MORAN AGENCY, Park West Station, P.O. Box 20191, New York NY 10025-1518. (212)222-3838. Fax: (212)531-3464. E-mail: maureenm@erols.com. **Contact:** Maureen Moran. Represents 30 clients. Currently handles: 100% novels.

● Prior to opening her agency, Ms. Moran worked for Donald MacCampbell (from whom she purchased the agency).

Represents: Novels.

○━ This agency specializes in women's book-length fiction in all categories. Does not want to receive science fiction, fantasy or juvenile books.

How to Contact: Query with outline and SASE; does not read unsolicited mss. Responds in 1 week to queries. Returns materials only with SASE.

Recent Sales: *Bed & Breakfast Mysteries*, by Mary Daheim (Avon); *Romance*, by Julianna Morris (Silhouette).

Terms: Agent receives 10% commission on domestic sales; 15-20% on foreign sales. Charges clients for extraordinary photocopying, courier and messenger, and bank wire fees, by prior arrangement with author.

Tips: "The agency does not handle unpublished writers."

HOWARD MORHAIM LITERARY AGENCY, 841 Broadway, Suite 604, New York NY 10003. Member of AAR. This agency did not respond to our request for information. Query before submitting.

WILLIAM MORRIS AGENCY, INC., 1325 Ave. of the Americas, New York NY 10019. (212)586-5100. West Coast Office: 151 El Camino Dr., Beverly Hills CA 90212. **Contact:** Mel Berger, vice president. Member of AAR.

Member Agents: Owen Laster; Mel Berger; Claudia Cross; Joni Evans; Tracy Fisher; Marcy Posner; Dan Strone; Bill Contardi; Peter Franklin; Samuel Liff; Gilbert Parker; George Lane.

Represents: Nonfiction books, novels.

How to Contact: Query with SASE. Does not accept queries by fax or e-mail.

Recent Sales: This agency prefers not to share information on specific sales.

Terms: Agent receives 10% commission on domestic sales; 20% on foreign sales.

HENRY MORRISON, INC., 105 S. Bedford Rd., Suite 306A, Mt. Kisco NY 10549. (914)666-3500. Fax: (914)241-7846. **Contact:** Henry Morrison. Estab. 1965. Signatory of WGA. Represents 48 clients. 5% of clients are new/previously unpublished writers. Currently handles: 5% nonfiction books; 5% juvenile books; 85% novels; 5% movie scripts.

Represents: Nonfiction books, novels. **Considers these nonfiction areas:** anthropology/archaeology; biography; government/politics/law; history; juvenile nonfiction. **Considers these fiction areas:** action/adventure; detective/police/crime; family saga.

How to Contact: Query with SASE. Responds in 2 weeks to queries; 3 months to mss. Obtains most new clients through recommendations from others.

Recent Sales: Sold 16 titles in the last year. *Legacy*, by Beverly Swerline (STS); *The Hades Factor*, by Robert Ludlum and Gayle Lynds (St. Martin's Press); *Pan Am 103*, by Susan and Daniel Cohen; *Untitled*, by David Morrell (Warner Books); *The Last Season*, by Ronald Florence (Forge Books); *Driftglass*, by Samuel R. Delany (Vintage Books). Other clients include Joe Gores, Eric Lusbader, Steve Samuel, Beverly Byrnne, Patricia Keneally-Morrison, Molly Katz.

Terms: Agent receives 15% commission on domestic sales; 25% on foreign sales. Charges clients for ms copies, bound galleys and finished books for submission to publishers, movie producers, foreign publishers.

MULTIMEDIA PRODUCT DEVELOPMENT, INC., 410 S. Michigan Ave., Suite 724, Chicago IL 60605-1465. (312)922-3063. Fax: (312)922-1905. E-mail: mpdinc@aol.com. **Contact:** Jane Jordan Browne, president. Estab. 1971. Member of AAR, RWA, MWA, SCBWI. Represents 175 clients. 2% of clients are new/previously unpublished writers. Currently handles: 60% nonfiction books; 39% novels; 1% movie scripts.

● Prior to opening her agency Ms. Browne served as the Managing Editor, then as head of the juvenile department for Hawthorn Books, Senior Editor for Thomas Y. Crowell, adult trade department and General Editorial and Production Manager for Macmillan Educational Services, Inc.

Member Agents: Scott A. Mendel (generalist); Janie McAdams (juvenile, romance).

Represents: Nonfiction books, novels. **Considers these nonfiction areas:** agriculture/horticulture; animals; anthropology/archaeology; biography/autobiography; business; child guidance/parenting; cooking/food/nutrition; crafts/hobbies; current affairs; ethnic/cultural issues; health/medicine; how-to; humor; juvenile nonfiction; memoirs; money/finance; nature; popular culture; psychology; religious/inspirational; science/technology; self-help/personal improvement; sociology; sports; travel; true crime/investigative; women's issues/women's studies. **Considers these fiction areas:** contemporary issues; detective/police/crime; ethnic; family saga; glitz; historical; juvenile; literary; mainstream; mystery/suspense; picture book; religious/inspirational; romance (contemporary, gothic, historical, regency, western); sports; thriller/espionage.

○━ "We are generalists looking for professional writers with finely honed skill in writing. We are partial to authors with promotion savvy. We work closely with our authors through the entire publishing process, from proposal to after publication." Actively seeking highly commercial mainstream fiction and nonfiction. Does not want to receive poetry, short stories, plays, screenplays, articles.

How to Contact: Query "by mail with SASE required." *"No unsolicited mss accepted."* Does not accept queries by e-mail or fax. Considers simultaneous queries; prefers to read solicited materials exclusively. Responds within 1 week to queries; 6 weeks to mss. Returns materials only with SASE. Obtains most new clients through "referrals, queries by professional, marketable authors."

Recent Sales: Sold 52 titles in the last year. *Lineage of Grace*, by Francine Rivers (Tyndale House); *Alice's Tulips*, by Sandra Dallas (St. Martin's Press); *Lord of the Nutcracker Men*, by Iain Lawrence (Random House); *The Complete Procastinator's Handbook*, by Rita Emmett (Walker); *American Folk Tales*, by Hugh Rawson (Overlook Press); *The Spy Wore Shades*, by Martha Freeman (HarperCollins).

Terms: Agent receives 15% commission on domestic sales; 20% on foreign sales. Offers written contract, binding for 2 years. Charges clients for photocopying, overseas postage, faxes, phone calls.

Writers' Conferences: BEA (Chicago, June); Frankfurt Book Fair (Frankfurt, October); RWA (Washington DC, July); CBA (New Orleans).

Tips: "If interested in agency representation, be well informed."

DEE MURA ENTERPRISES, INC., 269 W. Shore Dr., Massapequa NY 11758-8225. (516)795-1616. Fax: (516)795-8797. E-mail: samurai5@ix.netcom.com. **Contact:** Dee Mura, Ken Nyquist. Estab. 1987. Signatory of WGA. 50% of clients are new/previously unpublished writers. Currently handles: 25% nonfiction books; 10% scholarly books; 15% juvenile books; 25% novels; 25% movie scripts.

• Prior to opening her agency, Ms. Mura was a public relations executive with a roster of film and entertainment clients; and worked in editorial for major weekly news magazines.

Represents: Nonfiction books, scholarly books, juvenile books. **Considers these nonfiction areas:** agriculture/horticulture; animals; anthropology/archaeology; biography/autobiography; business; child guidance/parenting; computers/electronics; current affairs; education; ethnic/cultural interests; gay/lesbian issues; government/politics/law; health/medicine; history; how-to; humor; juvenile nonfiction; memoirs; military/war; money/finance/economics; nature/environment; science/technology; self-help/personal improvement; sociology; sports; travel; true crime/investigative; women's issues/women's studies. **Considers these fiction areas:** action/adventure; contemporary issues; detective/police/crime; ethnic; experimental; family saga; fantasy; feminist; gay; glitz; historical; humor/satire; juvenile; lesbian; literary; mainstream; mystery/suspense; psychic/supernatural; regional; romance (contemporary, gothic, historical, regency); science fiction; sports; thriller/espionage; westerns/frontier; young adult.

○→ "We work on everything, but are especially interested in literary fiction, commercial fiction and nonfiction, thrillers and espionage, true life stories, true crime, women's stories and issues." Actively seeking "unique nonfiction manuscripts and proposals; novelists who are great storytellers; contemporary writers with distinct voices and passion." Does not want to receive "ideas for sitcoms, novels, film, etc.; queries without SASEs."

Also Handles: Feature film, documentary, animation, TV MOW, miniseries, episodic drama, sitcom, variety show. **Considers these script subject areas:** action/adventure; cartoon/animation; comedy; contemporary issues; detective/police/crime; family saga; fantasy; feminist; gay; glitz; historical; horror; humor; juvenile; mainstream; mystery/suspense; psychic/supernatural; religious/inspirational; romantic comedy and drama; science fiction; sports; teen; thriller; western/frontier.

How to Contact: Query with SASE. Accepts queries by e-mail. Considers simultaneous queries. Responds in approximately 2 weeks to queries. Returns materials only with SASE. Obtains most new clients through recommendations from others and queries.

Recent Sales: Sold over 40 book titles and over 35 script projects in the last year.

Terms: Agent receives 15% commission on domestic sales; 20% on foreign sales. Offers written contract. Charges clients for photocopying, mailing expenses, overseas and long distance phone calls and faxes.

Tips: "Please include a paragraph on writer's background even if writer has no literary background and a brief synopsis of the project. We enjoy well-written query letters that tell us about the project and the author."

JEAN V. NAGGAR LITERARY AGENCY, 216 E. 75th St., Suite 1E, New York NY 10021. Member of AAR. This agency did not respond to our request for information. Query before submitting.

RUTH NATHAN, 53 E. 34th St., New York NY 10016. Member of AAR. This agency did not respond to our request for information. Query before submitting.

NATIONAL WRITERS LITERARY AGENCY, a division of GTR, Inc., 3140 S. Peoria #295, Aurora CO 80014. (720)851-1936. Fax: (720)851-1960. E-mail: aajwiii@aol.com. **Contact:** Andrew J. Whelchel III. Estab. 1987. Represents 52 clients. 20% of clients are new/previously unpublished writers. Currently handles: 60% nonfiction books; 20% juvenile books; 12% novels; 1% novellas; 1% poetry; 6% scripts.

TO LEARN MORE ABOUT THE PUBLISHING INDUSTRY, look for the helpful resources in **Books of Interest** and **Websites of Interest** listed in the back of this book.

Member Agents: Andrew J. Whelchel III (screenplays, nonfiction); Jason S. Cangialosi (nonfiction); Shayne Sharpe (novels, screenplays, fantasy).

Represents: Nonfiction books, juvenile books, textbooks. **Considers these nonfiction areas:** animals; biography/autobiography; child guidance/parenting; education; government/politics/law; how-to; juvenile nonfiction; popular culture; science/technology; sports; travel. **Considers these fiction areas:** action/adventure; juvenile; mainstream; science fiction; sports; young adult; suspense; mysteries.

　　O→ Actively seeking "music, business, cutting edge novels; pop culture, compelling true stories, science and technology." Does not want to receive "concept books, westerns, over published self-help topics."

How to Contact: Query with outline and SASE. Accepts queries by e-mail and fax. Considers simultaneous queries and submissions. Responds in 6 weeks to queries; 2 months to mss. Returns materials only with SASE. Obtains most new clients at conferences or over the transom.

Recent Sales: Sold 25 titles in the last year. *Joe Pickett*, 3 novels by first-time author C.J. Box (Putnam); *The After-Hours Trader*, by Mike Sincere (McGraw-Hill); *Escapade*, by Natalie Cosby (Orly Adelson Productions); *Love One Another* (3-book series), by Gloria Chisholm (Waterbrook Press/Random House).

Terms: Agent receives 15% commission on domestic sales; 20% on foreign sales; 10% on film. Offers written contract, binding for 1 year with 30-day termination notice.

Writers' Conferences: National Writers Association (Denver, CO, 2nd weekend in June); Sandpiper (Miami, FL, 1st weekend in October).

Reading List: Reads *Popular Mechanics*, *The Futurist*, *Industry Standard*, *Money*, *Rolling Stone*, *Maxim*, *Details*, *Spin* and *Buzz* to find new clients.

Tips: "Query letters should include a great hook just as if you only had a few seconds to impress us. A professional package gets professional attention. Always include return postage!"

■ ◎ **KAREN NAZOR LITERARY AGENCY**, Opera Plaza, PMB 124, 601 Van Ness Ave., Suite E, San Francisco CA 94102. (415)682-7676. Fax: (415)682-7666. E-mail: agentnazor@aol.com (queries only). **Contact:** Karen Nazor. Estab. 1991. Represents 35 clients. 15% of clients are new/previously unpublished writers. Currently handles: 75% nonfiction books; 10% electronic; 10% fiction.

　　● Prior to opening her agency, Ms. Nazor served a brief apprenticeship with Raines & Raines and was assistant to Peter Ginsberg, president of Curtis Brown Ltd.

Member Agents: Kris Ashley (literary and commercial fiction).

Represents: Nonfiction books, novels, novellas. **Considers these nonfiction areas:** biography; business; computers/electronics; current affairs; ethnic/cultural interests; government/politics/law; history; how-to; music/dance/theater/film; nature/environment; parenting; photography; popular culture; science/technology; sociology; sports; travel; women's issues/women's studies. **Considers these fiction areas:** cartoon/comic; contemporary issues; ethnic; feminist; literary; regional; women's.

　　O→ This agency specializes in "good writers! Mostly nonfiction—arts, culture, politics, technology, civil rights, etc."

How to Contact: Query (preferred) or send outline/proposal (accepted). Accepts queries by e-mail. Considers simultaneous queries. Responds in 2 weeks to queries; up to 2 months to mss. Returns materials only with SASE. Obtains most new clients from referrals from editors and writers; online; teaching classes on publishing; newspaper article on agency.

Recent Sales: Sold 12 titles in the last year. *The Secret Life of Dust*, by Hannah Holmes (John Wiley & Sons); *Childhood and Adolescent Obsessive Compulsive Disorder*, by Mitzi Waltz (O'Reilly).

Terms: Agent receives 15% commission on domestic sales; 20% on foreign sales. Offers written contract. Charges clients for express mail services, photocopying costs.

Tips: "I'm interested in writers who want a long term, long haul relationship. Not a one-book writer, but a writer who has many ideas, is productive, professional, passionate and meets deadlines!"

⊘ **THE CRAIG NELSON COMPANY**, 115 W. 18th St., 5th Floor, New York NY 10011. Member of AAR. This agency did not respond to our request for information. Query before submitting.

☑ ◎ **NEW CENTURY LITERARY AGENCY**, Box 7113, The Woodlands TX 77387-7113. (936)295-5357. Fax: (936)295-0409. E-mail: bookagts@lcc.net. Website: www.NewCenturyLitAgcy.com. **Contact:** Thomas Fensch or Sharon Wanslee. Estab. 1998. Represents 25 clients. 80% of clients are new/previously unpublished writers. Currently handles: 100% nonfiction books.

　　● Prior to opening heir agency, Mr. Fensch was an editor, book critic and professor; Ms. Wanslee was an editor and art therapy teacher.

Member Agents: Thomas Fensch; Sharon Wanslee.

Represents: Nonfiction books, juvenile books. **Considers these nonfiction areas:** animals; biography/autobiography; business; child guidance/parenting; cooking/food/nutrition; current affairs; education; ethnic/cultural interests; government/politics/law; history; how-to; humor; juvenile nonfiction; language/literature/criticism; memoirs; military/war; money/finance/economics; mustic/dance/theater/film; nature/environment; popular culture; psychology; self-help/personal improvement; sociology; sports; true crime/investigative; women's issues/women's studies.

　　O→ This agency specializes in general nonfiction. Actively seeking biographies/memoirs; business and personal success; communication/journalism; current affairs; parenting; popular culture; history; multi-cultural (Hispanic); how-to; southwestern and mountain states subjects; sports; trends; women's issues/women's health; selected children's books. Does not want to receive computer books; gothic romances; horror novels; poetry; science fiction; screenplays; westerns or anything of a nonbook-length nature.

How to Contact: Query with SASE. Does not accept queries by fax or e-mail. Considers simultaneous queries. Responds in 3 weeks to queries; 1 month to mss. Returns material only with SASE. Obtains most new clients through listings in reference books, conferences.

Recent Sales: *Nineteenth Century American Protest Poetry*, by Paul Christensen, (Oxford University Press); others.

Terms: Agent receives 15% commission on domestic sales; 20% on foreign sales. Offers written contract. Charges clients for photocopying, express mail and other office expenses if over $100.

Tips: "Be aware of the marketing potential of your book. Publishers won't ask, 'Is it well written?' (They assume it is.) They will ask, 'How can we sell it?' "

☑ ◐ **NEW ENGLAND PUBLISHING ASSOCIATES, INC.**, P.O. Box 5, Chester CT 06412-0645. (860)345-READ and (860)345-4976. Fax: (860)345-3660. E-mail: nepa@nepa.com. Website: www.nepa.com. **Contact:** Elizabeth Frost-Knappman, Edward W. Knappman, Kristine Schiavi, Ron Formica, or Victoria Harlow. Estab. 1983. Member of AAR, ASJA, Authors Guild, Connecticut Press Club. Represents over 100 clients. 15% of clients are new/previously unpublished writers.

Represents: Nonfiction books. **Considers these nonfiction areas:** biography/autobiography; business; child guidance/parenting; government/politics/law; health/medicine; history; language/literature/criticism; military/war; money/finance/economics; nature/environment; psychology; science/technology; personal improvement; sociology; true crime/investigative; women's issues/women's studies.

    ○➤ This agency specializes in adult nonfiction books of serious purpose.

How to Contact: Send outline/proposal with SASE. Considers simultaneous queries. Responds in 1 month to queries; 5 weeks to mss. Returns materials only with SASE.

Recent Sales: Sold 60 titles in the last year. *The Woman's Migraine Survival Handbook*, by Christina Peterson and Christine Adamec (HarperCollins); *Dreams in the Key of Blue, A Novel*, by John Philpin (Bantam); *Ice Blink: The Mysterious Fate of Sir John Franklin's Lost Polar Expedition*, by Scott Cookman (Wiley); *Susan Sontag*, by Carl Rollyson and Lisa Paddock (Norton).

Terms: Agent receives 15% commission on domestic sales; 20% foreign sales (split with overseas agent). Offers written contract, binding for 6 months.

Writers' Conferences: BEA (Chicago, June); ALA (San Antonio, January); ALA (New York, July).

Tips: "Check our website for tips on proposals and advice on how to market your book."

☑ ◐ **NINE MUSES AND APOLLO INC.**, 525 Broadway, Suite 201, New York NY 10012. (212)431-2665. **Contact:** Ling Lucas. Estab. 1991. Represents 50 clients. 10% of clients are new/previously unpublished writers. Currently handles: 90% nonfiction books; 10% novels.

    ● Ms. Lucas formerly served as a vice president, sales & marketing director and associate publisher of Warner Books.

Represents: Nonfiction books. **Considers these nonfiction areas:** animals; biography/autobiography; business; current affairs; ethnic/cultural interests; health/medicine; language/literature/criticism; psychology; spirituality; women's issues/women's studies. **Considers these fiction areas:** commercial; ethnic; literary.

    ○➤ This agency specializes in nonfiction. Does not want to receive children's and young adult material.

How to Contact: Send outline, 2 sample chapters and SASE. Responds in 1 month to mss.

Recent Sales: Sold 24 titles in the last year. *Reversing Adrenal Burnout*, Dr. Jesse Hanley & Nancy Deville (Putnam); *The Prayer Party*, by Carolyn Manji (Harmony); *Essential Spirituality*, by Roger Walsh M.D., Ph.D. (Wiley); and *Utne Reader's Visionaries*, by The Utne Reader (Morrow).

Terms: Agent receives 15% commission on domestic sales; 20-25% on foreign sales. Offers written contract. Charges clients for photocopying proposals and mss.

Tips: "Your outline should already be well developed, cogent, and reveal clarity of thought about the general structure and direction of your project."

◐ **THE BETSY NOLAN LITERARY AGENCY**, 224 W. 29th St., 15th Floor, New York NY 10001. (212)967-8200. Fax: (212)967-7292. **Contact:** Donald Lehr, president. Estab. 1980. Member of AAR. Represents 200 clients. 10% of clients are new/previously unpublished writers. Works with a small number of new/previously unpublished authors. Currently handles: 90% nonfiction books; 10% novels.

Member Agents: Donald Lehr; Carla Glasser.

Represents: Nonfiction books, novels.

How to Contact: Query with outline. Does not accept queries by fax. Considers simultaneous queries and submissions. Responds in 3 weeks to queries; 2 months to mss. Returns materials only with SASE.

Recent Sales: Sold 15 titles in the last year. *Mangia*, by Sasha Muniak/Ricardo Diaz (HarperCollins); *The Buttercup Bake Shop Cookbook*, by Jennifer Appel (Simon & Schuster); *Desperation Dinners*, by Beverly Mills and Alicia Ross (Workman); *Bridgehampton Weekends*, by Ellen Wright (William Morrow).

Terms: Agent receives 15% commission on domestic sales; 20% on foreign sales.

NONFICTION PUBLISHING PROJECTS, 12 Rally Court, Fairfax CA 94930. Member of AAR. This agency did not respond to our request for information. Query before submitting.

THE NORMA-LEWIS AGENCY, 311 W. 43rd St., Suite 602, New York NY 10036. (212)664-0807. **Contact:** Norma Liebert. Estab. 1980. 50% of clients are new/previously unpublished writers. Currently handles: 60% juvenile books; 40% adult books.
Represents: Juvenile and adult nonfiction and fiction. **Considers these nonfiction areas:** art/architecture/design; biography/autobiography; child guidance/parenting; cooking/food/nutrition; crafts/hobbies; current affairs; ethnic/cultural interests; government/politics/law; health/medicine; history; juvenile nonfiction; music/dance/theater/film; nature/environment; photography; popular culture; self-help/personal improvement; true crime/investigative; women's issues/women's studies. **Considers these fiction areas:** action/adventure; contemporary issues; detective/police/crime; family saga; historical; horror; humor/satire; juvenile; mainstream; mystery/suspense; picture book; romance (contemporary, gothic, historical, regency); thriller/espionage; westerns/frontier; young adult.
   O➔ This agency specializes in juvenile books (pre-school to high school).
Also Handles: Miniseries, documentaries, movie scripts, TV scripts, radio scripts, stage plays.
How to Contact: Query with SASE. Considers simultaneous queries; prefers to read ms submissions exclusively. Responds in 6 weeks. Returns materials only with SASE.
Recent Sales: *Viper Quarry* and *Pitchfork Hollow*, both by Dean Feldmeyer (Pocket Books).
Terms: Agent receives 15% commission on domestic sales; 20% on foreign sales.

HAROLD OBER ASSOCIATES, 425 Madison Ave., New York NY 10017. (212)759-8600. Fax: (212)759-9428. Estab. 1929. Member of AAR. Represents 250 clients. 10% of clients are new/previously unpublished writers. Currently handles: 35% nonfiction books; 15% juvenile books; 50% novels.
Member Agents: Phyllis Westberg; Wendy Schmalz; Emma Sweeney; Craig Tenney (not accepting new clients).
Represents: Nonfiction books, juvenile books, novels. **Considers all nonfiction and fiction subjects.**
How to Contact: Query letter *only* with SASE; "faxed queries are not read." Responds in 1 week to queries; 3 weeks to mss. Obtains most new clients through recommendations from others.
Recent Sales: This agency prefers not to share information on specific sales.
Terms: Agent receives 15% commission on domestic sales; 20% on foreign sales. Charges clients for photocopying and express mail or package services.

FIFI OSCARD AGENCY INC., 24 W. 40th St., New York NY 10018. (212)764-1100. **Contact:** Ivy Fischer Stone, Literary Department. Estab. 1956. Member of AAR, signatory of WGA. Represents 108 clients. 5% of clients are new/previously unpublished writers. Currently handles: 40% nonfiction books; 40% novels; 5% movie scripts; 10% stage plays; 5% TV scripts.
Member Agents: Carolyn French (plays).
Represents: Nonfiction books, novels, movie scripts, stage plays.
   O➔ This agency specializes in literary novels, commercial novels, mysteries and nonfiction, especially celebrity biographies and autobiographies.
How to Contact: Query with outline and SASE. *No unsolicited mss please.* Prefers to read materials exclusively. Responds in 1 week to queries if SASE enclosed. Returns materials only with SASE.
Recent Sales: *Dead Center*, by James MacGregor Burns and Georgia J. Sorenson (Scribner); *Get a Life*, by William Shatner (Pocket Books); *Elementary, My Dear Groucho*, by Ron Goulart (St. Martin's Press); *A Photographic Memory*, by William Claxton (Power House Books); **Movie/TV MOW scripts optioned/sold:** *Wit*, by Margaret Edson (The Wit L.L.C.).
Terms: Agent receives 15% commission on domestic sales; 10% on dramatic sales; 20% on foreign sales. Charges clients for photocopying expenses.
Tips: "Writer must have published articles or books in major markets or have screen credits if movie scripts, etc."

THE PALMER & DODGE AGENCY, One Beacon St., Boston MA 02108. (617)573-0100. Fax: (617)227-4420. E-mail: swilson@palmerdodge.com. Website: www.palmerdodge.com. **Contact:** Stephanie Wilson. Estab. 1990. Represents 100 clients. 5% of clients are new/previously unpublished writers. Currently handles: 80% nonfiction books; 20% novels.
Member Agents: John Taylor (Ike) Williams, director (books, film, TV); Jill Kneerim, managing director (books); Rob McQuilken, agent (books); Elaine Rogers, director of subsidiary rights (dramatic rights, foreign, audio).
Represents: Nonfiction books, novels. **Considers these nonfiction areas:** anthropology/archaeology; biography/autobiography; business; child guidance/parenting; current affairs; education; ethnic/cultural interests; gay/lesbian issues; government/politics/law; health/medicine; history; language/literature/criticism; money/finance/economics; music/dance/theater/film; nature/environment; New Age/metaphysics; popular culture; psychology; religous/inspirational; science/technology; self-help/personal improvement; sociology; women's issues/women's studies. **Considers these fiction areas:** contemporary issues; ethnic; feminist; gay; literary; mainstream.
   O➔ This agency specializes in trade nonfiction and quality fiction for adults. Dramatic rights for books and life story rights only. Does not want to receive genre fiction.
How to Contact: Query with outline/proposal. Responds in 1 month to queries; 3 months to mss. Obtains most new clients through recommendations from others.

Recent Sales: *The First Counsel*, by Brad Meltzer (Warner); *The Childhood Roots of Adult Happiness*, by Edward M. Hallowell (Ballantine); *The Wind Chill Factor*, by Norris Church Mailer (Random House).

Terms: Agent receives 15% commission on domestic sales; 20% on foreign sales. Offers written contract, with 4-month cancellation clause. Charges clients for direct expenses (postage, phone, photocopying, messenger service). 100% of business is derived from commissions on sales.

Tips: "We are taking very few new clients for representation."

⓿ ◎ **PARAVIEW, INC., (Specialized: spiritual/New Age)**, 1674 Broadway, Suite 4B, New York NY 10019. E-mail: paraview@inch.com. **Contact:** Sandra Martin. Estab. 1988. Represents 120 clients. 50% of clients are new/previously unpublished writers. Currently handles: 80% nonfiction books; 10% scholarly books; 10% fiction.

Member Agents: Sandra Martin (nonfiction self-help); Lisa Hagan (fiction and nonfiction self-help).

Represents: Nonfiction and fiction books. **Considers all nonfiction areas. Considers these fiction areas:** action/adventure; contemporary issues; ethnic; feminist; historical; literary; mainstream; psychic/supernatural; regional; romance; thriller/espionage.

   O→ This agency specializes in spiritual, New Age and paranormal.

How to Contact: Query with synopsis, author bio and SASE. Accepts queries by e-mail. Considers simultaneous queries and submissions. Responds in 1 month to queries; 3 months to mss. Obtains most new clients through recommendations from editors.

Recent Sales: Sold 30 titles in the last year. *Miracles in the Storm*, by Mark Macy (NAL); *Dream Magic*, by Sirona Knight (HarperSanFrancisco); *The Coming Global Superstorm*, by Art Bell and Whitley Strieber (Pocket Books); *UFOs, JFK & Elvis: Conspiracies You Don't Have to Be Crazy to Believe*, by Richard Belzer (Ballantine); *Writings On the Wall*, by Paula Roberts (Element).

Terms: Agent receives 15% commission on domestic sales; 20% on foreign sales.

Writers' Conferences: BEA (Chicago, June); E3—Electronic Entertainment Exposition.

Tips: "New writers should have their work edited, critiqued, and carefully reworked prior to submission. First contact should be via regular mail."

⓿ **THE RICHARD PARKS AGENCY**, 138 E. 16th St., 5th Floor, New York NY 10003. (212)254-9067. **Contact:** Richard Parks. Estab. 1988. Member of AAR. Currently handles: 50% nonfiction books; 5% young adult books; 40% novels; 5% short story collections.

   • Prior to opening his agency, Mr. Parks served as an agent with Curtis Brown, Ltd.

Represents: Nonfiction books, novels. **Considers these nonfiction areas:** animals; anthropology/archaeology; art/architecture/design; biography/autobiography; business; child guidance/parenting; cooking/food/nutrition; crafts/hobbies; current affairs; ethnic/cultural interests; gay/lesbian issues; government/politics; health/medicine; history; horticulture; how-to; humor; language/literature/criticism; memoirs; military/war; money/finance/economics; music/dance/theater/film; nature/environment; popular culture; psychology; science/technology; self-help/personal improvement; sociology; travel; women's issues/women's studies. **Considers fiction by referral only.**

   O→ Actively seeking narrative nonfiction. Does not want to receive unsolicited material.

How to Contact: Query by mail only with SASE. "No calls, faxes or e-mails, please. We will not accept any unsolicited material." Considers simultaneous queries and submissions, if advised in advance. Responds in 2 weeks to queries. Returns materials only with SASE. Obtains most new clients through recommendations and referrals.

Recent Sales: *A House Named Brazil*, by Audrey Schulman (William Morrow); *Exiting Nirvana*, by Clara Claiborne Park (Little, Brown); *One Bad Thing*, by Bill Eidson (TOR); *Double Date*, by Barbara Taylor McCafferty and Beverly Taylor Herald (Kensington); *All We Know of Heaven*, by Remy Rougeau (Houghton Mifflin); *Highwire Moon*, by Susan Straight (Houghton Mifflin); *The Sailor's Wife*, by Helen Benedict (Zoland); *The Spark*, by Dr. Glenn Gaesser and Karla Dougherty (Simon & Schuster); *Searching for John Ford*, by Joseph McBride (St. Martin's Press); *And Give You Peace*, by Jessica Treadway (Graywolf Press).

Terms: Agent receives 15% commission on domestic sales; 20% on foreign sales. Charges clients for photocopying or any unusual expense incurred at the writer's request.

✓ ◐ **KATHI J. PATON LITERARY AGENCY**, 19 W. 55th St., New York NY 10019-4907. (908)647-2117. E-mail: kpjlitbiz@aol.com. **Contact:** Kathi Paton. Estab. 1987. Currently handles: 65% nonfiction books; 35% fiction.

Represents: Nonfiction, novels, short story collections. **Considers these nonfiction areas:** business; child guidance/parenting; inspirational; personal investing; how-to; nature/environment; psychology; women's issues/women's studies. **Considers literary and mainstream fiction; short stories.**

   O→ This agency specializes in adult nonfiction.

How to Contact: For nonfiction, send proposal, sample chapter and SASE. For fiction, send first 40 pages, plot summary or 3 short stories and SASE. Accepts queries by e-mail. Considers simultaneous queries and submissions. Responds and returns materials only with SASE. Obtains most new clients through recommendations from other clients.

Recent Sales: *Future Wealth*, by McInerney and White (St. Martin's Press); *Unraveling the Mystery of Autism*, by Karyn Seroussi (Simon & Schuster).

Terms: Agent receives 15% commission on domestic sales; 20% on foreign sales. Offers written contract. Charges clients for photocopying.

Writers' Conferences: Attends major regional panels, seminars and conferences.

Tips: "Write well."

◔ RODNEY PELTER, 129 E. 61st St., New York NY 10021. (212)838-3432. **Contact:** Rodney Pelter. Estab. 1978. Represents 10 clients.
Represents: Nonfiction books, novels. **Considers all nonfiction areas. Considers most fiction areas.**
　　O→ Does not want to receive juvenile, romance, science fiction.
How to Contact: Query with SASE. No unsolicited mss. Responds in 3 months. Obtains most new clients through recommendations from others.
Recent Sales: This agency prefers not to share information on specific sales.
Terms: Agent receives 15% commission on domestic sales; 20% on foreign sales. Offers written contract. Charges clients for foreign postage, photocopying.

⒩ ◑ L. PERKINS ASSOCIATES, 1500 Arlington Ave., Riverdale NY 10471. (718)543-5344. Fax: (718)543-5354. E-mail: lperkinsagency@yahoo.com. **Contact:** Lori Perkins. Estab. 1990. Member of AAR. Represents 50 clients; 10% of clients are new/previously unpublished writers. Currently handles: nonfiction books; novels.
　　● Ms. Perkins has been an agent for 11 years. Her agency has an affiliate agency, Southern Literary Group. She is also the author of *The Insider's Guide to Getting an Agent* (Writer's Digest Books).
Represents: Nonfiction, novels. **Considers these nonfiction areas:** pop culture. **Considers these fiction areas:** fantasy; horror; science fiction; dark literary fiction.
　　O→ All of Ms. Perkins's clients write both fiction and nonfiction. "This combination keeps my clients publishing for years. I am also a published author so I know what it takes to write a book." Actively seeking a Latino *Gone With the Wind* and *Waiting to Exhale*, and urban ethnic horror. Does not want to receive "anything outside of the above categories, i.e., westerns, romance."
How to Contact: Query with SASE. Accepts queries by fax. Considers simultaneous queries and manuscripts. Responds in 6 weeks on queries; 3 months on mss. Returns materials only with SASE. Obtains most new clients through recommendations from others, queries/solicitations, conferences.
Recent Sales: Sold 100 titles in the last year. *An Unauthorized Biography of J.K. Rowling*, by Marc Shapiro; *An Unauthorized Guide to Dragonballz*, by Lois and Daniel Gresh; *Strangewood*, by Christopher Goldin; *Science of Star Wars*, by Jeanne Cavelors.
Terms: Agent receives 15% commission on domestic sales; 20% on foreign sales. No written contract. Charges clients for photocopying.
Writers' Conferences: Maui Writer's Conference, NECON, BEA, Horror Writers of America Conference.
Tips: "Research your field and contact professional writers' organizations to see who is looking for what. Finish your novel before querying agents. Read my book, *An Insider's Guide to Getting an Agent* to get a sense of how agents operate."

✓ ◑ STEPHEN PEVNER, INC., 248 W. 73rd St., 2nd Floor, New York NY 10023. (212)496-0474. Also: 100 N. Crescent Dr., Beverly Hills CA 90210. (310)385-4160. Fax: (310)385-6633. E-mail: spevner@aol.com. **Contact:** Stephen Pevner. Estab. 1991. Represents under 50 clients. 50% of clients are new/previously unpublished writers. Currently handles: 25% nonfiction books; 25% movie scripts; 25% novels; TV scripts; stage plays.
Represents: Nonfiction books, novels. **Considers these nonfiction areas:** biography/autobiography; ethnic/cultural interests; gay/lesbian issues; history; humor; language/literature/criticism; memoirs; music/dance/theater/film; New Age/metaphysics; photography; popular culture; religious/inspirational; sociology; travel. **Considers these fiction areas:** cartoon/comic; contemporary issues; erotica; ethnic; experimental; gay; glitz; horror; humor/satire; lesbian; literary; mainstream; psychic/supernatural; thriller/espionage; urban.
　　O→ This agency specializes in motion pictures, novels, humor, pop culture, urban fiction, independent filmmakers. Actively seeking urban fiction, popular culture, screenplays and film proposals.
Also Handles: Feature film, documentary, animation; TV MOW, TV scripts, miniseries, episodic drama; theatrical stage plays. **Considers these script subject areas:** comedy; contemporary issues; detective/police/crime; gay; glitz; horror; humor; lesbian; mainstream; romantic comedy and drama; teen; thriller.
How to Contact: Query with outline/proposal. Does not accept queries by e-mail or fax. Prefers to read materials exclusively. Responds in 2 weeks to queries; 1 month to mss. Obtains most new clients through recommendations from others.
Recent Sales: *Your Friends and Neighbors*, by Neil Labote; *The Vagina Monologues*, by Eve Ensler; *Guide to Life*, by The Five Lesbian Brothers; *Noise From the Underground*, by Michael Levine. Other clients include Richard Linklater (*Slacker, Dazed & Confused, Before Sunrise*); Gregg Araki (*The Living End, Doom Generation*); Tom DiCillo (*Living in Oblivion*); Genvieve Turner/Rose Troche (*Go Fish*); Todd Solondz (*Welcome to the Dollhouse*); Neil LaBute (*In the Company of Men*).
Terms: Agent receives 15% commission on domestic sales; 20% on foreign sales. Offers written contract, binding for 1 year, with 6-week cancellation clause. 100% of business is derived from commissions on sales.
Tips: "Be persistent but civilized."

✓ ◑ PINDER LANE & GARON-BROOKE ASSOCIATES, LTD., 159 W. 53rd St., Suite 14E, New York NY 10019-6005. (212)489-0880. E-mail: pinderl@interport.net. **Contact:** Robert Thixton. Member of AAR, signatory of WGA. Represents 80 clients. 20% of clients are new/previously unpublished writers. Currently handles: 25% nonfiction books; 75% novels.
Member Agents: Nancy Coffey (contributing agent); Dick Duane; Robert Thixton.

Represents: Nonfiction books, novels. **Considers these nonfiction areas:** biography/autobiography; child guidance/parenting; gay/lesbian issues; health/medicine; history; memoirs; military/war; music/dance/theater/film; psychology; self-help/personal improvement; true crime/investigative. **Considers these fiction areas:** contemporary issues; detective/police/crime; family saga; fantasy; gay; literary; mainstream; mystery/suspense; romance; science fiction.

O→ This agency specializes in mainstream fiction and nonfiction. Does not want to receive screenplays, TV series teleplays or dramatic plays.

How to Contact: Query with SASE. Accepts queries by e-mail. Prefers to read materials exclusively. Responds in 3 weeks to queries; 2 months to mss. Obtains most new clients through referrals and from queries.

Recent Sales: Sold 20 titles in the last year. *Nobody's Safe* and *The 4 Phaseman*, by Richard Steinberg (Doubleday); *The Kill Box* and *The Third Consequence*, by Chris Stewart (M. Evans); *Return to Christmas*, by Chris Heimerdinger (Ballantine); *Savage Desire*, by Rosemary Rogers (Mira Books).

Terms: Agent receives 15% on domestic sales; 30% on foreign sales. Offers written contract, binding for 3-5 years.

Tips: "With our literary and media experience, our agency is uniquely positioned for the current and future direction publishing is taking. Send query letter first giving the essence of the manuscript and a personal or career bio with SASE."

N⬤ JULIE POPKIN, 15340 Albright St., #204, Pacific Palisades CA 90272-2520. (310)459-2834. **Contact:** Julie Popkin. Estab. 1989. Represents 35 clients. 30% of clients are new/previously unpublished writers. Currently handles: 70% nonfiction books; 30% fiction.

● Prior to opening her agency, Ms. Popkin taught at the university level and did freelance editing and writing.

Member Agents: Julie Popkin; Margaret McCord (fiction, memoirs, biography).

Represents: Nonfiction books, novels, translations. **Considers these nonfiction areas:** art; criticism; feminist; history; politics. Represents a "wide variety of nonfiction." **Considers these fiction areas:** literary; mainstream; mystery.

O→ This agency specializes in selling book-length mss including fiction and nonfiction. Especially interested in social issues, ethnic and minority subjects, Latin American authors. Does not want to receive New Age, spiritual, romance, science fiction.

How to Contact: No fax submissions. "Must include SASE with query!" Responds in 1 month to queries; 2 months to mss. "Mostly clients find me through guides and personal contacts."

Recent Sales: Sold 15 titles in the last year. This agency prefers not to share information on specific sales.

Terms: Agent receives 15% commission on domestic sales; 10% on dramatic sales; 20% on foreign sales. Charges clients $150/year for photocopying, mailing, long distance calls.

Reading List: Reads "an assortment of literary journals—*Grand Street, Sewanee Review, Santa Monica Review*, book reviews, etc." to find new clients. Looks for "literary quality, unusual work."

Writers' Conferences: BEA (Los Angeles, June); Santa Barbara (June).

⬤ AARON M. PRIEST LITERARY AGENCY, 708 Third Ave., 23rd Floor, New York NY 10017. (212)818-0344. Fax: (212)573-9417. **Contact:** Aaron Priest or Molly Friedrich. Estab. 1974. Member of AAR. Currently handles: 25% nonfiction books; 75% fiction.

Member Agents: Lisa Erbach Vance; Paul Cirone; Aaron Priest; Molly Friedrich.

Represents: Nonfiction books, fiction.

How to Contact: Query only. SASE not required. If interested, will respond within 2 weeks of receipt of query. Will not respond if not interested. Does not accept queries by e-mail or fax. Unsolicited mss will be returned unread.

Recent Sales: *Aaron Priest: Saving Faith*, by David Baldacci (Warner); *Demolition Angel*, by Robert Crais (Doubleday); *The Saving Graces*, by Patricia Gaffney (HarperCollins). *Molly Friedrich*: *She is Me*, by Cathleen Schine (Little, Brown); *O is for Outlaw*, by Sue Grafton (Holt); *Horse Heaven*, by Jane Smiley (Knopf); *Lisa Erbach Vance: Darkest Fear*, by Harlan Coben (Delacorte); *The Magic of Ordinary Days*, by Ann Howard Creel (Viking); *Acid Test*, by Ross La Manina (Ballantine).

Terms: Agent receives 15% commission on domestic sales. Charges clients for photocopying, foreign postage expenses.

⬤ SUSAN ANN PROTTER LITERARY AGENT, 110 W. 40th St., Suite 1408, New York NY 10018. (212)840-0480. **Contact:** Susan Protter. Estab. 1971. Member of AAR. Represents 40 clients. 5% of clients are new/previously unpublished writers. Works with a very small number of new/previously unpublished authors. Currently handles: 50% nonfiction books; 50% novels; occasional magazine article or short story (for established clients only).

● Prior to opening her agency, Ms. Protter was associate director of subsidiary rights at Harper & Row Publishers.

Represents: Nonfiction books, novels. **Considers these nonfiction areas:** biography; health/medicine; memoirs; psychology; science. **Considers these fiction areas:** crime; mystery; science fiction, thrillers. **Also considers most general novel categories.**

O→ Writer must have book-length project or ms that is ready to be sold. Does not want to receive westerns, romance, fantasy, children's books, young adult novels, screenplays, plays, poetry, Star Wars or Star Trek.

VISIT WWW.WRITERSMARKET.COM to obtain a searchable database of agents and publishers, and to receive updates on your specific interests on your computer.

How to Contact: *Currently looking for limited number of new clients.* Send short query with SASE. Responds in 3 weeks to queries; 2 months to requested mss. "Please do not call; mail queries only. No bound manuscripts. Double-spaced and single-sided only."

Recent Sales: *Madeline Albright and the New American Diplomacy*, by Thomas W. Lippman (Westview Press); *In the Upper Room and Other Likely Stories*, by Terry Bissin (TOR); *Realware*, by Rudy Rucker (HarperCollins).

Terms: Agent receives 15% commission on domestic sales; 15% on TV, film and dramatic sales; 25% on foreign sales. "If we request to see your manuscript, there is a $10 minimum handling fee requested to cover cost of returning materials should they not be suitable." Charges clients for long distance, photocopying, messenger, express mail, airmail expenses.

Tips: "Please send neat and professionally organized queries. Make sure to include an SASE or we cannot reply. We receive approximately 200 queries a week and read them in the order they arrive. We usually reply within two weeks to any query. Please, do not call. If you are sending a multiple query, make sure to note that in your letter. I am looking for something outstanding in a large, difficult market."

◯ QUICKSILVER BOOKS—LITERARY AGENTS, 50 Wilson St., Hartsdale NY 10530-2542. Phone/fax: (914)946-8748. Website: www.artsnet.net. **Contact:** Bob Silverstein. Estab. 1973 as packager; 1987 as literary agency. Represents 50 clients. 50% of clients are new/previously unpublished writers. Currently handles: 75% nonfiction books; 25% novels.

● Prior to opening his agency, Mr. Silverstein served as senior editor at Bantam Books and Dell Books/Delacorte Press.

Represents: Nonfiction books, novels. **Considers these nonfiction areas:** anthropology/archaeology; biography; business; child guidance/parenting; cooking/food/nutrition; current affairs; ethnic/cultural interests; health/medicine; history; how-to; literature; memoirs; nature/environment; New Age/metaphysics; popular culture; psychology; inspirational; science/technology; self-help/personal improvement; sociology; sports; true crime/investigative; women's issues/women's studies. **Considers these fiction areas:** action/adventure; glitz; mystery/suspense; thrillers.

    0→ This agency specializes in literary and commercial mainstream fiction and nonfiction (especially psychology, New Age, holistic healing, consciousness, ecology, environment, spirituality, reference). Actively seeking commercial mainstream fiction and nonfiction in most categories. Does not want to receive "science fiction; pornography; poetry; single-spaced manuscripts!!"

How to Contact: Query with SASE. Authors are expected to supply SASE for return of mss and for query letter responses. Does not accept queries by e-mail or fax. Considers simultaneous queries and submissions. Responds in up to 2 weeks to queries; up to 1 month to mss. Returns materials only with SASE. Obtains most new clients through recommendations, listings in sourcebooks, solicitations, workshop participation.

Recent Sales: Sold over 20 titles in the last year. *Nature's Pharmacy for Kids*, by Lendon Smith, MD, Lynne Walker and Ellen H. Brown (Crown Publishers Inc.); *The Inextinguishable Symphony*, Martin Goldsmith (John Wiley & Sons, Inc.); *Look Great Naked*, by Brad Schoenfeld (Prentice Hall); *Healing Joint Pain Naturally*, by Ellen Brown (Doubleday); *Callous on My Soul Autobiography of Dick Gregory*, by Dick Gregory with Shelia Moses (Longstreet Press); *Earthwise*, by Victor Daniels (HarperCollins).

Terms: Agent receives 15% commission on domestic sales; 20% on foreign sales. Offers written contract, "only if requested. It is open ended, unless author requests time frame, usually one year." Charges clients for photocopying of mss and proposals ("we prefer that authors provide these copies"); and foreign mailings of books and mss.

Writers' Conferences: National Writers Union Conference (Dobbs Ferry NY, April).

◯ RAINES & RAINES, 71 Park Ave., Suite 44A, New York NY 10016. Estab. 1961. Member of AAR. **Contact:** Theron Raines, Joan Raines or Keith Korman. Represents 100 clients. 5% of clients are new/previously unpublished writers.

Members Agents: Theron Raines (fiction and nonfiction); Joan Raines (fiction and nonfiction); Keith Korman (fiction and nonfiction).

Represents: Nonfiction books and novels. **Considers all categories of nonfiction and fiction.**

How to Contact: Query with SASE. Does not accept queries by e-mail or fax. Prefers to read materials exclusively. Responds in 2 weeks to queries; 3 weeks to mss. Obtains most new clients through recommendations from others.

Recent Sales: *Taps*, by Willie Morris (Houghton Mifflin); *Quarrel & Quandry*, by Cynthia Ozick (Knopf); *Fox Eyes*, by Mordicai Gerstein (Golden Books); *Flying Cowboy*, by Fred Libby (Arcade). Other clients include Winston Groom, James Dickey, Raul Hilberg, and Bruno Bettelheim.

Terms: Charges 15% commission on domestic sales; 20% on foreign sales. Charges clients for photocopies and copies of books.

◯ CHARLOTTE CECIL RAYMOND, LITERARY AGENT, 32 Bradlee Rd., Marblehead MA 01945. **Contact:** Charlotte Cecil Raymond. Estab. 1983. Currently handles: 100% nonfiction books.

Represents: Nonfiction books. **Considers these nonfiction areas:** biography; current affairs; ethnic/cultural/gender interests; history; nature/environment; psychology; sociology.

    0→ Does not want to receive self-help/personal improvement.

How to Contact: Query with outline/proposal and SASE. Responds in 2 weeks to queries; 6 weeks to mss.

Recent Sales: This agency prefers not to share information on specific sales.

Terms: Agent receives 15% commission on domestic sales. 100% of business derived from commissions on ms sales.

☑ ◎ **HELEN REES LITERARY AGENCY**, 123 N. Washington St., 2nd Floor, Boston MA 02114. (617)723-5232, ext. 233 or 222. **Contact:** Joan Mazmanian. Estab. 1981. Member of AAR. Represents 50 clients. 50% of clients are new/previously unpublished writers. Currently handles: 60% nonfiction books; 40% novels.
Represents: Nonfiction books, novels. **Considers these nonfiction areas:** biography/autobiography; business; current affairs; government/politics/law; health/medicine; history; money/finance/economics; women's issues/women's studies. **Considers these fiction areas:** contemporary issues; historical; literary; mainstream; mystery/suspense; thriller/espionage.
   ○→ This agency specializes in general nonfiction, health, business, world politics, autobiographies, psychology, women's issues.
How to Contact: Query with outline plus 2 sample chapters and SASE. Does not accept queries by e-mail or fax. Prefers to read materials exclusively. Responds in 3 weeks to queries. Obtains most new clients through recommendations from others, solicitation, at conferences.
Recent Sales: Sold 15 titles in the last year. *The Mentor*, by Sebastian Stuart (Bantam); *Managing the Human Animal*, by Nigel Nicholson (Times Books); *Just Revenge*, by Alan Dershowitz (Warner).
Terms: Agent receives 15% commission on domestic sales; 20% on foreign sales.

◍ **JODY REIN BOOKS, INC.**, 7741 S. Ash Court, Littleton CO 80122. (303)694-4430. Website: http://JodyReinBo oks.com. **Contact:** Winnefred Dollar. Estab. 1994. Member of AAR and Authors Guild. Currently handles: 80% nonfiction books; 20% literary fiction.
   • Prior to opening an agency, Jody Rein worked for 13 years as an acquisitions editor for Contemporary Books, Bantam/Doubleday/Dell and Morrow/Avon.
Member Agents: Alexandra Philippe (screenwriting).
Represents: Nonfiction books; literary novels; some screenplays. **Considers these nonfiction areas:** animals; business; child guidance/parenting; current affairs; ethnic/cultural interests; government/politics/law; health/medicine; history; how-to; humor; music/dance/theater/film; nature/environment; popular culture; psychology; religious/inspirational; science/technology; self-help/personal improvement; sociology; women's issues/women's studies. **Considers these fiction areas:** literary, mainstream.
   ○→ This agency specializes in commercial nonfiction.
How to Contact: Query with SASE. Considers simultaneous queries. Responds in 6 weeks on queries; 2 months on mss. Obtains most new clients through recommendations from others.
Recent Sales: Sold 7 titles in the last year. *8 Simple Rules for Dating My Daughters*, by Bruce Cameron (Workman); *Think Like a Genius*, by Todd Siler (Bantam); *The ADDed Dimension*, by Kate Kelly (Scribner); *Beethoven's Hair*, by Russell Martin (Broadway Books); *Heart of Oak Sea Classics*, by Dean King (Holt); *Let the Wind Blow Through You*, by Joseph Marshall III (Viking Penguin).
Terms: Agent receives 15% commission on domestic sales; 25% on foreign sales. Offers a written contract. Charges clients for express mail, overseas expenses, photocopying ms.
Tips: "Do your homework before submitting. Make sure you have a marketable topic *and* the credentials to write about it. Well-written books on exciting nonfiction topics that have broad appeal. Authors must be well established in their fields and have strong media experience."

◎ **JODIE RHODES LITERARY AGENCY**, 8840 Villa La Jolla Dr., Suite 315, La Jolla CA 92037-1957. (858)625-0544. Website: www.writers.net.literaryagent.com. **Contact:** Jodie Rhodes, president. Estab. 1998. Represents 50 clients. 70% of clients are new/previously unpublished writers. Currently handles: 45% nonfiction books; 15% children's books; 40% novels.
   • Prior to opening her agency, Ms. Rhodes was a university level creative writing teacher, workshop director, published novelist and Vice President Media Director at the N.W. Ayer Advertising Agency.
Member Agents: Jodie Rhodes, president (memoirs, multicultural, African American, travel literature, medical-reference, women's books, literary fiction, military, mystery, suspense); Clark McCutcheon (fiction); Bob McCarter (nonfiction); Dan Press (electronic, film, television and foreign rights).
Represents: Nonfiction books, juvenile books, novels. **Considers these nonfiction areas:** animals, anthropology/archaeology; biography/autobiography; business; child guidance/parenting; computers/electronics; cooking/food/nutrition; current affairs; education; ethnic/cultural interests; gay/lesbian issues; government/politics/law; health/medicine; history; how-to; juvenile nonfiction; memoirs; military/war; money/finance/economics; music/dance/theater/film; nature/environment; popular culture; psychology; religious/inspirational; science/technology; sports; true crime/investigative; women's issues/women's studies; books that teach people how to use and benefit from the Internet. **Considers these fiction areas:** action/adventure; contemporary issues; detective/police/crime; ethnic; family saga; fantasy; feminist; gay/lesbian; historical; juvenile; literary; mainstream; mystery; psychic/supernatural; regional; romance; science fiction; sports; thriller/espionage; westerns/frontier; young adult.
   ○→ Actively seeking "writers passionate about their books with a talent for richly textured narrative and an eye for details." Does not want to receive erotica, horror, scholarly.
How to Contact: Query with brief synopsis, plus first 50 pages with SASE. Does not accept queries by fax or e-mail. Considers simultaneous queries and submissions. Responds in 10 days to queries; 1 month to mss. Returns materials only with SASE. Obtains most new clients through "agent sourcebooks, Internet websites, writers who read my magazine columns, conferences, recommendations."

insider report

Winds of change: the sale of a book *and* an author

When Joseph Marshall III set out to write *Let the Wind Blow Through You*—a collection of traditional Native American stories with a modern twist—he was no stranger to vivid imagery. Though this is his first book for the prestigious Viking Penguin's Arkana imprint, it is his fifth published work and his fifth book with Indian sensibilities.

A Sicangu Lakota Sioux, Marshall grew up on South Dakota's Rosebud Reservation where his elders were devoted to the meticulous preservation of family and tribal history via the most powerful medium of human communication—the spoken word. This strong oral tradition also played an important role when he and his agent, Jody Rein of Jody Rein Books, Inc., approached editors about *Let the Wind Blow Through You.*

Joseph Marshall III

Photo by Jim Evans of Jackson Hole News

"My grandfather's storytelling was so vivid, I felt I was almost there—150 years in the past," says Marshall. "Though the Lakota language has been preserved in writing, our culture is still largely oral. A generation ago, that's how our history was kept—passed on by memory alone. When something is committed to memory, it must be recalled just so. You can't deviate. You can't elaborate. It must be retold in exactly the same way. Storytelling is something you simply cannot do if you're lazy."

Lazy, he was not. Marshall finished high school, majored in English at the University of South Dakota, then went on to teach high school. "I grew up on the reservation," he says, proud of his home and his past. "But I knew if I stayed, I would never realize my dream of writing. I broke a lot of hearts when I left. But I had to."

Writing is not Marshall's only creative departure. He provided technical expertise in Hollywood (including work on NBC's *Lakota Moon*). He lectured extensively on college campuses and other public forums about Native American life. And he wrote, co-produced and starred in the educational video, *Hunter/Warriors of the High Plains*. According to Marshall, the film redefined the term "warrior" to mean a complete man—someone able to love, provide for, and protect his family. Every aspect of Marshall's career continues to point back to his tribal legacy.

Redefining misconceptions is a recurring Marshall theme. Three of his books published by Red Crane Books—*Winter of the Holy Iron* (1994); *On Behalf of the Wolf and the First Peoples* (1996); and *Dance House: Stories from Rosebud* (1998)—were heralded for their rejection of stereotypical characterizations. Critics say Marshall's writing shines with authenticity.

That truthful ring, according to Colorado agent Jody Rein, is part of what piqued her interest in Marshall. "He seemed an ideal client from the start," she says. "He has several books published by reputable small presses (which meant to me that he was talented but not yet known in the New York publishing scene). He has media connections. And he is a Native American writing about Native American issues, so he has credibility."

Chance also played a role in Rein's decision to take on Marshall as a client. "Luck always seems be an element in these things," Rein admits. "I had only recently begun to learn about the Lakota philosophies through other sources. So when Joe told me he wanted to write about Lakota teachings, I was personally—as well as professionally—intrigued."

After working closely with Marshall to develop an impressive book proposal, Rein set up meetings with editors. Though she's been in Colorado since opening her agency in the mid-1990s, Rein has important connections in New York made during her time as executive editor at Dell and Avon Books.

Once in Manhattan, Marshall deftly spoke for himself. "I spent two days talking to publishers," he says. "I explained my idea for the book, my plan to tell not only traditional stories but also to show how they serve a purpose today."

A man of quiet sophistication, Marshall wasn't sure how his Lakota wisdom and modern experience would play in New York. "I was intimidated, to a certain extent, by the environment of the city," he admits. "But once I walked into an office, once I looked an individual person in the eyes, any sense of intimidation vanished. Then it was up to me."

Janet Goldstein, executive editor and director of Arkana fully absorbed what Marshall had to say, and later made a six-figure, two-book offer.

"I was excited to send Joe's proposal to Janet Goldstein," says Rein, "because I have a great deal of respect for her. I'm always happy when I have a project I sense would be her cup of tea." Still, she insists it was Marshall who cinched the deal. "He is attractive, articulate, and a very powerful presence," Rein says. "He wowed them."

Indeed, Marshall believes modern authors must sell themselves along with their books. "If someone is interested to begin with and invites you to speak, that's a big open door. But then it's up to you to sell yourself. Eye-to-eye, one-on-one, the floor is yours. You make your project special by showing how you feel about it. If you're passionate, that's something they can see," he says.

Rein agrees. "With authors like Joe, I can comfortably tell publishers I am seeking a substantial offer. Doing things like calling first and sending an author to New York to meet with editors sends the 'big book' message quite clearly.

"I wouldn't (and don't) recommend that all authors go to New York and meet with publishers. But Joe really enhanced the value of the project, not only because he is so impressive, but also because we were going for a two-book deal. Editors needed to hear about the second book from Joe, since nothing was on paper yet." The second book is still in the planning stages.

Grab the agent, grab the editor, grab the reader—Marshall learned the lesson first hand. "There are so many people out there with unique, interesting, even outrageous things to say, it's become an 'in-your-face' kind of business. You have to find a way to capture a reader's attention," he says. "Being a good speaker and a good panelist is good for the book."

What about what's good for the author? Marshall maintains that the writer's job never has to change. "It's still about the story," he says. "I will write books mainly for the non-Indian community, so they will learn more about us—where we're coming from, what we've had to do to survive. These stories aren't just entertainment. They are life lessons. They are timeless."

—*Kelly Milner Halls*

Recent Sales: Sold 5 titles in the last year. *Infidelity*, by Ann Pearlman (MacAdam/Cage); *Combat Chaplain*, by Jim Johnson (movie rights optioned by Ribisi Entertainment Group) (University of Texas Press); *Farewell to Prague*, by Miriam Daruas (MacAdam/Cage).

Terms: Agent receives 15% commission on domestic sales; 20% on foreign sales. Offers written contract, binding for 1 year. 60-day written notice must be given to terminate contract. Charges clients for fax, photocopying, phone calls and postage. "Charges are itemized and sent to writer with submission report status."

Writers' Conferences: Southern California Writers Conference (San Diego, mid-February); SDSU Writers Conference (San Diego, mid-January).

Tips: "Think your book out before you write it. Do your research, know your subject matter intimately, write vivid specifics, not bland generalities. Care deeply about your book. Don't imitate other writers. Find your own voice. We never take on a book we done't believe in and we go the extra mile for our writers. We welcome talented new writers and work to build their careers."

■ ANGELA RINALDI LITERARY AGENCY, P.O. Box 7877, Beverly Hills CA 90212-7877. (310)842-7665. Fax: (310)837-8143. E-mail: e2arinaldi@aol.com. **Contact:** Angela Rinaldi. Estab. 1994. Member of AAR. Represents 50 clients. Currently handles: 50% nonfiction books; 50% novels.

  • Prior to opening her agency, Ms. Rinaldi was an editor at NAL/Signet, Pocket Books and Bantam, and the manager of book development of *The Los Angeles Times*.

Represents: Nonfiction books, novels, TV and motion picture rights. **Considers these nonfiction areas:** biography/autobiography; business; child guidance/parenting; food/nutrition; current affairs; health/medicine; money/finance/economics; popular culture; psychology; self-help/personal improvement; sociology; true crime/investigative; women's issues/women's studies. **Considers literary and commercial fiction.**

  ○━ Actively seeking commercial and literary fiction. Does not want to receive scripts, category romances, children's books, westerns, science fiction/fantasy, cookbooks.

How to Contact: For fiction, send the first 100 pages and brief synopsis. For nonfiction, query first or send outline/proposal, include SASE for both. Responds in 6 weeks. Accepts queries by e-mail. Considers simultaneous queries and submissions. "Please advise if this is a multiple submission to another agent." Returns materials only with SASE.

Recent Sales: *The Starlite Drive-In*, by Marjorie Reynolds (William Morrow & Co.); *Before Your Pregnancy*, by Amy Ogle and Lisa Mazzullo (Ballantine); *Breath of Confidence*, by Eben Perison (NAL/Signet); *The Thyroid Solution*, by Dr. Ridha Arem (Ballantine); *BlindSpot*, by Stephanie Kane (Bantam); *Who Moved My Cheese?*, by Dr. Spencer Johnson.

Terms: Agent receives 15% commission on domestic sales; 20% on foreign sales. Offers written contract. Charges clients for photocopying ("if client doesn't supply copies for submissions"). 100% of business is derived from commissions on sales. Foreign, TV and motion picture rights for clients only.

☑ ☻ ANN RITTENBERG LITERARY AGENCY, INC., 1201 Broadway, Suite 708, New York NY 10001. (212)684-6936. Fax: (212)684-6929. **Contact:** Ann Rittenberg, president. Associate: Susannah Susman. Estab. 1992. Member of AAR. Represents 35 clients. 40% of clients are new/previously unpublished writers. Currently handles: 50% nonfiction books; 50% novels.

Represents: Nonfiction, novels. **Considers these nonfiction areas:** biography; gardening; memoir; social/cultural history; travel; women's issues/women's studies. **Considers this fiction area:** literary.

  ○━ This agency specializes in literary fiction and literary nonfiction.

How to Contact: Send outline, 3 sample chapters and SASE. Considers simultaneous queries. Responds in 6 weeks to queries; 2 months to mss. Obtains most new clients largely through referrals from established writers and editors.

Recent Sales: Sold 15 titles in the last year. *Love for the Living*, by Dan Saferstein, Ph.D. (Hyperion 2000); *Someone Else's Child*, by Nancy Woodruff (Simon & Schuster 2000); *Mystic River*, by Dennis Lehane (Morrow 2001).

Terms: Agent receives 15% commission on domestic sales; 20% on foreign sales. Offers written contract. Charges clients for photocopying only.

☻ RIVERSIDE LITERARY AGENCY, 41 Simon Keets Rd., Leyden MA 01337. (413)772-0840. Fax: (413)772-0969. **Contact:** Susan Lee Cohen. Estab. 1991. Represents 40 clients. 20% of clients are new/previously unpublished writers.

Represents: Adult fiction and nonfiction. Very selective.

How to Contact: Query with outline and SASE. Does not accept queries by e-mail or fax. Considers simultaneous queries. Responds in 1 month. Obtains most new clients through referrals.

Recent Sales: Sold 14 titles in the last year. *Awakening the Buddhist Heart*, by Lama Surya Das (Doubleday Broadway); *Michio Kushi's Guide to Natural Healing*, by Michio Kushi and Alex Jack (Ballantine); *Awakening to the Sacred*, by Lama Surya Das (Broadway); *Jim Morrison's Adventures in the Afterlife*, by Mick Farren (St. Martin's Press).

Terms: Agent receives 15% commission. Offers written contract.

■ BJ ROBBINS LITERARY AGENCY, 5130 Bellaire Ave., North Hollywood CA 91607-2908. (818)760-6602. Fax: (818)760-6616. E-mail: robbinsliterary@aol.com. **Contact:** (Ms.) B.J. Robbins. Estab. 1992. Member of Board of Directors, PEN American Center West. Represents 40 clients. 50% of clients are new/previously unpublished writers. Currently handles: 50% nonfiction books; 50% novels.

Member Agents: Rob McAndrews (commercial fiction).

Represents: Nonfiction books, novels. **Considers these nonfiction areas:** biography/autobiography; child guidance/parenting; current affairs; ethnic/cultural interests; health/medicine; how-to; humor; memoirs; music/dance/theater/film; popular culture; psychology; self-help/personal improvement; sociology; sports; true crime/investigative; women's issues/women's studies. **Considers these fiction areas:** contemporary issues; detective/police/crime; ethnic; family saga; literary; mainstream; mystery/suspense; sports; thriller/espionage.
How to Contact: Send outline/proposal and 3 sample chapters with SASE. Considers simultaneous queries and submissions. Responds in 2 weeks to queries; 6 weeks to mss. Returns materials only with SASE. Obtains most new clients mostly through referrals, also at conferences.
Recent Sales: Sold 10 titles in the last year. *Please, Please, Please*, by Renée Swindle (Dial Press); *Katie.com*, by Katherine Tarbox (Dutton); *Quickening*, by Laura Catherine Brown (Random House); *Snow Mountain Passage*, by James D. Houston (Knopf); *Stone People Medicine*, by Manny Two Feathers (New World Library).
Terms: Agent receives 15% commission on domestic sales; 20% on foreign sales. Offers written contract, with 3 months notice to terminate if project is out on submission. Charges clients for postage and photocopying only. Writers charged for office fees only after the sale of ms. 100% of business is derived from commissions on sales.
Writers' Conferences: Squaw Valley Fiction Writers Workshop (Squaw Valley CA, August); Maui Writers Conference; SDSU Writers Conference.

THE ROBBINS OFFICE, INC., 405 Park Ave., New York NY 10022. (212)223-0720. Fax: (212)223-2535. **Contact:** Kathy P. Robbins, owner.
Member Agents: Bill Clegg.
Represents: Serious nonfiction, literary and commercial fiction and poetry. **Considers these nonfiction areas:** biography, political commentary; criticism; memoirs; investigative journalism.
  O— This agency specializes in selling serious nonfiction, poetry, commercial and literary fiction.
How to Contact: Accepts submissions by referral only.
Recent Sales: *King of the World*, by David Remnick (Random House); *Men in the Off Hours*, by Anne Carson (Knopf); *A Beautiful Mind*, by Sylvia Nasar (Simon & Schuster); *Dating Big Bird*, by Laura Zigman (The Dial Press); *War Boy*, by Kief Hillsbery (Rob Weisbach Books).
Terms: Agent receives 15% commission on all domestic, dramatic and foreign sales. Bills back specific expenses incurred in doing business for a client.

FLORA ROBERTS, 157 W. 57th St., Penthouse A, New York NY 10019. Member of AAR. This agency did not respond to our request for information. Query before submitting.

ROBINSON TALENT AND LITERARY MANAGEMENT, 1101 S. Robertson Blvd., Suite 210, Los Angeles CA 90035. (310)278-0801. Fax: (310)278-0807. **Contact:** Margaretrose Robinson. Estab. 1992. Signatory of WGA, franchised by DGA/SAG. Represents 150 clients. 10% of screenwriting clients are new/previously unpublished writers; all are WGA members. Currently handles; 15% novels; 40% movie scripts; 40% TV scripts; 5% stage plays.
  • See the expanded listing for this agency in Script Agents.

LINDA ROGHAAR LITERARY AGENCY, INC., 133 High Point Dr., Amherst MA 01002. (413)256-1921. Fax: (413)256-2636. E-mail: lroghaar@aol.com. Website: www.lindaroghaar.com. **Contact:** Linda L. Roghaar. Estab. 1996. Represents 31 clients. 50% of clients are new/previously unpublished writers. Currently handles: 90% nonfiction books; 10% novels.
  • Prior to opening her agency, Ms. Roghaar worked in retail bookselling for 5 years and as a publisher's sales rep for 15 years.
Represents: Nonfiction books, novels. **Considers these nonfiction areas:** animals; anthropology/archaeology; biography/autobiography; education; history; nature/environment; popular culture; religious/inspirational; self-help/personal improvement; women's issues/women's studies. **Considers these fiction areas:** mystery (amateur sleuth, cozy, culinary, malice domestic).
How to Contact: Query with SASE. Accepts queries by e-mail. Considers simultaneous queries. Responds in 1 month to queries; 3 months to mss.
Recent Sales: Sold 16 titles in the last year. *St. Disamus & The Toads*, by Molly Wolf (Doubleday); *Make Your Luck: How to Seize the Moments That Make Your Fortune*, by Peter Kash and Tom Monte (Prentice Hall); *Refrigerator Rights*, by Dr. Will Miller (Delacorte); *Love Always, Patsy* (Penguin Putnam/Berkley).
Terms: Agent receives 15% commission on domestic sales; negotiable on foreign sales. Offers written contract, binding for negotiable time.

CHECK THE INSIDER REPORTS throughout this section for first-hand information about working with agents.

N ○ ○ ROSE & ASSOCIATES LITERARY AGENCY, P.O. Box 906, Boulder CO 80306-0906. Phone/fax: (303)938-1905. E-mail: cerose88@aol.com. Website: http://rose&associates.com. **Contact:** Carl E. Rose. Estab. 1999. Represents 37 clients. 75% of clients are new/previously unpublished writers. Currently handles: 25% nonfiction books; 45% novels; 10% juvenile books; 5% scholarly books; 5% textbooks; 2.5% movie scripts; 7.5% other.

• Prior to becoming an agent, Mr. Rose was a sports writer with *The Denver Post* and an agent with another agency.

Member Agents: Carl Rose, owner (all specialties); Seymour Rose, agency counsel (legal and contractual matters, textbooks); Mr. Shannon Butler, agent (athletic, Native American and cultural topics).

Represents: Nonfiction books, novels, short story collections, novellas, juvenile books, scholarly books, textbooks. **Considers these nonfiction areas:** agriculture/horticulture; animals; anthropology/archaeology; art/architecture/design; biography/autobiography; business; child guidance/parenting; computers/electronics; cooking/food/nutrition; crafts/hobbies; current affairs; education; ethnic/cultural interests; government/politics/law; health/medicine; history; how-to; humor; interior design/decorating; juvenile nonfiction; language/literature/criticism; memoirs; military/war; money/finance/economics; multicultural; music/dance/theater/film; New Age/metaphysics; photography; popular culture; religious/inspirational; science/technology; self-help/personal improvement; sociology; sports; travel; true crime/investigative; women's issues/women's studies; young adult. **Considers these fiction areas:** action/adventure; cartoon/comic; confessional; detective/police/crime; erotica; ethnic; experimental; family saga; fantasy; feminist; glitz; historical; horror; humor/satire; juvenile; literary; mainstream; multicultural; mystery/suspense; New Age/metaphysical; picture book; psychic/supernatural; regional; religious/inspirational; romance; science fiction; sports; thriller/espionage; westerns/frontier; young adult.

O—π "We work well with a broad, sometimes eclectic range of fiction and nonfiction category interests. We enthusiastically welcome new authors and make a concerted effort to be available rather than distant. If something with great potential needs polish, one of us could be willing to offer some basic suggestions. However, if editing is needed, it is done from within or by the publisher—we do not refer work to any editorial services." Does not want to receive "extremely graphic violence or excessively pornographic sexual content, religious and philosophical extremists, attempts to justify any form of bigotry, slanderous materials with unproven allegations, collections of poems and short stories that have not had some of them individually published."

Also Handles: Episodic drama, poetry books, movie scripts, TV scripts, feature films, TV MOW, sitcom, animation, documentary, variety show, syndicated material. **Considers these script areas:** action/adventure; biography/autobiography; cartoon/animation; comedy; contemporary issues; detective/police/crime; erotica; ethnic; experimental; family saga; fantasy; feminist; glitz; historical; horror; juvenile; mainstream; multicultural; multimedia; mystery/suspense; psychic/supernatural; regional; religious/inspirational; romantic comedy; romantic drama; science fiction; sports; teen; thriller/espionage; western/frontier.

How to Contact: Query with SASE. Published authors send entire ms or send outline or proposal with SASE. Accepts queries by e-mail. Considers simultaneous queries and submissions. Responds in 2 weeks to queries; 5 weeks to mss. Returns materials only with SASE. Obtains most new clients through recommendations from others, queries/solicitations, advertisements, book festivals.

Recent Sales: Sold 1 title in the last year. *How to Make Money from Your Inventions and Patents*, by Steven Barbarich (Adams Media Corporation). Other clients include Janis Susan May, Riley Roam, Mike Costanza.

Terms: Agent receives 15% commission on domestic sales; 15% on foreign sales. Offers written contract, binding for 8-12 months. 30-60 day notice must be given to terminate contract. Asks first-time authors to submit photocopies and postage. Writers reimbursed after the sale of mss.

Writers' Conferences: BEA (Chicago, June); New York is Book Country (New York, September); San Francisco Bay Area Book Fest (San Francisco, November).

○ RITA ROSENKRANZ LITERARY AGENCY, 440 West End Ave., Suite 15D, New York NY 10024. (212)873-6333. **Contact:** Rita Rosenkranz. Estab. 1990. Member of AAR. Represents 30 clients. 20% of clients are new/previously unpublished writers. Currently handles: 98% nonfiction books; 2% novels.

• Prior to opening her agency, Rita Rosenkranz worked as an editor in major New York publishing houses.

Represents: Nonfiction. **Considers these nonfiction areas:** animals; anthropology/archaeology; art/architecture/design; biography/autobiography; business; child guidance/parenting; computers/electronics; cooking/food/nutrition; crafts/hobbies; current affairs; ethnic/cultural interests; gay/lesbian issues; government/politics/law; health/medicine; history; how-to; humor; interior design/decorating; language/literature/criticism; military/war; money/finance/economics; music/dance/theater/film; nature/environment; New Age/metaphysics; photography; popular culture; psychology; religious/inspirational; science/technology; self-help/personal improvement; sports; women's issues/women's studies.

O—π This "agency focuses on adult nonfiction. Stresses strong editorial development and refinement before submitting to publishers, and brainstorms ideas with authors." Actively seeking authors "who are well paired with their subject, either for professional or personal reasons."

How to Contact: Send outline/proposal with SASE. Does not accept queries by e-mail or fax. Considers simultaneous queries and submissions. Responds in 2 weeks to queries. Obtains most new clients through word of mouth, solicitations, conferences.

Recent Sales: Sold 35 titles in the last year. This agency prefers not to share information on specific sales.

Terms: Agent receives 15% commission on domestic sales; 20% on foreign sales. Offers written contract, binding for 3 years. 60-day written notice must be given to terminate contract. Charges clients for photocopying. Makes referrals to editing service. 100% of business is from commissions on sales.

Tips: "Identify the current competition for your project to make sure the project is valid. A strong cover letter is very important."

⊘ ROSENSTONE/WENDER, 3 E. 48th St., New York NY 10017. Member of AAR. This agency did not respond to our request for information. Query before submitting.

☑ ◎ THE GAIL ROSS LITERARY AGENCY, (formerly The Gail Rossman Literary Agency), 1666 Connecticut Ave. NW, #500, Washington DC 20009. (202)328-3282. Fax: (202)328-9162. **Contact:** Jennifer Manguera. Estab. 1988. Member of AAR. Represents 200 clients. 75% of clients are new/previously unpublished writers. Currently handles: 90% nonfiction books; 10% novels.
Member Agents: Gail Ross.
Represents: Nonfiction books, novels. **Considers these nonfiction areas:** anthropology/archaeology; biography/autobiography; business; cooking/food/nutrition; education; ethnic/cultural interests; gay/lesbian issues; government/politics/law; health/fitness; humor; money/finance/economics; nature/environment; psychology; religious/inspirational; science/technology; self-help/personal improvement; sociology; sports; true crime/investigative. **Considers these fiction areas:** ethnic; feminist; gay; literary.
 O─ This agency specializes in adult trade nonfiction.
How to Contact: Query with SASE. Responds in 1 month. Obtains most new clients through referrals.
Recent Sales: This agency prefers not to share information on specific sales.
Terms: Agent receives 15% commission on domestic sales; 25% on foreign sales. Charges clients for office expenses (i.e., postage, copying).

◙ ◎ CAROL SUSAN ROTH, LITERARY REPRESENTATION, (Specialized: self-help), 1824 Oak Creek Dr., Palo Alto CA 94304. (650)323-3795. E-mail: carol@authorsbest.com. **Contact:** Carol Susan Roth. Estab. 1995. Represents 30 clients. 10% of clients are new/previously unpublished writers. Currently handles: 100% nonfiction books.
 ● Prior to opening her agency, Ms. Roth was trained as a psychotherapist, motivational coach, conference producer and promoter for bestselling authors (e.g. Scott Peck, Bernie Siegal, John Gray) and the Heart of Business conference.
Represents: Nonfiction books. **Considers these nonfiction areas:** personal finance/investing; business; health/medicine; New Age/metaphysics; religious/inspirational; self help/personal improvement.
 O─ This agency specializes in spirituality, health, personal growth, personal finance, business. Actively seeking previously published authors—experts in health, spirituality, personal growth, business. Does not want to receive fiction.
How to Contact: Send proposal with SASE. Does not accept e-mail queries. Considers simultaneous queries. Responds in 1 week to queries. *"No phone calls please."* Returns materials only with SASE. Obtains most new clients through queries, current client referral.
Recent Sales: Sold 18 titles in the last year. *Healing Zen*, by Ellen Birx (Viking); *Celtic Flame*, by Mara Freeman (Harper Science Fiction); *Change Wave Investing*, by Tobin Smith (Bard); *Feng Shui for Dummies*, by David Kennedy; *The Bible for Dummies*, by Karl Schultz (IDG Books); The Everything Guides in Alternative Medicine & Online Investing (Adams Media).
Terms: Agent receives 15% commission on domestic sales; 20% on foreign sales. Offers written contract, binding for 3 years. 60-day notice must be given to terminate contract. This agency "asks the client to provide postage and do copying." Offers a proposal development and marketing consulting service on request. Charges $150/hour for service. Service is separate from agenting services.
Writers' Conferences: Maui Writer's Conference (Maui, HI, September).
Reading List: Reads *Yoga, New Age, People, Men's Health, Inquiring Mind, Fast Company* and *Red Herring* to find new clients. Looks for "ability to write and self-promote."
Tips: "Have charisma, content, and credentials—solve an old problem in a new way. I prefer clients with extensive seminar and media experience."

◙ JANE ROTROSEN AGENCY LLC, 318 E. 51st St., New York NY 10022. (212)593-4330. Fax: (212)935-6985. E-mail: jrotrosen@aol.com. **Contact:** Jane Rotrosen. Estab. 1974. Member of AAR and Authors Guild. Represents over 100 clients. Currently handles: 30% nonfiction books; 70% novels.
Member Agents: Andrea Cirillo; Ruth Kagle; Annelise Robey; Margaret Ruley; Stephanie Tade.
Represents: Nonfiction books, novels. **Considers these nonfiction areas:** biography/autobiography; business; child guidance/parenting; cooking/food/nutrition; current affairs; health/medicine; how-to; humor; money/finance/economics; nature/environment; popular culture; psychology; self-help/personal improvement; sports; true crime/investigative; women's issues/women's studies. **Considers these fiction areas:** action/adventure; detective/police/crime; family saga; historical; horror; mainstream; mystery; romance; thriller/espionage; women's fiction.
How to Contact: Query with SASE. Does not accept queries by fax or e-mail. Considers simultaneous queries and submissions. Responds in 2 weeks to queries; 7 weeks to mss. Returns materials only with SASE.
Recent Sales: Sold 120 titles in the last year. This agency prefers not to share information on specific sales.
Terms: Agent receives 15% commission on domestic sales; 20% on foreign sales. Offers written contract, binding for 3 years. 60-days notice must be given to terminate contract. Charges clients for photocopying, express mail, overseas postage, book purchases.

⊘ **THE DAMARIS ROWLAND AGENCY**, 510 E. 23rd St., #8-G, New York NY 10010-5020. Member of AAR. This agency did not respond to our request for information. Query before submitting.

☑ ⊘ **THE PETER RUBIE LITERARY AGENCY**, (formerly Perkins, Rubie & Associates), 240 W. 35th St., Suite 500, New York NY 10001. (212)279-1776. Fax: (212)279-0927. **Contact:** Peter Rubie, Jennifer DeChiarra or June Clark. Estab. 2000. Member of AAR. Represents 130 clients. 30% of clients are new/previously unpublished writers.
Member Agents: June Clark (New Age, pop culture, gay issues); Jennifer DeChiarra (children's books, theatre arts, literary fiction); Peter Rubie (crime, science fiction, fantasy, off-beat mysteries, history, literary fiction, thrillers, narrative nonfiction).
Represents: Nonfiction books, novels. **Considers these nonfiction areas:** narrative nonfiction; current affairs; commercial academic material; ethnic/cultural interests; music/dance/theater/film; science; TV. **Considers these fiction areas:** adventure; detective/police/crime; ethnic; historical; fantasy; literary; mainstream; mystery/suspense; science fiction; thriller.
How to Contact: Query with SASE. Responds in 2 months to queries with SASE; 3 months to mss. Obtains most new clients through recommendations from others, solicitation, at conferences.
Recent Sales: *Terrorists of Irustan*, by Louise Marley (Berkley); *Shooting at Midnight*, by Gregory Rucka (Bantam); *Violence Proof Your Kids* (Conari Press); *Toward Rational Exuberance* (Farrar, Straus & Giroux).
Terms: Agent receives 15% commission on domestic sales; 20% on foreign sales. Offers written contract "only if requested." Charges clients for photocopying.
Tips: "We look for writers who are experts and outstanding prose styles. Be professional. Read *Publishers Weekly* and genre-related magazines. Join writers' organizations. Go to conferences. Know your market, and learn your craft."

⊘ **PESHA RUBINSTEIN LITERARY AGENCY, INC.**, 1392 Rugby Rd., Teaneck NJ 07666-2839. (201)862-1174. Fax: (201)862-1180. E-mail: peshalit@aol.com. **Contact:** Pesha Rubinstein. Estab. 1990. Member of AAR, RWA, MWA, SCBWI. Represents 35 clients. 25% of clients are new/previously unpublished writers. Currently handles: 30% juvenile books; 70% novels.
• Prior to opening her agency, Ms. Rubenstein served as an editor at Zebra and Leisure Books.
Represents: Commercial fiction, juvenile books, picture book illustration. **Considers these nonfiction areas:** child guidance/parenting; contemporary issues. **Considers these fiction areas:** detective/police/crime; ethnic; glitz; humor; juvenile; mainstream; mystery/suspense; picture book; psychic/supernatural; romance (contemporary, historical); spiritual adventures.
  ○➔ This agency specializes in commercial fiction and nonfiction and children's books. Does not want to receive poetry or westerns.
How to Contact: Send query, first 10 pages and SASE. Responds in 2 weeks to queries; 6 weeks to requested mss. No weekend or collect calls accepted.
Recent Sales: *Freedom School*, by Amy Littlesugar (Philomel); *Excavation*, by James Rollins (Avon).
Terms: Agent receives 15% commission on domestic sales; 20% on foreign sales. Offers written contract. Charges clients for photocopying and overseas postage.
Tips: "Keep the query letter and synopsis short. Please send first ten pages of manuscript rather than selected chapters from the manuscript. I am a stickler for correct grammar, spelling and punctuation. The work speaks for itself better than any description can. Never send originals. A phone call after one month is acceptable. Always include a SASE covering return of the entire package with the submission."

⊘ **RUSSELL & VOLKENING**, 50 W. 29th St., #7E, New York NY 10001. (212)684-6050. Fax: (212)889-3026. **Contact:** Joseph Regal or Jennie Dunham. Estab. 1940. Member of AAR. Represents 140 clients. 10% of clients are new/previously unpublished writers. Currently handles: 40% nonfiction books; 5% juvenile books; 3% short story collections; 50% novels; 2% novellas.
Member Agents: Timothy Seldes (nonfiction, literary fiction); Joseph Regal (literary fiction, thrillers, nonfiction); Jennie Dunham (literary fiction, nonfiction, children's books).
Represents: Nonfiction books, novels, novellas, short story collections. **Considers these nonfiction areas:** anthropology/archaeology; art/architecture/design; biography/autobiography; business; cooking/food/nutrition; current affairs; education; ethnic/cultural interests; gay/lesbian issues; government/politics/law; health/medicine; history; language/literature/criticism; military/war; money/finance/economics; music/dance/theater/film; nature/environment; photography; popular culture; psychology; science/technology; sociology; sports; true crime/investigative; women's issues/women's studies. **Considers these fiction areas:** action/adventure; detective/police/crime; ethnic; literary; mainstream; mystery/suspense; picture book; sports; thriller/espionage.
  ○➔ This agency specializes in literary fiction and narrative nonfiction.
How to Contact: Query with SASE. Responds in 1 week to queries; 2 months to mss. Obtains most new clients by recommendation or occasionally through query letters.
Recent Sales: *The Many Aspects of Mobile Home Living*, by Martin Clark (Knopf); *The Special Prisoner*, by Jim Lehrer (Random); *The Visitor*, by Maeve Brennan (Counterpoint); *The Beatles in Rishikesh*, by Paul Saltzman (Viking Studio); *Lanterns*, by Marian Wright Edelman (Beacon); *Places in the Dark*, by Thomas H. Cook (Bantam); *Warriors of God*, by James Reston, Jr. (Doubleday); *The Obituary Writer*, by Porter Shreve (Houghton Mifflin).

Terms: Agent receives 15% commission on domestic sales; 20% on foreign sales. Charges clients for "standard office expenses relating to the submission of materials of an author we represent, e.g., photocopying, postage."
Tips: "If the query is cogent, well written, well presented and is the type of book we'd represent, we'll ask to see the manuscript. From there, it depends purely on the quality of the work."

☑ ◯ **THE SAGALYN AGENCY**, 4825 Bethesda Ave., Suite 302, Bethesda MD 20814. (301)718-6440. Fax: (301)718-6444. E-mail: agency@Sagalyn.com. Website: http://Sagalyn.com. **Contact:** Raphael Sagalyn. Estab. 1980. Member of AAR. Currently handles: 50% nonfiction books; 25% scholarly books; 25% novels.
　　○┐ Does not want to receive stage plays, screenplays, poetry, science fiction, romance, children's books or young adult books.
How to Contact: Send a query letter outlining your professional experience, a synopsis of your book, and a SASE. Does not accept queries by phone or fax. Accepts queries by e-mail but no attachments. Responds in 6 weeks.
Recent Sales: This agency prefers not to share information on specific sales.
Tips: "We receive between 1,000-1,200 queries a year, which in turn lead to two or three new clients."

☑ ◯ **VICTORIA SANDERS & ASSOCIATES**, (formerly Victoria Sanders Literary Agency), 241 Avenue of the Americas, New York NY 10014-4822. (212)633-8811. Fax: (212)633-0525. **Contact:** Victoria Sanders and/or Diane Dickensheid. Estab. 1993. Member of AAR, signatory of WGA. Represents 75 clients. 25% of clients are new/previously unpublished writers. Currently handles: 50% nonfiction books; 50% novels.
Member Agents: David Mayhew (lecture agent); Selena James (assistant literary agent).
Represents: Nonfiction, novels. **Considers these nonfiction areas:** biography/autobiography; current affairs; ethnic/cultural interests; gay/lesbian issues; govenment/politics/law; history; humor; language/literature/criticism; music/dance/theater/film; popular culture; psychology; translations; women's issues/women's studies. **Considers these fiction areas:** action/adventure; contemporary issues; ethnic; family saga; feminist; gay; lesbian; literary; thriller/espionage.
How to Contact: Query with SASE. Considers simultaneous queries. Responds in 1 week to queries; 1 month to mss. Returns materials only with SASE. Obtains most new clients through recommendations, "or I find them through my reading and pursue."
Recent Sales: Sold 20 titles in the last year. *Crowns: Portraits of Black Women in Church Hats*, by Cunningham & Marberry (Doubleday); *P.G. County*, by Connie Briscoe (Doubleday); *Daughter*, by Asha Bandgle (Scribner); *Blindsighted*, by Karin Slaughter (Morrow); *Redemption Song*, by Dr. Bertice Berry (Doubleday).
Terms: Agent receives 15% commission on domestic sales; 20% on foreign sales. Offers written contract, binding at will. Charges clients for photocopying, ms, messenger, express mail and extraordinary fees. If in excess of $100, client approval is required.
Tips: "Limit query to letter, no calls, and give it your best shot. A good query is going to get a good response."

◯ **SANDUM & ASSOCIATES**, 144 E. 84th St., New York NY 10028-2035. (212)737-2011. Fax number on request. **Contact:** Howard E. Sandum, managing director. Estab. 1987. Represents 35 clients. 20% of clients are new/previously unpublished writers. Currently handles: 80% nonfiction books; 20% novels.
Represents: Nonfiction books, literary novels.
　　○┐ This agency specializes in general nonfiction.
How to Contact: Query with proposal, sample pages and SASE. Do not send full ms unless requested. Responds in 2 weeks to queries.
Recent Sales: This agency prefers not to share information on specific sales.
Terms: Agent receives 15% commission. Agent fee adjustable on dramatic and foreign sales. Charges clients for photocopying, air express, long-distance telephone/fax.

◻ ◯ **SCHERF, INC. LITERARY MANAGAMENT**, P.O. Box 80180, Las Vegas NV 89180-0180. (702)243-4895. Fax: (702)243-7460. E-mail: ds@scherf.com. Website: www.scherf.com/literarymanagement.htm. **Contact:** Dietmar Scherf. Estab. 1999. Currently handles: 10% nonfiction books; 85% novels; 5% novellas.
　　● Prior to opening his agency, Mr. Scherf wrote several nonfiction books, and has been a publisher and editor since 1983.
Member Agents: Mr. Dietmar Scherf (fiction/nonfiction); Ms. Gail Kirby (fiction/nonfiction).
Represents: Nonfiction, novels, novellas. **Considers these nonfiction areas:** business; how-to; money/finance/economics; popular culture; psychology; religious/inspirational; self-help/personal improvement; true crime/investigative. **Considers these fiction areas:** action/adventure; literary; mainstream; mystery; religious/inspirational; thriller/espionage.
　　○┐ This agency specializes in discovering new authors, especially in the highly competitive fiction market. "As much as possible, we want to give every new author with a fresh voice a chance to find a publisher for their work. We also manage literary properties for established writers." Actively seeking well-written contemporary fiction with broad commercial appeal. Does not want to receive gay, lesbian, erotica, or anything with foul language.
How to Contact: Query with SASE. Does not accept queries by fax or e-mail. Considers simultaneous queries and submissions. Responds in 2 months to queries; 3 months to mss. Returns materials only with SASE. Obtains most new clients through recommendations from others, writing contests, unsolicited queries.
Recent Sales: This is a new agency with 1 recorded sale, *The Consultant*, by Alec Donzi.

Terms: Agent receives 10-15% commission on domestic sales; 15-20% on foreign sales (depending if new or established author). Offers written contract, binding on a case by case basis. 30-day notice must be given to terminate contract, if no sales are pending. Charges clients for postage, photocopying. Writers reimbursed for office fees after the sale of ms. May refer new writers to editing service. 0% of business is derived from referrals.

Tips: "Write the best manuscript, and polish it to the max. Write about a story that you love and are enthusiastic about. Learn good writing skills through books, seminars/courses, etc., especially regarding characterization, dialogue, plot, etc. in respect to novels. Know your competition well, and read books from authors that may fall into your category. In nonfiction, do the best research on your subject and be different from your competition with a new approach."

✓ ⬤ **SCHIAVONE LITERARY AGENCY, INC.**, 236 Trails End, West Palm Beach FL 33413-2135. Phone/fax: (561)966-9294. E-mail: profschia@aol.com. Website: www.freeyellow.com/members8/sciavone/index.html. **Contact:** James Schiavone, Ed.D. Estab. 1997. Member of the National Education Association. Represents 30 clients. 2% of clients are new/previously unpublished writers. Currently handles: 50% nonfiction books; 49% novels; 1% textbooks.
- Prior to opening his agency, Mr. Schiavone was a full professor of developmental skills at the City University of New York and author of 5 trade books and 3 textbooks.

Member Agents: Diane V. Jacques (film and TV rights; e-mail: jumpjupiter@aol.com).

Represents: Nonfiction books, juvenile books, scholarly books, novels, textbooks. **Considers these nonfiction areas:** animals; anthropology/archaeology; biography/autobiography; child guidance/parenting; current affairs; education; ethnic/cultural interests; gay/lesbian issues; government/politics/law; health/medicine; history; how-to; humor; juvenile nonfiction; language/literature/criticism; military/war; nature/environment; popular culture; psychology; science/technology; self-help/personal improvement; sociology; true crime/investigative. **Considers these fiction areas:** contemporary issues; ethnic; family saga; historical; horror; humor/satire; juvenile; literary; mainstream; science fiction; young adult.
- ○→ This agency specializes in celebrity biography and autobiography. Actively seeking serious nonfiction, literary fiction and celebrity biography. Does not want to receive poetry. "We have a newly established management division that handles motion picture and TV rights."

Also Handles: Moviescripts (feature film, TV MOW).

How to Contact: Send outline/proposal. Does not accept queries by e-mail or fax. Considers simultaneous queries and submissions. Responds in 2 weeks to queries; 6 weeks to mss. Returns materials only with SASE. Obtains most new clients through recommendations from others, solicitation, conferences.

Recent Sales: Sold 6 titles in the last year. Clients include Mark Littleton, Nickolae Gerstner, John Moffitt, George Mair.

Terms: Agent receives 15% commission on domestic sales; 20% on foreign sales. Offers a written contract. May be terminated by either party notifying the other in writing. Contract is on a "per project" basis. Charges clients for long distance, photocopying, postage, special handling. Dollar amount varies with each project depending on level of activity.

Writers' Conferences: Key West Literary Seminar (Key West FL, January).

Tips: "I prefer to work with published/established authors. I will consider marketable proposals from new/previously unpublished writers."

◎ ⬤ **SUSAN SCHULMAN, A LITERARY AGENCY (Specialized: self-help, women's issues)**, 454 W. 44th St., New York NY 10036-5205. Member of AAR. This agency did not respond to our request for information. Query before submitting.

◩ **LAURENS R. SCHWARTZ AGENCY**, 5 E. 22nd St., Suite 15D, New York NY 10010-5325. (212)228-2614. **Contact:** Laurens R. Schwartz. Estab. 1984. Represents 100 clients.

Represents: "General mix of nonfiction and fiction. Also handles movie and TV tie-ins, all licensing and merchandising. Works world-wide. *Very* selective about taking on new clients. Only takes on 2-3 new clients per year."

How to Contact: *No unsolicited mss.* Considers simultaneous queries. Responds in 1 month.

Recent Sales: This agency prefers not to share information on specific sales. "Have had 18 best-sellers."

Terms: Agent receives 15% commission on domestic sales; up to 25% on foreign sales. "No clients fees except for photocopying, and that fee is avoided by an author providing necessary copies or, in certain instances, transferring files on diskette—must be IBM compatible." Where necessary to bring a project into publishable form, editorial work and some rewriting provided as part of service. Works with authors on long-term career goals and promotion.

Tips: "I do not like receiving mass mailings sent to all agents. Be selective—do your homework. Do not send *everything* you have ever written. Choose *one* work and promote that. *Always* include an SASE. *Never* send your only copy. *Always* include a background sheet on yourself and a *one*-page synopsis of the work (too many summaries end up being as long as the work)."

⬤ **SCOVIL CHICHAK GALEN LITERARY AGENCY**, 381 Park Ave. South, Suite 1020, New York NY 10016. (212)679-8686. Fax: (212)679-6710. **Contact:** Russell Galen. Estab. 1993. Member of AAR. Represents 300 clients. Currently handles: 70% nonfiction; 30% fiction.

Member Agents: Russell Galen; Jack Scovil; Anna Ghosh; Alexander Smithline.

Recent Sales: *Last Man Standing*, by Jack Olsen; *Faith of the Fallen*, by Terry Goodkind (TOR); *Wides as the Waters Be*, by Benson Bobrick (Simon & Schuster); *The Burning Times*, by Jeanne Kalogridis (Simon & Schuster).

Terms: Charges clients for photocopying and postage.

☑ ◐ **SEBASTIAN LITERARY AGENCY**, The Towers, 172 E. Sixth St., #2005, St. Paul MN 55101. (651)224-6670. Fax: (651)224-6895. E-mail: harperlb@aol.com (query only—no attachments). **Contact:** Laurie Harper. Estab. 1985. Member of AAR. Represents approximately 50 clients.

● Prior to becoming an agent Laurie Harper was owner of a small regional publishing company selling mainly to retail bookstores, including B. Dalton and Waldenbooks. She was thus involved in editing, production, distribution, marketing and promotion. She came to publishing with a business and finance background, including eight years in banking.

Represents: Trade nonfiction, select literary fiction. **Considers these nonfiction areas:** biography; business; child guidance/parenting; consumer reference; current affairs; ethnic/cultural interests; health/medicine; money/finance/economics; psychology; self-help/personal improvement; sociology; women's issues/women's studies, and narrative nonfiction.

O→ Ms. Harper is known for working closely with her authors to plan and execute individual short-term and long-term goals. "A successful publishing experience is dependent upon closely coordinated efforts between the writer, the agent, the editor, the publisher's marketing group and sales force, and the booksellers. I give my authors as much advance information as possible so they can work most effectively with the publisher. An author needs every advantage he or she can have, and working closely with the agent can be one of those advantages." Does not want to receive scholarly work, children's or young adult work.

How to Contact: Taking new clients selectively; mainly by referral. Does not accept queries by e-mail or fax. Considers simultaneous queries and submissions. Responds in 3 weeks to queries; 6 weeks to mss. Obtains most new clients through "referrals from authors and editors, but some at conferences and some from unsolicited queries from around the country."

Recent Sales: Sold 25 titles in the last year. *Snapshots: 20th Century Mother-Daughter Fiction*, edited by Janet Berliner and Joyce Carol Oates (David R. Godine); *Latticework: The New Investing*, by Robert Hagstrom (Texere/Orion Publishing); *The 10 Smartest Decisions a Woman Can Make After Forty*, by Tina Tessina (Renaissance Books); *Forget Percent: You Deserve Better!*, by Lisa Earle with JoAnn Swan (Perigee Books); *The Other Side of Eden, Life with John Steinbeck*, by John Steinbeck IV and Nancy Steinbeck (Prometheus Books); *Champions of Silicon Valley: Visionary Thinking From Today's Technology Pioneers*, by Charles Sigismunc (John Wiley & Sons, Inc.).

Terms: Agent receives 15% commission on domestic sales; 20% on foreign sales. Offers written contract. No reading fees. Charges clients a one-time $100 administration fee and charges for photocopies of ms for submission to publisher.

Writers' Conferences: ASJA; and various independent conferences throughout the country.

☑ ◐ **SEDGEBAND LITERARY ASSOCIATES**, 7312 Martha Lane, Fort Worth TX 76112. (817)496-3652. Fax: (425)952-9518. E-mail: sedgeband@aol.com. Website: http://members.home.net/sedgeband. **Contact:** David Duperre or Ginger Norton. Estab. 1997. 80% of clients are new/previously unpublished writers. Currently handles: 90% novels; 10% novellas.

Member Agents: David Duperre (science fiction/fantasy, scripts, mystery, suspense); Ginger Norton (romance, horror, nonfiction, mainstream).

Represents: Nonfiction, novels, novellas. **Considers these nonfiction areas:** biography/autobiography; ethnic/cultural interests; history; true crime/investigative. **Considers these fiction areas:** action/adventure; contemporary issues; erotica; ethnic; experimental; fantasy; horror; literary; mainstream; mystery/suspense; psychic/supernatural; romance; science fiction.

O→ This agency is looking for new writers who have patience and are willing to work hard. Actively seeking science fiction, fantasy, all types of mystery.

How to Contact: Query with synopsis and SASE. Accepts queries by e-mail. Considers simultaneous queries. Responds in 3 weeks to queries; 3 months to mss. Returns materials only with SASE. Obtains most new clients through queries, the Internet, referrals.

Recent Sales: Sold 2 titles in the last year. *The Lord and Job Boudreaux*, by Dr. Tom Shafer (Picasso Publications); *Alias Jack the Ripper*, by R. Gordon (McFarland & Company Inc. Publishers).

Terms: Agent receives 15% commission on domestic sales; 20% on foreign sales. Offers written contract, binding for a year. Notice must be given to terminate contract. Charges clients for postage, photocopies, long distance calls, "until we make your first sale."

Tips: "We spend 18 hours a day working for our clients and we do not stop until we accomplish our goal. Simply put, we care about people and books, not just money. Do not send a rude query, it will get you rejected no matter how good of a writer you might be. And if we ask to review your work, don't wait to send it for several months. Send it as soon as possible. Also, it is better to wait for a contract offer before asking a lot of questions about publication and movie rights."

FOR INFORMATION ON THE CONFERENCES agents attend, refer to the **Writers' Conferences** section in this book.

☑ ◎ **LYNN SELIGMAN, LITERARY AGENT**, 400 Highland Ave., Upper Montclair NJ 07043. (973)783-3631. **Contact:** Lynn Seligman. Estab. 1985. Member of Women's Media Group. Represents 32 clients. 15% of clients are new/previously unpublished writers. Currently handles: 85% nonfiction books; 10% novels; 5% photography books.

● Prior to opening her agency, Ms. Seligman worked in the subsidiary rights department of Doubleday and Simon & Schuster, and served as an agent with Julian Bach Literary Agency (now IMG Literary Agency).

Represents: Nonfiction books, novels, photography books. **Considers these nonfiction areas:** anthropology/archaeology; art/architecture/design; biography/autobiography; business; child guidance/parenting; cooking/food/nutrition; current affairs; education; ethnic/cultural interests; government/politics/law; health/medicine; history; how-to; humor; interior design/decorating; language/literature/criticism; money/finance/economics; music/dance/theater/film; nature/environment; photography; popular culture; psychology; science/technology; self-help/personal improvement; sociology; translations; true crime/investigative; women's issues/women's studies. **Considers these fiction areas:** contemporary issues; detective/police/crime; ethnic; fantasy; feminist; gay; historical; horror; humor/satire; lesbian; literary; mainstream; mystery/suspense; romance (contemporary, gothic, historical, regency); science fiction.

○─ This agency specializes in "general nonfiction and fiction. I do illustrated and photography books and represent several photographers for books."

How to Contact: Query with letter or outline/proposal, 1 sample chapter and SASE. Does not accept queries by e-mail or fax. Considers simultaneous queries; prefers to read requested materials exclusively. Responds in 2 weeks to queries; 2 months to mss. Returns materials only with SASE. Obtains most new clients from other writers or editors.

Recent Sales: Sold 10 titles in the last year. *The Spark*, by Dr. Glenn Gaesser and Karla Dougherty (Simon & Schuster); *Resurrected Heart and Rebellious Heart*, by Barbara Pierce (Kensington); *Twins*, by Janet Seymour with Pamela Patrick Novotry (Pocket Books).

Terms: Agent receives 15% commission on domestic sales; 25% on foreign sales. Charges clients for photocopying, unusual postage or telephone expenses (checking first with the author), express mail.

▒Ⓝ▒ ◯ **SERENDIPITY LITERARY AGENCY, LLC.**, 732 Fulton St., Suite 3, Brooklyn NY 11238. Phone/fax: (718)230-4923. E-mail: serendipityla@hotmail.com. Website: www.serendipityla.com. **Contact:** Regina Brooks. Estab. 2000. Represents 12 clients; 20% of clients are new/previously unpublished writers.

● Prior to becoming an agent, Ms. Brooks was an acquisitions editor for John Wiley & Sons, Inc. and McGraw-Hill Companies.

Represents: Nonfiction, novels, juvenile books, scholarly books, textbooks. **Considers these nonfiction areas:** computers/electronics; education; ethnic/cultural interests; how-to; juvenile nonfiction; memoirs; money/finance/economics; multicultural; popular culture; psychology; religious/inspirational; science/technology; self-help/personal improvement; sports; women's issues/women's studies; young adult. **Considers these fiction areas:** action/adventure; confessional; ethnic; historical; juvenile; multicultural; picture book; romance; science fiction; thriller/espionage.

○─ Serendipity provides developmental editing. "We help build marketing plans for nontraditional outlets." Actively seeking African-American nonfiction, computer books (nonfiction), juvenile books. Does not want to receive poetry.

Also Handles: Scripts, multimedia. **Considers these script subject areas:** ethnic; fantasy; juvenile; multimedia. Also interested in children's CD/video projects; short films based on fantasy novels.

How to Contact: Send outline, 3 sample chapters, and SASE. Accepts queries by e-mail. Prefers to read materials exclusively. Responds in 10 days on queries; 2 months on mss. Returns materials only with SASE. Obtains most new clients through recommendations from others and conferences.

Recent Sales: This is a new agency with no recorded sales.

Terms: Agent receives 15% commission on domestic sales; 20% on foreign sales. Offers written contract. 60-day notice prior to expiration of the initial term must be given to terminate contract. Charges clients $200 upon signing for office fees or office fees will be taken from any advance. Marketing fees are project specific. "If author requests editing services, I can offer a list of potential services." 0% of business is derived from referral to editing services.

Tips: "We work aggressively to help you develop your ideas."

◎ **CHARLOTTE SHEEDY AGENCY**, 65 Bleecker St., New York NY 10012. This agency did not respond to our request for information. Query before submitting.

◎ **THE SHEPARD AGENCY**, Premier National Bank Bldg., Suite 3, 1525 Rt. 22, Brewster NY 10509. (914)279-2900 or (914)279-3236. Fax: (914)279-3239. E-mail: shepardagency-ldi@mindspring.com. **Contact:** Jean or Lance Shepard. Currently handles: 75% nonfiction books; 5% juvenile books; 20% novels.

Represents: Nonfiction books, scholarly books, juvenile books, novels. **Considers these nonfiction areas:** agriculture/horticulture; animals; biography/autobiography; business; child guidance/parenting; computers/electronics; cooking/food/nutrition; crafts/hobbies; current affairs; government/politics/law; health/medicine; history; interior design/decorating; juvenile nonfiction; language/literature/criticism; money/finance/economics; music/dance/theater/film; nature/environment; psychology; religious/inspirational; self-help/personal improvement; sociology; sports; women's issues/women's studies. **Considers these fiction areas:** contemporary issues; family saga; historical; humor/satire; literary; regional; sports; thriller/espionage.

○─ This agency specializes in "some fiction; nonfiction: business, biography, homemaking; inspirational; self-help."

How to Contact: Query with outline, sample chapters and SASE. Accepts queries by e-mail and fax. Considers simultaneous queries and submissions. Responds in 6 weeks to queries; 2 months to mss. Obtains most new clients through referrals and listings in various directories for writers and publishers.

Recent Sales: Sold 27 titles in the last year. Prefers not to share information on specific sales.

Terms: Agent receives 15% on domestic sales. Offers written contract. Charges clients for extraordinary postage, photocopying, long-distance and transatlantic phone calls.

Tips: "Provide information on those publishers who have already been contacted, seen work, accepted or rejected same. Provide complete bio and marketing information."

◧ THE ROBERT E. SHEPARD AGENCY, 4111 18th St., Suite 3, San Francisco CA 94114-2407. (415)255-1097. E-mail: query@shepardagency.com. Website: www.shepardagency.com. **Contact:** Robert Shepard. Estab. 1994. Authors Guild associate member. Represents 30 clients. 25% of clients are new/previously unpublished writers. Currently handles: 90% nonfiction books; 10% scholarly books.

  • Prior to opening his agency, Mr. Shepard "spent eight and a half years in trade publishing (both editorial and sales/marketing management). I also consulted to a number of major publishers on related subjects."

Represents: Nonfiction books. **Considers these nonfiction areas:** business; current affairs; ethnic/cultural interests; gay/lesbian issues; government/politics/law; history; money/finance/economics; popular culture; science/technology; sociology; sports; women's issues/women's studies.

  O─┐ This agency specializes in nonfiction, particularly key issues facing society and culture. Other specialties include personal finance, business, gay/lesbian subjects. Actively seeking "works in current affairs by recognized experts; also business, personal finance, and gay/lesbian subjects." Does not want to receive autobiography, highly visual works, fiction.

How to Contact: Query with SASE. E-mail encouraged; phone and fax strongly discouraged. Considers simultaneous queries and submissions. Responds in 1 month to queries; 6 weeks to mss and proposals. Returns materials only with SASE. Obtains most new clients through recommendations from others, solicitation.

Recent Sales: Sold 10 titles in the last year. *Coal: A Natural History*, by Barbara Freese (Perseus); *Wine and War*, by Donald and Petie Kladstrup (Broadway Books); *Word Freak*, by Stefan Fatsis (Houghton Mifflin Co.); *The Kitchen Table Investor*, by John F. Wasik (Henry Holt & Co.); *Talking Money With Jean Chatzky*, by Jean Sherman Chatzky (Warner Books); *Islam's Challenge*, by Anthony Shadid (Westview Press); *Between Sodom and Eden*, by Lee Walzer (Columbia University Press).

Terms: Agent receives 15% commission on domestic sales; 20% on foreign sales. Offers written contract, binding for term of project or until cancelled. 30-day notice must be given to terminate contract. Charges clients "actual expenses for phone/fax, photocopying, and postage only if and when project sells, against advance."

Reading List: Reads *Chronicle of Higher Education*, "certain professional publications and a wide range of periodicals" to find new clients. Looks for "a fresh approach to traditional subjects or a top credential in an area that hasn't seen too much trade publishing in the past. And, of course, superb writing."

Tips: "We pay attention to detail. We believe in close working relationships between author and agent and between author and editor. Regular communication is key. Please do your homework! There's no substitute for learning all you can about similar or directly competing books and presenting a well-reasoned competitive analysis. Don't work in a vacuum; visit bookstores, and talk to other writers about their own experiences."

▣ ◧ WENDY SHERMAN ASSOCIATES, INC., 450 Seventh Ave., Suite 3004, New York NY 10123. (212)279-9027. Fax: (212)279-8863. E-mail: wendy@wsherman.com. **Contact:** Wendy Sherman. Estab. 1999. Represents 20 clients. 30% of clients are new/previously unpublished writers. Currently handles: 50% nonfiction books; 50% novels.

  • Prior to becoming an agent, Ms. Sherman worked for Aaron Priest agency and was vice president, executive director of Henry Holt, and previous to that, associate publisher, subsidiary rights director, sales and marketing director.

Member Agents: Jessica Litchenstein (mystery and romance); Wendy Sherman.

Represents: Nonfiction books, novels. **Considers these nonfiction areas:** biography/autobiography; child guidance/parenting; ethnic/cultural interests; memoirs; psychology; self-help/personal improvement; true crime/investigative. **Considers these fiction areas:** literary fiction; contemporary issues; mainstream; mystery/suspense; romance; thriller/espionage.

  O─┐ "We specialize in developing new writers as well as working with more established writers. My experience as a publisher is a great asset to my clients."

How to Contact: Query with SASE or send outline/proposal and 1 sample chapter. Accepts queries by e-mail. Responds in 1 month to queries; 6 weeks to mss. Returns unwanted material only with SASE. Obtains most new clients through referrals from clients, writers, editors.

Recent Sales: Sold 12 titles in the last year. *The Judgment*, by D.W. Buffa (Warner Books); *Rescuing Jeffrey*, by Richard Galli (Algonquin); *These Granite Islands*, by Sarah Stonich (Little Brown); *Mad Dog in the Jungle*, by Alan Eisenstock (Pocket Books); *Crawling at Night*, by Nani Power (Grove/Atlantic); *Why Does He Do That?*, by Lundy Bancroft (Putnam); *The Silver Star*, by Howard Bahr (Henry Holt); *Big Book of Acting*, by Lise Friedman (Workman). Other clients include Howard Bahr, George Quesnelle, Lundy Bancroft, Lise Friedman, Tom Schweich.

Terms: Agent receives 15% commission on domestic sales; 20% on foreign sales. Offers written contract. Charges clients for photocopying of ms, messengers, FedEx, etc. (reasonable, standard expenses).

insider report

Agent guides writers through publishing process

For the last several months, you've labored painstakingly on your novel—crafting characters who captivate and prose that dazzles. Or, maybe you've poured all your efforts into your nonfiction book, and now you're confident that it far surpasses any other like it on the market. Writing your masterpiece has taken an *unbelievable* amount of time. And if you have to wait another second before it's on the shelves, you just might burst.

But everything in publishing seems to move at a snail's pace. Everyone is telling you to be realistic, but you don't know what qualifies as reasonable and what doesn't. That's where having an agent comes in handy. Not only do agents have personal connections with editors to help sell your book faster, but they are also advantageous to any writer trying to navigate the rocky waters of publishing. "The more I can share with my clients," says literary agent Wendy Sherman of Wendy Sherman Associates, Inc., "the better equipped they are to understand the publishing process and have realistic expectations. That includes how the process works from the moment you send in a book to when it's actually published and thereafter. A lot of authors get frustrated because they feel left in the dark. I feel it's my job to be with them through the entire process."

Although Sherman is new to agenting, her twenty years of publishing experience—including time as publisher at Henry Holt & Company—puts her in an excellent position to help her clients understand this process. "I always knew I wanted to be an agent," says Sherman, "because it allows me to use my publishing knowledge directly for the benefit of the writer."

When the opportunity to join the Aaron M. Priest Literary Agency arose, Sherman says, "I could not imagine a better place to work. I learned everything I possibly could—the basics of who to deal with and how things are done, how to run an agency and what editors are acquiring what kinds of books. It was good to work with people who are so professional and so good at what they do."

Nevertheless, after nine months at Aaron Priest, Sherman decided to open her own agency. "It became increasingly clear to me that I wanted to work for myself and fully devote my time to my own clients." And that client list grew quickly. "Becoming an agent has been a smooth transition for me. I worked with several authors at Holt who didn't have agents and who were happy to come with me." Those include legal suspense writer D.W. Buffa, whose next novel, *The Judgment*, Sherman sold to Warner Books; and Howard Bahr, author of *The Black Flower* and *The Year of Jubilo*, both published by Henry Holt & Company, Inc.

Working with an agent whose background is in publishing helps speed up the process once an editor accepts a book. Sherman explains, "I've sat in hundreds of editorial board meetings and dozens of sales conferences and marketing meetings. I know what issues come up. I can anticipate them and present my material in a way that makes it easier for my books to be acquired. An editor falling in love with a project is only the first step; they still have to convince other people. It's my job to give editors the tools and the information they need to allow that next step to happen."

Nevertheless, part of knowing how a publishing company works is having a realistic understanding of its limits. "Authors need to learn what publishers can and can't do for them," says Sherman. "Editors are incredibly overworked, and today, in many cases, authors have to do their own legwork to get their name out there. It's a collaborative effort."

There are even times when it's better to push the deadline for a book *back*—which can be difficult for an eager writer. Sherman encountered this situation when she sold *Rescuing Jeffery*, by Richard Galli, to Algonquin Books of Chapel Hill. "It's an incredible story about a father whose seventeen-year-old son is injured in a swimming pool accident. The book focuses on the ten days in the hospital after the accident when the father and family decide if they should allow the boy to live. The book was originally supposed to be published in March, but there was great interest from television and magazines who wanted to make the story a big event for Father's Day, so Algonquin pushed the publication back to June."

Sherman is also realistic when deciding who to take on as a client. "Obviously, I want to love the material and see that it has great potential to be sold. I look for writers who are substantive enough to have more than one book in them and who have a great story to tell—whether it's fiction or nonfiction."

An example of Sherman's dream client is novelist Sarah Stonich. "Everything attracted me to her book, *These Granite Islands*," she explains. "I fell in love with the manuscript instantly and was completely dazzled by her writing. While reading her manuscript, I found that I was pinching myself thinking I can't believe something this good has come my way so soon. We spent a lot of time on it—she is very hardworking. I was delighted with the response we got from publishers. Even the ones who didn't ultimately acquire the book loved it. It's been a dream from beginning to end. And now the book is one of Little, Brown's lead fall titles, and it's been sold to publishers around the world."

Sherman will read both nonfiction and fiction, but she says her tastes are varied. "My fiction tastes tend to be everywhere from upmarket quality fiction to somewhat literary to commercial. On the nonfiction side, I represent narrative nonfiction, memoir, and some broad self-help titles. I look for books that help you live your life better. I'm not looking for anything spiritual, and I'm not strong in the science fiction or horror genres."

Above all, Sherman looks for books she feels passionate enough about to back them every step of the way. And she looks for clients who understand the importance of this passion. "I was talking to a new client last week who said, 'I'm so glad I'm working with you because you really get my book.' When you write a book, you have a vision of what it is. What you want is an agent who reads it and says, 'Yes, I completely agree.' You want someone who has the same commitment and belief that you have."

—*Donya Dickerson*

THE SHUKAT COMPANY LTD., 340 W. 55th St., Suite 1A, New York NY 10019-3744. (212)582-7614. Fax: (212)315-3752. **Contact:** Patricia McLaughlin, Scott Shukat. Estab. 1972. Member of AAR. Currently handles: dramatic works.
How to Contact: Query with outline/proposal or 30 pages and SASE.

ROSALIE SIEGEL, INTERNATIONAL LITERARY AGENCY, INC., 1 Abey Dr., Pennington NJ 08534. (609)737-1007. Fax: (609)737-3708. **Contact:** Rosalie Siegel. Estab. 1977. Member of AAR. Represents 35 clients. 10% of clients are new/previously unpublished writers. Currently handles: 45% nonfiction books; 45% novels; 10% young adult books and short story collections for current clients.
Represents: Nonfiction, novels, young adult books, short story collections.
  ○─┐ This agency specializes in foreign authors, especially French, though diminishing.
How to Contact: Obtains most new clients through referrals from writers and friends.
Recent Sales: This agency prefers not to share information on specific sales.
Terms: Agent receives 15% commission on domestic sales; 20% on foreign sales. Offers written contract, with 60-day cancellation clause. Charges clients for photocopying.
Tips: "I'm not looking for new authors in an active way."

EVELYN SINGER LITERARY AGENCY INC., P.O. Box 594, White Plains NY 10602-0594. Fax: (914)948-5565. **Contact:** Evelyn Singer. Estab. 1951. Represents 30 clients. 10% of clients are new/previously unpublished writers.
  ● Prior to opening her agency, Ms. Singer served as an associate in the Jeanne Hale Literary Agency.
Represents: Nonfiction books, juvenile books (for over 4th grade reading level), novels. **Considers these nonfiction areas:** anthropology/archaeology; biography; business; child guidance; current affairs; ethnic/cultural interests; government/politics/law; health/medicine; how-to; juvenile nonfiction; money/finance/economics; nature/environment; psychology; inspirational; science; self-help; women's issues/women's studies. **Considers these fiction areas:** contemporary issues; ethnic; feminist; historical; literary; mainstream; mystery/suspense; regional; thriller/espionage.
  ○─┐ This agency specializes in nonfiction (adult/juvenile, adult suspense). Does not want to receive textbooks.
How to Contact: Query with SASE. Responds in 3 weeks to queries; 2 months to mss. "SASE must be enclosed for reply or return of manuscript." Obtains most new clients through recommendations only.
Recent Sales: *Cruel As The Grave*, by John Armistead (Recorded Books); *The Black Cowboy*, by Franklin Folsom (Editorial Cruïlla); *The $60.00 Summer*, by John Armistead.
Terms: Agent receives 15% commission on domestic sales; 20% on foreign sales. Offers written contract, binding for 3 years. Charges clients for long-distance phone calls, overseas postage ("authorized expenses only").
Tips: "I am accepting very few writers. Writers must have earned at least $20,000 from freelance writing. SASE must accompany all queries and material for reply and or return of ms. Enclose biographical material and double-spaced book outline or chapter outline. List publishers queried and publication credits."

IRENE SKOLNICK LITERARY AGENCY, 22 W. 23rd St., 5th Floor, New York NY 10010. (212)727-3648. Fax: (212)727-1024. E-mail: sirene35@aol.com. **Contact:** Irene Skolnick. Estab. 1993. Member of AAR. Represents 45 clients. 75% of clients are new/previously unpublished writers.
Represents: Adult nonfiction books, adult fiction. **Considers these nonfiction areas:** biography/autobiography; current affairs. **Considers these fiction areas:** contemporary issues; historical; literary.
How to Contact: Query with SASE, outline and sample chapter. *No unsolicited mss.* Accepts queries by fax. Considers simultaneous queries and submissions. Responds in 1 month to queries. Returns materials only with SASE.
Recent Sales: Sold 15 titles in the last year. *An Equal Music*, by Vikram Seth; *Kaaterskill Falls*, by Allegra Goodman; *Taking Lives*, by Michael Pye; *George Sand: A Woman's Life Writ Large*, by Belinda Jack; *The Temple of Optimism*, by James Fleming.
Terms: Agent receives 15% commission on domestic sales; 20% on foreign sales. Sometimes offers criticism service. Charges clients for international postage, photocopying over 40 pages.

SMITH-SKOLNIK LITERARY, 303 Walnut St., Westfield NJ 07090. Member of AAR. This agency specializes in literary fiction. Query with SASE before submitting.

MICHAEL SNELL LITERARY AGENCY, P.O. Box 1206, Truro MA 02666-1206. (508)349-3718. **Contact:** Michael Snell. Estab. 1978. Represents 200 clients. 25% of clients are new/previously unpublished authors. Currently handles: 90% nonfiction books; 10% novels.
  ● Prior to opening his agency, Mr. Snell served as an editor at Wadsworth and Addison-Wesley for 13 years.
Member Agents: Michael Snell (business, management, computers); Patricia Smith (nonfiction, all categories).
Represents: Nonfiction books. **Open to all nonfiction categories,** especially business, health, law, medicine, psychology, science, women's issues.
  ○─┐ This agency specializes in how-to, self-help and all types of business and computer books, from low-level how-to to professional and reference. Actively seeking "strong book proposals in any nonfiction area where a clear need exists for a new book. Especially self-help, how-to books on all subjects, from business to personal well-being." Does not want to receive "complete manuscripts; considers proposals only. No fiction. No children's books."

How to Contact: Query with SASE. Prefers to read materials exclusively. Responds in 1 week to queries; 2 weeks to mss. Obtains most new clients through unsolicited mss, word-of-mouth, *LMP* and *Guide to Literary Agents*.

Recent Sales: Sold 43 titles in the last year. *The Male Mind at Work*, by Deb Swiss (Perseus); *How to Say It to Your Kids*, by Paul Coleman (Prentice-Hall); *Topgrading: Hiring the Best People*, by Brad Smart (Prentice Hall); *A Good Night's Sleep*, by Frank Buda (Caroll).

Terms: Agent receives 15% on domestic sales; 15% on foreign sales.

Tips: "Send a half- to a full-page query, with SASE. Brochure 'How to Write a Book Proposal' available on request and SASE. We suggest prospective clients read Michael Snell's book, *From Book Idea to Bestseller* (Prima, 1997)."

◖ SOBEL WEBER ASSOCIATES, 146 E. 19th St., New York NY 10003. (212)420-8585. Fax:(212)505-1017. **Contact:** Nat Sobel, Judith Weber. Represents 125 clients. 15% of clients are new/previously unpublished writers.

    O⇥ "We edit every book before submitting it to publishers, even those of books under contract. For fiction, that may mean two or three drafts of the work. We are not interested in previously published authors, but pursue new talent wherever we find it."

◖ ELYSE SOMMER, INC., P.O. Box 71133, Forest Hills NY 11375. Member of AAR. This agency did not respond to our request for information. Query before submitting.

⟦N⟧ ◖ SOUTHERN LITERARY GROUP, a division of L. Perkins Associates, 43 Stamford Dr., Lakeview AK 72642. (870)431-7006. Fax: (870)431-8625. E-mail: bmay@mnthome.com. **Contact:** Beverly Maychuich. Estab. 2000. Represents 30 clients; 30% of clients are new/previously unpublished writers. Currently handles: nonfiction books; novels.

    ● Prior to becoming an agent, Ms. Maychuich was a real-estate agent. Her agency is affiliated with L. Perkins Associates.

Represents: Nonfiction, novels. **Considers these nonfiction areas:** current affairs; popular culture; women's issues/ women's studies. **Considers these fiction areas:** action/adventure; contemporary issues; detective/police/crime; ethnic; feminist; historical; horror; literary; mainstream; multicultural; mystery/suspense; regional; romance; thriller/espionage; young adult; women's fiction.

    O⇥ This agency is open to new writers. Does not want to receive material for children's books.

How to Contact: Query with SASE. Considers simultaneous queries and manuscripts. Responds in 1 week on queries; 3 months on mss. Returns materials only with SASE. Obtains most new clients through recommendations from others, the Internet.

Recent Sales: This is a new agency with no recorded sales.

Terms: Agent receives 15% commission on domestic sales; 20% on foreign sales. No written contract. Clients must provide 5 copies of ms.

Writers' Conferences: BEA.

Tips: "Care about your work. Belong to a writers' organization. Know your competition. The more you do your homework, the better your chance is of being sold."

◖ SPECTRUM LITERARY AGENCY, 111 Eighth Ave., Suite 1501, New York NY 10011. (212)691-7556. **Contact:** Eleanor Wood, president. Represents 75 clients. Currently handles: 90% fiction; 10% nonfiction books.

Member Agents: Lucienne Diver.

Represents: Nonfiction, novels. **Considers select nonfiction. Considers these fiction areas:** contemporary issues; fantasy; historical; romance; mainstream; mystery/suspense; science fiction.

How to Contact: Query with SASE. Responds in 2 months to queries. Obtains most new clients through recommendations from authors and others.

Recent Sales: This agency prefers not to share information on specific sales.

Terms: Agent receives 10% commission on domestic sales. Charges clients for photocopying and book orders.

◖ THE SPIELER AGENCY, 154 W. 57th St., 13th Floor, Room 135, New York NY 10019. (212)757-4439. Fax: (212)333-2019. **Contact:** Ada Muellner. Estab. 1981. Represents 160 clients. 2% of clients are new/previously unpublished writers.

    ● Prior to opening his agency, Mr. Spieler was a magazine editor.

Member Agents: Joe Spieler; John Thornton (nonfiction); Lisa M. Ross (fiction/nonfiction).

Represents: Nonfiction, literary fiction, children's books. **Considers these nonfiction areas:** biography/autobiography; business; child guidance/parenting; cooking/food/nutrition; current affairs; environmental issues; ethnic/cultural interests; gay/lesbian issues; government/politics/law; history; memoirs; money/finance/economics; sociology; travel; women's studies. **Considers these fiction areas:** ethnic; family saga; feminist; gay; humor/satire; lesbian; literary.

How to Contact: Query with SASE. Prefers to read materials exclusively. Responds in 2 weeks to queries; 5 weeks to mss. Returns materials only with SASE. Obtains most new clients through recommendations and occasionally through listing in *Guide to Literary Agents*.

Recent Sales: *Our Stolen Future*, by Theo Colburn, et. al. (Dutton); *The Dance of Change*, by Peter Senge, et. al. (Doubleday); *The Seventh Child: A Lucky Life*, by Freddie Mae Baxter and Gloria Miller (Knopf); *Orchid Fever*, by Eric Hansen (Pantheon); *In Code: A Mathematical Journey*, by Sarah and David Flannery (Workman); *A Natural History of the Rich*, by Richard Conniff (W.W. Norton).
Terms: Agent receives 15% commission on domestic sales. Charges clients for long distance phone/fax, photocopying, postage.
Writers' Conferences: London Bookfair; BEA.

Ø PHILIP G. SPITZER LITERARY AGENCY, 50 Talmage Farm Lane, East Hampton NY 11937. Member of AAR. This agency did not respond to our request for information. Query before submitting.

Ø STARS, THE AGENCY, (formerly ES Talent Agency), 777 Davis St., San Francisco CA 94111. (415)421-6272. Fax: (415)421-7620. **Contact:** Ed Silver. Estab. 1995. Represents 50-75 clients. 70% of clients are new/previously unpublished writers. Currently handles: 50% nonfiction books; 25% movie scripts; 25% novels.
  • See the expanded listing for this agency in Script Agents.

◐ NANCY STAUFFER ASSOCIATES, P.O. Box 1203, Darien CT 06820. (203)655-3717. Fax: (203)655-3704. E-mail: nanstauf@earthlink.net. **Contact:** Nancy Stauffer Cahoon. Estab. 1989. Member of Writers At Work and the Entrada Institute. 10% of clients are new/previously unpublished writers. Currently handles: 25% nonfiction books; 75% fiction.
Represents: Literary fiction, short story collections, nonfiction books. **Considers these nonfiction areas:** animals; biography/autobiography; current affairs; ethnic/cultural interests; popular culture; self-help/personal improvement; narrative nonfiction. **Considers these fiction areas:** contemporary issues; literary; mainstream; regional.
How to Contact: Fiction: Send query letter with first 20 pages. Nonfiction: Send query letter with table of contents. Does not accept queries by fax or e-mail. Considers simultaneous queries and submission. Returns materials only with SASE. Obtains most new clients primarily through referrals from existing clients.
Recent Sales: *The Toughest Indian in The World*, by Sherman Alexie (Grove/Atlantic); *Delirium of the Brave*, by William C. Harris (St. Martin's Press); *Where Rivers Change Direction*, by Mark Spragg (Riverhead Books); *Arroyo*, by Summer Wood (Chronicle).
Terms: Agent receives 15% commission on domestic sales; 20% on foreign and film/TV sales.
Writers' Conferences: Writers At Work and Entrada; Radcliffe Publishing Course.

N Ø STEELE-PERKINS LITERARY AGENCY, 26 Island Lane, Canandaigua NY 14424. (716)396-9290. Fax: (716)396-3579. E-mail: pattiesp@aol.com. **Contact:** Pattie Steele-Perkins. Member of AAR, RWA. Currently handles 100% novels.
  • Prior to becoming an agent, Ms. Steele-Perkins was a TV producer/writer for 15 years.
Represents: Novels. **Considers these nonfiction areas:** sports (specifically sailing). **Considers these fiction areas:** mainstream; multicultural; romance.
  ○━ The Steele-Perkins Literary Agency takes an active role in marketing their clients work including preparation for media appearances. They also develop with the author individual career plans. Actively seeking romance, women's fiction and multicultural works.
How to Contact: Send outline and 3 sample chapters, include SASE. Accepts queries by e-mail. Considers simultaneous queries. Reponds in 6 weeks. Returns materials only with SASE. Obtains most new clients through recommendations from others, queries/solicitations.
Recent Sales: This agency prefers not to share information on specific sales.
Terms: Agent receives 15% commission on domestic sales. Offers written contract, binding for 1 year. 30-day notice must be given to terminate contract.
Writers' Conferences: National Conference of Romance Writer's of America; Book Expo America Writers' Conferences.
Tips: "Be patient. E-mail rather than call. Make sure what you are sending is the best it can be."

FOR EXPLANATIONS OF THESE SYMBOLS,
SEE THE INSIDE FRONT AND BACK COVERS OF THIS BOOK

STERNIG & BYRNE LITERARY AGENCY, 3209 S. 55, Milwaukee WI 53219-4433. (414)328-8034. Fax: (414)328-8034. E-mail: jackbyrne@aol.com. **Contact:** Jack Byrne. Estab. 1950s. Member of SFWA, MWA. Represents 30 clients. 20% of clients are new/previously unpublished writers. Sold 17 titles in the last year. Currently handles: 5% nonfiction books; 40% juvenile books; 55% novels.

Member Agents: Jack Byrne.

Represents: Nonfiction books, juvenile books, novels. **Considers these nonfiction areas:** biography/autobiography; juvenile nonfiction; popular culture. **Considers these fiction areas:** action/adventure; fantasy; glitz; horror; juvenile; mystery/suspense; psychic/supernatural; science fiction; thriller/espionage; young adult.

> **O**→ "We have a small, friendly, personal, hands-on teamwork approach to marketing." Actively seeking science fiction/fantasy and mystery/suspense. Does not want to receive romance, poetry, textbooks, highly specialized nonfiction.

How to Contact: Query with SASE. Accepts queries by e-mail. Considers simultaneous queries; no simultaneous submissions. Responds in 3 weeks to queries; 3 months to mss. Returns materials only with SASE. "No SASE equals no return."

Recent Sales: Sold 17 titles in the last year. *The Beast That Was Max*, by Gerard Daniel Houarner (Leisure); *Mark of the Cat*, by Andre Norton (Meisha Merlin). Clients include Betty Ren Wright, Lyn McComchie.

Terms: Agent receives 15% commission on domestic sales; 20% on foreign sales. Offers written contract, open/nonbinding. 60-day notice must be given to terminate contract.

Reading List: Reads *Publishers Weekly, Locus, Science Fiction Chronicles*, etc. to find new clients. Looks for "whatever catches my eye."

Tips: "Don't send first drafts; have a professional presentation . . . including cover letter; know your field. Read what's been done . . . good and bad."

ROBIN STRAUS AGENCY, INC., 229 E. 79th St., New York NY 10021. (212)472-3282. Fax: (212)472-3833. E-mail: springbird@aol.com. **Contact:** Robin Straus. Estab. 1983. Member of AAR. Currently handles: 65% nonfiction books; 35% novels.

> ● Prior to becoming an agent, Robin Straus served as a subsidiary rights manager at Random House and Doubleday and worked in editorial at Little, Brown.

Represents: Nonfiction, novels. **Considers these nonfiction areas:** animals; anthropology/archaeology; art/architecture/design; biography/autobiography; child guidance/parenting; cooking/food/nutrition; current affairs; ethnic/cultural interests; government/politics/law; health/medicine; history; language/literature/criticism; music/dance/theater/film; nature/environment; popular culture; psychology; science/technology; sociology; women's issues/women's studies. **Considers these fiction areas:** contemporary issues; family saga; historical; literary; mainstream; thriller/espionage.

> **O**→ This agency specializes in high-quality fiction and nonfiction for adults. Does not want to receive genre fiction.

How to Contact: Nonfiction: query with proposal and sample pages. Fiction: brief synopsis and opening chapter or two. "Will not download e-mail inquiries." SASE ("stamps, not metered postage") required for response and return of material submitted. Responds in 1 month to queries and mss. Takes on very few new clients. Obtains most new clients through recommendations from others.

Recent Sales: This agency prefers not to share information on specific sales.

Terms: Agent receives 15% commission on domestic sales; 20% on foreign sales. Offers written contract when requested. Charges clients for "photocopying, UPS, messenger and foreign postage, etc. as incurred."

SUITE A MANAGEMENT, 1101 S. Robertson Blvd., Suite 210, Los Angeles CA 90035. (310)278-0801. Fax: (310)278-0807. E-mail: suite-a@juno.com. Website: www.suite-a-management.com. **Contact:** Lloyd D. Robinson. Estab. 1996. Represents 50 clients. 15% of clients are new/previously unpublished writers. Currently handles: 40% movie scripts; 20% novels; 10% animation; 15% TV scripts; 10% stage plays; 5% multimedia.

> ● See the expanded listing for this agency in Script Agents.

THE SWAYNE AGENCY LITERARY MANAGEMENT & CONSULTING, INC., 337 E. 54th St., New York NY 10022. (212)391-5438. E-mail: kexilus@swayneagency.com. Website: www.swayneagency.com. **Contact:** Karyn Exilus. Estab. 1997. Represents 100 clients. Currently handles: 100% nonfiction books.

Member Agents: Susan Barry (science, technology-related nonfiction, business, personal finance, memoir and sports); Lisa Swayne (technology-related and business nonfiction, women's issues, self help, health/fitness).

Represents: Nonfiction books, computer technology books. **Considers these nonfiction areas:** business; science; computers/electronics; current affairs; ethnic/cultural interests; gay/lesbian issues; how-to; popular culture; self-help/personal improvement; women's issues/women's studies.

> **O**→ This agency specializes in authors who participate in multimedia: book publishing, radio, movies and television, and information technology. Actively seeking technology-related nonfiction—particularly aimed at women or business. Does not want to receive westerns, romance novels, science fiction, children's books.

How to Contact: Query with outline/proposal and SASE. Accepts queries by e-mail. *No fax queries.* Considers simultaneous submissions. Responds in 6 weeks to all submissions. Obtains most new clients through recommendations from colleagues and clients.

Recent Sales: Sold 100 titles in the last year. *Net Slaves: True Tales of Working the Web*, by Steve Baldwin and Bill Lesscuel (McGraw Hill); *Spooked*, by Adam Penenberg (Perseus Books); *Slave Diaries*, by Michael Kinsley (Public Affairs); *Healing Mudras*, by Sabrina Mesko (Ballantine); *Citizen Greenspan*, by Justin Martin (Perseus Books); *Nurturing the Writer's Self*, by Bonni Goldberg (Penguin Putnam).

Terms: Agent receives 15% commission on domestic sales; 20% on foreign sales. Offers written contract, binding for 1 year. 60-day notice must be given to terminate contract.

Reading List: Reads *Red Herring*, *Business 2.0*, *Fast Company*, *Wall Street Journal*, *New York Observer*, *The Industry Standard*, to find new clients. Looks for cutting edge business, technology topics and trends and up and coming writers.

◢ SYDRA TECHNIQUES CORP., 481 Eighth Ave., E24, New York NY 10001. (212)631-0009. Fax: (212)631-0715. E-mail: sbuck@virtualnews.com. **Contact:** Sid Buck. Estab. 1988. Signatory of WGA. Represents 30 clients. 80% of clients are new/previously unpublished writers. Currently handles: 30% movie scripts; 10% novels; 30% TV scripts; 10% nonfiction books; 10% stage plays; 10% multimedia.
> • See the expanded listing for this agency in Script Agents.

◖ THE JOHN TALBOT AGENCY, 540 W. Boston Post Rd., PMB 266, Mamaroneck NY 10543-3437. (914)381-9463. **Contact:** John Talbot. Estab. 1998. Member of the Authors Guild. Represents 50 clients. 15% of clients are new/previously unpublished writers. Currently handles: 35% nonfiction books; 65% novels.
> • Prior to becoming an agent, Mr. Talbot was a book editor at Simon & Schuster and Putnam Berkley.

Represents: Nonfiction books, novels. **Considers these nonfiction areas:** general and narrative nonfiction. **Considers these fiction area:** literary; suspense.
> **O─π** This agency specializes in commercial suspense and literary fiction "by writers who are beginning to publish in magazines and literary journals." Also narrative nonfiction, especially outdoor adventure and spirituality. Does not want to receive children's books, science fiction, fantasy, westerns, poetry, screenplays.

How to Contact: Query with SASE. Does not accept queries by fax or e-mail. Considers simultaneous queries. Responds in 1 month to queries; 2 months to mss. Obtains most new clients usually through referrals.

Recent Sales: Sold 30 titles in the last year. *Inez*, by Clarence Major (John Wiley & Sons); *Frontera Street*, by Tanya Maria Barrientos (NAL); *Deep Sound Channel*, by Joe Buff (Bantam); *Lily of the Valley*, by Suzanne Strempek Shea (Pocket Books); *The Fuck-up*, by Arthur Nersesian (Pocket Books/MTV). Other clients include Doris Meredith, Peter Telep, Robert W. Walker.

Terms: Agent receives 15% commission on domestic sales; 20% on foreign sales. Offers written contract. 2-week notice must be given to terminate contract. Charges clients for photocopying, overnight delivery, additional copies of books needed for use in sale of subsidiary rights, and fees incurred for submitting mss or books overseas.

◔ ROSLYN TARG LITERARY AGENCY, INC., 105 W. 13th St., New York NY 10011. Member of AAR. This agency did not respond to our request for information. Query before submitting.

✔ ◔ REBECCA TAYLOR, LITERARY AGENT, 8491 Hospital Dr., PMB 196, Douglasville GA 30134. Phone/fax: (770)947-8263. E-mail: rebeccastaylor@aol.com. Website: www.writersadventures.com. **Contact:** Rebecca Taylor. Estab. 1998. Vice President of Board of Directors of Georgia Writers Inc. Represents 12 clients. 65% of clients are new/previously unpublished writers. Currently handles: 20% nonfiction books; 30% juvenile books; 60% novels.
> • Prior to opening her agency, Ms. Taylor was an administrative assistant and apprentice agent.

Represents: Nonfiction books, juvenile books, novels. **Considers these nonfiction areas:** cooking/food/nutrition; fitness; juvenile nonfiction; women's issues/women's studies. **Considers these fiction areas:** contemporary issues; family saga; feminist; juvenile; literary fiction; picture book; young adult.
> **O─π** Actively seeking women's and literary fiction. Does not want to receive screenplays, poetry or science fiction.

How to Contact: Send outline and 3-5 sample chapters. Does not accept queries by fax or e-mail. Considers simultaneous queries and submissions. Responds in 6 weeks to queries; 2 months to mss. Returns materials only with SASE. Obtains most new clients through recommendations from clients, conferences.

Recent Sales: *Sex, Dead Dogs and Me*, by Ed Williams (Elysian Publishing). Clients include Valerie Norris, Ed Williams, Laura Didio, Dr. Jeffrey Deal.

Terms: Agent receives 15% commission on domestic sales; 20% on foreign sales. Offers written contract. 30-day notice must be given to terminate contract.

Tips: "I am not afraid to break the rules when necessary, and I feel this industry needs that right now. I have found my previous experience and passion for what I do, coupled with my fresh attitude and unique perspective has been an advantageous distinction. I am currently looking for quality literary fiction and nonfiction, as well as women's fiction and nonfiction, all written with a fresh perspective and new ideas. I expect my clients to be flexible to constructive criticism, while remaining confident in their ability and attitude."

◖ PATRICIA TEAL LITERARY AGENCY, 2036 Vista Del Rosa, Fullerton CA 92831-1336. (714)738-8333. **Contact:** Patricia Teal. Estab. 1978. Member of AAR, RWA, Authors Guild. Represents 60 clients. Currently handles: 10% nonfiction books; 90% novels.

Represents: Nonfiction books, novels. **Considers these nonfiction areas:** animals; biography/autobiography; child guidance/parenting; health/medicine; how-to; psychology; self-help/personal improvement; true crime/investigative; women's issues. **Considers these fiction areas:** glitz, mainstream, mystery/suspense, romance (contemporary, histori-cal).

O➥ This agency specializes in women's fiction and commercial how-to and self-help nonfiction. Does not want to receive poetry, short stories, articles, science fiction, fantasy, regency romance.

How to Contact: *Published authors only.* Query with SASE. Does not accept queries by e-mail or fax. Considers simultaneous queries. Responds in 10 days to queries; 6 weeks to requested mss. Returns materials only with SASE. Obtains most new clients through recommendations from authors and editors or at conferences.

Recent Sales: Sold 45 titles in the last year. *Second to None*, by Muriel Jensen (Harlequin); *Found: His Perfect Wife*, by Marie Ferrarella (Silhouette).

Terms: Agent receives 10-15% commission on domestic sales; 20% on foreign sales. Offers written contract, binding for 1 year. Charges clients for photocopying.

Writers' Conferences: Romance Writers of America conferences; Asilomar (California Writers Club); Bouchercon; BEA (Chicago, June); California State University San Diego (January); Hawaii Writers Conference (Maui).

Reading List: Reads *Publishers Weekly*, *Romance Report* and *Romantic Times* to find new clients. "I read the reviews of books and excerpts from authors' books."

Tips: "Include SASE with all correspondence."

● **IRENE TIERSTEN LITERARY AGENCY**, 540 Ridgewood Rd., Maplewood NJ 07040. (973)762-4024. Fax: (973)762-0349. E-mail: tiersten@ix.netcom.com. **Contact:** Irene Tiersten. Prefers to work with published/established authors.

Represents: Adult fiction and nonfiction, young adult fiction and nonfiction.

O➥ Does not want to receive poetry.

How to Contact: Accepts queries by fax and e-mail. Considers simultaneous queries. Prefers to read materials exclusively. Responds in 2 weeks to queries; 1 month to mss.

Recent Sales: Sold 5 titles in the last year. *Traveling Light*, by Katrina Kittle (Warner Books); *Night Flyers* and *Watcher in the Piney Woods*, winner of 2000 Edgar Award, by Elizabeth Jones (Pleasant); *The Young Investor*, by Katherine Baterman (Chicago Review Press).

Terms: Agency receives 15% commission on domestic sales; 15% on dramatic sales; 25% on foreign and translation sales (split with co-agents abroad). Charges clients for international phone and postage expenses.

✓ ◐ **TOAD HALL, INC.**, RR 2, Box 2090, Laceyville PA 18623. (570)869-2942. Fax: (570)869-1031. E-mail: toadhallco@aol.com. Website: www.laceyville.com/Toad-Hall. **Contact:** Sharon Jarvis, Anne Pinzow. Estab. 1982. Member of AAR. Represents 35 clients. 10% of clients are new/previously unpublished writers. Currently handles: 50% nonfiction books; 40% novels; 5% movie scripts; 5% ancillary projects.

● Prior to becoming an agent, Ms. Jarvis was an acquisitions editor.

Member Agents: Sharon Jarvis (fiction, nonfiction); Anne Pinzow (TV, movies); Roxy LeRose (unpublished writers).

Represents: Nonfiction books. **Considers these nonfiction areas:** animals; anthropology/archaeology; business; child guidance/parenting; cooking/food/nutrition; crafts/hobbies; health/medicine; how-to; nature/environment; New Age/metaphysics; popular culture; religious/inspirational; self-help/personal improvement. **Considers these fiction areas:** historical; mystery/suspense; romance (contemporary, historical, regency); science fiction.

O➥ This agency specializes in popular nonfiction, some category fiction. Actively seeking New Age, paranormal—unusual but popular approaches. "We only handle scripts written by our clients who have published material agented by us." Does not want to receive poetry, short stories, essays, collections, children's books.

How to Contact: Query with SASE. "No fax or e-mail submissions considered." Responds in 3 weeks to queries; 3 months to mss. For scripts, send outline/proposal with query. Prefers to read materials exclusively. Responds in 3 weeks to queries; 3 months to mss. Obtains most new clients through recommendations from others, solicitation, at conferences.

Recent Sales: Sold 6 titles in the last year. *Against All Odds*, by Barbara Riefe (TOR); *Herbal Medicine*, by Mary Atwood (Sterling); *Blood on the Moon* by Sharman DiVono (movie option to ABC); *The Shag Harbour Incident*, by Ledger and Styles (Dell).

Terms: Agent receives 15% commission on domestic sales; 10% on foreign sales. Offers written contract, binding for 1 year. Charges clients for photocopying, bank fees and special postage (i.e., express mail). 100% of business is derived from commissions on sales.

Tips: "Pay attention to what is getting published. Show the agent you've done your homework!"

✓ ◐ ◎ **ANN TOBIAS—A LITERARY AGENCY FOR CHILDREN'S BOOKS, (Specialized: children's books)**, 2250 Clarendon Blvd., Suite 412, Arlington VA 22201. (703)312-4466. **Contact:** Ann Tobias. Estab. 1988. Member of Children's Book Guild of Washington, Women's National Book Association, SCBWI. Represents 25 clients. 50% of clients are new/previously unpublished writers. Currently handles: 100% juvenile books.

● Prior to opening her agency, Ms. Tobias worked as a children's book editor at Harper, William Morrow, Scholastic.

Represents: Juvenile books. **Considers this nonfiction area:** juvenile nonfiction. **Considers these fiction areas:** picture book texts; mid-level and young adult novels; poetry; illustrated mss.

O➥ This agency specializes in books for children. Actively seeking material for children.

How to Contact: Send entire ms with SASE. Considers simultaneous queries and submissions. Responds immediately to queries; in 2 months to mss. Returns materials only with SASE. Obtains most new clients through recommendations from editors.

Recent Sales: Sold 15 titles in the last year. This agency prefers not to share information on specific sales.

Terms: Agent receives 15% commission on domestic sales; 20% on foreign sales. No written contract. Charges clients for photocopying, overnight mail, foreign postage, foreign telephone.

Reading List: Reads *Horn Book, Bulletin for the Center of the Book* and *School Library Journal.* "These are review media and they keep me up to date on who is being published and by what company."

Tips: "As a former children's book editor I believe I am of special help to my clients, as I understand the practices of the children's book publishing field. Read a few books out of the library on how literary agents do business before approaching one."

◙ SUSAN TRAVIS LITERARY AGENCY, P.O. Box 3670, Burbank CA 91508-3670. (818)557-6538. Fax: (818)557-6549. **Contact:** Susan Travis. Estab. 1995. Represents 10 clients. 60% of clients are new/previously unpublished writers. Currently handles: 70% nonfiction books; 30% novels.
- Prior to opening her agency, Ms. Travis served as an agent with the McBride Agency and prior to that worked in the Managing Editors Department of Ballantine Books.

Represents: Nonfiction books, novels. **Considers these nonfiction areas:** business; child guidance/parenting; cooking/food/nutrition; ethnic/cultural interests; health/medicine; how-to; popular culture; psychology; self-help/personal improvement; women's issues/women's studies. **Considers these fiction areas:** contemporary issues; ethnic; historical; literary; mainstream; romance (historical).
- ◘ This agency specializes in mainstream fiction and nonfiction. Actively seeking mainstream nonfiction. Does not want to receive science fiction, poetry or children's books.

How to Contact: Query with SASE. Responds in 3 weeks to queries; 6 weeks to mss. Obtains most new clients through referrals from existing clients, and mss requested from query letters.

Recent Sales: This agency prefers not to share information on specific sales.

Terms: Agent receives 15% commission on domestic sales; 20% on foreign sales. Offers written contract, binding for 1 year, with 60-day cancellation clause. Charges clients for photocopying of mss and proposals if copies not provided by author. 100% of business is derived from commissions on sales.

☑ ◙ ◎ S©OTT TREIMEL NY, (Specialized: children's books), 434 Lafayette St., New York NY 10003. (212)505-8353. Fax: (212)505-0664. E-mail: mescottyt@earthlink.net. **Contact:** Scott Treimel. Estab. 1995. Member of AAR. Represents 26 clients. 15% of clients are new/previously unpublished writers. Currently handles: 100% juvenile books.
- Prior to becoming an agent, Mr. Treimel was a rights agent for Scholastic, Inc.; a book packager and rights agent for United Feature Syndicate; a freelance editor and a rights consultant for HarperCollins Children's Books; and the founding director of Warner Bros. Worldwide Publishing.

Represents: Concept books, picture books, middle grade, first chapter books, young adult. **Considers all juvenile fiction and nonfiction areas.**
- ◘ This agency specializes in children's books: tightly focused segments of the trade and educational markets. Actively seeking picture book illustrators, first chapter books, middle-grade fiction and young adult fiction.

How to Contact: "Do not contact if you are 'interviewing' agents." Query with SASE. For picture books, send entire ms, "no more than two." Does not accept queries by fax. Returns multiple submissions. Requires "30-day exclusive on requested manuscripts." Returns materials with SASE or discards upon rejection. Obtains most new clients through referrals and queries.

Recent Sales: Sold 21 titles in the last year to Hyperion, Harcourt, Harper, Simon & Schuster, Clarion, Random House, etc.

Terms: Agent receives 15% commission on domestic sales; 20% on foreign sales. Offers verbal or written contract, "binding on a book contract by contract basis." Charges clients for photocopying, overnight/express postage, messengers, and books ordered to sell foreign, film, etc. rights.

Writers' Conferences: "Can You Make a Living from Children's Books;" Society of Children's Book Writers & Illustrators (Los Angeles, August).

N ◘ ◙ PAIGE TURNER AGENCY, P.O. Box 730, Belleville MI 48112-0730. (734)699-4715. Fax: (734)697-5596. E-mail: Paigeturner777@aol.com. **Contact:** Paige Turner. Estab. 2000. Represents 28 clients. 50% of clients are new/previously unpublished writers. Currently handles: 25% nonfiction books; 75% novels.
- Prior to becoming an agent, Ms. Turner was an editor, marketing specialist, paralegal, book/movie reviewer, scriptwriter/co-producer for cable TV, author.

Represents: Nonfiction books, novels. **Considers these nonfiction areas:** biography/autobiography; business; how-to; money/finance/economics; New Age; popular culture; religious/inspirational; self-help/personal improvement; narrative nonfiction. **Considers these fiction areas:** action/adventure; detective/police/crime; fantasy; horror; literary; mainstream; multicultural; mystery/suspense; romance; science fiction; thriller/espionage; commercial fiction, women's fiction.
- ◘ This agency provides free minimal editing and career guidance to clients, and likes to get the author involved

with promotion/marketing. Actively seeking commercial fiction (all areas) especially suspense thrillers and romance/women's fiction. Does not want to receive gay/lesbian, pornography, cult-related works, novellas, poetry, short stories, or anything with excessive profanity or violence.

How to Contact: For nonfiction: send outline, author bio and 2 sample chapters. For fiction: query with SASE, 1- or 2-page synopsis and first 2 chapters. Accepts queries by e-mail (no attachments). Prefers to read materials exclusively. Responds in 2 weeks to queries; 1 months to mss. Returns materials only with SASE.

Recent Sales: This is a new agency with no recorded sales. Clients include Bill Linn, Joyce Weiss, George Lowe, Gianna Woods, Ariann Stone, Jack Mitchell, Timothy Smith, C.P. Emmons, Rod Miller, Phillip Tomasso, Janine Bruce, Cynthia Overton, Paul Barlin, A. Ispas and others.

Terms: Agent receives 15% commission on domestic sales; 20% on foreign sales. Offers written contract, binding for 1 year. 60-day notice must be given to terminate contract. Charges clients for photocopies, postage, long distance, galleys, books for foreign rights submissions. "$200 maximum—no advance payment necessary."

Writers' Conferences: Oakland University Writer's Conference (Rochester MI, October); Midland Writers Conference (Midland MI, June).

Tips: "Make sure manuscript is complete before contacting me. It should be properly formatted, typed, double-spaced, 12-point font, with one-inch margins, and unbound if I request to see it. Tell me the word count. No dot matrix. Do not send gifts. Please be professional, realistic and patient. Know your genre's competition. Keep studying the craft of writing."

2M COMMUNICATIONS LTD., 121 W. 27 St., #601, New York NY 10001. (212)741-1509. Fax: (212)691-4460. E-mail: morel@bookhaven.com. **Contact:** Madeleine Morel. Estab. 1982. Represents 50 clients. 20% of clients are new/previously unpublished writers. Currently handles: 100% nonfiction books.

• Prior to becoming an agent, Madeleine Morel worked at a publishing company.

Represents: Nonfiction books. **Considers these nonfiction areas:** biography/autobiography; child guidance/parenting; ethnic/cultural interests; gay/lesbian issues; health/medicine; memoirs; music/dance/theater/film; self-help/personal improvement; travel; women's issues/women's studies.

○━ This agency specializes in adult nonfiction.

How to Contact: Query with SASE. Send outline and 3 sample chapters. Accepts queries by e-mail and fax. Considers simultaneous queries. Responds in 1 week to queries; 1 month to submissions. Obtains most new clients through recommendations from others, solicitation.

Recent Sales: Sold 20 titles in the last year. *Kwanzaa*, by Harriette Cole (Hyperion); *A Woman's Guide to Treating Fibroids*, by Alan Warshowsky, MD (Pocket); *Safe Shopper's Bible for Kids* (Macmillan); *Dewey Beats Truman* (Avon); *Bone Density Program* (Berkley).

Terms: Agent receives 15% commission on domestic sales; 20% on foreign sales. Offers written contract, binding for 2 years. Charges clients for postage, photocopying, long distance calls, faxes.

UNITED TRIBES, 240 W. 35th St., #500, New York NY 10001. (212)534-7646. E-mail: janguerth@aol.com. Website: www.unitedtribes.com. **Contact:** Jan-Erik Guerth. Estab. 1998. Represents 40 clients. 10% of clients are new/previously unpublished writers. Currently handles: 99% nonfiction books, 1% novels.

• Prior to becoming an agent, Mr. Guerth was a comedian, journalist, radio producer and film distributor.

Represents: Nonfiction books. **Considers these nonfiction areas:** anthropology/archaeology; art/architecture/design; biography/autobiography; business; child guidance/parenting; cooking/food/nutrition; current affairs; education; ethnic/cultural interests; gay/lesbian issues; government/politics/law; health/medicine; history; how-to; language/literature/criticism; memoirs; money/finance/economics; music/dance/theater/film; nature/enviornment; popular culture; psychology; religious/inspirational; science/technology (popular); self-help/personal improvement; sociology; translations; women's issues/women's studies.

○━ This agency specializes in the "Spirituality of Everyday Life" and ethnic, social, gender and cultural issues; comparative religions; self-help and wellness; science and arts; history and politics; nature and travel; and any fascinating future trends.

How to Contact: Send outline and 3 sample chapters with SASE, include résumé. Accepts queries by e-mail. Prefers to read materials exlusively. Responds in 2 weeks to queries; 1 month to mss. Returns materials only with SASE. Obtains most new clients through recommendations from others, solicitations, conferences.

Recent Sales: *The Power of Negative Thinking*, by Tony Humphrey (The Crossing Press).

Terms: Agent receives 15% commission on domestic sales; 20% on foreign sales.

THE RICHARD R. VALCOURT AGENCY, INC., (Specialized: government issues), 177 E. 77th St., PHC, New York NY 10021-1934. Phone/fax: (212)570-2340. President: Richard R. Valcourt. Estab. 1995. Represents 50 clients. 20% of clients are new/previously unpublished writers. Currently handles: 100% nonfiction books.

ALWAYS INCLUDE a self-addressed, stamped envelope (SASE) for reply or return of your query or manuscript.

• Prior to opening his agency, Mr. Valcourt was a journalist, editor and college political science instructor. He is also editor-in-chief of the *International Journal of Intelligence* and a faculty member at American Military University in Virginia.

Represents: Nonfiction books, scholarly books. **Considers these nonfiction areas:** biography; current affairs; government/politics/law; history; memoirs; military/war.

O¬ This agency specializes in intelligence and other national security affairs; domestic and international politics. Represents exclusively academics, journalists and professionals in the categories listed.

How to Contact: Query with SASE. Does not accept queries by fax or e-mail. Prefers to read materials exclusively. Responds in 1 week to queries; 1 month to mss. Returns materials only with SASE. Obtains most new clients through active recruitment and recommendations from others.

Recent Sales: *Odd Man Out: Truman, Stalin, Mao and the Origins of the Korean War*, by Richard C. Thornton (Brassey's).

Terms: Agent receives 15% commission on domestic sales; 20% on foreign sales. Offers written contract. Charges clients for excessive photocopying, express mail, overseas telephone expenses.

Reading List: Reads *The New Republic, The Nation, The Weekly Standard, Commentary, International Journal of Intelligence* and *Intelligence and National Security* to find new clients. Looks for "expertise in my highly-specialized concentrations."

N: Ø ANNETTE VAN DUREN AGENCY, 11684 Ventura Blvd., #235, Studio City CA 91604. (818)752-6000. Fax: (818)752-6985. **Contact:** Annette Van Duren or Teena Portier. Estab. 1985. Signatory of WGA. Represents 12 clients. No clients are new/previously unpublished writers. Currently handles: 10% novels; 50% movie scripts; 40% TV scripts.

• See the expanded listing for this agency in Script Agents.

Ø RALPH VICIANANZA, LTD., 111 Eighth Ave., Suite 1501, New York NY 10011. (212)924-7090. Fax: (212)691-9644. Member of AAR. Represents 120 clients. 5% of clients are new/previously unpublished writers.

Member Agents: Ralph M. Viciananza; Chris Lotts; Chris Schelling.

Represents: Nonfiction, novels. **Considers these nonfiction areas:** history; business; science; biography; popular culture; inspirational. **Considers these fiction areas:** literary; fantasy; multicultural; science fiction; popular fiction; thrillers; women's fiction.

O¬ This agency is a foreign rights specialist.

How to Contact: Query with SASE. *No unsolicited mss.*

Recent Sales: This agency prefers not to share information on specific sales.

Terms: Agency receives 15% commission on domestic sales; 20% on foreign sales.

Ø DAVID VIGLIANO LITERARY AGENCY, 584 Broadway, Suite 809, New York NY 10012. Member of AAR. This agency did not respond to our request for information. Query before submitting.

✓ Ø THE VINES AGENCY, INC., 648 Broadway, Suite 901, New York NY 10012. (212)777-5522. Fax: (212)777-5978. E-mail: JV@Vinesagency.com. **Contact:** James C. Vines or Gary Neuwirth. Estab. 1995. Member of AAR; signatory of WGA. Represents 52 clients. 20% of clients are new/previously unpublished writers. Currently handles: 50% nonfiction books; 50% novels.

• Prior to opening his agency, Mr. Vines served as an agent with the Virginia Literary Agency.

Member Agents: James C. Vines (quality and commercial fiction and nonfiction); Gary Neuwirth; Ali Ryan (women's fiction and nonfiction, mainstream).

Represents: Nonfiction books, novels. **Considers these nonfiction areas:** business; biography/autobiography; current affairs; ethnic/cultural interests; history; how-to; humor; military/war; memoirs; money/finance/economics; nature/environment; New Age/metaphysics; photography; popular culture; psychology; religious/inspirational; science/technology; self help/personal improvement; sociology; sports; translations; travel; true crime/investigative; women's issues/women's studies. **Considers these fiction areas:** action/adventure; contemporary issues; detective/police/crime; ethnic; feminist; horror; humor/satire; experimental; family saga; gay; lesbian; historical; literary; mainstream; mystery/suspense; psychic/supernatural; regional; romance (contemporary, historical); science fiction; sports; thriller/espionage; westerns/frontier; women's fiction.

O¬ This agency specializes in mystery, suspense, science fiction, mainstream novels, screenplays, teleplays.

Also Handles: Feature film, TV scripts, stage plays. **Considers these script subject areas:** action/adventure; comedy; detective/police/crime; ethnic; experimental; feminist; gay; historical; horror; lesbian; mainstream; mystery/suspense; romance (comedy, drama); science fiction; teen; thriller; westerns/frontier.

How to Contact: Send outline and first 3 chapters with SASE. Accepts queries by e-mail and fax. "Maximum of one page by fax or e-mail." Considers simultaneous queries and submissions. Responds in 2 weeks to queries; 1 month to mss. Returns materials only with SASE. Obtains most new clients through query letters, recommendations from others, reading short stories in magazines, soliciting conferences.

Recent Sales: Sold 46 book titles and 5 script projects in the last year. *California Fire and Life*, by Don Winslow (Random House); *Sugar*, by Bernice McFadden (Doubleday). **Script(s) optioned/sold:** *Ninth Life*, by Jay Colvin (Miramax); *Hunting With Hemingway*, by Hilary Hemingway (Riverhead); *The Bottoms*, by Joe R. Lansdale (Mysterious Press); *Cross Dressing*, by Bill Fitzhugh (Morrow).

Terms: Agent receives 15% commission on domestic sales; 25% on foreign sales. Offers written contract, binding for 1 year, with 30 days cancellation clause. Charges clients for foreign postage, messenger services, photocopying. 100% of business is derived from commissions on sales.
Writers' Conferences: Maui Writer's Conference.
Tips: "Do not follow up on submissions with phone calls to the agency. The agency will read and respond by mail only. Do not pack your manuscript in plastic 'peanuts' that will make us have to vacuum the office after opening the package containing your manuscript. Always enclose return postage."

☑ MARY JACK WALD ASSOCIATES, INC., 111 E. 14th St., New York NY 10003. Member of AAR. This agency did not respond to our request for information. Query before submitting.

☑ ☑ WALES, LITERARY AGENCY, INC., 108 Hayes St., Seattle WA 98109-2808. (206)284-7114. Fax: (206)284-0190. E-mail: waleslit@aol.com. **Contact:** Elizabeth Wales or Nancy Shawn. Estab. 1988. Member of AAR, Pacific Northwest Writers' Conference, Book Publishers' Northwest. Represents 60 clients. 10% of clients are new/previously unpublished writers. Currently handles: 60% nonfiction books; 35% novels; 5% short story collections.
• Prior to becoming an agent, Ms. Wales worked at Oxford University Press and Viking Penguin.
Member Agents: Nancy Shawn (foreign rights/reprints); Elizabeth Wales.
Represents: Nonfiction books, novels, short story collections, novellas. **Considers these nonfiction areas:** animals; biography/autobiography; current affairs; ethnic/cultural interests; gay/lesbian issues; history; memoirs; multicultural; nature; popular culture; science; travel; women's issues/women's studies—open to creative or serious treatments of almost any nonfiction subject. **Considers these fiction areas:** contemporary issues; erotica; ethnic; family saga; feminist; gay/lesbian; literary; mainstream; multicultural; regional.
➤ This agency specializes in mainstream nonfiction and fiction, as well as narrative nonfiction and literary fiction.
How to Contact: Query with SASE. "To Query: Please send cover letter, writing sample (no more than 30 pp.) and SASE." Accepts queries by e-mail. "Only short e-mail queries, no attachments." Considers simultaneous queries and submissions. Responds in 3 weeks to queries; 6 weeks to mss. Returns materials only with SASE.
Recent Sales: Sold 20 titles in the last year. *The Rachel Book*, by Karen Brennan (Norton); *The Stars, the Snow, the Fire*, by John Haines (Graywolf); *Lessons of the Nordstrom Way*, by Robert Spector (John Wiley); *Things Worth Saving*, by David Masumoto (Norton).
Terms: Agent receives 15% commission on domestic sales; 20% on foreign sales. Offers written contract, binding on a book-by-book basis. "We make all our income from commissions. We offer editorial help for some of our clients and help some clients with the development of a proposal, but we do not charge for these services. We do charge clients, after a sale, for express mail, manuscript photocopying costs, foreign postage and outside USA telephone costs."
Writers' Conferences: Pacific NW Writers Conference (Seattle, July); Writers at Work (Salt Lake City); Writing Rendevous (Anchorage).

 CLOSE UP with Elizabeth Wales, Wales Literary Agency, Inc.

On running an agency in Seattle . . .

"My agency is located in Seattle for the simple reason that when I got the idea of founding an agency I was living in Seattle and had no intention of leaving. It seemed to me that with my contacts from working in New York publishing—at Oxford University Press and what was then Viking Penguin—and with the boom in Seattle, the time was ripe for a Seattle-based literary agency. It has worked.

"New York businesses, including publishers, are New York-centric. Agents outside New York, especially agents from a distance, bring work that often hasn't worked itself into the inner buzz-circle of publishing. West Coast, or 'Coast agents' as we have been called, are particularly adept at finding new writers, new voices, and writers with a new point of view. One of our clients, Dan Savage, was syndicated in more than a dozen papers outside New York before he appeared there in the *Village Voice*.

"I visit 'The City' and lunch with more than a hundred editors a year. We outsiders know we are on the outside, so we make a big effort to stay in touch. I closed a deal with Betsy Lerner—then of Doubleday, now an agent herself—and at the time that was the only deal she had closed with an agent in person. In other words, outsiders and New Yorkers talk on the phone all the time. Personal contact is very important but is periodic for most agent/editor relationships, regardless of where the agent lives and does business."

Tips: "We are interested in published and not-yet-published writers. Especially encourages writers living in the Pacific Northwest, West Coast, Alaska and Pacific Rim countries to submit work."

☑ ◍ **WALLACE LITERARY AGENCY, INC.**, 177 E. 70 St., New York NY 10021. (212)570-9090. Fax: (212)772-8979. E-mail: walliter@aol.com. **Contact:** Lois Wallace. Estab. 1988. Represents 50 clients. 0% of clients are new/previously unpublished writers.
Represents: Nonfiction books, novels. **Considers these nonfiction areas:** anthropology/archaeology, biography/autobiography, current affairs, history, literature. **Considers these fiction areas:** literary, mainstream, mystery/suspense.

    O→ This agency specializes in fiction and nonfiction by good writers. Does not want to receive children's books, cookbooks, how-to, photography, poetry, romance, science fiction, self-help.

How to Contact: Send outline, 1 (at the most 2) sample chapter, reviews of previously published books, curriculum vitae, return postage. Does not accept queries by e-mail or fax. Prefers to read materials exclusively, but will read simultaneous queries and submissions if writer notifies agency that it is being read by others at the same time. Responds in 3 weeks to queries with material. Obtains most new clients through "recommendations from editors and writers we respect."
Recent Sales: Sold 12-15 titles in the last year. *The Body Artist*, by Don Delillo (Scribner); *The First American*, by Stacy Schiff (Henry Holt).
Terms: Agent receives 10-15% commission on domestic sales; 20% on foreign sales. Offers written contract, binding until terminated with notice. Charges clients for photocopying, book shipping (or ms shipping) overseas, legal fees (if needed, with writer's approval), galleys and books needed for representation and foreign sales.

◍ **JOHN A. WARE LITERARY AGENCY**, 392 Central Park West, New York NY 10025-5801. (212)866-4733. Fax: (212)866-4734. **Contact:** John Ware. Estab. 1978. Represents 60 clients. 40% of clients are new/previously unpublished writers. Currently handles: 75% nonfiction books; 25% novels.

    • Prior to opening his agency, Mr. Ware served as a literary agent with James Brown Associates/Curtis Brown, Ltd. and as an editor for Doubleday & Company.

Represents: Nonfiction books, novels. **Considers these nonfiction areas:** animals; anthropology; biography; current affairs; social commentary; history (including oral history, Americana and folklore); investigative journalism; language; music; nature/environment; popular culture; psychology and health (academic credentials required); science; sports; travel; true crime; women's issues/women's studies; 'bird's eye' views of phenomena. **Considers these fiction areas:** accessible literate noncategory fiction; detective/police/crime; mystery/suspense; thriller/espionage.
How to Contact: Query by letter first only, include SASE. Does not accept queries by e-mail or fax. Considers simultaneous queries and submissions "with terms of multiple submissions to be agreed upon." Responds in 2 weeks to queries.
Recent Sales: *An Unreturned Pilgrim: Biography of Bishop James Pike*, by David Robertson (Knopf); *Taking Control: Harnessing the Drive of Addiction*, by Lance M. Dodes, M.D. (HarperCollins); *A Bishop's Tale*, by Craig Harline and Eddy Put (Yale). Other clients include Jon Krakauer, Jack Womack, Caroline Fraser.
Terms: Agent receives 15% commission on domestic sales; 15% on dramatic sales; 20% on foreign sales. Charges clients for messenger service, photocopying.
Tips: "Writers must have appropriate credentials for authorship of proposal (nonfiction) or manuscript (fiction); no publishing track record required. Open to good writing and interesting ideas by new or veteran writers."

∅ **HARRIET WASSERMAN LITERARY AGENCY**, 137 E. 36th St., New York NY 10016. Member of AAR. This agency did not respond to our request for information. Query before submitting.

⟦N⟧ ∅ **WATERSIDE PRODUCTIONS, INC.**, 2191 San Elijo Ave., Cardiff-by-the-Sea CA 92007-1839. (619)632-9190. Fax: (760)632-9295. E-mail: admin@waterside.com. Website: www.waterside.com. President: Bill Gladstone. **Contact:** Matt Wagner, Margot Maley. Estab. 1982. Represents 300 clients. 20% of clients are new/previously unpublished writers. Currently handles: 100% nonfiction.
Member Agents: Bill Gladstone (trade computer titles, business); Margot Maley (trade computer titles, nonfiction); Matthew Wagner (trade computer titles, nonfiction); Carole McClendon (trade computer titles); David Fugate (trade computer titles, business, general nonfiction, sports books); Chris Van Buren (trade computer titles, spirituality, self-help); Christian Crumlish (trade computer titles).
Represents: Nonfiction books. **Considers these nonfiction areas:** art/architecture/design; biography/autobiography; business; child guidance/parenting; computers/electronics; ethnic/cultural interests; health/medicine; humor; money/finance/economics; nature/environment; popular culture; psychology; sociology; sports.
How to Contact: Query with outline/proposal and SASE. Accepts queries by e-mail. Considers simultaneous queries and submissions. Responds in 2 weeks to queries; 2 months to mss. Obtains most new clients through recommendations from others.
Recent Sales: Sold 400 titles in the last year. *Just For the Fun of It*, by Linus Torvalds (Harper Business); *Windows 98 for Dummies*, by Andy Rathbone (IDG); *Mastering Visual Basic 5*, by Evangelos Petroutsos.
Terms: Agent receives 15% commission on domestic sales; 25% on foreign sales. Offers written contract. Charges clients for photocopying and other unusual expenses.
Writers' Conferences: "We host the Waterside Publishing Conference each spring in San Diego. Please check our website for details."

Tips: "For new writers, a quality proposal and a strong knowledge of the market you're writing for goes a long way towards helping us turn you into a published author."

✪ WATKINS LOOMIS AGENCY, INC., 133 E. 35th St., Suite 1, New York NY 10016. (212)532-0080. Fax: (212)889-0506. **Contact:** Katherine Fausset. Estab. 1908. Represents 150 clients.
Member Agents: Nicole Aragi (associate); Gloria Loomis (president); Katherine Fausset (assistant agent).
Represents: Nonfiction books, short story collections, novels. **Considers these nonfiction areas:** art/architecture/design; biography/autobiography; current affairs; ethnic/cultural interests; gay/lesbian issues; history; nature/environment; popular culture; science/technology; true crime/investigative; women's issues/women's studies; journalism. **Considers these fiction areas:** literary.
  ⚬➞ This agency specializes in literary fiction, nonfiction.
How to Contact: Query with SASE by mail only. Responds within 1 month to queries.
Recent Sales: This agency prefers not to share information on specific sales. Clients include Walter Mosley, Edwidge Danticat, Junot Díaz, Cornel West.
Terms: Agent receives 15% commission on domestic sales; 20% on foreign sales.

⊘ SANDRA WATT & ASSOCIATES, 1750 N. Sierra Bonita, Hollywood CA 90046-2423. (323)851-1021. Fax: (323)851-1046. E-mail: rondvart@aol.com. Estab. 1977. Represents 55 clients. 15% of clients are new/previously unpublished writers. Currently handles: 40% nonfiction books; 60% novels.
  ● Prior to opening her agency, Ms. Watt was vice president of an educational publishing company.
Member Agents: Sandra Watt (scripts, nonfiction, novels).
Represents: Nonfiction books, novels. **Considers these nonfiction areas:** agriculture/horticulture; animals; anthropology/archaeology; art/architecture/design; crafts/hobbies; current affairs; how-to; humor; language/literature/criticism; memoirs; nature/environment; New Age/metaphysics; popular culture; psychology; reference; religious/inspirational; self-help/personal improvement; sports; travel; true crime/investigative; women's issues/women's studies. **Considers these fiction areas:** contemporary issues; detective/police/crime; family saga; mainstream; mystery/suspense; regional; religious/inspirational; thriller/espionage; women's mainstream novels.
  ⚬➞ This agency specializes in "books to film" and scripts: film noir; family; romantic comedies; books: women's fiction, young adult, mystery, commercial nonfiction. Does not want to receive "first 'ideas' for finished work."
How to Contact: Query with SASE. Accepts queries by fax and e-mail. Considers simultaneous queries and submissions. Responds in 2 weeks to queries; 2 months to mss. Returns materials only with SASE. Obtains most new clients through recommendations from others, referrals and "from wonderful query letters. Don't forget the SASE!"
Recent Sales: Sold 6 titles in the last year. *Risk Factor*, by Charles Atkins (St. Martin's Press); *Love is the Only Answer* (Putnam).
Terms: Agent receives 15% commission on domestic sales; 25% on foreign sales. Offers written contract, binding for 1 year. Charges clients one-time nonrefundable marketing fee of $100 *for unpublished authors.*

✓ ⊘ SCOTT WAXMAN AGENCY, INC., 1650 Broadway, Suite 1011, New York NY 10019. (212)262-2388. Fax: (212)262-0119. E-mail: gracem@swagency.net. Website: www.swagency.net. **Contact:** Grace Madamba. Estab. 1997. Member of AAR. Represents 60 clients. 50% of clients are new/previously unpublished writers. Currently handles: 60% nonfiction books; 40% novels.
  ● Prior to opening his agency, Mr. Waxman was editor for five years at HarperCollins and an agent at the Literary Group International.
Member Agents: Scott Waxman (all categories of nonfiction, literary fiction, commercial fiction); Giles Anderson (literary fiction, commercial fiction, narrative nonfiction, spirituality).
Represents: Nonfiction books, novels. **Considers these nonfiction areas:** adventure/nature; biography/autobiography; business; ethnic/cultural interests; health/medicine; history; money/finance/economics; politics/current affairs; religious/inspirational; science/technology/new media; self-help/personal improvement; sports; true crime. **Considers these fiction areas:** action/adventure; ethnic; historical; literary; hard-boiled detective; religious/inspirational; romance (contemporary, historical); sports; suspense.
  ⚬➞ "Although we have specialized in spirituality/religion and sports, we are always very interested in looking at and expanding our list to include commercial and literary fiction (particularly by recent MFA graduates—Iowa, Johns Hopkins, etc.), as well as many categories of nonfiction. We encourage authors to visit our website for a better idea of the range of writing we represent." Actively seeking strong, high-concept commercial fiction, literary fiction and narrative nonfiction; very interested in women's commercial fiction.
How to Contact: Query with SASE. Accepts queries by e-mail. Considers simultaneous queries. Responds in 2 weeks to queries; 6 weeks to mss. Discards unwanted or unsolicited mss. Returns materials only with SASE and/or proper packaging. "Please view our website for submission requirements." Obtains most new clients through recommendations, writers conferences, Internet, magazines.
Recent Sales: Sold 40 titles in the last year. *A Separate Place*, by David Brill (Dutton Plume); *Survivor!*, by Mark Burnett (TV Books); *Black Mountain*, by Les Standiford (G.P. Putnam & Sons); *Fire On the Mountain*, by Daniel Glick (Public Affairs); *The Knight's Tour*, by J.C. Hallman (St. Martin's Press); *Endeavour*, by Martin Dsgard (Pocket); *Journal of the Dead*, by Jason Kersten (HarperCollins); *Kind of Blue*, by Ashley Kahn (Da Capo); *Leadership Ensemble*,

by Harvey Seifter-Orpheus Chamber Orchestra and Peter Economy (Henry Holt); *Six Steps to Affair-Proof Your Marriage*, by Gary Neuman (Crown); *Faster!*, by Bob Babbitt and Mike Gotfredson (Simon & Schuster); *The Last Frontier*, by Matthew Brzezinski (The Free Press); *A Still Small Voice*, by John Reed (Delacorte).
Terms: Agent receives 15% commission on domestic sales; 25% on foreign sales. Offers written contract. 60-day notice must be given to terminate contract. Charges clients for photocopying, express mail, messenger service, international postage, book orders. Refers to editing services for clients only. 0% of business is derived from editing service.
Writers' Conferences: Celebration of Writing in the Low Country (Beaufort SC, August 6-9, 1999); Golden Triangle Writers Guild Conference (Beaumont TX, October 1999); FIU/Seaside Writers Conference (FL, October).
Reading List: Reads *Witness*, *Boulevard*, *Literal Latté*, *Mississippi Review*, *Zoetrope*, as well as a variety of well-known periodicals such as *GQ*, *Vanity Fair*, *Harper's*, *Rolling Stone*, *Sports Illustrated*, *The Atlantic Monthly* and many others to find new clients.

WECKSLER-INCOMCO, 170 West End Ave., New York NY 10023. (212)787-2239. Fax: (212)496-7035. **Contact:** Sally Wecksler. Estab. 1971. Represents 25 clients. 50% of clients are new/previously unpublished writers. "However, I prefer writers who have had something in print." Currently handles: 60% nonfiction books; 15% novels; 25% juvenile books.

• Prior to becoming an agent, Ms. Wecksler was an editor at *Publishers Weekly*; publisher with the international department of R.R. Bowker; and international director at Baker & Taylor.

Member Agents: Joann Amparan (general, children's books), S. Wecksler (general, foreign rights/co-editions, fiction, illustrated books, children's books, business).
Represents: Nonfiction books, novels, juvenile books. **Considers these nonfiction areas:** art/architecture design; biography/autobiography; business; current affairs; history; juvenile nonfiction; literary; music/dance/theater/film; nature/environment; photography. **Considers these fiction areas:** contemporary issues; historical; juvenile; literary; mainstream; picture book.

O→ This agency specializes in nonfiction with illustrations (photos and art). Actively seeking "illustrated books for adults or children with beautiful photos or artwork." Does not want to receive "science fiction or books with violence."

How to Contact: Query with outline, brief bio and SASE. Responds in 1 month to queries; 2 months to mss. Obtains most new clients through recommendations from others, solicitations.
Recent Sales: Sold 11 titles in the last year. *Do's & Taboos—Women in International Business*, and *Do's & Taboos—Humor Around the World*, by Roger E. Axtell (Wiley); *Color Series*, by Candace Whitman (Abbeville).
Terms: Agent receives 15% commission on domestic sales; 20% on foreign sales. Offers written contract, binding for 3 years.
Tips: "Make sure a SASE is enclosed. Send three chapters and outline, clearly typed or word processed, double-spaced, written with punctuation and grammar in approved style. *No presentations by fax.*"

THE WENDY WEIL AGENCY, INC., 232 Madison Ave., Suite 1300, New York NY 10016. Member of AAR. This agency did not respond to our request for information. Query before submitting.

CHERRY WEINER LITERARY AGENCY, 28 Kipling Way, Manalapan NJ 07726-3711. (732)446-2096. Fax: (732)792-0506. E-mail: cherry8486@aol.com. **Contact:** Cherry Weiner. Estab. 1977. Represents 40 clients. 10% of clients are new/previously unpublished writers. Currently handles: 10-20% nonfiction books; 80-90% novels.

• This agency is not currently looking for new clients except by referral or by personal contact at writers' conferences.

Represents: Nonfiction books, novels. **Considers these nonfiction areas:** self-help/improvement, sociology. **Considers these fiction areas:** action/adventure; contemporary issues; detective/police/crime; family saga; fantasy; glitz; historical; mainstream; mystery/suspense; psychic/supernatural; romance; science fiction; thriller/espionage; westerns/frontier.

O→ This agency specializes in science fiction, fantasy, westerns, mysteries (both contemporary and historical), historical novels, Native American works, mainstream, all the genre romances.

How to Contact: Query with SASE. Does not accept queries by fax or e-mail. Prefers to read materials exclusively. Responds in 1 week to queries; 2 months to mss. Returns materials only with SASE or discards.
Recent Sales: Sold 30 titles in the last year. *7 Real People Series Books*, by Robert J. Conley (Oklahoma University Press); *Territorial Marshal Series*, by Dusty Richards (St. Martin's Press); *Problem of Evil Editor*, by Roberta Rogow (St. Martin's Press); *Little Bear*, by Tim McGuire (Dorchester Publishing); *Spanish Jack*, by Robert J. Conley (St. Martin's Press).
Terms: Agent receives 15% on domestic sales; 15% on foreign sales. Offers written contract. Charges clients for extra copies of mss "but would prefer author do it"; 1st class postage for author's copies of books; Express Mail for important document/manuscripts.
Writers' Conferences: Western Writers Convention; SF Conventions; Fantasy Conventions.
Tips: "Meet agents and publishers at conferences. Establish a relationship, then get in touch with them reminding them of meetings and conference."

THE WEINGEL-FIDEL AGENCY, 310 E. 46th St., 21E, New York NY 10017. (212)599-2959. **Contact:** Loretta Weingel-Fidel. Estab. 1989. Currently handles: 75% nonfiction books; 25% novels.

• Prior to opening her agency, Ms. Weingel-Fidel was a psychoeducational diagnostician.

insider report

Generating ideas: a creative agent/author partnership

Author Les Standiford has always been interested in Henry Flagler and the Key West connection of the Florida East Coast Railway. However, if it hadn't been for his agent, Scott Waxman of Scott Waxman, Inc., Standiford may have never pursued the story for his latest nonfiction project, *Last Train to Paradise* (Crown Publishers Inc.).

According to Standiford, Waxman was impressed by the story's potential when he heard about it at the Hemingway Home in Key West. "Hemingway had been involved in the aftermath of the hurricane that blew the railroad away in 1935," Standiford explains. "Scott had seen remnants of the railroad which still exist today. He thought there was a book in this story. I told him I'd be interested in writing it."

Although the "You write 'em—I sell 'em" philosophy is typical of some author/agent partnerships, Standiford describes his relationship with Waxman as "very creative." His agent's input and enthusiasm are important to him. "I credit Scott for making this project become a reality. He gave me a good topic to write about and then was instrumental in finding a publisher for it."

The upcoming *Last Train to Paradise*, which Standiford describes as "*Ragtime* meets *The Perfect Storm*," is the story of Standard Oil founder Flagler and his attempt to build a railroad linking Miami and Key West. "Flagler is one of the last of those old-time titans—men who thought they could do anything they set their minds to," says Standiford. "This is a man who at one time was John D. Rockefeller's boss and, tired of the oil business, moved to Florida and spent the last twenty-five years of his life developing one project or another." Flagler built hotels up and down the state's east coast, then built the railway to transport tourists to his resorts. His dream of building the Miami-Key West connection, which would span seven miles of open water en route, was called "Flagler's Folly."

"I take Flagler at his word when he said, 'I would have been a rich man if it hadn't been for Florida,' " says Standiford. "He became seduced by the tropics and is another in a long line of people drawn by the siren song of Paradise, then left to founder on the rocks. That's really the theme of this book. I think it's not only an exciting story but a profound story as well. That's why I wanted to do it."

Although Standiford is the author of such fictional thrillers as *Spill* (Atlantic Monthly Press), *Black Mountain* (Putnam Publishing Group), and the Deal series of crime novels (HarperCollins Publishers), he's written other nonfiction books as well. One, *Coral Gables: The City Beautiful* (Riverbend Books), is a history of Coral Gables and its builder, George Merrick, another man of epic dreams and personal drive. *Last Train to Paradise* is "somewhat more ambitious," says Standiford, whose academic background served him well during the whole undertaking. "By training, I'm a university professor. I have a Ph.D. in literature, and research is one of the things you learn how to do. In essence, the book combines those skills with the experience I really have, even though I'm mostly known for my fiction."

Did Standiford ever consider writing *Last Train to Paradise* as a fictional account? "No. I think there's too much drama in what really happened to change it from the truth."

Those writing skills helped Scott Waxman recognize that Standiford was just the man to tell the Flagler saga. "Les is a talented author who writes about characters and courageous, wonderful stories. I knew we had a great locale— his backyard is Key West. It was tailored just for him."

This isn't the first time Standiford has benefited from Waxman's inspiration and initiative. "He was also instrumental in developing *The Putt at the End of the World*, the concept book about golf in the tradition of *Naked Came the Manatee* (The Berkeley Publishing Group)." The book, team-written by thirteen top Florida authors, is a kind of round-robin mystery to which Standiford contributed. "That project was born of a conversation Scott had with an editor at Warner Books, where they were thinking about a serialized novel with golf as the central theme. Scott said, 'My client happens to be one of the people who was involved in making *Naked Came the Manatee*.' From that conversation, Scott was able to put together the deal that led to that book."

Standiford, who acted as editor, found the authors who participated and also wrote the first chapter of *The Putt at the End of the World*. He claims, "If it hadn't been for the conversation between Scott and that editor, the book never would have happened. I certainly never would have called up Scott or an editor at Warner Books out of the clear blue sky, and said, 'Hey, you guys want to do a book like that?' "

Waxman believes it's important for an agent to play as many roles as possible in an author's career. "It's not unusual for agents to be proactive during a time in publishing when ideas can lead to books. Agents are probably the closest relationship with someone in publishing an author has today. As editors change houses frequently, the agent becomes the one constant in the author's life. That relationship can take many shapes. It can be the financial advisor, it can be a support system, but it can also be a creative support."

Both Waxman and Standiford point out that such author/agent collaborations depend on the author's comfort level with that kind of interaction. "Some writers just want somebody to market their work once it's finished," says Standiford. "They don't want anyone meddling in their creative business. In terms of coming up with an interesting subject, I welcome that kind of input. I can always say no."

Waxman adds that it's important for writers to have chemistry with their agents, "to feel that they understand you as a writer and that they're not forcing their own ideas upon you. They need to work with you almost hand in glove as you develop ideas together.

"If authors like their agents," continues Waxman, "they should trust them and listen to them, because agents live in the world of publishing every day. If writers are going to follow through on this relationship, they need to have faith in what their agents are telling them." And for Standiford, his faith in Waxman's ideas has paid off wonderfully.

—*Nancy Breen*

Represents: Nonfiction books, novels. **Considers these nonfiction areas:** art/architecture/design; biography/autobiography; investigative; memoirs; music/dance/theater/film; psychology; science; sociology; women's issues/women's studies. **Considers these fiction areas:** contemporary issues; literary; mainstream.

   O→ This agency specializes in commercial, literary fiction and nonfiction. Actively seeking investigative journalism. Does not want to receive genre fiction, self-help, science fiction, fantasy.

How to Contact: Referred writers only. *No unsolicited mss.* Obtains most new clients through referrals.

Recent Sales: *The New Rabbi,* by Stephen Fried (Bantam); and *Brand New House,* by Katherine Salant (Clarkson Potter); *The V Book,* by Elizabeth G. Stewart, M.D. and Paula Spencer (Bantam).

Terms: Agent receives 15% on domestic sales; 20% on foreign sales. Offers written contract, binding for 1 year automatic renewal. Bills back to clients all reasonable expenses such as UPS, express mail, photocopying, etc.

Tips: "A very small, selective list enables me to work very closely with my clients to develop and nurture talent. I only take on projects and writers about which I am extremely enthusiastic."

◐ WEST COAST LITERARY ASSOCIATES, PMB 337, 1534 Plaza Lane, Burlingame CA 94010. E-mail: wstlit@aol.com. **Contact:** Richard Van Der Beets. Estab. 1986. Member of Authors League of America, Authors Guild. Represents 40 clients. 50% of clients are new/previously unpublished clients. Currently handles: 20% nonfiction books; 80% novels.

   • Prior to opening his agency, Mr. Van Der Beets served as a professor of English at San Jose State University.

Represents: Nonfiction books, novels. **Considers these nonfiction areas:** biography/autobiography; current affairs; ethnic/cultural interests; government/politics/law; history; language/literature/criticism; music/dance/theater/film; nature/environment; psychology; true crime/investigative; women's issues/women's studies. **Considers these fiction areas:** action/adventure; contemporary issues; detective/police/crime; experimental; historical; literary; mainstream; mystery/suspense; regional; romance (contemporary and historical); science fiction; thriller/espionage; westerns/frontier.

   O→ Actively seeking mystery, suspense, thriller. Does not want to receive self-help, humorous nonfiction.

How to Contact: Query first with SASE. *No phone calls.* Accepts queries by e-mail. Considers simultaneous queries and submissions. Responds in 2 weeks to queries; 1 month to mss. Returns materials only with SASE.

Recent Sales: Sold 2 titles in the last year. *Settler's Law,* by D.H. Eraldi (Berkley Books); *Johnny Ace,* by James Salem (Illinois University Press).

Terms: Agent receives 10% commission on domestic sales; 20% commission on foreign sales. Offers written contract, binding for 6 months. Charges clients $75-95 marketing and materials fee, depending on genre and length. Fees are refunded in full upon sale of the property.

Writers' Conferences: California Writer's Conference (Asilomar).

Tips: "Query with SASE for submission guidelines before sending material."

◖ RHODA WEYR AGENCY, 151 Bergen St., Brooklyn NY 11217. (718)522-0480. **Contact:** Rhoda A. Weyr, president. Estab. 1983. Member of AAR. Prefers to work with published/established authors.

   • Prior to starting her agency, Ms. Weyr was an agent at William Morris and a foreign correspondent.

Represents: Nonfiction books, novels.

   O→ This agency specializes in general nonfiction and fiction.

How to Contact: Query with SASE. *No unsolicited mss.*

Recent Sales: Sold over 21 titles in the last year. This agency prefers not to share information on specific sales.

Terms: Agent receives 15% commission on domestic sales; 20% on foreign sales. Charges clients for "heavy duty copying or special mailings (e.g., FedEx etc.)."

◖ WIESER & WIESER, INC., 25 E. 21 St., 6th Floor, New York NY 10010. (212)260-0860. **Contact:** Olga Wieser. Estab. 1975. 30% of clients are new/previously unpublished writers. Currently handles: 50% nonfiction books; 50% novels.

Member Agents: Jake Elwell (history, military, mysteries, romance, sports, thrillers); Olga Wieser (psychology, fiction, pop medical, literary fiction).

Represents: Nonfiction books, novels. **Considers these nonfiction areas:** business; cooking/food/nutrition; current affairs; health/medicine; history; money/finance/economics; nature/environment; psychology; sports; true crime/investigative. **Considers these fiction areas:** contemporary issues; detective/police/crime; historical; literary; mainstream; mystery/suspense; romance; thriller/espionage.

   O→ This agency specializes in mainstream fiction and nonfiction.

How to Contact: Query with outline/proposal and SASE. Responds in 2 weeks to queries. Obtains most new clients through queries, authors' recommendations and industry professionals.

Recent Sales: *Anatomy of Anorexia,* by Steven Levenkron (Norton); *Hocus Corpus,* by James N. Tucker, M.D. (Dutton/Signet); *A Little Traveling Music Please,* by Margaret Moseley (Berkley); *The Kamikazes,* by Edwin P. Hoyt (Burford Books); and *Angels & Demons,* by Dan Brown (Pocket); *Headwind,* by John Nance (Putnam).

Terms: Agent receives 15% commission on domestic sales; 20% on foreign sales. Offers written contract. Charges clients for photocopying and overseas mailing.

Writers' Conferences: BEA; Frankfurt Book Fair.

◑ AUDREY A. WOLF LITERARY AGENCY, 1001 Connecticut Ave. NW, Washington DC 20036. Member of AAR. This agency did not respond to our request for information. Query before submitting.

THE WONDERLAND PRESS, INC., 160 Fifth Avenue, Suite 723, New York NY 10010-7003. (212)989-2550. E-mail: litraryagt@aol.com. **Contact:** John Campbell. Estab. 1985. Member of the American Book Producers Association. Represents 24 clients. Currently handles: 90% nonfiction books; 10% novels.

• The Wonderland Press is also a book packager and "in a position to nurture strong proposals all the way from concept through bound books."

Represents: Nonfiction books, novels. **Considers these nonfiction areas:** art/architecture/design; biography/autobiography; enthnic/cultural interests; gay/lesbian issues; health/medicine; history; how-to; interior design/decorating; language/literature/criticism; photography; popular culture; psychology; self-help/personal improvement. **Considers these fiction areas:** action/adventure; literary; thriller.

○➤ This agency specializes in high-quality nonfiction, illustrated, reference, how-to and entertainment books. Does not want to receive poetry, memoir, children's fiction or category fiction.

How to Contact: Send outline/proposal with SASE. Accepts queries by e-mail or fax. Prefers to read materials exclusively. Responds in 5 days to queries; 2 weeks to mss. "Almost all of our new authors come to us by referral. Often they 'find' us by researching the books we have sold for our other clients."

Recent Sales: Sold 38 titles in the last year. *Nude Body Nude*, by Howard Schatz (HarperCollins); *The Essential*, by Dale Chihuly (Abrams).

Terms: Agent receives 15% commission on domestic sales. Offers written contract. 30-90 days notice must be given to terminate contract. Offers criticism service, included in 15% commission. Charges clients for photocopying, long-distance telephone, overnight express-mail, messengering.

Tips: "We welcome submissions from new authors, but proposals must be unique, of high commercial interest and well written. Follow your talent. Write with passion. Know your market. Submit polished work instead of apologizing for its mistakes, typos, incompleteness, etc. We want to see your best work."

N **PAMELA D. WRAY LITERARY AGENCY**, 1304 Dogwood Dr., Oxford AL 36203. (256)835-8008. E-mail: pxchange@hiwaay.net. Website: www.wrayagency.com. **Contact:** Pamela D. Wray. Estab. 1999. Represents 42 clients. 70% of clients are new/previously unpublished writers. Currently handles: 40% nonfiction books; 40% novels; 20% children's books.

• Prior to becoming an agent, Ms. Wray was CEO and President of her own marketing/design firm for 13 years.

Member Agents: Thomas R. Ray (technical, automotive, scientific); David Wray (sports, mechanical); Pamela Wray.

Represents: Nonfiction books, novels, children's. **Considers these nonfiction areas:** art/architecture/design; biography/autobiography; business; child guidance/parenting; computers/electronics; cooking/food/nutrition; current affairs; education; government/politics/law; health/medicine; how-to; humor; memoirs; military/war; money/finance/economics; religious/inspirational; science/technology; self-help/personal improvement; sociology; sports; travel. **Considers these fiction areas:** detective/police/crime; horror; humor/satire; mainstream; mystery/suspense; picture book; psychic/supernatural; thriller/espionage; young adult.

○➤ "My specialties are nonfiction (business, technical, medical and memoirs) and in fiction (mystery, suspense, thriller, horror and children's books). I have 25 years of personal experience and expertise in marketing, public relations, media consultant, advertising, contract negotiations, publishing and editorial services: freelance, contract and author. I am also a graphic designer and commercial artist. When an author signs with my agency, I personally read, edit and critique his/her manuscript and work with them as a development editor to get the manuscript in the best form for submission. I also develop a detailed marketing and publicity plan, author website, chat room and devise Internet marketing strategies for my clients. The best feature of my services, according to my clients, is that I answer telephone calls, return telephone calls and stay in touch with them by e-mail and actively seek author participation in managing their careers by working as a team." Actively seeking mystery, thriller, suspense, children's picture books, juvenile fiction, nonfiction: business, technical, medical, government. Does not want to receive hobbies or crafts, design or architecture, New Age, nature, photography, science fiction, fantasy, romance.

How to Contact: Send synopsis, author bio, first 3 chapters and last 3 chapters, SASE. Accepts queries by e-mail and fax. Prefers to read materials exclusively. Reponds in 3 days to queries; 1 month to mss. Returns materials only with SASE. Obtains most new clients through recommendations from others, queries/solicitations, conferences.

Recent Sales: This is a new agency with no recorded sales.

Terms: Agent receives 15% commission on domestic sales; 25% on foreign sales; 20% on performance rights. Offers written contract, binding on a book-to-book basis. 30-day notice must be given by author or agent to terminate contract.

Writers' Conference: Southeastern Booksellers Trade Show (Memphis TN, September 20-23, 2001); Book Expo America (Chicago IL, June 1-3, 2001); Boucheron World Mystery Convention (Washington DC, November 1-4, 2001).

THE PUBLISHING FIELD is constantly changing! Agents often change addresses, phone numbers, or even companies. If you're still using this book and it is 2002 or later, buy the newest edition of *Guide to Literary Agents* at your favorite bookstore or order directly from Writer's Digest Books at (800)289-0963.

Tips: "Please do not e-mail complete manuscripts because I do not have time to read them, just e-mail synopsis first, and I will respond with further information on what I would like to see concerning your manuscripts. When you send a manuscript, please make sure that you have proofread and edited for spelling and major grammatical errors before you submit to an agent. It is disheartening to know that the author has not taken the time to get their manuscripts in form and this lets me know that the author does not pay close attention to the smaller details and is not serious about their work or getting it published. Please send self-addressed, stamped envelopes if you want your work returned; otherwise it is discarded. Please don't submit manuscripts for subjects that I don't represent because I will return these."

ANN WRIGHT REPRESENTATIVES, 165 W. 46th St., Suite 1105, New York NY 10036-2501. (212)764-6770. Fax: (212)764-5125. **Contact:** Dan Wright. Estab. 1961. Signatory of WGA. Represents 23 clients. 30% of clients are new/previously unpublished writers. Prefers to work with published/established authors; works with a small number of new/previously unpublished authors. Currently handles: 50% novels; 40% movie scripts; 10% TV scripts.
  • See the expanded listing for this agency in Script Agents.

WRITERS HOUSE, 21 W. 26th St., New York NY 10010. (212)685-2400. Fax: (212)685-1781. Estab. 1974. Member of AAR. Represents 440 clients. 50% of clients were new/previously unpublished writers. Currently handles: 25% nonfiction books; 35% juvenile books; 40% novels.
Member Agents: Albert Zuckerman (major novels, thrillers, women's fiction, important nonfiction); Amy Berkower (major juvenile authors, women's fiction, popular and literary fiction); Merrilee Heifetz (major fantasy and science fiction authors, quality children's fiction, popular culture, literary fiction); Susan Cohen (juvenile and young adult fiction and nonfiction, juvenile illustrators, Judaism, women's issues); Susan Ginsburg (serious and popular fiction, narrative nonfiction, popular science and math, personality books, cookbooks); Fran Lebowitz (juvenile and young adult, popular culture); Michele Rubin (narrative nonfiction, history, biography, literary fiction, mysteries); Karen Solem (contemporary and historical romance, women's fiction, narrative nonfiction, horse and animal books); Robin Rue (commercial fiction and nonfiction, young adult fiction); Jennifer Lyons (literary, commercial fiction, international fiction, nonfiction and illustrated); Simon Lipskar (literary and commercial fiction, creative and narrative nonfiction, young writers).
Represents: Nonfiction books, juvenile books, novels. **Considers these nonfiction areas:** animals; art/architecture/design; biography/autobiography; business; child guidance/parenting; cooking/food/nutrition; health/medicine; history; interior design/decorating; juvenile nonfiction; military/war; money/finance/economics; music/dance/theater/film; nature/environment; psychology; science/technology; self-help/personal improvement; true crime/investigative; women's issues/women's studies. **Considers any fiction area.** "Quality is everything."
  O→ This agency specializes in all types of popular fiction and nonfiction. Does not want to receive scholarly work, professional, poetry, screenplays.
How to Contact: Query with SASE. Responds in 1 month to queries. Obtains most new clients through recommendations from others.
Recent Sales: *The New New Thing*, by Michael Lewis (Norton); *Middle of Nowhere*, by Ridley Pearson (Hyperion); *Into the Garden*, by V.C. Andrews (Pocket); *Carolina Moon*, by Nora Roberts (Putnam); *Code to Zero*, by Ken Follet (Dutton); *The Universe In a Nutshell, American Gods*, by Neil Gaimon (HarperCollins).
Terms: Agent receives 15% commission on domestic sales; 20% on foreign sales. Offers written contract, binding for 1 year.
Tips: "Do not send manuscripts. Write a compelling letter. If you do, we'll ask to see your work."

WRITERS HOUSE, (Specialized: young adult, children's books), (West Coast Office), 3368 Governor Dr. #224F, San Diego CA 92122. (858)678-8767. Fax: (858)678-8530. **Contact:** Steven Malk.
  • See Writers House listing above for more information.
Represents: Nonfiction, fiction, picture books, young adult, occasional adult books.

WRITERS' PRODUCTIONS, P.O. Box 630, Westport CT 06881-0630. (203)227-8199. **Contact:** David L. Meth. Estab. 1982. Represents 25 clients. Currently handles: 40% nonfiction books; 60% novels.
Represents: Nonfiction books, novels, literary quality fiction. "Especially interested in children's work that creates a whole new universe of characters and landscapes that goes across all media, i.e.—between Hobbits and Smurfs. Must be completely unique and original, carefully planned and developed."
  O→ This agency specializes in literary-quality fiction and nonfiction, and children's books. "I am not taking on new clients at this time."
How to Contact: Send query letter only with SASE. Responds in 1 week to queries; 1 month on mss. "No telephone calls, please." Obtains most new clients through word of mouth.
Recent Sales: This agency prefers not to share information on specific sales.
Terms: Agent receives 15% on domestic sales; 25% on foreign sales; 25% on dramatic sales; 25% on new media or multimedia sales. Offers written contract. Charges clients for electronic transmissions, long-distance calls, express or overnight mail, courier service, etc.
Tips: "Send only your best, most professionally prepared work. Do not send it before it is ready. We must have SASE for all correspondence and return of manuscripts."

☑ ◉ **WRITERS' REPRESENTATIVES, INC.**, 116 W. 14th St., 11th Floor, New York NY 10011-7305. (212)620-0023. E-mail: transom@writersreps.com. Website: www.writersreps.com. **Contact:** Glen Hartley or Lynn Chu. Estab. 1985. Represents 130 clients. 5% of clients are new/previously unpublished writers. Currently handles: 90% nonfiction books; 10% novels.

● Prior to becoming agents Ms. Chu was a lawyer, and Mr. Hartley worked at Simon & Schuster, Harper & Row and Cornell University Press.

Member Agents: Lynn Chu; Glen Hartley; Catherine Sprinkel.

Represents: Nonfiction books, novels. **Considers literary fiction.**

○➤ This agency specializes in serious nonfiction. Actively seeking serious nonfiction and quality fiction. Does not want to receive motion picture/television screenplays.

How to Contact: "Nonfiction submissions should include book proposal, detailed table of contents and sample chapter(s). For fiction submissions send sample chapters—not synopses. All submissions should include author biography and publication list. SASE required." Does not accept unsolicited mss. Prefers to read materials exclusively. Obtains most new clients through "recommendations from our clients."

Recent Sales: Sold 30 titles in the last year. *From Dawn to Decadence*, by Jacques Barun; *Bobos in Paradise*, by David Brooks; *The Mysteries Within*, by Sherwin B. Nuland, M.D.; *Genius and Genius*, by Harold Bloom (Warner Books); *Why There Are No Good Men Left*, by Barbara Dafoe Whitehead (Broadway Books).

Terms: Agent receives 15% commission on domestic sales; 20% on foreign sales. "We charge clients for out-of-house photocopying as well as messengers, courier services (e.g., Federal Express), etc."

Tips: "Always include a SASE that will ensure a response from the agent and the return of material submitted."

◉ **THE WRITERS SHOP**, (formerly The Virginia Barber Literary Agency, Inc.), 101 Fifth Ave., 11th Floor, New York NY 10003. (212)255-6515. Fax: (212)691-9418. Website: www.thewritersshop.com. **Contact:** Kristin Lewandowski. Member of AAR, signatory of WGA. Represents 100 clients. Currently handles 25% nonfiction books; 50% novels; 25% story collections.

Member Agents: Virginia Barber; Jennifer Rudolph Walsh; Jay Mandel.

Represents: Nonfiction books, novels, short story collections, scholarly books.

How to Contact: Query with SASE. Prefers to read materials exclusively. Reponds in 6 weeks. Returns materials only with SASE. Obtains most new clients through recommendations from others.

Recent Sales: This agency prefers not to share information on specific sales.

Terms: Agent receives 15% commission on domestic sales.

Writers' Conferences: Bread Loaf; Squaw Valley.

🅽 ◉ **WYLIE-MERRICK LITERARY AGENCY**, 1138 Webster, Kokomo IN 46902-6357. (765)459-8258 or (765)457-3783. E-mail: cwhimsy@netusa1.net. **Contact:** S.A. Martin. Estab. 1999. Member of SCBWI. Currently handles: 25% nonfiction books; 25% novels; 50% juvenile books.

● Ms. Martin holds a Master's degree in Language Education and is a writing and technology curriculum specialist.

Represents: Nonfiction, novels, juvenile books. **Considers these nonfiction areas:** computer/electronics; how-to; juvenile nonfiction; self-help/personal improvement; young adult. **Considers these fiction areas:** historical; juvenile; mainstream; picture book; young adult.

○➤ This agency specializes in children's and young adult literature as well as mainstream adult fiction. Actively seeking middle-grade/young adult fiction and nonfiction; and, in the future, adult fiction and nonfiction. Does not want to receive any subject not listed above—no erotica, religion, etc.

How to Contact: Query with SASE. Does not accept queries by e-mail or fax. Considers simultaneous queries and submissions. Responds in 1 month to queries; 3 months to mss. Returns materials only with SASE. Obtains most new clients through recommendations from others, queries/solicitations.

Recent Sales: This is a new agency with no recorded sales.

Terms: Agent receives 15% commission on domestic sales; 20% on foreign sales. Offers written contract. 30-day notice must be given to terminate contract. Charges clients for postage, photocopying.

Tips: "Potential clients should understand their subjects thoroughly and submit only error-free queries and manuscripts. We prefer to work with writers who show professionalism through their writing."

⊘ **MARY YOST ASSOCIATES, INC.**, 59 E. 54th St. 72, New York NY 10022. Member of AAR. This agency did not respond to our request for information. Query before submitting.

☑ ⊘ **ZACHARY SHUSTER HARMSWORTH**, (formerly Zachary Shuster Agency), Boston Office: 729 Boylston St., 5th Floor, Boston MA 02116. (617)262-2400. Fax: (617)262-2468. E-mail: toddshus@aol.com. **Contact:** Esmond Harrisworth. Also: New York Office: 888 Seventh Ave., 45th Floor, New York NY 10106. (212)765-6900. Fax: (212)765-6490. **Contact:** Todd Shuster, Jennifer Gates. Estab. 1996. Represents 75 clients. 20% of clients are new/previously unpublished writers. Currently handles: 45% nonfiction books; 5% scholarly books; 45% novels; 5% story collections.

● "Our principals include two former publishing and entertainment lawyers, a journalist and an editor/agent." Lane Zachary was an editor at Random House before becoming an agent.

Member Agents: Esmond Harmsworth (commercial fiction, history, science, adventure); Todd Shuster (narrative and prescriptive nonfiction, biography, memoirs); Lane Zachary (biography, memoirs, literary fiction); Jennifer Gates (literary fiction, nonfiction).

Represents: Nonfiction books, novels. **Considers these nonfiction areas:** animals; biography/autobiography; business; current affairs; gay/lesbian issues; government/politics/law; health/medicine; history; how-to; language/literature/criticism; memoirs; money/finance/economics; music/dance/theater/film; psychology; science/technology; self-help/personal improvement; sports; true crime/investigative; women's issues/women's studies. **Considers these fiction areas:** contemporary issues; detective/police/crime; ethnic; feminist; gay; historical; lesbian; literary; mainstream; mystery/suspense; thriller/espionage.

    O⊸ This agency specializes in journalist-driven narrative nonfiction, literary and commercial fiction. Actively seeking narrative nonfiction, mystery, commerical and literary fiction, memoirs, history, biographies. Does not want to receive poetry.

How to Contact: Send query letter and SASE and 50 page sample of ms. Accepts queries by e-mail and fax. Considers simultaneous queries. Responds in 3 months to mss. Obtains most new clients through recommendations from others, solicitation, conferences.

Recent Sales: Sold 15 titles in the last year. *The Last River*, by Todd Balf (Crown); *Lay That Trumpet in Our Hands*, by Susan McCarthy (Bantam); *Waiting*, by Ha Jin (Alfred A. Knopf—National Book Award winner); *Le Probleme avec Jane*, by Catherine Jenkins (Simon & Schuster). Other clients include Leslie Epstein, David Mixner.

Terms: Agent receives 15% commission on domestic sales; 20% on foreign sales. Offers written contract, binding for 1 work only. 30-day notice must be given to terminate contract. Charges clients for postage, copying, courier, telephone. "We only charge expenses if the manuscript is sold."

Tips: "We work closely with all our clients on all editorial and promotional aspects of their works."

⊘ **SUSAN ZECKENDORF ASSOC. INC.**, 171 W. 57th St., New York NY 10019. Member of AAR. This agency did not respond to our request for information. Query before submitting.

Additional Nonfee-charging Agents

    The following nonfee-charging agencies have indicated they are *primarily* interested in handling the work of scriptwriters, but also handle less than 10 to 15 percent book manuscripts. After reading the listing (you can find the page number in the Listings Index), send a query to obtain more information on needs and manuscript submissions policies.

Bohrman Agency, The
Circle of Confusion Ltd.
Communications Management
    Associates
Epstein-Wyckoff and Associates
Hart Literary Management
Larchmont Literary Agency

Management Company, The
Miller Co., The Stuart M.
Niad Management
Omniquest Entertainment
Picture of You, A
Preminger Agency, Jim
Robins & Associates, Michael D.

Shapiro-Lichtman
Sherman & Associates, Ken
Silver Screen Placements
Sorice Agency, Camille
Van Duren Agency, Annette
Wauhob Agency, Donna

Canadian/International Literary Agents: Nonfee-charging

For the first time, we've included the following section of Canadian/International literary agents. These are agents who make sales not only in the U.S. but also in their own and other foreign countries. Several of the agents listed here already have clients who live in the U.S. For many writers, having an agent in another country can be a wonderful opportunity, especially if the material you write appeals to a different sensibility than that held by most U.S. readers. Or, perhaps you even live outside the U.S. In that case, you may want to work with an agent in this section who is closer to home.

In a sense, working with a Canadian or International agent is similar to having an agent outside of New York. They may not be able to meet with New York editors every day, but when they do go to New York, or even London, editors give them priority over local agents. Many publishing companies are now found outside of New York and even the U.S., giving Canadian and International agents the same opportunity for contact as those agents in New York. And, of course, with e-mail, the Internet, and fax machines, communicating in the global community is just as easy as meeting your colleague next door for lunch.

Keep in mind, however, that there are a few downsides to working with a Canadian or International agent. For starters, the majority of the agent's contacts will be in his own country, and he may not be as well known by U.S. publishing houses as those abroad. While this fact can be good in terms of reaching foreign markets, it may mean your book will not be sold in the U.S. Meeting your agent may prove more difficult than if she lived in the U.S. And even though new technology makes communication easier, if you need to talk with your London agent, you'll have to pay close attention to the difference in time zones to avoid calling her in the middle of the night.

Only English-speaking agents are included in this section. Most agents—both in and outside the U.S.—prefer to work with "foreign co-agents" when dealing with nonEnglish-speaking publishers. Foreign co-agents are contacts that agents have in other countries, like Spain or Japan, who work directly with foreign publishers and translators. If you believe your book would appeal to an audience in a nonEnglish-speaking country, you may want to consider looking for a U.S. agent who has strong connections with foreign co-agents.

Just like U.S. agents, Canadian and International nonfee-charging agents receive payment from commissions on sales. Some agents in this section may charge office fees to their clients, but they do not charge reading or critiquing fees. Researching the agents in this section is just as important as researching any agent: you want to target your submission to ensure you reach a receptive agent, and you want to know the agent is well respected in the publishing industry and actively making sales.

When you send a Canadian or International agent a query, be sure to include an International Reply Coupon (IRC) with your self-addressed envelope. Regular U.S. postage is not valid in any country outside the U.S., and an agent outside the U.S. is unlikely to respond to your query without an IRC. Contact your local post office for more information about IRCs.

For a more detailed explanation of the information in the following listings, see the introduction to Literary Agents: Nonfee-charging on page 61 and "Reading the Listings in the *Guide to Literary Agents*" at the front of the book.

ACACIA HOUSE PUBLISHING SERVICES LTD., 51 Acacia Rd., Toronto, Ontario M4S 2K6 Canada. Phone/fax: (416)484-8356. **Contact:** (Ms.) Frances Hanna. Estab. 1985. Represents 30 clients. Works with a small number of new/unpublished authors. Currently handles: 30% nonfiction books; 70% novels.

   • Ms. Hanna has been in the publishing business for 30 years, first in London (UK) as a fiction editor with Barrie & Jenkins and Pan Books, and as a senior editor with a packager of mainly illustrated books. She was condensed books editor for 6 years for *Reader's Digest* in Montreal, senior editor and foreign rights manager for (the then) Wm. Collins & Sons (now HarperCollins) in Toronto.

Represents: Nonfiction books, novels. **Considers these nonfiction areas:** animals; biography/autobiography; language/literature/criticism; memoirs; military/war; music/dance/theater/film; nature/environment; travel. **Considers these fiction areas:** action/adventure; detective/police/crime; literary; mainstream; mystery/suspense; thriller/espionage.

   ○➥ This agency specializes in contemporary fiction: literary or commercial. Actively seeking "outstanding first novels with literary merit." Does not want to receive horror, occult, science fiction.

How to Contact: Query with outline and SASE. Does not accept queries by e-mail or fax. Prefers to read materials exclusively. *No unsolicited mss.* Responds in 6 weeks to queries. Returns materials only with SASE.

Recent Sales: Sold 20 titles in the last year and numerous international rights sales. Prefers not to share information on specific clients or sales.

Terms: Agent receives 15% commission on English language sales; 20% on dramatic sales; 25-30% on foreign language sales. Charges clients for photocopying.

Writers' Conferences: London International Book Fair (England); BEA (Chicago); Frankfurt Book Fair (Germany).

Tips: "I prefer that writers be previously published, with at least a few articles to their credit. Strongest consideration will be given to those with, say, three or more published books. However, I *would* take on an unpublished writer of outstanding talent."

ANUBIS LITERARY AGENCY, 79 Charles Gardner Rd., Leamington Spa, Warwickshire CV313BG Great Britain. Phone: 01926 832644. Fax: 01926 311607. **Contact:** Steve Calcutt. Estab. 1994. Represents 21 clients. 50% of clients are new/previously unpublished writers. Currently handles: 100% novels.

   • Prior to becoming an agent, Mr. Calcutt taught creative writing for Warwick University plus American history— US Civil War.

Member Agents: Maggie Heavey (crime); Steve Calcutt (horror/science fiction).

Represents: Novels. **Considers these fiction areas:** detective/police/crime; fantasy; historical; horror; science fiction.

   ○➥ "We are very keen on developing talented new writers. We give support, encouragement and editorial guidance." Actively seeking crime fiction. Does not want to receive children's, nonfiction, journalism or TV/film scripts.

How to Contact: Query with SASE or send outline/proposal with IRCs. Does not accept queries by e-mail or fax. Responds in 6 weeks to queries; 3 months to mss. Returns materials only with SASE and IRCs. Obtains most new clients through queries/solicitations.

Recent Sales: *Salt*, by Adam Roberts (Orion); *Tread Softly*, by Georgie Hale (Hodder & Stoughton); *The Nature of Balance*, by Tim Lebbon (Leisure/Dorchester). Other clients include Richard Irvine, Steve Savile, Lesley Asquith.

Terms: Agent receives 15% commission on domestic sales; 20% on foreign sales. No written contract.

CONTEMPORARY MANAGEMENT, Contemporary Communications Ltd., 1663 W. Seventh Ave., Vancouver, British Columbia V6J 1S4 Canada. (604)734-3663. Fax: (604)734-8906. E-mail: rmackwood@ccpr.com. **Contact:** Robert Mackwood. (2) Estab. 1974. Represents 59 clients. 20% of clients are new/previously unpublished writers. Currently handles: 84% nonfiction books; 9% novels; 1% TV scripts; 6% reference books website(s).

   • Prior to becoming an agent, Mr. Mackwood was a vice president, director of marketing and public relations for Bantam Doubleday Dell Toronto.

Member Agents: Robert Mackwood (co-director, nonfiction); Perry Goldsmith (co-director, nonfiction); Alma Lee (agent, fiction).

Represents: Nonfiction books, novels. **Considers these nonfiction areas:** anthropology/archaeology; art/architecture/design; biography/autobiography; business; child guidance/parenting; current affairs; education; government/politics/law; health/medicine; history; how-to; humor; money/finance/economics; photography; popular culture; psychology; science/technology; self-help/personal improvement; sports; travel; women's issues/women's studies. **Considers these fiction areas:** action/adventure; contemporary; literary; mystery/suspense; thriller/espionage.

   ○➥ This agency also owns Canada's largest speakers bureau (The National Speakers Bureau), a bureau in the US (Global Speakers) but it's a public relations division. "Many of our clients are also speakers (about 60%)— which makes our author agency unusual." Actively seeking good nonfiction/fiction projects. Does not want to receive poetry, short stories.

How to Contact: Send outline and 1 sample chapter. Accepts queries by e-mail. Prefers to read materials exclusively. Responds in 2 weeks to queries; 1 month to mss. Returns materials only with SASE. Obtains most new clients through recommendations from others. "We (sometimes) find a writer for a subject that we think is about to become popular."

Recent Sales: Sold 20 titles in the last year. *Untitled Modern History of the Bathroom*, by Holman Wang (Source Books [USA]); *Prototype*, by Bill Atkinson (Thomas Allen [Canada]); *Hot Sun, Cool Shadow: Savouring the Food History & Mystery of the Languedoc*, by Peter Matthews and Angela Murrills (Stoddart [Canada]); *The Debt Free Graduate*, by Murray Baker (Career Press [USA]). *Movie/TV MOW scripts optioned/sold:* CTV: *The Television Wars*, by Sue Gittens (Norfolk Productions Toronto).

Terms: Agent receives 15% commission on domestic sales; 25% on foreign sales. Offers written contract, binding for 3 years. Mutual agreement must be reached to terminate contract. Charges clients $200 (Canadian) expenses fee upon signing contract. May refer to editing service; 0% of business is derived from reading or criticism fee.

Writers' Conferences: Book Expo America (Chicago, June); Frankfurt Fair (Frankfurt); London (London, March).

N **⊕** **∅** **DORIAN LITERARY AGENCY**, Upper Thornehill, 27 Church Rd., St. Mary Church, Torquay, Devon TQ1 4Q4 England. Phone/fax: (0)1803 312095. **Contact:** Dorothy Lumley. Estab. 1986. Represents 40 clients. 10% of clients are new/previously unpublished writers. Currently handles: 5% nonfiction books; 85% novels; 10% story collections.

• Prior to becoming an agent, Ms. Lumley was a paperback editor.

Member Agents: Dorothy Lumley (popular adult fiction).

Represents: Nonfiction books, novels, short story collections. **Considers these nonfiction areas:** popular culture; self-help/personal improvement. **Considers these fiction areas:** detective/police/crime; family saga; fantasy; historical; horror; literary; mainstream; mystery/suspense; romance; science fiction; thriller/espionage; young adult.

    0→ This agency is a small specialist agency that offers personal service, and editorial input. Does not want to receive poetry, nonfiction of specialist type, autobiographies, plays, children's books.

How to Contact: Query with SASE and IRCs or send outline/proposal and 1-3 sample chapters. Does not accept queries by e-mail or fax. Considers simultaneous queries. Responds in 2 weeks to queries; 6 weeks to mss. Returns materials only with SASE and IRCs. Obtains most new clients through recommendations from others.

Recent Sales: Sold 30 titles in the last year. *Avengers/Defilers*, by B. Lumley (TOR); *Sand Reckoner/Wolf Hunt*, by G. Bradshaw (TOR); *Dark Terrors*, by S. Jones (Orion/Jollancy).

Terms: Agent receives 10% commission on domestic sales; 10% on foreign sales; 15% on sales to USA. No written contract. Charges clients for photocopying of mss, extra copies of book for rights sales.

Writers' Conferences: Winchester Writers' Conference; St. Hilda's Crime; Deansgate (crime); and Romantic Novelists/British Fantasy Society.

Tips: "My client list is officially 'full'—I may take on one or two new clients a year—and occasionally one is unpublished, e.g. an Irish family saga writer this spring."

N **⊕** **∅** **GREGORY AND RADICE AUTHORS' AGENTS**, 3 Barb Mews, London W6 7PA England. Phone: (020)7610-4676. Fax: (020)7610-4686. E-mail: info@gregoryradice.co.uk. **Contact:** Dr. Lisanne Radice, editorial; Jane Gregory, UK, US and film rights. Estab. 1987. Member of Association of Authors' Agents. Represents 60 clients. Currently handles: 10% nonfiction books; 90% novels.

• Prior to becoming an agent, Ms. Gregory was Rights Director (Caatto & Windus).

Member Agents: Jane Gregory (sales); Lisanne Radice (editorial); Jane Barlow (rights); Louee Beolene (translations).

Represents: Nonfiction books, novels. **Considers these nonfiction areas:** biography/autobiography; government/politics/law; history. **Considers these fiction areas:** action/adventure; commercial; detective/police/crime; historical; humor/satire; literary; mainstream; multicultural; romance; thriller/espionage.

    0→ This agency is "unusual as both partners look after every author. Editorial is handled by Dr. Lisanne Radice while Jane Gregory is successful in selling rights all over the world including film and television rights." Actively seeking well-written, accessible modern novels. Does not want to receive horror, science fiction, fantasy, children's books, TV scripts, poetry.

How to Contact: Query with SASE or send outline and 3 sample chapters and SASE. Does not accept mss by e-mail or fax. Considers simultaneous queries and submissions. Returns materials only with SASE. Obtains most new clients through recommendations, conferences.

Recent Sales: Sold 100 titles in the last year. *Birdman*, by Mo Hayder (Bantam, UK/Doubleday USA); *A Place of Execution*, by Vaol McDermid (HarperCollins UK/St. Martin's Press USA); *Shape of Snakes*, by Minette Walters (Fawcett UK/Putnam USA); *Dying Voices*, by Laura Wilson (Orion UK/Bantam USA).

Terms: Agent receives 15% commission on domestic sales; 20% on foreign sales. Offers written contract, binding on a book to book basis. 3-months notice must be given to terminate contract. Charges clients for photocopying of whole typescripts and books for selling purposes.

Writers' Conferences: CWA Conference (United Kingdom, Spring); Dead on Deansgate (Manchester, Autumn).

N **⊕** **◐** **LIMELIGHT MANAGEMENT**, 33 Newman St., London W1T 1PY England. Phone (00)44 207 637 2529. Fax: (00)44 207 637 2538. E-mail: limelightmanagement@virgin.net. Website: www.limelightmanagement.com. **Contact:** Fiona Lindsay. Estab. 1990. Member of Association of Authors' Agents. Represents 70 clients. Currently handles: 100% nonfiction books.

• Prior to becoming an agent, Ms. Lindsay was a public relations manager of the Dorchester and was working on her law degree.

Represents: Nonfiction, lifestyle TV. **Considers these nonfiction areas:** agriculture/horticulture; art/architecture/design; cooking/food/nutrition; crafts/hobbies; health/medicine; interior design/decorating; nature/environment; New Age/metaphysics; photography; self-help/personal improvement; sports; travel; gardening. Handles multimedia: electronic publishing, digital television, websites.

    0→ This agency specializes in lifestyle subject areas, especially celebrity chefs, gardeners and wine experts. Actively seeking health, cooking, gardening. Does not want to receive any subject not listed above.

How to Contact: Query, send outline/proposal with SASE/IRC. Accepts queries by e-mail and fax. Prefers to read materials exclusively. Responds in 1 week. Returns materials only with SASE. Obtains most new clients through recommendations from others.

Recent Sales: Sold 70 titles in the last year. Prefers not to share information on specific sales. Clients include Oz Clarke, Antony Worrall Thompson, David Stevens, David Joyce, John Bly.

Terms: Agent receives 15% commission on domestic sales; 20% on foreign sales. Offers written contract. 2-month notice must be given to terminate contract.

⟨N⟩ ⟨⟩ ⟨⟩ LIVINGSTON COOKE/CURTIS BROWN CANADA, 457A Danforth Ave., Suite 201, Toronto, Ontario M4K 1P1 Canada. (416)406-3390. Fax: (416)406-3389. E-mail: livcooke@idirect.ca. **Contact:** Suzanne Brandreth. Estab. 1992. Represents 200 clients. 30% of clients are new/previously unpublished writers. Currently handles: 50% nonfiction books; 30% novels; 10% movie scripts; 10% TV scripts.

- Prior to becoming an agent, Mr. Cooke was the publisher of Seal Books Canada.

Member Agents: David Johnston (film rights, literary fiction/nonfiction); Suzanne Brandreth (literary fiction, nonfiction); Duan Cooke (literary fiction, nonfiction).

Represents: Nonfiction books, novels, juvenile books. **Considers these nonfiction areas:** biography/autobiography; business; child guidance/parenting; current affairs; gay/lesbian issues; health/medicine; popular culture; science/technology; young adult. **Considers these fiction areas:** juvenile; literary.

- ⟳ Livingston Cooke represents some of the best Canadian writers in the world. "Through our contacts and sub-agents, we are building an international reputation for quality. Curtis Brown Canada is jointly owned by Dean Cooke and Curtis Brown New York. It represents Curtis Brown New York authors in Canada." Does not want to receive genre fiction.

How to Contact: Query with SASE. Accepts queries by e-mail and fax. Considers simultaneous queries. Responds in 1 month to queries; 6 weeks to mss. Returns materials only with SASE. Obtains most new clients through recommendations from others.

Recent Sales: Sold 40 titles and 4 script projects in the last year. *Spirit Cabinet*, by Paul Quarrington (Grove/Atlantic); *Lazarus and the Hurricane*, by S. Charton/T. Swinton (St. Martin's Press); *Latitudes of Melt*, by Joan Clark (Knopf Canada); *Brain Trust: Einstein's Lost Brain*, by Caroline Abraham (Penguin Canada). *Movie/TV MOW Scripts optioned/sold:* Englishman's Boy, by Guy Vanderhaeghe (Minds Eye); *Movie/TV MOW scripts in development:* Lazarus and the Hurricane, by T. Swinton and S. Chanton (Universal/Beacon). Other clients include Margaret Gibson, Richard Scrimger, Tony Hillerman, Robertson Davies, Brian Moore.

Terms: Agent receives 15% commission on domestic sales; 20% on foreign sales. Offers written contract. Charges clients for postage, photocopying, courier.

⟨N⟩ ⟨⊕⟩ ⟨⟩ ANDREW LOWNIE LITERARY AGENCY LTD., 17 Sutherland St., London SWIV 4JU England. Phone: (0207)828 1274. Fax: (0207)828 7608. E-mail: lownie@globalnet.co.uk. Website: www.andrewlownie.co.uk. **Contact:** Andrew Lownie. Estab. 1988. Member of Association of Author's Agents. Represents 130 clients. 50% of clients are new/previously unpublished writers. Currently handles: 90% nonfiction books; 10% novels.

- Prior to becoming an agent, Mr. Lownie was a journalist, bookseller, publisher, author of 12 books, and previously a Director of the Curtis Brown Agency.

Represents: Nonfiction books. **Considers these nonfiction areas:** anthropology/archaeology; biography/autobiography; current affairs; government/politics/law; history; memoirs; military/war; music/dance/theater/film; popular culture; true crime/investigative.

- ⟳ This agent has a wide publishing experience, extensive journalistic contacts, and a specialty in showbiz memoir and celebrities. Actively seeking showbiz memoirs, narrative histories and biographies. Does not want to receive poetry, short stories, children's fiction, scripts, academic.

How to Contact: Query with SASE and IRCs or send outline and 1 sample chapter. Accepts queries by e-mail and fax. Considers simultaneous queries and submissions. Responds in 1 week to queries; 1 month to mss. Returns materials only with SASE and IRCs. Obtains most new clients through recommendations from others.

Recent Sales: Sold 50 titles in the last year. *Still Memories*, by Sir John Mills (Hutchinson); *Memoirs*, by Alan Whaker (Deutsch); *Post-War Italy*, by Ken Murphy (Farrar Straus & Giroux); *Lost Civilizations*, by Richard Rudgley (Free Press). Other clients include Norma Major, Guy Bellamy, Joyce Cary Eslate, Lawrence James, Juliet Banker, Patrick McNee.

Terms: Agent receives 15% commission on domestic sales; 15% on foreign sales. Offers written contract, binding until author chooses to break it but contract valid while book in print. 30-day notice must be given to terminate contract. Charges clients for some copying, postage, copies of books for submission.

Tips: "I prefer submissions in writing by letter."

ALWAYS INCLUDE an International Reply Coupon (IRC) for reply or return of your material when sending query letters to non-U.S. countries.

N ⊕ ☑ JEFFREY SIMMONS LITERARY AGENCY, 10 Lowndes Square, London SWIX 9HA England. Phone: (020)7235 8852. Fax: (020)7235 9733. **Contact:** Jeffrey Simmons. Estab. 1978. Represents 46 clients. 50% of clients are new/previously unpublished writers. Currently handles: 60% nonfiction books; 40% novels.
• Prior to becoming an agent, Mr. Simmons was a publisher and he is also an author.
Represents: Nonfiction books, novels. **Considers these nonfiction areas:** biography/autobiography; current affairs; government/politics/law; history; language/literature/criticism; memoirs; music/dance/theater/film; popular culture; sociology; sports; translations; true crime/investigative. **Considers these fiction areas:** action/adventure; confessional; detective/police/crime; family saga; literary; mainstream; mystery/suspense; psychic/supernatural; thriller/espionage.
    O↴ This agency seeks to handle good books and promising young writers. "My long experience in publishing and as an author and ghostwriter means I can offer an excellent service all round, especially in terms of editorial experience where appropriate." Actively seeking quality fiction, biography, autobiography, showbiz, personality books, law, crime, politics, world affairs. Does not want to receive science fiction, horror, fantasy, juvenile, academic books, specialist subjects (i.e.: cooking, gardening, religious).
How to Contact: Send outline/proposal or send outline and sample chapters with SASE and IRCs. Accepts queries by fax. Prefers to read materials exclusively. Responds in 1 week to queries; 1 month to mss. Obtains most new clients through recommendations from others, queries/solicitations.
Recent Sales: Sold 21 titles in the last year. *Uncle Petros and Goldbach's Conjecture*, by Apostolos Doxiadis (Faber and Faber ([UK]/Bloomsbury); *The Director's Cut*, by Roy Ward Baker (Reynolds & Hearn [UK]); *Mango and Mimosa*, Suzanne St. Albans (Little, Brown [UK]); *Are You Being Served?*, by Richard Webber (Orion [UK]).
Terms: Agent receives 10-15% commission on domestic sales; net 15% on foreign sales. Offers written contract, binding for the lifetime of book in question or until it becomes out of print.
Tips: "When contacting us with an outline/proposal, include a brief biographical note (listing any previous publications, with publishers and dates). Preferably tell us if the book has already been offered elsewhere."

❖ ☻ BEVERLEY SLOPEN LITERARY AGENCY, 131 Bloor St. W., Suite 711, Toronto, Ontario M5S 1S3 Canada. (416)964-9598. Fax: (416)921-7726. E-mail: slopen@inforamp.net. Website: www.slopenagency.on.ca. **Contact:** Beverly Slopen. Estab. 1974. Represents 60 clients. 40% of clients are new/previously unpublished writers. Currently handles: 60% nonfiction books; 40% novels.
• Prior to opening her agency, Ms. Slopen worked in publishing and as a journalist.
Represents: Nonfiction books, scholarly books, novels, occasional college texts. **Considers these nonfiction areas:** anthropology/archaeology; biography/autobiography; business; child guidance/parenting; cooking/food/nutrition; current affairs; psychology; sociology; true crime/investigative; women's issues/women's studies. **Considers these fiction areas:** literary; mystery/suspense.
    O↴ This agency has a "strong bent towards Canadian writers." Actively seeking "serious nonfiction that is accessible and appealing to the general reader." Does not want to receive fantasy, science fiction or children's.
How to Contact: Query with SASE. Accepts queries by e-mail, "if short." Responds in 2 months. Returns materials only with SASE (or SAE with IRCs). Canadian postage only.
Recent Sales: Sold 25 titles in the last year. *Walking Since Daybreak*, by Modris Eksteins (Houghton Mifflin). Other clients include historians Modris Eksteins, Michael Marrus, Timothy Brook, critic Robert Fulford, novelists Donna Morrissey (*Kit's Law*), Howard Engel, Morley Torgov.
Terms: Agent receives 15% commission on domestic sales; 10% on foreign sales. Offers written contract, binding for 2 years. 90-day notice must be given to terminate contract.
Tips: "Please, no unsolicited manuscripts."

N ⊕ ☑ ROBERT SMITH LITERARY AGENCY, 12 Bridge Wharf, 156 Caledonian Rd., London NI 9UU England. Phone: (020) 7278 2444. Fax: (020) 7833 5680. E-mail: robertsmith.literaryagency@virgin.net. **Contact:** Robert Smith. Estab. 1997. Member of Association of Author's Agents. Represents 25 clients. 10% of clients are new/previously unpublished writers. Currently handles: 80% nonfiction books; 20% syndicated material.
• Prior to becoming an agent, Mr. Smith was a book publisher.
Member Agents: Robert Smith (all nonfiction); Renuka Harrison (mind/body/spirit).
Represents: Nonfiction books, syndicated material. **Considers these nonfiction areas:** biography/autobiography; cooking/food/nutrition; health/medicine; memoirs; music/dance/theater/film; New Age/metaphysics; popular culture; self-help/personal improvement; true crime/investigative.
    O↴ This agency offers clients full management service in all media. Clients are not necessarily book authors. "Our special expertise is in placing newspaper series internationally." Actively seeking autobiographies.
How to Contact: Send outline/proposal with SASE and IRCs. Accepts queries by fax. Prefers to read materials exclusively. Reponds in 1 week to proposals. Returns materials only with SASE and IRCs. Obtains most new clients through recommendations from others, direct approaches to prospective authors.
Recent Sales: Sold 25 titles in the last year. *The Truth At Last*, by Christine Keeler (Sidgwick & Jackson/Macmillan); *Presenting on Television*, by Joanne Zorian-Lynn (A&C Black); *Ron Kray*, by Laurie O'Leary (Headline); *The Ultimate Jack the Ripper Sourcebook*, by Stewart Evans and Keith Skinner (Constable Robinson). *Movie/TV MOW scripts optioned/sold: The Guv'nor*, by Lenny McLean & Peter Gerrard (Arrival Films). Other clients include Neil and Christine Hamilton, James Haspiel, Geoffrey Giuliano, Norman Parker, Mike Reid, Christopher Warwick, Rochelle Morton, Reg Kray, Julie Chrystyn.

Terms: Agent receives 15% commission on domestic sales; 20% on foreign sales. Offers written contract, binding for 3 months. 3-months notice must be given to terminate contract. Charges clients for couriers, overseas mailings of mss, subject to client authorization.

[N] [globe] [O] THE SUSIJN AGENCY, 820 Harrow Rd., London NWIO SSU England. Phone: (020)8968 7435. Fax: (020)8354 0415. E-mail: lsusijn@aol.com. Website: www.thesusijnagency.com. **Contact:** Laura Susijn. Estab. 1998. Represents 65 clients. 15% of clients are new/previously unpublished writers. Currently handles: 15% nonfiction books; 85% novels.
   • Prior to becoming an agent, Ms. Susijn was a rights director at Sheil Land Associates and Fourth Estate Ltd.
Member Agents: Laura Susijn.
Represents: Nonfiction books, novels, short story collections, novellas. **Considers these nonfiction areas:** biography/ autobiography; memoirs; multicultural; popular culture; science/technology; travel. **Considers these fiction areas:** literary.
   O─┐ This agency specializes in international works, selling world rights, representing nonEnglish-language writing as well as non-English with an emphasis on cross-cultural subjects. Does not want to receive self-help, romance, sagas, science fiction.
How to Contact: Send outline and 2 sample chapters with SASE and IRCs. Does not accept queries by e-mail or fax. Considers simultaneous queries and submissions. Responds in 1 month. Returns materials only with SASE and IRCs. Obtains most new clients through recommendations from others, via publishers in Europe and beyond.
Recent Sales: Sold 78 titles in the last year. *Mouthful of Glass*, by Henk Van Woerden (Granta); *Wild Numbers*, by Philibert Schogt (Gollancz); *Fragile Science*, by Robin Baker (Macmillan); *East of Acre Lane*, by Alex Wheatle (Fourth Estate). Other clients include Vassalluci, Podium, Atlas, De Ardeiderspers, Tiderne Skifter, MB Agency, Van Oorschot.
Terms: Agent receives 15% commission on domestic sales; 15-20% on foreign sales. Offers written contract. 6-week notice must be given to terminate contract. Charges clients for photocopying, buying copies only if sale is made.

[N] [figure] [O] CAROLYN SWAYZE LITERARY AGENCY, W.R.P.O. Box 39588, White Rock, British Columbia V4B 5L6 Canada. (604)538-3478. Fax: (604)531-3022. E-mail: cswayze@direct.ca. **Contact:** Carolyn Swayze. Also: P.O. Box 3976, Blaine WA USA 98231-3976. Estab. 1994. Represents 40 clients. 50% of clients are new/previously unpublished writers. Currently handles: 30% nonfiction books; 50% novels; 15% story collection; 5% juvenile books.
   • Prior to becoming an agent, Ms. Swayze was an intellectual property law lawyer, published biographer, novelist, columnist.
Member Agents: D. Barry Jones (military history, action-adventure); Carolyn Swayze (literary fiction, nonfiction).
Represents: Nonfiction books, novels. **Considers these nonfiction areas:** biography/autobiography; child guidance/ parenting; cooking/food/nutrition; ethnic/cultural interests; history; humor; memoirs; military/war; nature/environment; popular culture; self-help/personal improvement; sports; travel; true crime/investigative; women's issues/women's studies. **Considers these fiction areas:** contemporary issues; ethnic; family saga; historical; humor/satire; literary; mainstream; multicultural; mystery/suspense.
   O─┐ This agent has a diverse background, having sold advertising, practised law, written a biography, novels, columns and articles. "Our ratio of first novels and collections is very satisfying." Actively seeking solid proposals for accessible books on sciences, social sciences, philosophy, popular culture, psychology, history and ideas. Does not want to receive science fiction, religious, New Age, horror.
How to Contact: Query with SASE or send outline/proposal (nonfiction); send outline and 3 sample chapters (fiction). Accept queries by e-mail, if brief. Considers simultaneous queries and submissions. Responds in 3 weeks to queries; 6 weeks to mss. Returns materials only with SASE and IRCs. Obtains most new clients through recommendations from others, queries/solicitations.
Recent Sales: Sold 30 titles in the last year. *All the Seas of the World*, by Gayla Reid (Stoddart); *Niagara Falls*, by Kelli Deeth (Harper Flamingo); *Dummies Guide to Canadian History*, by Will Ferguson (CDG Books); *The Violent Child*, by Mike Sheridan (The Permanent Press). Other clients include W.P. Kinsella, Bill Gaston, Loranne Brown, Todd Babiak, Mark Zuehlke, Karen Rivers, Steven Galloway, Barbara Lambert, Teena Spencer, Wilf Cude, M.A.C. Farrant, Richard Van Camp, Marg Meikle, Taras Grescoe, Paul Grescoe, Miriam Toews, and four teams of co-authors.
Terms: Agent receives 15% commission on domestic sales; 20% on foreign sales. Offers written contract. "Termination upon receipt of notice, with up to twelve months to conclude negotiations on any outstanding submissions. Author or new agent free to market immediately." Charges clients for copying and courier expenses to a maximum of $200— always invoiced and often waived for new writers.
Writers' Conferences: Pacific Northwest Writers' Conference (Tacoma WA, July 13-16); Surrey Writers' Conference (Surrey BC, October). "I do numerous talks on copyright and publishing at colleges, universities, writers' workshops and Word on the Street, Vancouver."
Tips: "Please don't telephone to ask if I'm 'taking new writers.' Submit written material which will persuade me to call you."

Agents Specialties Index: Nonfee-charging

The subject index is divided into fiction and nonfiction subject categories for Nonfee-charging Literary Agents. Also included in this index are **Canadian/International** nonfee-charging agents. To find an agent interested in the type of manuscript you've written, see the appropriate sections under subject headings that best describe your work. Check the Listings Index for the page number of the agent's listing, then refer to the section of Nonfee-charging Literary Agents preceding this index. Agents who are open to most fiction, nonfiction, or script subjects appear under the "Open to all Categories" heading.

NONFEE-CHARGING LITERARY AGENTS/FICTION

Action/Adventure: Acacia House Publishing Services Ltd.; Agency West Entertainment; Alive Communications, Inc.; Allen Literary Agency, Linda; Allen, Literary Agent, James; Allred and Allred Literary Agents; AMG/Renaissance; Amsterdam Agency, Marcia; Authentic Creations Literary Agency; Baldi Literary Agency, Malaga; Barrett Books Inc., Loretta; Bial Agency, Daniel; Bova Literary Agency, The Barbara; Brandt & Brandt Literary Agents Inc.; Browne Ltd., Pema; Clark Associates, Wm; Communications and Entertainment, Inc.; Contemporary Management; Crawford Literary Agency; Donovan Literary, Jim; Ducas, Robert; Dupree/Miller and Associates Inc. Literary; Dystel Literary Management, Jane; Elmo Agency Inc., Ann; Farber Literary Agency Inc.; Fort Ross Inc. Russian-American Publishing Projects; Goldfarb & Associates; Goodman Associates; Grace Literary Agency, Carroll; Greenburger Associates, Inc., Sanford J.; Greene, Arthur B.; Gregory and Radice Authors' Agents; Halsey Agency, Reece; Halsey North, Reece; Harris Literary Agency; Harris Literary Agency, Inc., The Joy; Hawkins & Associates, Inc., John; Henshaw Group, Richard; Herner Rights Agency, Susan; Hogenson Agency, Barbara; Jabberwocky Literary Agency; JCA Literary Agency, Inc.; Jellinek & Murray Literary Agency; Joy Literary Agency; Kleinman, Esq., of Graybill & English L.L.C., Jeffrey M.; Klinger, Inc., Harvey; Koster Literary Agency, LLC, Elaine; Kraas Agency, Irene; Kritzer Productions, Eddie; Lampack Agency, Inc., Peter; Larken, Sabra Elliott; Larsen/Elizabeth Pomada Literary Agents, Michael; Lasher Agency, The Maureen; Levine Literary Agency, Paul S.; Lewis & Company, Karen; Lincoln Literary Agency, Ray; Literary Group, The; McBride Literary Agency, Margret; Michaels Literary Agency, Inc., Doris S.; Morrison, Inc., Henry; Mura Enterprises, Inc., Dee; National Writers Literary Agency; Norma-Lewis Agency, The; Paraview, Inc.; Pelter, Rodney; Pevner, Inc., Stephen; Quicksilver Books—Literary Agents; Rhodes Literary Agency, Jodie; Rose & Associates Literary Agency; Rotrosen Agency LLC, Jane; Russell & Volkening; Sanders & Associates, Victoria; Scherf, Inc. Literary Management; Sedgeband Literary Associates; Serendipity Literary Agency, LLC; Simmons Literary Agency, Jeffrey; Southern Literary Group; Stars, the Agency; Sternig & Byrne Literary Agency; Turner Agency, Paige; Vines Agency, Inc., The; Waxman Agency, Inc., Scott; Weiner Literary Agency, Cherry; West Coast Literary Associates; Wonderland Press, Inc., The; Wright Representatives, Ann

Cartoon/Comic: Agency West Entertainment; Bial Agency, Daniel; Communications and Entertainment, Inc.; Goodman Associates; Harris Literary Agency, Inc., The Joy; Hawkins & Associates, Inc., John; Jabberwocky Literary Agency; Kleinman, Esq., of Graybill & English L.L.C., Jeffrey M.; Levine Literary Agency, Paul S.; Literary Group, The; Nazor Literary Agency, Karen; Pelter, Rodney; Pevner, Inc., Stephen; Rose & Associates Literary Agency; Vines Agency, Inc., The; Wales, Literary Agency, Inc.

Confessional: Allred and Allred Literary Agents; Barrett Books Inc., Loretta; Goodman Associates; Harris Literary Agency, Inc., The Joy; Jellinek & Murray Literary Agency; Kritzer Productions, Eddie; Levine Literary Agency, Paul S.; March Tenth, Inc.; Pelter, Rodney; Rose & Associates Literary Agency; Serendipity Literary Agency, LLC; Simmons Literary Agency, Jeffrey

Contemporary Issues: Alive Communications, Inc.; Allen Literary Agency, Linda; Allred and Allred Literary Agents; Altshuler Literary Agency, Miriam; AMG/Renaissance; Authentic Creations Literary Agency; Authors Alliance Inc.; Baldi Literary Agency, Malaga; Barrett Books Inc., Loretta; Bedford Book Works, Inc., The; Bial Agency, Daniel; Boates Literary Agency, Reid; Books & Such; Bova Literary

Agency, The Barbara; Brandt & Brandt Literary Agents Inc.; Brandt Agency, The Joan; Brown Associates Inc., Marie; Browne Ltd., Pema; Castiglia Literary Agency; Charisma Communications, Ltd.; Clark Associates, Wm; Communications and Entertainment, Inc.; Connor Literary Agency; Contemporary Management; Dijkstra Literary Agency, Sandra; Doyen Literary Services, Inc.; Ducas, Robert; Dupree/Miller and Associates Inc. Literary; Dystel Literary Management, Jane; Elmo Agency Inc., Ann; Farber Literary Agency Inc.; Feigen/Parrent Literary Management; Flaherty, Literary Agent, Joyce A.; Frenkel & Associates, James; Goldfarb & Associates; Goodman Associates; Greenburger Associates, Inc., Sanford J.; Grosjean Literary Agency, Jill; Grosvenor Literary Agency, The; Halsey Agency, Reece; Halsey North, Reece; Harris Literary Agency, Inc., The Joy; Hawkins & Associates, Inc., John; Herner Rights Agency, Susan; Hogenson Agency, Barbara; Jabberwocky Literary Agency; JCA Literary Agency, Inc.; Jellinek & Murray Literary Agency; Jenks Agency, Carolyn; Joy Literary Agency; Kidde, Hoyt & Picard; Kleinman, Esq., of Graybill & English L.L.C., Jeffrey M.; Koster Literary Agency, LLC, Elaine; Kouts, Literary Agent, Barbara S.; Kritzer Productions, Eddie; Lampack Agency, Inc., Peter; Larken, Sabra Elliott; Larsen/Elizabeth Pomada Literary Agents, Michael; Lasher Agency, The Maureen; Levine Communications, Inc., James; Levine Literary Agency, Paul S.; Lincoln Literary Agency, Ray; Literary Group, The; Lowenstein Associates, Inc.; Markowitz Literary Agency, Barbara; Michaels Literary Agency, Inc., Doris S.; Multimedia Product Development, Inc.; Mura Enterprises, Inc., Dee; Nazor Literary Agency, Karen; Norma-Lewis Agency, The; Palmer & Dodge Agency, The; Paraview, Inc.; Pelter, Rodney; Pevner, Inc., Stephen; Pinder Lane & Garon-Brooke Associates, Ltd.; Rees Literary Agency, Helen; Rhodes Literary Agency, Jodie; Robbins Literary Agency, BJ; Sanders & Associates, Victoria; Schiavone Literary Agency, Inc.; Sedgeband Literary Associates; Seligman, Literary Agent, Lynn; Shepard Agency, The; Sherman Associates, Inc., Wendy; Singer Literary Agency Inc., Evelyn; Skolnick Literary Agency, Irene; Southern Literary Group; Spectrum Literary Agency; Stars, the Agency; Stauffer Associates, Nancy; Straus Agency, Inc., Robin; Swayze Literary Agency, Carolyn; Taylor, Literary Agent, Rebecca; Travis Literary Agency, Susan; Vines Agency, Inc., The; Watt & Associates, Sandra; Wecksler-Incomco; Weiner Literary Agency, Cherry; Weingel-Fidel Agency, The; West Coast Literary Associates; Wieser & Wieser, Inc.; Zachary Shuster Harmsworth Agency

Detective/Police/Crime: Acacia House Publishing Services Ltd.; Alive Communications, Inc.; Allen Literary Agency, Linda; Allen, Literary Agent, James; Allred and Allred Literary Agents; AMG/Renaissance; Amsterdam Agency, Marcia; Anubis Literary Agency; Appleseeds Management; Authentic Creations Literary Agency; Authors Alliance Inc.; Baldi Literary Agency, Malaga; Barrett Books Inc., Loretta; Bedford Book Works, Inc., The; Bial Agency, Daniel; Bleecker Street Associates, Inc.; Bova Literary Agency, The Barbara; Brandt & Brandt Literary Agents Inc.; Brandt Agency, The Joan; Browne Ltd., Pema; Charisma Communications, Ltd.; Collin Literary Agent, Frances; Connor Literary Agency; Core Creations, Inc.; Cypher, The Cypher Agency, James R.; DHS Literary, Inc.; Dijkstra Literary Agency, Sandra; Donovan Literary, Jim; Dorian Literary Agency; Ducas, Robert; Dupree/Miller and Associates Inc. Literary; Dystel Literary Management, Jane; Ellenberg Literary Agency, Ethan; Elmo Agency Inc., Ann; Fort Ross Inc. Russian-American Publishing Projects; Frenkel & Associates, James; Goldfarb & Associates; Goodman Associates; Grace Literary Agency, Carroll; Greenburger Associates, Inc., Sanford J.; Greene, Arthur B.; Gregory and Radice Authors' Agents; Grosvenor Literary Agency, The; Halsey Agency, Reece; Halsey North, Reece; Harris Literary Agency; Harris Literary Agency, Inc., The Joy; Hawkins & Associates, Inc., John; Henshaw Group, Richard; Herner Rights Agency, Susan; Hogenson Agency, Barbara; J de S Associates Inc.; Jabberwocky Literary Agency; JCA Literary Agency, Inc.; Jellinek & Murray Literary Agency; Kern Literary Agency, Natasha; Kidde, Hoyt & Picard; Klinger, Inc., Harvey; Koster Literary Agency, LLC, Elaine; Kraas Agency, Irene; Kritzer Productions, Eddie; Lampack Agency, Inc., Peter; Larken, Sabra Elliott; Larsen/Elizabeth Pomada Literary Agents, Michael; Lasher Agency, The Maureen; Levine Literary Agency, Paul S.; Lewis & Company, Karen; Lincoln Literary Agency, Ray; Literary Group, The; Lowenstein Associates, Inc.; Maass Literary Agency, Donald; Markowitz Literary Agency, Barbara; McBride Literary Agency, Margret; Morrison, Inc., Henry; Multimedia Product Development, Inc.; Mura Enterprises, Inc., Dee; Norma-Lewis Agency, The; Pelter, Rodney; Pinder Lane & Garon-Brooke Associates, Ltd.; Rhodes Literary Agency, Jodie; Robbins Literary Agency, BJ; Rose & Associates Literary Agency; Rotrosen Agency LLC, Jane; Rubie Literary Agency, The Peter; Rubinstein Literary Agency, Inc., Pesha; Russell & Volkening; Seligman, Literary Agent, Lynn; Simmons Literary Agency, Jeffrey; Singer Literary Agency Inc., Evelyn; Southern Literary Group; Stars, the Agency; Turner Agency, Paige; Vines Agency, Inc., The; Wallace Literary Agency, Inc.; Ware Literary Agency, John A.; Watt & Associates, Sandra; Weiner Literary Agency, Cherry; West Coast Literary Associates; Wieser & Wieser, Inc.; Wray Literary Agency, Pamela D.; Wright Representatives, Ann; Zachary Shuster Harmsworth

Erotica: Allred and Allred Literary Agents; Baldi Literary Agency, Malaga; Bial Agency, Daniel; Bleecker Street Associates, Inc.; Brandt & Brandt Literary Agents Inc.; DHS Literary, Inc.; Goodman Associates; Harris Literary Agency, Inc., The Joy; Jellinek & Murray Literary Agency; Kleinman, Esq., of Graybill & English L.L.C., Jeffrey M.; Levine Literary Agency, Paul S.; Lewis & Company, Karen; Lowenstein

Associates, Inc.; Pelter, Rodney; Pevner, Inc., Stephen; Rose & Associates Literary Agency; Sedgeband Literary Associates; Stars, the Agency

Ethnic: Agency West Entertainment; Allen Literary Agency, Linda; Allred and Allred Literary Agents; AMG/Renaissance; Amster Literary Enterprises, Betsy; Baldi Literary Agency, Malaga; Barrett Books Inc., Loretta; Bial Agency, Daniel; Bleecker Street Associates, Inc.; Book Deals, Inc.; Brandt & Brandt Literary Agents Inc.; Brown Associates Inc., Marie; Browne Ltd., Pema; Castiglia Literary Agency; Clark Associates, Wm; Collin Literary Agent, Frances; Connor Literary Agency; Daves Agency, Joan; Dawson Associates, Liza; DeFiore and Company; DHS Literary, Inc.; Dickens Group, The; Dijkstra Literary Agency, Sandra; Dupree/Miller and Associates Inc. Literary; Dystel Literary Management, Jane; Elmo Agency Inc., Ann; Eth Literary Representation, Felicia; Evans Inc., Mary; Frenkel & Associates, James; Goldfarb & Associates; Goodman Associates; Greenburger Associates, Inc., Sanford J.; Halsey Agency, Reece; Halsey North, Reece; Harris Literary Agency, Inc., The Joy; Hawkins & Associates, Inc., John; Henshaw Group, Richard; Herner Rights Agency, Susan; Hogenson Agency, Barbara; Jabberwocky Literary Agency; Jellinek & Murray Literary Agency; Jenks Agency, Carolyn; Kern Literary Agency, Natasha; Kleinman, Esq., of Graybill & English L.L.C., Jeffrey M.; Knight Agency, The; Koster Literary Agency, LLC, Elaine; Larken, Sabra Elliott; Larsen/Elizabeth Pomada Literary Agents, Michael; Levine Literary Agency, Paul S.; Lewis & Company, Karen; Lincoln Literary Agency, Ray; Literary Group, The; Lowenstein Associates, Inc.; March Tenth, Inc.; Markowitz Literary Agency, Barbara; McBride Literary Agency, Margret; Multimedia Product Development, Inc.; Mura Enterprises, Inc., Dee; Nazor Literary Agency, Karen; Nine Muses and Apollo Inc.; Palmer & Dodge Agency, The; Paraview, Inc.; Pelter, Rodney; Pevner, Inc., Stephen; Rhodes Literary Agency, Jodie; Robbins Literary Agency, BJ; Rose & Associates Literary Agency; Ross Literary Agency, The Gail; Rubie Literary Agency, The Peter; Rubinstein Literary Agency, Inc., Pesha; Russell & Volkening; Sanders & Associates, Victoria; Schiavone Literary Agency, Inc.; Sedgeband Literary Associates; Seligman, Literary Agent, Lynn; Serendipity Literary Agency, LLC; Singer Literary Agency Inc., Evelyn; Southern Literary Group; Spieler Agency, The; Swayze Literary Agency, Carolyn; Travis Literary Agency, Susan; Vines Agency, Inc., The; Wales, Literary Agency, Inc.; Waxman Agency, Inc., Scott; Zachary Shuster Harmsworth

Experimental: Baldi Literary Agency, Malaga; Barrett Books Inc., Loretta; Brandt & Brandt Literary Agents Inc.; Connor Literary Agency; Dupree/Miller and Associates Inc. Literary; Goodman Associates; Harris Literary Agency, Inc., The Joy; Hawkins & Associates, Inc., John; Kidd Agency, Inc., Virginia; Larken, Sabra Elliott; Larsen/Elizabeth Pomada Literary Agents, Michael; Levine Literary Agency, Paul S.; Manus & Associates Literary Agency; Mura Enterprises, Inc., Dee; Pelter, Rodney; Pevner, Inc., Stephen; Rhodes Literary Agency, Jodie; Rose & Associates Literary Agency; Sedgeband Literary Associates; Stars, the Agency; Vines Agency, Inc., The; Wales, Literary Agency, Inc.; West Coast Literary Associates

Family Saga: Agency West Entertainment; Alive Communications, Inc.; Allen, Literary Agent, James; Allred and Allred Literary Agents; AMG/Renaissance; Authentic Creations Literary Agency; Barrett Books Inc., Loretta; Bleecker Street Associates, Inc.; Boates Literary Agency, Reid; Books & Such; Bova Literary Agency, The Barbara; Brandt & Brandt Literary Agents Inc.; Brandt Agency, The Joan; Collin Literary Agent, Frances; Connor Literary Agency; Daves Agency, Joan; Dawson Associates, Liza; Dijkstra Literary Agency, Sandra; Dorian Literary Agency; Doyen Literary Services, Inc.; Ducas, Robert; Dupree/Miller and Associates Inc. Literary; Dystel Literary Management, Jane; Ellenberg Literary Agency, Ethan; Elmo Agency Inc., Ann; Feigen/Parrent Literary Management; Flaherty, Literary Agent, Joyce A.; Fredericks Literary Agency, Inc., Jeanne; Goodman Associates; Grace Literary Agency, Carroll; Greenburger Associates, Inc., Sanford J.; Grosvenor Literary Agency, The; Halsey Agency, Reece; Halsey North, Reece; Harris Literary Agency, Inc., The Joy; Hawkins & Associates, Inc., John; Henshaw Group, Richard; Herner Rights Agency, Susan; Jabberwocky Literary Agency; JCA Literary Agency, Inc.; Jellinek & Murray Literary Agency; Jenks Agency, Carolyn; Kleinman, Esq., of Graybill & English L.L.C., Jeffrey M.; Klinger, Inc., Harvey; Koster Literary Agency, LLC, Elaine; Kouts, Literary Agent, Barbara S.; Lampack Agency, Inc., Peter; Larken, Sabra Elliott; Larsen/Elizabeth Pomada Literary Agents, Michael; Lasher Agency, The Maureen; Levine Literary Agency, Paul S.; Lincoln Literary Agency, Ray; Literary Group, The; March Tenth, Inc.; Michaels Literary Agency, Inc., Doris S.; Morrison, Inc., Henry; Multimedia Product Development, Inc.; Mura Enterprises, Inc., Dee; Norma-Lewis Agency, The; Pelter, Rodney; Pinder Lane & Garon-Brooke Associates, Ltd.; Rhodes Literary Agency, Jodie; Robbins Literary Agency, BJ; Rose & Associates Literary Agency; Rotrosen Agency LLC, Jane; Sanders & Associates, Victoria; Schiavone Literary Agency, Inc.; Shepard Agency, The; Simmons Literary Agency, Jeffrey; Spieler Agency, The; Straus Agency, Inc., Robin; Swayze Literary Agency, Carolyn; Taylor, Literary Agent, Rebecca; Turner Agency, Paige; Vines Agency, Inc., The; Watt & Associates, Sandra; Weiner Literary Agency, Cherry

Fantasy: Agency West Entertainment; Allen, Literary Agent, James; Allred and Allred Literary Agents; AMG/Renaissance; Anubis Literary Agency; Appleseeds Management; Barbara's Literary Agency; Carvainis Agency, Inc., Maria; Collin Literary Agent, Frances; Communications and Entertainment, Inc.;

Dorian Literary Agency; Ellenberg Literary Agency, Ethan; Fleury Agency, B.R.; Fort Ross Inc. Russian-American Publishing Projects; Frenkel & Associates, James; Goodman Associates; Grace Literary Agency, Carroll; Hawkins & Associates, Inc., John; Henshaw Group, Richard; Herner Rights Agency, Susan; Jabberwocky Literary Agency; Kidd Agency, Inc., Virginia; Kleinman, Esq., of Graybill & English L.L.C., Jeffrey M.; Larsen/Elizabeth Pomada Literary Agents, Michael; Levine Literary Agency, Paul S.; Lincoln Literary Agency, Ray; Literary Group, The; Maass Literary Agency, Donald; Mura Enterprises, Inc., Dee; Pelter, Rodney; Perkins Associates, L.; Pinder Lane & Garon-Brooke Associates, Ltd.; Rhodes Literary Agency, Jodie; Rose & Associates Literary Agency; Rubie Literary Agency, The Peter; Sedgeband Literary Associates; Seligman, Literary Agent, Lynn; Spectrum Literary Agency; Sternig & Byrne Literary Agency; Turner Agency, Paige; Weiner Literary Agency, Cherry

Feminist: Allen Literary Agency, Linda; Allred and Allred Literary Agents; Axelrod Agency, The; Baldi Literary Agency, Malaga; Barrett Books Inc., Loretta; Bial Agency, Daniel; Bleecker Street Associates, Inc.; Brandt & Brandt Literary Agents Inc.; Brown Associates Inc., Marie; Browne Ltd., Pema; DHS Literary, Inc.; Dijkstra Literary Agency, Sandra; Dupree/Miller and Associates Inc. Literary; Elite Online; Elmo Agency Inc., Ann; Eth Literary Representation, Felicia; Feigen/Parrent Literary Management; Flaherty, Literary Agent, Joyce A.; Frenkel & Associates, James; Goldfarb & Associates; Goodman Associates; Greenburger Associates, Inc., Sanford J.; Harris Literary Agency, Inc., The Joy; Hawkins & Associates, Inc., John; Herner Rights Agency, Susan; Jellinek & Murray Literary Agency; Jenks Agency, Carolyn; Kern Literary Agency, Natasha; Kidd Agency, Inc., Virginia; Kidde, Hoyt & Picard; Kleinman, Esq., of Graybill & English L.L.C., Jeffrey M.; Koster Literary Agency, LLC, Elaine; Kouts, Literary Agent, Barbara S.; Larsen/Elizabeth Pomada Literary Agents, Michael; Lasher Agency, The Maureen; Levine Literary Agency, Paul S.; Lincoln Literary Agency, Ray; Literary Group, The; Lowenstein Associates, Inc.; Michaels Literary Agency, Inc., Doris S.; Mura Enterprises, Inc., Dee; Nazor Literary Agency, Karen; Palmer & Dodge Agency, The; Pelter, Rodney; Rhodes Literary Agency, Jodie; Rose & Associates Literary Agency; Ross Literary Agency, The Gail; Sanders & Associates, Victoria; Seligman, Literary Agent, Lynn; Singer Literary Agency Inc., Evelyn; Southern Literary Group; Spieler Agency, The; Taylor, Literary Agent, Rebecca; Vines Agency, Inc., The; Wales, Literary Agency, Inc.; Wright Representatives, Ann; Zachary Shuster Harmsworth

Gay/Lesbian: Allen Literary Agency, Linda; Allred and Allred Literary Agents; Baldi Literary Agency, Malaga; Barrett Books Inc., Loretta; Bial Agency, Daniel; Bleecker Street Associates, Inc.; Brandt & Brandt Literary Agents Inc.; Brown Associates Inc., Marie; Browne Ltd., Pema; Daves Agency, Joan; DeFiore and Company; DHS Literary, Inc.; Dupree/Miller and Associates Inc. Literary; Dystel Literary Management, Jane; Elite Online; Eth Literary Representation, Felicia; Feigen/Parrent Literary Management; Goodman Associates; Greenburger Associates, Inc., Sanford J.; Grosvenor Literary Agency, The; Harris Literary Agency, Inc., The Joy; Hawkins & Associates, Inc., John; Jabberwocky Literary Agency; Jellinek & Murray Literary Agency; Jenks Agency, Carolyn; Kidde, Hoyt & Picard; Kleinman, Esq., of Graybill & English L.L.C., Jeffrey M.; Larsen/Elizabeth Pomada Literary Agents, Michael; Levine Literary Agency, Paul S.; Lincoln Literary Agency, Ray; Literary Group, The; Lowenstein Associates, Inc.; Mura Enterprises, Inc., Dee; Palmer & Dodge Agency, The; Pelter, Rodney; Pevner, Inc., Stephen; Pinder Lane & Garon-Brooke Associates, Ltd.; Rhodes Literary Agency, Jodie; Ross Literary Agency, The Gail; Rubie Literary Agency, The Peter; Sanders & Associates, Victoria; Seligman, Literary Agent, Lynn; Spieler Agency, The; Vines Agency, Inc., The; Wales, Literary Agency, Inc.; Wright Representatives, Ann; Zachary Shuster Harmsworth

Glitz: Allen Literary Agency, Linda; Allen, Literary Agent, James; Allred and Allred Literary Agents; Authors Alliance Inc.; Barrett Books Inc., Loretta; Bova Literary Agency, The Barbara; Browne Ltd., Pema; Castiglia Literary Agency; Dupree/Miller and Associates Inc. Literary; Elmo Agency Inc., Ann; Goldfarb & Associates; Goodman Associates; Greenburger Associates, Inc., Sanford J.; Harris Literary Agency, Inc., The Joy; Hawkins & Associates, Inc., John; Henshaw Group, Richard; Herner Rights Agency, Susan; Jabberwocky Literary Agency; Jellinek & Murray Literary Agency; JLM Literary Agents; Kidd Agency, Inc., Virginia; Kidde, Hoyt & Picard; Kleinman, Esq., of Graybill & English L.L.C., Jeffrey M.; Klinger, Inc., Harvey; Larken, Sabra Elliott; Larsen/Elizabeth Pomada Literary Agents, Michael; Levine Literary Agency, Paul S.; Multimedia Product Development, Inc.; Mura Enterprises, Inc., Dee; Pelter, Rodney; Pevner, Inc., Stephen; Quicksilver Books—Literary Agents; Rose & Associates Literary Agency; Rubinstein Literary Agency, Inc., Pesha; Sternig & Byrne Literary Agency; Teal Literary Agency, Patricia; Weiner Literary Agency, Cherry

Historical: Alive Communications, Inc.; Allen, Literary Agent, James; Allred and Allred Literary Agents; Altair Literary Agency; AMG/Renaissance; Anubis Literary Agency; Authors Alliance Inc.; Baldi Literary Agency, Malaga; Barrett Books Inc., Loretta; Bleecker Street Associates, Inc.; Books & Such; Brandt & Brandt Literary Agents Inc.; Brown Associates Inc., Marie; Browne Ltd., Pema; Carvainis Agency, Inc., Maria; Clark Associates, Wm; Collin Literary Agent, Frances; Communications and Entertainment, Inc.;

Dawson Associates, Liza; DHS Literary, Inc.; Donovan Literary, Jim; Dorian Literary Agency; Doyen Literary Services, Inc.; Dupree/Miller and Associates Inc. Literary; Ellenberg Literary Agency, Ethan; Elmo Agency Inc., Ann; Flaherty, Literary Agent, Joyce A.; Fredericks Literary Agency, Inc., Jeanne; Frenkel & Associates, James; Goodman Associates; Grace Literary Agency, Carroll; Greenburger Associates, Inc., Sanford J.; Gregory and Radice Authors' Agents; Grosjean Literary Agency, Jill; Grosvenor Literary Agency, The; Halsey Agency, Reece; Halsey North, Reece; Harris Literary Agency, Inc., The Joy; Hawkins & Associates, Inc., John; Henshaw Group, Richard; Herner Rights Agency, Susan; Hogenson Agency, Barbara; Hopkins Literary Associates; J de S Associates Inc.; Jabberwocky Literary Agency; JCA Literary Agency, Inc.; Jellinek & Murray Literary Agency; Jenks Agency, Carolyn; Kern Literary Agency, Natasha; Kidd Agency, Inc., Virginia; Kidde, Hoyt & Picard; Kleinman, Esq., of Graybill & English L.L.C., Jeffrey M.; Koster Literary Agency, LLC, Elaine; Kouts, Literary Agent, Barbara S.; Lampack Agency, Inc., Peter; Larken, Sabra Elliott; Larsen/Elizabeth Pomada Literary Agents, Michael; Lasher Agency, The Maureen; Levine Literary Agency, Paul S.; Lincoln Literary Agency, Ray; Lowenstein Associates, Inc.; Maass Literary Agency, Donald; March Tenth, Inc.; Markowitz Literary Agency, Barbara; McBride Literary Agency, Margret; McHugh Literary Agency; Michaels Literary Agency, Inc., Doris S.; Multimedia Product Development, Inc.; Mura Enterprises, Inc., Dee; Norma-Lewis Agency, The; Paraview, Inc.; Pelter, Rodney; Rees Literary Agency, Helen; Rhodes Literary Agency, Jodie; Rose & Associates Literary Agency; Rotrosen Agency LLC, Jane; Rubie Literary Agency, The Peter; Schiavone Literary Agency, Inc.; Seligman, Literary Agent, Lynn; Serendipity Literary Agency, LLC; Shepard Agency, The; Singer Literary Agency Inc., Evelyn; Skolnick Literary Agency, Irene; Southern Literary Group; Spectrum Literary Agency; Stars, the Agency; Straus Agency, Inc., Robin; Swayze Literary Agency, Carolyn; Toad Hall, Inc.; Travis Literary Agency, Susan; Vines Agency, Inc., The; Waxman Agency, Inc., Scott; Wecksler-Incomco; Weiner Literary Agency, Cherry; West Coast Literary Associates; Wieser & Wieser, Inc.; Wylie-Merrick Literary Agency; Zachary Shuster Harmsworth

Horror: Allen Literary Agency, Linda; Allen, Literary Agent, James; Allred and Allred Literary Agents; Amsterdam Agency, Marcia; Anubis Literary Agency; Appleseeds Management; Connor Literary Agency; Core Creations, Inc.; Cypher, The Cypher Agency, James R.; Donovan Literary, Jim; Dorian Literary Agency; Dupree/Miller and Associates Inc. Literary; Elite Online; Fleury Agency, B.R.; Fort Ross Inc. Russian-American Publishing Projects; Goodman Associates; Grace Literary Agency, Carroll; Greene, Arthur B.; Hawkins & Associates, Inc., John; Henshaw Group, Richard; Herner Rights Agency, Susan; Jabberwocky Literary Agency; Jellinek & Murray Literary Agency; Kleinman, Esq., of Graybill & English L.L.C., Jeffrey M.; Levine Literary Agency, Paul S.; Literary Group, The; Maass Literary Agency, Donald; Norma-Lewis Agency, The; Perkins Associates, L.; Pevner, Inc., Stephen; Rose & Associates Literary Agency; Rotrosen Agency LLC, Jane; Rubie Literary Agency, The Peter; Schiavone Literary Agency, Inc.; Sedgeband Literary Associates; Seligman, Literary Agent, Lynn; Southern Literary Group; Sternig & Byrne Literary Agency; Turner Agency, Paige; Vines Agency, Inc., The; Wray Literary Agency, Pamela D.

Humor/Satire: Agency West Entertainment; Alive Communications, Inc.; Allred and Allred Literary Agents; AMG/Renaissance; Amsterdam Agency, Marcia; Barrett Books Inc., Loretta; Bial Agency, Daniel; Brandt & Brandt Literary Agents Inc.; Browne Ltd., Pema; Elite Online; Farber Literary Agency Inc.; Flannery Literary; Fleury Agency, B.R.; Goodman Associates; Greenburger Associates, Inc., Sanford J.; Gregory and Radice Authors' Agents; Grosjean Literary Agency, Jill; Harris Literary Agency; Henshaw Group, Richard; Hogenson Agency, Barbara; Jabberwocky Literary Agency; JCA Literary Agency, Inc.; Jellinek & Murray Literary Agency; Kidde, Hoyt & Picard; Kleinman, Esq., of Graybill & English L.L.C., Jeffrey M.; Larken, Sabra Elliott; Larsen/Elizabeth Pomada Literary Agents, Michael; Levine Literary Agency, Paul S.; Lincoln Literary Agency, Ray; Literary Group, The; March Tenth, Inc.; Markowitz Literary Agency, Barbara; McBride Literary Agency, Margret; Mura Enterprises, Inc., Dee; Norma-Lewis Agency, The; Pevner, Inc., Stephen; Rose & Associates Literary Agency; Rubinstein Literary Agency, Inc., Pesha; Schiavone Literary Agency, Inc.; Seligman, Literary Agent, Lynn; Spieler Agency, The; Stars, the Agency; Swayze Literary Agency, Carolyn; Vines Agency, Inc., The; Wray Literary Agency, Pamela D.; Wright Representatives, Ann

Juvenile: Agency West Entertainment; Alive Communications, Inc.; Allred and Allred Literary Agents; Barbara's Literary Agency; Books & Such; Briggs, M. Courtney; Brown Associates Inc., Marie; Brown Literary Agency, Inc., Andrea; Browne Ltd., Pema; Dwyer & O'Grady, Inc.; Elek Associates, Peter; Ellenberg Literary Agency, Ethan; Ellison Inc., Nicholas; Elmo Agency Inc., Ann; Farber Literary Agency Inc.; FitzGerald Literary Management; Flannery Literary; Fort Ross Inc. Russian-American Publishing Projects; Harris Literary Agency; Hawkins & Associates, Inc., John; Henshaw Group, Richard; J de S Associates Inc.; Kirchoff/Wohlberg, Inc., Authors' Representation Division; Kouts, Literary Agent, Barbara S.; Kroll Literary Agency Inc., Edite; Lincoln Literary Agency, Ray; Livingston Cooke/Curtis Brown Canada; Maccoby Literary Agency, Gina; Markowitz Literary Agency, Barbara; Multimedia Product Development, Inc.; Mura Enterprises, Inc., Dee; National Writers Literary Agency; Norma-Lewis Agency, The; Rhodes Literary Agency, Jodie; Rose & Associates Literary Agency; Rubinstein Literary Agency, Inc., Pesha; Russell & Volkening; Schiavone Literary Agency, Inc.; Serendipity Literary Agency, LLC; Sternig & Byrne Literary Agency; Taylor, Literary Agent, Rebecca; Tiersten Literary Agency, Irene; Tobias—A Literary Agency for Children's Books, Ann; Treimel NY, S©ott; Turner Agency, Paige; Vines Agency, Inc., The; Wecksler-Incomco; Writers' Productions; Wylie-Merrick Literary Agency

Literary: Acacia House Publishing Services Ltd.; Agency West Entertainment; Alive Communications, Inc.; Allen Literary Agency, Linda; Allred and Allred Literary Agents; Altair Literary Agency; Altshuler Literary Agency, Miriam; AMG/Renaissance; Amster Literary Enterprises, Betsy; Anubis Literary Agency; Authentic Creations Literary Agency; Authors Alliance Inc.; Baldi Literary Agency, Malaga; Barrett Books Inc., Loretta; Bial Agency, Daniel; Black Literary Agency, David; Bleecker Street Associates, Inc.; Book Deals, Inc.; Borchardt Inc., Georges; Brandt & Brandt Literary Agents Inc.; Brandt Agency, The Joan; Brown Associates Inc., Marie; Browne Ltd., Pema; Carvainis Agency, Inc., Maria; Castiglia Literary Agency; Clark Associates, Wm; Collin Literary Agent, Frances; Congdon Associates Inc., Don; Connor Literary Agency; Contemporary Management; Coover Agency, The Doe; Cypher, The Cypher Agency, James R.; Daves Agency, Joan; DeFiore and Company; DHS Literary, Inc.; Dickens Group, The; Dijkstra Literary Agency, Sandra; Donovan Literary, Jim; Dorian Literary Agency; Doyen Literary Services, Inc.; Ducas, Robert; Dupree/Miller and Associates Inc. Literary; Dystel Literary Management, Jane; Ellenberg Literary Agency, Ethan; Ellison Inc., Nicholas; Elmo Agency Inc., Ann; Eth Literary Representation, Felicia; Evans Inc., Mary; Farber Literary Agency Inc.; Feigen/Parrent Literary Management; Flannery Literary; Fleury Agency, B.R.; Fogelman Literary Agency, The; Franklin Associates, Ltd., Lynn C.; Fredericks Literary Agency, Inc., Jeanne; Gelfman Schneider Literary Agents, Inc.; Goldfarb & Associates; Goodman Associates; Grace Literary Agency, Carroll; Greenburger Associates, Inc., Sanford J.; Gregory and Radice Authors' Agents; Grosjean Literary Agency, Jill; Grosvenor Literary Agency, The; Halsey Agency, Reece; Halsey North, Reece; Harris Literary Agency, Inc., The Joy; Hawkins & Associates, Inc., John; Henshaw Group, Richard; Herner Rights Agency, Susan; Hill Associates, Frederick; Hogenson Agency, Barbara; J de S Associates Inc.; Jabberwocky Literary Agency; JCA Literary Agency, Inc.; Jellinek & Murray Literary Agency; Jenks Agency, Carolyn; Joy Literary Agency; Kidd Agency, Inc., Virginia; Kidde, Hoyt & Picard; Kleinman, Esq., of Graybill & English L.L.C., Jeffrey M.; Klinger, Inc., Harvey; Knight Agency, The; Koster Literary Agency, LLC, Elaine; Kouts, Literary Agent, Barbara S.; Lampack Agency, Inc., Peter; Larken, Sabra Elliott; Larsen/Elizabeth Pomada Literary Agents, Michael; Lasher Agency, The Maureen; Levine Communications, Inc., James; Levine Literary Agency, Paul S.; Levine Literary Agency, Inc., Ellen; Lewis & Company, Karen; Lincoln Literary Agency, Ray; Livingston Cooke/Curtis Brown Canada; Lowenstein Associates, Inc.; Maass Literary Agency, Donald; Maccoby Literary Agency, Gina; Mann Agency, Carol; Manus & Associates Literary Agency; March Tenth, Inc.; Markson Literary Agency, Elaine; McBride Literary Agency, Margret; McDonough, Literary Agent, Richard P.; Michaels Literary Agency, Inc., Doris S.; Multimedia Product Development, Inc.; Mura Enterprises, Inc., Dee; Nazor Literary Agency, Karen; Nine Muses and Apollo Inc.; Palmer & Dodge Agency, The; Paraview, Inc.; Paton Literary Agency, Kathi J.; Pelter, Rodney; Perkins Associates, L.; Pevner, Inc., Stephen; Pinder Lane & Garon-Brooke Associates, Ltd.; Popkin, Julie; Rees Literary Agency, Helen; Rein Books, Inc., Jody; Rhodes Literary Agency, Jodie; Rittenberg Literary Agency, Inc., Ann; Robbins Literary Agency, BJ; Rose & Associates Literary Agency; Ross Literary Agency, The Gail; Rubie Literary Agency, The Peter; Russell & Volkening; Sanders & Associates, Victoria; Sandum & Associates; Scherf, Inc. Literary Management; Schiavone Literary Agency, Inc.; Sebastian Literary Agency; Sedgeband Literary Associates; Seligman, Literary Agent, Lynn; Shepard Agency, The; Simmons Literary Agency, Jeffrey; Singer Literary Agency Inc., Evelyn; Skolnick Literary Agency, Irene; Slopen Literary Agency, Beverley; Southern Literary Group; Spieler Agency, The; Stars, the Agency; Stauffer Associates, Nancy; Straus Agency, Inc., Robin; Susijn Agency, The; Swayze Literary Agency, Carolyn; Talbot Agency, The John; Taylor, Literary Agent, Rebecca; Travis Literary Agency, Susan; Turner Agency, Paige; Vines Agency, Inc., The; Wales, Literary Agency, Inc.; Wallace Literary Agency, Inc.; Ware Literary Agency, John A.; Watkins Loomis Agency, Inc.; Waxman Agency, Inc., Scott; Wecksler-Incomco; Weingel-Fidel Agency, The; West Coast Literary Associates; Wieser & Wieser, Inc.; Wonderland Press, Inc., The; Wright Representatives, Ann; Writers' Productions; Writers' Representatives, Inc.; Zachary Shuster Harmsworth

Mainstream: Acacia House Publishing Services Ltd.; Agency West Entertainment; Agents Inc. for Medical and Mental Health Professionals; Alive Communications, Inc.; Allen Literary Agency, Linda; Allen, Literary Agent, James; Allred and Allred Literary Agents; Altshuler Literary Agency, Miriam; AMG/Renaissance; Amsterdam Agency, Marcia; Authentic Creations Literary Agency; Authors Alliance Inc.; Baldi Literary Agency, Malaga; Barrett Books Inc., Loretta; Bedford Book Works, Inc., The; Black Literary Agency, David; Boates Literary Agency, Reid; Book Deals, Inc.; Books & Such; Bova Literary Agency, The Barbara; Brandt & Brandt Literary Agents Inc.; Brandt Agency, The Joan; Briggs, M. Courtney; Brown Associates Inc., Marie; Browne Ltd., Pema; Carvainis Agency, Inc., Maria; Castiglia Literary Agency; Clark Associates, Wm; Collin Literary Agent, Frances; Coover Agency, The Doe; Crawford

Literary Agency; Cypher, The Cypher Agency, James R.; Daves Agency, Joan; DeFiore and Company; DHS Literary, Inc.; Dickens Group, The; Dijkstra Literary Agency, Sandra; Donovan Literary, Jim; Dorian Literary Agency; Doyen Literary Services, Inc.; Ducas, Robert; Dupree/Miller and Associates Inc. Literary; Dystel Literary Management, Jane; Ellenberg Literary Agency, Ethan; Ellison Inc., Nicholas; Elmo Agency Inc., Ann; Eth Literary Representation, Felicia; Farber Literary Agency Inc.; FitzGerald Literary Management; Flaherty, Literary Agent, Joyce A.; Flannery Literary; Fogelman Literary Agency, The; Franklin Associates, Ltd., Lynn C.; Frenkel & Associates, James; Gelfman Schneider Literary Agents, Inc.; Goldfarb & Associates; Goodman Associates; Grace Literary Agency, Carroll; Greenburger Associates, Inc., Sanford J.; Gregory and Radice Authors' Agents; Grosjean Literary Agency, Jill; Grosvenor Literary Agency, The; Halsey Agency, Reece; Halsey North, Reece; Harris Literary Agency; Harris Literary Agency, Inc., The Joy; Hawkins & Associates, Inc., John; Henshaw Group, Richard; Herner Rights Agency, Susan; Hill Associates, Frederick; Hogenson Agency, Barbara; Hopkins Literary Associates; J de S Associates Inc.; Jabberwocky Literary Agency; JCA Literary Agency, Inc.; Jellinek & Murray Literary Agency; Jenks Agency, Carolyn; Joy Literary Agency; Kern Literary Agency, Natasha; Kidd Agency, Inc., Virginia; Kidde, Hoyt & Picard; Kleinman, Esq., of Graybill & English L.L.C., Jeffrey M.; Klinger, Inc., Harvey; Knight Agency, The; Koster Literary Agency, LLC, Elaine; Kouts, Literary Agent, Barbara S.; Lampack Agency, Inc., Peter; Larken, Sabra Elliott; Larsen/Elizabeth Pomada Literary Agents, Michael; Lasher Agency, The Maureen; Levine Communications, Inc., James; Levine Literary Agency, Paul S.; Lewis & Company, Karen; Lincoln Literary Agency, Ray; Lipkind Agency, Wendy; Lowenstein Associates, Inc.; Maass Literary Agency, Donald; Maccoby Literary Agency, Gina; March Tenth, Inc.; Markowitz Literary Agency, Barbara; Markson Literary Agency, Elaine; McBride Literary Agency, Margret; McHugh Literary Agency; Michaels Literary Agency, Inc., Doris S.; Multimedia Product Development, Inc.; Mura Enterprises, Inc., Dee; National Writers Literary Agency; Nine Muses and Apollo Inc.; Norma-Lewis Agency, The; Palmer & Dodge Agency, The; Paraview, Inc.; Paton Literary Agency, Kathi J.; Pelter, Rodney; Pevner, Inc., Stephen; Pinder Lane & Garon-Brooke Associates, Ltd.; Popkin, Julie; Rees Literary Agency, Helen; Rein Books, Inc., Jody; Rhodes Literary Agency, Jodie; Robbins Literary Agency, BJ; Rose & Associates Literary Agency; Rotrosen Agency LLC, Jane; Rubie Literary Agency, The Peter; Rubinstein Literary Agency, Inc., Pesha; Russell & Volkening; Sandum & Associates; Scherf, Inc. Literary Management; Schiavone Literary Agency, Inc.; Sedgeband Literary Associates; Seligman, Literary Agent, Lynn; Sherman Associates, Inc., Wendy; Simmons Literary Agency, Jeffrey; Singer Literary Agency Inc., Evelyn; Southern Literary Group; Spectrum Literary Agency; Stars, the Agency; Stauffer Associates, Nancy; Steele-Perkins Literary Agency; Straus Agency, Inc., Robin; Swayze Literary Agency, Carolyn; Teal Literary Agency, Patricia; Travis Literary Agency, Susan; Turner Agency, Paige; Vines Agency, Inc., The; Wales, Literary Agency, Inc.; Wallace Literary Agency, Inc.; Ware Literary Agency, John A.; Watt & Associates, Sandra; Wecksler-Incomco; Weiner Literary Agency, Cherry; Weingel-Fidel Agency, The; West Coast Literary Associates; Wieser & Wieser, Inc.; Wray Literary Agency, Pamela D.; Wright Representatives, Ann; Wylie-Merrick Literary Agency; Zachary Shuster Harmsworth

Multicultural: Altshuler Literary Agency, Miriam; Black Literary Agency, David; Goodman Associates; Gregory and Radice Authors' Agents; Jellinek & Murray Literary Agency; Rose & Associates Literary Agency; Serendipity Literary Agency, LLC; Southern Literary Group; Steele-Perkins Literary Agency; Swayze Literary Agency, Carolyn; Turner Agency, Paige

Mystery/Suspense: Acacia House Publishing Services Ltd.; Agents Inc. for Medical and Mental Health Professionals; Alive Communications, Inc.; Allen Literary Agency, Linda; Allen, Literary Agent, James; Allred and Allred Literary Agents; AMG/Renaissance; Amsterdam Agency, Marcia; Appleseeds Management; Authentic Creations Literary Agency; Authors Alliance Inc.; Axelrod Agency, The; Baldi Literary Agency, Malaga; Barrett Books Inc., Loretta; Bedford Book Works, Inc., The; Bleecker Street Associates, Inc.; Bova Literary Agency, The Barbara; Brandt & Brandt Literary Agents Inc.; Brandt Agency, The Joan; Brown Associates Inc., Marie; Browne Ltd., Pema; Carvainis Agency, Inc., Maria; Castiglia Literary Agency; Charisma Communications, Ltd.; Collin Literary Agent, Frances; Connor Literary Agency; Contemporary Management; Dawson Associates, Liza; DeFiore and Company; DHS Literary, Inc.; Dickens Group, The; Dijkstra Literary Agency, Sandra; Donovan Literary, Jim; Dorian Literary Agency; Ducas, Robert; Dupree/Miller and Associates Inc. Literary; Ellenberg Literary Agency, Ethan; Elmo Agency Inc., Ann; Farber Literary Agency Inc.; Flaherty, Literary Agent, Joyce A.; Flannery Literary; Fort Ross Inc. Russian-American Publishing Projects; Frenkel & Associates, James; Goldfarb & Associates; Goodman Associates; Grace Literary Agency, Carroll; Greenburger Associates, Inc., Sanford J.; Greene, Arthur B.; Gregory and Radice Authors' Agents; Grosjean Literary Agency, Jill; Grosvenor Literary Agency, The; Halsey Agency, Reece; Halsey North, Reece; Harris Literary Agency; Harris Literary Agency, Inc., The Joy; Hawkins & Associates, Inc., John; Herner Rights Agency, Susan; Hogenson Agency, Barbara; J de S Associates Inc.; JCA Literary Agency, Inc.; Jellinek & Murray Literary Agency; Jenks Agency, Carolyn; JLM Literary Agents; Kern Literary Agency, Natasha; Kidd Agency, Inc., Virginia; Kidde, Hoyt & Picard; Kleinman, Esq., of Graybill & English L.L.C., Jeffrey M.; Koster Literary Agency, LLC, Elaine; Kouts,

Literary Agent, Barbara S.; Kraas Agency, Irene; Lampack Agency, Inc., Peter; Larken, Sabra Elliott; Larsen/Elizabeth Pomada Literary Agents, Michael; Lescher & Lescher Ltd.; Levine Literary Agency, Paul S.; Levine Literary Agency, Inc., Ellen; Lewis & Company, Karen; Lincoln Literary Agency, Ray; Lipkind Agency, Wendy; Literary Group, The; Love Literary Agency, Nancy; Lowenstein Associates, Inc.; Maass Literary Agency, Donald; Maccoby Literary Agency, Gina; Markowitz Literary Agency, Barbara; McBride Literary Agency, Margret; McHugh Literary Agency; Multimedia Product Development, Inc.; Mura Enterprises, Inc., Dee; Norma-Lewis Agency, The; Pelter, Rodney; Pinder Lane & Garon-Brooke Associates, Ltd.; Popkin, Julie; Protter Literary Agent, Susan Ann; Quicksilver Books—Literary Agents; Rees Literary Agency, Helen; Rhodes Literary Agency, Jodie; Robbins Literary Agency, BJ; Roghaar Literary Agency, Inc., Linda; Rose & Associates Literary Agency; Rotrosen Agency LLC, Jane; Rubie Literary Agency, The Peter; Rubinstein Literary Agency, Inc., Pesha; Russell & Volkening; Scherf, Inc. Literary Management; Sedgeband Literary Associates; Seligman, Literary Agent, Lynn; Sherman Associates, Inc., Wendy; Simmons Literary Agency, Jeffrey; Singer Literary Agency Inc., Evelyn; Slopen Literary Agency, Beverley; Southern Literary Group; Spectrum Literary Agency; Stars, the Agency; Sternig & Byrne Literary Agency; Swayze Literary Agency, Carolyn; Talbot Agency, The John; Teal Literary Agency, Patricia; Toad Hall, Inc.; Turner Agency, Paige; Vines Agency, Inc., The; Wallace Literary Agency, Inc.; Ware Literary Agency, John A.; Watt & Associates, Sandra; Waxman Agency, Inc., Scott; Weiner Literary Agency, Cherry; West Coast Literary Associates; Wieser & Wieser, Inc.; Wray Literary Agency, Pamela D.; Wright Representatives, Ann; Zachary Shuster Harmsworth

New Age/Metaphysical: Goodman Associates; Jellinek & Murray Literary Agency; Rose & Associates Literary Agency

Open to all Fiction Categories: Bernstein Literary Agency, Meredith; Brown Ltd., Curtis; Bykofsky Associates, Inc., Sheree; Circle of Confusion Ltd.; Congdon Associates Inc., Don; Curtis Associates, Inc., Richard; Fernandez Agent/Attorney, Justin E.; First Books; FitzGerald Literary Management; Goodman Associates; Hamilburg Agency, The Mitchell J.; Hoffman Literary Agency, Berenice; Lazear Agency Incorporated; Madsen Agency, Robert; Moran Agency, Maureen; Ober Associates, Harold; Raines & Raines; Schwartz Agency, Laurens R.; Writers House (NY)

Picture Book: Books & Such; Briggs, M. Courtney; Brown Literary Agency, Inc., Andrea; Browne Ltd., Pema; Dupree/Miller and Associates Inc. Literary; Dwyer & O'Grady, Inc.; Elek Associates, Peter; Ellenberg Literary Agency, Ethan; Flannery Literary; Harris Literary Agency, Inc., The Joy; Hawkins & Associates, Inc., John; Heacock Literary Agency, Inc.; Jellinek & Murray Literary Agency; Kouts, Literary Agent, Barbara S.; Kroll Literary Agency Inc., Edite; Levine Literary Agency, Paul S.; Multimedia Product Development, Inc.; Norma-Lewis Agency, The; Rose & Associates Literary Agency; Rubinstein Literary Agency, Inc., Pesha; Russell & Volkening; Serendipity Literary Agency, LLC; Taylor, Literary Agent, Rebecca; Turner Agency, Paige; Wecksler-Incomco; Wray Literary Agency, Pamela D.; Writers House (CA); Wylie-Merrick Literary Agency

Psychic/Supernatural: Allen Literary Agency, Linda; Allred and Allred Literary Agents; Appleseeds Management; Barrett Books Inc., Loretta; Bleecker Street Associates, Inc.; Brandt & Brandt Literary Agents Inc.; Browne Ltd., Pema; Collin Literary Agent, Frances; Doyen Literary Services, Inc.; Dupree/Miller and Associates Inc. Literary; Elite Online; Elmo Agency Inc., Ann; Fleury Agency, B.R.; Goodman Associates; Grace Literary Agency, Carroll; Greenburger Associates, Inc., Sanford J.; Harris Literary Agency, Inc., The Joy; Hawkins & Associates, Inc., John; Henshaw Group, Richard; Jabberwocky Literary Agency; Jellinek & Murray Literary Agency; JLM Literary Agents; Kleinman, Esq., of Graybill & English L.L.C., Jeffrey M.; Larsen/Elizabeth Pomada Literary Agents, Michael; Levine Literary Agency, Paul S.; Lincoln Literary Agency, Ray; Literary Group, The; Maass Literary Agency, Donald; Mura Enterprises, Inc., Dee; Paraview, Inc.; Pelter, Rodney; Pevner, Inc., Stephen; Rhodes Literary Agency, Jodie; Rose & Associates Literary Agency; Rubie Literary Agency, The Peter; Rubinstein Literary Agency, Inc., Pesha; Sedgeband Literary Associates; Simmons Literary Agency, Jeffrey; Sternig & Byrne Literary Agency; Vines Agency, Inc., The; Weiner Literary Agency, Cherry; Wray Literary Agency, Pamela D.

Regional: Allen Literary Agency, Linda; Allred and Allred Literary Agents; Baldi Literary Agency, Malaga; Bova Literary Agency, The Barbara; Brandt & Brandt Literary Agents Inc.; Collin Literary Agent, Frances; Dawson Associates, Liza; Elmo Agency Inc., Ann; Goodman Associates; Greenburger Associates, Inc., Sanford J.; Grosjean Literary Agency, Jill; Harris Literary Agency, Inc., The Joy; Hawkins & Associates, Inc., John; Jabberwocky Literary Agency; Jellinek & Murray Literary Agency; Kleinman, Esq., of Graybill & English L.L.C., Jeffrey M.; Koster Literary Agency, LLC, Elaine; Larken, Sabra Elliott; Levine Literary Agency, Paul S.; Lincoln Literary Agency, Ray; Manus & Associates Literary Agency; Mura Enterprises, Inc., Dee; Nazor Literary Agency, Karen; Paraview, Inc.; Pelter, Rodney; Rhodes Literary Agency, Jodie; Rose & Associates Literary Agency; Shepard Agency, The; Singer Literary Agency Inc.,

Evelyn; Southern Literary Group; Stauffer Associates, Nancy; Vines Agency, Inc., The; Watt & Associates, Sandra; West Coast Literary Associates

Religious/Inspirational: Agency West Entertainment; Alive Communications, Inc.; Allred and Allred Literary Agents; Barrett Books Inc., Loretta; BigScore Productions Inc.; Books & Such; Brandenburgh & Associates Literary Agency; Browne Ltd., Pema; Charisma Communications, Ltd.; Crawford Literary Agency; Dupree/Miller and Associates Inc. Literary; Goodman Associates; Harris Literary Agency, Inc., The Joy; Hawkins & Associates, Inc., John; Joy Literary Agency; Larsen/Elizabeth Pomada Literary Agents, Michael; Levine Literary Agency, Paul S.; Multimedia Product Development, Inc.; Pelter, Rodney; Rose & Associates Literary Agency; Scherf, Inc. Literary Management; Watt & Associates, Sandra; Waxman Agency, Inc., Scott

Romance: Allen, Literary Agent, James; Allred and Allred Literary Agents; Amsterdam Agency, Marcia; Authentic Creations Literary Agency; Axelrod Agency, The; Barrett Books Inc., Loretta; Bleecker Street Associates, Inc.; Books & Such; Bova Literary Agency, The Barbara; Brandt & Brandt Literary Agents Inc.; Browne Ltd., Pema; Carvainis Agency, Inc., Maria; Collin Literary Agent, Frances; Dorian Literary Agency; Ellenberg Literary Agency, Ethan; Elmo Agency Inc., Ann; Flaherty, Literary Agent, Joyce A.; Fogelman Literary Agency, The; Fort Ross Inc. Russian-American Publishing Projects; Goodman Associates; Grace Literary Agency, Carroll; Gregory and Radice Authors' Agents; Grosjean Literary Agency, Jill; Grosvenor Literary Agency, The; Harris Literary Agency, Inc., The Joy; Henshaw Group, Richard; Herner Rights Agency, Susan; Hogenson Agency, Barbara; Hopkins Literary Associates; Jenks Agency, Carolyn; JLM Literary Agents; Kern Literary Agency, Natasha; Kidde, Hoyt & Picard; Kleinman, Esq., of Graybill & English L.L.C., Jeffrey M.; Knight Agency, The; Larsen/Elizabeth Pomada Literary Agents, Michael; Levine Literary Agency, Paul S.; Lincoln Literary Agency, Ray; Literary Group, The; Lowenstein Associates, Inc.; Maass Literary Agency, Donald; McHugh Literary Agency; Multimedia Product Development, Inc.; Mura Enterprises, Inc., Dee; Norma-Lewis Agency, The; Paraview, Inc.; Pinder Lane & Garon-Brooke Associates, Ltd.; Rhodes Literary Agency, Jodie; Rose & Associates Literary Agency; Rotrosen Agency LLC, Jane; Rubinstein Literary Agency, Inc., Pesha; Sedgeband Literary Associates; Seligman, Literary Agent, Lynn; Serendipity Literary Agency, LLC; Sherman Associates, Inc., Wendy; Southern Literary Group; Steele-Perkins Literary Agency; Teal Literary Agency, Patricia; Toad Hall, Inc.; Travis Literary Agency, Susan; Turner Agency, Paige; Vines Agency, Inc., The; Waxman Agency, Inc., Scott; Weiner Literary Agency, Cherry; West Coast Literary Associates; Wieser & Wieser, Inc.; Wright Representatives, Ann

Science Fiction: Allen, Literary Agent, James; Allred and Allred Literary Agents; AMG/Renaissance; Amsterdam Agency, Marcia; Anubis Literary Agency; Appleseeds Management; Bova Literary Agency, The Barbara; Brandt & Brandt Literary Agents Inc.; Browne Ltd., Pema; Collin Literary Agent, Frances; Communications and Entertainment, Inc.; Core Creations, Inc.; Dorian Literary Agency; Elite Online; Ellenberg Literary Agency, Ethan; Fleury Agency, B.R.; Fort Ross Inc. Russian-American Publishing Projects; Frenkel & Associates, James; Goodman Associates; Halsey Agency, Reece; Halsey North, Reece; Harris Literary Agency; Hawkins & Associates, Inc., John; Henshaw Group, Richard; Herner Rights Agency, Susan; Jabberwocky Literary Agency; Kidd Agency, Inc., Virginia; Kleinman, Esq., of Graybill & English L.L.C., Jeffrey M.; Kraas Agency, Irene; Lawyer's Literary Agency, Inc.; Lewis & Company, Karen; Maass Literary Agency, Donald; Mura Enterprises, Inc., Dee; National Writers Literary Agency; Perkins Associates, L.; Pinder Lane & Garon-Brooke Associates, Ltd.; Protter Literary Agent, Susan Ann; Rhodes Literary Agency, Jodie; Rose & Associates Literary Agency; Rubie Literary Agency, The Peter; Schiavone Literary Agency, Inc.; Sedgeband Literary Associates; Seligman, Literary Agent, Lynn; Serendipity Literary Agency, LLC; Spectrum Literary Agency; Sternig & Byrne Literary Agency; Toad Hall, Inc.; Turner Agency, Paige; Vines Agency, Inc., The; Weiner Literary Agency, Cherry; West Coast Literary Associates

Sports: Agency West Entertainment; Allred and Allred Literary Agents; Authentic Creations Literary Agency; Authors Alliance Inc.; Barrett Books Inc., Loretta; Brandt & Brandt Literary Agents Inc.; Charisma Communications, Ltd.; Charlton Associates, James; DHS Literary, Inc.; Donovan Literary, Jim; Ducas, Robert; Dupree/Miller and Associates Inc. Literary; Goodman Associates; Greenburger Associates, Inc., Sanford J.; Greene, Arthur B.; Harris Literary Agency, Inc., The Joy; Hawkins & Associates, Inc., John; Henshaw Group, Richard; Jabberwocky Literary Agency; JCA Literary Agency, Inc.; Lasher Agency, The Maureen; Levine Literary Agency, Paul S.; Lincoln Literary Agency, Ray; Literary Group, The; Markowitz Literary Agency, Barbara; Multimedia Product Development, Inc.; Mura Enterprises, Inc., Dee; National Writers Literary Agency; Pelter, Rodney; Rhodes Literary Agency, Jodie; Robbins Literary Agency, BJ; Rose & Associates Literary Agency; Russell & Volkening; Shepard Agency, The; Turner Agency, Paige; Vines Agency, Inc., The; Waxman Agency, Inc., Scott; Wright Representatives, Ann

Thriller/Espionage: Acacia House Publishing Services Ltd.; Agents Inc. for Medical and Mental Health

Professionals; Alive Communications, Inc.; Allen Literary Agency, Linda; Allred and Allred Literary Agents; Altshuler Literary Agency, Miriam; AMG/Renaissance; Amsterdam Agency, Marcia; Authentic Creations Literary Agency; Authors Alliance Inc.; Baldi Literary Agency, Malaga; Barrett Books Inc., Loretta; Bedford Book Works, Inc., The; Bleecker Street Associates, Inc.; Boates Literary Agency, Reid; Bova Literary Agency, The Barbara; Brandt & Brandt Literary Agents Inc.; Brandt Agency, The Joan; Browne Ltd., Pema; Carvainis Agency, Inc., Maria; Clark Associates, Wm; Communications and Entertainment, Inc.; Contemporary Management; Crawford Literary Agency; Dawson Associates, Liza; DeFiore and Company; DHS Literary, Inc.; Dickens Group, The; Dijkstra Literary Agency, Sandra; Donovan Literary, Jim; Dorian Literary Agency; Ducas, Robert; Dupree/Miller and Associates Inc. Literary; Dystel Literary Management, Jane; Ellenberg Literary Agency, Ethan; Elmo Agency Inc., Ann; Eth Literary Representation, Felicia; Farber Literary Agency Inc.; Flaherty, Literary Agent, Joyce A.; Fleury Agency, B.R.; Fort Ross Inc. Russian-American Publishing Projects; Frenkel & Associates, James; Goldfarb & Associates; Goodman Associates; Grace Literary Agency, Carroll; Greenburger Associates, Inc., Sanford J.; Greene, Arthur B.; Gregory and Radice Authors' Agents; Grosjean Literary Agency, Jill; Grosvenor Literary Agency, The; Halsey Agency, Reece; Halsey North, Reece; Harris Literary Agency; Harris Literary Agency, Inc., The Joy; Hawkins & Associates, Inc., John; Henshaw Group, Richard; Herner Rights Agency, Susan; Hogenson Agency, Barbara; Jabberwocky Literary Agency; JCA Literary Agency, Inc.; Jellinek & Murray Literary Agency; Jenks Agency, Carolyn; Kidde, Hoyt & Picard; Kleinman, Esq., of Graybill & English L.L.C., Jeffrey M.; Klinger, Inc., Harvey; Koster Literary Agency, LLC, Elaine; Lampack Agency, Inc., Peter; Larken, Sabra Elliott; Lasher Agency, The Maureen; Lawyer's Literary Agency, Inc.; Levine Literary Agency, Paul S.; Levine Literary Agency, Inc., Ellen; Lewis & Company, Karen; Lincoln Literary Agency, Ray; Literary Group, The; Love Literary Agency, Nancy; Lowenstein Associates, Inc.; Maass Literary Agency, Donald; Maccoby Literary Agency, Gina; Manus & Associates Literary Agency; Markowitz Literary Agency, Barbara; McBride Literary Agency, Margret; McHugh Literary Agency; Multimedia Product Development, Inc.; Mura Enterprises, Inc., Dee; Norma-Lewis Agency, The; Paraview, Inc.; Pelter, Rodney; Pevner, Inc., Stephen; Protter Literary Agent, Susan Ann; Quicksilver Books—Literary Agents; Rees Literary Agency, Helen; Rhodes Literary Agency, Jodie; Robbins Literary Agency, BJ; Rose & Associates Literary Agency; Rotrosen Agency LLC, Jane; Rubie Literary Agency, The Peter; Russell & Volkening; Sanders & Associates, Victoria; Scherf, Inc. Literary Management; Serendipity Literary Agency, LLC; Shepard Agency, The; Sherman Associates, Inc., Wendy; Simmons Literary Agency, Jeffrey; Singer Literary Agency Inc., Evelyn; Southern Literary Group; Stars, the Agency; Sternig & Byrne Literary Agency; Straus Agency, Inc., Robin; Turner Agency, Paige; Vines Agency, Inc., The; Ware Literary Agency, John A.; Watt & Associates, Sandra; Weiner Literary Agency, Cherry; West Coast Literary Associates; Wieser & Wieser, Inc.; Wonderland Press, Inc., The; Wray Literary Agency, Pamela D.; Wright Representatives, Ann; Zachary Shuster Harmsworth

Westerns/Frontier: Alive Communications, Inc.; Allred and Allred Literary Agents; Amsterdam Agency, Marcia; Brandt & Brandt Literary Agents Inc.; DHS Literary, Inc.; Donovan Literary, Jim; Frenkel & Associates, James; Goodman Associates; Grace Literary Agency, Carroll; Hawkins & Associates, Inc., John; J de S Associates Inc.; Jellinek & Murray Literary Agency; Jenks Agency, Carolyn; Kern Literary Agency, Natasha; Levine Literary Agency, Paul S.; Literary Group, The; McBride Literary Agency, Margret; Mura Enterprises, Inc., Dee; Norma-Lewis Agency, The; Pelter, Rodney; Rhodes Literary Agency, Jodie; Rose & Associates Literary Agency; Vines Agency, Inc., The; Weiner Literary Agency, Cherry; West Coast Literary Associates; Wright Representatives, Ann

Young Adult: Agency West Entertainment; Alive Communications, Inc.; Allen, Literary Agent, James; Allred and Allred Literary Agents; Amsterdam Agency, Marcia; Brandt & Brandt Literary Agents Inc.; Briggs, M. Courtney; Brown Literary Agency, Inc., Andrea; Browne Ltd., Pema; Carvainis Agency, Inc., Maria; Dorian Literary Agency; Dwyer & O'Grady, Inc.; Ellenberg Literary Agency, Ethan; Elmo Agency Inc., Ann; Farber Literary Agency Inc.; FitzGerald Literary Management; Flannery Literary; Fort Ross Inc. Russian-American Publishing Projects; Frenkel & Associates, James; Harris Literary Agency; Harris Literary Agency, Inc., The Joy; Henshaw Group, Richard; J de S Associates Inc.; Kidd Agency, Inc., Virginia; Kirchoff/Wohlberg, Inc., Authors' Representation Division; Kleinman, Esq., of Graybill & English L.L.C., Jeffrey M.; Kouts, Literary Agent, Barbara S.; Levine Literary Agency, Paul S.; Lincoln Literary Agency, Ray; Literary Group, The; Maccoby Literary Agency, Gina; Markowitz Literary Agency, Barbara; Mura Enterprises, Inc., Dee; National Writers Literary Agency; Norma-Lewis Agency, The; Rhodes Literary Agency, Jodie; Rose & Associates Literary Agency; Russell & Volkening; Schiavone Literary Agency, Inc.; Southern Literary Group; Stars, the Agency; Sternig & Byrne Literary Agency; Taylor, Literary Agent, Rebecca; Tiersten Literary Agency, Irene; Tobias—A Literary Agency for Children's Books, Ann; Treimel NY, Sⓒott; Turner Agency, Paige; Watt & Associates, Sandra; Wray Literary Agency, Pamela D.; Writers House (CA); Wylie-Merrick Literary Agency

NONFEE-CHARGING LITERARY AGENTS/NONFICTION

Agriculture/Horticulture: Amster Literary Enterprises, Betsy; Baldi Literary Agency, Malaga; Brandt & Brandt Literary Agents Inc.; Casselman Literary Agency, Martha; Ellison Inc., Nicholas; ForthWrite Literary Agency; Fredericks Literary Agency, Inc., Jeanne; Gartenberg, Literary Agent, Max; Goodman Associates; Hawkins & Associates, Inc., John; Kleinman, Esq., of Graybill & English L.L.C., Jeffrey M.; Larken, Sabra Elliott; Lieberman Associates, Robert; Limelight Management; Lincoln Literary Agency, Ray; Multimedia Product Development, Inc.; Mura Enterprises, Inc., Dee; Parks Agency, The Richard; Rose & Associates Literary Agency; Shepard Agency, The; Watt & Associates, Sandra

Animals: Acacia House Publishing Services Ltd.; Baldi Literary Agency, Malaga; Balkin Agency, Inc.; Barbara's Literary Agency; Bial Agency, Daniel; Bleecker Street Associates, Inc.; Boates Literary Agency, Reid; Boston Literary Group, The; Brandt & Brandt Literary Agents Inc.; Briggs, M. Courtney; Castiglia Literary Agency; DH Literary, Inc.; Ducas, Robert; Dystel Literary Management, Jane; Ellison Inc., Nicholas; Eth Literary Representation, Felicia; Flaherty, Literary Agent, Joyce A.; Fredericks Literary Agency, Inc., Jeanne; Gartenberg, Literary Agent, Max; Goodman Associates; Greene, Arthur B.; Grosvenor Literary Agency, The; Hawkins & Associates, Inc., John; Henshaw Group, Richard; Jellinek & Murray Literary Agency; Jenks Agency, Carolyn; Kern Literary Agency, Natasha; Kleinman, Esq., of Graybill & English L.L.C., Jeffrey M.; Kritzer Productions, Eddie; Larken, Sabra Elliott; Lasher Agency, The Maureen; Levine Communications, Inc., James; Lincoln Literary Agency, Ray; Literary Group, The; Love Literary Agency, Nancy; Lowenstein Associates, Inc.; McHugh Literary Agency; Multimedia Product Development, Inc.; Mura Enterprises, Inc., Dee; National Writers Literary Agency; New Century Literary Agency; Nine Muses and Apollo Inc.; Parks Agency, The Richard; Rein Books, Inc., Jody; Rhodes Literary Agency, Jodie; Roghaar Literary Agency, Inc., Linda; Rose & Associates Literary Agency; Rosenkranz Literary Agency, Rita; Schiavone Literary Agency, Inc.; Shepard Agency, The; Stauffer Associates, Nancy; Straus Agency, Inc., Robin; Teal Literary Agency, Patricia; Toad Hall, Inc.; Wales, Literary Agency, Inc.; Ware Literary Agency, John A.; Watt & Associates, Sandra; Writers House (NY); Zachary Shuster Harmsworth

Anthropology/Archaeology: Allen Literary Agency, Linda; Allred and Allred Literary Agents; Altair Literary Agency; Authentic Creations Literary Agency; Baldi Literary Agency, Malaga; Balkin Agency, Inc.; Bial Agency, Daniel; Bleecker Street Associates, Inc.; Boates Literary Agency, Reid; Borchardt Inc., Georges; Boston Literary Group, The; Brandt & Brandt Literary Agents Inc.; Casselman Literary Agency, Martha; Castiglia Literary Agency; Collin Literary Agent, Frances; Contemporary Management; Coover Agency, The Doe; DH Literary, Inc.; Dijkstra Literary Agency, Sandra; Dystel Literary Management, Jane; Educational Design Services, Inc.; Elek Associates, Peter; Ellison Inc., Nicholas; Elmo Agency Inc., Ann; Eth Literary Representation, Felicia; Fredericks Literary Agency, Inc., Jeanne; Fullerton Associates, Sheryl B.; Goodman Associates; Grosvenor Literary Agency, The; Hawkins & Associates, Inc., John; Herner Rights Agency, Susan; Hochmann Books, John L.; James Peter Associates, Inc.; JCA Literary Agency, Inc.; Jellinek & Murray Literary Agency; Kellock Company, Inc., The; Kern Literary Agency, Natasha; Kleinman, Esq., of Graybill & English L.L.C., Jeffrey M.; Lampack Agency, Inc., Peter; Larken, Sabra Elliott; Larsen/Elizabeth Pomada Literary Agents, Michael; Lasher Agency, The Maureen; Levine Literary Agency, Inc., Ellen; Lieberman Associates, Robert; Lincoln Literary Agency, Ray; Literary Group, The; Lowenstein Associates, Inc.; Lownie Literary Agency Ltd., Andrew; Mann Agency, Carol; McHugh Literary Agency; Miller Agency, The; Morrison, Inc., Henry; Multimedia Product Development, Inc.; Mura Enterprises, Inc., Dee; Palmer & Dodge Agency, The; Parks Agency, The Richard; Quicksilver Books—Literary Agents; Rhodes Literary Agency, Jodie; Roghaar Literary Agency, Inc., Linda; Rose & Associates Literary Agency; Rosenkranz Literary Agency, Rita; Ross Literary Agency, The Gail; Russell & Volkening; Schiavone Literary Agency, Inc.; Seligman, Literary Agent, Lynn; Singer Literary Agency Inc., Evelyn; Slopen Literary Agency, Beverley; Straus Agency, Inc., Robin; Toad Hall, Inc.; United Tribes; Wallace Literary Agency, Inc.; Ware Literary Agency, John A.; Watt & Associates, Sandra

Art/Architecture/Design: Ajlouny Literary Agency, Joseph; Allen Literary Agency, Linda; Allred and Allred Literary Agents; Altair Literary Agency; Baldi Literary Agency, Malaga; Boates Literary Agency, Reid; Boston Literary Group, The; Brandt & Brandt Literary Agents Inc.; Brown Associates Inc., Marie; Clark Associates, Wm; Contemporary Management; Donnaud & Associates, Inc., Janis A.; Ellison Inc., Nicholas; Elmo Agency Inc., Ann; ForthWrite Literary Agency; Fredericks Literary Agency, Inc., Jeanne; Gartenberg, Literary Agent, Max; Goodman Associates; Grace Literary Agency, Carroll; Grosjean Literary Agency, Jill; Grosvenor Literary Agency, The; Hawkins & Associates, Inc., John; Heacock Literary Agency, Inc.; Hochmann Books, John L.; Hogenson Agency, Barbara; James Peter Associates, Inc.; Jellinek & Murray Literary Agency; Kellock Company, Inc., The; Kidde, Hoyt & Picard; Kleinman, Esq., of Graybill & English L.L.C., Jeffrey M.; Lampack Agency, Inc., Peter; Larken, Sabra Elliott; Larsen/Elizabeth Pomada Literary Agents, Michael; Lasher Agency, The Maureen; Levine Communications, Inc., James; Levine Literary Agency, Paul S.; Lieberman Associates, Robert; Limelight Management; Lincoln Literary Agency,

Ray; Mann Agency, Carol; Miller Agency, The; Norma-Lewis Agency, The; Parks Agency, The Richard; Popkin, Julie; Rose & Associates Literary Agency; Rosenkranz Literary Agency, Rita; Rubie Literary Agency, The Peter; Russell & Volkening; Seligman, Literary Agent, Lynn; Straus Agency, Inc., Robin; United Tribes; Waterside Productions, Inc.; Watkins Loomis Agency, Inc.; Watt & Associates, Sandra; Wecksler-Incomco; Weingel-Fidel Agency, The; Wonderland Press, Inc., The; Wray Literary Agency, Pamela D.; Writers House (NY)

Biography/Autobiography: Acacia House Publishing Services Ltd.; Agency West Entertainment; Ajlouny Literary Agency, Joseph; Alive Communications, Inc.; Allen Literary Agency, Linda; Allred and Allred Literary Agents; Altair Literary Agency; Altshuler Literary Agency, Miriam; AMG/Renaissance; Amster Literary Enterprises, Betsy; Andrews & Associates Inc., Bart; Authentic Creations Literary Agency; Authors Alliance Inc.; Baldi Literary Agency, Malaga; Balkin Agency, Inc.; Bedford Book Works, Inc., The; Bial Agency, Daniel; Black Literary Agency, David; Bleecker Street Associates, Inc.; Boates Literary Agency, Reid; Borchardt Inc., Georges; Boston Literary Group, The; Bova Literary Agency, The Barbara; Brandt & Brandt Literary Agents Inc.; Briggs, M. Courtney; Brown Associates Inc., Marie; Bykofsky Associates, Inc., Sheree; Carvainis Agency, Inc., Maria; Casselman Literary Agency, Martha; Castiglia Literary Agency; Charisma Communications, Ltd.; Clark Associates, Wm; Clausen, Mays & Tahan, LLC; Collin Literary Agent, Frances; Contemporary Management; Coover Agency, The Doe; Crawford Literary Agency; Cypher, The Cypher Agency, James R.; Daves Agency, Joan; Dawson Associates, Liza; DeFiore and Company; DH Literary, Inc.; DHS Literary, Inc.; Dickens Group, The; Dijkstra Literary Agency, Sandra; Donnaud & Associates, Inc., Janis A.; Donovan Literary, Jim; Ducas, Robert; Dystel Literary Management, Jane; Ellenberg Literary Agency, Ethan; Elmo Agency Inc., Ann; Eth Literary Representation, Felicia; Evans Inc., Mary; Feigen/Parent Literary Management; Fogelman Literary Agency, The; Fort Ross Inc. Russian-American Publishing Projects; ForthWrite Literary Agency; Franklin Associates, Ltd., Lynn C.; Fredericks Literary Agency, Inc., Jeanne; Frenkel & Associates, James; Gartenberg, Literary Agent, Max; Goodman Associates; Grace Literary Agency, Carroll; Gregory and Radice Authors' Agents; Grosvenor Literary Agency, The; Halsey Agency, Reece; Halsey North, Reece; Harris Literary Agency; Hawkins & Associates, Inc., John; Heacock Literary Agency, Inc.; Henshaw Group, Richard; Herner Rights Agency, Susan; Hill Associates, Frederick; Hochmann Books, John L.; Hogenson Agency, Barbara; J de S Associates Inc.; Jabberwocky Literary Agency; James Peter Associates, Inc.; JCA Literary Agency, Inc.; Jellinek & Murray Literary Agency; Jenks Agency, Carolyn; JLM Literary Agents; Joy Literary Agency; Kellock Company, Inc., The; Kern Literary Agency, Natasha; Ketz Agency, Louise B.; Kidde, Hoyt & Picard; Kleinman, Esq., of Graybill & English L.L.C., Jeffrey M.; Klinger, Inc., Harvey; Knight Agency, The; Koster Literary Agency, LLC, Elaine; Kouts, Literary Agent, Barbara S.; Kritzer Productions, Eddie; Lampack Agency, Inc., Peter; Larken, Sabra Elliott; Larsen/Elizabeth Pomada Literary Agents, Michael; Lasher Agency, The Maureen; Lawyer's Literary Agency, Inc.; Levine Communications, Inc., James; Levine Literary Agency, Paul S.; Levine Literary Agency, Inc., Ellen; Lincoln Literary Agency, Ray; Lipkind Agency, Wendy; Literary and Creative Artists, Inc.; Literary Group, The; Livingston Cooke/Curtis Brown Canada; Love Literary Agency, Nancy; Lowenstein Associates, Inc.; Lownie Literary Agency Ltd., Andrew; Maccoby Literary Agency, Gina; Mann Agency, Carol; Manus & Associates Literary Agency; March Tenth, Inc.; Markowitz Literary Agency, Barbara; McBride Literary Agency, Margret; McCauley, Gerard; McHugh Literary Agency; Michaels Literary Agency, Inc., Doris S.; Miller Agency, The; Morrison, Inc., Henry; Multimedia Product Development, Inc.; Mura Enterprises, Inc., Dee; National Writers Literary Agency; Nazor Literary Agency, Karen; New Century Literary Agency; New England Publishing Associates, Inc.; Nine Muses and Apollo Inc.; Norma-Lewis Agency, The; Palmer & Dodge Agency, The; Parks Agency, The Richard; Pevner, Inc., Stephen; Pinder Lane & Garon-Brooke Associates, Ltd.; Protter Literary Agent, Susan Ann; Quicksilver Books—Literary Agents; Raymond, Literary Agent, Charlotte Cecil; Rees Literary Agency, Helen; Rhodes Literary Agency, Jodie; Rinaldi Literary Agency, Angela; Rittenberg Literary Agency, Inc., Ann; Robbins Literary Agency, BJ; Robbins Office, Inc., The; Roghaar Literary Agency, Inc., Linda; Rose & Associates Literary Agency; Rosenkranz Literary Agency, Rita; Ross Literary Agency, The Gail; Rotrosen Agency LLC, Jane; Russell & Volkening; Sanders & Associates, Victoria; Schiavone Literary Agency, Inc.; Sebastian Literary Agency; Sedgeband Literary Associates; Seligman, Literary Agent, Lynn; Shepard Agency, The; Sherman Associates, Inc., Wendy; Simmons Literary Agency, Jeffrey; Singer Literary Agency Inc., Evelyn; Skolnick Literary Agency, Irene; Slopen Literary Agency, Beverley; Smith Literary Agency, Robert; Spieler Agency, The; Stauffer Associates, Nancy; Sternig & Byrne Literary Agency; Straus Agency, Inc., Robin; Susijn Agency, The; Swayze Literary Agency, Carolyn; Teal Literary Agency, Patricia; Turner Agency, Paige; 2M Communications Ltd.; United Tribes; Valcourt Agency, Inc., The Richard R.; Vines Agency, Inc., The; Wales, Literary Agency, Inc.; Wallace Literary Agency, Inc.; Ware Literary Agency, John A.; Waterside Productions, Inc.; Watkins Loomis Agency, Inc.; Waxman Agency, Inc., Scott; Wecksler-Incomco; Weingel-Fidel Agency, The; West Coast Literary Associates; Wonderland Press, Inc., The; Wray Literary Agency, Pamela D.; Writers House (NY); Zachary Shuster Harmsworth

Business: Alive Communications, Inc.; Allen Literary Agency, Linda; Altair Literary Agency; Amster Literary Enterprises, Betsy; Authors Alliance Inc.; Baldi Literary Agency, Malaga; Bedford Book Works, Inc., The; Bial Agency, Daniel; Black Literary Agency, David; Bleecker Street Associates, Inc.; Boates Literary Agency, Reid; Book Deals, Inc.; Boston Literary Group, The; Bova Literary Agency, The Barbara; Brandt & Brandt Literary Agents Inc.; Brown Associates Inc., Marie; Browne Ltd., Pema; Bykofsky Associates, Inc., Sheree; Carvainis Agency, Inc., Maria; Castiglia Literary Agency; Connor Literary Agency; Contemporary Management; Coover Agency, The Doe; Cypher, The Cypher Agency, James R.; Dawson Associates, Liza; DeFiore and Company; DHS Literary, Inc.; Dickens Group, The; Dijkstra Literary Agency, Sandra; Donovan Literary, Jim; Ducas, Robert; Dystel Literary Management, Jane; Educational Design Services, Inc.; Ellenberg Literary Agency, Ethan; Ellison Inc., Nicholas; Elmo Agency Inc., Ann; Eth Literary Representation, Felicia; Feigen/Parrent Literary Management; Fogelman Literary Agency, The; ForthWrite Literary Agency; Fredericks Literary Agency, Inc., Jeanne; Fullerton Associates, Sheryl B.; Goodman Associates; Grosvenor Literary Agency, The; Hawkins & Associates, Inc., John; Henshaw Group, Richard; Herman Agency LLC, The Jeff; Herner Rights Agency, Susan; J de S Associates Inc.; Jabberwocky Literary Agency; James Peter Associates, Inc.; JCA Literary Agency, Inc.; Jellinek & Murray Literary Agency; JLM Literary Agents; Kellock Company, Inc., The; Kern Literary Agency, Natasha; Ketz Agency, Louise B.; Kleinman, Esq., of Graybill & English L.L.C., Jeffrey M.; Knight Agency, The; Konner Literary Agency, Linda; Koster Literary Agency, LLC, Elaine; Kritzer Productions, Eddie; Lampack Agency, Inc., Peter; Larken, Sabra Elliott; Larsen/Elizabeth Pomada Literary Agents, Michael; Lasher Agency, The Maureen; Levine Communications, Inc., James; Levine Literary Agency, Paul S.; Lieberman Associates, Robert; Lincoln Literary Agency, Ray; Literary and Creative Artists, Inc.; Literary Group, The; Livingston Cooke/Curtis Brown Canada; Lowenstein Associates, Inc.; Mann Agency, Carol; Manus & Associates Literary Agency; McBride Literary Agency, Margret; McHugh Literary Agency; Menza Literary Agency, Claudia; Michaels Literary Agency, Inc., Doris S.; Miller Agency, The; Multimedia Product Development, Inc.; Mura Enterprises, Inc., Dee; Nazor Literary Agency, Karen; New Century Literary Agency; New England Publishing Associates, Inc.; Nine Muses and Apollo Inc.; Palmer & Dodge Agency, The; Parks Agency, The Richard; Paton Literary Agency, Kathi J.; Quicksilver Books—Literary Agents; Rees Literary Agency, Helen; Rein Books, Inc., Jody; Rhodes Literary Agency, Jodie; Rinaldi Literary Agency, Angela; Rose & Associates Literary Agency; Rosenkranz Literary Agency, Rita; Ross Literary Agency, The Gail; Roth, Literary Representation, Carol Susan; Rotrosen Agency LLC, Jane; Russell & Volkening; Scherf, Inc. Literary Management; Sebastian Literary Agency; Seligman, Literary Agent, Lynn; Shepard Agency, The; Shepard Agency, The Robert E.; Singer Literary Agency Inc., Evelyn; Slopen Literary Agency, Beverley; Snell Literary Agency, Michael; Spieler Agency, The; Swayne Agency Literary Management & Consulting, Inc., The; Toad Hall, Inc.; Travis Literary Agency, Susan; Turner Agency, Paige; United Tribes; Vines Agency, Inc., The; Wales, Literary Agency, Inc.; Waterside Productions, Inc.; Waxman Agency, Inc., Scott; Wecksler-Incomco; Wieser & Wieser, Inc.; Wray Literary Agency, Pamela D.; Writers House (NY); Zachary Shuster Harmsworth

Child Guidance/Parenting: Agency West Entertainment; Alive Communications, Inc.; Allen Literary Agency, Linda; Amster Literary Enterprises, Betsy; Amsterdam Agency, Marcia; Authentic Creations Literary Agency; Authors Alliance Inc.; Bial Agency, Daniel; Bleecker Street Associates, Inc.; Boates Literary Agency, Reid; Books & Such; Boston Literary Group, The; Brandt & Brandt Literary Agents Inc.; Browne Ltd., Pema; Bykofsky Associates, Inc., Sheree; Castiglia Literary Agency; Charlton Associates, James; Connor Literary Agency; Contemporary Management; Coover Agency, The Doe; DeFiore and Company; DH Literary, Inc.; DHS Literary, Inc.; Dijkstra Literary Agency, Sandra; Donovan Literary, Jim; Dystel Literary Management, Jane; Educational Design Services, Inc.; Elek Associates, Peter; Ellenberg Literary Agency, Ethan; Ellison Inc., Nicholas; Elmo Agency Inc., Ann; Eth Literary Representation, Felicia; Farber Literary Agency Inc.; Flaherty, Literary Agent, Joyce A.; Flannery Literary; Fogelman Literary Agency, The; ForthWrite Literary Agency; Fredericks Literary Agency, Inc., Jeanne; Gartenberg, Literary Agent, Max; Goodman Associates; Grosvenor Literary Agency, The; Hawkins & Associates, Inc., John; Henshaw Group, Richard; Herner Rights Agency, Susan; James Peter Associates, Inc.; Jellinek & Murray Literary Agency; Kellock Company, Inc., The; Kern Literary Agency, Natasha; Kleinman, Esq., of Graybill & English L.L.C., Jeffrey M.; Knight Agency, The; Konner Literary Agency, Linda; Koster Literary Agency, LLC, Elaine; Kouts, Literary Agent, Barbara S.; Larsen/Elizabeth Pomada Literary Agents, Michael; Lasher Agency, The Maureen; Levine Communications, Inc., James; Levine Literary Agency, Paul S.; Lincoln Literary Agency, Ray; Literary Group, The; Livingston Cooke/Curtis Brown Canada; Love Literary Agency, Nancy; Lowenstein Associates, Inc.; Mann Agency, Carol; Manus & Associates Literary Agency; McBride Literary Agency, Margret; McHugh Literary Agency; Miller Agency, The; Multimedia Product Development, Inc.; Mura Enterprises, Inc., Dee; National Writers Literary Agency; Nazor Literary Agency, Karen; New Century Literary Agency; New England Publishing Associates, Inc.; Norma-Lewis Agency, The; Palmer & Dodge Agency, The; Parks Agency, The Richard; Paton Literary Agency, Kathi J.; Pinder Lane & Garon-Brooke Associates, Ltd.; Quicksilver Books—Literary Agents; Rein Books, Inc., Jody; Rhodes Literary Agency, Jodie; Rinaldi Literary Agency, Angela; Robbins Literary Agency, BJ; Rose &

Associates Literary Agency; Rosenkranz Literary Agency, Rita; Rotrosen Agency LLC, Jane; Rubinstein Literary Agency, Inc., Pesha; Schiavone Literary Agency, Inc.; Sebastian Literary Agency; Seligman, Literary Agent, Lynn; Shepard Agency, The; Sherman Associates, Inc., Wendy; Singer Literary Agency Inc., Evelyn; Slopen Literary Agency, Beverley; Spieler Agency, The; Straus Agency, Inc., Robin; Swayze Literary Agency, Carolyn; Teal Literary Agency, Patricia; Toad Hall, Inc.; Travis Literary Agency, Susan; Turner Agency, Paige; 2M Communications Ltd.; United Tribes; Waterside Productions, Inc.; Wray Literary Agency, Pamela D.; Writers House (NY)

Computers/Electronics: Allen Literary Agency, Linda; Authors Alliance Inc.; Bleecker Street Associates, Inc.; DHS Literary, Inc.; Dickens Group, The; Ellison Inc., Nicholas; Elmo Agency Inc., Ann; Evans Inc., Mary; ForthWrite Literary Agency; Goodman Associates; Henshaw Group, Richard; Herman Agency LLC, The Jeff; Jellinek & Murray Literary Agency; Kleinman, Esq., of Graybill & English L.L.C., Jeffrey M.; Knight Agency, The; Kritzer Productions, Eddie; Levine Communications, Inc., James; Levine Literary Agency, Paul S.; Lieberman Associates, Robert; Manus & Associates Literary Agency; Mura Enterprises, Inc., Dee; Nazor Literary Agency, Karen; Rhodes Literary Agency, Jodie; Rose & Associates Literary Agency; Rosenkranz Literary Agency, Rita; Serendipity Literary Agency, LLC; Shepard Agency, The; Swayne Agency Literary Management & Consulting, Inc., The; Waterside Productions, Inc.; Wray Literary Agency, Pamela D.; Wylie-Merrick Literary Agency

Cooking/Food/Nutrition: Agency West Entertainment; Agents Inc. for Medical and Mental Health Professionals; Allred and Allred Literary Agents; Authors Alliance Inc.; Baldi Literary Agency, Malaga; Bial Agency, Daniel; Bleecker Street Associates, Inc.; Book Deals, Inc.; Bova Literary Agency, The Barbara; Brandt & Brandt Literary Agents Inc.; Browne Ltd., Pema; Bykofsky Associates, Inc., Sheree; Casselman Literary Agency, Martha; Castiglia Literary Agency; Clausen, Mays & Tahan, LLC; Connor Literary Agency; Coover Agency, The Doe; DeFiore and Company; DHS Literary, Inc.; Dickens Group, The; Dijkstra Literary Agency, Sandra; Donnaud & Associates, Inc., Janis A.; Dystel Literary Management, Jane; Ellenberg Literary Agency, Ethan; Ellison Inc., Nicholas; Elmo Agency Inc., Ann; Farber Literary Agency Inc.; Flaherty, Literary Agent, Joyce A.; ForthWrite Literary Agency; Fredericks Literary Agency, Inc., Jeanne; Goodman Associates; Grace Literary Agency, Carroll; Hawkins & Associates, Inc., John; Henshaw Group, Richard; Herner Rights Agency, Susan; Hill Associates, Frederick; Hochmann Books, John L.; Jabberwocky Literary Agency; Jellinek & Murray Literary Agency; Joy Literary Agency; Kleinman, Esq., of Graybill & English L.L.C., Jeffrey M.; Klinger, Inc., Harvey; Knight Agency, The; Konner Literary Agency, Linda; Koster Literary Agency, LLC, Elaine; Kritzer Productions, Eddie; Larken, Sabra Elliott; Larsen/Elizabeth Pomada Literary Agents, Michael; Lasher Agency, The Maureen; Lescher & Lescher Ltd.; Levine Communications, Inc., James; Levine Literary Agency, Paul S.; Limelight Management; Lincoln Literary Agency, Ray; Literary and Creative Artists, Inc.; Literary Group, The; Love Literary Agency, Nancy; McBride Literary Agency, Margret; McHugh Literary Agency; Miller Agency, The; Multimedia Product Development, Inc.; New Century Literary Agency; Norma-Lewis Agency, The; Parks Agency, The Richard; Quicksilver Books—Literary Agents; Rhodes Literary Agency, Jodie; Rinaldi Literary Agency, Angela; Robbins Literary Agency, BJ; Rose & Associates Literary Agency; Rosenkranz Literary Agency, Rita; Ross Literary Agency, The Gail; Rotrosen Agency LLC, Jane; Russell & Volkening; Seligman, Literary Agent, Lynn; Shepard Agency, The; Slopen Literary Agency, Beverley; Smith Literary Agency, Robert; Spieler Agency, The; Straus Agency, Inc., Robin; Swayze Literary Agency, Carolyn; Taylor, Literary Agent, Rebecca; Toad Hall, Inc.; Travis Literary Agency, Susan; United Tribes; Wieser & Wieser, Inc.; Wray Literary Agency, Pamela D.; Writers House (NY)

Crafts/Hobbies: Agency West Entertainment; Ajlouny Literary Agency, Joseph; Allred and Allred Literary Agents; Authentic Creations Literary Agency; Authors Alliance Inc.; Brandt & Brandt Literary Agents Inc.; Connor Literary Agency; Ellison Inc., Nicholas; Elmo Agency Inc., Ann; ForthWrite Literary Agency; Fredericks Literary Agency, Inc., Jeanne; Goodman Associates; Grace Literary Agency, Carroll; Hawkins & Associates, Inc., John; Kellock Company, Inc., The; Kleinman, Esq., of Graybill & English L.L.C., Jeffrey M.; Levine Literary Agency, Paul S.; Limelight Management; Lincoln Literary Agency, Ray; Literary Group, The; Lowenstein Associates, Inc.; Multimedia Product Development, Inc.; Norma-Lewis Agency, The; Parks Agency, The Richard; Rose & Associates Literary Agency; Rosenkranz Literary Agency, Rita; Shepard Agency, The; Toad Hall, Inc.; Watt & Associates, Sandra

Current Affairs: Ajlouny Literary Agency, Joseph; Allred and Allred Literary Agents; Authentic Creations Literary Agency; Authors Alliance Inc.; Baldi Literary Agency, Malaga; Balkin Agency, Inc.; Bedford Book Works, Inc., The; Bial Agency, Daniel; Bleecker Street Associates, Inc.; Boates Literary Agency, Reid; Borchardt Inc., Georges; Boston Literary Group, The; Brandt & Brandt Literary Agents Inc.; Bykofsky Associates, Inc., Sheree; Castiglia Literary Agency; Charisma Communications, Ltd.; Clark Associates, Wm; Connor Literary Agency; Contemporary Management; Cypher, The Cypher Agency, James R.; DH Literary, Inc.; DHS Literary, Inc.; Dickens Group, The; Dijkstra Literary Agency, Sandra; Donnaud & Associates, Inc., Janis A.; Donovan Literary, Jim; Ducas, Robert; Dystel Literary Management, Jane;

Educational Design Services, Inc.; Ellenberg Literary Agency, Ethan; Ellison Inc., Nicholas; Elmo Agency Inc., Ann; Eth Literary Representation, Felicia; Evans Inc., Mary; Feigen/Parrent Literary Management; Flaming Star Literary Enterprises; Fogelman Literary Agency, The; Franklin Associates, Ltd., Lynn C.; Fredericks Literary Agency, Inc., Jeanne; Fullerton Associates, Sheryl B.; Gartenberg, Literary Agent, Max; Goodman Associates; Grosvenor Literary Agency, The; Halsey Agency, Reece; Halsey North, Reece; Hawkins & Associates, Inc., John; Henshaw Group, Richard; Herner Rights Agency, Susan; Hill Associates, Frederick; Hochmann Books, John L.; J de S Associates Inc.; Jabberwocky Literary Agency; James Peter Associates, Inc.; JCA Literary Agency, Inc.; Jellinek & Murray Literary Agency; JLM Literary Agents; Kellock Company, Inc., The; Kern Literary Agency, Natasha; Ketz Agency, Louise B.; Kidde, Hoyt & Picard; Kleinman, Esq., of Graybill & English L.L.C., Jeffrey M.; Knight Agency, The; Koster Literary Agency, LLC, Elaine; Kouts, Literary Agent, Barbara S.; Lampack Agency, Inc., Peter; Larken, Sabra Elliott; Larsen/Elizabeth Pomada Literary Agents, Michael; Lasher Agency, The Maureen; Levine Literary Agency, Paul S.; Levine Literary Agency, Inc., Ellen; Lincoln Literary Agency, Ray; Lipkind Agency, Wendy; Literary Group, The; Livingston Cooke/Curtis Brown Canada; Love Literary Agency, Nancy; Lowenstein Associates, Inc.; Lownie Literary Agency Ltd., Andrew; Maccoby Literary Agency, Gina; Mann Agency, Carol; Manus & Associates Literary Agency; March Tenth, Inc.; Markowitz Literary Agency, Barbara; McBride Literary Agency, Margret; McCauley, Gerard; McHugh Literary Agency; Menza Literary Agency, Claudia; Michaels Literary Agency, Inc., Doris S.; Miller Agency, The; Multimedia Product Development, Inc.; Mura Enterprises, Inc., Dee; Nazor Literary Agency, Karen; New Century Literary Agency; Nine Muses and Apollo Inc.; Norma-Lewis Agency, The; Palmer & Dodge Agency, The; Parks Agency, The Richard; Quicksilver Books—Literary Agents; Raymond, Literary Agent, Charlotte Cecil; Rees Literary Agency, Helen; Rein Books, Inc., Jody; Rhodes Literary Agency, Jodie; Rinaldi Literary Agency, Angela; Robbins Literary Agency, BJ; Rose & Associates Literary Agency; Rosenkranz Literary Agency, Rita; Rotrosen Agency LLC, Jane; Rubie Literary Agency, The Peter; Russell & Volkening; Sanders & Associates, Victoria; Schiavone Literary Agency, Inc.; Sebastian Literary Agency; Seligman, Literary Agent, Lynn; Shepard Agency, The; Shepard Agency, The Robert E.; Simmons Literary Agency, Jeffrey; Singer Literary Agency Inc., Evelyn; Skolnick Literary Agency, Irene; Slopen Literary Agency, Beverley; Southern Literary Group; Spieler Agency, The; Stauffer Associates, Nancy; Straus Agency, Inc., Robin; Swayne Agency Literary Management & Consulting, Inc., The; United Tribes; Valcourt Agency, Inc., The Richard R.; Vines Agency, Inc., The; Wales, Literary Agency, Inc.; Wallace Literary Agency, Inc.; Ware Literary Agency, John A.; Watkins Loomis Agency, Inc.; Watt & Associates, Sandra; Wecksler-Incomco; West Coast Literary Associates; Wieser & Wieser, Inc.; Wray Literary Agency, Pamela D.; Zachary Shuster Harmsworth

Education: Agency West Entertainment; Allred and Allred Literary Agents; Contemporary Management; Dystel Literary Management, Jane; Elmo Agency Inc., Ann; Fogelman Literary Agency, The; Goodman Associates; Grace Literary Agency, Carroll; Joy Literary Agency; Kellock Company, Inc., The; Kern Literary Agency, Natasha; Kleinman, Esq., of Graybill & English L.L.C., Jeffrey M.; Larken, Sabra Elliott; Levine Literary Agency, Paul S.; Lieberman Associates, Robert; Literary Group, The; Lowenstein Associates, Inc.; Menza Literary Agency, Claudia; Mura Enterprises, Inc., Dee; National Writers Literary Agency; New Century Literary Agency; Palmer & Dodge Agency, The; Rhodes Literary Agency, Jodie; Roghaar Literary Agency, Inc., Linda; Rose & Associates Literary Agency; Ross Literary Agency, The Gail; Russell & Volkening; Schiavone Literary Agency, Inc.; Seligman, Literary Agent, Lynn; Serendipity Literary Agency, LLC; United Tribes; Wales, Literary Agency, Inc.; Wray Literary Agency, Pamela D.

Ethnic/Cultural Interests: Agency West Entertainment; Allen Literary Agency, Linda; Allred and Allred Literary Agents; Altair Literary Agency; Altshuler Literary Agency, Miriam; Amster Literary Enterprises, Betsy; Baldi Literary Agency, Malaga; Bial Agency, Daniel; Bleecker Street Associates, Inc.; Boates Literary Agency, Reid; Book Deals, Inc.; Boston Literary Group, The; Brandt & Brandt Literary Agents Inc.; Brown Associates Inc., Marie; Browne Ltd., Pema; Bykofsky Associates, Inc., Sheree; Castiglia Literary Agency; Clark Associates, Wm; Connor Literary Agency; Coover Agency, The Doe; Cypher, The Cypher Agency, James R.; DH Literary, Inc.; DHS Literary, Inc.; Dijkstra Literary Agency, Sandra; Dystel Literary Management, Jane; Educational Design Services, Inc.; Ellison Inc., Nicholas; Eth Literary Representation, Felicia; Fogelman Literary Agency, The; Fullerton Associates, Sheryl B.; Goodman Associates; Hawkins & Associates, Inc., John; Herner Rights Agency, Susan; J de S Associates Inc.; James Peter Associates, Inc.; Jellinek & Murray Literary Agency; Jenks Agency, Carolyn; Kellock Company, Inc., The; Kern Literary Agency, Natasha; Kidde, Hoyt & Picard; Kleinman, Esq., of Graybill & English L.L.C., Jeffrey M.; Knight Agency, The; Koster Literary Agency, LLC, Elaine; Kouts, Literary Agent, Barbara S.; Larken, Sabra Elliott; Larsen/Elizabeth Pomada Literary Agents, Michael; Lasher Agency, The Maureen; Levine Literary Agency, Paul S.; Lewis & Company, Karen; Lincoln Literary Agency, Ray; Literary Group, The; Love Literary Agency, Nancy; Lowenstein Associates, Inc.; Maccoby Literary Agency, Gina; Mann Agency, Carol; Manus & Associates Literary Agency; McBride Literary Agency, Margret; Menza Literary Agency, Claudia; Michaels Literary Agency, Inc., Doris S.; Miller Agency, The; Multimedia Product

Development, Inc.; Mura Enterprises, Inc., Dee; Nazor Literary Agency, Karen; New Century Literary Agency; Nine Muses and Apollo Inc.; Norma-Lewis Agency, The; Palmer & Dodge Agency, The; Parks Agency, The Richard; Pevner, Inc., Stephen; Quicksilver Books—Literary Agents; Raymond, Literary Agent, Charlotte Cecil; Rein Books, Inc., Jody; Rhodes Literary Agency, Jodie; Robbins Literary Agency, BJ; Rose & Associates Literary Agency; Rosenkranz Literary Agency, Rita; Ross Literary Agency, The Gail; Rubie Literary Agency, The Peter; Russell & Volkening; Sanders & Associates, Victoria; Schiavone Literary Agency, Inc.; Sebastian Literary Agency; Sedgeband Literary Associates; Seligman, Literary Agent, Lynn; Serendipity Literary Agency, LLC; Shepard Agency, The Robert E.; Sherman Associates, Inc., Wendy; Singer Literary Agency Inc., Evelyn; Spieler Agency, The; Stauffer Associates, Nancy; Straus Agency, Inc., Robin; Swayne Agency Literary Management & Consulting, Inc., The; Swayze Literary Agency, Carolyn; Travis Literary Agency, Susan; 2M Communications Ltd.; United Tribes; Vines Agency, Inc., The; Wales, Literary Agency, Inc.; Waterside Productions, Inc.; Watkins Loomis Agency, Inc.; Waxman Agency, Inc., Scott; West Coast Literary Associates; Wonderland Press, Inc., The

Gay/Lesbian Issues: Allen Literary Agency, Linda; Altair Literary Agency; Baldi Literary Agency, Malaga; Bial Agency, Daniel; Bleecker Street Associates, Inc.; Brandt & Brandt Literary Agents Inc.; Browne Ltd., Pema; Bykofsky Associates, Inc., Sheree; Core Creations, Inc.; Cypher, The Cypher Agency, James R.; Daves Agency, Joan; DeFiore and Company; DHS Literary, Inc.; Ducas, Robert; Dystel Literary Management, Jane; Eth Literary Representation, Felicia; Evans Inc., Mary; Feigen/Parent Literary Management; Fullerton Associates, Sheryl B.; Goodman Associates; Hawkins & Associates, Inc., John; Henshaw Group, Richard; Herner Rights Agency, Susan; Hochmann Books, John L.; Jabberwocky Literary Agency; James Peter Associates, Inc.; Jellinek & Murray Literary Agency; Jenks Agency, Carolyn; Kidde, Hoyt & Picard; Kleinman, Esq., of Graybill & English L.L.C., Jeffrey M.; Konner Literary Agency, Linda; Larsen/Elizabeth Pomada Literary Agents, Michael; Levine Communications, Inc., James; Levine Literary Agency, Paul S.; Lewis & Company, Karen; Lincoln Literary Agency, Ray; Literary Group, The; Livingston Cooke/Curtis Brown Canada; Lowenstein Associates, Inc.; McBride Literary Agency, Margret; Miller Agency, The; Mura Enterprises, Inc., Dee; Palmer & Dodge Agency, The; Parks Agency, The Richard; Pevner, Inc., Stephen; Pinder Lane & Garon-Brooke Associates, Ltd.; Rhodes Literary Agency, Jodie; Rosenkranz Literary Agency, Rita; Ross Literary Agency, The Gail; Rubie Literary Agency, The Peter; Russell & Volkening; Sanders & Associates, Victoria; Schiavone Literary Agency, Inc.; Shepard Agency, The Robert E.; Spieler Agency, The; Swayne Agency Literary Management & Consulting, Inc., The; 2M Communications Ltd.; United Tribes; Wales, Literary Agency, Inc.; Watkins Loomis Agency, Inc.; Wonderland Press, Inc., The; Zachary Shuster Harmsworth

Government/Politics/Law: Agents Inc. for Medical and Mental Health Professionals; Allen Literary Agency, Linda; Altair Literary Agency; Authors Alliance Inc.; Baldi Literary Agency, Malaga; Bial Agency, Daniel; Black Literary Agency, David; Bleecker Street Associates, Inc.; Boates Literary Agency, Reid; Boston Literary Group, The; Brandt & Brandt Literary Agents Inc.; Charisma Communications, Ltd.; Connor Literary Agency; Contemporary Management; Cypher, The Cypher Agency, James R.; DH Literary, Inc.; Dickens Group, The; Dijkstra Literary Agency, Sandra; Ducas, Robert; Dystel Literary Management, Jane; Educational Design Services, Inc.; Ellison Inc., Nicholas; Eth Literary Representation, Felicia; Evans Inc., Mary; Feigen/Parent Literary Management; Flaming Star Literary Enterprises; Fogelman Literary Agency, The; Goodman Associates; Gregory and Radice Authors' Agents; Grosvenor Literary Agency, The; Hawkins & Associates, Inc., John; Henshaw Group, Richard; Herman Agency LLC, The Jeff; Herner Rights Agency, Susan; Hill Associates, Frederick; Hochmann Books, John L.; J de S Associates Inc.; Jabberwocky Literary Agency; James Peter Associates, Inc.; JCA Literary Agency, Inc.; Jellinek & Murray Literary Agency; Kellock Company, Inc., The; Kleinman, Esq., of Graybill & English L.L.C., Jeffrey M.; Lampack Agency, Inc., Peter; Larken, Sabra Elliott; Larsen/Elizabeth Pomada Literary Agents, Michael; Lasher Agency, The Maureen; Lawyer's Literary Agency, Inc.; Levine Literary Agency, Paul S.; Lincoln Literary Agency, Ray; Literary and Creative Artists, Inc.; Literary Group, The; Love Literary Agency, Nancy; Lowenstein Associates, Inc.; Lownie Literary Agency Ltd., Andrew; Mann Agency, Carol; McBride Literary Agency, Margret; Morrison, Inc., Henry; Mura Enterprises, Inc., Dee; National Writers Literary Agency; Nazor Literary Agency, Karen; New Century Literary Agency; New England Publishing Associates, Inc.; Norma-Lewis Agency, The; Palmer & Dodge Agency, The; Parks Agency, The Richard; Popkin, Julie; Rees Literary Agency, Helen; Rein Books, Inc., Jody; Rhodes Literary Agency, Jodie; Robbins Office, Inc., The; Rose & Associates Literary Agency; Rosenkranz Literary Agency, Rita; Ross Literary Agency, The Gail; Russell & Volkening; Sanders & Associates, Victoria; Schiavone Literary Agency, Inc.; Seligman, Literary Agent, Lynn; Shepard Agency, The; Shepard Agency, The Robert E.; Simmons Literary Agency, Jeffrey; Singer Literary Agency Inc., Evelyn; Snell Literary Agency, Michael; Spieler Agency, The; Straus Agency, Inc., Robin; United Tribes; Valcourt Agency, Inc., The Richard R.; Ware Literary Agency, John A.; West Coast Literary Associates; Wray Literary Agency, Pamela D.; Zachary Shuster Harmsworth

Health/Medicine: Agents Inc. for Medical and Mental Health Professionals; Allred and Allred Literary Agents; Altair Literary Agency; Amster Literary Enterprises, Betsy; Authors Alliance Inc.; Baldi Literary Agency, Malaga; Balkin Agency, Inc.; Bedford Book Works, Inc., The; Black Literary Agency, David; Bleecker Street Associates, Inc.; Boates Literary Agency, Reid; Book Deals, Inc.; Boston Literary Group, The; Brandt & Brandt Literary Agents Inc.; Briggs, M. Courtney; Browne Ltd., Pema; Bykofsky Associates, Inc., Sheree; Carvainis Agency, Inc., Maria; Casselman Literary Agency, Martha; Castiglia Literary Agency; Charlton Associates, James; Clausen, Mays & Tahan, LLC; Collin Literary Agent, Frances; Connor Literary Agency; Contemporary Management; Coover Agency, The Doe; Cypher, The Cypher Agency, James R.; Dawson Associates, Liza; DeFiore and Company; DH Literary, Inc.; Dickens Group, The; Dijkstra Literary Agency, Sandra; Donnaud & Associates, Inc., Janis A.; Donovan Literary, Jim; Ducas, Robert; Dystel Literary Management, Jane; Ellenberg Literary Agency, Ethan; Ellison Inc., Nicholas; Elmo Agency Inc., Ann; Eth Literary Representation, Felicia; Feigen/Parrent Literary Management; Flaherty, Literary Agent, Joyce A.; Flaming Star Literary Enterprises; Fleury Agency, B.R.; Fogelman Literary Agency, The; ForthWrite Literary Agency; Franklin Associates, Ltd., Lynn C.; Fredericks Literary Agency, Inc., Jeanne; Fullerton Associates, Sheryl B.; Gartenberg, Literary Agent, Max; Goodman Associates; Grace Literary Agency, Carroll; Grosvenor Literary Agency, The; Harris Literary Agency; Hawkins & Associates, Inc., John; Henshaw Group, Richard; Herman Agency LLC, The Jeff; Herner Rights Agency, Susan; Hochmann Books, John L.; J de S Associates Inc.; Jabberwocky Literary Agency; James Peter Associates, Inc.; JCA Literary Agency, Inc.; Jellinek & Murray Literary Agency; Joy Literary Agency; Kellock Company, Inc., The; Kern Literary Agency, Natasha; Kleinman, Esq., of Graybill & English L.L.C., Jeffrey M.; Klinger, Inc., Harvey; Knight Agency, The; Konner Literary Agency, Linda; Koster Literary Agency, LLC, Elaine; Kouts, Literary Agent, Barbara S.; Kritzer Productions, Eddie; Lampack Agency, Inc., Peter; Larken, Sabra Elliott; Larsen/Elizabeth Pomada Literary Agents, Michael; Lasher Agency, The Maureen; Levine Communications, Inc., James; Levine Literary Agency, Paul S.; Levine Literary Agency, Inc., Ellen; Lieberman Associates, Robert; Limelight Management; Lincoln Literary Agency, Ray; Lipkind Agency, Wendy; Literary and Creative Artists, Inc.; Literary Group, The; Livingston Cooke/Curtis Brown Canada; Love Literary Agency, Nancy; Lowenstein Associates, Inc.; Mann Agency, Carol; Manus & Associates Literary Agency; March Tenth, Inc.; McBride Literary Agency, Margret; McHugh Literary Agency; Menza Literary Agency, Claudia; Michaels Literary Agency, Inc., Doris S.; Miller Agency, The; Multimedia Product Development, Inc.; Mura Enterprises, Inc., Dee; New England Publishing Associates, Inc.; Nine Muses and Apollo Inc.; Norma-Lewis Agency, The; Palmer & Dodge Agency, The; Parks Agency, The Richard; Pinder Lane & Garon-Brooke Associates, Ltd.; Protter Literary Agent, Susan Ann; Quicksilver Books—Literary Agents; Rees Literary Agency, Helen; Rein Books, Inc., Jody; Rhodes Literary Agency, Jodie; Rinaldi Literary Agency, Angela; Robbins Literary Agency, BJ; Rose & Associates Literary Agency; Rosenkranz Literary Agency, Rita; Ross Literary Agency, The Gail; Roth, Literary Representation, Carol Susan; Rotrosen Agency LLC, Jane; Russell & Volkening; Schiavone Literary Agency, Inc.; Sebastian Literary Agency; Seligman, Literary Agent, Lynn; Shepard Agency, The; Singer Literary Agency Inc., Evelyn; Smith Literary Agency, Robert; Snell Literary Agency, Michael; Straus Agency, Inc., Robin; Taylor, Literary Agent, Rebecca; Teal Literary Agency, Patricia; Toad Hall, Inc.; Travis Literary Agency, Susan; Turner Agency, Paige; 2M Communications Ltd.; United Tribes; Wales, Literary Agency, Inc.; Ware Literary Agency, John A.; Waterside Productions, Inc.; Waxman Agency, Inc., Scott; Wieser & Wieser, Inc.; Wonderland Press, Inc., The; Wray Literary Agency, Pamela D.; Writers House (NY); Zachary Shuster Harmsworth

History: Ajlouny Literary Agency, Joseph; Allen Literary Agency, Linda; Allen, Literary Agent, James; Allred and Allred Literary Agents; Altair Literary Agency; Altshuler Literary Agency, Miriam; AMG/Renaissance; Amster Literary Enterprises, Betsy; Authentic Creations Literary Agency; Authors Alliance Inc.; Baldi Literary Agency, Malaga; Balkin Agency, Inc.; Bedford Book Works, Inc., The; Bial Agency, Daniel; Black Literary Agency, David; Bleecker Street Associates, Inc.; Boates Literary Agency, Reid; Book Deals, Inc.; Borchardt Inc., Georges; Boston Literary Group, The; Brandt & Brandt Literary Agents Inc.; Brown Associates Inc., Marie; Bykofsky Associates, Inc., Sheree; Castiglia Literary Agency; Clark Associates, Wm; Clausen, Mays & Tahan, LLC; Collin Literary Agent, Frances; Communications and Entertainment, Inc.; Contemporary Management; Coover Agency, The Doe; Cypher, The Cypher Agency, James R.; Dawson Associates, Liza; DH Literary, Inc.; Dickens Group, The; Dijkstra Literary Agency, Sandra; Donovan Literary, Jim; Ducas, Robert; Dystel Literary Management, Jane; Educational Design Services, Inc.; Ellenberg Literary Agency, Ethan; Ellison Inc., Nicholas; Elmo Agency Inc., Ann; Eth Literary Representation, Felicia; Evans Inc., Mary; Fort Ross Inc. Russian-American Publishing Projects; ForthWrite Literary Agency; Franklin Associates, Ltd., Lynn C.; Fredericks Literary Agency, Inc., Jeanne; Gartenberg, Literary Agent, Max; Goodman Associates; Grace Literary Agency, Carroll; Gregory and Radice Authors' Agents; Grosvenor Literary Agency, The; Halsey Agency, Reece; Halsey North, Reece; Hawkins & Associates, Inc., John; Herman Agency LLC, The Jeff; Herner Rights Agency, Susan; Hochmann Books, John L.; Hogenson Agency, Barbara; J de S Associates Inc.; Jabberwocky Literary Agency; James Peter Associates, Inc.; JCA Literary Agency, Inc.; Jellinek & Murray Literary Agency; Jenks Agency,

Carolyn; Kellock Company, Inc., The; Ketz Agency, Louise B.; Kidde, Hoyt & Picard; Kleinman, Esq., of Graybill & English L.L.C., Jeffrey M.; Knight Agency, The; Koster Literary Agency, LLC, Elaine; Kouts, Literary Agent, Barbara S.; Lampack Agency, Inc., Peter; Larken, Sabra Elliott; Larsen/Elizabeth Pomada Literary Agents, Michael; Lasher Agency, The Maureen; Levine Literary Agency, Paul S.; Levine Literary Agency, Inc., Ellen; Lincoln Literary Agency, Ray; Lipkind Agency, Wendy; Literary Group, The; Love Literary Agency, Nancy; Lowenstein Associates, Inc.; Lownie Literary Agency Ltd., Andrew; Maccoby Literary Agency, Gina; Mann Agency, Carol; March Tenth, Inc.; McBride Literary Agency, Margret; McCauley, Gerard; McHugh Literary Agency; Menza Literary Agency, Claudia; Michaels Literary Agency, Inc., Doris S.; Morrison, Inc., Henry; Mura Enterprises, Inc., Dee; Nazor Literary Agency, Karen; New Century Literary Agency; New England Publishing Associates, Inc.; Norma-Lewis Agency, The; Palmer & Dodge Agency, The; Parks Agency, The Richard; Pevner, Inc., Stephen; Pinder Lane & Garon-Brooke Associates, Ltd.; Popkin, Julie; Quicksilver Books—Literary Agents; Raymond, Literary Agent, Charlotte Cecil; Rees Literary Agency, Helen; Rein Books, Inc., Jody; Rhodes Literary Agency, Jodie; Rittenberg Literary Agency, Inc., Ann; Roghaar Literary Agency, Inc., Linda; Rose & Associates Literary Agency; Rosenkranz Literary Agency, Rita; Russell & Volkening; Sanders & Associates, Victoria; Schiavone Literary Agency, Inc.; Sedgeband Literary Associates; Seligman, Literary Agent, Lynn; Shepard Agency, The; Shepard Agency, The Robert E.; Simmons Literary Agency, Jeffrey; Spieler Agency, The; Straus Agency, Inc., Robin; Swayze Literary Agency, Carolyn; United Tribes; Valcourt Agency, Inc., The Richard R.; Vines Agency, Inc., The; Wallace Literary Agency, Inc.; Ware Literary Agency, John A.; Watkins Loomis Agency, Inc.; Waxman Agency, Inc., Scott; Wecksler-Incomco; West Coast Literary Associates; Wieser & Wieser, Inc.; Wonderland Press, Inc., The; Writers House (NY); Zachary Shuster Harmsworth

How-to: Agency West Entertainment; Ajlouny Literary Agency, Joseph; Alive Communications, Inc.; Allred and Allred Literary Agents; Altair Literary Agency; Amster Literary Enterprises, Betsy; Authentic Creations Literary Agency; Authors Alliance Inc.; Balkin Agency, Inc.; Bedford Book Works, Inc., The; Bial Agency, Daniel; Bleecker Street Associates, Inc.; Bova Literary Agency, The Barbara; Browne Ltd., Pema; Bykofsky Associates, Inc., Sheree; Charlton Associates, James; Clausen, Mays & Tahan, LLC; Connor Literary Agency; Contemporary Management; Core Creations, Inc.; Crawford Literary Agency; Cypher, The Cypher Agency, James R.; Dawson Associates, Liza; DH Literary, Inc.; Elmo Agency Inc., Ann; Feigen/Parrent Literary Management; Flaherty, Literary Agent, Joyce A.; Fleury Agency, B.R.; Fredericks Literary Agency, Inc., Jeanne; Fullerton Associates, Sheryl B.; Goodman Associates; Grace Literary Agency, Carroll; Grosvenor Literary Agency, The; Harris Literary Agency; Heacock Literary Agency, Inc.; Henshaw Group, Richard; Herman Agency LLC, The Jeff; Herner Rights Agency, Susan; Jellinek & Murray Literary Agency; Joy Literary Agency; Kellock Company, Inc., The; Kleinman, Esq., of Graybill & English L.L.C., Jeffrey M.; Knight Agency, The; Konner Literary Agency, Linda; Koster Literary Agency, LLC, Elaine; Kritzer Productions, Eddie; Larken, Sabra Elliott; Larsen/Elizabeth Pomada Literary Agents, Michael; Lasher Agency, The Maureen; Levine Literary Agency, Paul S.; Limelight Management; Literary and Creative Artists, Inc.; Literary Group, The; Love Literary Agency, Nancy; Lowenstein Associates, Inc.; Manus & Associates Literary Agency; McBride Literary Agency, Margret; McHugh Literary Agency; Menza Literary Agency, Claudia; Michaels Literary Agency, Inc., Doris S.; Multimedia Product Development, Inc.; Mura Enterprises, Inc., Dee; National Writers Literary Agency; Nazor Literary Agency, Karen; New Century Literary Agency; Parks Agency, The Richard; Paton Literary Agency, Kathi J.; Quicksilver Books—Literary Agents; Rein Books, Inc., Jody; Rhodes Literary Agency, Jodie; Robbins Literary Agency, BJ; Rose & Associates Literary Agency; Rosenkranz Literary Agency, Rita; Rotrosen Agency LLC, Jane; Scherf, Inc. Literary Management; Schiavone Literary Agency, Inc.; Seligman, Literary Agent, Lynn; Serendipity Literary Agency, LLC; Singer Literary Agency Inc., Evelyn; Swayne Agency Literary Management & Consulting, Inc., The; Teal Literary Agency, Patricia; Toad Hall, Inc.; Travis Literary Agency, Susan; Turner Agency, Paige; United Tribes; Vines Agency, Inc., The; Watt & Associates, Sandra; Wonderland Press, Inc., The; Wray Literary Agency, Pamela D.; Wylie-Merrick Literary Agency; Zachary Shuster Harmsworth

Humor: Agency West Entertainment; Ajlouny Literary Agency, Joseph; Allred and Allred Literary Agents; Amsterdam Agency, Marcia; Bedford Book Works, Inc., The; Bial Agency, Daniel; Bleecker Street Associates, Inc.; Books & Such; Bykofsky Associates, Inc., Sheree; Charlton Associates, James; Clausen, Mays & Tahan, LLC; Connor Literary Agency; Contemporary Management; Core Creations, Inc.; Donnaud & Associates, Inc., Janis A.; Dystel Literary Management, Jane; Fleury Agency, B.R.; Goodman Associates; Grosjean Literary Agency, Jill; Harris Literary Agency; Henshaw Group, Richard; Jabberwocky Literary Agency; Kellock Company, Inc., The; Kleinman, Esq., of Graybill & English L.L.C., Jeffrey M.; Kritzer Productions, Eddie; Larsen/Elizabeth Pomada Literary Agents, Michael; Levine Literary Agency, Paul S.; Literary Group, The; Lowenstein Associates, Inc.; March Tenth, Inc.; Multimedia Product Development, Inc.; Mura Enterprises, Inc., Dee; New Century Literary Agency; Parks Agency, The Richard; Pevner, Inc., Stephen; Rein Books, Inc., Jody; Robbins Literary Agency, BJ; Rose & Associates Literary Agency;

Rosenkranz Literary Agency, Rita; Ross Literary Agency, The Gail; Rotrosen Agency LLC, Jane; Sanders & Associates, Victoria; Schiavone Literary Agency, Inc.; Seligman, Literary Agent, Lynn; Swayze Literary Agency, Carolyn; Vines Agency, Inc., The; Waterside Productions, Inc.; Watt & Associates, Sandra; Wray Literary Agency, Pamela D.

Interior Design/Decorating: Allred and Allred Literary Agents; Baldi Literary Agency, Malaga; Brandt & Brandt Literary Agents Inc.; Connor Literary Agency; Ellison Inc., Nicholas; ForthWrite Literary Agency; Fredericks Literary Agency, Inc., Jeanne; Goodman Associates; Grace Literary Agency, Carroll; Grosjean Literary Agency, Jill; Hawkins & Associates, Inc., John; Hogenson Agency, Barbara; Kellock Company, Inc., The; Kleinman, Esq., of Graybill & English L.L.C., Jeffrey M.; Larsen/Elizabeth Pomada Literary Agents, Michael; Levine Literary Agency, Paul S.; Limelight Management; Lincoln Literary Agency, Ray; Rose & Associates Literary Agency; Rosenkranz Literary Agency, Rita; Seligman, Literary Agent, Lynn; Shepard Agency, The; Wonderland Press, Inc., The; Writers House (NY)

Juvenile Nonfiction: Agency West Entertainment; Allred and Allred Literary Agents; Bleecker Street Associates, Inc.; Books & Such; Brandt & Brandt Literary Agents Inc.; Briggs, M. Courtney; Brown Associates Inc., Marie; Brown Literary Agency, Inc., Andrea; Browne Ltd., Pema; Dwyer & O'Grady, Inc.; Educational Design Services, Inc.; Elek Associates, Peter; Ellenberg Literary Agency, Ethan; Ellison Inc., Nicholas; Elmo Agency Inc., Ann; Flannery Literary; ForthWrite Literary Agency; Hawkins & Associates, Inc., John; Henshaw Group, Richard; Joy Literary Agency; Kirchoff/Wohlberg, Inc., Authors' Representation Division; Kouts, Literary Agent, Barbara S.; Lewis & Company, Karen; Lincoln Literary Agency, Ray; Literary Group, The; Maccoby Literary Agency, Gina; Markowitz Literary Agency, Barbara; Morrison, Inc., Henry; Multimedia Product Development, Inc.; Mura Enterprises, Inc., Dee; National Writers Literary Agency; New Century Literary Agency; Norma-Lewis Agency, The; Rhodes Literary Agency, Jodie; Rose & Associates Literary Agency; Rubinstein Literary Agency, Inc., Pesha; Russell & Volkening; Schiavone Literary Agency, Inc.; Serendipity Literary Agency, LLC; Shepard Agency, The; Singer Literary Agency Inc., Evelyn; Sternig & Byrne Literary Agency; Taylor, Literary Agent, Rebecca; Tiersten Literary Agency, Irene; Tobias—A Literary Agency for Children's Books, Ann; Treimel NY, S©ott; Wecksler-Incomco; Writers House (NY); Wylie-Merrick Literary Agency

Language/Literature/Criticism: Acacia House Publishing Services Ltd.; Ajlouny Literary Agency, Joseph; Allred and Allred Literary Agents; Altshuler Literary Agency, Miriam; Authors Alliance Inc.; Baldi Literary Agency, Malaga; Balkin Agency, Inc.; Bial Agency, Daniel; Boates Literary Agency, Reid; Brandt & Brandt Literary Agents Inc.; Castiglia Literary Agency; Connor Literary Agency; Coover Agency, The Doe; Cypher, The Cypher Agency, James R.; DH Literary, Inc.; Dijkstra Literary Agency, Sandra; Educational Design Services, Inc.; Ellison Inc., Nicholas; Goodman Associates; Grosvenor Literary Agency, The; Halsey Agency, Reece; Halsey North, Reece; Hawkins & Associates, Inc., John; Herner Rights Agency, Susan; Hill Associates, Frederick; Jabberwocky Literary Agency; James Peter Associates, Inc.; JCA Literary Agency, Inc.; Jenks Agency, Carolyn; Kidde, Hoyt & Picard; Kleinman, Esq., of Graybill & English L.L.C., Jeffrey M.; Larken, Sabra Elliott; Larsen/Elizabeth Pomada Literary Agents, Michael; Levine Literary Agency, Paul S.; Lincoln Literary Agency, Ray; Literary Group, The; Lowenstein Associates, Inc.; March Tenth, Inc.; Miller Agency, The; New Century Literary Agency; New England Publishing Associates, Inc.; Nine Muses and Apollo Inc.; Palmer & Dodge Agency, The; Parks Agency, The Richard; Pevner, Inc., Stephen; Popkin, Julie; Quicksilver Books—Literary Agents; Robbins Office, Inc., The; Rose & Associates Literary Agency; Rosenkranz Literary Agency, Rita; Russell & Volkening; Sanders & Associates, Victoria; Schiavone Literary Agency, Inc.; Seligman, Literary Agent, Lynn; Shepard Agency, The; Simmons Literary Agency, Jeffrey; Straus Agency, Inc., Robin; Turner Agency, Paige; United Tribes; Wales, Literary Agency, Inc.; Wallace Literary Agency, Inc.; Ware Literary Agency, John A.; Watt & Associates, Sandra; West Coast Literary Associates; Wonderland Press, Inc., The; Zachary Shuster Harmsworth

Memoirs: Acacia House Publishing Services Ltd.; Agency West Entertainment; Altshuler Literary Agency, Miriam; Authors Alliance Inc.; Baldi Literary Agency, Malaga; Bial Agency, Daniel; Black Literary Agency, David; Bleecker Street Associates, Inc.; Borchardt Inc., Georges; Clark Associates, Wm; Clausen, Mays & Tahan, LLC; Coover Agency, The Doe; Cypher, The Cypher Agency, James R.; Dawson Associates, Liza; Ducas, Robert; Feigen/Parrent Literary Management; Flaherty, Literary Agent, Joyce A.; Fort Ross Inc. Russian-American Publishing Projects; Franklin Associates, Ltd., Lynn C.; Goodman Associates; Halsey North, Reece; James Peter Associates, Inc.; JCA Literary Agency, Inc.; Jellinek & Murray Literary Agency; Kidde, Hoyt & Picard; Kleinman, Esq., of Graybill & English L.L.C., Jeffrey M.; Larsen/Elizabeth Pomada Literary Agents, Michael; Levine Literary Agency, Paul S.; Levine Literary Agency, Inc., Ellen; Lieberman Associates, Robert; Literary and Creative Artists, Inc.; Literary Group, The; Love Literary Agency, Nancy; Lowenstein Associates, Inc.; Lownie Literary Agency Ltd., Andrew; Manus & Associates Literary Agency; Multimedia Product Development, Inc.; Mura Enterprises, Inc., Dee; New Century Literary Agency; Parks Agency, The Richard; Pevner, Inc., Stephen; Pinder Lane & Garon-Brooke Associates,

Ltd.; Popkin, Julie; Protter Literary Agent, Susan Ann; Quicksilver Books—Literary Agents; Rhodes Literary Agency, Jodie; Rittenberg Literary Agency, Inc., Ann; Robbins Literary Agency, BJ; Robbins Office, Inc., The; Rose & Associates Literary Agency; Serendipity Literary Agency, LLC; Sherman Associates, Inc., Wendy; Simmons Literary Agency, Jeffrey; Smith Literary Agency, Robert; Spieler Agency, The; Susijn Agency, The; Swayze Literary Agency, Carolyn; Turner Agency, Paige; 2M Communications Ltd.; United Tribes; Valcourt Agency, Inc., The Richard R.; Vines Agency, Inc., The; Wales, Literary Agency, Inc.; Watt & Associates, Sandra; Weingel-Fidel Agency, The; Wray Literary Agency, Pamela D.; Zachary Shuster Harmsworth

Military/War: Acacia House Publishing Services Ltd.; Allred and Allred Literary Agents; Authors Alliance Inc.; Bial Agency, Daniel; Black Literary Agency, David; Bleecker Street Associates, Inc.; Boston Literary Group, The; Brandt & Brandt Literary Agents Inc.; Browne Ltd., Pema; Charisma Communications, Ltd.; Charlton Associates, James; Dijkstra Literary Agency, Sandra; Donovan Literary, Jim; Ducas, Robert; Dystel Literary Management, Jane; Educational Design Services, Inc.; Ellison Inc., Nicholas; Gartenberg, Literary Agent, Max; Goodman Associates; Grosvenor Literary Agency, The; Hawkins & Associates, Inc., John; Henshaw Group, Richard; Hochmann Books, John L.; J de S Associates Inc.; Jabberwocky Literary Agency; James Peter Associates, Inc.; JCA Literary Agency, Inc.; Jellinek & Murray Literary Agency; Kellock Company, Inc., The; Ketz Agency, Louise B.; Levine Literary Agency, Paul S.; Literary Group, The; Lownie Literary Agency Ltd., Andrew; McCauley, Gerard; McHugh Literary Agency; Mura Enterprises, Inc., Dee; New Century Literary Agency; New England Publishing Associates, Inc.; Parks Agency, The Richard; Pinder Lane & Garon-Brooke Associates, Ltd.; Rhodes Literary Agency, Jodie; Rose & Associates Literary Agency; Rosenkranz Literary Agency, Rita; Russell & Volkening; Schiavone Literary Agency, Inc.; Swayze Literary Agency, Carolyn; Valcourt Agency, Inc., The Richard R.; Vines Agency, Inc., The; Wray Literary Agency, Pamela D.; Writers House (NY)

Money/Finance/Economics: Altair Literary Agency; Amster Literary Enterprises, Betsy; Authors Alliance Inc.; Baldi Literary Agency, Malaga; Bedford Book Works, Inc., The; Bial Agency, Daniel; Black Literary Agency, David; Bleecker Street Associates, Inc.; Book Deals, Inc.; Boston Literary Group, The; Bova Literary Agency, The Barbara; Brandt & Brandt Literary Agents Inc.; Brown Associates Inc., Marie; Browne Ltd., Pema; Castiglia Literary Agency; Clausen, Mays & Tahan, LLC; Connor Literary Agency; Contemporary Management; Coover Agency, The Doe; Cypher, The Cypher Agency, James R.; DeFiore and Company; DH Literary, Inc.; Dijkstra Literary Agency, Sandra; Donnaud & Associates, Inc., Janis A.; Donovan Literary, Jim; Ducas, Robert; Dystel Literary Management, Jane; Educational Design Services, Inc.; Ellison Inc., Nicholas; Elmo Agency Inc., Ann; Feigen/Parrent Literary Management; Fleury Agency, B.R.; ForthWrite Literary Agency; Fredericks Literary Agency, Inc., Jeanne; Gartenberg, Literary Agent, Max; Goodman Associates; Grosvenor Literary Agency, The; Hawkins & Associates, Inc., John; Henshaw Group, Richard; Jabberwocky Literary Agency; James Peter Associates, Inc.; JCA Literary Agency, Inc.; Jellinek & Murray Literary Agency; Kellock Company, Inc., The; Ketz Agency, Louise B.; Kleinman, Esq., of Graybill & English L.L.C., Jeffrey M.; Knight Agency, The; Konner Literary Agency, Linda; Koster Literary Agency, LLC, Elaine; Lampack Agency, Inc., Peter; Larken, Sabra Elliott; Larsen/Elizabeth Pomada Literary Agents, Michael; Levine Communications, Inc., James; Levine Literary Agency, Paul S.; Lieberman Associates, Robert; Lincoln Literary Agency, Ray; Literary Group, The; Lowenstein Associates, Inc.; Mann Agency, Carol; Manus & Associates Literary Agency; McBride Literary Agency, Margret; Michaels Literary Agency, Inc., Doris S.; Multimedia Product Development, Inc.; Mura Enterprises, Inc., Dee; New Century Literary Agency; New England Publishing Associates, Inc.; Palmer & Dodge Agency, The; Parks Agency, The Richard; Rees Literary Agency, Helen; Rhodes Literary Agency, Jodie; Rinaldi Literary Agency, Angela; Rose & Associates Literary Agency; Rosenkranz Literary Agency, Rita; Ross Literary Agency, The Gail; Rotrosen Agency LLC, Jane; Russell & Volkening; Scherf, Inc. Literary Management; Sebastian Literary Agency; Seligman, Literary Agent, Lynn; Serendipity Literary Agency, LLC; Shepard Agency, The; Shepard Agency, The Robert E.; Singer Literary Agency Inc., Evelyn; Spieler Agency, The; Turner Agency, Paige; United Tribes; Vines Agency, Inc., The; Waterside Productions, Inc.; Waxman Agency, Inc., Scott; Wieser & Wieser, Inc.; Wray Literary Agency, Pamela D.; Writers House (NY); Zachary Shuster Harmsworth

Multicultural: Altshuler Literary Agency, Miriam; Black Literary Agency, David; DeFiore and Company; Goodman Associates; Menza Literary Agency, Claudia; Rose & Associates Literary Agency; Serendipity Literary Agency, LLC; Writers House (NY)

Multimedia: Elek Associates, Peter; Jenks Agency, Carolyn; Kellock Company, Inc., The

Music/Dance/Theater/Film: Acacia House Publishing Services Ltd.; Agency West Entertainment; Ajlouny Literary Agency, Joseph; Allen Literary Agency, Linda; Allred and Allred Literary Agents; Altair Literary Agency; Altshuler Literary Agency, Miriam; AMG/Renaissance; Andrews & Associates Inc., Bart; Appleseeds Management; Authors Alliance Inc.; Baldi Literary Agency, Malaga; Balkin Agency, Inc.; Bial

Agency, Daniel; Brandt & Brandt Literary Agents Inc.; Brown Associates Inc., Marie; Bykofsky Associates, Inc., Sheree; Clark Associates, Wm; Communications and Entertainment, Inc.; Cypher, The Cypher Agency, James R.; Donovan Literary, Jim; Ellison Inc., Nicholas; Elmo Agency Inc., Ann; Farber Literary Agency Inc.; Feigen/Parrent Literary Management; Fort Ross Inc. Russian-American Publishing Projects; Gartenberg, Literary Agent, Max; Goodman Associates; Greene, Arthur B.; Grosvenor Literary Agency, The; Hawkins & Associates, Inc., John; Heacock Literary Agency, Inc.; Henshaw Group, Richard; Hochmann Books, John L.; Hogenson Agency, Barbara; Jabberwocky Literary Agency; James Peter Associates, Inc.; JCA Literary Agency, Inc.; Jenks Agency, Carolyn; JLM Literary Agents; Kellock Company, Inc., The; Kleinman, Esq., of Graybill & English L.L.C., Jeffrey M.; Knight Agency, The; Kouts, Literary Agent, Barbara S.; Lampack Agency, Inc., Peter; Larken, Sabra Elliott; Larsen/Elizabeth Pomada Literary Agents, Michael; Levine Literary Agency, Paul S.; Lieberman Associates, Robert; Lincoln Literary Agency, Ray; Literary Group, The; Lowenstein Associates, Inc.; Lownie Literary Agency Ltd., Andrew; March Tenth, Inc.; Markowitz Literary Agency, Barbara; McBride Literary Agency, Margret; Menza Literary Agency, Claudia; Michaels Literary Agency, Inc., Doris S.; Nazor Literary Agency, Karen; New Century Literary Agency; Norma-Lewis Agency, The; Palmer & Dodge Agency, The; Parks Agency, The Richard; Pevner, Inc., Stephen; Pinder Lane & Garon-Brooke Associates, Ltd.; Rein Books, Inc., Jody; Rhodes Literary Agency, Jodie; Robbins Literary Agency, BJ; Rose & Associates Literary Agency; Rosenkranz Literary Agency, Rita; Rubie Literary Agency, The Peter; Russell & Volkening; Sanders & Associates, Victoria; Seligman, Literary Agent, Lynn; Shepard Agency, The; Simmons Literary Agency, Jeffrey; Smith Literary Agency, Robert; Straus Agency, Inc., Robin; Susijn Agency, The; 2M Communications Ltd.; United Tribes; Ware Literary Agency, John A.; Wecksler-Incomco; Weingel-Fidel Agency, The; West Coast Literary Associates; Writers House (NY); Zachary Shuster Harmsworth

Nature/Environment: Acacia House Publishing Services Ltd.; Allen Literary Agency, Linda; Altair Literary Agency; Altshuler Literary Agency, Miriam; Authors Alliance Inc.; Baldi Literary Agency, Malaga; Balkin Agency, Inc.; Bial Agency, Daniel; Bleecker Street Associates, Inc.; Boates Literary Agency, Reid; Boston Literary Group, The; Brandt & Brandt Literary Agents Inc.; Browne Ltd., Pema; Castiglia Literary Agency; Collin Literary Agent, Frances; Coover Agency, The Doe; Cypher, The Cypher Agency, James R.; DH Literary, Inc.; Dijkstra Literary Agency, Sandra; Donovan Literary, Jim; Ducas, Robert; Elek Associates, Peter; Ellison Inc., Nicholas; Eth Literary Representation, Felicia; Evans Inc., Mary; Flaherty, Literary Agent, Joyce A.; Flaming Star Literary Enterprises; ForthWrite Literary Agency; Fredericks Literary Agency, Inc., Jeanne; Gartenberg, Literary Agent, Max; Goodman Associates; Grosjean Literary Agency, Jill; Grosvenor Literary Agency, The; Hawkins & Associates, Inc., John; Heacock Literary Agency, Inc.; Henshaw Group, Richard; Herner Rights Agency, Susan; Jabberwocky Literary Agency; JCA Literary Agency, Inc.; Jellinek & Murray Literary Agency; Jenks Agency, Carolyn; JLM Literary Agents; Joy Literary Agency; Kellock Company, Inc., The; Kern Literary Agency, Natasha; Kleinman, Esq., of Graybill & English L.L.C., Jeffrey M.; Koster Literary Agency, LLC, Elaine; Kouts, Literary Agent, Barbara S.; Larken, Sabra Elliott; Larsen/Elizabeth Pomada Literary Agents, Michael; Lasher Agency, The Maureen; Levine Communications, Inc., James; Levine Literary Agency, Paul S.; Lieberman Associates, Robert; Limelight Management; Lincoln Literary Agency, Ray; Literary Group, The; Love Literary Agency, Nancy; Lowenstein Associates, Inc.; Manus & Associates Literary Agency; Markowitz Literary Agency, Barbara; McHugh Literary Agency; Michaels Literary Agency, Inc., Doris S.; Multimedia Product Development, Inc.; Mura Enterprises, Inc., Dee; Nazor Literary Agency, Karen; New Century Literary Agency; New England Publishing Associates, Inc.; Norma-Lewis Agency, The; Palmer & Dodge Agency, The; Parks Agency, The Richard; Paton Literary Agency, Kathi J.; Quicksilver Books—Literary Agents; Raymond, Literary Agent, Charlotte Cecil; Rein Books, Inc., Jody; Rhodes Literary Agency, Jodie; Roghaar Literary Agency, Inc., Linda; Rosenkranz Literary Agency, Rita; Ross Literary Agency, The Gail; Rotrosen Agency LLC, Jane; Russell & Volkening; Schiavone Literary Agency, Inc.; Seligman, Literary Agent, Lynn; Shepard Agency, The; Singer Literary Agency Inc., Evelyn; Straus Agency, Inc., Robin; Swayze Literary Agency, Carolyn; Toad Hall, Inc.; Travis Literary Agency, Susan; United Tribes; Vines Agency, Inc., The; Wales, Literary Agency, Inc.; Ware Literary Agency, John A.; Waterside Productions, Inc.; Watkins Loomis Agency, Inc.; Watt & Associates, Sandra; Wecksler-Incomco; West Coast Literary Associates; Wieser & Wieser, Inc.; Writers House (NY)

New Age/Metaphysics: Altair Literary Agency; Authors Alliance Inc.; Bial Agency, Daniel; Bleecker Street Associates, Inc.; Browne Ltd., Pema; Castiglia Literary Agency; Dystel Literary Management, Jane; Ellenberg Literary Agency, Ethan; Ellison Inc., Nicholas; Flaming Star Literary Enterprises; Fleury Agency, B.R.; Franklin Associates, Ltd., Lynn C.; Fullerton Associates, Sheryl B.; Goodman Associates; Grosvenor Literary Agency, The; Hawkins & Associates, Inc., John; Heacock Literary Agency, Inc.; Henshaw Group, Richard; Herner Rights Agency, Susan; J de S Associates Inc.; Jellinek & Murray Literary Agency; Kern Literary Agency, Natasha; Koster Literary Agency, LLC, Elaine; Larsen/Elizabeth Pomada Literary Agents, Michael; Levine Communications, Inc., James; Levine Literary Agency, Paul S.; Lewis & Company, Karen; Limelight Management; Literary Group, The; Love Literary Agency, Nancy; Lowenstein Associates, Inc.;

Miller Agency, The; Palmer & Dodge Agency, The; Pevner, Inc., Stephen; Quicksilver Books—Literary Agents; Rose & Associates Literary Agency; Rosenkranz Literary Agency, Rita; Roth, Literary Representation, Carol Susan; Smith Literary Agency, Robert; Toad Hall, Inc.; Turner Agency, Paige; Vines Agency, Inc., The; Wales, Literary Agency, Inc.; Watt & Associates, Sandra

Open to all Nonfiction Categories: Ajlouny Literary Agency, Joseph; Barrett Books Inc., Loretta; Bernstein Literary Agency, Meredith; Brown Ltd., Curtis; Circle of Confusion Ltd.; Congdon Associates Inc., Don; Curtis Associates, Inc., Richard; Doyen Literary Services, Inc.; Dupree/Miller and Associates Inc. Literary; Fernandez Agent/Attorney, Justin E.; Fleming Agency, Peter; Ghosts & Collaborators International; Goldfarb & Associates; Goodman Associates; Greenburger Associates, Inc., Sanford J.; Hamilburg Agency, The Mitchell J.; Hoffman Literary Agency, Berenice; Lake Agency, The Candace; Lazear Agency Incorporated; Madsen Agency, Robert; Ober Associates, Harold; Paraview, Inc.; Pelter, Rodney; Raines & Raines; Sandum & Associates; Schwartz Agency, Laurens R.; Snell Literary Agency, Michael; Talbot Agency, The John; Wales, Literary Agency, Inc.

Photography: Allred and Allred Literary Agents; Altair Literary Agency; Baldi Literary Agency, Malaga; Boston Literary Group, The; Connor Literary Agency; Contemporary Management; Donnaud & Associates, Inc., Janis A.; Ellison Inc., Nicholas; Elmo Agency Inc., Ann; ForthWrite Literary Agency; Fredericks Literary Agency, Inc., Jeanne; Goodman Associates; Grace Literary Agency, Carroll; Grosvenor Literary Agency, The; Hawkins & Associates, Inc., John; Kleinman, Esq., of Graybill & English L.L.C., Jeffrey M.; Larken, Sabra Elliott; Larsen/Elizabeth Pomada Literary Agents, Michael; Levine Literary Agency, Paul S.; Limelight Management; Menza Literary Agency, Claudia; Nazor Literary Agency, Karen; Norma-Lewis Agency, The; Pevner, Inc., Stephen; Rose & Associates Literary Agency; Rosenkranz Literary Agency, Rita; Russell & Volkening; Seligman, Literary Agent, Lynn; Vines Agency, Inc., The; Wecksler-Incomco; Wonderland Press, Inc., The

Popular Culture: Ajlouny Literary Agency, Joseph; Allen Literary Agency, Linda; Allred and Allred Literary Agents; Altair Literary Agency; Altshuler Literary Agency, Miriam; Amster Literary Enterprises, Betsy; Amsterdam Agency, Marcia; Balkin Agency, Inc.; Bedford Book Works, Inc., The; Bial Agency, Daniel; Bleecker Street Associates, Inc.; Book Deals, Inc.; Browne Ltd., Pema; Bykofsky Associates, Inc., Sheree; Charlton Associates, James; Clark Associates, Wm; Connor Literary Agency; Contemporary Management; Cypher, The Cypher Agency, James R.; Daves Agency, Joan; DeFiore and Company; DH Literary, Inc.; DHS Literary, Inc.; Dickens Group, The; Donovan Literary, Jim; Dorian Literary Agency; Dystel Literary Management, Jane; Elek Associates, Peter; Ellenberg Literary Agency, Ethan; Elmo Agency Inc., Ann; Eth Literary Representation, Felicia; Evans Inc., Mary; Flaherty, Literary Agent, Joyce A.; Fogelman Literary Agency, The; Fullerton Associates, Sheryl B.; Goodman Associates; Grosvenor Literary Agency, The; Halsey Agency, Reece; Halsey North, Reece; Henshaw Group, Richard; Herner Rights Agency, Susan; Hogenson Agency, Barbara; Jabberwocky Literary Agency; James Peter Associates, Inc.; JCA Literary Agency, Inc.; Jellinek & Murray Literary Agency; JLM Literary Agents; Kellock Company, Inc., The; Kern Literary Agency, Natasha; Kidde, Hoyt & Picard; Kleinman, Esq., of Graybill & English L.L.C., Jeffrey M.; Knight Agency, The; Konner Literary Agency, Linda; Koster Literary Agency, LLC, Elaine; Lampack Agency, Inc., Peter; Larken, Sabra Elliott; Larsen/Elizabeth Pomada Literary Agents, Michael; Lasher Agency, The Maureen; Levine Literary Agency, Paul S.; Levine Literary Agency, Inc., Ellen; Literary Group, The; Livingston Cooke/Curtis Brown Canada; Love Literary Agency, Nancy; Lowenstein Associates, Inc.; Lownie Literary Agency Ltd., Andrew; Maccoby Literary Agency, Gina; Manus & Associates Literary Agency; March Tenth, Inc.; Markowitz Literary Agency, Barbara; McBride Literary Agency, Margret; Multimedia Product Development, Inc.; National Writers Literary Agency; Nazor Literary Agency, Karen; New Century Literary Agency; Norma-Lewis Agency, The; Palmer & Dodge Agency, The; Parks Agency, The Richard; Perkins Associates, L.; Pevner, Inc., Stephen; Quicksilver Books—Literary Agents; Rein Books, Inc., Jody; Rhodes Literary Agency, Jodie; Rinaldi Literary Agency, Angela; Robbins Literary Agency, BJ; Roghaar Literary Agency, Inc., Linda; Rose & Associates Literary Agency; Rosenkranz Literary Agency, Rita; Rotrosen Agency LLC, Jane; Rubie Literary Agency, The Peter; Russell & Volkening; Sanders & Associates, Victoria; Scherf, Inc. Literary Management; Schiavone Literary Agency, Inc.; Seligman, Literary Agent, Lynn; Serendipity Literary Agency, LLC; Shepard Agency, The Robert E.; Simmons Literary Agency, Jeffrey; Smith Literary Agency, Robert; Southern Literary Group; Stauffer Associates, Nancy; Sternig & Byrne Literary Agency; Straus Agency, Inc., Robin; Susijn Agency, The; Swayne Agency Literary Management & Consulting, Inc., The; Swayze Literary Agency, Carolyn; Toad Hall, Inc.; Travis Literary Agency, Susan; Turner Agency, Paige; United Tribes; Vines Agency, Inc., The; Wales, Literary Agency, Inc.; Ware Literary Agency, John A.; Waterside Productions, Inc.; Watkins Loomis Agency, Inc.; Watt & Associates, Sandra; Waxman Agency, Inc., Scott; Wonderland Press, Inc., The

Psychology: Agents Inc. for Medical and Mental Health Professionals; Allen Literary Agency, Linda; Allred and Allred Literary Agents; Altair Literary Agency; Altshuler Literary Agency, Miriam; Amster

Literary Enterprises, Betsy; Authors Alliance Inc.; Baldi Literary Agency, Malaga; Bedford Book Works, Inc., The; Bial Agency, Daniel; Bleecker Street Associates, Inc.; Boates Literary Agency, Reid; Book Deals, Inc.; Boston Literary Group, The; Brandt & Brandt Literary Agents Inc.; Brown Associates Inc., Marie; Browne Ltd., Pema; Bykofsky Associates, Inc., Sheree; Castiglia Literary Agency; Clausen, Mays & Tahan, LLC; Contemporary Management; Coover Agency, The Doe; Core Creations, Inc.; Cypher, The Cypher Agency, James R.; Dawson Associates, Liza; DeFiore and Company; DH Literary, Inc.; Dijkstra Literary Agency, Sandra; Donnaud & Associates, Inc., Janis A.; Dystel Literary Management, Jane; Ellenberg Literary Agency, Ethan; Ellison Inc., Nicholas; Elmo Agency Inc., Ann; Eth Literary Representation, Felicia; Farber Literary Agency Inc.; Feigen/Parrent Literary Management; Flaherty, Literary Agent, Joyce A.; Fogelman Literary Agency, The; Fort Ross Inc. Russian-American Publishing Projects; ForthWrite Literary Agency; Franklin Associates, Ltd., Lynn C.; Fredericks Literary Agency, Inc., Jeanne; Fullerton Associates, Sheryl B.; Gartenberg, Literary Agent, Max; Goodman Associates; Grosvenor Literary Agency, The; Harris Literary Agency; Hawkins & Associates, Inc., John; Heacock Literary Agency, Inc.; Henshaw Group, Richard; Herman Agency LLC, The Jeff; Herner Rights Agency, Susan; James Peter Associates, Inc.; Jellinek & Murray Literary Agency; JLM Literary Agents; Kellock Company, Inc., The; Kern Literary Agency, Natasha; Kidde, Hoyt & Picard; Kleinman, Esq., of Graybill & English L.L.C., Jeffrey M.; Klinger, Inc., Harvey; Knight Agency, The; Konner Literary Agency, Linda; Koster Literary Agency, LLC, Elaine; Kouts, Literary Agent, Barbara S.; Larken, Sabra Elliott; Larsen/Elizabeth Pomada Literary Agents, Michael; Lasher Agency, The Maureen; Levine Communications, Inc., James; Levine Literary Agency, Inc., Ellen; Levine Literary Agency, Paul S.; Lieberman Associates, Robert; Lincoln Literary Agency, Ray; Literary Group, The; Love Literary Agency, Nancy; Lowenstein Associates, Inc.; Mann Agency, Carol; Manus & Associates Literary Agency; McBride Literary Agency, Margret; Menza Literary Agency, Claudia; Miller Agency, The; Multimedia Product Development, Inc.; New Century Literary Agency; New England Publishing Associates, Inc.; Nine Muses and Apollo Inc.; Palmer & Dodge Agency, The; Parks Agency, The Richard; Paton Literary Agency, Kathi J.; Pinder Lane & Garon-Brooke Associates, Ltd.; Protter Literary Agent, Susan Ann; Quicksilver Books—Literary Agents; Raymond, Literary Agent, Charlotte Cecil; Rein Books, Inc., Jody; Rhodes Literary Agency, Jodie; Rinaldi Literary Agency, Angela; Robbins Literary Agency, BJ; Rosenkranz Literary Agency, Rita; Ross Literary Agency, The Gail; Rotrosen Agency LLC, Jane; Russell & Volkening; Sanders & Associates, Victoria; Scherf, Inc. Literary Management; Schiavone Literary Agency, Inc.; Sebastian Literary Agency; Seligman, Literary Agent, Lynn; Serendipity Literary Agency, LLC; Shepard Agency, The; Sherman Associates, Inc., Wendy; Singer Literary Agency Inc., Evelyn; Slopen Literary Agency, Beverley; Snell Literary Agency, Michael; Straus Agency, Inc., Robin; Teal Literary Agency, Patricia; Travis Literary Agency, Susan; United Tribes; Vines Agency, Inc., The; Wales, Literary Agency, Inc.; Ware Literary Agency, John A.; Waterside Productions, Inc.; Watt & Associates, Sandra; Weingel-Fidel Agency, The; West Coast Literary Associates; Wieser & Wieser, Inc.; Wonderland Press, Inc., The; Writers House (NY); Zachary Shuster Harmsworth

Religious/Inspirational: Agency West Entertainment; Alive Communications, Inc.; Allred and Allred Literary Agents; Altair Literary Agency; Authors Alliance Inc.; Bial Agency, Daniel; BigScore Productions Inc.; Bleecker Street Associates, Inc.; Books & Such; Brandenburgh & Associates Literary Agency; Brown Associates Inc., Marie; Browne Ltd., Pema; Bykofsky Associates, Inc., Sheree; Castiglia Literary Agency; Clark Associates, Wm; Clausen, Mays & Tahan, LLC; Crawford Literary Agency; DeFiore and Company; Dystel Literary Management, Jane; Ellenberg Literary Agency, Ethan; Ellison Inc., Nicholas; ForthWrite Literary Agency; Franklin Associates, Ltd., Lynn C.; Goodman Associates; Grosvenor Literary Agency, The; Herner Rights Agency, Susan; Jellinek & Murray Literary Agency; JLM Literary Agents; Joy Literary Agency; Knight Agency, The; Larsen/Elizabeth Pomada Literary Agents, Michael; Levine Communications, Inc., James; Levine Literary Agency, Paul S.; Literary Group, The; Lowenstein Associates, Inc.; McBride Literary Agency, Margret; Multimedia Product Development, Inc.; Nine Muses and Apollo Inc.; Palmer & Dodge Agency, The; Pevner, Inc., Stephen; Quicksilver Books—Literary Agents; Rein Books, Inc., Jody; Rhodes Literary Agency, Jodie; Roghaar Literary Agency, Inc., Linda; Rose & Associates Literary Agency; Rosenkranz Literary Agency, Rita; Ross Literary Agency, The Gail; Roth, Literary Representation, Carol Susan; Scherf, Inc. Literary Management; Serendipity Literary Agency, LLC; Shepard Agency, The; Singer Literary Agency Inc., Evelyn; Toad Hall, Inc.; Turner Agency, Paige; Vines Agency, Inc., The; Watt & Associates, Sandra; Waxman Agency, Inc., Scott; Wray Literary Agency, Pamela D.

Science/Technology: Agents Inc. for Medical and Mental Health Professionals; Ajlouny Literary Agency, Joseph; Allred and Allred Literary Agents; Altair Literary Agency; Authentic Creations Literary Agency; Baldi Literary Agency, Malaga; Balkin Agency, Inc.; Bedford Book Works, Inc., The; Bial Agency, Daniel; Bleecker Street Associates, Inc.; Boates Literary Agency, Reid; Book Deals, Inc.; Boston Literary Group, The; Brandt & Brandt Literary Agents Inc.; Carvainis Agency, Inc., Maria; Castiglia Literary Agency; Clark Associates, Wm; Contemporary Management; Cypher, The Cypher Agency, James R.; DH Literary, Inc.; Dickens Group, The; Dijkstra Literary Agency, Sandra; Ducas, Robert; Dystel Literary Management, Jane; Educational Design Services, Inc.; Elek Associates, Peter; Ellenberg Literary Agency,

Ethan; Ellison Inc., Nicholas; Eth Literary Representation, Felicia; Evans Inc., Mary; Flaming Star Literary Enterprises; ForthWrite Literary Agency; Fredericks Literary Agency, Inc., Jeanne; Gartenberg, Literary Agent, Max; Goodman Associates; Grosvenor Literary Agency, The; Harris Literary Agency; Hawkins & Associates, Inc., John; Heacock Literary Agency, Inc.; Henshaw Group, Richard; Herner Rights Agency, Susan; Jabberwocky Literary Agency; JCA Literary Agency, Inc.; Jellinek & Murray Literary Agency; Jenks Agency, Carolyn; Kern Literary Agency, Natasha; Ketz Agency, Louise B.; Kleinman, Esq., of Graybill & English L.L.C., Jeffrey M.; Klinger, Inc., Harvey; Larken, Sabra Elliott; Larsen/Elizabeth Pomada Literary Agents, Michael; Lasher Agency, The Maureen; Levine Communications, Inc., James; Levine Literary Agency, Paul S.; Levine Literary Agency, Inc., Ellen; Lieberman Associates, Robert; Lincoln Literary Agency, Ray; Lipkind Agency, Wendy; Literary Group, The; Livingston Cooke/Curtis Brown Canada; Love Literary Agency, Nancy; Lowenstein Associates, Inc.; Manus & Associates Literary Agency; McBride Literary Agency, Margret; McHugh Literary Agency; Multimedia Product Development, Inc.; Mura Enterprises, Inc., Dee; National Writers Literary Agency; Nazor Literary Agency, Karen; New England Publishing Associates, Inc.; Palmer & Dodge Agency, The; Parks Agency, The Richard; Pevner, Inc., Stephen; Protter Literary Agent, Susan Ann; Quicksilver Books—Literary Agents; Rein Books, Inc., Jody; Rhodes Literary Agency, Jodie; Rose & Associates Literary Agency; Rosenkranz Literary Agency, Rita; Ross Literary Agency, The Gail; Rubie Literary Agency, The Peter; Russell & Volkening; Schiavone Literary Agency, Inc.; Seligman, Literary Agent, Lynn; Serendipity Literary Agency, LLC; Shepard Agency, The Robert E.; Singer Literary Agency Inc., Evelyn; Snell Literary Agency, Michael; Straus Agency, Inc., Robin; Susijn Agency, The; Swayne Agency Literary Management & Consulting, Inc., The; United Tribes; Vines Agency, Inc., The; Wales, Literary Agency, Inc.; Ware Literary Agency, John A.; Watkins Loomis Agency, Inc.; Weingel-Fidel Agency, The; Wray Literary Agency, Pamela D.; Writers House (NY); Zachary Shuster Harmsworth

Self-help/Personal Improvement: Agency West Entertainment; Agents Inc. for Medical and Mental Health Professionals; Alive Communications, Inc.; Allred and Allred Literary Agents; Altair Literary Agency; Amster Literary Enterprises, Betsy; Amsterdam Agency, Marcia; Authentic Creations Literary Agency; Authors Alliance Inc.; Bial Agency, Daniel; BigScore Productions Inc.; Bleecker Street Associates, Inc.; Boates Literary Agency, Reid; Book Deals, Inc.; Books & Such; Bova Literary Agency, The Barbara; Brandt & Brandt Literary Agents Inc.; Briggs, M. Courtney; Brown Associates Inc., Marie; Browne Ltd., Pema; Bykofsky Associates, Inc., Sheree; Castiglia Literary Agency; Client First—A/K/A Leo P. Haffey Agency; Connor Literary Agency; Contemporary Management; Crawford Literary Agency; Cypher, The Cypher Agency, James R.; Dawson Associates, Liza; DeFiore and Company; DH Literary, Inc.; Dijkstra Literary Agency, Sandra; Dorian Literary Agency; Ellenberg Literary Agency, Ethan; Elmo Agency Inc., Ann; Feigen/Parrent Literary Management; Flaherty, Literary Agent, Joyce A.; Flaming Star Literary Enterprises; Fleury Agency, B.R.; Fort Ross Inc. Russian-American Publishing Projects; Franklin Associates, Ltd., Lynn C.; Fredericks Literary Agency, Inc., Jeanne; Fullerton Associates, Sheryl B.; Gartenberg, Literary Agent, Max; Goodman Associates; Grosvenor Literary Agency, The; Harris Literary Agency; Hawkins & Associates, Inc., John; Heacock Literary Agency, Inc.; Henshaw Group, Richard; Herman Agency LLC, The Jeff; Herner Rights Agency, Susan; J de S Associates Inc.; James Peter Associates, Inc.; Jellinek & Murray Literary Agency; JLM Literary Agents; Joy Literary Agency; Kellock Company, Inc., The; Kern Literary Agency, Natasha; Kidde, Hoyt & Picard; Kleinman, Esq., of Graybill & English L.L.C., Jeffrey M.; Klinger, Inc., Harvey; Knight Agency, The; Konner Literary Agency, Linda; Koster Literary Agency, LLC, Elaine; Kouts, Literary Agent, Barbara S.; Kritzer Productions, Eddie; Larsen/Elizabeth Pomada Literary Agents, Michael; Lasher Agency, The Maureen; Levine Communications, Inc., James; Levine Literary Agency, Paul S.; Lewis & Company, Karen; Limelight Management; Lincoln Literary Agency, Ray; Literary and Creative Artists, Inc.; Literary Group, The; Love Literary Agency, Nancy; Lowenstein Associates, Inc.; Mann Agency, Carol; Manus & Associates Literary Agency; McBride Literary Agency, Margret; McHugh Literary Agency; Menza Literary Agency, Claudia; Michaels Literary Agency, Inc., Doris S.; Miller Agency, The; Multimedia Product Development, Inc.; Mura Enterprises, Inc., Dee; New Century Literary Agency; New England Publishing Associates, Inc.; Norma-Lewis Agency, The; Palmer & Dodge Agency, The; Parks Agency, The Richard; Pinder Lane & Garon-Brooke Associates, Ltd.; Quicksilver Books—Literary Agents; Rein Books, Inc., Jody; Rinaldi Literary Agency, Angela; Robbins Literary Agency, BJ; Roghaar Literary Agency, Inc., Linda; Rose & Associates Literary Agency; Rosenkranz Literary Agency, Rita; Ross Literary Agency, The Gail; Roth, Literary Representation, Carol Susan; Rotrosen Agency LLC, Jane; Scherf, Inc. Literary Management; Schiavone Literary Agency, Inc.; Sebastian Literary Agency; Seligman, Literary Agent, Lynn; Serendipity Literary Agency, LLC; Shepard Agency, The; Sherman Associates, Inc., Wendy; Singer Literary Agency Inc., Evelyn; Smith Literary Agency, Robert; Stauffer Associates, Nancy; Swayne Agency Literary Management & Consulting, Inc., The; Swayze Literary Agency, Carolyn; Teal Literary Agency, Patricia; Toad Hall, Inc.; Travis Literary Agency, Susan; Turner Agency, Paige; 2M Communications Ltd.; United Tribes; Vines Agency, Inc., The; Wales, Literary Agency, Inc.; Watt & Associates, Sandra; Waxman Agency, Inc., Scott; Weiner Literary

Agency, Cherry; Wonderland Press, Inc., The; Wray Literary Agency, Pamela D.; Writers House (NY); Wylie-Merrick Literary Agency; Zachary Shuster Harmsworth

Sociology: Agents Inc. for Medical and Mental Health Professionals; Allen Literary Agency, Linda; Allred and Allred Literary Agents; Altair Literary Agency; Altshuler. Literary Agency, Miriam; Amster Literary Enterprises, Betsy; Baldi Literary Agency, Malaga; Balkin Agency, Inc.; Bial Agency, Daniel; Bleecker Street Associates, Inc.; Boston Literary Group, The; Bova Literary Agency, The Barbara; Brandt & Brandt Literary Agents Inc.; Castiglia Literary Agency; Clark Associates, Wm; Coover Agency, The Doe; Cypher, The Cypher Agency, James R.; Dawson Associates, Liza; Dijkstra Literary Agency, Sandra; Educational Design Services, Inc.; Ellison Inc., Nicholas; Eth Literary Representation, Felicia; Flaherty, Literary Agent, Joyce A.; ForthWrite Literary Agency; Goodman Associates; Grosvenor Literary Agency, The; Hawkins & Associates, Inc., John; Henshaw Group, Richard; Herner Rights Agency, Susan; Hochmann Books, John L.; J de S Associates Inc.; Jabberwocky Literary Agency; JCA Literary Agency, Inc.; Jenks Agency, Carolyn; JLM Literary Agents; Joy Literary Agency; Kellock Company, Inc., The; Kidde, Hoyt & Picard; Kleinman, Esq., of Graybill & English L.L.C., Jeffrey M.; Larsen/Elizabeth Pomada Literary Agents, Michael; Lasher Agency, The Maureen; Levine Communications, Inc., James; Levine Literary Agency, Paul S.; Lieberman Associates, Robert; Lincoln Literary Agency, Ray; Lipkind Agency, Wendy; Literary Group, The; Love Literary Agency, Nancy; Lowenstein Associates, Inc.; Mann Agency, Carol; McBride Literary Agency, Margret; Multimedia Product Development, Inc.; Mura Enterprises, Inc., Dee; Nazor Literary Agency, Karen; New Century Literary Agency; New England Publishing Associates, Inc.; Palmer & Dodge Agency, The; Parks Agency, The Richard; Pevner, Inc., Stephen; Quicksilver Books—Literary Agents; Raymond, Literary Agent, Charlotte Cecil; Rein Books, Inc., Jody; Rinaldi Literary Agency, Angela; Rittenberg Literary Agency, Inc., Ann; Robbins Literary Agency, BJ; Rose & Associates Literary Agency; Ross Literary Agency, The Gail; Russell & Volkening; Schiavone Literary Agency, Inc.; Sebastian Literary Agency; Seligman, Literary Agent, Lynn; Shepard Agency, The; Shepard Agency, The Robert E.; Simmons Literary Agency, Jeffrey; Slopen Literary Agency, Beverley; Spieler Agency, The; Straus Agency, Inc., Robin; United Tribes; Vines Agency, Inc., The; Waterside Productions, Inc.; Weiner Literary Agency, Cherry; Weingel-Fidel Agency, The; Wray Literary Agency, Pamela D.

Sports: Agency West Entertainment; Agents Inc. for Medical and Mental Health Professionals; Ajlouny Literary Agency, Joseph; Alive Communications, Inc.; Allred and Allred Literary Agents; Altair Literary Agency; Authentic Creations Literary Agency; Authors Alliance Inc.; Bedford Book Works, Inc., The; Bial Agency, Daniel; Black Literary Agency, David; Bleecker Street Associates, Inc.; Boates Literary Agency, Reid; Brandt & Brandt Literary Agents Inc.; Browne Ltd., Pema; Connor Literary Agency; Contemporary Management; Cypher, The Cypher Agency, James R.; DeFiore and Company; DHS Literary, Inc.; Dijkstra Literary Agency, Sandra; Donovan Literary, Jim; Ducas, Robert; Flaming Star Literary Enterprises; Fogelman Literary Agency, The; Fredericks Literary Agency, Inc., Jeanne; Gartenberg, Literary Agent, Max; Goodman Associates; Greene, Arthur B.; Hawkins & Associates, Inc., John; Henshaw Group, Richard; J de S Associates Inc.; Jabberwocky Literary Agency; JCA Literary Agency, Inc.; Kellock Company, Inc., The; Ketz Agency, Louise B.; Klinger, Inc., Harvey; Knight Agency, The; Larsen/Elizabeth Pomada Literary Agents, Michael; Lasher Agency, The Maureen; Levine Communications, Inc., James; Levine Literary Agency, Paul S.; Limelight Management; Lincoln Literary Agency, Ray; Literary Group, The; Lowenstein Associates, Inc.; Markowitz Literary Agency, Barbara; McBride Literary Agency, Margret; McCauley, Gerard; Michaels Literary Agency, Inc., Doris S.; Miller Agency, The; Multimedia Product Development, Inc.; Mura Enterprises, Inc., Dee; National Writers Literary Agency; Nazor Literary Agency, Karen; New Century Literary Agency; Quicksilver Books—Literary Agents; Rhodes Literary Agency, Jodie; Robbins Literary Agency, BJ; Rose & Associates Literary Agency; Rosenkranz Literary Agency, Rita; Ross Literary Agency, The Gail; Rotrosen Agency LLC, Jane; Russell & Volkening; Serendipity Literary Agency, LLC; Shepard Agency, The; Shepard Agency, The Robert E.; Simmons Literary Agency, Jeffrey; Steele-Perkins Literary Agency; Swayze Literary Agency, Carolyn; Vines Agency, Inc., The; Ware Literary Agency, John A.; Waterside Productions, Inc.; Watt & Associates, Sandra; Waxman Agency, Inc., Scott; Wieser & Wieser, Inc.; Wray Literary Agency, Pamela D.; Zachary Shuster Harmsworth

Translations: Balkin Agency, Inc.; Clark Associates, Wm; Daves Agency, Joan; Ellison Inc., Nicholas; Grosvenor Literary Agency, The; J de S Associates Inc.; JCA Literary Agency, Inc.; Jenks Agency, Carolyn; Kleinman, Esq., of Graybill & English L.L.C., Jeffrey M.; Sanders & Associates, Victoria; Seligman, Literary Agent, Lynn; Simmons Literary Agency, Jeffrey; United Tribes; Vines Agency, Inc., The

Travel: Acacia House Publishing Services Ltd.; Baldi Literary Agency, Malaga; Balkin Agency, Inc.; Bial Agency, Daniel; Borchardt Inc., Georges; Contemporary Management; Coover Agency, The Doe; Cypher, The Cypher Agency, James R.; Ducas, Robert; Flaherty, Literary Agent, Joyce A.; Goodman Associates; Grosjean Literary Agency, Jill; Hawkins & Associates, Inc., John; James Peter Associates, Inc.; Jellinek & Murray Literary Agency; Larsen/Elizabeth Pomada Literary Agents, Michael; Limelight Management; Love Literary Agency, Nancy; Lowenstein Associates, Inc.; Multimedia Product Development, Inc.; Mura

Enterprises, Inc., Dee; National Writers Literary Agency; Nazor Literary Agency, Karen; Parks Agency, The Richard; Pevner, Inc., Stephen; Rittenberg Literary Agency, Inc., Ann; Rose & Associates Literary Agency; Spieler Agency, The; Susijn Agency, The; 2M Communications Ltd.; Vines Agency, Inc., The; Ware Literary Agency, John A.; Watt & Associates, Sandra; Wray Literary Agency, Pamela D.

True Crime/Investigative: Agency West Entertainment; Allen, Literary Agent, James; Allred and Allred Literary Agents; AMG/Renaissance; Appleseeds Management; Authentic Creations Literary Agency; Authors Alliance Inc.; Baldi Literary Agency, Malaga; Balkin Agency, Inc.; Bial Agency, Daniel; Bleecker Street Associates, Inc.; Boates Literary Agency, Reid; Boston Literary Group, The; Bova Literary Agency, The Barbara; Brandt & Brandt Literary Agents Inc.; Browne Ltd., Pema; Bykofsky Associates, Inc., Sheree; Charisma Communications, Ltd.; Clausen, Mays & Tahan, LLC; Collin Literary Agent, Frances; Connor Literary Agency; Coover Agency, The Doe; Core Creations, Inc.; Cypher, The Cypher Agency, James R.; DH Literary, Inc.; DHS Literary, Inc.; Dickens Group, The; Dijkstra Literary Agency, Sandra; Donovan Literary, Jim; Ducas, Robert; Dystel Literary Management, Jane; Elek Associates, Peter; Ellenberg Literary Agency, Ethan; Ellison Inc., Nicholas; Elmo Agency Inc., Ann; Eth Literary Representation, Felicia; Fleury Agency, B.R.; Fogelman Literary Agency, The; Fort Ross Inc. Russian-American Publishing Projects; Frenkel & Associates, James; Gartenberg, Literary Agent, Max; Goodman Associates; Grace Literary Agency, Carroll; Grosvenor Literary Agency, The; Halsey Agency, Reece; Halsey North, Reece; Henshaw Group, Richard; Herner Rights Agency, Susan; Jabberwocky Literary Agency; JCA Literary Agency, Inc.; Jellinek & Murray Literary Agency; JLM Literary Agents; Kleinman, Esq., of Graybill & English L.L.C., Jeffrey M.; Klinger, Inc., Harvey; Kritzer Productions, Eddie; Lampack Agency, Inc., Peter; Larken, Sabra Elliott; Larsen/Elizabeth Pomada Literary Agents, Michael; Lasher Agency, The Maureen; Lawyer's Literary Agency, Inc.; Levine Literary Agency, Paul S.; Literary Group, The; Love Literary Agency, Nancy; Lowenstein Associates, Inc.; Lownie Literary Agency Ltd., Andrew; McBride Literary Agency, Margret; McHugh Literary Agency; Multimedia Product Development, Inc.; Mura Enterprises, Inc., Dee; New Century Literary Agency; New England Publishing Associates, Inc.; Norma-Lewis Agency, The; Pinder Lane & Garon-Brooke Associates, Ltd.; Quicksilver Books—Literary Agents; Rhodes Literary Agency, Jodie; Rinaldi Literary Agency, Angela; Robbins Literary Agency, BJ; Robbins Office, Inc., The; Rose & Associates Literary Agency; Ross Literary Agency, The Gail; Rotrosen Agency LLC, Jane; Russell & Volkening; Scherf, Inc. Literary Management; Schiavone Literary Agency, Inc.; Sedgeband Literary Associates; Seligman, Literary Agent, Lynn; Sherman Associates, Inc., Wendy; Simmons Literary Agency, Jeffrey; Slopen Literary Agency, Beverley; Smith Literary Agency, Robert; Swayze Literary Agency, Carolyn; Teal Literary Agency, Patricia; Vines Agency, Inc., The; Ware Literary Agency, John A.; Watkins Loomis Agency, Inc.; Watt & Associates, Sandra; Weingel-Fidel Agency, The; West Coast Literary Associates; Wieser & Wieser, Inc.; Writers House (NY); Zachary Shuster Harmsworth

Women's Issues/Women's Studies: Agency West Entertainment; Alive Communications, Inc.; Allen Literary Agency, Linda; Allred and Allred Literary Agents; Altair Literary Agency; Altshuler Literary Agency, Miriam; Amster Literary Enterprises, Betsy; Authentic Creations Literary Agency; Baldi Literary Agency, Malaga; Barbara's Literary Agency; Bial Agency, Daniel; Bleecker Street Associates, Inc.; Boates Literary Agency, Reid; Books & Such; Borchardt Inc., Georges; Boston Literary Group, The; Bova Literary Agency, The Barbara; Brandt & Brandt Literary Agents Inc.; Brown Associates Inc., Marie; Browne Ltd., Pema; Bykofsky Associates, Inc., Sheree; Carvainis Agency, Inc., Maria; Casselman Literary Agency, Martha; Castiglia Literary Agency; Clausen, Mays & Tahan, LLC; Connor Literary Agency; Contemporary Management; Coover Agency, The Doe; Crawford Literary Agency; Cypher, The Cypher Agency, James R.; Daves Agency, Joan; Dawson Associates, Liza; DH Literary, Inc.; Dijkstra Literary Agency, Sandra; Dystel Literary Management, Jane; Educational Design Services, Inc.; Ellison Inc., Nicholas; Elmo Agency Inc., Ann; Eth Literary Representation, Felicia; Feigen/Parrent Literary Management; Flaherty, Literary Agent, Joyce A.; Fogelman Literary Agency, The; ForthWrite Literary Agency; Fredericks Literary Agency, Inc., Jeanne; Fullerton Associates, Sheryl B.; Gartenberg, Literary Agent, Max; Goodman Associates; Grace Literary Agency, Carroll; Grosjean Literary Agency, Jill; Grosvenor Literary Agency, The; Halsey Agency, Reece; Halsey North, Reece; Hawkins & Associates, Inc., John; Heacock Literary Agency, Inc.; Henshaw Group, Richard; Herner Rights Agency, Susan; Hill Associates, Frederick; Jabberwocky Literary Agency; James Peter Associates, Inc.; JCA Literary Agency, Inc.; Jellinek & Murray Literary Agency; Jenks Agency, Carolyn; JLM Literary Agents; Joy Literary Agency; Kellock Company, Inc., The; Kern Literary Agency, Natasha; Kidde, Hoyt & Picard; Kleinman, Esq., of Graybill & English L.L.C., Jeffrey M.; Klinger, Inc., Harvey; Konner Literary Agency, Linda; Koster Literary Agency, LLC, Elaine; Kouts, Literary Agent, Barbara S.; Kroll Literary Agency Inc., Edite; Lampack Agency, Inc., Peter; Larken, Sabra Elliott; Larsen/Elizabeth Pomada Literary Agents, Michael; Lasher Agency, The Maureen; Levine Communications, Inc., James; Levine Literary Agency, Paul S.; Levine Literary Agency, Inc., Ellen; Lewis & Company, Karen; Lincoln Literary Agency, Ray; Lipkind Agency, Wendy; Literary Group, The; Love Literary Agency, Nancy; Lowenstein Associates, Inc.; Maccoby Literary Agency, Gina; Mann Agency, Carol; Manus & Associates Literary Agency; Markowitz Literary Agency, Barbara; McBride Literary

Agency, Margret; Michaels Literary Agency, Inc., Doris S.; Miller Agency, The; Multimedia Product Development, Inc.; Mura Enterprises, Inc., Dee; Nazor Literary Agency, Karen; New Century Literary Agency; New England Publishing Associates, Inc.; Nine Muses and Apollo Inc.; Norma-Lewis Agency, The; Palmer & Dodge Agency, The; Parks Agency, The Richard; Paton Literary Agency, Kathi J.; Popkin, Julie; Quicksilver Books—Literary Agents; Rees Literary Agency, Helen; Rein Books, Inc., Jody; Rhodes Literary Agency, Jodie; Rinaldi Literary Agency, Angela; Rittenberg Literary Agency, Inc., Ann; Robbins Literary Agency, BJ; Roghaar Literary Agency, Inc., Linda; Rose & Associates Literary Agency; Rosenkranz Literary Agency, Rita; Rotrosen Agency LLC, Jane; Russell & Volkening; Sanders & Associates, Victoria; Sebastian Literary Agency; Seligman, Literary Agent, Lynn; Serendipity Literary Agency, LLC; Shepard Agency, The; Shepard Agency, The Robert E.; Singer Literary Agency Inc., Evelyn; Slopen Literary Agency, Beverley; Snell Literary Agency, Michael; Southern Literary Group; Spieler Agency, The; Straus Agency, Inc., Robin; Swayne Agency Literary Management & Consulting, Inc., The; Swayze Literary Agency, Carolyn; Taylor, Literary Agent, Rebecca; Teal Literary Agency, Patricia; Travis Literary Agency, Susan; 2M Communications Ltd.; United Tribes; Vines Agency, Inc., The; Wales, Literary Agency, Inc.; Ware Literary Agency, John A.; Watkins Loomis Agency, Inc.; Watt & Associates, Sandra; Weingel-Fidel Agency, The; West Coast Literary Associates; Writers House (NY); Zachary Shuster Harmsworth

Young Adult Nonfiction: Briggs, M. Courtney; Livingston Cooke/Curtis Brown Canada; Rose & Associates Literary Agency; Serendipity Literary Agency, LLC; Treimel NY, S©ott; Wylie-Merrick Literary Agency

Literary Agents:
Fee-charging

This section contains literary agencies that charge a fee to writers in addition to taking a commission on sales. Several agencies charge fees only under certain circumstances, generally for previously unpublished writers. These agencies are indicated by a briefcase (💼) symbol. Most agencies will consider you unpublished if you have subsidy publishing, electronic publishing, or local or small press publication credits only; check with a prospective agency before sending material to see if you fit its definition of a published author.

Some agents in this section also charge for office expenses such as photocopying, foreign postage, long distance phone calls, or express mail services. Often your agent will deduct such expenses from your advance or royalties. We've asked agents listing in this section to disclose what office expenses they charge. Make sure you have a clear understanding of what these expenses are before signing any agency agreement. While a one-time office expense charge is fairly common, be wary of agents who request yearly, quarterly, or even monthly reimbursements. As a client, you have the right to request copies of all receipts received for any office expense you are required to pay.

This year, we've included—for the first time—a section of Canadian/International fee-charging literary agents. To learn more about the pros and cons of using an agent outside the United States, read the introduction to this section on page 239.

When reading through this section, keep in mind the following information specific to the fee-charging listings:

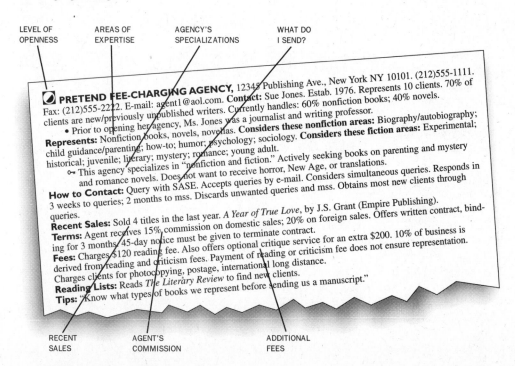

LEVEL OF OPENNESS

AREAS OF EXPERTISE

AGENCY'S SPECIALIZATIONS

WHAT DO I SEND?

💼 **PRETEND FEE-CHARGING AGENCY,** 12345 Publishing Ave., New York NY 10101. (212)555-1111. Fax: (212)555-2222. E-mail: agent1@aol.com. **Contact:** Sue Jones. Estab. 1976. Represents 10 clients. 70% of clients are new/previously unpublished writers. Currently handles: 60% nonfiction books; 40% novels.
  • Prior to opening her agency, Ms. Jones was a journalist and writing professor.
Represents: Nonfiction books, novels, novellas. **Considers these nonfiction areas:** Biography/autobiography; child guidance/parenting; how-to; humor; psychology; sociology. **Considers these fiction areas:** Experimental; historical; juvenile; literary; mystery; romance; young adult.
  ○→ This agency specializes in "nonfiction and fiction." Actively seeking books on parenting and mystery and romance novels. Does not want to receive horror, New Age, or translations.
How to Contact: Query with SASE. Accepts queries by e-mail. Considers simultaneous queries. Responds in 3 weeks to queries; 2 months to mss. Discards unwanted queries and mss. Obtains most new clients through queries.
Recent Sales: Sold 4 titles in the last year. *A Year of True Love*, by J.S. Grant (Empire Publishing).
Terms: Agent receives 15% commission on domestic sales; 20% on foreign sales. Offers written contract, binding for 3 months/45-day notice must be given to terminate contract.
Fees: Charges $120 reading fee. Also offers optional critique service for an extra $200. 10% of business is derived from reading and criticism fees. Payment of reading or criticism fee does not ensure representation. Charges clients for photocopying, postage, international long distance.
Reading Lists: Reads *The Literary Review* to find new clients.
Tips: "Know what types of books we represent before sending us a manuscript."

RECENT SALES

AGENT'S COMMISSION

ADDITIONAL FEES

Quick Reference Icons

At the beginning of some listings, you will find one or more of the following symbols for quick identification of features particular to that listing.

N: Agency new to this edition.

✓ Change in address, contact information, or phone number from last year's edition.

$ Agents who charge fees to previously unpublished writers only.

■ Agents who make sales to electronic publishers. For more information on this topic, see "The Flight to Quantity: Will the Internet Ruin It for Everybody?" on page 51.

✂ Canadian agency.

⊕ International agency.

Level of Openness

Each agency has an icon indicating its openness to submissions. Before contacting any agency, check the listing to make sure it is open to new clients.

◻ Newer agency actively seeking clients.

◗ Agency seeking both new and established writers.

◔ Agency prefers to work with established writers, mostly obtains new clients through referrals.

◎ Agency handling only certain types of work or work by writers under certain circumstances.

⊘ Agency not currently seeking new clients. We include these agencies to let you know they are currently not open to new clients. *Unless you have a strong recommendation from someone well respected in the field, our advice is to avoid approaching these agents.*

For quick reference, a chart of these icons and their meanings is printed on the inside covers of this book.

For a detailed explanation of the agency listings and for more information on approaching agents, read "Reading the Listings in the *Guide to Literary Agents*" and "How to Find the Right Agent." Other informative articles included in the front of the book explain the process to follow during your search for a literary agent.

SUBHEADS FOR QUICK ACCESS TO INFORMATION

Each listing is broken down into subheads to make locating specific information easier. In the first section, you'll find contact information for each agency, including the agency's address, phone number, e-mail, and website address. Any trade or writers' organizations an agent belongs to is listed. (An explanation of all organizations' acronyms is available on page 366.) Also provided here is information on an agency's size, its willingness to work with new or previously unpublished writers, and a percentage breakdown of its general areas of interest.

Member Agents: To help you locate the best person for your writing, agencies with more than one agent list member names and their individual specialties.

Represents: Here agencies specify what nonfiction and fiction subjects they consider. Only query agents who represent the type of material you write. To help narrow your search, check the **Agents Specialties Index** immediately after the Canadian/International fee-charging listings.

⚷ Look for the key icon to quickly ascertain an agent's areas of specialization or specific strengths (i.e., editorial or marketing experience, sub-rights expertise, etc.). Agents also mention here what specific areas they are currently seeking as well as subjects they do *not* wish to receive.

How to Contact: Most agents prefer initially to receive a query letter briefly describing your work. (See "Queries That Made It Happen" on page 31.) Some agents ask for an outline and a number of sample chapters, but send these only if requested to do so. Here agents also indicate if they accept queries by fax or e-mail, if they are receptive to simultaneous submission, and their preferred way of meeting new clients.

Recent Sales: Agents provide specific titles they've sold to give a sense of the types of material they represent. Looking at the publisher of those titles also can tell you the caliber of publishing contacts the agent has developed. Just having an agent is not enough—*you want an agent who can sell your work.* If an agent expresses interest in representing you, it is permissible to ask for the names of other clients. An unwillingness to share such information with a prospective client could be an indication that an agent isn't actively making sales.

Terms: The sales commissions are the same as those taken by nonfee-charging agents: 10 to 15 percent for domestic sales, 15 to 20 percent for foreign or dramatic sales, with the difference going to the co-agent. Details about contracts are also given here.

Fees: On top of their commission, agents in this section charge writers various fees. Often, payment of reading or critique fees does not ensure representation. In order to understand what services are provided for the different fees and to learn the issues surrounding fee-charging agents, read the following side bar, "Reading Fees and Critique Services." Also listed under this subhead are any additional office expenses the agent charges to clients.

Writers' Conferences: Here agents list the writers' conferences they attend to discover new talent. For more information about a specific conference, check the **Writers' Conferences** section starting on page 333.

Reading List: Learn what magazines and journals agents read to discover potential clients.

Tips: Agents offer advice for writers and additional instructions about submitting to their agency.

SPECIAL INDEXES TO HELP YOUR SEARCH

Additional Fee-charging Agents: Many literary agents are also interested in scripts; many script agents will also consider book manuscripts. Fee-charging script agents who primarily sell scripts but also handle at least 10 to 15 percent book manuscripts appear among the listings in this section, with the contact information, breakdown of work currently handled, and a note to check the full listing in the script section. Fee-charging script agencies that sell scripts and less than 10 to 15 percent book manuscripts appear at the end of this section on page 238. Complete listings for these agents appear in the Script Agents section.

Agents Specialties Index: Immediately following the section **Canadian/International Fee-charging Literary Agents** is an index which organizes agencies according to the subjects they are interested in receiving. This index should help you compose a list of agents specializing in your areas. Cross-referencing categories and concentrating on agents interested in two or more aspects of your manuscript might increase your chances of success. Agencies open to all nonfiction or fiction topics are grouped under the subject heading "open."

Agencies Indexed by Openness to Submissions: This index lists agencies according to their receptivity to new clients.

Geographic Index: For writers looking for an agent close to home, this index lists agents state-by-state.

Agents Index: Often you will read about an agent who is an employee of a larger agency and you may not be able to locate her business phone or address. Starting on page 379 is a list of agents' names in alphabetical order along with the name of the agency they work for. Find the name of the person you would like to contact, and then check the agency listing.

Listing Index: This index lists all agencies, independent publicists, and writers' conferences listed in the book.

Reading Fees and Critique Services

The issue of agents charging reading fees is controversial in the publishing industry. While some agents dismiss the concept as inherently unethical and a scam, others see merit in the system, provided an author goes into it with open eyes. Some writers spend hundreds of dollars for an "evaluation" that consists of a poorly written critique full of boilerplate language that says little, if anything, about their individual work. Others have received the helpful feedback they needed to get their manuscript in shape and have gone on to publish their work successfully.

Since January 1, 1996, however, all members of the AAR have been prohibited from directly charging reading fees. Until that time some members were allowed to continue to charge fees, provided they adhered to guidelines designed to protect the client. (For more information on the AAR's stance, read "Agents & Ethics: Getting Published without Losing Your Shirt," on page 13.) A copy of the AAR's Canon of Ethics may be obtained for $7 and a 99¢ SAE. The address is listed in Professional Organizations toward the end of this book.

Be wary of an agent who refers you to a specific book doctor. While the relationship may be that the agent trusts that professional editor's work, it is too hard to tell if there are other reasons the agent is working with him (for instance, the agent is receiving a kickback for the referral). As with the AAR, the Writers Guild of America, which franchises literary agencies dealing largely in scripts, prohibits their signatories from such recommendations simply because it is open to abuse.

Researching agents

In discussing consideration of a fee-charging agent, we must underscore the importance of research. Don't be bowled over by an impressive brochure or an authoritative manner. At the same time, overly aggressive skepticism may kill your chances with a legitimate agent. Business-like, professional behavior will help you gather the material you need to make an informed decision.

- **Ask questions about the fees.** Obtain a fee schedule, making sure you understand what the fees cover and what to expect for your money.
- **Request a sample critique.** Looking at what the agent has done for another person's manuscript is the best way to decide if the critique is worth the price. Are the suggestions helpful and specific? Do they offer advice you couldn't get elsewhere, such as in writing groups, conferences, seminars, or reference books?
- **Ask for recent sales an agent has made.** Many agents have a pre-printed list of sales they can send you. If there haven't been any sales made in the past two years, what is the agent living on? An agent's worth to you, initially, is who they know and their ability to get your book published. In the listings, we provide information on the percentage of income an agency receives from commissions on sales and the percentage from reading or critique fees.
- **Verify a few of these sales.** To verify the publisher has a book by that title, check *Books in Print*. To verify the agent made the sale, call the contracts department of the publisher and ask who the agent of record is for a particular title.

Recently, there has been a trend among a few agents to recommend contracts with subsidy publishers that ask the writer to pay from $3,500 to $6,000 toward the cost of publication. These deals are open to writers directly, without the intermediating "assistance" of an agent. Your best defense is to carefully examine the list of an agent's recent sales and investigate some of the publishers. We chose not to include agents who work with subsidy publishers.

Don't hesitate to ask the questions that will help you decide. The more you know about an agent and her abilities, the fewer unpleasant surprises you'll receive.

Different types of fees

Fees range from one agency to another in nomenclature, price and purpose. Here are some of the more frequent services and their generally accepted definitions.

- **Reading fee.** This is charged for reading a manuscript (most agents do not charge to look at queries alone). Often the fee is paid to outside readers. It is generally a one-time, nonrefundable fee, but some agents will return the fee or credit it to your account if they decide to take you on as a client. Often an agent will offer to refund the fee upon sale of the book, but that isn't necessarily a sign of good faith. If the agency never markets your manuscript no sale would ever be made and the fee never refunded.
- **Evaluation fee.** Sometimes a reading fee includes a written evaluation, but many agents charge for this separately. An evaluation may be a one-paragraph report on the marketability of a manuscript or a several-page evaluation covering marketability along with flaws and strengths of the manuscript. Be sure you have a clear understanding of the critique's length and scope before paying any money.
- **Marketing fees.** Usually a one-time charge to offset the costs of handling work, marketing fees cover a variety of expenses and may include initial reading or evaluation. Beware of agencies charging a monthly marketing fee; there is nothing to compel them to submit your work in a timely way if they are getting paid anyway.
- **Critiquing service.** Although "critique" and "evaluation" are sometimes used interchangeably, a critique is usually more extensive, with suggestions on ways to improve the manuscript. Many agents offer critiques as a separate service and have a standard fee scale, based on a per-page or word-length basis. Some agents charge fees based on the extent of the service required, ranging from overall review to line-by-line commentary.
- **Editing service.** While we do not list businesses whose primary source of income is from editing, we do list agencies who also offer this service. Many do not distinguish between critiques and edits, but we define editing services as critiques that include detailed suggestions on how to improve the work and reduce weaknesses. Editing services can be charged on similar bases as critiquing services.
- **Other services.** Depending on an agent's background and abilities, the agent may offer a variety of other services to writers including ghostwriting, typing, copyediting, proofreading, translating, book publicity, and legal advice.

Be forewarned that payment of a critique or editing fee does *not* ensure an agent will take you on as a client. However, if you feel you need more than sales help and do not mind paying for an evaluation or critique from a professional, the agents listed in this section may interest you.

FEE-CHARGING AGENTS

N **ABS LITERARY AGENCY**, 1731 Ashland St., Ashland OR 97520-2328. (541)488-6934. Fax: (541)488-6937. E-mail: AGENT@abs-book.com. Website: www.abs-book.com. **Contact:** Gail Manchur. Estab. 1998. 25% of clients are new/unpublished writers. Currently handles: 20% nonfiction books, 60% novels, 20% creative nonfiction.

   ● Prior to becoming an agent, Ms. Manchur was a professional editor.

Member Agents: Christine George, associate editor (history, Native American, nonfiction, mystery); Gail Manchur, president (mystery, suspense/thriller, science fiction).

Represents: Nonfiction books, novels. **Considers these nonfiction areas:** child guidance/parenting; computers/electronics; health/medicine; history; memoirs; religious/inspirational; women's issues/women's studies. **Considers these fiction areas:** action/adventure; historical; mystery/suspense; science fiction; thriller/science.

   O→ Does not want to receive erotica, pornography, children's, young adult, poetry, romance.

How to Contact: Query with SASE. Accepts queries by e-mail. Does not accept queries by fax. Prefers to read materials exclusively. Responds in 2 months to queries; 6 months to mss. Returns materials only with SASE. Obtains most new clients through queries/solicitations.

Recent Sales: Sold 3 titles in the last year. *Debugging Java*, by Will D. Mitchell (Osborne/McGraw-Hill); *Japanese Home Cooking*, by Rina Goto-Nance and Ron Nance (Hippocrene Books, Inc.).

Terms: Agent receives 15% commission on domestic sales; 20% on foreign sales. Offers written contract. 30-day notice must be given to terminate contract.

Fees: Charges clients certain fees (postage, etc.) to be reimbursed only if ms is sold. Monthly cap on expenses of $25 in contract.

Tips: "Don't send query, synopsis or other materials if they include spelling errors, etc. If you are a sloppy writer, we aren't interested. Don't tell us how many friends 'loved' your work unless those friends are acquisitions editors. Visit our website for detailed guidelines, and follow them closely.

☑ 💲 ⬭ **AEI/ATCHITY EDITORIAL/ENTERTAINMENT INTERNATIONAL, Literary Management & Motion Picture Production**, 9601 Wilshire Blvd., Box 1202, Beverly Hills CA 90210. (323)932-0407. Fax: (323)932-0321. E-mail: webaei@aol.com. Website: www.aeionline.com. **Contact:** Kenneth Atchity. Estab. 1996. Represents 50 clients. 75% of clients are new/previously unpublished writers. Currently handles: 30% nonfiction books; 40% novels; 30% movie scripts.

● Prior to opening his agency, Dr. Atchity was a professor of comparative literature at Occidental College, a Fullbright Professor at University of Bologna, and an instructor from 1970-1987 at the UCLA writers' program. He is the author of 13 books and has produced 20 films for video, television and theater. He was also co-editor of *Dreamworks*, a quarterly devoted to the relationship between art and dreams.

Member Agents: Kenneth Atchity (President); Chi-Li Wong (Partner and Vice President of Development and Production); Vincent Atchity (Associate Manager, Executive Vice President of Writers Lifeline); Kendra Mitchell (associate manager); Margo Hamilton (associate manager); Elizabeth Fujiwara (Honolulu); Lenny Cavellero (Boston); Mai-Ding Wong (New York); Andrea McKeown (Vice President); David Angsten (Vice President Development); Julie Mooney (senior editor), Lori Needleman (creative executive); Brenna Lui (development).

Represents: Nonfiction books, novels. **Considers these nonfiction areas:** biography/autobiography; business; government/politics/law; money/finance/economics; New Age/metaphysics; popular culture; self-help/personal improvement; true crime/investigative; women's issues/women's studies. **Considers these fiction areas:** action/adventure; contemporary issues; erotica; historical; horror; literary; mainstream; mystery/suspense; romance; science fiction; thriller/espionage.

O━ This agency specializes in novel film tie-ins. "We also specialize in taking successfully self-published books to the national market. We are always looking for true, heroic, *contemporary* women's stories for both book and television. We have a fondness for thrillers (both screenplays and novels), romantic comedies, as well as for mainstream nonfiction appealing to everyone today. We rarely do 'small audience' books." Does not want to receive "episodic" scripts, treatments, or ideas; no "category" fiction of any kind. Nothing drug-related, fundamental religious. No poetry, children's books, "interior" confessional fiction or novelty books.

Also Handles: Feature film, movie scripts, TV scripts, TV MOW, no episodic. **Considers these script subject areas:** action/adventure; comedy; contemporary issues; detective/police/crime; erotica; horror; mainstream; mystery/suspense; psychic/supernatural; romantic comedy and drama; science fiction; teen; thriller.

How to Contact: Send query letter, including synopsis and first 50 pages/3 sample chapters, with SASE. "Nothing, including scripts, will be returned without the SASE. Please send a professional return envelope and sufficient postage. Make your cover letter to the point and focused, your synopsis compelling and dramatic." Accepts queries by fax and e-mail. Prefers to be only reader. For books, reports in 2 weeks on queries; 2 months on mss. For scripts, reports in 1 month on queries; 2 months on mss. Returns materials only with SASE. Obtains most new clients through referrals, directories.

Recent Sales: Sold 16 book titles and 7 script projects in the last year. *The Adams Financial and Accounting Dictionary*, by Howard Bonham (Adams); *I Don't Have To Make Everything All Better*, by Gary and Joy Lundberg (Viking); *I Ain't Got Time to Bleed*, by Jesse Ventura; *A Midnight Carole*, by Patricia Davis (St. Martin's Press). *Movie script(s) optioned/sold: Life, or Something Like It* (New Regency); *Eulogy for Joseph Way* (Warner Brothers); *Henry's List of Wrongs* (New Line Cinema).

Terms: For books, agent receives 15% commission on domestic sales; 30% on foreign sales. Offers written contract, binding for 1 year, with 30 day cancellation clause. For scripts, agent receives 15% commission; (0% when produce).

Fees: No reading fee. $150 one-time advance against expenses, upon signing, for previously unpublished writers. Offers criticism service through "AEI Writers Lifeline," with fees ranging from $250-750. "We offer this service to writers

---

THE PUBLISHING FIELD is constantly changing! Agents often change addresses, phone numbers, or even companies. If you're still using this book and it is 2002 or later, buy the newest edition of *Guide to Literary Agents* at your favorite bookstore or order directly from Writer's Digest Books at (800)289-0963.

requesting specific feedback for their careers or seeking to enter our Lifeline Program for one-on-one coaching. The Writers Lifeline Program offers proposal, rewriting and ghostwriting services." 10% of revenue is derived from reading fees or criticism service. Payment of criticism or reading fee does not ensure representation.

Tips: "Take writing seriously as a career, which requires disciplined time and full attention (as described in *The Mercury Transition* and *A Writer's Time* by Kenneth Atchity). Most submissions, whether fiction or nonfiction, are rejected because the writing is not at a commercially competitive dramatic level. Our favorite client is one who has the desire and talent to develop both a novel and a film career and who is determined to learn everything possible about the business of writing, publishing, and producing. Dream big. Risk it. Never give up. Go for it! The rewards in this career are as endless as your imagination, and the risks, though real, are not greater than the risk of suffocating on a more secure career path. Begin by learning all you can about the business of writing, publishing and producing, and recognizing that as far-off and exalted as they may seem, the folks in these professions are as human as anyone else. We're enthusiasts, like you. Make us enthused."

THE AHEARN AGENCY, INC., 2021 Pine St., New Orleans LA 70118-5456. (504)861-8395. Fax: (504)866-6434. E-mail: pahearn@aol.com. **Contact:** Pamela G. Ahearn. Estab. 1992. Member of RWA. Represents 25 clients. 20% of clients are new/previously unpublished writers. Currently handles: 15% nonfiction books; 85% novels.

● Prior to opening her agency, Ms. Ahearn was an agent for eight years and an editor with Bantam Books.

Represents: Nonfiction books, novels, short story collections (if stories previously published). **Considers these nonfiction areas:** animals; biography; business; child guidance/parenting; current affairs; ethnic/cultural interests; gay/lesbian issues; health/medicine; history; juvenile nonfiction; music/dance/theater/film; popular culture; self-help/personal improvement; true crime/investigative; women's issues/women's studies. **Considers these fiction areas:** action/adventure; contemporary issues; detective/police/crime; ethnic; family saga; fantasy; feminist; gay; glitz; historical; horror; humor/satire; juvenile; lesbian; literary; mainstream; mystery/suspense; psychic/supernatural; regional; romance (contemporary, gothic, historical, regency); science fiction; thriller/espionage; westerns/frontier.

○━ This agency specializes in historical romance; also very interested in mysteries and suspense fiction. Does not want to receive category romance.

How to Contact: Query with SASE. Accepts queries by e-mail, but no attachments. Considers simultaneous queries. Responds in 1 month to queries; 10 weeks to mss. Obtains most new clients "through listings such as this one, client recommendations and sometimes at conferences."

Recent Sales: *The Concubine's Tattoo*, by Laura Joh Rowland (St. Martin's Press); *A Prince Among Men*, by Kate Moore (Avon Books); *In the Dark*, by Meagan McKinney (Kensington).

Terms: Agent receives 15% commission on domestic sales; 20% on foreign sales. Offers written contract, binding for 1 year; renewable by mutual consent.

Fees: "I charge a reading fee to previously unpublished authors, based on length of material. Fees range from $125-400 and are nonrefundable. When authors pay a reading fee, they receive a three- to five-page single-spaced critique of their work, addressing writing quality and marketability." Critiques written by Pamela G. Ahearn. Charges clients for photocopying. 10% of business derived from reading fees or criticism services. Payment of reading fee does not ensure representation.

Writers' Conferences: Midwest Writers Workshop, Moonlight & Magnolias, RWA National conference (Orlando); Virginia Romance Writers (Williamsburg, VA); Florida Romance Writers (Ft. Lauderdale, FL); Golden Triangle Writers Conference; Bouchercon (Monterey, November).

Tips: "Be professional! Always send in exactly what an agent/editor asks for, no more, no less. Keep query letters brief and to the point, giving your writing credentials and a very brief summary of your book. If one agent rejects you, keep trying—there are a lot of us out there!"

ALP ARTS CO., (Specialized: juvenile), 221 Fox Rd., Suite 7, Golden CO 80403. Phone/fax: (303)582-5189. E-mail: sffuller@alparts.com. **Contact:** Ms. Sandy Ferguson Fuller. Estab. 1994. Member of SCBWI. Represents 40 clients. 55% of clients are new/previously unpublished writers. Currently handles: 90% juvenile or young adult proposals; selective adult.

● Prior to becoming an agent, Ms. Fuller worked for 25 years in all aspects of children's book publishing, including international work, editorial, sales, marketing, retailing, wholesale buying, consulting. She is also a published author/illustrator.

Member Agents: Sandy Ferguson Fuller, director; Lynn Volkens, administrative assistant.

Represents: Juvenile and young adult books, all types, selective adult fiction and nonfiction. **Considers juvenile nonfiction. Considers juvenile and young adult fiction, picture books.**

○━ This agency specializes in children's books and works with picture book authors and illustrators, also middle-grade and YA writers, nonfiction and fiction. "Actively seeking children's/YA—all books and related media products, including scripts and licensing programs." Does not want to receive any adult material.

Also Handles: Scripts. "Will co-agent." **Considers these script areas:** juvenile (all); teen (all). Query with SASE. Responds in 3 weeks to queries; 2 months to mss.

How to Contact: Query with SASE. For picture books and easy readers send entire ms. Responds in 3 weeks to queries; 10 weeks to mss. Obtains most new clients from referrals, solicitation and at conferences.

Recent Sales: *Morning Dance*, Hannert (Chronicle); *Moose*, by Fredericks (Northword); *Geo Almanac*, by Siegel/McLoone (Blackbirch); *This Is the Sea That Feeds Us*, by Baldwin (Dawn). Other clients include Holly Huth, Kathy Johnson-Clarke, Pattie Schnetzler, Roberta Collier Morales, Frank Kramer, John Denver (Estate), Bonnie Turner, Hazel Krantz, Janice Leotti-Bachem.

Terms: 10-15% commission on domestic sales. 20% illustration only. Offers written contract, with 30 day cancellation clause.

Fees: Basic consultation is $70/picture books, easy readers; $100 middle grade or young adult proposal. Contract custom to client's needs. Charges clients for postage, photocopying costs and fee for submissions ($25 each) for nonpublished authors. Long-distance phone consultation at $60/hour plus phone bill. Consultation in person: $60/hour. Will prorate. Receipts supplied to client for all of the above. 30% of business derived from criticism fees.

Writers' Conferences: PPWC (Colorado Springs, CO, April); BEA (Chicago, June); SCBWI (October).

Reading List: Reads *Publishers Weekly*; *Booklist*; *Horn Book*; *SCBWI Bulletin*; *Children's Writer*; etc. to find new clients.

Tips: "Agency representation is not for everyone. Some aspiring or published authors and/or illustrators have more confidence in their own abilities to target and market work. Others are 'territorial' or prefer to work directly with the publishers. The best agent/client relationships exist when complete trust is established prior to representation. I recommend at least one (or several) consultations via phone or in person with a prospective agent. References are important. Also, the author or illustrator should have a clear idea of the agent's role i.e., editorial/critiquing input, 'post-publication' responsibilities, exclusive or non-exclusive representation, fees, industry reputation, etc. Each author or illustrator should examine his or her objectives, talents, time constraints, and perhaps more important, personal rapport with an individual agent prior to representation."

☑ ◪ **AMBER LITERARY**, 1956 Homestead Duquesne Rd., W. Mifflin PA 15122. (412)469-8293. E-mail: kathyo@amberliterary.com. Website: www.amberliterary.com. **Contact:** Jerome E. Laycak. Estab. 1999. Represents 3 clients. 75% of clients are new/unpublished writers. Currently handles: 5% nonfiction books; 5% juvenile books; 70% novels; 10% novellas; 10% poetry.

• Prior to becoming an agent, Mr. Laycak was a newspaper columnist, magazine staff editor and freelance writer.

Member Agents: Jerome Laycak (all areas); William Ray (mainstream fiction); Jeri Spang (poetry, scholarly books, history); Beverly Browe (romance); Elizabeth G. Crowe (romance); Kathleen O'Malley (acquisition editor).

Represents: Nonfiction books, juvenile books, scholarly books, novels, novellas, poetry books, short story collections. **Considers these nonfiction areas:** anthropology/archaeology; art/architecture/design; biography/autobiography; child guidance/parenting; computers/electronics; current affairs; education; government/politics/law; history; how-to; humor; juvenile nonfiction; military/war; music/dance/theater/film; psychology; religious/inspirational; sociology; true crime/investigative; women's issues/women's studies. **Considers these fiction areas:** action/adventure; contemporary issues; detective/police/crime; family saga; fantasy; historical; horror; humor/satire; juvenile; literary; mainstream; mystery; romance; religious/inspirational; science fiction; thriller/espionage; westerns/frontier; young adult.

➜ Actively seeking all types of mainstream fiction. Does not want to receive movies, TV, scripts, erotica or pornography.

How to Contact: Query with SASE or e-mail synopsis. Accepts queries by e-mail. Does not accept queries by fax. Considers simultaneous queries and submissions. Responds in 2 weeks. Returns materials only with SASE. Obtains most new clients through submissions.

Recent Sales: Sold 4 titles in the last year. *State of the Union*, by Tom Colarossi (Den Mark); *Michael Patrick*, by Victoria Thompson (Steele Press). Clients include Thomas Rohosky, Jarrod Davis, Linda S. Bingham.

Terms: Agent receives 15% commission on domestic sales; 20% on foreign sales. Offers written contract. 30-day notice must be given to terminate contract. Charges clients $10 office handling fee. Charges $50 server fee to post ms on website.

Tips: "Clarity in synopsis is important. Many first-time writers have excellent story lines but are weak in sentence structure and basic grammar."

◪ **THE AUTHOR'S AGENCY**, P.O. Box 16590, Boise ID 83715-6590. (208)376-5477. E-mail: rjwinchell@aol.com. **Contact:** R.J. Winchell. Estab. 1995. Represents 40 clients. 35% of clients are new/previously unpublished writers. Currently handles: 50% nonfiction books; 50% novels.

• Prior to opening her agency, Ms. Winchell taught writing and wrote book reviews. Ms. Winchell is a summa cum laude graduate of Pacific Lutheran University and a nationally publisher writer.

Represents: Nonfiction books, novels, movie scripts, TV scripts. **Considers these nonfiction areas:** animals; anthropology/archaeology; biography/autobiography; business; child guidance/parenting; cooking/food/nutrition; crafts/hobbies; current affairs; education; ethnic/cultural interests; government/politics/law; health/medicine; history; how-to; humor; interior design/decorating; language/literature/criticism; memoirs; military/war; money/finance/economics; music/dance/theater/film; nature/environment; New Age/metaphysics; photography; popular culture; psychology; religious/inspirational; science/technology; self-help/personal improvement; sociology; sports; translations; travel; true crime/investigative; women's issues/women's studies. **Considers "any fiction supported by the author's endeavor to tell a story with excellent writing."**

➜ "We specialize in high concepts which have a dramatic impact."

Also Handles: Feature film, animation, TV MOW, miniseries, episodic drama, animation. **Considers all script subject areas.** "We represent very few scripts but we are open to them."

How to Contact: Query or send 3 chapters with SASE. Accepts queries by e-mail. "But, they must be to the point." Considers simultaneous queries and submissions. Responds in 6 weeks. Returns materials only with SASE. Obtains most new clients through "speaking engagements and referrals such as this book."

Recent Sales: *"What If Our World Is Their Heaven?" conversations with Philip K. Dick* (Overlook Press); Johnny Rutherford autobiography, by Johnny Rutherford with David Craft (Triumph Books).

Terms: Agent receives 15% commission on domestic sales; 15% on foreign sales. Offers written contract on project-by-project basis.

Fees: Occasionally provides an editing service, charges $450 *minimum* for service. Editing service does not ensure representation. "No reading fee, ever." Charges clients for expenses (photocopying, etc.). 90% of business is derived from commissions on sales.

Tips: "We obtain writers through speaking engagements, and referrals such as this book. We believe writers make a valuable contribution to society. As such, we offer encouragement and support to writers, whether we represent them or not. Publishing continues to be competitive industry. Writers need not only talent but patience with the process in order to see their work in print."

✔ ◎ **ELIZABETH H. BACKMAN**, P.O. Box 762, 86 Johnnycake Hollow Rd., Pine Plains NY 12567. (518)398-9344. Fax: (518)398-6368. E-mail: bethcountry@idsi.net. **Contact:** Elizabeth H. Backman. Also: 60 Sutton Place S., New York NY 10022. Estab 1981. Represents 50 clients. Currently handles: 33-60% nonfiction books; 40% fiction.

Represents: Nonfiction, novels. **Considers these nonfiction areas:** biography/memoirs; business; child guidance/parenting; cooking/food/nutrition; sports; current affairs; dance; ethnic/cultural interests; government/politics/law; health/medicine; history; photography; pop science; psychology; inspirational; self-help/personal improvement; sports; women's issues/women's studies. **Considers these fiction areas:** ethnic; fantasy; historical; mystery/suspense; regional; science fiction; thriller/espionage; men's adventure and suspense; women's contemporary fiction.

➙ This agency specializes in nonfiction, women's interest and positive motivation.

How to Contact: Query with sample ms and SASE. Responds in 6 weeks to queries and mss.

Recent Sales: *Stress for Success*, by James Loehr; *Digital Hood & Other Stories*, by Peter Rondinone (Picador).

Terms: Agent receives 15% commission on domestic sales; commission between 10-20% on foreign sales. Offers written contract on request, binding for 1-3 years.

Fees: Charges $50 reading fee for proposal/3 sample chapters, $100 for complete ms. Offers criticism service. Charges clients for photocopying, postage, telephone, fax, typing, editing, special services.

Writers' Conference: International Women's Writing Guild conferences.

Tips: Obtains new clients through referrals from other editors. "I help writers prepare their proposals in best possible shape so they can get best possible deal with publisher. May not be the highest advance but best overall deal."

◎ **JOSEPH A. BARANSKI LITERARY AGENCY**, 214 North 2100 Rd., Lecompton KS 66050. (785)887-6010. Fax: (785)887-6263. **Contact:** D.A. Baranski. Estab. 1975. Represents over 50 clients. Currently handles 25% nonfiction books; 15% movie scripts; 50% novels; 5% TV scripts; 2% syndicated material; 2% textbooks; 1% stage plays.

• Prior to becoming an agent, Mr. Baranski was a lawyer.

Represents: Nonfiction, novels, scripts, textbooks, plays.

➙ "We handle both film and publishing clients."

How to Contact: Query with SASE. Responds in 2 weeks to queries. Obtains most new clients through recommendations from others. Prefers to work with established writers.

Recent Sales: This agency prefers not to share information on specific sales.

Terms: Agent receives 10% commission on domestic sales; 20% on foreign sales. Offers written contract, binding for 1 year with options. 30-day notice must be given to terminate contract.

Fees: "Writers without recommendation or substantial previous sales shall be assessed a $100 fee to consider completed manuscript. Nonreturnable. No guarantee." Payment of reading fee does not ensure representation.

Tips: "Be careful. The sharks are always cruising."

⦿ ◎ **BAWN PUBLISHERS INC.—LITERARY AGENCY**, 2515 Losantiville Ave., Cincinnati OH 45237. (513)841-9664. Fax: (513)841-9667. E-mail: bawn@compuserve.com. Website: www.BawnAgency.com. **Contact:** Willie E. Nason or Beverly A. Nason. Estab. 1994. Represents 75 clients. 50% of clients are new/unpublished writers. Currently handles: 40% nonfiction books; 30% movie scripts; 30% novels.

• Prior to opening his agency, Mr. Nason was a screenwriting consultant for several major producers for over 15 years in Los Angeles.

Member Agents: Willie E. Nason (nonfiction, scripts); Beverly A. Nason (literary/fiction-nonfiction); Lishawn Scott (literary fiction).

Represents: Nonfiction books, movie scripts, scholarly books, novels, textbooks, novellas. **Considers these nonfiction areas:** agriculture; anthropology/archaeology; biography/autobiography; business; computers/electronics; cooking/food/

CHECK THE AGENT SPECIALTIES INDEX to find agents who are interested in your specific nonfiction or fiction subject area.

nutrition; current affairs; education; ethnic/cultural interests; gay/lesbian issues; government/politics/law; health/medicine; history; how-to; humor; language/literature/criticism; military/war; money/finance/economics; music/dance/theater/film; New Age/metaphysics; popular crime; psychology; religious/inspirational; science/technology; self-help/personal improvement; sociology; sports; translations; true crime/investigative; women's issues/women's studies. **Considers these fiction areas:** action/adventure; confessional; contemporary issues; detective/police/crime; erotica; ethnic; experimental; family saga; fantasy; feminist; gay/lesbian; historical; horror; humor/satire; literary; mainstream; mystery (amateur sleuth, malice domestic); psychic/supernatural; religious/inspirational; romance (contemporary, gothic, historical, regency); science fiction; suspense; thriller/espionage; young adult.

O→ BAWN is the only US literary agency which translates languages in French, Spanish, Italian, German, Portuguese, Chinese, Japanese, Russian and several other foreign languages. Does not want to receive poetry, children's books, picture books.

Also Handles: Feature film, episodic drama, TV MOW. **Considers these script areas:** action/adventure; comedy; detective/police/crime; erotica; ethnic; family saga; fantasy; horror; mystery/suspense; romance (comedy, drama); science fiction; thriller.

How to Contact: Query with outline/proposal and SASE. Responds in 1 month to queries; 3 months to mss. Obtains most new clients through website, referrals.

Recent Sales: Sold 10 titles in the last year. *Unemployment in the New Millenium*, by Anthony Stith (Warwick Publishing); *More Than They Promised*, by Thomas A. Boswall (Stanford University Press); *Movie Script(s) optioned sold: Coal of the Heart*, by George Foster (Skylark Films); *Different Words*, by Kenneth Hawsen (CPC Entertainment).

Terms: Agent receives 15% commission on domestic sales; 20% on foreign sales. Offers written contract, binding for 1 year. 90-day notice must be given to terminate contract.

Fees: Offers criticism service, fee negotiable. Payment of criticism fee ensures representation.

Tips: "Always follow the instructions given or required by the agency. Do not assume they will want to review your manuscript, if they say they do not want certain types of work. When you sign with any agency, patience is very important. It isn't easy. If you can't be patient, find a new hobby."

N $ ✒ BETHEL AGENCY, 311 W. 43rd St., Suite 602, New York NY 10036. (212)664-0455. **Contact:** Lewis R. Chambers. Estab. 1967. Represents 25+ clients.

Represents: Fiction, nonfiction. **Considers these nonfiction areas:** agriculture/horticulture; animals; anthropology/archaeology; art/archirecture/design; biography/autobiography; business; child guidance/parenting; cooking/food/nutrition; crafts/hobbies; current affairs; ethnic/cultural interests; gay/lesbian issues; government/politics/law; health/medicine; history; interior design/decorating; juvenile nonfiction; language/literature/criticism; military/war; money/finance/economics; music/dance/theater/film; nature/environment; photography; psychology; religious/inspirational; science/technology; self-help/personal improvement; sociology; sports; translations; true crime/investigative; women's issues/women's studies. **Considers these fiction areas:** action/adventure; confessional; contemporary issues; detective/police/crime; ethnic; family saga; fantasy; feminist; gay; glitz; historical; humor/satire; juvenile; lesbian; literary; mainstream; mystery/suspense; picture book; psychic/supernatural; regional; religious/inspiration; romance (contemporary, gothic, historical, regency); sports; teen; thriller/espionage; westerns/frontier.

How to Contact: Query with outline plus 1 sample chapter and SASE. Responds in 2 months to queries. Obtains new clients through recommendations from others.

Recent Sales: *The Viper Quarry* (nominated for an Edgar); *Pitchfork Hollow*, both by Dean Feldmeyer (Pocket Books); *Hamburger Heaven*, by Jeffrey Tennyson (Hyperion); *Words Can Tell*, by Christina Ashton.

Terms: Agent receives 15% commission on domestic sales; 20% on foreign sales. Offers written contract, binding for 6-12 months.

Fees: Charges reading fee only to unpublished authors; writer will be contacted on fee amount.

✒ ◎ JIM BUCHAN LITERARY SERVICE, (Specialized: religious/Christian), 1422 Longleaf Ct., Matthews NC 28104. (704)708-8151. Fax: (704)708-8155. E-mail: buchanj@aol.com. Website: www.crosslinknet.org. **Contact:** Jim Buchan. Estab. 1998. Represents 15 clients. 90% of clients are new/previously unpublished writers. Currently handles: 10% nonfiction books; 20% juvenile books; 60% novels; 10% textbooks.

● Prior to becoming an agent, Mr. Buchan was an attorney, a pastor, and an editor at *Ministries Today* magazine.

Represents: Nonfiction books, juvenile books, novels. **Considers these nonfiction areas:** biography/autobiography; business; child guidance/parenting; cooking/food/nutrition; current affairs; government/politics/law; health/medicine; history; how-to; humor; music/dance/theater film; religious/inspirational; self-help/personal improvement; sports; leadership topics. **Considers these fiction areas:** action/adventure; cartoon/comic; family saga; fantasy; historical; humor/satire; juvenile; mystery; picture book; religious/inspirational; science fiction; sports; thriller/espionage; young adult.

O→ This agency specializes in books for the Christian market but covers a variety of genres: fiction, nonfiction, children's books, science fiction, devotional materials, etc.

How to Contact: Send entire ms or outline/proposal. Accepts queries by fax and e-mail. Considers simultaneous queries and submissions. Responds in 2 months to queries. Returns material only with SASE. Obtains most new clients through recommendations from other authors and at conferences.

Recent Sales: Sold 1 title in the last year. Prefers not to share information on specific sales.

Terms: Agent receives 20% commission on domestic sales; 25% on foreign sales. Offers written contract, binding for 9 months. 1-month notice must be given to terminate contract.

Fees: Charges $75 for ms evaluation, "refundable if I agree to represent the author. Fee applies to all authors." Charges $75 critique fee. Critique deals with writing style, marketability, etc. and is done by Jim Buchan. 5% of business is derived from reading fees or criticism service. Payment of reading or critique fees does not ensure representation. Charges clients for postage, photocopying and other directly related expenses.

Tips: "We have provided free initial phone consultation for many first-time authors."

◑ THE CATALOG™ LITERARY AGENCY, P.O. Box 2964, Vancouver WA 98668-2964. Phone/fax: (360)694-8531. Contact: Douglas Storey. Estab. 1986. Represents 30 clients. 50% of clients are new/previously unpublished writers. Currently handles: 60% nonfiction books; 20% juvenile books; 20% novels.

● Prior to opening his agency, Mr. Storey was a business planner—"especially for new products." He has Masters degrees in both business and science.

Represents: Nonfiction books, juvenile books, novels. **Considers these nonfiction areas:** agriculture/horticulture; animals; anthropology/archaeology; biography/autobiography; business; child guidance/parenting; computers/electronics; cooking/food/nutrition; crafts/hobbies; education; ethnic/cultural interests; health/medicine; history; how-to; juvenile nonfiction; military/war; money/finance/economics; nature/environment; photography; popular culture; psychology; science/technology; self-help/personal improvement; sociology; sports; women's issues/women's studies. **Considers these fiction areas:** action/adventure; family saga; horror; juvenile; literary; mainstream; romance; thriller/espionage; young adult.

    ○┰ This agency specializes in business, health, psychology, money, science, how-to, self-help, technology, parenting, women's interest. Does not want to receive poetry, short stories or religious works.

How to Contact: Query with SASE. Accepts queries by fax; no e-mail queries. Considers simultaneous queries and submissions. Responds in 2 weeks to queries; 3 weeks to mss. Returns materials only with SASE. Obtains most new clients through recommendations from others, queries.

Recent Sales: Sold 1 title in the last year. *The Simplified Classroom Aquarium*, by Ed Stansbury (Charles C. Thomas, Publisher); *Seven Story Tower*, by Hoffman (Plenum Publishing). Clients include Martin Pall, Ken Boggs, Ken Hutchins and Bruce Dierenfield.

Terms: Agent receives 15% on domestic sales; 20% on foreign sales. Offers written contract, binding for about 9 months.

Fees: Does not charge a reading fee. Charges an upfront handling fee from $85-250 that covers photocopying, telephone and postage expense.

🔳 ◉ COLLIER ASSOCIATES, P.O. Box 20149, W. Palm Beach FL 33416-1361. (561)697-3541. Fax: (561)478-4316. Contact: Dianna Collier. Estab. 1976. Member of MWA. Represents over 200 clients. 20% of clients are new/previously unpublished writers. Currently handles: 50% nonfiction books; 50% novels.

Member Agents: Dianna Collier (food, history, self help, women's issues, most fiction, especially mystery, romance); Bill Vassilopoulos (financial, biography, autobiography, most fiction especially mystery).

Represents: Nonfiction, novels. **Considers these nonfiction areas:** biography/autobiography of well-known people; exposés; business and investment books for general audience; cooking/food/nutrition (by prominent people/chefs); crafts/hobbies; popular works of political subjects and history; popular reference; how-to; self-help/personal improvement; true crime/investigative; women's issues/women's studies. **Considers these fiction areas:** action/adventure; detective/police/crime; historical; mainstream; mystery/suspense; romance (contemporary, historical); thriller/espionage.

    ○┰ This agency specializes in "adult fiction and nonfiction books directed at general audience, and novelization rights to screenplays under contract to producers only. This is a small agency that rarely takes on new clients because of the many authors it represents already. We do not handle textbooks, plays, screenplays, children's books, novelties, cartoon books, Star Trek novels, books of trivia, newspaper columns, articles, short stories, novellas, pamphlets nor pornography."

How to Contact: Query with SASE. Does not accept queries by e-mail or fax. Prefers to read materials exclusively. Responds in 2 months to queries; 4 months "or longer" to mss. Rejection may be much quicker Obtains most new clients through recommendations from others.

Recent Sales: This agency prefers not to share information on specific sales.

Terms: Agent receives 15% commission on domestic sales; 20% on foreign sales and dramatic rights. Offers written contract.

Fees: Charges $75 reading fee for unpublished trade book authors. "Reserves the right to charge a reading fee on manuscripts submitted by unpublished authors." Charges clients for mailing expenses, photocopying and express mail, "if requested, with author's consent, and for copies of author's published books used for rights sales."

Writers' Conferences: BEA (Los Angeles, April); Florida Mystery Writers (Ft. Lauderdale, March); Key West Mystery Weekend (September).

Reading Lists: Reads *Business Week, Publishers Weekly, New York Times, Palm Beach Post, Food & Wine, Cooking Light, Travel & Leisure* and others to find new clients. "An article may spark an idea for a new project or may find a writer for an existing project."

Tips: "ALWAYS submit query first with description and biographical information. No telephone calls or unsolicited mss, please! For fiction, query first with outline, first three chapters or 50 pages. If you want material returned, send check or money order for exact amount of postage with word count and submission history. Same for nonfiction, though chapter selection can be random; include audience and how project is different from competition. Manuscript should be 12-point typeface, double-spaced, one and one-half-inch margins, edited and clean!"

◑ **CREATIVE LITERARY AGENCY**, P.O. Box 506, Birmingham MI 48009-0506. (248)932-0441. **Contact:** Michele Rooney. Represents 15 clients. 20% of clients are new/previously unpublished writers. Currently handles: 10% nonfiction books; 20% juvenile books; 5% scholarly books; 50% novels; 5% syndicated material; 5% textbooks; 5% poetry.

  • Prior to opening her agency, Ms. Rooney received a degree in journalism, worked as a newspaper reporter and editor, and was a book editor and editing consultant.

Represents: Nonfiction books, juvenile books, scholarly books, novels, textbooks, poetry books, short story collections. **Considers these nonfiction areas:** animals; art/architecture/design; biography/autobiography; business; child guidance/parenting; computers/electronics; cooking/food/nutrition; crafts/hobbies; current affairs; education; government/politics/law; health/medicine; history; how-to; humor; interior design/decorating; juvenile nonfiction; language/literature/criticism; memoirs; money/finance/economics; music/dance/theater/film; nature/environment; New Age/metaphysics; photography; popular culture; psychology; religious/inspirational; science/technology; self-help/personal improvement; sociology; sports; true crime/investigative; women's studies; travel. **Considers these fiction areas:** action/adventure; contemporary issues; detective/police/crime; family saga; fantasy; feminist; glitz; historical; horror; humor/satire; juvenile; literary; mainstream; mystery; psychic/supernatural; regional; romance; religious/inspirational; science fiction; sports; thriller/espionage; westerns/frontier; young adult.

  ⦿ Actively seeking travel books, cookbooks, fiction from promising new authors. Does not want to receive TV or movie scripts.

How to Contact: Query with SASE. Does not accept queries by fax or e-mail. Considers simultaneous queries. Responds in 2 weeks to queries; 6 weeks to mss. Returns materials only with SASE. Obtains most new clients through conferences, recommendations, query letters.

Recent Sales: *A New Day Dawning*, by Julie Burg (Electric Works); *Baby Milton Detective*, by Mary Ellen (Scholastic).

Terms: Agent receives 10% commission on domestic sales; 15% on foreign sales. Offers written contract, binding for 60 days.

Fees: "We have an annual marketing fee of $300 for representing book length projects. There's no reading or critiquing fee."

Tips: "You can't succeed unless you try. Your manuscript will never sell if you leave it in a drawer gathering dust. Seize the day and begin the important work of marketing your ms today! The internet and electronic publishing are creating new publishing opportunities daily. There has never been a better time to be a writer."

◐ **CS INTERNATIONAL LITERARY AGENCY**, 43 W. 39th St., New York NY 10018-3811. (212)921-1610. E-mail: csliterary@aol.com. **Contact:** Cynthia Neesemann. Estab. 1996. Represents 25 clients. Currently handles: 33% nonfiction books; 33% movie and TV scripts; 33% novels.

  • Prior to opening her agency, Ms. Neesemann worked with another literary agency and also as a real estate broker—residential and commercial—and a foreign correspondent.

Represents: Nonfiction books, juvenile books, novels. **Considers all nonfiction areas. Considers all fiction areas.** "Must see queries to decide on subjects."

  ⦿ This agency specializes in full-length fiction, nonfiction, and screenplays (no pornography). "We prefer feature film scripts. Clients think we give very good critiques."

Also Handles: Feature film, TV MOW, sitcom, animation, documentary. **Considers these script areas:** action/adventure; cartoon/animation; comedy; contemporary issues; detective/police/crime; ethnic; family saga; fantasy; feminist; historical; juvenile; mainstream; mystery/suspense; psychic/supernatural; religious/inspirational; romance (comedy, drama); science fiction; sports; thriller; westerns/frontier. "Must see queries to decide on all subjects."

How to Contact: Query with SASE. Accepts queries by e-mail. Considers simultaneous queries. Responds in 2 weeks to queries; 3 weeks to mss. Returns materials only with SASE. Obtains most new clients through recommendations, solicitation and at conferences.

Recent Sales: This agency prefers not to share information on specific sales.

Terms: Agent receives 10-15% commission on domestic sales; variable percentage on foreign sales. Sometimes offers written contract.

Fees: Charges reading fee for unestablished writers. Offers criticism service for varied fees. Fee depends upon length of manuscript. Average fee is $75 for each 100 pages submitted (partial mss considered). "We usually read and write critiques of one or two pages in length. Fee for average length screenplay is $75." Critique may be done through a written letter or through a phone conversation. Payment of critique fee does not ensure representation. Charges for marketing, office expenses, long distance phone calls, postage and photocopying depending on amount of work involved.

Tips: "Professional but friendly, we are interested in helping beginning writers to improve their writing skills and style with suggestions for better plotting and structure where needed. Manuscript analysis and evaluation of nonfiction, fiction, screennplays, and plays as well as research available for a reasonable fee."

🅽 ◯ **JOËLLE DELBOUNGO ASSOCIATES, INC.**, 450 Seventy Ave., Suite 3004, New York NY 10123. (212)279-9027. Fax: (212)279-8863. E-mail: jdelboungo.com. **Contact:** Joëlle Delboungo. Estab. 1999. Represents 15 clients; 35% of clients are new/previously unpublished writers. Currently handles: 50% nonfiction books; 45% novels; 5% short story collections.

  • Prior to becoming an agent, Ms. Delboungo was an editor and publishing executive for over 25 years, most recently as Senior VP and Editor-in-Chief at HarperCollins.

Member Agents: Joëlle Delboungo (serious and commercial nonfiction, history, psychology, medicine, health, politics, science, literary fiction); Jessica Lichtenstein (commercial fiction, thrillers, romance, mysteries).

Represents: Nonfiction, novels, short story collections. **Considers these nonfiction areas:** animals; anthropology/archaeology; biography/autobiography; business; child guidance/parenting; cooking/food/nutrition; current affairs; education; ethnic/cultural interests; government/politics/law; health/medicine; history; how-to; humor; interior design/decorating; language/literature/criticism; memoirs; military/war; money/finance/economics; multicultural; music/dance/theater/film; nature/environment; New Age/metaphysics; photography; popular culture; psychology; religious/inspirational; science/technology; self-help/personal improvement; sociology; sports; travel; true crime/investigative; women's issues/women's studies. **Considers these fiction areas:** contemporary issues; detective/police/crime; family saga; historical; literary; mainstream; multicultural; mystery/suspense; thriller/espionage.

> **O—** "We are a quality agency as opposed to volume of work. Our long-term editorial and publishing expertise makes us distinct. I have 25 years 'insider' experience. I know what publishers want and I'm also an expert marketer who works with authors to develop their platforms." Actively seeking narrative nonfiction, history, serious works, literary fiction. Does not want to receive genre fiction or light humor.

How to Contact: Query with SASE or send outline and 2 sample chapters. Accepts queries by e-mail and fax. Considers simultaneous queries. Prefers to read mss exclusively. Responds in 3 weeks on queries; 1 month on mss. Returns materials only with SASE. Obtains most new clients through recommendations from others, solicitations of authors.

Recent Sales: Sold 8 titles in the last 8 months. *Moon Women*, by Pamela Duncan (Bantam Dell); *The Speed of Light*, by Elizabeth Rosney (Ballentine); *When Someone You Love Needs Nursing Care*, by Robert Bornstein and Mary Langurrand (New Market Press); *The Cosmos without Him*, by Harold Bloomfield (Hampton Road). Other clients include Gay Courter, Richard de Combrah, Noah Ben Shea, Laura Berman, John Culhane.

Terms: Agent receives 15% commission on domestic sales; 20% on foreign sales. Offers written contract.

Fees: Offers editing service for $50/hour on selected projects for agency clients and serious prospective clients.

◐ ◎ THE WILSON DEVEREUX COMPANY, (Specialized: science), P.O. Box 3517, 915 Bay Ridge Ave. Annapolis MD 21403. (410)263-0880. Fax: (410)263-1479. E-mail: bdb4@wildev.com. Website: www.wildev.com. **Contact:** B.D. Barker. Represents 25 clients. 10% of clients are new/unpublished writers. Currently handles: 95% nonfiction books, 5% scholarly books.

> • Prior to becoming an agent, B.D. Barker was a senior financial professional.

Represents: Nonfiction books. **Considers these nonfiction areas:** biography/autobiography; how-to; science/technology.

> **O—** This agency specializes in popular trade science books and the "For Dummies" line published by IDG Books Worldwide. Actively seeking science writers, proposals for trade science books, "For Dummies" proposals in math, science, history, hobbies. Does not want to receive fiction, religious material or children's books.

How to Contact: Query with SASE. Accepts queries by e-mail. Considers simultaneous queries. Responds in 1 week to queries; 6 weeks to mss. Returns materials only with SASE. "Rapid response to queries by e-mail." Obtains most new clients through referrals (from current clients), website, conferences.

Recent Sales: This agency prefers not to share information on specific sales.

Terms: Agent receives 15% commission on domestic sales; 15% on foreign sales. Offers written contract.

Fees: Charges for direct expenses with a limit of $500.

[N] [$] ◐ FRIEDA FISHBEIN ASSOCIATES, P.O. Box 723, Bedford NY 10506. (914)234-7232. **Contact:** Heidi Carlson. Estab. 1928. Represents 18 clients. 40% of clients are new/previously unpublished writers. Currently handles: 20% novels; 20% movie scripts; 60% stage plays.

Member Agents: Heidi Carlson (literary and contemporary); Douglas Michael (play and screenplay scripts); Janice Fishbein (consultant).

Represents: Novels, comic books. **Considers these fiction areas:** action/adventure; contemporary issues; detective/police/crime; family saga; fantasy; feminist; historical; humor/satire; mainstream; mystery/suspense; romance (contemporary, historical, regency); science fiction; thriller/espionage; young adult.

> **O—** Actively seeking playwrights. "Particularly new and unproduced playwrights or writers from another medium adapting their work for stage or screen." Does not want to receive young adult, poetry, memoirs or New Age.

Also Handles: Movie scripts, stage plays.

How to Contact: Query letter a must before sending ms, including SASE. Responds in 2 months to queries; 2 months to mss accepted for evaluation. Obtains most new clients through recommendations from others.

Recent Sales: Sold 17 titles in the last year. *Last Wish Baby*, by Wm. Seebring (Applause Theatre Books); *Detail of A Larger Work*, by Lisa Dillman (Smith & Krause); *Two and a Half Jews*, by Alan Brandt (Production).

Terms: Agent receives 10% commission on domestic sales; 15% on foreign sales. Offers written contract, binding for 30 days, cancellable by either party, except for properties being marketed or already sold.

Fees: No fee for reading. Critique service available. Charges for critique: $80 plus $1/1,000 words after 50,000 words. "We hire readers and pay them 80% of our fee. This service is offered but rarely suggested. However, some writers want a reading critique, and we try to ensure they get a good one at a fair price. Sometimes specific staff readers may refer to associates for no charge for additional readings if warranted." Charges marketing fees. "New writers pay most costs associated with marketing their work. Specific amount agreed upon based on the scope of the sales effort and refunded upon sale or significant production."

Tips: "*Always* submit a query letter first with an SASE. Manuscripts should be done in large type, double-spaced and one and one-half-inch margins, clean copy and edited for typos, etc."

FRAN LITERARY AGENCY, 7235 Split Creek, San Antonio TX 78238-3627. (210)684-1659. **Contacts:** Fran Rathmann, Kathy Kenney. Estab. 1993. Signatory of WGA and member of ASCAP. Represents 25 clients. 60% of clients are new/previously unpublished writers. Currently handles: 15% nonfiction books; 15% juvenile books; 40% novels; 5% novellas; 5% poetry books; 20% teleplays/screenplays.
Represents: Nonfiction and fiction. **Considers these nonfiction areas:** agriculture/horticulture; animals; anthropology/archaeology; art/architecture/design; biography/autobiography; business; child guidance/parenting; cooking/food/nutrition; crafts/hobbies; current affairs; education; ethnic/cultural interests; government/politics/law; health/medicine; history; how-to; humor; interior design/decorating; juvenile nonfiction; memoirs; music/dance/theater/film; military/war; nature/environment; religious/inspirational; self-help/personal improvement; sports; true crime/investigative; women's issues/women's studies. **Considers these fiction areas:** action/adventure; cartoon/comic; contemporary issues; detective/police/crime; family saga; fantasy; glitz; historical; horror; humor/satire; juvenile; literary; mainstream; mystery/suspense; picture book; regional; religious/inspirational; romance (gothic, regency); science fiction; sports; thriller/espionage; westerns/frontier; young adult.

O── "This agency is very interested in *Star Trek* novels. If you write for *Star Trek*, please follow the Pocket Books guidelines on the Internet."

Also Handles: Feature film, documentary, animation, TV MOW, sitcom, miniseries, syndicated material, animation, episodic drama. **Considers these script subject areas:** action/adventure; cartoon/animation; comedy; contemporary issues; detective/police/crime; ethnic; family saga; fantasy; historical; horror; humor; juvenile; mainstream; mystery/suspense; religious/inspirational; romantic comedy and drama; science fiction; sports; teen; thriller; westerns/frontier.
How to Contact: For books, send entire ms with SASE. For scripts, please query before sending ms. Considers simultaneous queries and submissions. Responds in 2 weeks to queries; 2 months to mss. "Please send SASE or Box!" Obtains most clients through referrals, yellow pages.
Recent Sales: Sold 15 titles and 4 script projects in the last year. *The Year the Oil Ended*, by Frederick Wilkins (Signet).
Terms: Agent receives 15% commission on domestic sales; 20% on foreign sales and performance sales. Needs "letter of agreement," usually binding for 2 years.
Fees: Charges $25 processing fee, credit after sale. Written criticism service $150, average 4 pages. "Critique includes corrections/comments/suggestions on mechanics, grammar, punctuation, plot, characterization, dialogue, marketability, etc." 90% of business is derived from commissions on mss sales. Payment of fee does not ensure representation.
Writers' Conferences: SAWG (San Antonio, spring).

$ ◯ **THE LAYA GELFF AGENCY**, 16133 Ventura Blvd., Suite 700, Encino CA 91436. (818)996-3100. Estab. 1985. Signatory of WGA. Represents many clients. Currently handles: 40% movie scripts; 40% TV scripts; 20% book mss.
  • See the expanded listing for this agency in Script Agents.

✓ $ ◯ **THE SEBASTIAN GIBSON AGENCY**, P.O. Box 13350, Palm Desert CA 92255-3350. (760)322-2446. Fax: (760)322-3857. E-mail: SGibsonEsq@aol.com. **Contact:** Sebastian Gibson. Estab. 1995. 100% of clients are new/previously unpublished writers.
Represents: Nonfiction books, novels. **Considers these nonfiction areas:** animals; anthropology/archaeology; biography/autobiography; business; cooking/food/nutrition; current affairs; government/politics/law; health/medicine; history; military/war; music/dance/theater/film; nature/environment; photography; popular culture; psychology; science/technology; sociology; sports; travel; true crime/investigative; women's issues/women's studies. **Considers these fiction areas:** action/adventure; contemporary issues; detective/police/crime; ethnic; experimental; family saga; glitz; historical; mainstream; regional; romance (contemporary, gothic, historical, regency); science fiction; sports; thriller/espionage.

O── This agency specializes in fiction. Actively seeking sports books, thrillers, contemporary fiction, detective/police/crime and psychological suspense, as well as business and financial books. Does not want to receive autobiographies, poetry, short stories, pornography.

How to Contact: Send outline, 3 sample chapters, "$10 bush-league, small-potato, hardly-worth-mentioning handling fee is requested as each year we receive more and more submissions and we wish to give each of them the time they

**FOR EXPLANATIONS OF THESE SYMBOLS,
SEE THE INSIDE FRONT AND BACK COVERS OF THIS BOOK**

deserve." SASE required for a response. No fax or e-mail queries. Considers simultaneous queries and submissions. Responds in 3 weeks. "Writers should not be overly demanding or with unrealistic time constraints." Returns materials only with SASE. Obtains most new clients through advertising, queries and book proposals, and through the representation of entertainment clients.

Recent Sales: This agency prefers not to share information on specific sales.

Terms: Agent receives 15% commission on domestic sales; 20% on foreign sales and film rights. Offers written contract, with 30 day cancellation notice. Charges clients for postage, photocopying and express mail fees charged only against sales. Authors are not charged upfront for these costs.

Writers' Conference: BEA (Chicago, June); Book Fair (Frankfurt); London International Book Fair (London).

Tips: "We look for manuscripts with fresh characters whose dialogue and pacing jump off the page. With the well-edited book that contains new and exciting story lines, and locations that grab at the imagination of the reader, we can see that you become a published author. No bribes necessary, just brilliant writing. We're also interested in nonfiction business and financial books, books for investors and books by industry leaders. Consider hiring a freelance editor to make corrections and assist you in preparing book proposals. Try to develop unusual characters in your novels, and novel approaches to nonfiction. Manuscripts should be clean and professional looking and without errors. Do not send unsolicited manuscripts or disks. Save your money and effort for redrafts. Don't give up. We want to help you become published. But your work must be very readable without plot problems or gramatical errors. Do not send sample chapters or book proposals until you've completed at least your fourth draft. Unless you're famous, don't send autobiographies. We are looking primarily for all categories of fiction with unusual characters, new settings and well-woven plots. Key tip: Make the first page count and your first three chapters your best chapters. An author should have something to say that either pulls on your emotions, or sparks you interest in such a way as to have a profound effect on the reader."

✔️ 🅞 **GLADDEN UNLIMITED**, 3808 Georgia St., #301, San Diego CA 92103. **Contact:** Carolan Gladden. Estab. 1987. Represents 30 clients. 95% of clients are new/previously unpublished writers. Currently handles: 5% nonfiction; 95% novels.

● Prior to becoming an agent Ms. Gladden worked as an editor, writer, and real estate and advertising agency representative.

Represents: Novels, nonfiction. **Considers these nonfiction areas:** celebrity biography; business; how-to; self-help; true crime/investigative. **Considers these fiction areas:** action/adventure; detective/police/crime; ethnic; glitz; horror; thriller.

○┐ Does not want to receive romance, mystery, children's or short fiction.

How to Contact: Query only with synopsis by mail with SASE. Responds in 2 weeks to queries; 2 months to mss.

Recent Sales: This agency prefers not to share information on specific sales.

Terms: Agent receives 10% commission on domestic sales; 20% on foreign sales.

Fees: Does not charge a reading fee. Charges clients refundable evaluation fee. Marketability evaluation: $100 (manuscript to 400 pages), $200 (over 400 pages). "Offers six to eight pages of diagnosis and specific recommendations to turn the project into a saleable commodity. Also includes a copy of the book *Be a Successful Writer*, dedicated to helping new authors learn skills necessary to achieve publication."

💲 🅞 **THE CHARLOTTE GUSAY LITERARY AGENCY**, 10532 Blythe, Los Angeles CA 90064-3312. (310)559-0831. E-mail: gusay1@aol.com. Website: www.mediastudio.com/gusay. **Contact:** Charlotte Gusay. Estab. 1988. Member of Authors Guild and PEN, signatory of WGA. Represents 30 clients. 50% of clients are new/previously unpublished writers.

● Prior to opening her agency, Ms. Gusay was a vice president for an audiocassette producer and also a bookstore owner.

Represents: Nonfiction books, scholarly books, juvenile books, travel books, novels. **Considers all nonfiction areas and most fiction areas.** No romance, short stories, science fiction or horror.

○┐ This agency specializes in fiction, nonfiction, children's (multicultural, nonsexist), children's illustrators, screenplays, books to film. Actively seeking "the next *English Patient*." Does not want to receive poetry, science fiction, horror.

Also Handles: Feature film. **Considers these script subject areas:** action/adventure; comedy; detective/police/crime; ethnic; experimental; family saga; feminist; gay/lesbian; historical; humor; mainstream; mystery/suspense; romantic (comedy, drama); sports; thriller; western/frontier.

How to Contact: SASE always required for response. "Queries only, *no* unsolicited manuscripts. Initial query should be 1- to 2-page synopsis with SASE." Responds in 6 weeks to queries; 10 weeks to mss; 10 weeks to scripts. Obtains most new clients through referrals and queries.

Recent Sales: *Bye-Bye*, by Jane Ransom (Pocket Books/Simon & Schuster); *Loteria and Other Stories*, by Ruben Mendoza (St. Martin's Press); *Ten Pearls of Wisdom*, by Eleanor Jacobs (Kadansha); *A Place Called Waco: A Survivor's Story*, by David Thibodeau and Leon Whiteson (Public Affairs/Perseus Book Group/film rights optioned by SRG Productions for Fox Television); *Imperial Mongolian Cooking: Recipes from the Kingdoms of the Genghis Khan*, by Marc Cramer (Hippocrene Books); *Love, Groucho: Letters from Groucho Marx to His Daughter Miriam*, edited by Miriam Marx Allen (previously published by Faber & Faber Publishers/film rights optioned by SRG Productions for CBS Television); *Changing the Rules: A Corporate Woman Inside the Playboy Empire*, by Stephanie Wells-Walper (optioned by SRG Productions); *Ishi's Journey* (optioned by Moll/Beallor/SKG Dreamworks).

Terms: Agent receives 15% commission on domestic sales; 10% on dramatic sales; 25% on foreign sales. Offers written contract, binding for "usually 1 year." Shares out-of-pocket expenses such as long distance phone calls, fax, express mail, postage, etc.

Fees: Charges $35 processing fee to certain writers.

Writers' Conferences: Writers Connection (San Jose, CA); Scriptwriters Connection (Studio City, CA); National Women's Book Association (Los Angeles), California Writers Conference (Monterey, CA), San Diego Writers Conference, Maui Writers Conference.

Tips: "Please be professional."

$ ☻ HARTLINE LITERARY AGENCY, 123 Queenston Dr., Pittsburgh PA 15235-5429. (412)829-2495 or 2483. Fax: (412)829-2450. E-mail: jachart@aol.com. Website: www.hartlinemarketing.com/. **Contact:** Joyce A. Hart. Estab. 1990. Represents 7 clients. 30% of clients are new/previously unpublished writers. Currently handles: 40% nonfiction books; 60% novels.

Member Agents: Joyce A. Hart (adult/fiction); Mary Busha (adult/fiction).

Represents: Nonfiction books, novels. **Considers these nonfiction subject areas:** business; child guidance/parenting; cooking/food/nutrition; money/finance/economics; religious/inspirational; self-help/personal improvement; women's issues. **Considers these fiction subject areas:** action/adventure; contemporary issues; family saga; historical; literary; mystery (amateur sleuth, cozy); regional; religious/inspirational; romance (contemporary, gothic, historical, regency); thriller/espionage.

    ☛ This agency specializes in the Christian bookseller market. Actively seeking adult fiction, self-help, nutritional books, devotional, business. Does not want to receive science fiction, erotica, gay and lesbian, fantasy, horror, etc.

How to Contact: Send outline and 3 sample chapters. Accepts queries by fax or e-mail. Considers simultaneous queries and submissions. Responds in 1 month to queries; 2 months to mss. Returns materials only with SASE. Obtains most new clients through recommendations from others.

Recent Sales: Sold 5 titles in the last year. *Men Are Clams, Women are Crow Bars*, by Dr. David Clarke (Promise Press); *No Eye Can See*, by Jane Kirkpatrick (Waterbrooke); *Little White Lies*, by Ron and Janet Benrey (Broadman & Halman).

Terms: Agent receives 15% commission on domestic sales. Offers written contract.

Fees: Offers criticism service to freelance editor for first-time writers. Charges $20-25/hour. 10% of business is derived from criticism service. Payment of criticism fee does not ensure representation. Charges clients for photocopying and postage.

$ ☻ THE EDDY HOWARD AGENCY, % 732 Coral Ave., Lakewood NJ 08701. (732)942-1023. **Contact:** Eddy Howard Pevovar, N.D., Ph.D. Estab. 1986. Member of Author's Guild. Represents 20 clients. 10% of clients are new/previously unpublished writers. Currently handles: 15% nonfiction books; 15% scholarly books; 15% juvenile books; 15% novels; 20% stage plays; 15% short story collections; 1% syndicated material; 4% other.

Member Agents: Eddy Howard Pevovar, N.D., Ph.D. (agency executive), Francine Gales (director of comedy development); Tracey Jones (agent).

Represents: Nonfiction books, scholarly books, textbooks, juvenile books, novels, novellas, short story collections, stage plays, syndicated material. **Considers these nonfiction areas:** art/architecture; biography/autobiography; business; child guidance/parenting; computers/electronics; government/politics/law; history; how-to; language/literature/criticism; sociology; educational books (math, science, history, geology and the arts). **Considers these fiction areas:** cartoon/comic; contemporary issues; family saga; historical; fantasy; humor/satire; juvenile; literary; mainstream; picture book; regional; sports.

    ☛ This agency specializes in film, sitcom and literary works.

How to Contact: Query with outline and letter—include phone number. Prefers to be only reader. Responds in 5 days to queries; up to 1 month to mss. Returns materials only with SASE. Obtains most new clients through recommendations from others and by submissions.

Recent Sales: Sold 9 book titles in the last year. Prefers not to share information on specific sales.

Terms: Agent receives 10% commission on domestic sales; 15% on foreign sales. Offers written contract.

Fees: No reading fees. Offers criticism service: corrective—style, grammar, punctuation, spelling, format. Technical critical evaluation with fee (saleability, timeliness, accuracy). Offers complete editorial and research services now. "We can also offer ghostwriting services."

Writers' Conferences: Instructor—Writers Workshops at Brookdale College; Community Education Division; Barnes & Noble Bookstores (1 night seminars).

Tips: "I was rejected 12 times before I ever had my first book published and I was rejected 34 times before my first magazine article was published. Stick to what you believe in. . . . Don't give up! Never give up! Take constructive criticism for whatever it's worth and keep yourself focused. Each rejection a beginner receives is one step closer to the grand finale—acceptance. It's sometimes good to get your manuscript peer reviewed. I think it's a great idea to hire an editor and have them correct your manuscript if you're a new author, or if you've written something technical or even historical. I personally use media services for my work. This is one way to obtain objective analysis of your work, and see what others think about it. Remember, if it weren't for new writers . . . there'd be *no* writers."

Ø INDEPENDENT PUBLISHING AGENCY: A LITERARY AND ENTERTAINMENT AGENCY, P.O. Box 176, Southport CT 06490-0176. Phone/fax: (203)332-7629. E-mail: henryberry@aol.com. **Contact:** Henry Berry. Estab. 1990. Represents 40 clients. 50% of clients are new/previously unpublished writers. Currently handles: 70% nonfiction books; 10% juvenile books; 20% novels and short story collections.

• Prior to opening his agency, Mr. Berry was a book reviewer, writing instructor, publishing consultant. Mr. Cherici has more than 10 years experience as an independent publisher, publishing consultant, agent.

Represents: Nonfiction books, juvenile books, novels, short story collections. **Considers these nonfiction areas:** anthropology/archaeology; art/architecture/design; biography/autobiography; business; child guidance/parenting; cooking/food/nutrition; crafts/hobbies; current affairs; ethnic/cultural interests; government/politics/law; history; juvenile nonfiction; language/literature/criticism; military/war; money/finance/economics; music/dance/theater/film; nature/environment; photography; popular culture; psychology; religious; science/technology; self-help/personal improvement; sociology; sports; true crime/investigative; women's issues/women's studies. **Considers these fiction areas:** action/adventure; cartoon/comic; confessional; contemporary issues; crime; erotica; ethnic; experimental; fantasy; feminist; historical; humor/satire; juvenile; literary; mainstream; mystery/suspense; picture book; psychic/supernatural; thriller/espionage; young adult.

○➤ This agency is especially interested in topical nonfiction (historical, political, social topics, cultural studies, health, business), and literary and genre fiction.

How to Contact: Send synopsis/outline plus 2 sample chapters. Accepts queries by e-mail. Considers simultaneous queries. Responds in 2 weeks to queries; 6 weeks to mss. Obtains most new clients through referrals from clients, queries.

Recent Sales: Sold 4 titles in the last year. Recent sales available upon request to prospective clients.

Terms: Agent receives 15% commission on domestic sales; 20% on foreign sales and film rights with co-agent involved. Offers "agreement that spells out author-agent relationship."

Fees: No fee for queries with sample chapters; $250 reading fee for evaluation/critique of complete ms. Offers criticism service, if requested. Written critique averages 3 pages—includes critique of the material, suggestions on how to make it marketable and advice on marketing it. Charges clients $25/month for marketing costs. 10% of business is derived from criticism services.

Tips: Looks for "proposal or chapters professionally presented, with clarification of the distinctiveness of the project and grasp of intended readership."

N Ø JANUS LITERARY AGENCY, 43 Lakeman's Lane, Ipswich MA 01938. (508)356-0909. **Contact:** Lenny Cavallaro, Eva Wax. Estab. 1980. Currently handles: 100% nonfiction books.

Represents: Nonfiction books. **Considers these nonfiction areas:** biography/autobiography; business; crafts/hobbies; current affairs; education; government/politics/law; health/medicine; history; how-to; money/finance/economics; New Age/metaphysics; self-help/personal improvement; sports; true crime/investigative.

○➤ "We work primarily as a referral agency, sending only the most promising materials to other firms. We rarely act as agents ourselves and appear to be phasing out."

How to Contact: Call, write or e-mail to query. Responds in 1 week to queries; 2 weeks to mss. Obtains most new clients through LMP and referrals.

Recent Sales: This agency prefers not to share information on specific sales.

Terms: Agent receives 15% commission on domestic sales; 20% on foreign sales. Offers written contract, binding for "usually less than 1 year."

Fees: Charges handling fees, "usually $100-200 to defray costs."

Tips: "Not actively seeking clients, but will consider outstanding nonfiction proposals."

✓ Ø JOHNSON WARREN LITERARY AGENCY, 115 W. California Blvd., Suite 173, Pasadena CA 91105. (909)625-8400. Fax: (909)624-3930. E-mail: jwla@aol.com. **Contact:** Billie Johnson. Signatory of WGA. Represents 15 clients. 95% of clients are new/previously unpublished writers. Currently handles: 10% movie scripts; 50% novels; 40% nonfiction books.

• Prior to becoming an agent, Billie Johnson worked 25 years in accounting and project management.

Represents: Feature film, TV MOW. **Considers these script subject areas:** action/adventure; contemporary issues; detective/police/crime; mainstream; mystery/suspense; romance (comedy, drama); thriller/espionage.

○➤ Actively seeking nonfiction projects. Does not want to receive science fiction, horror, children's, religious material.

How to Contact: Query with SASE. Accepts queries by e-mail. Responds in 1 month to queries; 4 months to mss. Obtains most new clients through solicitations via reference books and internet registry.

Recent Sales: Sold 7 projects in the last year. Prefers not to share information on specific sales.

Terms: Agent receives 15% commission on domestic sales; 20% on foreign sales; 10% on scripts. Offers written contract. 30-day notice must be given to terminate contract.

Fees: Offers criticism service. 10% of business is derived from criticism service. Payment of criticism fees does not ensure representation. Charges clients for actual costs reimbursements.

Writers' Conferences: Romance Writers of America National Conference (Anaheim); Bouchercon (Philadelphia); Sisters in Crime (L.A.).

Tips: "This agency is open to new writers and enjoys a teamwork approach to projects. We prefer queries via e-mail or snail mail. No phone queries please."

$ ⊘ **LITERARY GROUP WEST**, 746 W. Shaw, Suite 127, Clovis CA 93612. (209)297-9409. Fax: (209)225-5606. **Contact:** Ray Johnson or Alyssa Williams. Estab. 1993. Represents 6 clients. 50% of clients are new/previously unpublished writers. Currently handles: 20% nonfiction books; 70% novels; 10% novellas.

Member Agents: B.N. Johnson, Ph.D. (English literature).

Represents: Nonfiction books, novels. **Considers these nonfiction areas:** current affairs; ethnic/cultural interests; military/war; true crime/investigative. **Considers these fiction areas:** action/adventure; detective/police/crimes; historical; mainstream; thriller/espionage.

⊶ This agency specializes in novels.

How to Contact: Query with SASE. Responds in 1 week to queries; 1 month to mss. Does not want to receive unsolicited mss. Obtains most new clients through queries and referrals.

Recent Sales: This agency prefers not to share information on specific sales.

Terms: Agent receives 15% commission on domestic sales; 20% on foreign sales. Offers written contract.

Fees: Charges expense fees to unpublished authors. Deducts expenses from sales of published authors.

Writers' Conferences: Fresno County Writers Conference.

Tips: "Query first with strong letter. Please send SASE with query letter."

$ ◖ **MEWS BOOKS LTD.**, 20 Bluewater Hill, Westport CT 06880. (203)227-1836. Fax: (203)227-1144. E-mail: mewsbooks@aol.com. **Contact:** Sidney B. Kramer. Estab. 1972. Represents 35 clients. Prefers to work with published/established authors; works with small number of new/previously unpublished authors "producing professional work." Currently handles: 20% nonfiction books; 10% novels; 20% juvenile books; 10% electronic; 40% miscellaneous.

Member Agents: Fran Pollak (assistant); Sidney B. Kramer.

Represents: Nonfiction books, novels, juvenile books, character merchandising and video and TV use of illustrated published books.

⊶ This agency specializes in juvenile (preschool through young adult), cookery, self-help, adult nonfiction and fiction, parenting, technical and medical and electronic publishing.

How to Contact: Query with précis, outline, character description, a few pages of sample writing and author's bio. Does not accept queries by fax or e-mail. Considers simultaneous queries. Returns materials only with SASE.

Recent Sales: Sold 10 titles in the last year. *Jane Butel's Quick and Easy Southwestern Cookbook*, by Jane Butel (Harmony Books); *Dr. Susan Love's Breast Book*, (Revised) (Perseus Books); *Prospect*, by Bill Littlefield (Houghton Mifflin); *To The Moon: An Engineer's Adventure*, by Thomas Kelly (Smithsonian Institute Press); *Master Math*, by Debra Ross (Career Press).

Terms: Agent receives 15% commission on domestic sales; 20% on foreign sales.

Fees: Does not charge a reading fee. "If material is accepted, agency asks for $350 circulation fee (4-5 publishers), which will be applied against commissions (waived for published authors)." Charges clients for photocopying, postage expenses, telephone calls and other direct costs.

Tips: "Principle agent is an attorney and former publisher. Offers consultation service through which writers can get advice on a contract or on publishing problems."

☑ ⊘ **BK NELSON LITERARY AGENCY & LECTURE BUREAU**, 84 Woodland Rd., Pleasantville NY 10570-1322. (914)741-1322. Fax: (914)741-1324. Also: 1500 S. Palm Canyon Dr., Suites 7 & 9, Palm Springs CA 92262. (760)318-2773. Fax: (760)318-2774. E-mail: bknelson4@cs.com. Website: www.bknelson.com. **Contact:** B.K. Nelson, John Benson, Chip Ashbach or Erv Rosenfeld. Estab. 1980. Member of NACA, Author's Guild, NAFE, ABA, AAUW. Represents 62 clients. 40% of clients are new/previously unpublished writers. Currently handles: 30% nonfiction books; 5% CD-ROM/electronic products; 30% novels; 20% movie scripts; 10% TV scripts; 10% stage plays.

● Prior to opening her agency, Ms. Nelson worked for Eastman and Dasilva, a law firm specializing in entertainment law, and at American Play Company, a literary agency.

Member Agents: B.K. Nelson (business books, self help); John Benson (Director of Lecture Bureau, sports); Erv Rosenfeld (TV scripts); Chip Ashbach (novels); Jean Rejaunier (biography, theatrical).

Represents: Nonfiction books, CD-ROM/electronic products, business books, novels, plays and screenplays. **Considers these nonfiction areas:** anthropology/archaeology; art/architecture/design; biography/autobiography; business; child guidance/parenting; computers/electronics; cooking/food/nutrition; crafts/hobbies; current affairs; education; ethnic/cultural interests; government/politics/law; health/medicine; history; how-to; language/literature/criticism; memoirs; military/war; money/finance/economics; music/dance/theater/film; nature/environment; popular culture; psychology; religious/inspirational; science/technology; self-help/personal improvement; sociology; sports; travel; true crime/

investigative; women's issues/women's studies. **Considers these fiction areas:** action/adventure; cartoon/comic; contemporary issues; detective/police/crime; family saga; fantasy; feminist; glitz; historical; horror; literary; mainstream; mystery/suspense; psychic/supernatural; romance (contemporary, historical); science fiction; sports; thriller/espionage; westerns/frontier.

Oπ This agency specializes in business, self-help, how-to, novels, screenplays, biographies. Actively seeking screenplays. Does not want to receive unsolicited material.

Also Handles: Feature film, documentary, animation, TV MOW, episodic drama, sitcom, variety show, miniseries, animation, stage plays. **Considers these script subject areas:** action/adventure; cartoon; comedy; contemporary issues; detective/police/crime; family saga; fantasy; historical; horror; mainstream; psychic/supernatural; romantic comedy and drama; thriller; westerns/frontier.

How to Contact: Query with SASE. Accepts queries by e-mail or fax. Prefers to read materials exclusively. Responds in 2 weeks to queries; 1 month to ms. Obtains most new clients through referrals and reputation with editors.

Recent Sales: Sold 40 titles in the last year. *How to, I do,* by Christine Cudance and Holly Lefevre; *Oktoberfest: Cooking with Beer,* by Armand Vanderstigchel. Other clients include Arthur Pell, Robert W. Bly, Antony Mora, Leon Katz, Ph.D., Professor Emeritus Drama Yale, Anne Marie Baugh, Lilly Walters, Branden Ward, Paula Moulton, Bill Green, Jason and Edith Marks. ***Plays optioned for off-Broadway:*** *Gianni Schicchi,* by John Morogiello; *Obediently Yours, Orson Welles,* by Richard France. ***TV scripts optioned/sold:*** *American Harvest,* by Brandon Ward (starring Johnny Depp); *Nellie Bly,* by Jason Marks (Brandon Ward for TNT).

Terms: Agent receives 20% on domestic sales; 25% on foreign sales. Offers written contract, exclusive for 8-12 months.

Fees: Charges $450 reading fee for mss; $375 for screenplays; $4/page for proposals. "It is not refundable. We usually charge for the first reading only. The reason for charging in addition to time/expense is to determine if the writer is saleable and thus a potential client." Offers editorial services ranging from book query critiques for $50 to ghost writing a corporate book for $100,000. "After sale, charge any expenses over $50 for FedEx, long distance, travel or luncheons. We always discuss deducting expenses with author before deducting."

Tips: "We handle the business aspect of the literary and lecture fields. We handle careers as well as individual book projects. If the author has the ability to write and we are harmonious, success is certain to follow with us handling the selling/business."

$ ⊘ PELHAM LITERARY AGENCY, 2290 E. Fremont Ave., Suite C, Littleton CO 80122. (303)347-0623. **Contact:** Howard Pelham. Estab. 1994. Represents 10 clients. 50% of clients are new/previously unpublished writers. Currently handles: 20% nonfiction books; 80% novels.

• Prior to opening his agency, Mr. Pelham worked as a writer and college professor.

Member Agents: Howard Pelham; Jim Meals.

Represents: Novels, short story collections. **Considers these fiction areas:** action/adventure; detective/police/crime; fantasy; horror; literary; mainstream; romance (contemporary, gothic, historical); science fiction; sports; thriller/espionage; westerns/frontier.

Oπ This agency specializes in genre fiction. Actively seeking all adult genre fiction. Does not want to receive movie scripts, children's mss, young adult fiction.

How to Contact: Send outline and sample chapters or query with description of novel or manuscript. Considers simultaneous queries and submissions. Responds in 3 weeks to queries; 2 months to mss. Returns materials only with SASE. "Most of my clients have been from recommendation by other writers."

Recent Sales: *The Passenger,* by Patrick A. Davis (Putnam); *Blowout,* by Robert Howarth (Intermedia); *The Colonel,* by Patrick A. Davis (Penguin Putnam).

Terms: Agent receives 15% commission on domestic sales; 20% on foreign sales. Offers written contract, with 30 day cancellation clause.

Fees: Charges $95 reading fee to unpublished writers. Offers criticism service. 90% of business is derived from commissions on sales.

Writers' Conferences: Rocky Mountain Book Fair.

N ⊘ PENMARIN BOOKS, 2011 Ashridge Way, Granite Bay CA 95746. (916)771-5869. Fax: (916)771-5879. E-mail: penmarin@aol.com. **Contact:** Hal Lockwood, President. Estab. 1987. Represents 20 clients. 80% of clients are new/unpublished writers. Currently represents: general trade nonfiction, illustrated books, fiction.

• Prior to opening his agency, Mr. Lockwood served as an editorial assistant at Stanford University Press, an editor with Painter/Hopkins Publishing, and in editorial production with Presidio Publishing.

Represents: Nonfiction books, fiction.

Oπ "No previous publication is necessary. We do expect authoritative credentials in terms of history, politics, science and the like."

How to Contact: For nonfiction books, query with outline and SASE. For fiction, query with outline, sample chapters and SASE. Will read submissions at no charge, but may charge a criticism fee or service charge for work performed after the initial reading. Responds in 2 weeks to queries; 1 month to mss.

Recent Sales: *Smokescreen: A Novel of Medical Intrigue,* by Vernon Avile (Bookmark); *The Quiet Revolutionary: An Oral History of Carl Rogers,* by Carl Rogers with David Russell (Columbia University Press).

Terms: Agent receives 15% commission on domestic sales; 15% on dramatic sales; 15% on foreign sales.

Fees: "We normally do not provide extensive criticism as part of our reading but, for a fee, will prepare guidance for editorial development. Charges $200/300 pages. Our editorial director writes critiques. These may be two to ten pages long. They usually include an overall evaluation and then analysis and recommendations about specific sections, organization or style."

PINKHAM LITERARY AGENCY, 418 Main St., Amesbury MA 01913. (978)388-4210. Fax: (978)388-4221. E-mail: jnoblepink@aol.com. Website: www.pinkhamliterary.com. **Contact:** Joan Noble Pinkham. Estab. 1996. Currently handles: 20% movie scripts; 20% nonfiction books; 60% novels.
   ● Ms. Pinkham is a published author, ghost writer, public relations executive, and broadcaster. She writes for TV in London and Boston. In addition, Ms. Pinkham owns Sea & Coast Films.
Member Agents: Edward P. Mannix (contract law, entertainment).
Represents: Feature film, TV movie of the week, novels, mysteries. **Considers these script subject areas:** action/adventure; comedy; detective/police/crime; historical; mystery/suspense; psychic/supernatural; thriller/espionage.
   ○━ This agency specializes in novels, how-tos, mysteries, screenplays. Actively seeking new writers. Does not want to receive horror, children's material or stage plays.
How to Contact: Query with SASE. Responds immediately to queries; 2 months to mss. Returns materials only with SASE. Obtains most new clients through website.
Recent Sales: This agency prefers not to share information on specific sales.
Terms: Agent receives 15% commission on domestic sales; 20% on foreign sales. Offers written contract, binding for 1 year. 90-day notice must be given to terminate contract.
Fees: Charges reading fee of $1/page to new writers. Does not charge a reading fee to WGA members. Offers criticism service. Criticism service: "$400 and up for several detailed pages." Editing fee: $400 and up. Charges $50, reserved in client's name, for expenses. "Any expenses are deducted as they occur or are billed to us, postage, phone calls, copies, etc."
Tips: "We work with our writers in development and consult on marketing. We are all writers; also winners of national awards. We are developing new writers. This area of Massachusetts is host to many talented writers and artists, as well as craftsmen. We are taking our time with these people—knowing the time and patience it takes. We regularly do business in Hollywood and are listed in *Hollywood Agents & Managers Directory*, *Writer's Guide to Hollywood* and *Kempers-London*."

✓ ◐ PMA LITERARY AND FILM MANAGEMENT, INC., 45 W. 21st St., 6th Floor, New York NY 10010. (212)929-1222. Fax: (212)206-0238. E-mail: pmalitfilm@aol.com. Website: www.pmalitfilm.com. **Contact:** Peter Miller, president. Estab. 1975. Represents 80 clients. 50% of clients are new/unpublished writers. Currently handles: 50% fiction; 25% nonfiction; 25% screenplays.
   ● 1997 marked Mr. Miller's 25th anniversary as an agent.
Member Agents: Delin Cormeny, vice president (fiction and narrative nonfiction); Peter Miller, president (fiction, nonfiction and motion picture properties); Elaine Gartner, development associate (fiction/nonfiction); Kate Garrick, development assistant (fiction/nonfiction).
Represents: Fiction, nonfiction, film scripts. **Considers these nonfiction areas:** animals; biography/autobiography; business; child guidance/parenting; cooking/food/nutrition; current affairs; ethnic/cultural interests; government/politics/law; history; money/finance/economics; music/dance/theater/film; popular culture; travel; true crime/investigative; women's issues/women's studies. **Considers these fiction areas:** action/adventure; contemporary issues; detective/police/crime; ethnic; family saga; gay; historical; humor/satire; lesbian; literary; mainstream; mystery/suspense; romance (historical); science fiction; thriller/espionage; westerns/frontier.
   ○━ This agency specializes in commercial fiction and nonfiction, thrillers, and "fiction with *real* motion picture and television potential." Actively seeking professional journalists, first-time novelists, ethnic and female writers.
Also Handles: Feature film, TV MOW, miniseries. **Considers these script areas:** action/adventure; comedy; contemporary issues; detective/police/crime; family saga; historical; mainstream; mystery/suspense; psychic/supernatural; romantic comedy; romantic drama; science fiction; thriller; westerns/frontier.
How to Contact: Query with outline and/or sample chapters. *No unsolicited mss.* Accepts queries by fax or e-mail. Considers simultaneous queries and submissions. Writers' guidelines for 5×8½ SASE with 2 first-class stamps. Responds in 3 weeks to queries; 2 months to ms. Submissions and queries without SASE will not be returned.
Recent Sales: Sold 30 titles. *Chocolate for a Woman's Heart* series (7 books total), by Kay Allenbaugh (Simon & Schuster); *The Unwanted*, by Kien Nguyen (Little, Brown); *Buried Evidence* and *Conflict of Interest*, by Nancy Taylor Rosenberg (Hyperion); *Higher Purpose*, by Tom Whittaker and Johnny Dodd (Regency). Other clients include Vincent Bugliosi, John Glatt, Michael Eberhardt, Kay Allenbaugh, Ann B. Ross, Nancy Taylor Rosenberg, Chris Rogers, James Dallesandro.
Terms: Agent receives 15% commission on domestic sales; 20-25% on foreign sales.
Fees: Does not charge a reading fee. Offers sub-contracted criticism service. "Fee varies on the length of the manuscript from $150-500. Publishing professionals/critics are employed by PMA to write five- to eight-page reports." Charges clients for photocopying.
Writers' Conferences: Romance Writer's Conference (Chicago, October); North Carolina Writers Network Conference (Wilmington, November); Charleston Writers Conference (March).

◐ **PUDDINGSTONE LITERARY AGENCY**, Affiliate of SBC Enterprises Inc., 11 Mabro Dr., Denville NJ 07834-9607. (201)366-3622. **Contact:** Alec Bernard or Eugenia Cohen. Estab. 1972. Represents 25 clients. 80% of clients are new/previously unpublished writers. Currently handles: 10% nonfiction books; 70% novels; 20% movie scripts.
- Prior to becoming a agent, Mr. Bernard was a motion picture/television story editor and an executive managing editor for a major publishing house.

Represents: Nonfiction books, novels, movie scripts. **Considers these nonfiction areas:** business; how-to; language/literature/criticism; military/war; true crime/investigative. **Considers these fiction areas:** action/adventure; detective/police/crime; horror; science fiction; thriller/espionage.
How to Contact: Query first with SASE including $1 cash processing fee, "which controls the volume and eliminates dilettantism among the submissions." Responds immediately to queries; 1 month to mss "that are requested by us." Obtains most new clients through referrals and listings.
Recent Sales: Sold 2 titles in the last year. *The Action-Step Plan to Owning And Operating A Small Business*, by E. Toncré (Prentice-Hall).
Terms: Agent receives 10-15% sliding scale (decreasing) on domestic sales; 20% on foreign sales. Offers written contract, binding for 1 year with renewals.
Fees: Charges reading fee for unsolicited mss over 20 pages. Negotiated fees for market analysis available. Charges clients for photocopying for foreign sales.

▨ ⑤ ◐ **QCORP LITERARY AGENCY**, P.O. Box 8, Hillsboro OR 97123-0008. (800)775-6038. E-mail: qcorp @qcorplit.com. Website: www.qcorplit.com. **Contact:** William C. Brown. Estab. 1990. Represents 25 clients. 75% of clients are new/previously unpublished writers. Currently handles: 30% nonfiction books; 60% fiction books; 10% scripts.
- Prior to opening his agency, Mr. Brown was a physicist/engineer and university professor.

Member Agent: William C. Brown.
Represents: Fiction and nonfiction books, including textbooks, scholarly books, novels, novellas, short story collections. **Considers all nonfiction areas. Considers all areas of fiction.**
Also Handles: TV and feature film scripts. **Considers all script subject areas.**
How to Contact: Query with SASE. Accepts queries by e-mail. Considers simultaneous queries and submissions. Will request script, if interested. Responds in 2 weeks to queries. Obtains new clients through recommendations, advertisements, the Web, reference books and from critique service.
Recent Sales: Sold 2 titles. *Evolutionary Science of Extraterrestrial Life*, by William C. Brown (Wyndam Hall Press); and *Ella!*, by J. Wilfred Johnson (McFarland and Company).
Terms: Agent receives 10% commission on domestic sales; 20% on foreign sales. Offers written contract, binding for 6 months, automatically renewed unless cancelled by author.
Fees: Consult web page for critique services and information on free first chapter critique.
Tips: "New authors should use our critique service and its free, no obligation first chapter critique to introduce themselves. Call, write or consult our website for details. Our critique service is serious business, line-by-line and comprehensive. Established writers should call or send résumé."

⑤ ◐ **DIANE RAINTREE LITERARY AGENCY**, 360 W. 21st St., New York NY 10011-3305. (212)242-2387. **Contact:** Diane Raintree. Estab. 1977. Represents 6-8 clients.
- Prior to opening her agency, Ms. Raintree was a reader for Avon Books and a senior editor for Dial Press.

Represents: Nonfiction, novels, children's books. **Considers most fiction areas.**
○┱ This agency specializes in novels, film and TV scripts, memoirs, plays, poetry and children's books.
Also Handles: Feature film, TV MOW, sitcom. **Considers these script areas:** action/adventure; comedy; contemporary issues; detective/police/crime; ethnic; family saga; historical; juvenile; mainstream; mystery/suspense; psychic/supernatural; romance; science fiction; teen; thriller/suspense.
How to Contact: Phone first. Send entire script with SASE if requested. Responds in 1 week to queries; 3 months to mss.
Recent Sales: This agency prefers not to share information on specific sales.
Terms: Agent receives 10% on domestic sales. "Writer should engage an entertainment lawyer for negotiations of film and TV option and contract."
Fees: May charge reading fee. "Amount varies from year to year."

▨ ⑤ ♡ **JACK SCAGNETTI TALENT & LITERARY AGENCY**, 5118 Vineland Ave., #102, North Hollywood CA 91601. (818)762-3871. **Contact:** Jack Scagnetti. Estab. 1974. Signatory of WGA, member of Academy of Television Arts and Sciences. Represents 50 clients. 50% of clients are new/previously unpublished writers. Currently handles: 20% nonfiction books; 70% movie scripts; 10% TV scripts.
- See the expanded listing for this agency in Script Agents.

✔ ◐ ⑤ **THE SEYMOUR AGENCY**, 475 Miner St. Rd., Canton NY 13617. (315)386-1831. Fax: (315)386-1037. E-mail: mseymour@slic.com. Website: www.pages.slic.com/mseymour. **Contact:** Mary Sue Seymour or Mike Seymour. Estab. 1992. Represents 75 clients. 20% of clients are new/previously unpublished writers. Currently handles: 30% nonfiction books; 5% scholarly books; 5% textbooks; 50% novels.

• Ms. Seymour is retired NYS certified teacher. Mr. Seymour has an M.A. from St. Lawrence University in Canton.

Represents: Fiction and nonfiction. **Considers all nonfiction areas. Considers these fiction areas:** action/adventure; detective/police/crime; ethnic; glitz; historical; horror; humor/satire; mainstream; mystery/suspense; religious/inspirational; romance (contemporary, gothic, historical, medieval, regency); vampire; westerns/frontier. Will read well-thought-out nonfiction proposals and good fiction in any genre.

O━ Actively seeking nonfiction and well-written novels. Does not want to receive screenplays, short stories, poetry.

How to Contact: Query with first 50 pages and synopsis. Does not accept queries by fax. Considers simultaneous queries and submissions. Responds in 1 month to queries; 3 months to mss. Returns materials only with SASE.

Recent Sales: Sold 27 titles in the last year. *Wild Rose of York*, by Betty Davidson (Berkley/Jove); *Lord Langdon's Tudor*, by Laura Paquet (Kensington Publishing Corp.); *Eye of the Cat*, by Donna MacQuigg (Kensington Publishing Corp.).

Terms: Agent receives 12½% (published authors) to 15% (unpublished authors) commission on domestic sales; 20% on foreign sales. Offers written contract, binding for 1 year.

Fees: Offers criticism service for prospective clients only. Seymour Agency offers inhouse editing for first 50 pages of selected mss. Editing fee is $50. Author is encouraged to resubmit after rewrite. Charges unpublished cients $5/house postage fee. Writers reimbursed for office fees after the sale of ms.

Tips: "Send query, synopsis and first 50 pages. If you don't hear from us, you didn't send SASE. We are looking for nonfiction and romance—women in jeopardy, suspense, contemporary, historical, some regency and any well-written fiction and nonfiction."

🖉 **JACQUELINE SIMENAUER LITERARY AGENCY**, P.O. Box 1039, Barnegat NJ 08005. (609)607-1780. Fax: (609)607-1780. E-mail: jhs223@aol.com. **Contact:** Jacqueline Simenauer. Estab. 1990. Member of Authors Guild, Authors League, NASW. Represents 30-35 clients. 40% of clients are new/previously unpublished writers. Currently handles: 95% nonfiction books; 5% novels.

• Prior to opening her agency, Ms. Simenauer co-authored several books for Doubleday, Simon & Schuster and Times Books.

Members Agents: Jacqueline Simenauer (nonfiction/medical/how-to); Fran Pardi (fiction); Doris Walfield (New Age/alternative medicine/spirituality).

Represents: Nonfiction books, novels. **Considers these nonfiction areas:** child guidance/parenting; current affairs; education; health/medicine; how-to; money/finance; New Age/metaphysics; nutrition; popular culture; psychology; religious/inspirational; self-help/personal improvement; true crime/investigative; travel; women's issues/women's studies. **Considers these fiction areas:** contemporary issues; family saga; feminist; gay; glitz; historical; literary; mainstream; mystery/suspense; psychic/supernatural; romance (contemporary); thriller/espionage.

O━ This agency specializes in strong commercial nonfiction such as popular psychology, health/medicine, self-help/personal improvement, women's issues, how-to. Actively seeking strong commercial nonfiction, but "will look at some fiction." Does not want to receive poetry, crafts, children's books.

How to Contact: Query with SASE. Responds in 6 weeks to queries. Does not accept queries by e-mail or fax. Obtains most new clients through recommendations from others; advertising in various journals, newsletters, publications and professional conferences.

Recent Sales: Sold 21 titles in the last year. *The Thyroid Guide*, by Beth Ann Ditkoff/Paul Lo Gerfo (HarperCollins); *Defeating Insulin Resistance*, by Dr. Cheryl Hart/Mary Grossman R.D. (Contemporary Books).

Terms: Agent receives 15% commission on domestic sales; 20% on foreign sales.

Fees: "There are no reading fees. However, we have a special Breakthrough Program for the first-time author who would like an in-depth critique of his/her work by our freelance editorial staff. There is a charge of $2 per page for this service, and it is completely optional." Charges clients for postage, photocopying, phone, fax. 5% of business is derived from reading or criticism fees.

🖉 **SLC ENTERPRISES**, 852 Highland Place, Highland Park IL 60035. (847)432-7553. Fax: (847)432-7554. **Contact:** Ms. Carole Golin. Estab. 1985. Represents 40 clients. 50% of clients are new/previously unpublished writers. Currently handles: 75% nonfiction books; 25% novels.

Member Agent: Stephen Casari (sports).

Represents: Nonfiction books, juvenile books, novels, short story collections. **Considers these nonfiction areas:** biography/autobiography, business, cooking/food/nutrition; current affairs; history; memoirs; sports; women's issues/women's studies; Holocaust studies. **Considers these fiction areas:** feminist; historical; literary; regional; sports.

How to Contact: Query with outline/proposal and SASE. Accepts queries by fax. Prefers to read materials exclusively. Responds in 2 weeks to queries; 1 months to mss. Returns materials only with SASE.

Recent Sales: Sold 3 titles in the last year. *The Raiders—A History*, by John Lombardo (Contemporary).

CONTACT THE EDITOR of *Guide to Literary Agents* by e-mail at literaryagents @fwpubs.com with your questions and comments.

Terms: Agent receives 15% commission on domestic sales. Offers written contract, binding for 9 months.
Fees: Charges $150 reading fee for entire ms; $75-150 for children's, depending on length and number of stories. Reading fee includes overall critique plus specifics. No line editing for grammar etc. Charges no other fees. 20% of business is derived from reading and criticism fees.

☑ ◐ **MICHAEL STEINBERG LITERARY AGENCY**, P.O. Box 274, Glencoe IL 60022. Phone/fax: (847)835-8881. **Contact:** Michael Steinberg. Estab. 1980. Represents 27 clients. 5% of clients are new/previously unpublished writers. Currently handles: 75% nonfiction books; 25% novels.
Represents: Nonfiction books, novels. **Considers these nonfiction areas:** biography; business; computers; law; history; how-to; money/finance/economics; self-help/personal improvement. **Considers these fiction areas:** action/adventure; contemporary issues; detective/police/crime; erotica; mainstream; mystery/suspense; science fiction; thriller/espionage.
○→ This agency specializes in business and general nonfiction, mysteries, science fiction.
How to Contact: Query for guidelines with SASE. No unsolicited mss. Does not accept queries by e-mail or fax. Considers simultaneous queries and submissions. Responds in 2 weeks to queries; 6 weeks to mss. Returns materials only with SASE. Obtains most new clients through unsolicited inquiries and referrals from editors and authors.
Recent Sales: *Guide to Investing, 3rd ed.*, by Michael Steinberg (Prentice-Hall); *Euro Trading*, by Jake Bernstein (Prentice-Hall); *Day Trading Stocks Electronically*, by Jake Bernstein (McGraw-Hill).
Terms: Agent receives 15% on domestic sales; 15-20% on foreign sales. Offers written contract, which is binding, "but at will."
Fees: Charges $75 reading fee for outline and chapters 1-3; $200 for a full ms to 100,000 words. Criticism included in reading fee. Charges clients actual phone and postage, which is billed back quarterly. 5% of business derived from reading fees or criticism services.
Writers' Conferences: BEA (Chicago).
Tips: "We do not solicit new clients. Do not send generically addressed, photocopied query letters."

$ ◐ **MARIANNE STRONG LITERARY AGENCY**, 65 E. 96th St., New York NY 10128. (212)249-1000. Fax: (212)831-3241. **Contact:** Marianne Strong. Estab. 1978. Represents 15 clients. Currently handles: 80% nonfiction books; 5% scholarly books; 5% novels; 10% TV scripts.
Member Agents: Mai D. Wong; Marianne Strong.
Represents: Nonfiction books, novels, TV scripts, syndicated material. **Considers these nonfiction areas:** art/architecture/design; biography/autobiography; business; child guidance/parenting; cooking/food/nutrition; current affairs; education; health/medicine; history; how-to; interior design/decorating; juvenile nonfiction; military/war; money/finance/economics; religious/inspirational; self-help/personal improvement; true crime; women's issues/women's studies. **Considers these fiction areas:** action/adventure; contemporary issues; detective/police/crime; family saga; glitz; historical; literary; mainstream; religious/inspirational; romance (contemporary, gothic, historical, regency); thriller/espionage; western/frontier.
○→ This agency specializes in biographies.
How to Contact: Send complete outline plus 4-6 sample chapters. Accepts queries by e-mail or fax. Considers simultaneous queries. Responds "fairly soon" to queries; 2 months to mss. Obtains most new clients through recommendations from others.
Recent Sales: Sold 10 titles in the last year. *All American and British Theaters in the Past 20 Years*, by Clive Barnes (Watson-Guptill).
Terms: Agent receives 15% commission on domestic sales; 20% on foreign sales. Offers written contract, binding for the life of book or play.
Fees: Charges a reading fee for unpublished writers only, "refundable when manuscript sold." Offers criticism service. "If using outside freelance writers and editors, entire fee goes to them unless specified. Critiques prepared by freelance writers and editors who receive entire fee and pay small commission." Charges clients for long distance calls.
Tips: "Submit a totally professional proposal with a story line that elucidates the story from A to Z plus several perfectly typed or word processed chapters. No disks, please. Also include background information on the author, especially literary or journalistic references. Author must supply copies of ms. Agency does not make copies of chapters, only the proposal."

N ○ **TAHOE SIERRAS AGENCY**, P.O. Box 2179, Dayton NV 89403. (775)241-0881. Fax: (775)241-0413. E-mail: tahoesierras@aol.com. Website: www.cuebon.com/tahoesierras. **Contact:** Ed Oversen. Estab. 1999. 80% of clients are new/unpublished writers. Currently handles: 50% novels, 40% movie scripts, 10% TV scripts.
Member Agents: Ed Oversen (agent/editor, books); Linda Heater (agent/editor, books); Deb Oversen (agent/editor, scripts, books).
Represents: Nonfiction books, novels, short story collections, novellas, juvenile books. **Considers these nonfiction areas:** biography/autobiography; gay/lesbian issues; how-to; humor; juvenile nonfiction; music/dance/theater/film; self-help/personal improvement; true crime/investigative; women's issues/women's studies; young adult. **Considers these fiction areas:** action/adventure; confessional; detective/police/crime; family saga; fantasy; gay/lesbian; historical; horror; humor/satire; juvenile; mainstream; mystery/suspense; psychic/supernatural; science fiction; thriller/espionage; young adult.

O→ This agency specializes in originality. "We are also a consulting firm for scriptwriting. We offer editorial services for novels and script polish with rewrites." Actively seeking horror, mystery/suspense, psychological horror/drama, romance/drama, action adventure.

Also Handles: Episodic drama, movie scripts, TV scripts, feature film, TV movie of the week, documents, miniseries. **Considers these script subject areas:** action/adventure; biography/autobiography; comedy; contemporary issues; detective/police/crime; family saga; fantasy; historical; horror; mystery/suspense; psychic/supernatural; romantic comedy; romantic drama; science fiction; sports; teen; thriller/espionage; western/frontier.

How to Contact: Query with SASE. Accepts queries by e-mail and fax. Considers simultaneous queries and submissions. Responds in 1 month to queries; 3 months to mss. Returns materials only with SASE. Obtains most new clients through recommendations from others.

Recent Sales: Sold 1 title in the last year. *Another Side of Evil*, by Jax Laffer (Yard Dog Press). Other clients include Paul Carlson, Jeff Hughes, Selina Rosen, Sarah Hoffer, Cara Kelly.

Terms: Agent receives 10% commission on domestic sales; 20% on foreign sales. Offers written contract, binding for 1 year.

Fees: Charges for several types of critiquing services on scripts only ranging from $25-300.

Writers' Conferences: Science Fiction Conference (Kansas City, KS, summer).

Tips: "Since publishers do so little editing anymore, it's best to submit the best possible manuscripts available. Make sure novels are in correct format, no typos and correct spelling. Scripts must be in a correct format and written on a script format software program. Be patient, and allow us time to do our job correctly."

DAWSON TAYLOR LITERARY AGENCY, 4722 Holly Lake Dr., Lake Worth FL 33463-5372. (561)965-4150. Fax: (561)641-9765. **Contact:** Dawson Taylor, attorney at law. Estab. 1974. Represents 34 clients. 80% of clients are new/previously unpublished writers. Currently handles: 80% nonfiction; 5% scholarly books; 15% novels.

● Prior to opening his agency, Mr. Taylor served as book editor at the *National Enquirer* from 1976-1983, and book editor at the *Globe* from 1984-1991.

Represents: Nonfiction books, textbooks, scholarly books, novels. **Considers all nonfiction areas.** Specializes in nonfiction on sports, especially golf. **Considers these fiction areas:** detective/police/crime; mystery/suspense; thriller/espionage.

O→ This agency specializes in nonfiction, fiction, sports (especially golf), military history.

How to Contact: Query with outline and SASE. Does not accept queries by fax. Prefers to read materials exclusively. Responds in 5 days to queries; 10 days to mss. Returns materials only with SASE. Obtains most new clients through "recommendations from publishers and authors who are presently in my stable."

Recent Sales: Sold 5 titles in the last year. *Life & Times of Jack Nicklaus* (Sleeping Bear); *Picture Perfect Golf* (NTC Contemporary).

Terms: Agent receives 15% or 20% commission "depending upon editorial help." Offers written contract, indefinite, but cancellable on 60-day notice by either party.

Fees: "Reading fees are subject to negotiation, usually $100 for normal length manuscript, more for lengthy ones. Reading fee includes critique and sample editing. Criticism service subject to negotiation, from $100. Critiques are on style and content, include editing of manuscript, and are written by myself." 10% of business is derived from reading fees or criticism services. Payment of reading or criticism fee does not ensure representation.

N ◑ LYNDA TOLLS LITERARY AGENCY, 2415 NW Awbrey Rd., Bend OR 97701. Phone/fax: (541)388-3510. **Contact:** Lynda Tolls Swarts. Estab. 1995. Agency represents 16 clients. 30% of clients are new/unpublished writers. Currently handles: 40% nonfiction books; 50% novels; 10% novellas.

Represents: Nonfiction books, scholarly books, novels. **Considers these nonfiction areas:** biography/autobiography; business; current affairs; education; ethnic/cultural interests; history; money/finance/economics; religious/inspirational; self-help/personal improvement; sociology; true crime/investigative; women's issues/women's studies. **Considers these fiction areas:** contemporary issues; detective/police/crime; ethnic; historical; literary; mystery/suspense.

O→ This agency specializes in adult commercial and literary fiction and nonfiction.

How to Contact: For nonfiction, query with proposal. For fiction, synopsis with first 50 pages. Responds in 2 months. Obtains most new clients through recommendations from others.

Recent Sales: This agency prefers not to share information on specific sales.

Terms: Agent receives 15% commission on domestic sales; 20% on foreign sales. Offers written contract, binding until terminated. 60-day notice must be given to terminate contract.

Fees: No reading fee.

Writers' Conferences: Williamette Writers' Conference, Surrey Writers' Conference.

$ ◐ JEANNE TOOMEY ASSOCIATES, 95 Belden St., Falls Village CT 06031-1113. (860)824-0831/5460. Fax: (860)824-5460. **Contact:** Jeanne Toomey, president. Assistant: Peter Terranova. Estab. 1985. 50% of clients are new/previously unpublished writers. Currently handles: 45% nonfiction books; 20% novels; 35% movie scripts.

● Prior to opening her agency, Ms. Toomey was a newspaper reporter—"worked all over the country for AP, NY Journal-American, Brooklyn Daily Eagle, Orlando Sentinel, Stamford Advocate, Asbury Park Press, News Tribune (Woodbridge, NJ)."

Member Agents: Peter Terranova (religion, epigraphy); Jeanne Toomey (crime, media, nature, animals).

Represents: Nonfiction books, novels, short story collections, movie scripts. **Considers these nonfiction areas:** agriculture/horticulture; animals; anthropology/archaeology; art/architecture/design; biography/autobiography; government/politics/law; history; interior design/decorating; money/finance/economics; nature/environment; true crime/investigative. **Considers these fiction areas:** detective/police/crime; psychic/supernatural; thriller/espionage.

O→ This agency specializes in "nonfiction; biographies of famous men and women; history with a flair—murder and detection. We look for local history books—travel guides, as well as religion, crime and media subjects— as of special interest to us. No children's books, no poetry, no Harlequin-type romances." Actively seeking already published authors. Does not want to receive poetry, children's books, Harlequin type romance, science fiction or sports. Exploring internet publishing possibilities.

How to Contact: Send outline plus 3 sample chapters and SASE. "Query *first*, please!" Accepts queries by fax. Prefers to read materials exclusively. Responds in 1 month. Returns materials only with SASE.

Recent Sales: Sold 1 book title in the last year. *Beyond the Brooklyn Bridge*, by Bernice Carton (Sunstone Press).

Terms: Agent receives 15% commission on domestic sales; 10% on foreign sales.

Fees: Charges $100 reading fee for unpublished authors; no fee for published authors. "The $100 covers marketing fee, office expenses, postage, photocopying. We absorb those costs in the case of published authors."

Writers' Conferences: Mystery Weekend (Mohonk, NY).

☑ ⬤ **PHYLLIS TORNETTA AGENCY**, 4 Kettle Lane, Mashpee MA 02649. (508)529-8821. E-mail: phyl4@cap ecod.net. **Contact:** Phyllis Tornetta, president. Estab. 1979. Represents 22 clients. 35% of clients are new/previously unpublished writers. Currently handles: 100% novels.

Represents: Novels and juvenile.

O→ This agency specializes in romance, contemporary.

How to Contact: Query with outline and SASE. No unsolicited mss. Prefers to read materials exclusively. Responds in 1 month.

Recent Sales: Sold 7 titles in the last year. Prior sales: *Heart of the Wolf*, by Sally Dawson (Leisure); *Jennie's Castle*, by Elizabeth Sinclair (Silhouette).

Terms: Agent receives 15% commission on domestic sales; 20% on foreign sales.

Fees: Charges a $100 reading fee for full mss.

☑ 💲 ⬤ ◎ **VISIONS PRESS, (Specialized: educational issues)**, P.O. Box 4904, Valley Village CA 91617-0904. (805)722-8241. **Contact:** Allen Brown. Estab. 1991. Currently handles: 50% newspaper columns and magazine features; 50% nonfiction novels.

Represents: Novels, newspaper columns and magazine features. **Considers these novel and magazine areas:** ethnic/cultural interests; women's issues/women's studies.

O→ "We prefer to support writers who concentrate on public school issues."

How to Contact: Send outline and 2 sample chapters and author bio. Responds in 2 weeks to queries; 1 month to mss. Obtains most new clients through recommendations from others and through inquiries.

Recent Sales: Available upon request. "Primarily represents the works of Diana Beard-Williams, an advocate for change in the area of public education. Looking for other dynamic clients."

Terms: Agent receives 10% commission on domestic sales; 15% on foreign sales. Offers written contract, specific length of time depends on type of work—novel newspaper column or magazine feature.

Fees: Charges $150 reading fee. Offers critique service. "Same as for the reading fee. Both the reading fee and the critique fee entitle the author to a critique of his/her work by one of our editors. We are interested in everyone who has a desire to be published . . . to hopefully realize their dream. To that end, we provide very honest and practical advice on what needs to be done to correct a manuscript." Additional fees "will be negotiated with the author on a project by project basis. Often there is a one-time fee charged that covers all office expenses associated with the marketing of a manuscript." 10% of business is derived from reading fees or critique services. Payment of critique fee does not ensure representation.

Writers' Conferences: "We do not usually attend writing conferences. Most of our contacts are made through associations with groups that promote consciousness-raising activities."

Tips: "We believe the greatest story ever told has yet to be written! For that reason we encourage every writer to uninhibitedly pursue his/her dream of becoming published. A no from us should simply be viewed as a temporary setback that can be overcome by another attempt to meet our high expectations. Discouraged, frustrated, and demoralized are words we have deleted from our version of the dictionary. An aspiring writer must have the courage to press on and believe in his/her talent."

💲 ⬤ **WINDFALL MANAGEMENT**, 4084 Mandeville Canyon Rd., Los Angeles CA 90049-1032. (310)471-6317. Fax: (310)471-4577. E-mail: windfall@deltanet.com. **Contact:** Jeanne Field. Represents 20 clients. Currently handles: 20% novels; 50% movie scripts; 25% TV scripts; 5% stage plays.

VISIT WWW.WRITERSMARKET.COM to obtain a searchable database of agents and publishers, and to receive updates on your specific interests on your computer.

• See the expanded listing for this agency in Script Agents.

☑ 🄢 ◎ **WOLCOTT LITERARY AGENCY**, P.O. Box 7493, Shawnee Mission KS 66207-7493. (913)327-1440. Fax: (419)791-2197. E-mail: nordwolc@oz.sunflower.org. Website: http://oz.sunflower.org/~nordwolc. **Contact:** Chris Wolcott. Estab. 1996. Member of Kansas City Professional Writer's Group. Represents over 10 clients. 90% of clients are new/previously unpublished writers. Currently handles: 10% movie scripts, 90% novels.
Represents: Novels, novellas, short story collections. **Considers these fiction areas:** action/adventure; detective/police/crime; erotica; experimental; fantasy; historical; horror; humor/satire; literary; mainstream; memoirs; mystery/suspense; psychic/supernatural; romance (gothic, historical); science fiction; thriller/espionage; westerns/frontier; young adult.
   O─╖ This agency specializes in mass-market genre fiction, science fiction, fantasy, horror, romance, erotica, etc. Actively seeking wide spectrum of fiction and pertinent nonfiction. Does not want to receive poetry.
Also Handles: Movie scripts. **Considers these script subject areas:** documentary screenplays only.
How to Contact: Query with short explanation of storyline and SASE. Accepts queries by e-mail or fax. "We accept e-mail queries for faster responses." Considers simultaneous queries and submissions. Responds in 3 weeks to queries; 7 weeks to mss; 5 days to e-mail queries. Returns materials only with SASE. Obtains most new clients through recommendations from others, conferences, unsolicited queries and from Website.
Recent Sales: Sold 5 titles in the last year. *The Storm Adventures*, by John Leon (Westport Press); *Only Once*, by Shelia Wirst (Tri Perf Book). Other clients include Eleanor Witherspoon Miller, Helen Folsom, Mark Carey, Robert Heinen and John Altman.
Terms: Agent receives 10% commission on domestic sales; 20% on foreign sales. Offers written contract, binding for 1 year, with a 30-day termination clause.
Fees: Reading fee: $150 for outline and full ms to 100,000 words; $50 for short stories to 10,000 words. Fee is for new/previously unpublished writers only, includes a critique of all works they agree to review. Criticism service: all works reviewed receive a detailed critique. The critiques, written by the agents, focus on story flow, content and format, not necessarily punctuation and grammar, and advise as to the proper format for submissions. Charges clients for postage on submissions to publishers. "There are no hidden fees." 10% of business is derived from reading fees or criticism service.
Reading List: Reads *Publishers Weekly* to find new clients. Looks for "freshness and, most importantly, marketability."
Tips: "We form a strategy to help new authors get their name into the market so approaching the larger houses is made easier. We want you to succeed. It all starts with a simple query letter. Drop us a line, we'd like to hear from you."

☑ ◉ **KAREN GANTZ ZAHLER LITERARY AGENCY**, 860 Fifth Ave., Suite 7J, New York NY 10021. Fax: (212)734-0057. E-mail: karengantz@hotmail.com. **Contact:** Karen Gantz Zahler. Estab. 1990. Represents 40 clients. Currently handles: 70% nonfiction books; 20% novels; 10% movie scripts.
   • Ms. Gantz is also an entertainment and literary property lawyer.
Represents: Nonfiction books, novels, movie scripts. **Considers all nonfiction and fiction areas;** "anything great."
   O─╖ This agency specializes in nonfiction, cookbooks.
How to Contact: Query with SASE. Accepts queries by e-mail and fax. Considers simultaneous submissions. Responds in 2 months. Prefers to obtain new clients through recommendations.
Recent Sales: Sold 15 titles in the last year. *Photo Diary of Britney Spears*, by Felicia Culotta (Penguin); *Design Diary: Secrets of the Decorator*, by Noel Jeffrey (Rizzoli); *Testing 1, 2, 3*, by Stanley Kaplan (Simon & Schuster).
Terms: Agent receives 15% commission on domestic sales; 20% commission on foreign sales. Offers written contract, binding for 1 year.
Fees: Offers a ms analysis service for $450.
Writers' Conferences: BEA.
Tips: "I'm a literary property lawyer and provide excellent negotiating services and exploitation of subsidiary rights. I take only one or two unsolicited clients annually."

Additional Fee-charging Agents

   The following fee-charging agencies have indicated they are *primarily* interested in handling the work of scriptwriters. However, they also handle less than 10 to 15 percent book manuscripts. After reading the listing (you can find the page number in the Listings Index), send a query to obtain more information on needs and manuscript submissions policies.

Camejo & Assoc., Suzanna
Gelff Agency, The Laya
Legacies

Canadian/International Literary Agents: Fee-charging

For the first time, we've included the following section of Canadian/International literary agents. These are agents who make sales not only in the U.S. but also in their own and other foreign countries. Several of the agents listed here already have clients who live in the U.S. For many writers, having an agent in another country can be a wonderful opportunity, especially if the material you write appeals to a different sensibility than that held by most U.S. readers. Or, perhaps you even live outside the U.S. In that case, you may want to work with an agent in this section who is closer to home.

In a sense, working with a Canadian or International agent is similar to having an agent outside of New York. They may not be able to meet with New York editors every day, but when they do go to New York, or even London, editors give them priority over local agents. Many publishing companies are now found outside of New York and even the U.S., giving Canadian and International agents the same opportunity for contact as those agents in New York. And, of course, with e-mail, the Internet, and fax machines, communicating in the global community is just as easy as meeting your colleague next door for lunch.

Keep in mind, however, that there are a few downsides to working with a Canadian or International agent. For starters, the majority of the agent's contacts will be in his own country, and he may not be as well known by U.S. publishing houses as those abroad. While this fact can be good in terms of reaching foreign markets, it may mean your book will not be sold in the U.S. market. Meeting your agent may prove more difficult than if she lived in the U.S. And even though new technology makes communication easier, if you need to talk with your London agent, you'll have to pay close attention to the difference in time zones to avoid calling her in the middle of the night.

Only English-speaking agents are included in this section. Most agents—both in and outside the U.S.—prefer to work with "foreign co-agents" when dealing with nonEnglish-speaking publishers. Foreign co-agents are contacts that agents have in other countries, like Spain or Japan, who work directly with foreign publishers and translators. If you believe your book would appeal to an audience in a nonEnglish-speaking country, you may want to consider looking for a U.S. agent who has strong connections with foreign co-agents.

Just like fee-charging agents in the U.S., the agents in this section charge fees in addition to the commission they receive on sales. Always understand what you will receive for any reading or critiquing fee before you pay anything. Keep in mind, too, that payment of any fee does not automatically ensure representation. For more information about fees, see "Reading Fees and Critique Services" on page 216.

Some agents in this section may also charge office fees to their clients. Researching the agents in this section is just as important as researching any agent: you want to target your submission to ensure you reach a receptive agent, and you want to know the agent is well respected in the publishing industry and actively making sales.

When you send a Canadian or International agent a query, be sure to include an International Reply Coupon (IRC) with your self-addressed envelope. Regular U.S. postage is not valid in any country outside the U.S., and an agent outside the U.S. is unlikely to respond to your query without an IRC. Contact your local post office for more information about IRCs.

For a more detailed explanation of the information in the following listings, see the introduction to Literary Agents: Fee-charging on page 213 and "Reading the Listings in the *Guide to Literary Agents*" at the front of the book.

☑ ✂ ▣ ⏺ **AUTHOR AUTHOR LITERARY AGENCY LTD.**, P.O. Box 56534, Lougheed Mall R.P.O., Burnaby, British Columbia V3J 7W2 Canada. (604)415-0056. Fax: (604)415-0076. E-mail: authorauthor@home.com. **Contact:** Joan Rickard, president. Assistant: Eileen McGaughey. Estab. 1992. Member of Writers' Guild of Alberta, Federation of British Columbia Writers and CAA. Represents 35 clients. Currently handles: 20% nonfiction books; 5% scholarly books; 25% juvenile books; 45% novels; 5% short story collections.
Represents: Book-length fiction and nonfiction, adult and juvenile (of every genre except poetry, screenplays or magazine stories/articles).
  ○─┐ This agency "welcomes new writers."
How to Contact: "Authors may submit partial or entire manuscripts. Hard copy (paper) only. No disk, faxed or e-mailed submissions." Considers simultaneous queries and submissions. Due to publishers' constraints, book proposals should rarely exceed 125,000 words. Please ensure manuscripts are properly formatted: unbound; allow 1″ borders on all sides; double-space throughout manuscript (no extra double-spaces between paragraphs); indent paragraphs five character spaces; print size should provide about 250 words/page. Include a brief synopsis of your proposal (*high impact*, as displayed on the back of books' covers), and your author's bio. Each may be shorter than, but not exceed, 100 words (double-space, indent paragraphs). For response to inquiries and/or return of submissions, writers must enclose adequate means. *Note: stamps are not valid for mailing beyond a country's borders!* Send Canadian postage, IRCs, certified checks or international (if non-Canadian) money order. If you wish acknowledgment of your proposal's arrival, include SASE and pretyped letter or form." Accepts queries by mail, fax and e-mail. Considers simultaneous queries and submissions. Responds in about 1 month to queries; about 3 months to submissions.
Recent Sales: Sold 4 titles in the last year. *Heavenly Delicacies*, by Ingrid Born (Macmillan); *Your Plate or Mine?*, by Andrew Berry (Macmillan); *The Evil That We Do*, by Anne Barton (Elwood eBooks); *Rowers*, by John Cruise (Ellwood eBooks).
Terms: Agent receives 15% commission on domestic (Canadian) sales; 20% on foreign (non-Canadian) sales. Offers written contract.
Fees: "No fee for authors published in the same genre as their current endeavors. No fee to view book synopses and outlines. Otherwise, to partially defray our time and disbursements in studying and responding to submissions, a nominal entry fee of US $75 per proposal is charged: certified checks or international (if nonCanadian money order) money orders only. If agency agrees to represent, no further fees are required. Charges only for usual marketing disbursements: photocopying of manuscripts, long-distance telephone/fax, and express of proposals to/from publishers. Long distance inquiries via phone or fax are returned collect. Confers with and reports promptly to authors on marketing communications. Consulting fees to non-clients (e.g., self-marketing or self-sold book, contractual advice, etc.): $65/hr. Office hours: 9-5, Monday-Friday."
Tips: "Whether writing fiction or nonfiction, for adults or children, study your chosen genre thoroughly to learn style/technique and what publishers are contracting. It's a very tight, competitive market. Be professional with your presentation's appearance. Form *and* substance sell proposals. The initial impact sets the stage for agents and editors in anticipating the caliber of your literary ability. If undistracted by mechanical flaws, your audience may focus upon your proposal's content. For your guidance, our 22-page booklet, *"CRASH COURSE" for Proposals to Book and Magazine Publishers: Business Letters, Basic Punctuation/Information Guidelines & Manuscript Formatting*, is available for US $8.95 (includes postage/handling). Certified checks or international (if nonCanadian) money orders only."

✂ 💲 ⏺ **AUTHORS MARKETING SERVICES LTD.**, 55 Kennedy Ave., Toronto, Ontario M6S 2X6 Canada. (416)763-8797. Fax: (416)763-1504. E-mail: Authors_LHoffman@compuserve.com. **Contact:** Larry Hoffman. Estab. 1978. Represents 20 clients. 25% of clients are new/previously unpublished writers. Currently handles: 65% nonfiction books; 10% juvenile books; 25% novels.
  • Prior to becoming an agent, L. Hoffman worked for a bookstore chain.
Member Agents: Antonia Hoffman (nonfiction); Sharon DeWynter (romance).
Represents: Nonfiction books, novels. **Considers these nonfiction areas:** biography/autobiography; business; child guidance/parenting; cooking/food/nutrition; education; current affairs; health/medicine; history; how-to; military/war; popular culture; psychology; self-help/personal improvement; sports; travel; true crime/investigative; women's issues/women's studies. **Considers these fiction areas:** action/adventure; cartoon/comic; detective/police/crime; family saga; fantasy; historical; horror; literary; mainstream; mystery/suspense; romance; science fiction; thriller/espionage.
  ○─┐ This agency specializes in commercial books.
How to Contact: Send outline and 1 sample chapter with SASE. Accepts queries by e-mail or fax. Consider simultaneous queries. Responds in 1 week to queries; 2 months to mss. Returns materials only with SASE. Obtains most new clients through recommendations from others.
Recent Sales: Sold 6 titles in the last year. *Euromarket Day Finder*, by R. Lauers (Pearson); *The Banks*, by L. Whittington (Stoddart); *EDF for Windows*, by R. Lavers (Pearson Professional); *Firesale*, by L. Whittington (HarperCollins); *Confidentially Yours*, by Julia Dow (McClellan & Stewart).
Terms: Agent receives 15% commission on domestic sales; 20% on foreign sales. Offers written contract, negotiable.

Fees: Charges $295 reading fee to new and unpublished novelists only. "A reading/evaluation fee of $395 applies only to unpublished authors, and the fee must accompany the completed manuscript. Criticism service is included in the reading fee. The critique averages three to four pages in length, and discusses strengths and weaknesses of the execution, as well as advice aimed at eliminating weakness." 5% of business is derived from criticism service. Payment of criticism fee does not ensure representation.

N 🌐 ⊘ FRENCH'S, 9 Elgin Mews S., London W91JZ England. **Contact:** Mark Taylor. Represents 40 clients. 15% of clients are new/previously unpublished writers. Currently handles: 20% nonfiction books; 50% novels; 20% movie scripts; 20% TV scripts.
   • Prior to becoming an agent, Mr. Taylor was an assistant in another literary agency.
Represents: Nonfiction books, novels. **Considers these nonfiction areas:** biography/autobiography; current affairs; government/politics/law; history; memoirs; popular culture; true crime/investigative. **Considers these fiction areas:** action/adventure; contemporary issues; detective/police/crime; erotica; fantasy; historical; horror; mystery/suspense; science fiction; thriller/espionage.
Also Handles: Episodic drama, movie scripts, TV scripts, feature film, TV movie of the week, sitcom. **Considers these script subject areas:** action/adventure; biography/autobiography; comedy; contemporary issues; detective/police/crime; erotica; family saga; fantasy; horror; mainstream; psychic/supernatural; science fiction; thriller/espionage.
How to Contact: Query with SASE or IRC or send outline and sample chapters. Accepts queries by fax. Considers simultaneous queries. Responds in 3 weeks to queries; 1 month to mss. Returns materials only with SASE. Obtains most new clients through recommendations from others. Returns material only with SASE.
Recent Sales: Sold 35 titles in the last year. Prefers not to share information on specific sales.
Terms: Agent receives 10% commission on domestic sales; 15% on foreign sales. No written contract.
Fees: Offers critique service for mss "where we consider work needs to be done." Charges £65 up to 100,000 words. £80 above for critique, money is refunded once ms is sold. 10% of business is derived from reading or criticism fees. Payment of criticism fee does not ensure representation.

N 🌐 ◐ LITOPIA CORPORATION LTD., 186 Bickenhall Mansions, London W1H 3DE United Kingdom. Phone (+44)20 7224 1748. Fax: (+44)20 7224 1802. E-mail: info@litopia.com. Website: www.litopia.com. **Contact:** Peter Cox. Estab. 1995. Represents 18 clients. 30% of clients are new/previously unpublished writers. Currently handles: 60% nonfiction books; 20% novels; 10% story collections; 10% textbooks.
   • Prior to becoming an agent, Mr. Cox was an author.
Member Agents: Peter Cox; Peggy Brusequ; Jane Mountbatten.
Represents: Nonfiction books, novels, short story collections, textbooks. **Considers these nonfiction areas:** animals; anthropology/archaeology; art/architecture/design; biography/autobiography; business; child guidance/parenting; cooking/food/nutrition; current affairs; education; gay/lesbian issues; government/politics/law; health/medicine; history; how-to; humor; interior design/decorating; language/literature/criticism; memoirs; military/war; money/finance/economics; multicultural; music/dance/theater/film; nature/environment; New Age/metaphysics; popular culture; psychology; religious/inspirational; science/technology; self-help/personal improvement; sociology; travel; true crime/investigative; women's issues/women's studies. **Considers these fiction areas:** action/adventure; confessional; contemporary issues; detective/police/crime; experimental; family saga; fantasy; feminist; gay/lesbia; glitz; historical; horror; humor/satire; literary; mainstream; mystery/suspense; New Age/metaphysical; psychic/supernatural; religious/inspirational; romance; science fiction; thriller/espionage.
   ☛ This agency's misison "is to provide the world's best management for the world's most creative people. Please refer to our website for an updated list of what we are actively seeking and what we do not want to receive."
How to Contact: "Follow submission guidelines on our website." Accepts queries by e-mail. Considers simultaneous queries. Responds in 6 weeks. Returns materials only with SASE. Obtains most new clients through recommendations from others.
Recent Sales: Sold 14 titles in the last year. *Stop Teaching Kids to Kill*, by De Gaetano (Crown); *Without Charity*, by Paver (Bantam); *Love Food Lose Weight*, by Twigg (Dutton); *Musician's Handbook*, Collis (Penguin). Other clients include Senator Orrin Hatch, Scott Jones, USN, Jeffrey Kottler, Michael J. Nelson, Professor Jane Plant.
Terms: Commission is negotiable. Offers written contract. 6-month notice must be given to terminate contract.
Fees: "No fees charged for standard submissions. If a Reader's Report is requested, this is charged at $50."
Tips: "Read our website and follow the simple submission guidelines."

🔳 ◯ JANIS RENAUD, LITERARY AGENT, Dept. 341, 20465 Douglas Crescent, Langley, British Columbia V3A 4B6 Canada. E-mail: jrliterary25@hotmail.com. Website: www3.telus.net/literary1/literary1.html. **Contact:** Janis Renaud. Estab. 1998.
   • Prior to opening her agency, Ms. Renaud worked as an independent television producer, casting director and writer (MOWs, documentary).

ALWAYS INCLUDE an International Reply Coupon (IRC) for reply or return of your material when sending query letters to non-U.S. countries.

Represents: Nonfiction books, juvenile books, scholarly books, novels, textbooks, novellas, short story collections. **Considers these nonfiction areas:** agriculture/horticulture; animals; anthropology/archaeology; art/architecture/design; biography/autobiography; business; child guidance/parenting; cooking/food/nutrition; crafts/hobbies; current affairs; education; ethnic/cultural interests; government/politics/law; health/medicine; history; how-to; humor; interior design/ decorating; juvenile nonfiction; language/literature/criticism; money/finance/economics; music/dance/theater/film; nature/environment; New Age/metaphysics; popular culture; psychology; religious/inspirational; science/technology; self-help/personal improvement; sociology; sports; true crime/ investigative; women's issues/women's studies. **Considers these fiction areas:** contemporary issues; ethnic; experimental; historical; horror; humor/satire; juvenile; literary; mainstream; mystery (amateur sleuth); suspense; psychic/supernatural; regional; religious/inspirational; romance (contemporary, gothic, historical, regency); sports; thriller/espionage; young adult.

O⟶ Actively seeking all genres and writers willing to work hard at their craft. The following are of particular interest: literary fiction, women's issues, mystery, suspense, thrillers, true crime, young adult, romance, health, parapsychology, show business and how-to books. Does not want to receive any graphic violence or pornographic material, poetry, anthologies, westerns, science fiction, adventure or erotica.

How to Contact: Query with SASE (writers outside Canada must include IRCs). "Fiction should include a short synopsis, first 3 chapters, and approximate word count. A half page bio is also helpful. Nonfiction should include a chapter outline, author credentials, research done, meaning, audience, competition, and how you think your book is different. Approximate word count." Accepts queries by e-mail, "maximum of one page. No attachments." Considers simultaneous queries and submissions. *No telephone or faxed queries, please.* Returns materials only with SASE. Obtains most new clients through advertising, referrals and conferences.

Recent Sales: Prefers not to share information on specific sales.

Terms: Agent receives 15% commission on domestic sales; 20% on foreign sales. Offers written contract, binding for 1 year, with renewals. Book by book basis. 60-day written notice must be given to terminate contract.

Fees: Charges one-time flat marketing fee to defer costs. Cost is $225, minimum of 8-10 targeted publishers.

Writers' Conferences: Writer's World (British Columbia, fall).

Agents Specialties Index: Fee-charging

The subject index is divided into fiction and nonfiction subject categories for Fee-charging Literary Agents. Also included in this index are the **Canadian/International** fee-charging agents. To find an agent interested in the type of manuscript you've written, see the appropriate sections under subject headings that best describe your work. Check the Listings Index for the page number of the agent's listing, then look for that listing in the section of Fee-charging Literary Agents preceding this index. Agents who are open to most fiction, nonfiction, or script subjects appear under the "Open to all Categories" heading.

FEE-CHARGING LITERARY AGENTS/FICTION

Action/Adventure: ABS Literary Agency; AEI/Atchity Editorial/Entertainment International; Ahearn Agency, Inc., The; Amber Literary; Authors Marketing Services Ltd.; BAWN Publishers Inc.—Literary Agency; Bethel Agency; Buchan Literary Service, Jim; Catalog Literary Agency, The; Collier Associates; Creative Literary Agency; Fishbein Associates, Frieda; Fran Literary Agency; French's; Gibson Agency, The Sebastian; Gladden Unlimited; Gusay Literary Agency, The Charlotte; Hartline Literary Agency; Independent Publishing Agency: A Literary and Entertainment Agency; Literary Group West; Litopia Corporation Ltd.; Nelson Literary Agency & Lecture Bureau, BK; Pelham Literary Agency; PMA Literary and Film Management, Inc.; Puddingstone Literary Agency; Scagnetti Talent & Literary Agency, Jack; Seymour Agency, The; Steinberg Literary Agency, Michael; Strong Literary Agency, Marianne; Tahoe Sierras Agency; Wolcott Literary Agency

Cartoon/Comic: Authors Marketing Services Ltd.; Buchan Literary Service, Jim; Fran Literary Agency; Gusay Literary Agency, The Charlotte; Howard Agency, The Eddy; Independent Publishing Agency: A Literary and Entertainment Agency; Nelson Literary Agency & Lecture Bureau, BK

Confessional: BAWN Publishers Inc.—Literary Agency; Bethel Agency; Gusay Literary Agency, The Charlotte; Independent Publishing Agency: A Literary and Entertainment Agency; Tahoe Sierras Agency

Contemporary Issues: AEI/Atchity Editorial/Entertainment International; Ahearn Agency, Inc., The; Amber Literary; BAWN Publishers Inc.—Literary Agency; Bethel Agency; Creative Literary Agency; Fishbein Associates, Frieda; Fran Literary Agency; French's; Gibson Agency, The Sebastian; Gusay Literary Agency, The Charlotte; Hartline Literary Agency; Howard Agency, The Eddy; Independent Publishing Agency: A Literary and Entertainment Agency; Litopia Corporation Ltd.; Nelson Literary Agency & Lecture Bureau, BK; PMA Literary and Film Management, Inc.; Renaud, Literary Agent, Janis; Scagnetti Talent & Literary Agency, Jack; Simenauer Literary Agency, Jacqueline; Steinberg Literary Agency, Michael; Strong Literary Agency, Marianne; Tolls Literary Agency, Lynda; Tornetta Agency, Phyllis

Detective/Police/Crime: Ahearn Agency, Inc., The; Amber Literary; Authors Marketing Services Ltd.; Bethel Agency; Collier Associates; Creative Literary Agency; Fishbein Associates, Frieda; Fran Literary Agency; French's; Gibson Agency, The Sebastian; Gladden Unlimited; Gusay Literary Agency, The Charlotte; Independent Publishing Agency: A Literary and Entertainment Agency; Literary Group West; Litopia Corporation Ltd.; Nelson Literary Agency & Lecture Bureau, BK; Pelham Literary Agency; PMA Literary and Film Management, Inc.; Puddingstone Literary Agency; Scagnetti Talent & Literary Agency, Jack; Seymour Agency, The; Steinberg Literary Agency, Michael; Strong Literary Agency, Marianne; Tahoe Sierras Agency; Taylor Literary Agency, Dawson; Tolls Literary Agency, Lynda; Toomey Associates, Jeanne; Wolcott Literary Agency

Erotica: AEI/Atchity Editorial/Entertainment International; BAWN Publishers Inc.—Literary Agency; French's; Gusay Literary Agency, The Charlotte; Independent Publishing Agency: A Literary and Entertainment Agency; Steinberg Literary Agency, Michael; Wolcott Literary Agency

Ethnic: Ahearn Agency, Inc., The; Backman, Elizabeth H.; BAWN Publishers Inc.—Literary Agency;

Bethel Agency; Gibson Agency, The Sebastian; Gladden Unlimited; Gusay Literary Agency, The Charlotte; Independent Publishing Agency: A Literary and Entertainment Agency; PMA Literary and Film Management, Inc.; Renaud, Literary Agent, Janis; Seymour Agency, The; Tolls Literary Agency, Lynda

Experimental: BAWN Publishers Inc.—Literary Agency; Gibson Agency, The Sebastian; Gusay Literary Agency, The Charlotte; Independent Publishing Agency: A Literary and Entertainment Agency; Litopia Corporation Ltd.; Renaud, Literary Agent, Janis; Wolcott Literary Agency

Family Saga: Ahearn Agency, Inc., The; Amber Literary; Authors Marketing Services Ltd.; BAWN Publishers Inc.—Literary Agency; Bethel Agency; Buchan Literary Service, Jim; Catalog Literary Agency, The; Creative Literary Agency; Fishbein Associates, Frieda; Fran Literary Agency; Gibson Agency, The Sebastian; Gusay Literary Agency, The Charlotte; Hartline Literary Agency; Howard Agency, The Eddy; Litopia Corporation Ltd.; Nelson Literary Agency & Lecture Bureau, BK; PMA Literary and Film Management, Inc.; Scagnetti Talent & Literary Agency, Jack; Simenauer Literary Agency, Jacqueline; Strong Literary Agency, Marianne; Tahoe Sierras Agency

Fantasy: Ahearn Agency, Inc., The; Amber Literary; Authors Marketing Services Ltd.; Backman, Elizabeth H.; Bethel Agency; Buchan Literary Service, Jim; Creative Literary Agency; Fishbein Associates, Frieda; Fran Literary Agency; French's; Gusay Literary Agency, The Charlotte; Howard Agency, The Eddy; Independent Publishing Agency: A Literary and Entertainment Agency; Litopia Corporation Ltd.; Nelson Literary Agency & Lecture Bureau, BK; Pelham Literary Agency; Tahoe Sierras Agency; Wolcott Literary Agency

Feminist: Ahearn Agency, Inc., The; BAWN Publishers Inc.—Literary Agency; Bethel Agency; Creative Literary Agency; Fishbein Associates, Frieda; Gusay Literary Agency, The Charlotte; Independent Publishing Agency: A Literary and Entertainment Agency; Litopia Corporation Ltd.; Nelson Literary Agency & Lecture Bureau, BK; Simenauer Literary Agency, Jacqueline; SLC Enterprises

Gay/Lesbian: Ahearn Agency, Inc., The; BAWN Publishers Inc.—Literary Agency; Bethel Agency; Gusay Literary Agency, The Charlotte; Litopia Corporation Ltd.; PMA Literary and Film Management, Inc.; Simenauer Literary Agency, Jacqueline; Tahoe Sierras Agency

Glitz: Ahearn Agency, Inc., The; Bethel Agency; Creative Literary Agency; Fran Literary Agency; Gibson Agency, The Sebastian; Gladden Unlimited; Gusay Literary Agency, The Charlotte; Litopia Corporation Ltd.; Nelson Literary Agency & Lecture Bureau, BK; Seymour Agency, The; Simenauer Literary Agency, Jacqueline; Strong Literary Agency, Marianne

Historical: ABS Literary Agency; AEI/Atchity Editorial/Entertainment International; Ahearn Agency, Inc., The; Amber Literary; Authors Marketing Services Ltd.; Backman, Elizabeth H.; BAWN Publishers Inc.—Literary Agency; Bethel Agency; Buchan Literary Service, Jim; Collier Associates; Creative Literary Agency; Fishbein Associates, Frieda; Fran Literary Agency; French's; Gibson Agency, The Sebastian; Gusay Literary Agency, The Charlotte; Hartline Literary Agency; Howard Agency, The Eddy; Independent Publishing Agency: A Literary and Entertainment Agency; Literary Group West; Litopia Corporation Ltd.; Nelson Literary Agency & Lecture Bureau, BK; PMA Literary and Film Management, Inc.; Renaud, Literary Agent, Janis; Scagnetti Talent & Literary Agency, Jack; Seymour Agency, The; Simenauer Literary Agency, Jacqueline; SLC Enterprises; Strong Literary Agency, Marianne; Tahoe Sierras Agency; Tolls Literary Agency, Lynda; Wolcott Literary Agency

Horror: Ahearn Agency, Inc., The; Amber Literary; Authors Marketing Services Ltd.; BAWN Publishers Inc.—Literary Agency; Catalog Literary Agency, The; Creative Literary Agency; Fran Literary Agency; French's; Gladden Unlimited; Litopia Corporation Ltd.; Nelson Literary Agency & Lecture Bureau, BK; Pelham Literary Agency; Puddingstone Literary Agency; Renaud, Literary Agent, Janis; Seymour Agency, The; Tahoe Sierras Agency; Wolcott Literary Agency

Humor/Satire: Amber Literary; BAWN Publishers Inc.—Literary Agency; Bethel Agency; Buchan Literary Service, Jim; Creative Literary Agency; Fishbein Associates, Frieda; Fran Literary Agency; Gusay Literary Agency, The Charlotte; Howard Agency, The Eddy; Independent Publishing Agency: A Literary and Entertainment Agency; Litopia Corporation Ltd.; PMA Literary and Film Management, Inc.; Renaud, Literary Agent, Janis; Seymour Agency, The; Tahoe Sierras Agency; Wolcott Literary Agency

Juvenile: Alp Arts Co.; Amber Literary; Author Author Literary Agency Ltd.; Bethel Agency; Buchan Literary Service, Jim; Catalog Literary Agency, The; Creative Literary Agency; Fran Literary Agency; Gusay Literary Agency, The Charlotte; Howard Agency, The Eddy; Independent Publishing Agency: A Literary and Entertainment Agency; Mews Books Ltd.; Renaud, Literary Agent, Janis; Tahoe Sierras Agency

Literary: Ahearn Agency, Inc., The; Amber Literary; Authors Marketing Services Ltd.; BAWN Publishers Inc.—Literary Agency; Bethel Agency; Catalog Literary Agency, The; Creative Literary Agency; Fran Literary Agency; Gusay Literary Agency, The Charlotte; Hartline Literary Agency; Howard Agency, The Eddy; Independent Publishing Agency: A Literary and Entertainment Agency; Litopia Corporation Ltd.; Nelson Literary Agency & Lecture Bureau, BK; Pelham Literary Agency; PMA Literary and Film Management, Inc.; Renaud, Literary Agent, Janis; Simenauer Literary Agency, Jacqueline; SLC Enterprises; Strong Literary Agency, Marianne; Tolls Literary Agency, Lynda; Wolcott Literary Agency

Mainstream: Ahearn Agency, Inc., The; Amber Literary; BAWN Publishers Inc.—Literary Agency; Bethel Agency; Catalog Literary Agency, The; Collier Associates; Creative Literary Agency; Fishbein Associates, Frieda; Fran Literary Agency; Gibson Agency, The Sebastian; Gusay Literary Agency, The Charlotte; Howard Agency, The Eddy; Independent Publishing Agency: A Literary and Entertainment Agency; Literary Group West; Litopia Corporation Ltd.; Nelson Literary Agency & Lecture Bureau, BK; Pelham Literary Agency; PMA Literary and Film Management, Inc.; Renaud, Literary Agent, Janis; Scagnetti Talent & Literary Agency, Jack; Seymour Agency, The; Simenauer Literary Agency, Jacqueline; Steinberg Literary Agency, Michael; Strong Literary Agency, Marianne; Tahoe Sierras Agency; Wolcott Literary Agency

Mystery/Suspense: ABS Literary Agency; AEI/Atchity Editorial/Entertainment International; Ahearn Agency, Inc., The; Amber Literary; Authors Marketing Services Ltd.; Backman, Elizabeth H.; BAWN Publishers Inc.—Literary Agency; Bethel Agency; Buchan Literary Service, Jim; Collier Associates; Creative Literary Agency; Fishbein Associates, Frieda; Fran Literary Agency; French's; Gusay Literary Agency, The Charlotte; Hartline Literary Agency; Independent Publishing Agency: A Literary and Entertainment Agency; Litopia Corporation Ltd.; Nelson Literary Agency & Lecture Bureau, BK; PMA Literary and Film Management, Inc.; Renaud, Literary Agent, Janis; Scagnetti Talent & Literary Agency, Jack; Seymour Agency, The; Simenauer Literary Agency, Jacqueline; Steinberg Literary Agency, Michael; Tahoe Sierras Agency; Taylor Literary Agency, Dawson; Tolls Literary Agency, Lynda; Tornetta Agency, Phyllis; Wolcott Literary Agency

New Age/Metaphysical: Litopia Corporation Ltd.

Open to all Fiction Categories: Author Author Literary Agency Ltd.; Author's Agency, The; CS International Literary Agency; QCorp Literary Agency; Raintree Literary Agency, Diane; Zahler Literary Agency, Karen Gantz

Picture Book: Alp Arts Co.; Bethel Agency; Buchan Literary Service, Jim; Fran Literary Agency; Gusay Literary Agency, The Charlotte; Howard Agency, The Eddy; Independent Publishing Agency: A Literary and Entertainment Agency; Scagnetti Talent & Literary Agency, Jack

Psychic/Supernatural: Ahearn Agency, Inc., The; BAWN Publishers Inc.—Literary Agency; Bethel Agency; Creative Literary Agency; Gusay Literary Agency, The Charlotte; Independent Publishing Agency: A Literary and Entertainment Agency; Litopia Corporation Ltd.; Nelson Literary Agency & Lecture Bureau, BK; Renaud, Literary Agent, Janis; Simenauer Literary Agency, Jacqueline; Tahoe Sierras Agency; Toomey Associates, Jeanne; Wolcott Literary Agency

Regional: Ahearn Agency, Inc., The; Backman, Elizabeth H.; Bethel Agency; Creative Literary Agency; Fran Literary Agency; Gibson Agency, The Sebastian; Gusay Literary Agency, The Charlotte; Hartline Literary Agency; Howard Agency, The Eddy; Renaud, Literary Agent, Janis; SLC Enterprises

Religious/Inspirational: Amber Literary; BAWN Publishers Inc.—Literary Agency; Bethel Agency; Buchan Literary Service, Jim; Creative Literary Agency; Fran Literary Agency; Gusay Literary Agency, The Charlotte; Hartline Literary Agency; Litopia Corporation Ltd.; Renaud, Literary Agent, Janis; Seymour Agency, The; Strong Literary Agency, Marianne

Romance: AEI/Atchity Editorial/Entertainment International; Ahearn Agency, Inc., The; Amber Literary; BAWN Publishers Inc.—Literary Agency; Bethel Agency; Catalog Literary Agency, The; Collier Associates; Creative Literary Agency; Fishbein Associates, Frieda; Fran Literary Agency; Gibson Agency, The Sebastian; Hartline Literary Agency; Litopia Corporation Ltd.; Nelson Literary Agency & Lecture Bureau, BK; Pelham Literary Agency; PMA Literary and Film Management, Inc.; Renaud, Literary Agent, Janis; Scagnetti Talent & Literary Agency, Jack; Seymour Agency, The; Simenauer Literary Agency, Jacqueline; Strong Literary Agency, Marianne; Tahoe Sierras Agency; Tornetta Agency, Phyllis; Wolcott Literary Agency

Science Fiction: ABS Literary Agency; AEI/Atchity Editorial/Entertainment International; Ahearn Agency, Inc., The; Amber Literary; Authors Marketing Services Ltd.; Backman, Elizabeth H.; BAWN

Publishers Inc.—Literary Agency; Buchan Literary Service, Jim; Creative Literary Agency; Fishbein Associates, Frieda; Fran Literary Agency; French's; Gibson Agency, The Sebastian; Litopia Corporation Ltd.; Nelson Literary Agency & Lecture Bureau, BK; Pelham Literary Agency; PMA Literary and Film Management, Inc.; Puddingstone Literary Agency; Steinberg Literary Agency, Michael; Tahoe Sierras Agency; Wolcott Literary Agency

Sports: Backman, Elizabeth H.; Bethel Agency; Buchan Literary Service, Jim; Creative Literary Agency; Fran Literary Agency; Gibson Agency, The Sebastian; Gusay Literary Agency, The Charlotte; Howard Agency, The Eddy; Nelson Literary Agency & Lecture Bureau, BK; Pelham Literary Agency; Renaud, Literary Agent, Janis; Scagnetti Talent & Literary Agency, Jack; SLC Enterprises

Thriller/Espionage: ABS Literary Agency; AEI/Atchity Editorial/Entertainment International; Ahearn Agency, Inc., The; Amber Literary; Authors Marketing Services Ltd.; Backman, Elizabeth H.; BAWN Publishers Inc.—Literary Agency; Bethel Agency; Buchan Literary Service, Jim; Catalog Literary Agency, The; Collier Associates; Creative Literary Agency; Fishbein Associates, Frieda; Fran Literary Agency; French's; Gibson Agency, The Sebastian; Gladden Unlimited; Gusay Literary Agency, The Charlotte; Hartline Literary Agency; Independent Publishing Agency: A Literary and Entertainment Agency; Literary Group West; Litopia Corporation Ltd.; Nelson Literary Agency & Lecture Bureau, BK; Pelham Literary Agency; PMA Literary and Film Management, Inc.; Puddingstone Literary Agency; Renaud, Literary Agent, Janis; Scagnetti Talent & Literary Agency, Jack; Simenauer Literary Agency, Jacqueline; Steinberg Literary Agency, Michael; Strong Literary Agency, Marianne; Tahoe Sierras Agency; Taylor Literary Agency, Dawson; Toomey Associates, Jeanne; Wolcott Literary Agency

Westerns/Frontier: Ahearn Agency, Inc., The; Amber Literary; Bethel Agency; Creative Literary Agency; Fran Literary Agency; Gusay Literary Agency, The Charlotte; Nelson Literary Agency & Lecture Bureau, BK; Pelham Literary Agency; PMA Literary and Film Management, Inc.; Scagnetti Talent & Literary Agency, Jack; Seymour Agency, The; Strong Literary Agency, Marianne; Wolcott Literary Agency

Young Adult: Alp Arts Co.; Amber Literary; BAWN Publishers Inc.—Literary Agency; Bethel Agency; Buchan Literary Service, Jim; Catalog Literary Agency, The; Creative Literary Agency; Fishbein Associates, Frieda; Fran Literary Agency; Gusay Literary Agency, The Charlotte; Independent Publishing Agency: A Literary and Entertainment Agency; Mews Books Ltd.; Renaud, Literary Agent, Janis; Tahoe Sierras Agency; Wolcott Literary Agency

FEE-CHARGING LITERARY AGENTS/NONFICTION

Agriculture/Horticulture: BAWN Publishers Inc.—Literary Agency; Bethel Agency; Catalog Literary Agency, The; Fran Literary Agency; Renaud, Literary Agent, Janis; Toomey Associates, Jeanne

Animals: Ahearn Agency, Inc., The; Author's Agency, The; Bethel Agency; Catalog Literary Agency, The; Creative Literary Agency; Fran Literary Agency; Gibson Agency, The Sebastian; Litopia Corporation Ltd.; PMA Literary and Film Management, Inc.; Renaud, Literary Agent, Janis; Toomey Associates, Jeanne

Anthropology/Archaeology: Amber Literary; Author's Agency, The; BAWN Publishers Inc.—Literary Agency; Bethel Agency; Catalog Literary Agency, The; Fran Literary Agency; Gibson Agency, The Sebastian; Independent Publishing Agency: A Literary and Entertainment Agency; Litopia Corporation Ltd.; Nelson Literary Agency & Lecture Bureau, BK; Renaud, Literary Agent, Janis; Toomey Associates, Jeanne

Art/Architecture/Design: Amber Literary; Bethel Agency; Creative Literary Agency; Fran Literary Agency; Howard Agency, The Eddy; Independent Publishing Agency: A Literary and Entertainment Agency; Litopia Corporation Ltd.; Nelson Literary Agency & Lecture Bureau, BK; Renaud, Literary Agent, Janis; Strong Literary Agency, Marianne; Toomey Associates, Jeanne

Biography/Autobiography: AEI/Atchity Editorial/Entertainment International; Ahearn Agency, Inc., The; Amber Literary; Author's Agency, The; Authors Marketing Services Ltd.; Backman, Elizabeth H.; BAWN Publishers Inc.—Literary Agency; Bethel Agency; Buchan Literary Service, Jim; Catalog Literary Agency, The; Collier Associates; Creative Literary Agency; Devereux Company, The Wilson; Fran Literary Agency; French's; Gibson Agency, The Sebastian; Gladden Unlimited; Howard Agency, The Eddy; Independent Publishing Agency: A Literary and Entertainment Agency; Janus Literary Agency; Litopia Corporation Ltd.; Nelson Literary Agency & Lecture Bureau, BK; PMA Literary and Film Management, Inc.; Renaud, Literary Agent, Janis; Scagnetti Talent & Literary Agency, Jack; SLC Enterprises; Steinberg Literary Agency, Michael; Strong Literary Agency, Marianne; Tahoe Sierras Agency; Tolls Literary Agency, Lynda; Toomey Associates, Jeanne

Business: AEI/Atchity Editorial/Entertainment International; Ahearn Agency, Inc., The; Author's Agency,

The; Authors Marketing Services Ltd.; Backman, Elizabeth H.; BAWN Publishers Inc.—Literary Agency; Bethel Agency; Buchan Literary Service, Jim; Catalog Literary Agency, The; Collier Associates; Creative Literary Agency; Fran Literary Agency; Gibson Agency, The Sebastian; Gladden Unlimited; Hartline Literary Agency; Howard Agency, The Eddy; Independent Publishing Agency: A Literary and Entertainment Agency; Janus Literary Agency; Litopia Corporation Ltd.; Nelson Literary Agency & Lecture Bureau, BK; Puddingstone Literary Agency; Renaud, Literary Agent, Janis; SLC Enterprises; Steinberg Literary Agency, Michael; Strong Literary Agency, Marianne; Tolls Literary Agency, Lynda

Child Guidance/Parenting: ABS Literary Agency; Ahearn Agency, Inc., The; Amber Literary; Author's Agency, The; Authors Marketing Services Ltd.; Backman, Elizabeth H.; Bethel Agency; Buchan Literary Service, Jim; Catalog Literary Agency, The; Creative Literary Agency; Fran Literary Agency; Hartline Literary Agency; Howard Agency, The Eddy; Independent Publishing Agency: A Literary and Entertainment Agency; Litopia Corporation Ltd.; Nelson Literary Agency & Lecture Bureau, BK; PMA Literary and Film Management, Inc.; Renaud, Literary Agent, Janis; Simenauer Literary Agency, Jacqueline; Strong Literary Agency, Marianne

Computers/Electronics: ABS Literary Agency; Amber Literary; BAWN Publishers Inc.—Literary Agency; Catalog Literary Agency, The; Creative Literary Agency; Howard Agency, The Eddy; Nelson Literary Agency & Lecture Bureau, BK; Steinberg Literary Agency, Michael

Cooking/Food/Nutrition: Author's Agency, The; Authors Marketing Services Ltd.; Backman, Elizabeth H.; BAWN Publishers Inc.—Literary Agency; Bethel Agency; Buchan Literary Service, Jim; Catalog Literary Agency, The; Collier Associates; Creative Literary Agency; Fran Literary Agency; Gibson Agency, The Sebastian; Hartline Literary Agency; Independent Publishing Agency: A Literary and Entertainment Agency; Litopia Corporation Ltd.; Mews Books Ltd.; Nelson Literary Agency & Lecture Bureau, BK; PMA Literary and Film Management, Inc.; Renaud, Literary Agent, Janis; Scagnetti Talent & Literary Agency, Jack; Simenauer Literary Agency, Jacqueline; SLC Enterprises; Strong Literary Agency, Marianne

Crafts/Hobbies: Author's Agency, The; Bethel Agency; Catalog Literary Agency, The; Collier Associates; Creative Literary Agency; Fran Literary Agency; Independent Publishing Agency: A Literary and Entertainment Agency; Janus Literary Agency; Nelson Literary Agency & Lecture Bureau, BK; Renaud, Literary Agent, Janis

Current Affairs: Ahearn Agency, Inc., The; Amber Literary; Author's Agency, The; Authors Marketing Services Ltd.; Backman, Elizabeth H.; BAWN Publishers Inc.—Literary Agency; Bethel Agency; Buchan Literary Service, Jim; Creative Literary Agency; Fran Literary Agency; French's; Gibson Agency, The Sebastian; Independent Publishing Agency: A Literary and Entertainment Agency; Janus Literary Agency; Literary Group West; Litopia Corporation Ltd.; Nelson Literary Agency & Lecture Bureau, BK; PMA Literary and Film Management, Inc.; Renaud, Literary Agent, Janis; Scagnetti Talent & Literary Agency, Jack; Simenauer Literary Agency, Jacqueline; SLC Enterprises; Strong Literary Agency, Marianne; Tolls Literary Agency, Lynda

Education: Amber Literary; Author's Agency, The; Authors Marketing Services Ltd.; BAWN Publishers Inc.—Literary Agency; Catalog Literary Agency, The; Creative Literary Agency; Fran Literary Agency; Janus Literary Agency; Litopia Corporation Ltd.; Nelson Literary Agency & Lecture Bureau, BK; Renaud, Literary Agent, Janis; Simenauer Literary Agency, Jacqueline; Strong Literary Agency, Marianne; Tolls Literary Agency, Lynda

Ethnic/Cultural Interests: Ahearn Agency, Inc., The; Author's Agency, The; Backman, Elizabeth H.; BAWN Publishers Inc.—Literary Agency; Bethel Agency; Catalog Literary Agency, The; Fran Literary Agency; Independent Publishing Agency: A Literary and Entertainment Agency; Literary Group West; Nelson Literary Agency & Lecture Bureau, BK; PMA Literary and Film Management, Inc.; Renaud, Literary Agent, Janis; Tolls Literary Agency, Lynda; Visions Press

Gay/Lesbian Issues: Ahearn Agency, Inc., The; BAWN Publishers Inc.—Literary Agency; Bethel Agency; Litopia Corporation Ltd.; Tahoe Sierras Agency

Government/Politics/Law: AEI/Atchity Editorial/Entertainment International; Amber Literary; Author's Agency, The; Backman, Elizabeth H.; BAWN Publishers Inc.—Literary Agency; Bethel Agency; Buchan Literary Service, Jim; Catalog Literary Agency, The; Creative Literary Agency; Fran Literary Agency; French's; Gibson Agency, The Sebastian; Howard Agency, The Eddy; Independent Publishing Agency: A Literary and Entertainment Agency; Janus Literary Agency; Litopia Corporation Ltd.; Nelson Literary Agency & Lecture Bureau, BK; PMA Literary and Film Management, Inc.; Renaud, Literary Agent, Janis; Steinberg Literary Agency, Michael; Toomey Associates, Jeanne

Health/Medicine: ABS Literary Agency; Ahearn Agency, Inc., The; Author's Agency, The; Authors Marketing Services Ltd.; Backman, Elizabeth H.; BAWN Publishers Inc.—Literary Agency; Bethel Agency; Buchan Literary Service, Jim; Catalog Literary Agency, The; Creative Literary Agency; Fran Literary Agency; Gibson Agency, The Sebastian; Janus Literary Agency; Litopia Corporation Ltd.; Mews Books Ltd.; Nelson Literary Agency & Lecture Bureau, BK; Renaud, Literary Agent, Janis; Scagnetti Talent & Literary Agency, Jack; Simenauer Literary Agency, Jacqueline; Strong Literary Agency, Marianne

History: ABS Literary Agency; Ahearn Agency, Inc., The; Amber Literary; Author's Agency, The; Authors Marketing Services Ltd.; Backman, Elizabeth H.; BAWN Publishers Inc.—Literary Agency; Bethel Agency; Buchan Literary Service, Jim; Catalog Literary Agency, The; Collier Associates; Creative Literary Agency; Fran Literary Agency; French's; Gibson Agency, The Sebastian; Howard Agency, The Eddy; Independent Publishing Agency: A Literary and Entertainment Agency; Janus Literary Agency; Litopia Corporation Ltd.; Nelson Literary Agency & Lecture Bureau, BK; PMA Literary and Film Management, Inc.; Renaud, Literary Agent, Janis; SLC Enterprises; Steinberg Literary Agency, Michael; Strong Literary Agency, Marianne; Tolls Literary Agency, Lynda; Toomey Associates, Jeanne

How-to: Amber Literary; Author's Agency, The; Authors Marketing Services Ltd.; BAWN Publishers Inc.—Literary Agency; Buchan Literary Service, Jim; Catalog Literary Agency, The; Collier Associates; Creative Literary Agency; Devereux Company, The Wilson; Fran Literary Agency; Gladden Unlimited; Howard Agency, The Eddy; Janus Literary Agency; Litopia Corporation Ltd.; Nelson Literary Agency & Lecture Bureau, BK; Puddingstone Literary Agency; Renaud, Literary Agent, Janis; Scagnetti Talent & Literary Agency, Jack; Simenauer Literary Agency, Jacqueline; Steinberg Literary Agency, Michael; Strong Literary Agency, Marianne; Tahoe Sierras Agency

Humor: Amber Literary; Author's Agency, The; BAWN Publishers Inc.—Literary Agency; Buchan Literary Service, Jim; Creative Literary Agency; Fran Literary Agency; Litopia Corporation Ltd.; Renaud, Literary Agent, Janis; Tahoe Sierras Agency

Interior Design/Decorating: Author's Agency, The; Bethel Agency; Creative Literary Agency; Fran Literary Agency; Litopia Corporation Ltd.; Renaud, Literary Agent, Janis; Strong Literary Agency, Marianne; Toomey Associates, Jeanne

Juvenile Nonfiction: Ahearn Agency, Inc., The; Alp Arts Co.; Amber Literary; Author Author Literary Agency Ltd.; Bethel Agency; Catalog Literary Agency, The; Creative Literary Agency; Fran Literary Agency; Independent Publishing Agency: A Literary and Entertainment Agency; Mews Books Ltd.; Renaud, Literary Agent, Janis; Strong Literary Agency, Marianne; Tahoe Sierras Agency

Language/Literature/Criticism: Author's Agency, The; BAWN Publishers Inc.—Literary Agency; Bethel Agency; Creative Literary Agency; Howard Agency, The Eddy; Independent Publishing Agency: A Literary and Entertainment Agency; Litopia Corporation Ltd.; Nelson Literary Agency & Lecture Bureau, BK; Puddingstone Literary Agency; Renaud, Literary Agent, Janis

Memoirs: ABS Literary Agency; Author's Agency, The; Creative Literary Agency; Fran Literary Agency; French's; Litopia Corporation Ltd.; Nelson Literary Agency & Lecture Bureau, BK; SLC Enterprises; Wolcott Literary Agency

Military/War: Amber Literary; Author's Agency, The; Authors Marketing Services Ltd.; BAWN Publishers Inc.—Literary Agency; Bethel Agency; Catalog Literary Agency, The; Fran Literary Agency; Gibson Agency, The Sebastian; Independent Publishing Agency: A Literary and Entertainment Agency; Literary Group West; Litopia Corporation Ltd.; Nelson Literary Agency & Lecture Bureau, BK; Puddingstone Literary Agency; Scagnetti Talent & Literary Agency, Jack; Strong Literary Agency, Marianne

Money/Finance/Economics: AEI/Atchity Editorial/Entertainment International; Author's Agency, The; BAWN Publishers Inc.—Literary Agency; Bethel Agency; Catalog Literary Agency, The; Creative Literary Agency; Hartline Literary Agency; Independent Publishing Agency: A Literary and Entertainment Agency; Janus Literary Agency; Litopia Corporation Ltd.; Nelson Literary Agency & Lecture Bureau, BK; PMA Literary and Film Management, Inc.; Renaud, Literary Agent, Janis; Simenauer Literary Agency, Jacqueline; Steinberg Literary Agency, Michael; Strong Literary Agency, Marianne; Tolls Literary Agency, Lynda; Toomey Associates, Jeanne

Multicultural: Litopia Corporation Ltd.

Multimedia:: Nelson Literary Agency & Lecture Bureau, BK

Music/Dance/Theater/Film: Ahearn Agency, Inc., The; Amber Literary; Author's Agency, The; Backman, Elizabeth H.; BAWN Publishers Inc.—Literary Agency; Bethel Agency; Buchan Literary Service,

Jim; Creative Literary Agency; Fran Literary Agency; Gibson Agency, The Sebastian; Independent Publishing Agency: A Literary and Entertainment Agency; Litopia Corporation Ltd.; Nelson Literary Agency & Lecture Bureau, BK; PMA Literary and Film Management, Inc.; Renaud, Literary Agent, Janis; Scagnetti Talent & Literary Agency, Jack; Tahoe Sierras Agency; Author's Agency, The

Nature/Environment: Bethel Agency; Catalog Literary Agency, The; Creative Literary Agency; Fran Literary Agency; Gibson Agency, The Sebastian; Independent Publishing Agency: A Literary and Entertainment Agency; Litopia Corporation Ltd.; Nelson Literary Agency & Lecture Bureau, BK; Renaud, Literary Agent, Janis; Toomey Associates, Jeanne

New Age/Metaphysics: AEI/Atchity Editorial/Entertainment International; Author's Agency, The; BAWN Publishers Inc.—Literary Agency; Creative Literary Agency; Janus Literary Agency; Litopia Corporation Ltd.; Renaud, Literary Agent, Janis; Simenauer Literary Agency, Jacqueline

Open to all Nonfiction Categories: Author Author Literary Agency Ltd.; CS International Literary Agency; Gusay Literary Agency, The Charlotte; QCorp Literary Agency; Seymour Agency, The; Zahler Literary Agency, Karen Gantz

Photography: Author's Agency, The; Backman, Elizabeth H.; Bethel Agency; Catalog Literary Agency, The; Creative Literary Agency; Gibson Agency, The Sebastian; Independent Publishing Agency: A Literary and Entertainment Agency

Popular Culture: AEI/Atchity Editorial/Entertainment International; Ahearn Agency, Inc., The; Author's Agency, The; Authors Marketing Services Ltd.; BAWN Publishers Inc.—Literary Agency; Catalog Literary Agency, The; Creative Literary Agency; French's; Gibson Agency, The Sebastian; Independent Publishing Agency: A Literary and Entertainment Agency; Litopia Corporation Ltd.; Nelson Literary Agency & Lecture Bureau, BK; PMA Literary and Film Management, Inc.; Renaud, Literary Agent, Janis; Simenauer Literary Agency, Jacqueline

Psychology: Amber Literary; Author's Agency, The; Authors Marketing Services Ltd.; Backman, Elizabeth H.; BAWN Publishers Inc.—Literary Agency; Bethel Agency; Catalog Literary Agency, The; Creative Literary Agency; Gibson Agency, The Sebastian; Independent Publishing Agency: A Literary and Entertainment Agency; Litopia Corporation Ltd.; Nelson Literary Agency & Lecture Bureau, BK; Renaud, Literary Agent, Janis; Simenauer Literary Agency, Jacqueline

Religious/Inspirational: ABS Literary Agency; Amber Literary; Author's Agency, The; Backman, Elizabeth H.; BAWN Publishers Inc.—Literary Agency; Bethel Agency; Buchan Literary Service, Jim; Creative Literary Agency; Fran Literary Agency; Hartline Literary Agency; Independent Publishing Agency: A Literary and Entertainment Agency; Litopia Corporation Ltd.; Nelson Literary Agency & Lecture Bureau, BK; Renaud, Literary Agent, Janis; Simenauer Literary Agency, Jacqueline; Strong Literary Agency, Marianne; Tolls Literary Agency, Lynda

Science/Technology: Author's Agency, The; Backman, Elizabeth H.; BAWN Publishers Inc.—Literary Agency; Bethel Agency; Catalog Literary Agency, The; Creative Literary Agency; Devereux Company, The Wilson; Gibson Agency, The Sebastian; Independent Publishing Agency: A Literary and Entertainment Agency; Litopia Corporation Ltd.; Mews Books Ltd.; Nelson Literary Agency & Lecture Bureau, BK; Renaud, Literary Agent, Janis

Self-help/Personal Improvement: AEI/Atchity Editorial/Entertainment International; Ahearn Agency, Inc., The; Author's Agency, The; Authors Marketing Services Ltd.; Backman, Elizabeth H.; Bethel Agency; Buchan Literary Service, Jim; Catalog Literary Agency, The; Collier Associates; Creative Literary Agency; Fran Literary Agency; Gladden Unlimited; Hartline Literary Agency; Independent Publishing Agency: A Literary and Entertainment Agency; Janus Literary Agency; Litopia Corporation Ltd.; Mews Books Ltd.; Nelson Literary Agency & Lecture Bureau, BK; Renaud, Literary Agent, Janis; Scagnetti Talent & Literary Agency, Jack; Simenauer Literary Agency, Jacqueline; Steinberg Literary Agency, Michael; Strong Literary Agency, Marianne; Tahoe Sierras Agency; Tolls Literary Agency, Lynda

Sociology: Amber Literary; Author's Agency, The; Bethel Agency; Catalog Literary Agency, The; Creative Literary Agency; Gibson Agency, The Sebastian; Howard Agency, The Eddy; Independent Publishing Agency: A Literary and Entertainment Agency; Litopia Corporation Ltd.; Nelson Literary Agency & Lecture Bureau, BK; Renaud, Literary Agent, Janis; Tolls Literary Agency, Lynda

Sports: Author's Agency, The; Authors Marketing Services Ltd.; Backman, Elizabeth H.; BAWN Publishers Inc.—Literary Agency; Bethel Agency; Buchan Literary Service, Jim; Catalog Literary Agency, The; Creative Literary Agency; Gibson Agency, The Sebastian; Independent Publishing Agency: A Literary and

Entertainment Agency; Janus Literary Agency; Nelson Literary Agency & Lecture Bureau, BK; Renaud, Literary Agent, Janis; Scagnetti Talent & Literary Agency, Jack; SLC Enterprises; Taylor Literary Agency, Dawson

Translations: Author's Agency, The; BAWN Publishers Inc.—Literary Agency; Bethel Agency

Travel: Author's Agency, The; Authors Marketing Services Ltd.; Creative Literary Agency; Gibson Agency, The Sebastian; Nelson Literary Agency & Lecture Bureau, BK; PMA Literary and Film Management, Inc.; Simenauer Literary Agency, Jacqueline

True Crime/Investigative: AEI/Atchity Editorial/Entertainment International; Ahearn Agency, Inc., The; Amber Literary; Author's Agency, The; Authors Marketing Services Ltd.; BAWN Publishers Inc.—Literary Agency; Bethel Agency; Collier Associates; Creative Literary Agency; French's; Gibson Agency, The Sebastian; Gladden Unlimited; Independent Publishing Agency: A Literary and Entertainment Agency; Janus Literary Agency; Literary Group West; Litopia Corporation Ltd.; Nelson Literary Agency & Lecture Bureau, BK; PMA Literary and Film Management, Inc.; Puddingstone Literary Agency; Renaud, Literary Agent, Janis; Scagnetti Talent & Literary Agency, Jack; Simenauer Literary Agency, Jacqueline; Strong Literary Agency, Marianne; Tahoe Sierras Agency; Tolls Literary Agency, Lynda; Toomey Associates, Jeanne

Women's Issues/Women's Studies: ABS Literary Agency; AEI/Atchity Editorial/Entertainment International; Ahearn Agency, Inc., The; Amber Literary; Author's Agency, The; Authors Marketing Services Ltd.; Backman, Elizabeth H.; BAWN Publishers Inc.—Literary Agency; Bethel Agency; Catalog Literary Agency, The; Collier Associates; Creative Literary Agency; Gibson Agency, The Sebastian; Hartline Literary Agency; Independent Publishing Agency: A Literary and Entertainment Agency; Litopia Corporation Ltd.; Nelson Literary Agency & Lecture Bureau, BK; PMA Literary and Film Management, Inc.; Renaud, Literary Agent, Janis; Scagnetti Talent & Literary Agency, Jack; Simenauer Literary Agency, Jacqueline; SLC Enterprises; Strong Literary Agency, Marianne; Tahoe Sierras Agency; Tolls Literary Agency, Lynda; Visions Press

Young Adult Nonfiction: Mews Books Ltd.; Tahoe Sierras Agency

Script Agents

Making it as a screenwriter takes time. For starters, a good script takes time. It takes time to write. It takes time to rewrite. It takes time to write the four or five scripts that precede the really great one. The learning curve from one script to the next is tremendous, and you'll probably have a drawer full of work before you're ready to approach an agent. Your talent has to show on the page, and the page has to excite people.

You'll need both confidence and insecurity at the same time. Confidence to enter the business at all. For a twenty-two-week season, a half-hour sitcom buys two freelance scripts. There are less than 300 network television movies and less than 100 big screen feature films produced each year. Nevertheless, in recent years the number of cable channels buying original movies has grown, independent film houses have sprouted up all over the country, and more studios are buying direct to video scripts—all of which offer a wide range of opportunities for emerging scriptwriters. If you're good and you persevere, you will find work.

Use your insecurity to spur you and your work on to become better. Accept that, at the beginning, you know little. Then go out and learn. Read all the books you can find on scriptwriting, from format to dramatic structure. Learn the formulas, but don't become formulaic. Observe the rules, but don't be predictable. Absorb what you learn, and make it your own.

And finally, you'll need a good agent. In this book we call agents handling screenplays or teleplays script agents, but in true West Coast parlance they are literary agents, since they represent writers as opposed to actors or musicians. Most studios, networks, and production companies will return unsolicited manuscripts unopened for legal protection. An agent has the entree to get your script on the desk of a story analyst or development executive.

The ideal agent understands what a writer writes, is able to explain it to others, and has credibility with individuals who are in a position to make decisions. An agent sends out material, advises what direction a career should take, and makes the financial arrangements. And how do you get a good agent? By going back to the beginning—great scripts.

THE SPEC SCRIPT

There are two sides to an agent's representation of a scriptwriter: finding work on an existing project and selling original scripts. Most writers break in with scripts written on "spec," that is, on speculation without a specific sale in mind. A spec script is a calling card that demonstrates skills, and gets your name and abilities before influential people. Movie spec scripts are always original, not for a sequel. Spec scripts for TV are always based on existing TV shows, not for an original concept.

More often than not, a spec script will not be made. An original movie spec can either be "optioned" or "bought" outright, with the intention of making a movie, or it can attract rewrite work on a script for an existing project. For TV, on the basis of the spec script, a writer can be invited in to pitch five or six ideas to the producers. If an idea is bought, the writer is paid to flesh out the story to an outline. If that is acceptable, the writer can be commissioned to write the script. At that point the in-house writing staff comes in, and in a lot of cases, rewrites the script. But it's a sale, and the writer receives the residuals every time that episode is shown anywhere in the world. The goal is to sell enough scripts so you are invited to join the writing staff.

What makes a good spec script? Good writing for a start. Write every single day. Talk to as many people you can find who are different from you. Take an acting class to help you really hear dialogue. Take a directing class to see how movies are put together. If you are just getting started, working as an assistant to an established screenwriter can be beneficial. You get excellent experience, and as your name becomes attached to scripts, you'll have more assets to bring with you as you start to approach agents.

Learn the correct dramatic structure, and internalize those rules. Then throw them away and write intuitively. The three-act structure is basic and crucial to any dramatic presentation. Act 1—get your hero up a tree. Act 2—throw a rock at him. Act 3—get him down. Some books will tell you that certain events have to happen by a certain page. What they're describing is not a template but a rhythm. Good scriptwriting is good storytelling.

Spec scripts for movies

If you're writing for movies, explore the different genres until you find one you feel comfortable writing. Read and study scripts for movies you admire to find out what makes them work. Choose a premise for yourself, not "the market." What is it you care most about? What is it you know the most about? Write it. Know your characters and what they want. Know what the movie is about, and build a rising level of tension that draws the reader in and makes her care about what happens.

For feature films, you'll need two or three spec scripts, and perhaps a few long-form scripts (miniseries, movies of the week or episodics) as well. Your scripts should depict a layered story with characters who feel real, each interaction presenting another facet of their personalities.

Although you should write from your heart, keep in mind that Hollywood follows trends like no other industry. A script on a hot topic means more money for the studio. Current big genres are teen movies with edge, *Sixth Sense*-type thrillers, family-oriented stories, and real-life dramas. Instead of trying to write to a trend, use your stellar script to start one of your own.

Spec scripts for TV

If you want to write for TV, watch a lot of it. Tape several episodes of a show, and analyze them. Where do the jokes fall? Where do the plot points come? How is the story laid out? Read scripts of a show to find out what professional writers do that works. (Script City, (800)676-2522, and Book City, (800)4-CINEMA, have thousands of movie and TV scripts for sale.)

Your spec script will demonstrate your knowledge of the format and ability to create believable dialogue. Choosing a show you like with characters you're drawn to is important. Current hot shows for writers include *3rd Rock From the Sun*, *Everybody Loves Raymond*, *Law and Order*, *Will & Grace*, and *Felicity*. Newer shows may also be good bets, such as *Popular* and *The Hughleys*. If a show has been on three or more years, a lot of story lines have already been done, either on camera or in spec scripts. Your spec should be for today's hits, not yesterday's.

Television shows where the cast is predominantly composed of teenagers continue to be extremely popular. Shows like *Buffy the Vampire Slayer* and *Dawson's Creek* appealed so strongly to both adult and teen audiences that almost every network raced to add similar shows to their fall lineup. Animated sitcoms like *The Simpsons*, which are aimed at adult audiences, also remain favorites. Most networks now have animated shows in prime-time slots.

You probably already want to write for a specific program. Paradoxically, to be considered for that show your agent will submit a spec script for a different show, because—to protect themselves from lawsuits—producers do not read scripts written for their characters. So pick a show similar in tone and theme to the show you really want to write for. If you want to write for *Dharma & Greg*, submit a spec script for *Two Guys and a Girl*. The hour-long dramatic shows are more individual in nature. You practically would have had to attend med school to write for *ER*, but *Law and Order* and *NYPD Blue* have a number of things in common that would make them good specs for one another. Half-hour shows generally have a writing staff and only occasionally buy freelance scripts. Hour-long shows are more likely to pick up scripts written by freelancers.

In writing a spec script, you're not just writing an episode. You're writing an *Emmy-winning* episode. You are not on staff yet; you have plenty of time. Make this the episode the staff writers wish they had written. But at the same time, certain conventions must be observed. The regular characters always have the most interesting story line. Involve all the characters in the episode. Don't introduce important new characters.

SELLING YOURSELF TO THE SALESPEOPLE

Scriptwriting is an art and craft. Marketing your work is salesmanship, and it's a very competitive world. Read the trades, attend seminars, stay on top of the news. Make opportunities for yourself.

But at the same time, your writing side always has to be working, producing pages for the selling side to hawk. First you sell yourself to an agent. Then the agent sells herself to you. If you both feel the relationship is mutually beneficial, the agent starts selling you to others.

All agents are open to third-party recommendations, referrals from a person whose opinion is trusted. To that end, you can pursue development people, producers' assistants, anyone who will read your script. Mail room employees at the bigger agencies are agents in training. They're looking for the next great script that will earn them a raise and a promotion to the next rung.

The most common path, however, is through a query letter. In one page you identify yourself, what your script is about and why you're contacting this particular agent. Show that you've done some research, and make the agent inclined to read your script. Find a connection to the agent like "we both attended the same college," or mention recent sales you know through your reading the agent has made. Give a three- or four-line synopsis of your screenplay, with some specific plot elements, not just a generic premise. You can use comparisons as shorthand. *Men in Black* could be described as "*Ghostbusters* meets *Alien*" and lets the reader into the story quickly, through something she's familiar with already. Be sure to include your name, return address, and telephone number in your letter, as well as a SASE. If the response is positive, the agent probably will want to contact you by phone to let you know of her interest, but she will need the SASE to send you a release form that must accompany your script.

Your query might not be read by the agent but by an assistant. That's okay. There are few professional secretaries in Hollywood, and assistants are looking for material that will earn them the step up they've been working for.

To be taken seriously, your script must be presented professionally. You must follow predetermined script formats. Few agents have time to develop talent. A less than professional script will be read only once. If it's not ready to be seen, you may have burned that bridge. Putting the cart before the horse, or the agent before the script, will not get you to where you want to go.

Read everything you can about scripting and the industry. As in all business ventures, you must educate yourself about the market to succeed. There are a vast number of books to read. Samuel French Bookstores [(323)876-0570] offers an extensive catalog of books for scriptwriters. *From Script to Screen*, by Linda Seger and Edward Jay Whetmore, J. Michael Straczynski's *The Complete Book of Scriptwriting* and Richard Walter's *Screenwriting* are highly recommended books on the art of scriptwriting. Study the correct format for your type of script. Cole and Haag's *Complete Guide to Standard Script Formats* is a good source for the various formats. Newsletters such as *Hollywood Scriptwriter* are good sources of information. Trade publications such as *The Hollywood Reporter*, *Premiere*, *Variety* and *Written By* are invaluable as well. A number of smaller magazines have sprung up in the last few years, including *Script Magazine* and *New York Screenwriter*. See the "Books & Publications of Interest" section for more information.

When Should a Screenwriter Get an Agent?

BY CHARLES DEEMER

Beginning screenwriters invariably worry about getting an agent too early in their development. Not only are there important skills to learn before an agent is necessary (including marketing skills), but too-early contact with important agencies can prematurely—and permanently—close doors that might open a few years down the road. It's crucial that young screenwriters jump through the career hoops in the proper order.

Even before learning the craft, you must know what you are getting into. Screenwriting is unlike any other form of writing in several important ways.

For example, perhaps in no other writing field are language skills less important. A mediocre writer who masters the special craft of filmic storytelling will be more successful than a brilliant writer with mediocre storytelling skills. Screenwriting requires writing with great economy, and a screenplay is more a blueprint for a movie than a literary document to be read. Writers in love with language may be discouraged by how irrelevant their rhetorical skills can be in this world.

Screenwriting is also more collaborative than other forms of writing. The goal of a screenwriter is to sell a script so it may become a movie, and the first step of this process is to put the screenplay into development. What this really means is that the writer, who created the story, no longer determines what happens. The vision of a producer, director, or actor becomes much more important. The writer is reduced to a hired hand, making changes dictated by others.

In this context, the contrast between playwriting and screenwriting is striking. Whereas a playwright forever owns his material and changes in a script cannot be made without the writer's permission, a screenwriter relinquishes ownership once the contract is signed. This reality is hard for many writers to accept, and such writers should not pursue a career in screenwriting.

LEARN THE CRAFT

For those who can accept these first two obstacles, learning the craft is the highest priority. There are many ways to do this, from reading books and taking classes to studying scripts and videos of movies. The following essential skills must be mastered before approaching an agent with your script:

Format

Screenplays are written in a special format which has evolved in such a way that the writer no longer "calls the shots" of the camera. This format must be followed.

Language

Screenplays are written in sparse, compressed prose with little rhetorical dressing or complexity (even something as common as a complex sentence is rare in a tight screenplay). There is

CHARLES DEEMER *is the author of* Screenwright: The Craft of Screenwriting *(Xlibris Corporation) and* Seven Come Eleven: Stories and Plays, 1969-1999 *(Writers Club Press). Over three dozen of his plays have been produced and six of his screenplays optioned. He teaches undergraduate and graduate screenwriting courses at Portland State University and since 1994 has been the webmaster of the Screenwriters and Playwrights Home Page at www.screenwright.com.*

so much "white space" on the page that the compressed language of a 100-page screenplay would become only 25 or 30 pages of prose. Think of a screenplay as a thirty-page novel, in which only the essentials of the story are written.

Plot

Screenplay stories have a clear main character or hero who has a clear goal with clear obstacles standing in the way of reaching it. Most complexity and subtlety in a film come from the filmmaker and visual effects, not from the writer and story effects. In screenwriting, simplicity is a virtue.

Structure

Screenplay stories have a very clear beginning, middle, and end, or what is called the "classic three-act structure." There are almost no exceptions to this structure in the Hollywood film industry (including independent films), no matter what genre of story is being told. *Titanic, Dead Poet's Society, True Lies, Carrie, North By Northwest, Bird Cage, E.T.*, and even *My Dinner with Andre* all have classic three-act structures.

Pace

Screenplay narrative is driven by a strong sense of "what happens next." Dramatic movement in a screenplay is constant and intense no matter what kind of story is being told, or whether physical or psychological action drives the narrative. There should be no lapses in story interest, no time for the audience to run out for popcorn.

Timing

Scenes in a screenplay are short and efficient. Every scene over a page in length must be defended. There are no wasted moments in a screenplay.

BEFORE YOU CONTACT AN AGENT

Once the craft of screenwriting is mastered, there are three steps to take before seeking an agent: entering contests, querying independent producers without an agent, and deciding whether or not to move to Southern California.

Contests

Several contests have become important clearing houses for discovering new screenwriting talent. The two most important of these contests are the Nicholl Fellowships in Screenwriting and the Austin Heart of Film Screenwriting Contest. The serious young screenwriter should enter each annually. Many other contests are out there—the list growing almost monthly—but none have the prestige and practical advantages of these two. Even reaching the quarter-finals in the Nicholl or Austin will open doors to agents and producers. However, be forewarned that about five thousand people enter these contests each year, and that number keeps growing. (For information on Nicholl, go to www.oscars.org/nicholl/basics.html; for Austin, call (800)310-3378.)

Independent producers

Many independent producers will accept "queries" from unagented screenwriters. A query is a short letter—never over a page—in which you "pitch" your story and briefly summarize what credentials you may have. If producers are interested, they will request a script. If a producer becomes interested enough to want to "option" your screenplay, you then have leverage with which to seek an agent. (An option gives the producer temporary legal ownership of the script during a time period, usually a year, in which to try to finance the movie. In the past, scripts were optioned for 10 percent of the purchase price, but a trend distressing to writers has been the appearance of the "free option," which speaks to the crowded "buyers' market" business climate in Hollywood.)

Several tools are helpful in this self-marketing process. The most important is the *Hollywood Creative Directory* (*HCD*), which is available in print three times a year or online (updated weekly at www.hcdonline.com). This directory contains virtually every production company in the movie business, and there are hundreds of them. Facing the *HCD* can be overwhelming, so you need a strategy. I suggest this one, which requires a connection to the Internet. If you don't have one, get one—it will save you hours of research.

First, make a list of movies meeting the following criterion: "The producers of such-and-such would do a really good job on my script." Try to think of as many movies as you can.

Take this list to The Internet Movie Database (www.imdb.com), and look up each one in turn. Go to the movie credits, and write down all of the producers and production companies listed, especially the smaller companies you've never heard of (as opposed to Warner Bros. or Columbia Pictures) who probably originated the project. These unknown companies are the ones most receptive to beginning screenwriters.

Next take this information to the online *HCD*, and look up each production company and producer. If you find an e-mail address, use it; if not, use the postal address. If you use the latter, look for the name of the person with "development" after his title, and direct the letter there. If sending an e-mail, put "Pitch" in the subject line, and it will be directed to the right person.

E-mail or postage-mail your *brief* query letter. Any good screenwriting book will have examples of these. I suggest you do something else before sending out your queries: get your own 800 number. This is not expensive, and having your own 800 number will invite producers, who live on the phone (but who do *not* like unsolicited phone calls!), to respond to you.

Once you've exhausted your list of producers and companies, go back to the *HCD* and contact anyone who looks appropriate (that is, they don't specialize in genre movies inappropriate for your script). Self-marketing is a numbers game. Several hundred query letters may be sent out before interest is obtained. Nevertheless, a 10 percent response rate (one of ten requesting a script) is good.

Moving to Los Angeles

As you market your script, give serious thought to your goals as a screenwriter. There are two basic kinds of screenwriters: those who live in Los Angeles and are full-time writers, making most of their money on assignments; and everyone else. The latter, wherever they live (usually out of Los Angeles), write what are called "spec scripts," which are scripts written "on speculation" and marketed after they are written. These writers usually support themselves with other work, such as teaching or other kinds of writing.

All established, full-time screenwriters, on the other hand, get paid first and write second. They take assignments but also pitch their own ideas, seldom writing anything they don't first get paid to write.

If you want to join the ranks of the mainstream, you must live in Los Angeles. Period. It's where meetings are held and decisions are made; it's where networking happens and assignments are taken. If this is your goal, then you must decide how to survive in Los Angeles while paying your professional dues there.

If you don't want to live in Los Angeles, then accept the fact that your screenwriting career will be part time; you still must make a living.

As you market your script yourself, you immediately begin another. A serious screenwriter always has a new script in the works. There are no exceptions to this drive.

APPROACHING AGENTS

Finally, once you have producer interest in a script or have placed well in a contest, it is time to approach agents. If you live in Los Angeles, agents will be delighted to see a local return address on your query letter and will be more curious to meet you. They may even invite you to their office for a meeting.

At any rate, only query agents on the Writers Guild of America signatory list (available at www.wga.org). Agents on this list agree to abide by certain standards and rules set by the Writers Guild of America, the screenwriters' union. For example, these agents don't charge reading fees to Guild members—and if you find an agent who charges fees, run. Once you sell a script, you'll be required to join the union yourself.

Anyone who knows a working screenwriter will hear horror stories. They are true. This field is neither nice nor respectful to writers. That is why most career screenwriters graduate to directing, where they have more artistic control, and from there to producing, where they control the purse strings and, therefore, everything.

But this information should not surprise you once you think about it. Can you name a screenwriter who isn't also a director? On the other hand, can you name a director of stage plays? In theater, the playwright is the artist; in film, the director is the artist.

Despite these challenges and unpleasantries, many of us have screenwriting in our blood. If you do as well, welcome to the strangest, most frustrating arena a writer can find. Despite everything, you're going to love what you do.

Using an Agent to Launch a Career Outside Los Angeles

BY JANICE M. PIERONI

When Boston-based Pulitzer Prize-winning playwright and screenwriter David Mamet (*Glengarry Glen Ross*) spent the day with students and faculty at Boston's Emerson College, he spoke of a colleague who'd been getting lead roles on the Chicago stage but then moved to Los Angeles only to land tiny roles. When Mamet suggested that his friend return to Chicago where he had been playing lead roles, he exclaimed, "I can't do that! Los Angeles is where the jobs are!"

I have found much wisdom in this exchange. There are many writers and actors who believe they must live in Los Angeles to succeed in the entertainment industry. Nevertheless, many people have proved this idea wrong. Mamet is one writer who has worked steadily outside the Hollywood system, writing and directing films that he shoots mostly in and around New England. In the next town over from him, educational software developer Tom Snyder of Tom Snyder Productions produces the award-winning Comedy Central show, *Dr. Katz, Professional Therapist*. In nearby Roxbury, screenwriter Robert Patton-Spruill's first feature, *Squeeze*, was sold to Miramax. He also directed Showtime's *Body Count*.

These three examples of successful creators making film and television projects outside the Hollywood system are just the tip of the iceberg. In years to come, living where you want to live may become the norm for screenwriters and television writers, too.

LOCATION IS AN OPTION

For some, the romance of the Los Angeles screen scene is irresistible. The palm trees are intoxicating, playing tennis outdoors in winter feels like "hooky," and there is a giddy, "insider" feel to the realization that even the lowliest "development girls (or boys)" yield corporate credit like Samurai swords, and thus one need never buy or cook breakfast, lunch, or dinner again. Moreover, even if success proves elusive, as one writer put it, "If I'm going to be unemployed, I'd rather be in a place where I can surf most of the year."

For others, it's nice to have a buffer.

You may have work or family commitments that make it difficult if not nearly impossible to move. Fear of freeways, earthquakes, or fast-talking, film industry "suits" may be enough to convince you to stay away. Or, like many of us, you've lived in Los Angeles already and decided it's not for you. Perhaps your city or town is your muse and your inspiration. Your town is to you what Baltimore is to Barry Levinson or New York is to Martin Scorsese—it gets your mind dancing and your fingers flying.

If, for whatever reason, you decide to write screenplays while living outside of Los Angeles, revel in your choice! Be proactive about it, not defensive!

JANICE PIERONI is a former Universal Studios executive who launched her career working as Martin Scorsese's assistant, and has also worked for Warner Bros. and WNET, New York's public broadcasting station. Pieroni specializes in developing stories and screenplays and negotiating deals and is also an adjunct faculty member at Emerson College. She is admitted to practice law in both California and Massachusetts.

Turning a con into a pro

You can turn the liability of living outside Los Angeles into an asset—if not your greatest asset. To do so, you must create a Los Angeles presence without actually living there. One way to accomplish this goal is to enchant industry insiders with the unique charm of the world in which you actually live.

When I was an executive for Universal Studios, I was continually struck by how little most writers understand the link between purchases of stories and writers' personalities. Writers are storytellers. They tend to remember this idea when writing but forget it when speaking—especially when speaking about themselves. Agents, executives, and producers are looking for great scripts first and foremost, but if they can find a great script that comes packaged with a person who also fires them up, they are particularly appreciative. Writers living outside the Los Angeles area should be particularly mindful of this connection, and should use the uniqueness of their environment to their advantage when searching for agents and producers.

Agents can be your greatest allies in helping you create a Los Angeles presence when you live out of town. They (and in some instances, managers or entertainment attorneys) are the gatekeepers of the film and television industry. It is difficult to submit work to studios or production companies without them.

You may get the most mileage out of an agent, manager, or entertainment attorney who is based in Los Angeles or New York. However, many cities, including Boston, San Francisco, and Washington, D.C., have effective agents who have industry experience and insider contacts. Wherever he may work, the best agent is one who believes in you, connects with you, is willing to fight for you, and puts your interests first—no matter where you live.

But how can you compete with Los Angeles-based writers in attracting an agent?

Use your town to attract an agent

Try putting yourself in an agent's shoes. Most agents are bored at the prospect of reading one more Los Angeles-based screenplay written by a Los Angeles-based writer. They also tire of scripts inspired by news stories that were splattered across *The Los Angeles Times* eight weeks ago which spawned some 300 similar scripts.

As an out-of-towner, you have a distinct advantage. You are exposed to different media, different stories. Take agents into a fresh world—your world—and they will thank the screenwriting "gods" for sending you to them.

You can lure an agent by offering stories or news clips about events or persons living in your area. Is there an interesting lawsuit, feud, or project in your city that might make a good feature film, television movie, or television series? The ten seconds you spent clipping a news story (which is public domain material) could earn you a screenplay assignment and a producing deal. With a project in development, you become a "hot commodity" which boosts the sales prospects of your original script.

You can also offer to be the agent's "eyes and ears" in your part of the country. Without distracting yourself too much from your work as a writer, you can make it your business to know about emerging literary talent in your area. Is there a local novelist, playwright, screenwriter, short story writer, or journalist who has created a work that would make a wonderful movie, television movie, or series? If so, let your agent know.

This approach has additional benefits for you. You can, after optioning the rights, attach yourself to such projects as a producer and potentially earn a producing credit and fee if the project gets made. (Don't worry too much if you've never produced anything—Hollywood gives out producing credits like candy.) Your discovery might also be a good project for you to adapt as a screenwriter, perhaps working in collaboration with the original writer. You will, of course, need to secure permission from the writer.

USING AN AGENT TO LAUNCH YOUR CAREER FROM AFAR

What can an agent with knowledge and contacts in the entertainment industry do for you?

An agent has contacts

An agent can do much more than just try to sell your script. A good agent can offer solid advice on changes necessary to make a script marketable. Agents set up pitch meetings, or meetings in which you verbally present your screenplay ideas to a studio or production company. If you live far away, an agent can set up several meetings each time you visit Los Angeles. Agents can also get you paid rewrites or polishes of your own or another writer's work, sometimes known as "script doctoring." They can help you land staff writing deals on television shows or pilot writing assignments. They can sometimes get you a day job or freelance work in the industry to tide you over, such as work as a script reader. If you live outside Los Angeles, agents can help connect you with companies located near you.

Agents are known for having a lot of information that hasn't yet hit the trades and for leaking it—eager to show off their insider's knowledge. They often hear news about musical chairs within the industry, and projects that have been "green-lighted" (given a go-ahead) or placed into "turnaround" (been "killed" and are thus available for placement at another studio or production company). They also know what projects actors and directors are seeking to develop—sitcoms or one-hour episodic shows, comedies or dramas, young or mature demographics, etc.

You may wind up being a direct beneficiary of such an insider tip and get a job you would never have known about, all because your agent learned another writer had been fired from a project that morning. Since most producers will be sent a sample of your work before any face-to-face meeting, you will be at no particular disadvantage in securing such work if you don't live in Los Angeles as long as you can get there quickly and stay for at least a few days if necessary. This means your day job should be flexible enough to accommodate taking advantage of such opportunities on relatively short notice.

An agent can spread your name around

Perhaps the strongest skill any agent can offer a writer is the ability to create recognition of your name and appreciation for your work.

While agents are spreading the latest industry news or gossip, hopefully they are also building the legend of you! If you are a lawyer turned writer who lives in Anchorage, you may find yourself re-billed as an avalanche survivor who wrote an entire screenplay in your head while buried eyeball-to-eyeball with a moose under thirty feet of snow.

Based on my experiences at Universal Studios, discussions with agents, and my own hectic schedule now as I service clients all over New England and beyond, I would estimate that very active agents get about thirty-five or more calls a day, as well as e-mails and faxes. If you assume that five are personal, that leaves about thirty or more industry-related calls. If you are discussed in even 10 percent of their calls, in a week's time, about fifteen "introductions" will have been made. Why, you'll be taking Los Angeles by storm even while literally holed up in a blizzard writing your next screenplay from your Anchorage home (or cabin, as your agent will romantically refer to it).

OTHER WAYS TO BE AN INSIDER FROM THE OUTSIDE

Besides working with an agent, there are other ways to boost your career's potential without making a permanent move to Los Angeles.

Consider a writing partner

Another effective way to create a Los Angeles presence while living elsewhere is by having a Los Angeles-based writing partner. For starters, a Los Angeles-based partner can be beneficial because if you don't have an agent, often the agent of your collaborator will agree to take you on, too. And having a shared credit on a project that gets produced is far preferable to sole credit on a project that remains in your desk drawer.

Because you are exposed to different stories through local media, friends, neighbors, and work, you can bring stories to your partner that he might otherwise never encounter. He can then quickly rewrite them (busy Los Angeles writers are so on "automatic pilot" that they sometimes literally can't think of ideas but can often write up existing ideas practically in their sleep), make them more marketable, and then pitch them—in most instances without requiring you to fly to Los Angeles. If a deal is struck, you will share writing and possibly production credits. If a deal is struck for a television series, the experienced writer will probably executive produce the show, and you more likely than not will get a position as a staff writer, story editor, or co-producer, plus a series royalty, etc. Of course, in order to work on staff on a television show, you would most likely be required to move to where the show is shot in order to work directly with the production executives, actors, directors, and other writers. If you don't want to do this, you would still receive a portion, presumably 50 percent, of the buy-out rights to the project, as well as an ongoing series royalty.

How would you find such a partner? Which screenwriters do you most admire? If you are responding to their work, they will likely respond to your work as well. I'd approach these writers first. Ask to send a sample and to set up a pitch meeting. The partnership can evolve over time. If you do this, you should probably be prepared to meet face-to-face at least once or twice a year. However, keep in mind you don't need to meet in Los Angeles.

Try a part-time Los Angeles lifestyle

For several years, one of my favorite clients as an artists' consultant and entertainment attorney was a talented, prolific young Boston-area screenwriter named Nat Damon (yes, he is related). Like most screenwriters living away from Los Angeles, he wrestled with the idea of moving there. After numerous meetings in which we weighed the pros and cons, I hit him with the obvious: "Nat, you're a teacher. You get four months off a year—including your entire summer. Why not live in both places?"

It was a simple solution. Too simple and too logical. After making several trips to Los Angeles, Damon decided to move there. For him, it was the right time and the right place.

Living in Los Angeles for part of the year sounds extravagant, but it can be accomplished more easily than you might imagine. You may, for example, be able to swap apartments or houses—particularly if you live in a vacation destination. Or you can use corporate relocation apartments, which are fully furnished and have short-term rental agreements. A third possibility is renting a room in a house, either for the year or just periodically, giving you the added advantage of a Los Angeles address.

I would say that, at a minimum, you should try to make one trip to Los Angeles every year. However, if doing this is not possible for you, compensate by staying in touch more frequently with those Los Angeles contacts you do make through e-mails, phone calls, faxes, end-of-the-year holiday cards, and, most of all, by being a prolific writer with great ideas.

The importance of conferences

How will you compete against Los Angeles-based writers for the attention of studio executives? After all, those writers can show up for a meeting in an hour. Actually, more and more, it is possible to meet with agents, executives, producers, directors, and actors outside of Los Angeles. You might be able to meet quite a few industry professionals if you arrange your visits to coincide with major industry events or seminars offered in Los Angeles. Consult the Writers Guild of America and writers' magazines for lists of such events, or look for scriptwriting conferences in the **Writers' Conferences** section starting on page 333. Don't be intimidated to ask for meetings with studios or production companies who might be interested in producing your work.

The abundance of writers' conferences, retreats, film festivals, and other industry events sponsored all over the country now provides ample opportunities to meet such persons on your own turf, or at least closer to it than Los Angeles, and often in a much more casual and approachable atmosphere. Take advantage of these opportunities. We often forget that many of those important agents, executives, producers, directors, and actors didn't always live in Los Angeles. More than you might think might hail from your city or state, and still visit on holidays and special occasions. For example, people who have recently come to New England to work on films or plays include Oliver Stone, Danny De Vito, Quentin Tarantino, John Travolta, Steve Martin, Goldie Hawn, Michael Caine, and Natalie Portman (who is also a student in the area). With the right approach, it might be possible to meet such people when they are visiting in your own backyard.

Although Los Angeles will remain the nerve center of the film and television industry for the foreseeable future, there has been a truly remarkable decentralization of this industry within the last ten years, with pockets of independent production companies and local financing springing up all over the country. You can launch a film from your hometown without ever leaving it. The "if you build it, they will come" theory from *Field of Dreams* applies to screenwriters. If you write a richly textured and beautifully layered screenplay with characters and a sense of place rooted in your town, most Hollywood producers will bring a production team your way.

Managers vs. Agents— The Changing Role in Hollywood

BY RON SUPPA

If you don't have direct contacts in the movie and television industry you must partner with someone who does. Traditionally, the answer was clear: hire an agent! An agent can get exposure not only for your script but also for *you* which leads to writing assignments, the lifeline of the freelance screenwriter.

Photo by Eric Harrington

Ron Suppa

But the position of the agent as the primary sales force for the writer is changing. With many new markets to cover and a heavy concentration on packaging clients as a means of circumventing the straight 10 percent screenwriter commission, agencies are left with little time for grooming new writers or nurturing an existing client's career. The result is a black hole into which armies of untended writers have fallen. And where such a vacuum exists, someone will fill it. That someone is the literary manager. Some view managers as a welcome addition to the writer's sales force, but others see them as just a new percentage drain on a writer's sweat-income. As with anything new, the role of a literary manager is somewhat controversial. Ultimately, the question is, *what can a literary manager do for you and do you really want one?*

The role of an agent

Agents spend their days cultivating relationships with movie producers and studio executives. Those same people love agents because, although agents may not have infallible taste, they can be counted upon to distinguish a professionally formatted and potentially viable screenplay from one that is not up to marketable standards. Working with agents saves potential buyers piles of money on "coverage" (i.e., having your work read, summarized, and critiqued). Later the agent can also act as a buffer zone between producers and clients—a service that becomes more and more indispensable to writers as their cherished works climb the rocky path of development.

Agents also confer instant credibility to the new writer: if you have one, *you belong.* In addition, regardless of the individual egos that comprise it, film is a collaborative art, and the business of screenwriting is ultimately about the writer developing into someone with whom others in the business will want to work. When bonds form, assignments can follow and careers can become established.

RON SUPPA *is a member of the Writers Guild of America, west and a former entertainment lawyer. He is also a published author, a produced screenwriter, an international script consultant, the producer of ten feature motion pictures, and a regular contributor to* Creative Screenwriting Magazine. *A Senior Instructor in the UCLA Extension Writers Program, Suppa is currently Visiting Professor of Screenwriting at the University of Miami School of Communication. Portions of this article have been excerpted from his book,* This Business of Screenwriting *(Lone Eagle Publishing Co.).*

How managers fit into the picture

Sometimes it seems you need an agent to get an agent. As one agent bluntly put it: "Let new writers do the work, find a prominent person in the film business, have them read the work first and personally recommend it to me, and then, and only then, will I read it." This attitude can be frustrating for writers, especially in the new Hollywood hustle where the "blockbuster" mentality rules. It can seem that agents are so busy cultivating writers with proven track records and a steady income stream that they hardly have time to read work by new writers.

Enter the literary manager. While talent management is not a novel concept, what was once hands-on career guidance for highly successful actors is now seen as a viable support base for, and income source from, writers as well. The financial carrot is there: a film agent is limited by law to 10 percent of a client's gross income and cannot produce or otherwise involve himself directly in a client's film. Managers have free reign to take a 15, 25, or even 50 percent commission if the client so agrees, and can negotiate freely for credits or employment on a client's film.

And, anyone can declare himself to be a literary manager—no training, no tests, no licensing required. Similar to the New York publishing industry, entertainment industry background and contacts will do for experience. In California, agents must be licensed to procure employment and negotiate deals, while personal managers are neither regulated nor franchised. By law, their work is strictly limited to advise and counsel. Many managers, however, ignore these regulations, and solicit jobs for their clients with or without the help of an agent. And because the money is better, former agents seem to take to the management business like a fish to water.

This mass exodus has ruffled more than a few feathers in the agency business. When a key agent at United Talent Agency left to form a management company, many of his writing clients went with him. More recently, former superagent Michael Ovitz announced the formation of his management company, Artists Management Group; his former client, Robin Williams, promptly exited Creative Artists Agency (with his then agent) to join him. Such developments have left agents wondering out loud whether managers are acting as *de facto* agents. In fact, the argument in California has reached Sacramento, where legislation is being introduced that would oblige managers to labor under substantially the same rules as agents.

The benefits of working with a literary manager

Why do writers need a manager at all? Simply put, writers want work. And despite the legal constraint in California against managers seeking or obtaining work for their clients, a manager can help a writer find more work.

In practice, a manager can gain employment for his clients and still remain within the law. For example, he can help obtain agency representation or switch the writer to an agent who will market the writer and his work more aggressively. He can prod the agent to action with calls a writer may be loath to make himself. He can help the agent arrange meetings with producers, production company executives, and others in order to more widely expose the writer and his work to the film community.

Managers can also help build the rest of the writer's support team, finding him a publicist, entertainment attorney, business manager, or industry-savvy accountant. He may even help a blocked writer find a writing partner to get the creative juices flowing again.

Creatively, a manager can help identify the current needs of the marketplace and serve as a critical reader of the writer's work before it is sent to potential agents or buyers. A manager can even act as a test audience for a writer's pitch. And, in a business in which truth is in short supply, managers can make discreet inquiries to production companies and receive valuable feedback on what worked or didn't work at those pitch meetings. Perhaps most important for the writer who feels isolated at his computer, the manager can serve as a sounding board for the writer's concerns about the day-to-day activities of the film business and his place in it. A good manager keeps in constant touch with his client, unlike an agent who may speak with his client only upon the delivery of a new spec script to market.

As if all that was not enough bang for your buck, remember the manager often toils long and hard far in advance of any money changing hands. Many managers have small client lists and charge as little as 5 percent of the client's gross income (though 10 or 15 percent is more the norm) for developing a client's career.

Sometimes, the legal limits on a manager's role makes for curious justice. As a young lawyer, I represented a country-and-western singer suing her manager of ten years after a personal falling out. Her complaint, ironically enough, was that the manager had solicited bookings for her during a rough period when her agent had let her career simmer on the back burner. Though the manager's efforts were, at that time, well intentioned and encouraged, the judge ordered all of his hard-earned commissions forfeited.

Managers are best found via personal recommendations. Or try contacting one listed in this book or *The Hollywood Agents and Managers Directory* (Hollywood Creative Directory).

The problem with managers

If you are considering finding someone to manage your career, your next question will likely be: *What's the downside?"*

The manager/client bond is often the closest of all professional relationships in the entertainment industry, and there is much to recommend it. But, any seasoned veteran knows that abuse is possible when money can be made from the exploitation of talent.

The manager being attached to a client's project—as a producer, for example—is a common development in the manager/client association. And not, necessarily, an unwelcome one. For the writer, having a manager may mean acquiring an instant producer for a new screenplay as well as a chance to be in business with a trusted ally. For the manager, having a writer for a client is like getting a free option on good screen material as well as providing a means to profit from the alliance in a way prohibited to agents (who are barred by law from involvement in the production of their client's work).

Nevertheless, this kind of close relationship can also lead to conflict of interest that you, the writer, must vigilantly monitor. Ask yourself: is the manager working primarily for you or for him? If a studio wants to bid one million dollars for your spec screenplay but views your manager-cum-producer as excess baggage, he could actually hold up your deal with his own demands. Horror stories have been known to happen, especially if a management contract expressly gives permission for your manager to act as the producer of your projects.

How to protect yourself

The core of any management relationship is built on trust even though a writer will most likely have to sign a management contract. Ideally when the arrangement is no longer working, the parties should be able to shake hands and go their separate ways. But ours is not an ideal world; experience dictates that it's best if the terms of the association are set forth as specifically as possible.

Unlike an agency contract, which allows the writer to quit the agency if no work is obtained within a ninety-day period, a typical management pact is harder to exit gracefully. A writer can find himself contractually bound to a failing relationship or a vague notion of what services are expected on his behalf. Forewarned is forearmed; let the following caveats serve as a guideline for your agreement:

1. Be certain that the contract clearly spells out the duties of the manager and the responsibilities of the writer over the term of the contract. These duties can be so specific as to set forth the "meet and greet" contacts the manager will arrange, the number of times a week the manager will contact the writer, and the circumstances under which both parties can be released from the contract.

2. Presumably you will want a personal manager who is held in high esteem in the industry and who gives you the personal attention that sparked your interest in the manager to begin with. Therefore, you do not want the manager to be free to delegate or assign his duties to third parties without your approval. Similarly, while you may want help in finding an agent or lawyer, you do not want to grant the manager the right to form these associations *without your prior consent.*

3. Finally, be very wary of giving your manager power of attorney over any of your affairs, particularly the incurring of debt, the signing of contracts on your behalf, or the right to endorse and cash checks payable to you. Also, be careful about granting your manager the right to act, be credited, or paid as a "producer" of your work on the screen.

Although problems can arise as in any business relationship, when a writer and manager respect and value the other's contribution to the relationship, they can form a winning combination that's hard to beat.

Script Agents:
Nonfee-charging and Fee-charging

This section contains agents who sell feature film scripts, television scripts, and theatrical stage plays. The listings in this section differ slightly from those in the literary agent sections. Nonfee-charging and fee-charging script agencies are listed together. Fee-charging script agents are indicated by a clapper ($) symbol. A breakdown of the types of scripts each agency handles is included in the listing.

Many of the script agents listed here are signatories to the Writers Guild of America Artists' Manager Basic Agreement. They have paid a membership fee and agreed to abide by the WGA's standard code of behavior. Agents who are WGA signatories are not permitted to charge a reading fee to WGA members, but are allowed to do so to nonmembers. They are permitted to charge for critiques and other services, but they may not refer you to a particular script doctor. Enforcement is uneven, however. Although a signatory can, theoretically, be stripped of its signatory status, this rarely happens.

For the first time, we've included a section of Canadian/International Script Agents. To learn more about the pros and cons of using an agent outside the United States, read the introduction to this section on page 303.

When reading through this section, keep in mind the following information specific to the script agent listings:

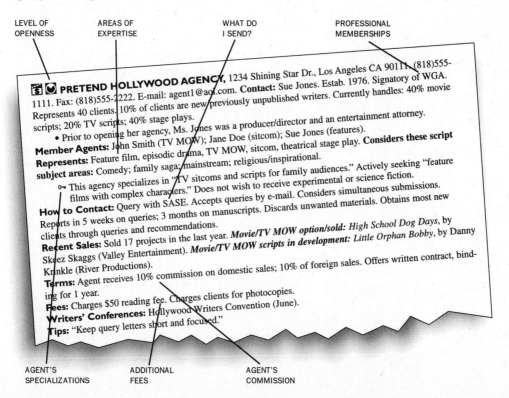

LEVEL OF OPENNESS
AREAS OF EXPERTISE
WHAT DO I SEND?
PROFESSIONAL MEMBERSHIPS

$ ✓ **PRETEND HOLLYWOOD AGENCY,** 1234 Shining Star Dr., Los Angeles CA 90111, (818)555-1111. Fax: (818)555-2222. E-mail: agent1@aol.com. **Contact:** Sue Jones. Estab. 1976. Signatory of WGA. Represents 40 clients. 10% of clients are new/previously unpublished writers. Currently handles: 40% movie scripts; 20% TV scripts; 40% stage plays.
 • Prior to opening her agency, Ms. Jones was a producer/director and an entertainment attorney.
Member Agents: John Smith (TV MOW); Jane Doe (sitcom); Sue Jones (features).
Represents: Feature film, episodic drama, TV MOW, sitcom, theatrical stage play. **Considers these script subject areas:** Comedy; family saga; mainstream; religious/inspirational.
  o→ This agency specializes in "TV sitcoms and scripts for family audiences." Actively seeking "feature films with complex characters." Does not wish to receive experimental or science fiction.
How to Contact: Query with SASE. Accepts queries by e-mail. Considers simultaneous submissions. Reports in 5 weeks on queries; 3 months on manuscripts. Discards unwanted materials. Obtains most new clients through queries and recommendations.
Recent Sales: Sold 17 projects in the last year. *Movie/TV MOW option/sold: High School Dog Days*, by Skeez Skaggs (Valley Entertainment). *Movie/TV MOW scripts in development: Little Orphan Bobby*, by Danny Krinkle (River Productions).
Terms: Agent receives 10% commission on domestic sales; 10% of foreign sales. Offers written contract, binding for 1 year.
Fees: Charges $50 reading fee. Charges clients for photocopies.
Writers' Conferences: Hollywood Writers Convention (June).
Tips: "Keep query letters short and focused."

AGENT'S SPECIALIZATIONS
ADDITIONAL FEES
AGENT'S COMMISSION

Quick Reference Icons

At the beginning of some listings, you will find one or more of the following symbols for quick identification of features particular to that listing.

- **N** Agency new to this edition.
- ✓ Change in address, contact information or phone number from last year's edition.
- **$** Fee-charging script agent.
- ▢ Agents who make sales to electronic publishers.
- ✦ Canadian agency.
- 🌐 International agency.

Level of Openness

Each agency has an icon indicating its openness to submissions. Before contacting any agency, check the listing to make sure it is open to new clients.

- ▢ Newer agency actively seeking clients.
- ▣ Agency seeking both new and established writers.
- ▣ Agency prefers to work with established writers, mostly obtains new clients through referrals.
- ◎ Agency handling only certain types of work or work by writers under certain circumstances.
- ⊘ Agency not currently seeking new clients. We include these agencies to let you know they are currently not open to new clients. *Unless you have a strong recommendation from someone well respected in the field, our advice is to avoid approaching these agents.*

For quick reference, a chart of these icons and their meanings is printed on the inside covers of this book.

A few of the listings in this section are actually management companies. The role of managers is quickly changing in Hollywood—they were once only used by actors, or "talent," and the occasional writer. Now many managers are actually selling scripts to producers. To gain a better understanding of this changing role, read "Managers vs. Agents—The Changing Role in Hollywood" starting on page 263.

It's a good idea to register your script before sending it out, and the WGA offers a registration service to members and nonmembers alike. Membership in the WGA is earned through the accumulation of professional credits and carries a number of significant benefits. Write the Guild for more information on specific agencies, script registration, and membership requirements.

Like the literary agents listed in the nonfee-charging and fee-charging sections of this book, some script agencies ask that clients pay for some or all of the office fees accrued when sending out scripts. Some agents ask for a one-time "handling" fee up front, while others deduct office expenses after a script has been sold. Always have a clear understanding of any fee an agent asks you to pay.

SUBHEADS FOR QUICK ACCESS TO INFORMATION

Each listing is broken down into subheads to make locating specific information easier. In the first section, you'll find contact information for each agency. You'll also learn if the agent is a WGA signatory or a member of any other professional organizations. (An explanation of all organizations' acronyms is available on page 366.) Further information is provided which indicates an agency's size, its willingness to work with a new or previously unpublished writer, and a percentage breakdown of the general types of scripts the agency will consider.

Member Agents: Agencies comprised of more than one agent list member agents and their individual specialties to help you determine the most appropriate person for your query letter.

Represents: Make sure you query only agents who represent the type of material you write. To help you narrow your search, we've included an **Agents Specialties Index** and the **Script Agents Format Index** immediately after the Canadian/International script agent listings.

☞ Look for the key icon to quickly learn an agent's areas of specializations and individual strengths. Agents also mention here what specific areas they are currently seeking as well as subjects they do *not* wish to receive.

How to Contact: Most agents open to submissions prefer initially to receive a query letter briefly describing your work. Script agents usually discard material sent without a SASE. Here agents also indicate if they accept queries by fax or e-mail, if they consider simultaneous submissions, and their preferred way of meeting new clients.

Recent Sales: Reflecting the different ways scriptwriters work, agents list scripts optioned or sold, and scripting assignments procured for clients. The film industry is very secretive about sales, but you may be able to get a list of clients or other references upon request—especially if the agency is interested in representing your work.

Terms: Most agents' commissions range from 10 to 15 percent, and WGA signatories may not earn over 10 percent from WGA members.

Fees: Agencies who charge some type of fee (for reading, critiques, consultations, promotion, marketing, etc.) are indicated with a clapper (🎬) symbol by their name. Also listed here are any additional office fees the agent asks the client to pay.

Writers' Conferences: For screenwriters unable to move to Los Angeles, writers' conferences provide another venue for meeting agents. For more information about a specific conference, check the **Writers' Conferences** section starting on page 333.

Tips: Agents offer advice and additional instructions for writers looking for representation.

SPECIAL INDEXES TO HELP YOUR SEARCH

Additional Script Agents: Many script agents are also interested in book manuscripts; many literary agents will also consider scripts. Agents who primarily sell books but also handle at least 10 to 15 percent scripts appear among the listings in this section, with the contact information, breakdown of work currently handled and a note to check the full listing in either the Nonfee-charging or Fee-charging sections. Those literary agents who sell mostly books and less than 10 to 15 percent scripts appear at the end of this section on page 302. Complete listings for these agents also appear in either the Nonfee-charging or Fee-charging sections.

Agents Specialties Index: Immediately following the section of Canadian/International Script Agents is an index divided into various subject areas specific to scripts, such as mystery, romantic comedy, and teen. This index should help you compose a list of agents specializing in your areas. Cross-referencing categories and concentrating on agents interested in two or more aspects of your manuscript might increase your chances of success. Agencies open to all categories are grouped under the subject heading "open."

Script Agents Format Index: Following the **Agents Specialties Index** is an index organizing agents according to the script types they consider: such as TV movie of the week (MOW), sitcom, or episodic drama.

Agencies Indexed by Openness to Submissions: This index lists agencies according to their receptivity to new clients.

Geographic Index: For writers looking for an agent close to home, this index lists agents state-by-state.

Agents Index: Often you will read about an agent who is an employee of a larger agency and you may not be able to locate her business phone or address. Starting on page 379, is a list of agents' names in alphabetical order along with the name of the agency they work for. Find the name of the person you would like to contact and then check the agency listing.

Listing Index: This index lists all agencies, independent publicists, and writers' conferences listed in the book.

For More Information

For a detailed explanation of the agency listings and for more information on approaching agents, read "Reading the Listings in the *Guide to Literary Agents*" on page 4 and "How to Find the Right Agent" on page 20. Also, take note of the articles dealing specifically with contacting—and working with—script agents that start on page 251.

SCRIPT AGENTS

ABOVE THE LINE AGENCY, 9200 Sunset Blvd., #804, Los Angeles CA 90069. (310)859-6115. Fax: (310)859-6119. **Contact:** Bruce Bartlett. Owner: Rima Bauer Greer. Estab. 1994. Signatory of WGA. Represents 35 clients. 10% of clients are new/previously unpublished writers. Currently handles: 95% movie scripts; 5% TV scripts.
• Prior to starting her own agency, Ms. Greer served as president with Writers & Artists Agency.
Represents: Feature film, TV MOW, animation, writers and directors.
How to Contact: Query by mail with SASE. Responds in 1 month to queries.
Recent Sales: Sold 25 projects in the last year. *Movie scripts sold*: *3 Stooges*, by Matheson (Columbia); *Charlie's Angels*, by Ryan Rowe (Columbia); *Constantine*, by Frank Cappello (Warner Bros.); *Dracula 2000*, by Saison (Dimension/Miramax). *Scripting assignments: Mephisto in Onyx*, by Greg Widen (Miramax); *Prometheus Project*, by Engelbach and Wolff (Fox).
Terms: Agent receives 10% commission on domestic sales; 10% on foreign sales.

ABRAMS ARTISTS AGENCY, (formerly The Tantleff Office), 275 Seventh Ave., 26th Floor, New York NY 10001. (646)486-4600. Fax: (646)486-0100. **Contact:** Jack Tantleff. Estab. 1986. Signatory of WGA, member of AAR.
Member Agents: Jack Tantleff (theater, TV, film); Charmaine Ferenczi (theater); John Santoianni (TV, film, theater).
Represents: Feature film, soap opera, episodic drama, theatrical stage play, sitcom, animation (TV), musicals. **Considers these script subject areas:** comedy; contemporary issues; mainstream; mystery/suspense; romantic comedy; romantic drama.
Oᵣ This agency specializes in theater, film, TV.
How to Contact: Query with outline and SASE. Accepts queries by fax. Returns material only with SASE.
Recent Sales: This agency prefers not to share information on specific sales.
Terms: Agent receives 10% commission on domestic sales; 10% on dramatic sales; 10% on foreign sales.

ACME TALENT & LITERARY, 6310 San Vicente Blvd., #520, Los Angeles CA 90048. (323)954-2263. Fax: (323)954-2262. **Contact:** Lisa Lindo Lieblein. Also: 875 Ave. of the Americas, Suite 2108, New York NY 10001. (212)328-0388. Fax: (212)328-0391. Estab. 1993. Signatory of WGA. Represents 12 clients. Currently handles: movie scripts; TV; Internet rights.
Member Agents: Lisa Lindo Lieblein (feature film specs); "also nine additional agents handling talent in Los Angeles, and three agents in New York."
Represents: Feature film. **Considers all script subject areas.** "Prefer high-concept well-written literate work."
Oᵣ This agency specializes in "feature films, completed specs or pitches by established produced writers and new writers." Actively seeking great feature scripts. Does not want to receive unsolicited material.
How to Contact: Query. Accepts queries by fax. Considers simultaneous queries. Responds in 1 week to queries; 2 months on mss. Returns unwanted materials only with SASE. Obtains most new clients through recommendations from established industry contacts, production companies of note, and reputable entertainment attorneys.
Recent Sales: "Since the beginning of this year, Acme has become a major player in the Internet/original content world of dot coms with websodes on Pop, Mediatrip, Z, Icebox, Voxxy, Reelshots, etc.)"
Terms: Agent receives 10% commission on domestic sales; 10% on foreign sales. Offers written contract, binding for 1 year.
Tips: We are very hands on, work developmentally with specs in progress. Individual attention due to low number of clients. All sales have been major 6-7 figures."

AEI/ATCHITY EDITORIAL/ENTERTAINMENT INTERNATIONAL, Literary Management & Motion Picture Production, 9601 Wilshire Blvd., Box 1202, Beverly Hills CA 90210. (323)932-0407. Fax:

(323)932-0321. E-mail: webaei@aol.com. Website: www.aeionline.com. **Contact:** Kenneth Atchity. Estab. 1996. Represents 50 clients. 75% of clients are new/previously unpublished writers. Currently handles: 30% nonfiction books; 40% novels; 30% movie scripts.
- See the expanded listing for this agency in Literary Agents: Fee-charging.

[N] [icon] AGENCY WEST ENTERTAINMENT, 6255 W. Sunset Blvd., #908, Hollywood CA 90028. (323)468-9470. Fax: (323)468-0867. **Contact:** Dackeyia Q. Simmons. Estab. 1995. Signatory of WGA. Represents 10 clients. 25% of clients are new/previously unpublished writers. Currently handles: 10% nonfiction books; 5% juvenile books; 5% novels; 40% movie script; 40% TV scripts.
- Prior to becoming an agent, Ms. Simmons was a writer and worked in personal management.

Member Agents: Holly Davis; Nancy Chaidez; Sheba Williams (youth division); J. Renee Colquit (youth division).
Represents: Movie scripts, feature film, novels, TV scripts, TV movie of the week, sitcom, miniseries, animation. **Considers these script subject areas:** action/adventure; biography/autobiography; cartoon/animation; comedy; ethnic; family saga; fantasy; juvenile; mainstream; religious/inspirational; romantic comedy; romantic drama; science fiction; sports; teen; thriller/espionage.
- Agency West Entertainment specializes in the theatrical development and representation of urban musical and literary artists in television and film.

Also Handles: Nonfiction books, juvenile books. **Considers these nonfiction areas:** biography/autobiography; child guidance/parenting; cooking/food/nutrition; crafts/hobbies; education; ethnic/cultural interests; how-to; humor; juvenile nonfiction; memoirs; music/dance/theater/film; religious/inspirational; self-help/personal improvement; sports; true crime/investigative; women's issues/women's studies. **Considers these fiction areas:** action/adventure; cartoon/comic; ethnic; family saga; fantasy; humor/satire; juvenile; literary; mainstream; religious/inspirational; sports; young adult.
How to Contact: Query with SASE. Prefers to read materials exclusively. Responds in 1 month to queries; 6 weeks to mss. Returns materials only with SASE. Obtains most new clients through recommendations from colleagues, conferences and festivals.
Recent Sales: This agency prefers not to share information on specific sales.
Terms: Agent receives 10% commission on domestic sales; 15% on foreign sales. Offers written contract.
Writers' Conferences: Book Expo America.
Tips: "Make sure your submission is your absolute best work before you send it to us. (No typos, correct grammar, proper script or manuscript format, etc.)."

[N] [icon] JOSEPH AJLOUNY LITERARY AGENCY, (Specialized: humor, popular culture and reference), Federal Bureau of Entertainment, 29205 Greening Blvd., Farmington Hills MI 48334-2945. (248)932-0090. Fax: (248)932-8763. E-mail: jsapub@aol.com. Website: www.the-feds.com. **Contact:** Joseph Ajlouny, director. Estab. 1988. Signatory of WGA; member of Mid-America Publishers Association, Michigan Publishers Association. Represents 80 clients. 20% of clients are new/previously unpublished writers. Currently handles: 60% nonfiction books; 20% stage plays; 5% syndicated material; 15% licensing.
- See the expanded listing for this agency in Literary Agents: Nonfee-charging.

[icon] ALLRED AND ALLRED, LITERARY AGENTS, 7834 Alabama Ave., Canoga Park CA 91304-4905. (818)346-4313. **Contact:** Robert Allred. Estab. 1991. Represents 5 clients. 100% of clients are new/previously unpublished writers. Currently handles: books, movie scripts, TV scripts.
- See the expanded listing for this agency in Literary Agents: Nonfee-charging.

[N] [icon] THE ALPERN GROUP, 15645 Royal Oak Rd., Encino CA 91436. (818)528-1111. Fax: (818)528-1110. Estab. 1994. **Contact:** Jeff Alpern. Signatory of WGA. Represents 50 clients. 10% of clients are new/previously unpublished writers. Currently handles: 30% movie scripts; 60% TV scripts; 10% stage plays.
Member Agents: Jeff Alpern (president); Liz Wise; Jeff Aghassi.
- Prior to opening his agency, Mr. Alpern served as an agent with William Morris.

Represents: Movie scripts (feature film), TV scripts (TV MOW, miniseries, episodic drama). **Considers all script areas.**
How to Contact: Query with SASE. Responds in 1 month.
Recent Sales: This agency prefers not to share information on specific sales.
Terms: Agent receives 10% commission on domestic sales. Offers written contract.

[check] [icon] AMG/RENAISSANCE LITERARY AGENCY, (formerly Renaissance Literary Agency), 9220 Sunset Blvd., Suite 302, Los Angeles CA 90069. (310)858-5365. **Contact:** Joel Gotler. Member of SAG, AFTRA, DGA. Represents 350 clients. 10% of clients are new/previously unpublished writers. Currently handles: 90% novels; 10% movie and TV scripts.
- See the expanded listing for this agency in Literary Agents: Nonfee-charging.

[icon] MARCIA AMSTERDAM AGENCY, 41 W. 82nd St., New York NY 10024-5613. (212)873-4945. **Contact:** Marcia Amsterdam. Estab. 1970. Signatory of WGA. Currently handles: 15% nonfiction books; 70% novels; 10% movie scripts; 5% TV scripts.
- See the expanded listing for this agency in Literary Agents: Nonfee-charging.

AUTHORS ALLIANCE INC., 25 Claremont Ave., Suite 3C, New York NY 10027. Phone/fax: (212)662-9788. E-mail: camp544@aol.com. **Contact:** Chris Cane. Represents 25 clients. 10% of clients are new/previously unpublished writers. Currently hands: 40% nonfiction books, 30% movie scripts, 30% novels.
• See the expanded listing for this agency in Literary Agents: Nonfee-charging.

JOSEPH A BARANSKI LITERARY AGENCY, 214 North 2100 Rd., Lecompton KS 66050. (785)887-6010. Fax: (785)887-6263. **Contact:** D.A. Baranski. Estab. 1975. Represents over 50 clients. Currently handles: 25% nonfiction books; 15% movie scripts; 50% novels; 5% TV scripts; 2% syndicated material; 2% textbooks; 1% stage plays.
• See expanded listing for this agency in Literary Agents: Fee-charging.

BASKOW AGENCY, 2948 E. Russell Rd., Las Vegas NV 89120. (702)733-7818. Fax: (702)733-2052. E-mail: jaki@baskow.com. **Contact:** Jaki Baskow. Estab. 1976. Represents 8 clients. 40% of clients are new/previously unpublished writers. Currently handles: 20% movie scripts; 70% TV scripts; 5% novels; 5% nonfiction books.
Member Agents: Crivolus Sarulus (scripts); Jaki Baskou.
Represents: Feature film, episodic drama, TV movie of the week, sitcom, documentary, variety show, miniseries. **Considers these script subject areas:** action/adventure; comedy; contemporary issues; family saga; glitz; biography/autobiography; mystery/suspense; religious/inspirational; romance (comedy, drama); science fiction (juvenile only); thriller/espionage.
• Actively seeking unique scripts/all American true stories, kids projects and movie of the weeks. Does not want to receive heavy violence.
How to Contact: Send outline/proposal and treatments. Responds in 1 month. Accepts queries by e-mail and fax. Obtains most new clients through recommendations.
Recent Sales: Sold 3 projects in the last year. *Movie/TV MOW scripts: Malpractice*, by Larry Leirketen (Blakely); *Angel of Death* (CBS). Other clients include Cheryl Anderson, Camisole Prods, Michael Store.
Terms: Agent receives 10% commission on domestic sales; 10% on foreign sales. Offers written contract.

BAWN PUBLISHERS INC.—LITERARY AGENCY, 2515 Losantiville Ave., Cincinnati OH 45237. (513)841-9664. Fax: (513)841-9667. E-mail: bawn@compuserve.com. Website: http://ourworld.compuserve.com/home pages/BAWN. **Contact:** Willie E. Nason or Beverly A. Nason. Estab. 1994. Represents 75 clients. 50% of clients are new/previously unpublished writers. Currently handles: 40% nonfiction books; 30% movie scripts; 30% novels.
• See the expanded listing for this agency in Literary Agents: Fee-charging.

THE BENNETT AGENCY, 150 S. Barrington Ave., Suite #1, Los Angeles CA 90049. (310)471-2251. Fax: (310)471-2254. **Contact:** Carole Bennett. Estab. 1984. Signatory of WGA, DGA. Represents 15 clients. 2% of clients are new/previously unpublished writers. Currently handles: 5% movie scripts; 95% TV scripts.
Member Agents: Carole Bennett (owner); Tanna Herr (features).
Represents: Feature film, sitcom. **Considers these script subject areas:** comedy; family saga; mainstream.
• This agency specializes in TV sitcoms.
How to Contact: Query with SASE. Responds in 2 months to queries if SASE included. Accepts queries by fax. Considers simultaneous queries. Returns materials only with SASE. Obtains most new clients through recommendations from others.
Recent Sales: *Scripting assignments:* "Most of our clients are on the writing staff of such half-hour sitcoms as *Friends* and *Dharma & Greg*."
Terms: Agent receives 10% commission on domestic sales. Offers written contract.

BERMAN BOALS AND FLYNN INC., 208 W. 30th St., #401, New York NY 10001. (212)868-1068. **Contact:** Judy Boals or Jim Flynn. Estab. 1995. Member of AAR; signatory of WGA. Represents about 35 clients.
Represents: Feature film, TV scripts, stage plays.
• This agency specializes in dramatic writing for stage, film, TV.
How to Contact: Query with SASE. Obtains most new clients through recommendations from others.
Recent Sales: This agency prefers not to share information on specific sales.
Terms: Agent receives 10% commission.

THE BOHRMAN AGENCY, 8899 Beverly Blvd., Suite 811, Los Angeles CA 90048. (310)550-5444; Fax: (310)550-5445. **Contact:** Michael Hruska, Caren Bohrman or Rob Seitzner, literary assistant. Signatory of WGA.

THE PUBLISHING FIELD is constantly changing! Agents often change addresses, phone numbers, or even companies. If you're still using this book and it is 2002 or later, buy the newest edition of *Guide to Literary Agents* at your favorite bookstore or order directly from Writer's Digest Books at (800)289-0963.

Represents: Feature film, TV scripts, theatrical stage play. **Considers all script subject areas.** Also represents novels.
How to Contact: Query with SASE. *Does not read unsolicited mss.* Obtains clients by referral only.
Recent Sales: This agency prefers not to share information on specific sales.

CURTIS BROWN LTD., 10 Astor Place, New York NY 10003-6935. (212)473-5400. Member of AAR; signatory of WGA. **Contact:** Perry Knowlton, chairman emeritus; Timothy Knowlton, CEO. Queries to Blake Peterson. Also: 1750 Montgomery St., San Francisco CA 94111. (415)954-8566. **Contact:** Peter L. Ginsberg, president.
• See the expanded listing for this agency in Literary Agents: Nonfee-charging.

[N:] **DON BUCHWALD AND ASSOCIATES, INC.**, 6500 Wilshire Blvd., Suite 2200, Los Angeles CA 90048. (323)655-7400. Estab. 1977. Signatory of WGA. Represents 50 literary clients.
Represents: Movie scripts (feature film, documentary; manuscripts); TV scripts (TV MOW, miniseries, episodic drama, sitcom); stage play (adult fiction).
How to Contact: Query with SASE only. Obtains most new clients through other authors, agents.
    ⚬┅ This agency represents talent and literary clients.

KELVIN C. BULGER AND ASSOCIATES, 11 E. Adams St., Suite 604, Chicago IL 60603. (312)692-1002. E-mail: kcbwoi@aol.com. **Contact:** Kelvin C. Bulger. Estab. 1992. Signatory of WGA. Represents 25 clients. 90% of clients are new/previously unpublished writers. Currently handles: 75% movie scripts; 25% TV scripts.
Represents: Feature film, documentary, TV MOW, syndicated material. **Considers these script subject areas:** action/adventure; cartoon/animation; comedy; contemporary issues; ethnic; family saga; religious/inspirational.
How to Contact: Query with SASE. Responds in 3 weeks to queries; 2 months to mss. "If material is to be returned, writer must enclose SASE." Obtains most new clients through solicitations and recommendations.
Recent Sales: This agency prefers not to share information on specific sales.
Terms: Agent receives 10% commission on domestic sales; 10% on foreign sales. Offers written contract, binding for 6 months-1 year.
Tips: "Proofread before submitting to agent. We only reply to letter of inquiries if SASE is enclosed."

[$] **[◎]** **SUZANNA CAMEJO & ASSOC.**, 3000 W. Olympic Blvd., Santa Monica CA 90404. (310)449-4064. Fax: (310)449-4026. E-mail: scamejo@earthlink.net. **Contact:** Elizabeth Harris. Estab. 1992. Represents 10 clients. 30% of clients are new/previously unpublished writers. Currently handles: 80% movie scripts; 5% novels; 10% TV scripts; 5% life stories.
Member Agents: Suzanna Camejo (issue oriented); Elizabeth Harris (creative associate).
Represents: Feature film, novels, TV scripts, life stories. **Considers these script areas:** contemporary issues; ethnic; family saga; feminist; historical; romantic comedy; romantic drama; science fiction; thriller; environmental.
    ⚬┅ This agency specializes in environmental issues, animal rights, women's stories, art-oriented, children/family. Does not want to receive action/adventure, violence.
Also Handles: Nonfiction, novels. **Considers these nonfiction areas:** animals; nature/environment; women's issues/ women's studies. **Considers these fiction areas:** ethnic; family saga; romance (comedy); environmental; animal.
How to Contact: Send outline/proposal. Does not accept e-mail queries. Considers simultaneous queries. Returns materials only with SASE. Obtains most new clients through recommendations from others and queries.
Recent Sales: *Primal Scream*, by John Shirley (Showtime); *The Christmas Project*, by Joe Hindy (Ganesha Partners).
Terms: Agent receives 10% commission on domestic sales; 10% on foreign sales. Offers written contract, binding for 1 year, with 3 weeks cancellation clause.
Fees: Charges $20 reading fee (per script or ms). Critiques of storyline, subplot, backstory, pace, characterization, dialogue, marketability, commerciality by professional readers. Charges postage for returned scripts.
Writers' Conferences: Cannes Film Festival (France, May); Telluride Film Festival (Colorado, September); Sundance Film Festival (Utah, January); AFM (Los Angeles, February).
Tips: "If the feature script is well written (three acts, backstory, subplot), with good characters and dialogue, the material is moving, funny or deals with important issues and is nonviolent (no war stories, please), we will read it and consider it for representation."

THE MARSHALL CAMERON AGENCY, 19667 NE 20th Lane, Lawtey FL 32058. Phone/fax: (904)964-7013. E-mail: marshall_cameron@hotmail.com. **Contact:** Margo Prescott. Estab. 1986. Signatory of WGA. Currently handles: 100% movie scripts.
Member Agents: Margo Prescott; Ashton Prescott; John Pizzo (New York co-agent).
Represents: Feature film. **Considers these script subject areas:** action/adventure; comedy; detective/police/crime; drama (contemporary); mainstream; thriller/espionage.
    ⚬┅ This agency specializes in feature films.
How to Contact: Query with SASE. No phone queries. Accepts queries by e-mail. Considers simultaneous queries. Responds in 1 week to queries; 2 months to mss. Returns materials only with SASE. "Must be referred by someone known to us in the industry. No unsolicited material."
Recent Sales: This agency prefers not to share information on specific sales.
Terms: Agent receives 10% commission on domestic sales; 20% on foreign sales. Offers written contract, binding for 1 year.

Tips: "Often professionals in film will recommend us to clients. Always enclose SASE with your query."

☑ ◖◗ **CEDAR GROVE AGENCY ENTERTAINMENT**, P.O. Box 1692, Issaquah WA 98027-0068. (425)837-1687. Fax: (425)391-7907. E-mail: cedargroveagency@juno.com. Website: http://freeyellow.com/members/cedargrove/index.html. **Contact:** Renée MacKenzie or Samantha Powers. Estab. 1995. Member of Cinema Seattle. Represents 7 clients. 100% of clients are new/previously unpublished writers. Currently handles: 90% movie scripts; 10% TV scripts.
   • Prior to becoming agents, Ms. Taylor worked for the stock brokerage firm, Morgan Stanley Dean Witter; Ms. Powers was a customer service/office manager; Ms. MacKenzie was an office manager and recently a Production Manager.
Member Agents: Amy Taylor (Senior Vice President-Motion Picture Division); Samantha Powers (Executive Vice President—Motion Picture Division); and Renée MacKenzie (Story Editor).
Represents: Feature film, TV MOW, sitcom. **Considers these script subject areas:** action/adventure; comedy; detective/police/crime; family saga; biography/autobiography; juvenile; mystery/suspense; romance (comedy); science fiction; sports; thriller/espionage; western/frontier.
   ○┯ Cedar Grove Agency Entertainment was formed in the Pacific Northwest to take advantage of the rich and diverse culture as well as the many writers who reside there. Does not want to receive period pieces, horror genres, children scripts dealing with illness, or scripts with excessive substance abuse.
How to Contact: Query with 1 page synopsis and SASE. "E-mail okay." Responds in 10 days to queries; 2 months to mss. *"Please! No phone calls!"* Obtains most new clients through referrals and website.
Recent Sales: This agency prefers not to share information on specific sales.
Terms: Agent receives 10% commission on domestic sales. Offers written contract, binding for 6-12 months. 30-day notice must be given to terminate contract.
Tips: "We focus on finding that rare gem, the undiscovered, multi-talented writer, no matter where they live. Write, write, write! Find time everyday to write. Network with other writers when possible, and write what you know. Learn the craft through books. Read scripts of your favorite movies. Enjoy what you write!"

☑ ○ **CHADWICK & GROS LITERARY AGENCY**, Lessman@Screenplay Pkwy 671, Baton Rouge LA 70806-5426. (225)338-9861. Fax: (775)206-1180. E-mail: chadgros@aol.com. Website: http://colorpro.com/chadwick-gros/. Director: Anna Piazza, director. **Contact:** Tony Seigan, associate director/overseas officer. Estab. 1998. Represents 30 clients. 95% of clients are new/previously unpublished writers. Currently handles: 90% movie scripts; 10% TV scripts.
   • Prior to becoming an agent, Ms. Piazza was a talent scout for Rinehart & Associates.
Member Agents: Tony Seigan (associate director/overseas officer); David J. Carubba (business manager); C.J. Myerson (president of Institute of Baton Rouge Qford Writers [I-BROWS] colony); Theron T. Jacks (business advisor).
Represents: Feature film, episodic drama, soap opera, TV MOW sitcom, documentary, variety show, miniseries, animation. **Considers all script subject areas.**
   ○┯ Actively seeking "good attitudes; tough-minded, sure-footed, potential pros."
How to Contact: E-mail for guidelines. "Study our website thoroughly before querying via e-mail." Accepts queries by fax and e-mail. Considers simultaneous queries and submissions. Returns material only with SASE. Accepts queries during February, July and October. "All material is returned critiqued." Obtains most new clients through website and listings in directories.
Recent Sales: Sold 16 script projects in the last year. *Movie/TV MOW scripts optioned/sold: Carrot Tips,* by J. Seivers (Generation X); *The Author; The Ouida Link; Whorehouse Roux.*
Terms: Agent receives 10% commission on domestic sales; 15% on foreign sales. Offers written contract, binding for 1-2 years. 6-month notice must be given to terminate contract. Charges clients for all communications with C&G—phone, fax, postage and handling—fees fall to queries/clients; that is, office expenses, postage, photocopying, but NO MARKETING FEE.
Tips: "Be most businesslike when you tap on an agency's door. Agencies are business offices, and every exchange costs money, time, effort, grief or joy."

☑ ◎ **CHARISMA COMMUNICATIONS, LTD. (Specialized: organizations)**, 250 W. 54th St., Suite 806 New York NY 10019. (212)832-3020. Fax: (646)227-0828. E-mail: charismcomm@aol.com. **Contact:** James W. Grau. Estab. 1972. Represents 10 clients. 20% of clients are new/previously unpublished writers. Currently handles: 50% nonfiction books; 20% movie scripts; 20% TV scripts; 10% other.
   • See the expanded listing for this agency in Literary Agents: Nonfee-charging.

☑ ○ **CIRCLE OF CONFUSION LTD.**, 575 Lexington Ave., 4th Floor, New York NY 10022. (212)527-7579. Fax: (212)527-8304. E-mail: circleltd@aol.com. **Contact:** Lawrence Mattis, Trisha Smith, Jessica G. Estab. 1990. Signatory of WGA. Represents 25 clients. 60% of clients are new/previously unpublished writers. Currently handles: 90% movie scripts; 5% novels; 5% other.
Member Agents: Lawrence Mattis; John Sherman; Trisha Smith; Jessica G.
Represents: Feature film. **Considers all script subject areas.**
   ○┯ This literary management company specializes in screenplays for film and TV.
Also Handles: Nonfiction books, novels, novellas, short story collections. **Considers all nonfiction and fiction areas.**
How to Contact: Send query letter. Responds in 1 month to queries; 2 months to mss. Obtains most new clients through queries, recommendations and writing contests.

Recent Sales: *Movie/TV MOW scripts optioned/sold:* The Matrix, by Wachowski Brothers (Warner Brothers); *Ghosts of October,* by Chabot/Peterka (Dreamworks); *Blood of the Gods,* by Jaswinski (Warner Brothers); *Droid,* by Massa (Warner Brothers); *Extinction,* by Herkrom and Leane (Sony).

Terms: Agent receives 10% commission on domestic sales; 10% on foreign sales. Offers written contract, binding for 1 year.

Tips: "We look for screenplays and other material for film and television."

CLIENT FIRST—A/K/A LEO P. HAFFEY AGENCY, P.O. Box 128049, Nashville TN 37212-8049. (615)463-2388. E-mail: c1@nashville.net. Website: www.c-1st.com or www.nashville.net/~c1. **Contact:** Robin Swensen. Estab. 1990. Signatory of WGA. Represents 21 clients. 25% of clients are new/previously unpublished writers. Currently handles: 40% novels; 60% movie scripts.

Member Agent: Leo Haffey (attorney/agent in the motion picture industry).

Represents: Feature film, animation. **Considers these script subject areas:** action/adventure; cartoon; animation; comedy; contemporary issues; detective/police/crime; family saga; historical; mystery/suspense; romance (contemporary, historical); science fiction; sports; thriller/espionage; westerns/frontier.

○━ This agency specializes in movie scripts and novels for sale to motion picture industry.

Also Handles: Novels, novellas, short story collections, and self-help books.

How to Contact: Query with SASE. Accepts queries by e-mail. Considers simultaneous queries. Responds in 1 week to queries; 2 months to mss. Returns materials only with SASE. Obtains most new clients through referrals.

Recent Sales: This agency prefers not to share information on specific sales.

Terms: Offers written contract, binding for a negotiable length of time.

Tips: "The motion picture business is a numbers game like any other. The more you write the better your chances are of success. Please send a SASE along with your query letter."

COMMUNICATIONS AND ENTERTAINMENT, INC., 2851 South Ocean Blvd. #5K, Boca Raton FL 33432-8407. (561)391-9575. Fax: (561)391-7922. E-mail: jlbearde@bellsouth.net. **Contact:** James L. Bearden. Estab. 1989. Represents 10 clients. 50% of clients are new/previously unpublished writers. Currently handles: 5% juvenile books; 40% movie scripts; 10% novels; 40% TV scripts.

● Prior to opening his agency, Mr. Bearden worked as a producer/director and an entertainment attorney.

Member Agents: James Bearden (TV/film); Roslyn Ray (literary).

Represents: Movie scripts, TV scripts, syndicated material.

○━ This agency specializes in TV, film and print media. Actively seeking "synopsis, treatment or summary." Does not want to receive "scripts/screenplays unless requested."

Also Handles: Novels, juvenile books. **Considers these nonfiction areas:** history; music/dance/theater/film. **Considers these fiction areas:** action/adventure; cartoon/comic; contemporary issues; fantasy; historical; science fiction; thriller/espionage.

How to Contact: For scripts, query with SASE. For books, query with outline/proposal or send entire ms. Responds in 1 month to queries; 3 months to mss. Obtains most new clients through referrals and recommendations.

Recent Sales: This agency prefers not to share information on specific sales.

Terms: Agent receives 10% commission on domestic sales; 5% on foreign sales. Offers written contract, varies with project.

Tips: "Be patient."

COMMUNICATIONS MANAGEMENT ASSOCIATES, 1129 Sixth Ave., #1, Rockford IL 61104-3147. (815)964-1335. Fax: (815)964-3061. **Contact:** Thomas R. Lee. Estab. 1989. Represents 30 clients. 50% of clients are new/previously unpublished writers. Currently handles: 10% novels; 80% movie scripts; 5% TV scripts; 5% nonfiction.

Represents: Feature film; TV MOW; animation; documentary; miniseries. **Considers these fiction areas:** action/adventure; biography/autobiography; cartoon/animation; comedy; contemporary issues; detective/police/crime; erotica; fantasy; historical; horror; juvenile; mainstream; psychic/supernatural; religious; romantic comedy; romantic drama; science fiction; teen; thriller/espionage; western/frontier.

○━ This agency specializes in research, editing and financing.

Also Handles: Novels, short story collections, nonfiction books, juvenile books, scholarly books, novellas, poetry books. **Considers these fiction areas:** action/adventure; contemporary issues; detective/police/crime; erotica; fantasy; historical; horror; juvenile; mainstream; mystery/suspense; picture book; romance (historical, regency); science fiction; thriller/espionage; westerns/frontier; young adult.

How to Contact: Query with outline/proposal, 3 sample chapters and a release. Accepts queries by fax and e-mail. Considers simultaneous queries and submissions. Responds to queries "if interested." Discards unwanted queries/mss. Obtains new clients through referrals only.

Recent Sales: This agency prefers not to share information. Send query for list of credits.

Terms: Agent receives 10% commission on domestic sales; 15% on foreign sales. Offers written contract binding for 2-4 months with 60-day cancellation clause. Charges clients for postage, photocopying and office expenses.

Writers' Conferences: BEA.

Tips: "Don't let greed or fame-seeking, or anything but a sincere love of writing push you into this business."

CS INTERNATIONAL LITERARY AGENCY, 43 W. 39th St., New York NY 10018-3811. (212)921-1610. **Contact:** Cynthia Neesemann. Estab. 1996. Represents 25 clients. Currently handles: 33% nonfiction books; 33% movie and TV scripts; 33% novels.

> ● See the expanded listing for this agency in Literary Agents: Fee-charging.

DOUROUX & CO., 815 Manhattan Ave., Suite D, Manhattan Beach CA 90266-5541. E-mail: douroux@rela ypoint.net. **Contact:** Michael E. Douroux. Estab. 1985. Signatory of WGA, member of DGA. 20% of clients are new/previously unpublished writers. Currently handles: 50% movie scripts; 50% TV scripts.
Member Agents: Michael E. Douroux (chairman/CEO).
Represents: Movie scripts, feature film, TV scripts, TV MOW, episodic drama, sitcom, animation. **Considers these script subject areas:** action/adventure; comedy; detective/police/crime; family saga; fantasy; historical; mainstream; mystery/suspense; romantic comedy and drama; science fiction; thriller/espionage; westerns/frontier.
How to Contact: Query with SASE. Accepts queries by e-mail.
Recent Sales: This agency prefers not to share information on specific sales.
Terms: Agent receives 10% commission. Offers written contract, binding for 2 years. Charges clients for photocopying only.

DRAMATIC PUBLISHING (Specialized: theatrical works), 311 Washington St., Woodstock IL 60098. (815)338-7170. Fax: (815)338-8981. E-mail: plays@dramaticpublishing.com. Website: ww.dramaticpublishing.com. **Contact:** Linda Habjan. Estab. 1885. Currently handles: 2% textbooks; 98% stage plays.
Represents: Stage plays.
> ⚬━ This agency specializes in a full range of stage plays, musicals, adaptations, and instructional books about theater.
How to Contact: Query with SASE. Responds in 6 months.
Recent Sales: This agency prefers not to share information on specific sales.

EPSTEIN-WYCKOFF AND ASSOCIATES, 280 S. Beverly Dr., #400, Beverly Hills CA 90212-3904. (310)278-7222. Fax: (310)278-4640. **Contact:** Karin Wakefield. Estab. 1993. Signatory of WGA. Represents 15 clients. Currently handles: 1% nonfiction books; 1% novels; 60% movie scripts; 30% TV scripts; 2% stage plays.
Member Agents: Karin Wakefield (literary); Craig Wyckoff (talent); Gary Epstein (talent).
Represents: Feature film, TV MOW, miniseries, episodic drama, sitcom, animation, soap opera, stage plays. **Considers these script subject areas:** action/adventure; comedy; contemporary issues; detective/police/crime; erotica; family saga; feminist; gay/lesbian; historical; juvenile; mainstream; mystery/suspense; romantic comedy and drama; teen; thriller.
> ⚬━ This agency specializes in features, TV, books and stage plays.
Also Handles: Nonfiction books, novels.
How to Contact: Responds in 1 month to solicited mss. Obtains new clients through recommendations only.
Recent Sales: This agency prefers not to share information on specific sales.
Terms: Agent receives 15% commission on domestic sales of books, 10% on scripts; 20% on foreign sales. Offers written contract, binding for 1 year. Charges clients for photocopying.
Writers' Conferences: Book Expo America.

ESQ. MANAGEMENT, P.O. Box 16194, Beverly Hills CA 90209-2194 (310)252-9879. **Contact:** Patricia E. Lee, Esq. Estab. 1996. Member of Motion Picture Editors Guild. Represents 2 clients. 0% of clients are new/previously unpublished writers. Currently handles: 100% movie scripts.
> ● Prior to opening her agency, Ms. Lee was a film editor.
Represents: Feature film, TV MOW, sitcom, animation, miniseries. **Considers these script subject areas:** action/adventure; cartoon/animation; comedy; contemporary issues; detective/police/crime; erotica; ethnic; fantasy; feminist; gay/lesbian; historical; horror; biography/autobiography; juvenile; mystery/suspense; psychic/supernatural; religious/inspirational; romance (comedy, drama); science fiction; teen; thriller/espionage; western/frontier.
> ⚬━ This management company specializes in representing people who are working professionals in more than one area. Actively seeking writers who have been optioned and/or have made at least one sale previously.
How to Contact: Query with 1-page synopsis. Considers simultaneous queries and submissions. Discards unwanted queries; returns mss. Obtains most new clients through listings in agents/managers directories; print ads; referrals.
Recent Sales: This management company prefers not to share information on specific sales.
Terms: Agent receives 9% commission on domestic sales; 9% on foreign sales. Offers written contract, binding for 2 years. "During the two-year period, contract can only be terminated under certain specified circumstances."
Fees: "No reading fee unless material submitted for our critiquing/proofreading service." Criticism services: "Rates vary from $150-450 depending on length of report." 10% of business is derived from criticism fees. Payment of criticism fee does not ensure representation. Charges clients $30/month for postage, photocopying, etc.

CHECK THE AGENT SPECIALTIES INDEX to find agents who are interested in your specific nonfiction or fiction subject area.

Tips: "Make sure you've got a good query letter. Enclose a résumé or a bio."

☑ ◐ **FEIGEN/PARRENT LITERARY MANAGEMENT**, 10158 Hollow Glen Circle, Bel Air CA 90077-2112. (310)271-4722. Fax: (310)274-0503. E-mail: reellifewomen@compuserve.com. **Contact:** Brenda Feigen, Joanne Parrent. Estab. 1995. Member of PEN USA West, Authors Guild, and LA County Bar Association. Represents 35-40 clients. 20-30% of clients are new/previously unpublished writers. Currently handles: 40% nonfiction books; 25% movie scripts; 30% novels; 5% TV scripts.
• See the expanded listing for this agency in Literary Agents: Nonfee-charging.

N ◐ **FILM ARTISTS ASSOCIATES**, 13563 Ventura Blvd., 2nd Floor, Sherman Oaks CA 91423 (818)386-9669. Fax: (818)386-9363. E-mail: ronsin@ix.netcom.com. **Contact:** Ron Singer. Signatory of WGA. Represents 6 clients. 75% of clients are new/previously unpublished writers. Currently handles: 80% movie scripts; 5% multimedia; 15% stage plays.
• Prior to becoming an agent, Mr. Singer was a manager for writers and performers.
Represents: Movie scripts, feature film, theatrical stage play, stage plays. **Considers these script subject areas:** action/adventure; biography/autobiography; comedy; historical; horror; mainstream; multimedia; mystery/suspense; romantic comedy; science fiction; military war.
☛ This agency represents writers, new or established, on the basis of their material and how they are able to develop and market it. "We give feedback on all submissions as we receive them." Actively seeking contemporary dramas and comedies. Strong characters, unique plots, underlying pulse and smart writing. Does not want to receive clichés, dirty laundry, self-aggrandizement.
How to Contact: Query with SASE. Accepts queries by e-mail. Considers simultaneous queries. Responds in 1 week to queries; 1 month to mss. Returns materials only with SASE. Obtains most new clients through recommendations.
Recent Sales: Sold 3 script projects in the last year. *Movie/TV MOW script(s) optioned/sold: The Replicant, Straight Blast* and *Eye of the Storm*, by Larry Riggins. Other clients include Joeseph Scott Kierland, Ted Farrell, Kevin Walsh, Jesse Vint, Farrin Rosenthal.
Terms: Agent receives 10% commission on domestic sales; 10% on foreign sales. Offers written contract, binding for 1 year. After 6 months, 1-month notice must be given to terminate contract.
Tips: "Know your craft, know your market, submit accordingly and professionally. Be receptive to criticism and feedback."

◐ **FILMWRITERS LITERARY AGENCY**, 4932 Long Sahdow Dr., Midlothian VA 23112. (804)744-1718. **Contact:** Helene Wagner. Signatory of WGA.
• Prior to opening her agency, Ms. Wagner was director of the Virginia Screenwriters' Forum for 7 years and taught college level screenwriting classes. "As a writer myself, I have won or been a finalist in most major screenwriting competitions throughout the country and have a number of my screenplays optioned. Through the years I have enjoyed helping and working with other writers. Some have gone on to have their movies made, their work optioned, and won national contests."
Represents: Feature film, TV MOW, miniseries. **Considers these script subject areas:** action/adventure; comedy; contemporary issues; detective/police/crime; historical; juvenile; mystery/suspense; psychic/supernatural; romantic comedy; romantic drama; teen; thriller/espionage.
☛ This agency is seeking "original and intelligent writing; professional in caliber, correctly formatted and crafted with strong characters and storytelling." Does not want to receive "clones of last year's big movies, somebody's first screenplay that's filled with 'talking heads,' camera directions, real life 'chit-chat' that doesn't belong in a movie, or a story with no conflict or drama in it."
How to Contact: Obtains new clients only through recommendations from others.
Recent Sales: Movie/TV MOW script(s) optioned/sold: *Between Heaven & Hell*, by Charles Deemer (Never a Dull Moment Productions) and others that are under consideration.
Terms: Agent receives 10% commission on domestic sales; 10% on foreign sales. Offers written contract. Clients supply photocopying and postage. Writers reimbursed for office fees after the sale of ms.
Tips: "Professional writers should wait until they have at least four drafts done before they send out their work because they know it takes that much hard work to make a story and characters work. Show me something I haven't seen before with characters that I care about, that jump off the page. I not only look at writer's work, I look at the writer's talent. If I believe in a writer, even though a piece may not sell, I'll stay with the writer and help nurture that talent which a lot of the big agencies won't do."

☑ ◑ **FIRST LOOK TALENT AND LITERARY AGENCY**, 264 S. La Cienega, Suite 1068, Beverly Hills CA 90211. (310)967-5761. Also: 511 Avenue of the Americas, Suite 3000, New York NY 10011. (212)216-9522. E-mail: afirstlook@aol.com or firstlookla@firstlookagency.com or firstlookny@firstlookagency.com. Website: www.firstlookagency.com or afirstlook@aol.com. **Contact:** Burt Avalone. Estab. 1997. Represents 18 clients. 30% of clients are new/previously unpublished writers. Currently handles: 70% movie scripts; 5% stage plays; 25% TV scripts.
• Prior to becoming agents, Burt Avalone and Ken Richards were agents at other agencies. Harry Nolan was vice president of development for a major production company.
Member Agents: Burt Avalone (NY, all literary); Ken Richards (LA, features, TV); Harry Nolan (LA, Features, TV); Julie Stein (LA, TV MOW).

Represents: Feature film, TV MOW, TV scripts, stage plays, "anything that screams movie." **Considers these script subject areas:** action/adventure, cartoon/animation, comedy, contemporary issues, family saga, fantasy, historical, horror, juvenile, mainstream, military/war, mystery/suspense, psychic/supernatural, romance, science fiction, sports, teen, thriller/espionage, westerns/frontier.

○┐ Actively seeking fresh, new ideas.

How to Contact: Query or electronic query via website. Responds in 10 days to queries; 1 months to mss. Obtains most new clients through referrals.

Recent Sales: Sold 6 projects in the last year. Prefers not to share information on specific sales.

Terms: Agent receives 10% commission on domestic sales; 10% on foreign sales. Offers written contract, binding for 1 year.

Tips: "We're willing to consider ideas for features and TV that haven't been scripted yet. If we're excited about the idea, we'll help with its development. We've even made the pitching easier for completed scripts or script ideas via the easy-to-follow instructions on our website. Don't spend six months or more of your life writing something you're not excited about. For better or worse, Hollywood responds more quickly to a great idea with mediocre execution than the other way around."

N̲ $ ⊘ FRIEDA FISHBEIN ASSOCIATES, P.O. Box 723, Bedford NY 10506. (914)234-7132. **Contact:** Heidi Carlson. Estab. 1928. Represents 18 clients. 80% of clients are new/previously unpublished writers. Currently handles: 20% novels; 20% movie scripts; 60% stage plays.

● See the expanded listing for this agency in Literary Agents: Fee-charging.

⊘ FITZGERALD LITERARY MANAGEMENT, 84 Monte Alto Rd., Santa Fe NM 87505. Phone/fax: (505)466-1186. **Contact:** Lisa FitzGerald. Estab. 1994. Represents 12 clients. 75% of clients are new/previously unpublished writers. Currently represents: 75% movie scripts; 15% film rights to novels; 5% TV scripts; 5% film rights to stage plays.

● Prior to opening her agency, Ms. FitzGerald headed development at Universal Studios for Bruce Evans and Raynold Gideon, Oscar-nominated writer-producers. She also served as Executive Story Analyst at CBS, and held positions at Curtis Brown Agency in New York and Adams, Ray & Rosenberg Talent Agency in Los Angeles.

Represents: Feature film, TV MOW. **Considers these script subject areas:** action/adventure; comedy; contemporary issues; detective/police/crime; erotica; ethnic; family saga; fantasy; historical; horror; biography/autobiography; juvenile; mainstream; mystery/suspense; psychic/supernatural; romance (comedy, drama); science fiction; sports; teen; thriller/espionage; western/frontier. "Any subject, if the query sounds of interest."

○┐ This agency specializes in screenwriters and selling film rights to novels. Actively seeking mainstream feature film scripts. Does not want to receive true stories.

Also Handles: Novels. **Considers these fiction areas:** children's books, young adult novels and mainstream novels with film potential.

How to Contact: Query with 1 page synopsis and SASE. Prefers to be read materials exclusively. "Will not respond if no SASE included. No faxed queries, please." Responds in 2 weeks to queries; 6 weeks to mss. Returns materials only with SASE. Obtains most new clients through referrals from other clients or business contacts, writers conferences, screenplay contests, queries.

Recent Sales: Sold 7 book titles and 5 script projects in the last year. Prefers not to share information on specific sales.

Terms: Agent receives 10-15% commission on domestic sales. Offers written contract, binding for 1-2 years. Charges clients for photocopying and postage.

Tips: "Know your craft. Read produced screenplays. Enter screenplay contests. Educate yourself on the business in general (read *The Hollywood Reporter* or *Daily Variety*). Learn how to pitch. Keep writing and don't be afraid to get your work out there."

⊘ B.R. FLEURY AGENCY, P.O. Box 149352, Orlando FL 32814-9352. (407)895-8494. Fax: (407)898-3923. E-mail: brfleuryagency@juno.com. **Contact:** Blanche or Margaret. Estab. 1994. Signatory of WGA. Currently handles: 70% books; 30% scripts.

● See the expanded listing for this agency in Literary Agents: Nonfee-charging.

$ ♥ FRAN LITERARY AGENCY, 7235 Split Creek, San Antonio TX 78238-3627. (210)684-1569. **Contact:** Fran Rathmann, Kathy Kenney. Estab. 1993. Signatory of WGA, member of ASCAP. Represents 25 clients. 60% of clients are new/previously unpublished writers. Currently handles: 15% nonfiction books; 15% juvenile books; 40% novels; 5% novellas; 5% poetry books; 20% teleplays/screenplays.

IF YOU'RE LOOKING for a particular agent, check the Agents Index to find the specific agency where the agent works. Then check the listing for that agency in the appropriate section.

● See the expanded listing for this agency in Literary Agents: Fee-charging.

THE BARRY FREED CO., 2040 Ave. of the Stars, #400, Los Angeles CA 90067. (310)277-1260. Fax: (310)277-3865. E-mail: blfreed@aol.com. **Contact:** Barry Freed. Signatory of WGA. Represents 15 clients. 95% of clients are new/previously unpublished writers. Currently represents: 100% movie scripts.
● Prior to opening his agency, Mr. Freed worked for ICM.
Represents: Feature film, TV MOW. **Considers these script subject areas:** action/adventure; comedy; contemporary issues; detective/police/crime; ethnic; family saga; horror; mainstream; mystery/suspense.
○┯ Actively seeking adult drama, comedy, romantic comedy. Does not want to receive period pieces, westerns.
How to Contact: Query with SASE. Responds immediately to queries; in 3 months to mss. Accepts queries via e-mail and fax. Prefers to read materials exclusively. Obtains most new clients through recommendations from others.
Recent Sales: This agency prefers not to share information on specific sales.
Terms: Offers written contract, binding for 2 years.
Tips: "Our clients are a highly qualified small roster of writers who write comedy, action adventure/thrillers, adult drama, romantic comedy."

ROBERT A. FREEDMAN DRAMATIC AGENCY, INC., 1501 Broadway, Suite 2310, New York NY 10036. (212)840-5760. **Contact:** Robert A. Freedman, president; Selma Luttinger, vice president; Marta Praeger and Robin Kaver, associates. Estab. 1928. Member of AAR; signatory of WGA.
● Robert Freedman has served as vice president of the dramatic division of AAR.
Represents: Movie scripts, TV scripts, stage plays.
○┯ This agency prefers to work with established authors; works with a small number of new authors. Specializes in plays, movie scripts and TV scripts.
How to Contact: Query with SASE. No unsolicited mss. Usually responds in 2 weeks to queries; 3 months to mss.
Recent Sales: "We will speak directly with any prospective client concerning sales that are relevant to his/her specific script."
Terms: Agent receives 10% on dramatic sales; "and, as is customary, 20% on amateur rights." Charges clients for photocopying.

SAMUEL FRENCH, INC., (Specialized: plays), 45 W. 25th St., New York NY 10010-2751. (212)206-8990. Fax: (212)206-1429. **Contact:** Lawrence Harbison, editor. Estab. 1830. Member of AAR.
Member Agents: Brad Lohrenz; Alleen Hussung; Linda Kirland; Charles R. Van Nostrand.
Represents: Theatrical stage play, musicals, variety show. **Considers these script subject areas:** comedy; contemporary issues; detective/police/crime; ethnic; experimental; fantasy; horror; mystery/suspense; religious/inspirational; thriller.
○┯ This agency specializes in representing *plays* which it publishes for production rights.
How to Contact: Query or send entire ms with SASE. Responds "immediately" to queries; decision in 2-8 months regarding publication. "Enclose SASE."
Recent Sales: This agency prefers not to share information on specific sales.
Terms: Agent usually receives 10% professional production royalties; variable amateur production royalties.

THE GAGE GROUP, 9255 Sunset Blvd., Suite 515, Los Angeles CA 90069. (310)859-8777. Fax: (310)859-8166. Estab. 1976. Signatory of WGA. Represents 34 clients.
Represents: Movies scripts (feature film), TV scripts, theatrical stage play. **Considers all script subject areas.**
How to Contact: Query with SASE. Responds in 1 month to queries and mss.
Recent Sales: This agency prefers not to share information on specific sales.
Terms: Agent receives 10% commission on domestic sales; 10% commission on foreign sales.

GEDDES AGENCY, 8430 Santa Monica Blvd., #200, West Hollywood CA 90069. (323)848-2700. **Contact:** Literary Department. Estab. 1983 in L.A., 1967 in Chicago. Signatory of WGA, SAG, AFTRA. Represents 15 clients.
Member Agents: Ann Geddes; Dana Wright.
Represents: Feature film, miniseries, variety show, episodic drama, TV MOW, sitcom. **Considers these script areas:** action/adventure; comedy; contemporary issues; detective/police/crime; ethnic; experimental; family saga; fantasy; horror; mainstream; mystery/suspense; psychic/supernatural; romance (comedy, drama); science fiction; teen; thriller.
How to Contact: Query with synopsis and SASE. Responds in 2 months to mss only if interested. Obtains most new clients through recommendations from others and through mailed-in synopses.
Recent Sales: This agency prefers not to share informationon specific sales.
Terms: Agent receives 10% commission on domestic sales. Offers written contract, binding for 1 year. Charges for "handling and postage for a script to be returned—otherwise it is recycled."
Tips: "Send in query—say how many scripts you have available for representation. Send synopsis of each one. Mention something about yourself."

THE LAYA GELFF AGENCY, 16133 Ventura Blvd., Suite 700, Encino CA 91436. (818)996-3100. Estab. 1985. Signatory of WGA. Represents many clients. Currently handles: 40% movie scripts; 20% book mss.
Represents: Feature film. TV scripts.

O—n This agency specializes in TV and film scripts; WGA members preferred. "Also represents writers to publishers."

How to Contact: Query with SASE. Responds in 2 weeks to queries; 1 month to mss. "Must have SASE for reply." Obtains new clients through recommendations from others.

Recent Sales: This agency prefers not to share information on specific sales.

Terms: Agent receives 10% commission on domestic sales; 10% on foreign sales. Offers standard WGA contract.

Fees: Changes reading fee for book representation only.

THE SEBASTIAN GIBSON AGENCY, P.O. Box 13350, Palm Desert CA 92255-3350. (760)837-3726. Fax: (619)322-3857. **Contact:** Sebastian Gibson. Estab. 1995. 100% of clients are new/previously unpublished writers. Specializes in fiction.

• See the expanded listing for this agency in Literary Agents: Fee-charging.

GRAHAM AGENCY, 311 W. 43rd St., New York NY 10036. (212)489-7730. **Contact:** Earl Graham, owner. Estab. 1971. Represents 40 clients. 30% of clients are new/previously unpublished writers. Currently handles: movie scripts, stage plays.

Represents: Theatrical stage play, feature film.

O—n This agency specializes in playwrights and screenwriters only. "We're interested in commercial material of quality." Does not want to receive one-acts or material for children.

How to Contact: "We consider on the basis of the letters of inquiry." Writers *must* query before sending any material for consideration. Responds in 3 months to queries; 6 weeks to mss. Obtains most new clients through queries, referrals.

Recent Sales: This agency prefers not to share information on specific sales.

Terms: Agent receives 10% commission.

Tips: "Write a concise, intelligent letter giving the gist of what you are offering."

ARTHUR B. GREENE, 101 Park Ave., 26th Floor, New York NY 10178. (212)661-8200. Fax: (212)370-7884. **Contact:** Arthur Greene. Estab. 1980. Represents 20 clients. 10% of clients are new/previously unpublished writers. Currently handles: 25% novels; 10% novellas; 10% short story collections; 25% movie scripts; 10% TV scripts; 10% stage plays; 10% other.

Represents: Feature film, TV MOW, stage play. **Considers these script subject areas:** action/adventure; detective/police/crime; horror; mystery/suspense.

O—n This agency specializes in movies, TV, fiction.

Also Handles: Novels. **Considers these nonfiction areas:** animals; music/dance/theater/film; sports. **Considers these fiction areas:** action/adventure; detective/police/crime; horror; mystery/suspense; sports; thriller/espionage.

How to Contact: Query with SASE. Responds in 2 weeks to queries. No written contract, 30 day cancellation clause. 100% of business is derived from commissions on sales. Obtains most new clients through recommendations from others.

Recent Sales: This agency prefers not to share information on specific sales.

Terms: Agent receives 10% commission on domestic sales; 20% on foreign sales.

THE SUSAN GURMAN AGENCY, #15A, 865 West End Ave., New York NY 10025-8403. (212)749-4618. Fax: (212)864-5055. **Contact:** Susan Gurman. Estab. 1993. Signatory of WGA. 28% of clients are new/previously unpublished writers. Currently handles: 70% movie scripts; 30% stage plays.

Member Agent: Gail Eisenberg (associate agent); Susan Gurman.

Represents: Feature film, theatrical stage play, TV MOW. **Considers these script areas:** true stories; comedy; detective/police/crime; family saga; horror; mainstream; mystery/suspense; romantic comedy; romantic drama; thriller.

O—n This agency specializes in referred screenwriters and playwrights.

Also Handles: Considers these nonfiction areas: biography/autobiography; true crime/investigative. **Considers these fiction areas:** action/adventure; detective/police/crime; family saga; fantasy; horror; literary; mainstream; mystery/suspense; picture book; thriller/espionage.

How to Contact: Obtains most new clients *through referral only*. Responds in 2 weeks to queries; 2 months to mss.

Recent Sales: This agency prefers not to share information on specific sales.

Terms: Agent receives 10% commission on domestic sales; 10% on foreign sales.

H.W.A. TALENT REPRESENTATIVE, (formerly Preferred Artists Talent Agency), 3500 W. Olive Ave., Suite 1400, Burbank CA 91505. (818)972-4310. Fax: (818)972-4313. **Contact:** Kimber Wheeler. Estab. 1985. Signatory of WGA. 90% of clients are new/previously unpublished writers. Currently handles: 90% movie scripts, 10% novels.

Represents: Movie scripts, television material, novels. **Considers these script areas:** action/adventure; biography/autobiography; cartoon/comic; comedy; contemporary issues; detective/police/crime; ethnic; family saga; fantasy; feminist; gay; horror; lesbian; mystery/suspense; psychic/supernatural; romance; science fiction; sports; thriller/espionage.

How to Contact: Query with outline/proposal. Accepts queries by fax. Considers simultaneous queries.

Recent Sales: This agency prefers not to share information on specific sales.

Terms: Agent receives 10% commission on domestic sales. Offers written contract, binding for 1 year. WGA rules on termination apply.

Tips: "A good query letter is important. Use any relationship you have in the business to get your material read."

N ○ HART LITERARY MANAGEMENT, 3541 Olive St., Santa Ynez CA 93460 Phone/fax: (805)686-7912. E-mail: tibicen@silcom.com. Website: www.silcom.com/~tibicen/. **Contact:** Susan Hart. Estab. 1997. Represents 35 clients. 95% of clients are new/previously unpublished writers. Currently handles: 2% nonfiction books; 98% movie scripts.

● Prior to becoming an agent, Ms. Hart was a screenwriter.

Represents: Movie scripts, feature film, movie of the week. **Considers these script subject areas:** biography/autobiography; family saga; horror; juvenile; mainstream; science fiction; teen.

○→ This management company likes to "have clients from all over the world to give them a chance to get a script optioned/sold to Hollywood." Actively seeking teen, family adventure, based on actual events (not historical); earth-based science fiction. Does not want to receive erotica, too much sex or violence.

Also Handles: Nonfiction books for film rights only. **Considers these nonfiction areas:** biography/autobiography; popular culture; true crime/investigative.

How to Contact: Queries with SASE. Accepts queries by e-mail and fax. Considers simultaneous queries and submissions. Responds in 2 weeks. Returns materials only with SASE. Obtains most new clients through queries/solicitations.

Recent Sales: *Movie/TV MOW script(s) optioned/sold: Annus Horribilis*, by J. McIluaine (Millbrook Farm Productions/Showtime); *Franklin vs. God*, by Mark Blaisefallon (Pacifica Entertainment).

Terms: Agent receives 10% commission on domestic sales on gross income written any source. Offers written contract, binding for 1 year, "but can be cancelled at anytime by either party." Charges clients for photocopies and postage: $6 domestic, $10 Canadian and $12 international.

Tips: "I want a great story spell-checked, formatted, and "typed" in industry standard 12 point Courier or Courier New only, between 95-120 pages maximum. No overt gore, sex, violence."

N $ ○ GIL HAYES & ASSOCIATES, 5125 Barry Rd., Memphis TN 38117. (901)818-0086. **Contact:** Gil Hayes. Estab. 1992. Represents 10 clients. 40% of clients are new/previously unpublished writers. Currently handles: 100% movie scripts.

Member Agent: Gil Hayes.

Represents: Movie scripts. **Considers these script subject areas:** biography/autobiography; comedy; current affairs; family saga; mainstream; mystery/suspense.

○→ This agency specializes in serious scripts.

How to Contact: Query with outline/proposal and SASE. Responds in 3 months to queries; 6 months to mss. Obtains most new clients through "recommendations from others—contacts at tape and film commission offices around the nation. Absolutely no queries via fax, e-mail or phone calls."

Recent Sales: This agency prefers not to share information on specific sales.

Terms: Agent receives 10% commission on script sales. Offers written contract, binding for variable length of time, usually 2 years.

Fees: Criticism service: $50 for script, $100 if requesting written notes in advance. "Published writers write and review all critiques. Some major input from writers I already represent if area is appropriate. Writers must provide bound copies, usually five to ten at a time if I represent them." Payment of criticism fee does not ensure representation.

Tips: "Always register with WGA or copyright material before sending to anyone."

○ CAROLYN HODGES AGENCY, 1980 Glenwood Dr., Boulder CO 80304-2329. (303)443-4636. Fax: (303)443-4636. E-mail: hodgesc@earthlink.net. **Contact:** Carolyn Hodges. Estab. 1989. Signatory of WGA. Represents 12 clients. 75% of clients are new/previously unpublished writers. Currently handles: 15% movie scripts; 45% TV scripts.

● Prior to opening her agency, Ms. Hodges was a freelance writer and founded the Writers in the Rockies Screenwriting Conference.

Represents: Movie scripts; feature film; TV scripts, TV MOW. **Considers these script subject areas:** action/adventure; comedy; contemporary issues; horror; mainstream; mystery/suspense; psychic/supernatural; romance (comedy, drama).

○→ This agency represents only screenwriters for film and TV MOW.

How to Contact: Query with 1-page synopsis and SASE. Accepts queries by e-mail. Considers simultaneous queries and submissions. Responds in 1 week to queries; 2 months to mss. *"Please, no queries by phone."* Returns materials only with SASE. Obtains most new clients by referral only.

Recent Sales: Sold 3 script projects in the last year. *Movie/TV MOW scripts optioned/sold: Fantasy Land*, by Robert Lilly (Gallus Enterprises); *Ribit*, by Janie Norris (K. Peterson); *Two Hour Layover*, by Steven Blake (River Road Enterprises).

Terms: Agent receives 10% on domestic sales; foreign sales "depend on each individual negotiation." Offers written contract, standard WGA. No charge for criticism. "I always try to offer concrete feedback, even when rejecting a piece of material." Charges clients for postage. "Sometimes we request reimbursement for long-distance phone and fax charges."

Writers' Conferences: Director and founder of Writers in the Rockies Film Screenwriting Conference (Boulder CO, August).

Tips: "Become proficient at your craft. Attend all workshops accessible to you. READ all the books applicable to your area of interest. READ as many 'produced' screenplays as possible. Live a full, vital, and rewarding life so your writing will have something to say. Get involved in a writers' support group. Network with other writers. Receive 'critiques' from your peers and consider merit of suggestions. Don't be afraid to re-examine your perspective."

BARBARA HOGENSON AGENCY, 165 West End Ave., Suite 19-C, New York NY 10023. (212)874-8084. Fax: (212)362-3011. **Contact:** Barbara Hogenson. Estab. 1994. Member of AAR, signatory of WGA. Represents 60 clients. 5% of clients are new/previously unpublished writers. Currently handles: 35% nonfiction books; 15% novels; 15% movie scripts; 35% stage plays.
  ● Prior to opening her own agency, Ms. Hogenson was with the prestigious Lucy Kroll Agency for 10 years.
Represents: Feature film, soap opera, theatrical stage play, TV MOW, sitcom.
Also Handles: Nonfiction books, novels. **Considers these nonfiction areas:** biography/autobiography; history; interior design/decorating; music/dance/theater/film; popular culture. **Considers these fiction areas:** action/adventure; contemporary issues; detective/police/crime; ethnic; historical; humor/satire; literary; mainstream; mystery/suspense; romance (contemporary); thriller/espionage.
How to Contact: Query with outline and SASE. No unsolicited mss. Responds in 1 month. Obtains most new clients strictly by referral.
Recent Sales: *Daniel Plainway*, by Van Reid; *Life Lessons*, by Elisabeth Kubler-Ross; *South Mountain Road*, by Hesper Anderson (Simon & Schuster). ***Movie/TV MOW scripts optioned/sold:*** *The Eighth Day*, by Thornton Wilder (Hallmark).
Terms: Agent receives 10% on film and TV sales; 15% commission on domestic sales of books; 20% on foreign sales of books. Offers written contract.

HUDSON AGENCY, 3 Travis Lane, Montrose NY 10548. (914)737-1475. Fax: (914)736-3064. E-mail: hudagency@juno.com. Website: www.hudsonagency.net. **Contact:** Susan or Pat Giordano. Estab. 1994. Signatory of WGA. Represents 30 clients. 50% of clients are new/previously unpublished writers. Currently handles: 50% movie scripts; 50% TV scripts and TV animation.
Member Agents: Sue Giordano (features and TV animation); Michele Perri (books); Cheri Santone (animation); Sunny Bik (Canada contact).
Represents: Feature film, documentary, animation, TV MOW, miniseries, sitcom; PG or PG-13 only. **Considers these script subject areas:** action/adventure; cartoon/animation; comedy; contemporary issues; detective/police/crime; family saga; fantasy; juvenile; mystery/suspense; romantic comedy and drama; teen; westerns/frontier.
  ○▪ This agency specializes in feature film, TV, and animation writers. Actively seeking "writers with television and screenwriting education or workshops under their belts." Does not want to receive "R-rated material, occult, or writers who haven't taken at least one screenwriting workshop."
How to Contact: Send outline and sample pages. Accepts queries by e-mail and via website. Considers simultaneous queries. Responds in 1 week to queries; 3 weeks to mss. Returns material only with SASE. Obtains most new clients through recommendations from others and listing on WGA agency list.
Recent Sales: Sold 2 script projects in the last year. *Becoming Dick*, by Rick Gitelson (E Television); *Tell*, by Michael Stern (Studio Hamburg).
Terms: Agent receives 10% commission on domestic sales; 10% on foreign sales; 20% if using a book agent.
Tips: "Yes, we may be small, but we work very hard for our clients. Any script we are representing gets excellent exposure to producers. Our network has over 2,000 contacts in the business and growing rapidly. We are GOOD salespeople. Ultimately it all depends on the quality of the writing and the market for the subject matter. Do not query unless you have taken at least one screenwriting course and read all of Syd Field's books."

INTERNATIONAL CREATIVE MANAGEMENT, 8942 Wilshire Blvd., Beverly Hills CA 90211. (310)550-4000. Fax: (310)550-4100. East Coast office: 40 W. 57th St., New York NY 10019. (212)556-5600. Fax: (212)556-5665. Signatory of WGA, member of AAR.
  ● See expanded listing for this agency in Literary Agents: Nonfee-charging.

INTERNATIONAL LEONARDS CORP., 3612 N. Washington Blvd., Indianapolis IN 46205-3534. (317)926-7566. **Contact:** David Leonards. Estab. 1972. Signatory of WGA. Currently handles: 50% movie scripts; 50% TV scripts.
Represents: Feature film, animation, TV MOW, sitcom, variety show. **Considers these script subject areas:** action/adventure; cartoon/animation; comedy; contemporary issues; detective/police/crime; horror; mystery/suspense; romantic comedy; science fiction; sports; thriller.
How to Contact: Query with SASE. Prefers to read materials exclusively. Responds in 1 month to queries; 6 months to mss. Returns materials only with SASE. Obtains most new clients through recommendations and queries.
Recent Sales: This agency prefers not to share information on specific sales.
Terms: Agent receives 10% commission on domestic sales; 10% on foreign sales. Offers written contract, following "WGA standards," which "vary."

▐N▌ JARET ENTERTAINMENT, 220 Main St., Venice CA 90272. (310)450-7544. Fax: (310)664-0871. E-mail: ssullyentertain@aol.com. Website: www.Jaretentertainment.com. **Contact:** Susan Sullivan. Represents 20 clients. 20% of clients are new/previously unpublished writers. Currently handles: 75% movie scripts; 25% TV scripts.
Represents: Movie scripts, TV scripts, TV movie of the week, animation. **Considers these script subject areas:** action/adventure; biography/autobiography; cartoon/animation; comedy; mystery/suspense; psychic/supernatural; romantic comedy; romantic drama; science fiction; sports; thriller/espionage.
  ○▪ This management company specializes in creative, out-of-the-box thinking. "We're willing to take a chance

Talent plus a good agent land first-time screenwriter in the *Sauce*

Monique Johnson had no intention of selling her script when she started writing *Sauce*, the story of two grandchildren from rivaling barbecue monarchies who fall in love when they're paired as kitchen mates at an elite culinary institute. She'd seen a lot of mediocre scripts come across her desk while working as an assistant to Warner Bros.'s producer Michael Andreen, and she just wanted to see if she could do better. From all accounts, it looks like she succeeded. With the help of Andreen and agent Todd Feldman of International Creative Management (ICM), she's landed a deal with New Line Cinema to turn her first script into a movie, starring Grammy award-winning musician, Lauryn Hill.

"I gave the script to a friend who said, 'I think Lauryn Hill would like this, and I'm close friends with her producer,'" Johnson explains. "Well, people say that kind of stuff all the time, so I didn't take it too seriously."

Within two weeks, the friend came back, saying she'd pitched the idea to Hill's producer, Karen Bell, who liked it and wanted to read the script. At the same time, Andreen moved to a new position as a vice president at New Line Cinema. He, too, liked the script and wanted to take it with him. When word came that Hill was interested, a two-month period of intense communication followed to determine who should get the script—Warner Bros. or New Line. Working hard to hammer out the details was Johnson's agent, Todd Feldman.

"I knew Todd," says Johnson. "He covered Warner Bros., and he was my favorite—always likable, really smart. He's an upright guy, and he made a fantastic deal for me." Johnson and Feldman ultimately decided to go with New Line Cinema.

Although she'd met many agents through her job at the studio, this was Johnson's first time working with an agent to sell her own work. During the negotiating period, she was on the phone with Feldman several times a day. Currently, they check in with each other once or twice a week.

She is quick to sing praises about how much he's helped her: "There's no way I could negotiate a deal. He's great at it. He's very aggressive. He's a big agent with ICM, so he has connections with everyone. And he knows what projects are going on at the different studios and which one I would be right for. Because of him, no one's going to be sending me their writing assignments willy-nilly."

When asked if it's necessary for a scriptwriter to have an agent, Johnson hedges only a little. "I think it's almost necessary," she replies. "Studios don't accept work from unsolicited sources. You can get an attorney to send in your script, but that's like saying, 'Amateur—put it at the bottom of the barrel.' If it's really great, it might get covered, but there's no guarantee."

Johnson believes the best way to find an agent is to begin at the top and work your way down. "You should start with the William Morrises and the ICMs because if you get one of their great agents, you will get coverage. Your stuff will be out there."

Of course, it's not easy to get an agent to look at your work if this is your first time stepping up to the plate. Johnson recommends getting to know the assistants at studios or agencies. They can be very helpful, if shown respect. "I did a lot for people I didn't even know," she remembers, "but who, for whatever reason, went out of their way to meet an assistant like me. Assistants in these places are generally not lifers. They want to become producers or agents. They want to go to their boss and say, 'Wow, look what I found. Look at this great script.' If the script gets sold, that can boost an assistant's career and help her jump to the next level."

Reading the trades is another way to scout out an agent. Johnson advises newcomers to check what spec scripts have been sold and who sold them. Make note of which agents are representing first-time scriptwriters. Call that agency, and pitch your idea to the assistant. And here's an important tip: don't ever say you've sent your script to other agencies and have been turned down, even if you've been turned down by everyone. Always act as if this is the first time you've sent it out.

For now, Johnson is busy working on her next script. She knows she is incredibly lucky because talent isn't enough to make it in this industry. So much of it depends on being in the right place at the right time and having good connections. She cautions first-timers not to count their chickens before they're hatched. "Nothing is real until everything is signed and things are happening. Don't go spending your money. Don't count on anything. Studios buy tons and tons of scripts, but the percentage of scripts that get made into movies is very small."

In the meantime, she hopes to beat the odds and see *Sauce* make it to the big screen. According to Johnson, "Lauryn Hill is so intelligent and great at articulating her vision. People will want to work with her, so that will help in getting a better cast—and a great sound track."

Johnson may not be counting her chickens, but she definitely has a lot to crow about.

—Cindy Duesing

---

on well-written materials." Actively seeking science fiction, romantic comedy. Does not want to receive any projects with unnecessary violence, westerns, or anything you've seen before—studio programmers, black comedy or period pieces that drag out and are boring."

How to Contact: Query with SASE. "If we don't respond, we're not interested." Accepts queries by e-mail and fax. Considers simultaneous queries. Discards unwanted material. Obtains most new clients through recommendations from others.

Recent Sales: Sold 5 script projects in the last year. This agency prefers not to share information on specific sales.

Terms: Agent receives 10% commission on domestic sales. Offers written contract, binding for 10-24 months.

✔ ◑ JOHNSON WARREN LITERARY AGENCY, 115 W. California Blvd., Suite 173, Pasadena CA 91105. (909)625-8400. Fax: (909)624-3930. E-mail: jwa@aol.com. **Contact:** Billie Johnson. Signatory of WGA. Represents 15 clients. 95% of clients are new/previously unpublished writers. Currently handles: 10% movie scripts; 50% novels; 40% nonfiction books.

• See the expanded listing for this agency in the Literary Agents: Fee-charging.

✔ ◑ LESLIE KALLEN AGENCY, 15760 Ventura Blvd., Suite #700, Encino CA 91436. (818)906-2785. Fax: (818)906-8931. Website: www.lesliekallen.com. **Contact:** J.R. Gowan. Estab. 1988. Signatory of WGA, DGA. Specializes in feature films and MOWs.

Represents: Feature film, TV MOW.

How to Contact: Query. "No phone inquiries for representation."

Recent Sales: This agency prefers not to share information on specific sales.

Terms: Agent receives 10% commission on domestic sales.

Tips: "Write a two- to three-paragraph query that makes an agent excited to read the material."

N ⬤ **KERIN-GOLDBERG ASSOCIATES**, 155 E. 55th St., #5D, New York NY 10022. (212)838-7373. Fax: (212)838-0774. **Contact:** Charles Kerin. Estab. 1984. Signatory of WGA. Represents 29 clients. Currently handles: 30% movie scripts; 30% TV scripts; 40% stage plays.
Represents: Movie scripts, feature film, TV scripts, TV MOW, miniseries, episodic drama, sitcom, variety show, syndicated material, stage plays. **Considers all script subject areas.**
   ⌒ This agency specializes in theater plays, screenplays, teleplays.
How to Contact: Query. Responds in 1 month to queries; 2 months to scripts. "Scripts are not returned." Obtains most new clients through recommendations from others.
Recent Sales: This agency prefers not to share information on specific sales.
Terms: Agent receives 10% commission on domestic sales; 10% commission on foreign sales. Offers written contract.

N ⬤ **WILLIAM KERWIN AGENCY**, 1605 N. Cahuenga, Suite 202, Hollywood CA 90028. (323)469-5155. **Contact:** Al Wood and Bill Kerwin. Estab. 1979. Signatory of WGA. Represents 5 clients. Currently handles: 100% movie scripts.
Represents: Movie scripts. **Considers these script subject areas:** mystery/suspense; romance; science fiction; thriller/espionage.
How to Contact: Query with SASE. Responds in 1 day to queries; 1 month to mss. Obtains most new clients through recommendations and solicitation.
Recent Sales: HBO or TMC film *Steel Death*, starring Jack Scalia.
Terms: Agent receives 10% commission on domestic sales; 10% on foreign sales. Offers written contract, binding for 1-2 years, with 30-day cancellation clause. Offers free criticism service.
Tips: "Listen. Be nice."

N ⬤ **THE JOYCE KETAY AGENCY**, 1501 Broadway, Suite 1908, New York NY 10036. (212)354-6825. Fax: (212)354-6732. **Contact:** Joyce Ketay, Carl Mulert, Wendy Streeter. Member of WGA.
Member Agents: Joyce Ketay; Carl Mulert; Wendy Streeter.
Represents: Feature film, TV MOW, episodic drama, sitcom, theatrical stage play. **Considers these script subject areas:** action/adventure; comedy; contemporary issues; detective/police/crime; ethnic; experimental; family saga; fantasy; feminist; gay; glitz; historical; juvenile; lesbian; mainstream; mystery/suspense; psychic/supernatural; romantic comedy and drama; thriller; westerns/frontier.
   ⌒ This agency specializes in playwrights and screenwriters only. Does not want to receive novels.
Recent Sales: This agency prefers not to share information on specific sales.

N ⬤ **KICK ENTERTAINMENT**, 1934 E. 123rd St., Cleveland OH 44106-1912. Phone/fax: (216)791-2515. **Contact:** Sam Klein. Estab. 1992. Signatory of WGA. Represents 8 clients. 100% of clients are new/previously unpublished writers. Currently handles: 100% movie scripts.
Member Agents: Geno Trunzo (president-motion picture division); Ms. Palma Trunzo (director-creative affairs); Fred Landsmann (TV); Gia Leonardi (creative executive).
Represents: Movie scripts (feature film). **Considers these script subject areas:** action/adventure; comedy; detective/police/crime; fantasy; horror; mainstream; mystery/suspense; psychic/supernatural; romantic comedy and drama; science fiction; thriller/espionage.
How to Contact: Query. Responds in 2 weeks to queries; 2 months to mss.
Recent Sales: This agency prefers not to share information on specific sales.
Terms: Agent receives 10% commission on domestic sales; 10% on foreign sales. Offers written contract, binding for 1 or 2 years.
Tips: "Always send a query letter first, and enclose a SASE. We now presently represent clients in six states."

◎ **PAUL KOHNER, INC., (Specialized: film rights)**, 9300 Wilshire Blvd., Suite 555, Beverly Hills CA 90212-3211. (310)550-1060. **Contact:** Stephen Moore. Estab. 1938. Member of ATA, signatory of WGA. Represents 150 clients. 10% of clients are new/previously unpublished writers.
Represents: Film/TV rights to published books; feature film, documentary, animation, TV MOW, miniseries, episodic drama, sitcom, variety show, animation; soap opera, stage plays. **Considers these script subject areas:** action/adventure; comedy; detective/police/crime; family saga; historical; mainstream; mystery/suspense; romantic comedy and drama.
   ⌒ This agency specializes in film and TV rights sales and representation of film and TV writers.
How to Contact: "All unsolicited material is automatically discarded unread."
Recent Sales: This agency prefers not to share information on specific sales.
Terms: Agent receives 10% commission on domestic sales; 10% on foreign sales. Offers written contract, binding for 1-3 years. "We charge clients for copying manuscripts or scripts for submission unless a sufficient quantity is supplied by the author."

N ⬤ **EDDIE KRITZER PRODUCTIONS**, 8484 Wilshire Blvd., Suite 205, Beverly Hills CA 90211. (323)655-5696. Fax: (323)655-5173. E-mail: producedby@aol.com. Website: www.eddiekritzer.com. **Contact:** Clair Weer, executive story editor. Estab. 1995. Represents 20 clients. 50% of clients are new/previously unpublished writers. Currently handles: 25% nonfiction books; 5% novels; 10% movie scripts; 15% TV scripts; 1% stage plays; 1% syndicated material.
   • See the expanded listing for this agency in Literary Agents: Nonfee-charging.

☑ ⦿ **THE CANDACE LAKE AGENCY**, 9200 Sunset Blvd., Suite 820, Los Angeles CA 90069. (310)247-2115. Fax: (310)247-2116. E-mail: clagency@earthlink.net. **Contact:** Candace Lake. Estab. 1977. Signatory of WGA, member of DGA. 50% of clients are new/previously unpublished writers. Currently handles: 20% novels; 40% movie scripts; 40% TV scripts.

Member Agents: Candace Lake (president/agent).

Represents: Feature film, TV MOW, episodic drama, sitcom. **Considers all script subject areas.**

    O━┓ This agency specializes in screenplay and teleplay writers.

Also Handles: Novels. **Considers all fiction types.**

How to Contact: Query with SASE. *No unsolicited material.* Responds in 1 month to queries; 3 months to scripts. Accepts queries by fax. Considers simultaneous queries. Returns materials only with SASE or else discards. Obtains most new clients through referrals.

Recent Sales: This agency prefers not to share information on specific sales.

Terms: Agent receives 10% commission on domestic sales; 10% on foreign sales. Offers written contract, binding for 2 years. Charges clients for photocopying.

⦿ **LARCHMONT LITERARY AGENCY**, 444 N. Larchmont Blvd., Suite 200, Los Angeles CA 90004. (323)856-3070. Fax: (323)856-3071. E-mail: agent@larchmontlit.com. **Contact:** Joel Millner. Estab. 1998. Signatory of WGA, member of DGA. Currently handles: 5% novels, 90% movie scripts, 5% cable or TV films.

    • Prior to becomming an agent, Mr. Millner attended NYU Film School and participated in The William Morris agent training program.

Represents: Movie scripts, feature film. **Considers these script subject areas:** action/adventure; biography/autobiography; animation; comedy; contemporary issues; detective/police/crime; fantasy; historical; horror; mainstream; mystery/suspense; psychic/supernatural; romantic comedy; romantic drama; science fiction; sports; thriller/espionage.

    O━┓ This agency specializes in feature writers and feature writer/directors. "We maintain a small, highly selective client list and offer a long-term career management style of agenting that larger agencies can't provide." Actively seeking spec feature scripts or established feature writers.

Also Handles: Novels. **Considers these fiction areas:** action/adventure; contemporary issues; detective/police crime; family saga; fantasy; historical; horror; humor/satire; juvenile; literary; mainstream; mystery; psychic/supernatural; romance; science fiction; sports; thriller/espionage.

How to Contact: Query with SASE. Accepts queries by e-mail. Prefers to read materials exclusively. Responds in 2 weeks. *No unsolicited scripts.* Discards unwanted queries and mss. Obtains most new clients through recommendations from current clients, producers, studio execs, university writing programs, national writing contests.

Recent Sales: This agency prefers not to share information on specific sales.

Terms: Agent receives 10% commission on domestic sales. No written contract.

Writers' Conferences: NYU Film School (Los Angeles, June).

Tips: "Please do not send a script until it is in its best possible draft."

⦿ **LEGACIES**, 501 Woodstork Circle, Bradenton FL 34209-7393. (941)792-9159. **Contact:** Mary Ann Amato, executive director. Estab. 1993. Signatory of WGA, member of Florida Motion Picture & Television Association, Board of Talent Agents, Dept. of Professional Regulations License No. TA 0000404. 50% of clients are new/previously unpublished writers. Currently handles: 10% fiction books; 80% screenplays; 10% stage plays.

Represents: Feature film. **Considers these script subject areas:** comedy; contemporary issues; family saga; feminist; historical.

    O━┓ This agency specializes in screenplays.

How to Contact: Query by mail. Enclose SASE. Does not accept e-mail or phone queries. Considers simultaneous queries. Responds in 2 weeks to queries; 6 weeks to mss.

Recent Sales: Sold 2 script projects in the last year. *Movie sold:* "Untitled," by Patricia A. Friedberg; *Movie optioned: Progress of the Sun*, by Patricia A. Friedberg; *Death's Parallel*, by Dr. Oakley Jordan (Rainbow Books).

Terms: Agent receives 15% commission on domestic sales; 20% on foreign sales (WGA percentages on member sales). Offers written contract.

Tips: "New writers should purchase script writing computer programs, or read and apply screenplay format before submitting."

☑ ⦿ **PAUL S. LEVINE LITERARY AGENCY**, 1054 Superba Ave., Venice CA 90291-3940. (310)450-6711. Fax: (310)450-0181. E-mail: pslevine@ix.netcom.com. Website: www.netcom.con/~pslevine/lawliterary.html. **Contact:** Paul S. Levine. Estab. 1996. Member of the Attorney-State Bar of California. Represents over 100 clients. 75% of clients are new/previously unpublished writers. Currently handles: 30% nonfiction books; 30% novels; 10% movie scripts; 30% TV scripts.

    • See the expanded listing for this agency in Literary Agents: Nonfee-charging.

N ⦿ **THE LUEDTKE AGENCY**, 1674 Broadway, Suite 7A, New York NY 10019. (212)765-9564. Fax: (212)765-9582. **Contact:** Elaine Devlin. Estab. 1997. Signatory of WGA. Represents 35 clients. 20% of clients are new/previously unpublished writers. Currently handles: 70% movie scripts; 20% TV scripts; 10% stage plays.

    • Prior to becoming an agent, Penny Luedtke was in classical music management; Elaine Devlin was in film development, story editing; Marcia Weiss was an attorney, owner of a music agency.

Member Agents: Penny Luedtke (primarily represents talent—some special project writers); Elaine Devlin (screenwriters, playwrights); Marcia Weiss (screenwriters, television writers).
Represents: Movie scripts, TV scripts, feature film, TV movie of the week; sitcom, soap opera, theatrical stage play, miniseries, stage plays. **Considers these script subject areas:** action/adventure, biography/autobiography, cartoon/animation; comedy; contemporary issues; detective/police/crime; ethnic; family saga; fantasy; feminist; gay/lesbian; historical; horror; juvenile; mainstream; multicultural; multimedia; mystery/suspense; psychic/supernatural; regional; religious/inspirational; romantic comedy; romantic drama; science fiction; sports; teen; thriller/espionage; western/frontier.

> ○➥ "We are a small shop and like it that way. We work closely with our writers developing projects and offer extensive editorial assistance." Actively seeking well-written material. Does not want to receive any project with graphic or explicit violence against women or children.

How to Contact: Query with SASE. Does not accept queries by e-mail or fax. Considers simultaneous queries and submissions. Responds in 1 month to queries; 2 months to mss. Returns materials only with SASE. Obtains most new clients through recommendations from others.
Recent Sales: This agency prefers not to share information on specific sales.
Terms: Agent receives 10% commission on domestic sales; 15% on foreign sales. Offers written contract, binding per WGA standards. Charges clients for reimbursement of expenses for couriers, messengers, international telephone and photocopying.

◑ ROBERT MADSEN AGENCY, 1331 E. 34th St., Suite #1, Oakland CA 94602-1032. (510)223-2090. Agent: Robert Madsen. Senior Editor: Liz Madsen. Estab. 1992. Represents 5 clients. 100% of clients are new/previously unpublished writers. Currently handles: 25% nonfiction books; 25% fiction books; 25% movie scripts; 25% TV scripts.

> • See the expanded listing for this agency in Literary Agents: Nonfee-charging.

◐ MAJOR CLIENTS AGENCY, 345 N. Maple Dr., #395, Beverly Hills CA 90210. (310)205-5000. (310)205-5099. **Contact:** Donna Williams Fontno. Estab. 1985. Signatory of WGA. Represents 200 clients. 0% of clients are new/previously unpublished writers. Currently handles: 30% movie scripts; 70% TV scripts.
Represents: Movie scripts; feature films; TV scripts; TV MOW; sitcom. **Considers these script subject areas:** detective/police/crime; erotica; family saga; horror; mainstream; mystery/suspense; sports; thriller/espionage.

> ○➥ This agency specializes in TV writers, creators, directors, film writers/directors.

How to Contact: Send outline/proposal with SASE. Responds in 2 weeks to queries; 1 month to scripts.
Recent Sales: This agency prefers not to share information on specific sales.
Terms: Agent receives 10% commission on domestic sales; 10% on foreign sales. Offers written contract.

🆖 ◑ THE MANAGEMENT COMPANY, 1337 Ocean Ave., Suite F, Santa Monica CA 90401. (310)664-9044. E-mail: tjk915@aol.com. **Contact:** Tom Klassen. Represents 15 clients.

> • Prior to becoming an agent, Mr. Klassen was an agent with International Creative Management (ICM).

Member Agents: Tom Klassen; F. Miguel Valenti; Jacob Vonk; Helene Taber; Paul Davis.
Represents: Episodic drama; movie scripts; TV scripts; feature film; sitcom; miniseries; also children's books.

> ○➥ Actively seeking "real good comedies." Does not want to receive horror scripts.

How to Contact: Query with SASE. Does not accept queries by e-mail or fax. Responds in 2 weeks to queries. Returns materials only with SASE. Obtains most new clients through recommendations from others and conferences.
Recent Sales: This agency sold 7 script projects in the last year.
Terms: Agent receives 10% commission on domestic sales; 10% on foreign sales. Offers written contract, binding for 2 years.
Writers' Conferences: Sundance Film Festival.
Tips: "We only accept query letters with a short, one-page synopsis. We will request full manuscript with a SASE if interested. We rarely take on nonreferred material, but do review query letters and occasionally take on new writers."

◑ MANUS & ASSOCIATES LITERARY AGENCY, INC., 417 E. 57th St., Suite 5D, New York NY 10022. (212)644-8020. Fax: (212)644-3374. **Contact:** Janet Manus. Also: 375 Forest Ave. Palo Alto CA 94301. (650)470-5151. Fax: (650)470-5159. **Contact:** Jillian Manus. Estab. 1985. Member of AAR. Represents 75 clients. 15% of clients are new/previously unpublished writers. Currently handles: 60% nonfiction books; 10% juvenile books; 30% novels (sells 40% of material into TV/film markets).

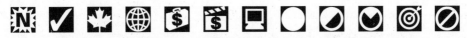

**FOR EXPLANATIONS OF THESE SYMBOLS,
SEE THE INSIDE FRONT AND BACK COVERS OF THIS BOOK**

● See the expanded listing for this agency in Literary Agents: Nonfee-charging.

THE STUART M. MILLER CO., 11684 Ventura Blvd., #225, Studio City CA 91604-2699. (818)506-6067. Fax: (818)506-4079. E-mail: smmco@aol.com. **Contact:** Stuart Miller. Estab. 1977. Signatory of WGA, member of DGA. Currently handles: 40% multimedia; 10% novels; 50% movie scripts.
Represents: Movie scripts. **Considers these script subject areas:** action/adventure; biography/autobiography; cartoon/animation; comedy; contemporary issues; detective/police/crime; family saga; historical; mainstream; multimedia; mystery/suspense; romantic comedy; romantic drama; science fiction; sports; teen; thriller/espionage.
Also Handles: Nonfiction books, novels. **Considers these nonfiction areas:** biography/autobiography; computers/electronics; current affairs; government/politics/law; health/medicine; history; how-to; memoirs; military/war; self-help/personal improvement; true crime/investigative. **Considers these fiction areas:** action/adventure; contemporary issues; detective/police/crime; historical; literary; mainstream; mystery; science fiction; sports; thriller/espionage.
How to Contact: Query with SASE, include outline/proposal. Accepts queries by fax and e-mail. Considers simultaneous queries. Responds in 3 days to queries; 6 weeks to mss. Returns material only with SASE.
Recent Sales: This agency prefers not to share information on specific sales.
Terms: Agent receives 10% commission on domestic sales; 15-20% on foreign sales. Offers written contract, binding for 2 years. Follows WGA standards for contract termination.
Tips: "Always include SASE, e-mail address, or fax number with query letters. Make it easy to respond."

MOMENTUM MARKETING, (Specialized: Arizona-based writers), 1112 E. Laguna Dr., Tempe AZ 85282-5516. (480)777-0365. Fax: (480)756-0019. E-mail: klepage@concentric.net. **Contact:** Kerry LePage. Estab. 1995. Signatory of WGA. Represents Arizona/based writers only.
● Prior to opening her agency, Ms. LePage was a marketing consultant and actress.
Represents: Feature film, episodic drama, TV MOW, sitcom. **Considers these script subject areas:** action/adventure; biography/autobiography; cartoon/animation; comedy; contemporary/issues; detective/police/crime; ethnic; experimental; family saga; fantasy; feminist; gay/lesbian; historical; horror; juvenile; mainstream; mystery/suspense; psychic/supernatural; religious/inspirational; romance (comedy, drama); science fiction; sports; teen; thriller/espionage; western/frontier.
O─ "Focusing on Arizona-based writers and projects which can be locally produced."
How to Contact: "Not accepting new writers ar this time—queries will be returned. Personal referrals only."
Recent Sales: This agency prefers not to share information on specific sales.
Terms: Agent receives 10% commission on domestic sales; 10% on foreign sales. Offers written contract, binding for 1 year. 10-day written notice will be given to terminate contract. Charges clients for postage, long distance—no more than $50/writer will be charged without their prior approval.
Tips: "We are currently looking at internet-based projects and doing what we can for film in Arizona."

MONTEIRO ROSE AGENCY, 17514 Ventura Blvd., #205, Encino CA 91316. (818)501-1177. Fax: (818)501-1194. E-mail: monrose@ix.netcom.com. Website: www.monteiro-rose.com. **Contact:** Milissa Brockish. Estab. 1987. Signatory of WGA. Represents over 50 clients. Currently handles: 40% movie scripts; 20% TV scripts; 40% animation.
Member Agents: Candace Monteiro (literary); Fredda Rose (literary); Milissa Brockish (literary); Jason Dravis (literary).
Represents: Feature film, animation, TV MOW, episodic drama. **Considers these script subjects:** action/adventure; cartoon/animation; comedy; contemporary issues; detective/police/crime; ethnic; family saga; historical; juvenile; mainstream; mystery/suspense; psychic/supernatural; romantic comedy and drama; science fiction; teen; thriller.
O─ This agency specializes in scripts for animation, TV and film.
How to Contact: "Currently, we are only accepting established writers." Query with SASE. Accepts queries by fax, "but cannot guarantee reply without SASE." Responds in 1 week to queries; 2 months to mss. Returns materials only with SASE. Obtains most new clients through recommendations from others in the entertainment business and query letters.
Recent Sales: This agency prefers not to share information on specific sales.
Terms: Agent receives 10% commission on domestic sales. Offers standard WGA 2-year contract, with 90-day cancellation clause. Charges clients for photocopying.
Tips: "It does no good to call and try to speak to an agent before they have read your material, unless referred by someone we know. The best and only way, if you're a new writer, is to send a query letter with a SASE. If agents are interested, they will request to read your script. Also enclose a SASE with the script if you want it back."

DEE MURA ENTERPRISES, INC., 269 W. Shore Dr., Massapequa NY 11758-8225. (516)795-1616. Fax: (516)795-8757. E-mail: samurai5@ix.netcom.com. **Contact:** Dee Mura, Ken Nyquist. Estab. 1987. Signatory of WGA. 50% of clients are new/previously published writers. Currently handles: 25% nonfiction books; 10% scholarly books; 15% juvenile books; 25% novels; 25% movie scripts.
● See the expanded listing for this agency in Literary Agents: Nonfee-charging.

BK NELSON LITERARY AGENCY & LECTURE BUREAU, 84 Woodland Rd., Pleasantville NY 10570-1322. (914)741-1322. Fax: (914)741-1324. Also: 1500 S. Palm Canyon Dr., Suites 7 & 9, Beverly Hills CA 92262. (760)318-2773. Fax: (760)318-2774. E-mail: bknelson4@cs.com. Website: www.bknelson.com. **Contact:** B.K.

Nelson, John Benson, Chip Ashbach or Erv Rosenfeld. Estab. 1980. Member of NACA, Author's Guild, NAFE, ABA, AAUW. Represents 62 clients. 40% of clients are new/previously unpublished writers. Currently handles: 30% nonfiction books; 5% CD-ROM/electronic products; 30% novels; 20% movie scripts; 10% TV scripts; 10% stage plays.
- See the expanded listing for this agency in Literary Agents: Fee-charging.

N: ◐ NIAD MANAGEMENT, 3465 Coy Dr., Sherman Oaks CA 91423. (818)981-2505. Fax: (818)386-2082. E-mail: wniad@aol.com. **Contact:** Wendi Niad. Estab. 1997. Represents 15 clients. 2% of clients are new/previously unpublished writers. Currently handles: 1% novels; 95% movie scripts; 2% TV scripts; 1% multimedia; 1% stage plays.
Represents: Movie scripts, TV scripts, feature film, TV movie of the week, theatrical stage play, miniseries, stage plays. **Considers these script subject areas:** action/adventure; biography/autobiography; comedy; contemporary issues; detective/police/crime; ethnic; family saga; historical; horror; mainstream; multicultural; mystery/suspense; psychic/supernatural; romantic comeday; romantic drama; sports; teen; thriller/espionage.
Also Handles: Novels, nonfiction. **Considers these nonfiction areas:** biography/autobiography. **Considers these fiction areas:** action/adventure; contemporary issues; detective/police/crime; ethnic; family saga; literary; mainstream; multicultural; mystery/suspense; psychic/supernatural; romance; thriller/espionage.
How to Contact: Query with SASE. Accepts queries by e-mail and fax. Considers simultaneous queries. Responds in 1 week to queries; 1 month to mss. Returns materials only with SASE. Obtains most new clients through recommendations from others.
Recent Sales: Sold 5 script projects in the last year. *Movie/TV MOW script(s) optioned/sold: Flying in Place*, by Susan Sandler (Columbia/TriStar TV); *Blessed Virgins*, by Sarah Kelly (Avenue Pictures) *Movie/TV MOW script(s) in development: Florence Greenberg*, by Story Susan Sandler (TNT); *Preying On Puritans*, by Joshua Rebell (Lincoln Stalmaster); *Corcovado*, by Claudia Salter (Fox Anaimation). Other clients include Steve Copling, Peter Egan, Karen Kelly, Jim McGlynn, Debra Mooradian, Don Most, Brian Rousso, Fernando Fragata.
Terms: Agent receives 10-15% commission on domestic sales. Offers written contract, binding for 1 year. 30-day notice must be given to terminate contract.

N: ◐ OMNIQUEST ENTERTAINMENT, 843 Berkeley St., Santa Monica CA 90403-2503. (310)453-6549. Fax: (310)453-2523. E-mail: info@omniquestmedia.com. Website: www.omniquestmedia.com. **Contact:** Michael Kaliski. Estab. 1997. Currently handles: 5% novels; 5% juvenile books; 40% movie scripts; 10% TV scripts; 20% multimedia; 15% stage plays.
Represents: Episodic drama, movie scripts, TV scripts, feature film, TV movie of the week, sitcom, theatrical stage play, miniseries, stage plays, syndicated material. **Considers these script subject areas:** action/adventure; biography/ autobiography; comedy; contemporary issues; detective/police/crime; experimental; family saga; fantasy; historical; mainstream; multimedia; mystery/suspense; psychic/supernatural; romantic comedy; romantic drama; science fiction; thriller/espionage. Also handles DV shorts for Internet.
    ○─ Actively seeking books that can be adapted for film and scripts. Does not want to receive erotic material.
Also Handles: Novels, short story collections, novellas. **Considers these fiction areas:** action/adventure; detective/ police/crime; experimental; family saga; fantasy; literary; psychic/supernatural; romance; science fiction; thriller/espionage.
How to Contact: Query with SASE or send outline and 2-3 sample chapters. Accepts queries by e-mail. Considers simultaneous queries. Returns materials only with SASE or recycles unwanted materials. Obtains most new clients through recommendations from others.
Recent Sales: This agency prefers not to share information on specific sales.
Terms: Agent receives 15% commission on domestic sales; 15% on foreign sales. Offers written contract.

◪ FIFI OSCARD AGENCY INC., 24 W. 40th St., New York NY 10018. (212)764-1100. **Contact:** Ivy Fischer Stone, Literary Department. Estab. 1956. Member of AAR, signatory of WGA. Represents 108 clients. 5% of clients are new/previously unpublished writers. Currently handles: 40% nonfiction books; 40% novels; 5% movie scripts; 10% stage plays; 5% TV scripts.
- See the expanded listing for this agency in Literary Agents: Nonfee-charging.

◐ DOROTHY PALMER, 235 W. 56 St., New York NY 10019. Phone/fax: (212)765-4280 (press *51 for fax). Estab. 1990. Signatory of WGA. Represents 12 clients. Works with published writers only. Currently handles: 70% movie scripts, 30% TV scripts.
- In addition to being a literary agent, Ms. Palmer has worked as a talent agent for 30 years.
Represents: Feature film, TV MOW, episodic drama, sitcom, miniseries. **Considers these script subject areas:** action/ adventure; comedy; contemporary issues; detective/police/crime; family saga; feminist; mainstream; mystery/suspense; romantic comedy; romantic drama; thriller/espionage.
    ○─ This agency specializes in screenplays, TV. Actively seeking successful, published writers (screenplays only). Does not want to receive work from new or unpublished writers.
How to Contact: Query with SASE. "Published writers *only*." Prefers to read materials exclusively. Returns materials only with SASE. Obtains most new clients through recommendations from others.
Recent Sales: This agency prefers not to share information on specific sales.
Terms: Agent receives 10% commission on domestic sales; 10% on foreign sales. Offers written contract, binding for 1 year. Charges clients for postage, photocopies.

Tips: "Do *not* telephone. When I find a script that interests me, I call the writer. Calls to me are a turn-off because they cut into my reading time."

⊘ **PANDA TALENT**, 3721 Hoen Ave., Santa Rosa CA 95405. (707)576-0711. Fax: (707)544-2765. **Contact:** Audrey Grace. Estab. 1977. Signatory of WGA, SAG, AFTRA, Equity. Represents 10 clients. 80% of clients are new/previously unpublished writers. Currently handles: 5% novels; 40% TV scripts; 50% movie scripts; 5% stage plays.
Story Readers: Steven Grace (science fiction/war/action); Vicki Lima (mysteries/romance); Cleo West (western/true stories).
Represents: Feature film, TV MOW, episodic drama, sitcom. **Considers these script subject areas:** action/adventure; animals; comedy; detective/police/crime; ethnic; family saga; military/war; mystery/suspense; romantic comedy and drama; science fiction; true crime/investigative; westerns/frontier.
How to Contact: Query with treatment and SASE. Responds in 3 weeks to queries; 2 months to mss. Must include SASE.
Recent Sales: This agency prefers not to share information on specific sales.
Terms: Agent receives 10% commission on domestic sales; 10% on foreign sales.

[N] ⊘ **THE PARTOS COMPANY**, 6363 Wilshire Blvd., Suite 227, Los Angeles CA 90048. (323)951-1320. Fax: (323)951-1324. **Contact:** Jim Barquette. Estab. 1991. Signatory of WGA. Represents 20 clients. 50% of clients are new/previously unpublished writers. Currently handles: 90% movie scripts; 10% TV scripts (features only).
Member Agents: Walter Partos (below the line and literary); Jim Barquette (literary); Cynthia Guber (actors).
Represents: Movie scripts (feature film); TV scripts (TV MOW).
○→ This agency specializes in independent features.
How to Content: Query with SASE. Responds in 1 month to queries; 3 months to scripts. Currently not considering new clients.
Recent Sales: This agency prefers not to share information on specific sales.
Terms: Agent receives 10% commission on domestic sales; 10% on foreign sales. Offers written contract, binding for 1 year plus WGA Rider W.

☑ ⊘ **BARRY PERELMAN AGENCY**, 9200 Sunset Blvd., #1201, Los Angeles CA 90069. (310)274-5999. Fax: (310)274-6445. **Contact:** Marina D'Amico. Estab. 1982. Signatory of WGA, DGA. Represents 40 clients. 15% of clients are new/previously unpublished writers. Currently handles: 99% movie scripts; 1% stage plays.
Member Agents: Barry Perelman (motion picture/packaging); Marina D'Amico (television).
Represents: Movie scripts. **Considers these script areas:** action/adventure; biography/autobiography; contemporary issues; detective/police/crime; historical; horror; mystery/suspense; romance; science fiction; thriller/espionage.
○→ This agency specializes in motion pictures/packaging.
How to Contact: Send outline/proposal with query. Responds in 1 month. Obtains most new clients through recommendations and query letters.
Recent Sales: This agency prefers not to share information on specific sales.
Terms: Agent receives 10% commission on domestic sales; 10% on foreign sales. Offers written contract, binding for 1-2 years. Charges clients for postage and photocopying.

☑ ⊘ **STEPHEN PEVNER, INC.**, 248 W. 73rd St., 2nd Floor, New York NY 10023. (212)496-0474. Also: 100 N. Crescent Dr., Beverly Hills CA 90210. (310)385-4160. Fax: (310)385-6633. E-mail: spevner@aol.com. **Contact:** Stephen Pevner. Estab. 1991. Member of AAR. Represents under 50 clients. 50% of clients are new/previously unpublished writers. Currently handles: 25% nonfiction books; 25% novels; TV scripts; stage plays.
● Mr. Pevner represents a number of substantial independent writer/directors. See the expanded listing for this agency in Literary Agents: Nonfee-charging.

⊘ **A PICTURE OF YOU**, 1176 Elizabeth Dr., Hamilton OH 45013-3507. Phone/fax: (513)863-1108. E-mail: apoy1 @aol.com. **Contact:** Lenny Minelli. Estab. 1993. Signatory of WGA. Represents 40 clients. 50% of clients are new/previously unpublished writers. Currently handles: 80% movie scripts; 10% TV scripts; 10% syndicated material.
● Prior to opening his agency, Mr. Minelli was an actor/producer for 10 years. Also owned and directed a talent agency and represented actors and actresses from around the world.
Member Agents: Michelle Chang (fiction/nonfiction books).
Represents: Feature film, animation, miniseries, documentary, TV MOW, sitcom, episodic drama, syndicated material. **Considers all script subject areas.**
○→ This agency specializes in screenplays and TV scripts.
Also Handles: Nonfiction books, novels, novellas, short story collections. **Considers these nonfiction areas:** gay/lesbian issues; history; juvenile nonfiction; music/dance/theatre/film; religious/inspirational; self-help/personal. **Considers these fiction areas:** action/adventure; detective/police/crime; erotica; ethnic; family saga; fantasy; gay/lesbian; glitz; historical; horror; literary; mainstream; mystery/suspense; religious; romance (contemporary, gothic, historical); thriller/espionage; westerns/frontier; young adult.
How to Contact: Query with SASE first. Accepts queries by e-mail. Considers simultaneous queries. Responds in 3 weeks to queries; 1 month to scripts. Obtains most new clients through recommendations and queries.

Recent Sales: *Movie/TV MOW scripts optioned/sold: Stranglehold*, by L.I. Isgro; *Bodyslams in the Boardroom*, by Gary M. Cappetta; *Mainstay*, by David L. Carpenter. **Scripting assignments:** *The Governor*, by Gary M. Cappetta.
Terms: Agent receives 10% commission on domestic sales; 15% on foreign sales. Offers written contract, binding for 1 year, with 90 day cancellation clause. Charges clients for postage/express mail and long distance calls.
Tips: "Make sure that the script is the best it can be before seeking an agent."

PINKHAM LITERARY AGENCY, 418 Main St., Amesbury MA 01913. (978)388-4210: Fax: (978)388-4221. E-mail: jnoblepink@aol.com. Website: www.pinkhamliterary.com. **Contact:** Joan Noble Pinkham. Estab. 1996. Currently handles: 20% movie scripts; 20% nonfiction books; 60% novels.
• See the expanded listing for this agency in Literary Agents: Fee-charging.

PMA LITERARY AND FILM MANAGEMENT, INC., 45 W. 21st St., 6th Floor, New York NY 10010. (212)929-1222. Fax: (212)206-0238. E-mail: pmalitfilm@aol.com. Website: www.pmalitfilm.com. **Contact:** Peter Miller. Estab. 1975. Represents 80 clients. 50% of clients are new/previously unpublished writers. Currently handles: 50% fiction; 25% nonfiction; 25% screenplays.
• See the expanded listing for this agency in Literary Agents: Fee-charging.

JIM PREMINGER AGENCY, 450 N. Roxbury, PH 1050, Beverly Hills CA 90210. (310)860-1116. Fax: (310)860-1117. E-mail: general@premingeragency.com. Estab. 1980. Signatory of WGA, DGA. Represents 55 clients. 20% of clients are new/previously unpublished writers. Currently represents 47% movie scripts; 1% novels; 50% TV scripts; 1% nonfiction books; 1% stage plays.
Member Agents: Jim Preminger (television and features); Dean Schramm (features and television); Ryan L. Saul (features and television); Melissa Read (television and features).
Represents: Feature film, episodic drama, TV MOW, sitcom, miniseries, Internet.
  ⚬→ This agency specializes in representing showrunners for television series, writers for television movies, as well as directors and writers for features.
How to Contact: Query with SASE. Responds in 2 months to queries; 3 months to mss. "No unsolicited material." Obtains most new clients through recommendations.
Recent Sales: This agency prefers not to share information on specific sales.
Terms: Agent receives 10% commission on domestic sales; 10% on foreign sales. Offers written contract.

PUDDINGSTONE LITERARY AGENCY, Affiliate of SBC Enterprises Inc., 11 Mabro Dr., Denville NJ 07834-9607. (201)366-3622. **Contact:** Alec Bernard or Eugenia Cohen. Estab. 1972. Represents 25 clients. 80% of clients are new/previously unpublished writers. Currently handles: 10% nonfiction books; 70% novels; 20% movie scripts.
• See the expanded listing for this agency in Literary Agents: Fee-charging.

QCORP LITERARY AGENCY, P.O. Box 8, Hillsboro OR 97123-0008. (800)775-6038. E-mail: qcorp @qcorplit.com. Website: www.qcorplit.com. **Contact:** William C. Brown. Estab. 1990. Represents 25 clients. 75% of clients are new/previously unpublished writers. Currently handles: 30% nonfiction books; 60% fiction books; 10% scripts.
• See the expanded listing for this agency in Literary Agents: Fee-charging.

THE QUILLCO AGENCY, 3104 W. Cumberland Court, Westlake Village CA 91362. (805)495-8436. Fax: (805)373-9868. E-mail: quillcoagency@aol.com. **Contact:** Sandy Mackey (owner). Estab. 1993. Signatory of WGA. Represents 40 clients.
Represents: Feature film, documentary, animation/TV MOW.
How to Contact: Not accepting query letters at this time. Prefers to read materials exclusively. Returns materials only with SASE.
Recent Sales: This agency prefers not to share information on specific sales.
Terms: Agent receives 10% commission on domestic sales; 10% on foreign sales.

DAN REDLER ENTERTAINMENT, 18730 Hatteras St., #8, Tarzana CA 91356 (818)776-0938. Fax: (818)705-6870. **Contact:** Dan Redler. Represents 10 clients. Currently handles: 100% movie scripts.
• Prior to opening his management company, Mr. Redler was a production executive.
Represents: Movie scripts, feature film. **Considers these script subject areas:** action/adventure; biography/autobiography; comedy; contemporary issues; detective/police/crime; ethnic; family saga; fantasy; feminist; historical; horror; juvenile; mainstream; mystery/suspense; psychic/supernatural; romantic comedy; romantic drama; science fiction; sports; teen; thriller/espionage.
  ⚬→ Actively seeking mainstream and contemporary scripts. Does not want to receive small noncommercial stories.
How to Contact: Query with SASE. Accepts queries by fax. Prefers to read materials exclusively. Responds in 2 weeks to queries; 1 month to mss. Returns materials only with SASE.
Recent Sales: This agency prefers not to share information on specific sales.

Terms: Agent receives 10% commission on domestic sales; 10% on foreign sales and subagent fees. Offers written contract, binding for 2 years. Client must supply all copies of scripts.
Tips: "We offer personal service, indepth career guidance, and aggressive sales efforts."

REDWOOD EMPIRE AGENCY, P.O. Box 1946, Guerneville CA 95446-1146. (707)869-1146. E-mail: redemp @sonic.net. **Contact:** Jim Sorrells or Rodney Shull. Estab. 1992. Represents 10 clients. 90% of clients are new/previously unpublished writers. Currently handles: 100% movie scripts.
Represents: Feature film, animation (movie), TV MOW. **Considers these script subject areas:** comedy; contemporary issues; erotica; family saga; feminist; gay; mainstream; mystery/suspense; romantic comedy; romantic drama; thriller.
    Oм This agency specializes in screenplays, big screen or TV.
How to Contact: Query with 1 page synopsis and SASE. Responds in 1 week to queries; 1 month to mss. Obtains most new clients through word of mouth, letter in *Hollywood Scriptwriter*.
Recent Sales: This agency prefers not to share information on specific sales.
Terms: Agent receives 10% commission on domestic sales; 10% on foreign sales. Offers criticism service: structure, characterization, dialogue, format style. No fee for criticism service.
Tips: "Most interested in ordinary people confronting real-life situations."

MICHAEL D. ROBINS & ASSOCIATES, 23241 Ventura Blvd., #300, Woodland Hills CA 91364. (818)343-1755. Fax: (818)343-7355. E-mail: mdr2@msn.com. **Contact:** Michael D. Robins. Estab. 1991. Signatory of WGA; member of DGA. 10% of clients are new/previously unpublished writers. Currently handles: 5% nonfiction books; 5% novels; 20% movie scripts; 60% TV scripts; 10% syndicated material.
    • Prior to becoming an agent, Mr. Robins was a literary agent at a mid-sized agency.
Represents: Episodic drama, movie scripts, TV scripts, feature film, TV movie of the week, animation, miniseries, stage plays, syndicated material. **Considers all script subject areas.**
Also Handles: Nonfiction books, novels. **Considers these nonfiction areas:** history; humor; memoirs; military/war; popular culture; science/technology; true crime/investigative; urban lifestyle. **Considers these fiction areas:** action/ adventure; cartoon/comic; contemporary issues; detective/police/crime; family saga; fantasy; gay/lesbian; historical; mainstream; mystery/suspense; psychic/supernatural; romance; science fiction; thriller/espionage; westerns/frontier; young adult.
How to Contact: Query with SASE. Accepts queries by e-mail and fax. Considers simultaneous queries. Responds in 1 week to queries; 1 month to mss. Obtains most new clients through recommendations from others.
Recent Sales: This agency prefers not to share information on specific sales.
Terms: Agent receives 10% commission on domestic sales; 10% on foreign sales. Offers written contract, binding for 2 years. 4-month notice must be given to terminate contract.

ROBINSON TALENT AND LITERARY MANAGEMENT, 1101 S. Robertson Blvd., Suite 210, Los Angeles CA 90035. (310)278-0801. Fax: (310)278-0807. **Contact:** Margaretrose Robinson. Estab. 1992. Franchised by DGA/ SAG. Represents 150 clients. 10% of screenwriting clients are new/previously unpublished writers; all are WGA members. Currently handles: 15% novels; 40% movie scripts; 40% TV scripts; 5% stage plays.
    • Prior to becoming an agent, Ms. Robinson worked as a designer.
Member Agents: Margaretrose Robinson (adaptation of books and plays for development as features or TV MOW); Kevin Douglas (scripts for film and TV).
Represents: Feature film, documentary, TV MOW, miniseries, episodic drama, variety show, stage play, CD-ROM. **Considers these script subject areas:** action/adventure; cartoon/animation; comedy; contemporary issues; detective/ police/crime; erotica; ethnic; experimental; family saga; fantasy; mainstream; mystery/suspense; psychic/supernatural; religious/inspirational; romantic comedy and drama; science fiction; sports; teen; thriller; western/frontier.
    Oм "We represent screenwriters, playwrights, novelists and producers, directors."
How to Contact: Send outline/proposal, synopsis or log line. Obtains most new clients only through referral.
Recent Sales: This agency prefers not to share information on specific sales. Clients include Steve Edelman, Merryln Hammond, Michael Hennessey.
Terms: Agent receives 10% commission on domestic sales; 10% on foreign sales. Offers written contract, binding for 2 years minimum. Charges clients for photocopying, messenger, FedEx, and postage when required.
Tips: "We are a talent agency specializing in the copyright business. Fifty percent of our clients generate copyright— screenwriters, playwrights and novelists. Fifty percent of our clients service copyright—producers, directors and cinematographers. We represent only produced, published and/or WGA writers who are eligible for staff TV positions as well as novelists and playwrights whose works may be adapted for film on television."

JACK SCAGNETTI TALENT & LITERARY AGENCY, 5118 Vineland Ave., #102, North Hollywood CA 91601. (818)762-3871. **Contact:** Jack Scagnetti. Estab. 1974. Signatory of WGA, member of Academy of Television Arts and Sciences. Represents 50 clients. 50% of clients are new/previously unpublished writers. Currently handles: 20% nonfiction books; 70% movie scripts; 10% TV scripts.
    • Prior to opening his agency, Mr. Scagnetti wrote nonfiction books and magazine articles on movie stars, sports
      and health subjects and was a magazine and newspaper editor.
Member Agents: Janet Brown (books); Karen Disner (books).

insider report

Agents and the world of sitcom writing

Steve Young

Steve Young has been writing scripts for television for more than seven years. When he got his first taste of the business, "it was all about comedy, trying to make people laugh," he says. In the late 1970s, Young owned comedy clubs called The Comedy Works in the Philadelphia area where then up-and-coming comics like Eddie Murphy, Jay Leno, and Jerry Seinfeld performed. Young also got the chance to take the stage himself on occasion.

In the late 1980s, Young decided to give "it" a shot in Los Angeles. "I wasn't sure what 'it' was," he says, "but I knew Los Angeles was where I had to go." Since he found writing, he says, "I can't do anything else. I didn't know I could write until I was forty because I have attention deficit disorder and have a hard time reading. Finding out I could write was pretty amazing." Now Young fits in his writing time around the schedules of his two youngest kids, ages five and six, often setting his alarm clock for 4:30 a.m. so he can work before the little ones are awake.

He says breaking into the television writing business is tough and staying in is even tougher. In television, "you better have a very good friend who is running the show." Here he talks about the business, his work, and his experience with agents.

What are some of the programs you've written for? Have your scripts won awards?
Most of the shows I've worked for have been prime time and on major networks. I've written for *Boy Meets World, Cybill, Maybe This Time, Smart Guy,* HBO's *Crashbox,* to name but a few. One of my *Smart Guy* scripts won the 2000 PRISM Award and has also been nominated for the 2000 Humanitas Prize. Both awards recognize the ability to portray important social issues through television and film.

How does the world of television writing work? Does writing for this area of the entertainment business differ from writing feature films? Do agents work differently in these two areas?
When I talk about television, I mean writing for sitcoms or "episodics." To get an agent and to prove to a show or network that you can write, you usually create two samples of scripts for shows presently on the air. If your work gets read and they are bowled over by your talent, they might want to meet with you. If they're considering you for a staff job that season, they'll want to get an idea of your "chemistry" with them. Or, if they are having you "pitch" for a particular show, you should come in with three ideas they haven't done yet but are completely in sync with the show's ideals and characters.

In the sitcom world, if they like one of your ideas, they'll ask you (and have to pay you) to write a "step treatment," then the script, and then one rewrite. If you're on staff, you'll spend a lot of time in a room with a bunch of people shouting out lines and ideas, each attempting to get the executive producer's ear. There is a definite pecking order.

In television, you are usually writing for shows and characters that already exist. In film, you're creating a world and characters that never existed before. Of course, you're also writing 115 pages with much of it single spaced, while in television, it's approximately 45 double-spaced pages.

While all agents attempt to build "heat" about your ability, the television agent has the tougher job. He must first get someone at the show who has a say in hiring to read your sample script and actually pay attention to it when there are literally thousands of writers vying for, maybe, less than 100 openings. With experienced writers, friends, and relatives lining up, getting someone to pay attention to an unknown writer is not an easy job.

A film agent, on the other hand, must have some clout to get his client's script to the right people at production companies or studios, but they're not pitching a writer as much as they're pitching an idea for a film. If the agent gets a bite, then the completed script is submitted. The daunting process from reader on up to decision maker often knocks 99 percent of the scripts out of the box.

Briefly describe the schedule you follow to complete a single episode.

Once I receive a "go" on a particular story idea, I'll work up a treatment in a few days. Then I'll meet with the producers to flesh it out. I go home, apply those notes, and return to the producer a few days later. With final notes, I will be given two weeks to write the script. I write rather quickly and usually finish in a week. I turn that draft in, receive more notes, and then turn in a revision in another week. At that point, I'm finished. The script is turned over to the entire staff, or "the room," where they'll probably rewrite the entire script from page one.

What does an agent do for a writer who works in television?

Ideally, they keep their finger on the pulse of all potential buyers—whether it's NBC or Nickelodeon—finding out what they're looking for and making sure you know what tools (i.e., sample scripts, ideas) he'll need in order to sell you.

For staff positions, contracts for new writers are pretty much set by the Writers Guild of America (WGA). Contracts for cable, the Internet, and most animation shows are still rather loose. They want to pay the writer as little as they have to.

An agent should make sure the writer he represents is knowledgeable of *all* opportunities, no matter how seemingly small. An agent only interested in a big commission will often ignore jobs that a writer struggling to stay off welfare would gladly take.

Do you have to live in Los Angeles to work on a television show?

If you are working on a staff, you definitely need to live in Los Angeles, although there are a few shows that shoot in New York or Chicago. With communications as they are today, you may be able to live out of town if you are writing a single script.

You've written a number of scripts for younger viewers. How do you stay hip and up-to-date on your audience's interests?

I have children in their twenties and thirties and also a five- and six-year old so my experience with kids is spread all over the map. Even so, by the time something you write hits the air, the things that were hip are no longer so. I try to write from the inside out. Hip references tend to be overused and have no shelf life. I'd rather be funny than hip. I'm active in the PTA, I mentor kids and teens in writing, and I watch bad teen movies, so I get a feel for what's happening in their lives.

A while back, there was some controversy over a *Smart Guy* episode you wrote. Would you share the details of that incident?
The script had to do with minors drinking. The Federal Office of Drug Control Policy (ONDCP) looked at the script to see if the network, The WB, would qualify to receive financial credit because of the episode. Prior to the show getting on the air, ONDCP was saying, "Here's an idea you might want to use. You might want to do a little more of this, a little heavier-handed here." In the long run, it didn't change anything I wrote. They offered several thoughts, all of which fell within the realm of the script's intent. In fact, their comments ended up resurrecting some of my material from the first draft.

Since then, the government has changed their approach. They don't take a look at the script until after it airs, so there's no danger of them stepping in and changing anything.

The episode—which aired during sweeps—was selected by the Entertainment Industries Council for its 2000 PRISM Award and has been nominated for the prestigious Humanitas Prize. I was interviewed for CNN, ABC, etc., which gave me fifteen minutes of fame, but the awards meant a lot.

You've had some unsatisfying relationships with agents in the past. What's your advice to other writers about using an agent?
I truly believe agents are real people who are asked to take on much more than a human should be able to deal with. With that said, it would be hard to give all your clients equal or sufficient time. Therefore, the less credited and "nonhot" are often left by the wayside, and newer, younger talent soon replace them. If you can take the ignoring and lack of connection with your agent, stay with him until you can get another one.

I'm always searching for a better agent. They're always searching for better clients. I don't necessarily need an agent. There are certain networks and production companies I can go to directly. They know me better than they know my agent, and I can just pick up the phone and call them.

In this business, if you can have an agent, you should. You'll get in a lot of doors just by saying you have an agent. Much of the time you can only submit through an agent, and in that way, you can at least have them cover the cost for photocopying and postage. My suggestion is to find smaller, hungrier agents who show a real passion for your work. If you can't get someone like that and you can't get work on your own, take whomever you can get.

—Alice Pope

Represents: Feature film, miniseries, episodic drama, animation (movie), TV MOW, sitcom. **Considers these script subject areas:** action/adventure; comedy; detective/police/crime; family saga; historical; horror; mainstream; mystery/suspense; romantic comedy and drama; sports; thriller.
Also Handles: Nonfiction, novels. **Considers these nonfiction areas:** biography/autobiography; cooking/food/nutrition; health; current affairs; how-to; military/war; music/dance/theater/film; self-help/personal; sports; true crime/investigative; women's issues/women's studies. **Considers these fiction areas:** action/adventure; contemporary issues; detective/police/crime; family saga; historical; mainstream; mystery/suspense; picture book; romance (contemporary); sports; thriller/espionage; westerns/frontier.
　　O⟶ This agency specializes in film books with many photographs. Actively seeking books and screenplays. Does not want to receive TV scripts for existing shows.
How to Contact: Query with outline/proposal and SASE. Considers simultaneous queries. Responds in 1 month to script queries; 2 months to mss. Returns materials only with SASE. "No queries by phone or fax." Obtains most new clients through "referrals by others and query letters sent to us."
Recent Sales: *Movie/TV MOW scripts optioned/sold: Kastner's Cutthroats (44 Blue Prod.). Movie/TV MOW scripts in development: Pain,* by Charles Pickett (Concorde-New Horizons).
Terms: Agent receives 15% commission on domestic sales; 15% on foreign sales. Offers written contract, binding for 6 months-1 year. Charges clients for postage and photocopies.
Fees: Offers criticism service (books only). "Fee depends upon condition of original copy and number of pages."
Tips: "Write a good synopsis, short and to the point and include marketing data for the book."

☑ Ⓜ **SHAPIRO-LICHTMAN,** (formerly Shapiro-Lichtman-Stein), Shapiro-Lichtman Building, 8827 Beverly Blvd., Los Angeles CA 90048. Fax: (310)859-7153. **Contact:** Martin Shapiro. Estab. 1969. Signatory of WGA. 10% of clients are new/previously unpublished writers.
Represents: Feature film, miniseries, variety show, soap opera, episodic drama, animation (movie), theatrical stage play, TV MOW, sitcom, animation (TV). **Considers these script areas:** action/adventure; cartoon/animation; comedy; contemporary issues; detective/police/crime; ethnic; family saga; historical; horror; mainstream; mystery/suspense; romance (comedy, drama); science fiction; teen; thriller; westerns/frontier.
Also Handles: Nonfiction books, novels, novellas. **Considers all nonfiction areas. Considers all fiction areas.**
How to Contact: Query with SASE. Accepts queries by fax. Considers simultaneous queries. Responds in 10 days to queries. Returns materials only with SASE. Obtains most new clients through recommendations from others.
Recent Sales: This agency prefers not to share information on specific sales.
Terms: Agent receives 10% commission on domestic sales; 20% on foreign sales. Offers written contract, binding for 2 years.

☑ Ⓜ **KEN SHERMAN & ASSOCIATES,** 9507 Santa Monica Blvd. Beverly Hills CA 90210. (310)273-3840. Fax: (310)271-2875. **Contact:** Ken Sherman. Estab. 1989. Member of DGA, BAFTA, PEN Int'l, signatory of WGA. Represents approx. 50 clients. 10% of clients are new/previously unpublished writers. Currently handles: fiction; nonfiction books; juvenile books; movie scripts; TV scripts.
　　• Prior to opening his agency, Mr. Sherman was with the William Morris Agency, The Lantz Office, and Paul Kohner, Inc.
Represents: Nonfiction, fiction, movie scripts, TV scripts, film and television rights to books. **Considers all script subjects, nonfiction and fiction areas.**
　　O⟶ This agency specializes in solid writers for film, TV, books and rights to books for film and TV.
How to Contact: *Contact by referral only please.* Responds in approximately 1 month to mss.
Recent Sales: Sold over 25 projects in the last year. *Priscilla Salyers Story,* Andrea Baynes (ABC); *Toys of Glass,* by Martin Booth (ABC/Saban Ent.); *Brazil,* by John Updike (film rights to Glaucia Carmagos); *Fifth Sacred Thing,* by Starhawk (Bantam); *Questions From Dad,* by Dwight Twilly (Tuttle); *Snow Falling on Cedars,* by David Guterson (Universal Pictures); *The Witches of Eastwick—The Musical,* by John Updike (Cameron Macintosh, Ltd.).
Terms: Agent receives 15% commission on domestic book sales, 10% for WGA projects. Offers written contract only. Charges clients for office expenses, postage, photocopying, negotiable expenses.
Writers' Conferences: Maui; Squaw Valley; Santa Barbara; Sante Fe, Aspen Institute, Aspen Writers Foundation.

☑ Ⓒ **SILVER SCREEN PLACEMENTS,** 602 65th St., Downers Grove IL 60516-3020. (630)963-2124. Fax: (630)963-1998. E-mail: silverscreen@mediaone.net. **Contact:** William Levin. Estab. 1990. Signatory of WGA. Represents 11 clients. 100% of clients are new/previously unpublished writers. Currently handles: 10% juvenile books, 10% novels, 80% movie scripts.
　　• Prior to opening his agency, Mr. Levin did product placement for motion pictures/TV.
Represents: Movie scripts; feature film. **Considers these script subject areas:** action/adventure; comedy; contemporary issues; detective/police/crime; family saga; fantasy; historical; juvenile; mainstream; mystery/suspense; science fiction; thriller/espionage; young adult.
　　O⟶ Actively seeking "screenplays for young adults, 17-30." Does not want to receive "horror, religious, X-rated."
Also Handles: Juvenile books, novels. **Considers these nonfiction areas:** education; juvenile nonfiction; language/literature/criticism. **Consider these fiction areas:** action/adventure; contemporary issues; detective/police/crime; family saga; fantasy; historical; humor/satire; juvenile; mainstream; mystery/suspense; science fiction; thriller/espionage; young adult.

How to Contact: Brief query with outline/proposal and SASE. Responds in 2 weeks to queries; 2 months to mss. Obtains most new clients through recommendations from other parties, as well as being listed with WGA and *Guide to Literary Agents*.

Recent Sales: Sold 3 projects plus 2 options in the last year. Prefers not to share information on specific sales. Clients include Jean Hurley, Charles Geier, Robert Smola, August Tonne, Michael Jeffries and Yair Packer.

Terms: Agent receives 10% commission on screenplay/teleplay sales; 15% on foreign and printed media sales. Offers written contract, binding for 2 years. May make referrals to freelance editors. Use of editors does not ensure representation. 0% of business is derived from referrals to editing service.

Tips: "Advise against 'cutsie' inquiry letters."

✔ ⊘ **SISTER MANIA PRODUCTIONS, INC.**, 916 Penn St., Brackenridge PA 15014. (412)226-2964. E-mail: ceo@sistermania.com. Website: www.sistermania.com. **Contact:** Literary Department. Estab. 1978. Signatory of WGA. Represents 12 clients. 20% of clients are new/previously unpublished writers. Currently handles: 50% movie scripts and 50% mss for publication.

Represents: Feature film, TV scripts, syndicated material. **Considers these script subject areas:** action/adventure; comedy; detective/police/crime; experimental; family saga; horror; romance; thriller/espionage; true crime/investigative.

   O→ "We also package, develop and produce."

Also Handles: Nonfiction books, juvenile books, scholarly books, novels. **Considers these nonfiction areas:** biography/autobiography; business; computers/electronics; history; humor; juvenile nonfiction; military/war; money/finance/economics; music/dance/theater/film; New Age metaphysics; science/technology; self-help/personal improvement; women's issues/women's studies. **Considers these fiction areas:** action/adventure; contemporary issues; detective/police/crime; ethnic; family saga; fantasy; historical; horror; humor/satire; juvenile; literary; mainstream; mystery/suspense; picture book; romance (contemporary); science fiction; thriller/espionage.

How to Contact: Query. Accepts queries by e-mail. Considers simultaneous queries. Responds in up to 1 month to queries; 2 months to mss. Returns materials only with SASE. Obtains most new clients through "very creative query with project creative and executive appeal in maintaining integrity through quality products."

Recent Sales: Sold 1 ms in the last year. *Movie/TV MOW scripts optioned/sold:* The Pope, by Sam Walker and Darleen Pusey; *Happytime Manor*, by Gordon Webb; *Movie/TV MOW scripts in development:* Accidentally On Purpose and *Mind Fodder. Scripting assignments:* biography on Bonnie Consolo.

Terms: Offers written contract. Offers criticism service, no fees for clients.

⊘ **CAMILLE SORICE AGENCY**, 13412 Moorpark St., #C, Sherman Oaks CA 91423. (818)995-1775. **Contact:** Camille Sorice. Estab. 1988. Signatory of WGA.

Represents: Feature film. **Considers these script subject areas:** action/adventure; comedy; detective/police/crime; family saga; historical; mystery/suspense; romantic comedy and drama; westerns/frontier.

How to Contact: Send query letter with synopsis. Does not accept queries by e-mail or fax. Prefers to read materials exclusively. Responds in 6 weeks to mss. "I now also represent novels." Query with 1-page synopsis.

Recent Sales: This agency prefers not to share information on specific sales.

Tips: "No calls. Query letters accepted."

$ ⊘ **STANTON & ASSOCIATES LITERARY AGENCY**, 4413 Clemson Dr., Garland TX 75042-5246. (972)276-5427. Fax: (972)276-5426. E-mail: preston8@onramp.net. Website: www.grahamcomputers.com/stanton.html. **Contact:** Henry Stanton, Harry Preston. Estab. 1990. Signatory of WGA. Represents 36 clients. 90% of clients are new screenwriters. Currently handles: 50% movie scripts; 40% TV scripts; 10% books.

   ● Prior to joining the agency, Mr. Preston was with the MGM script department and an author and screenwriter for 40 years.

Represents: Feature film, TV MOW. **Considers these script subject areas:** action/adventure; comedy; romantic comedy; romantic drama; thriller.

   O→ This agency specializes in screenplays. Does not want to see science fiction, fantasy or horror.

How to Contact: Query with SASE. Accepts queries by fax or e-mail. Considers simultaneous queries. Responds in 1 week to queries; 1 month to screenplays (review). Returns materials only with SASE. Obtains most new clients through WGA listing, *Hollywood Scriptwriter*, word of mouth (in Dallas).

Recent Sales: Sold 2 script projects in the last year. *A Tale Worth Telling (The Life of Saint Patrick)*, (Angelic Entertainment); *Chipita* (uprize Productions); *Today I Will Nourish My Inner Martyr* (Prima Press); *Barbara Jordan, The Biography* (Golden Touch Press).

Terms: Agent receives 15% commission on domestic sales. Offers written contract, binding for 2 years on individual screenplays. Returns scripts with reader's comments.

Fees: "We have writers available to edit or ghostwrite screenplays and books. Fees vary dependent on the writer."

CONTACT THE EDITOR of *Guide to Literary Agents* by e-mail at literaryagents @fwpubs.com with your questions and comments.

Tips: "All writers should always please enclose a SASE with any queries."

✅ 🖉 **STARS, THE AGENCY,** (formerly ES Talent Agency), 777 Davis St., San Francisco CA 94111. (415)421-6272. Fax: (415)421-7620. **Contact:** Ed Silver. Estab. 1995. Represents 50-75 clients. 70% of clients are new/previously unpublished writers. Currently handles: 50% nonfiction books; 25% movie scripts; 25% novels.
- Prior to opening his agency, Mr. Silver was an entertainment business manager.
Member Agent: Ed Silver.
Represents: Feature film, TV MOW. Considers these script areas: action/adventure; comedy; contemporary issues; detective/police/crime; erotica; ethnic; experimental; family saga; mainstream; mystery/suspense; romantic comedy; romantic drama; sports; thriller.
   O➤ This agency specializes in theatrical screenplays, MOW and miniseries. Actively seeking "anything good and distinctive."
Also Handles: Nonfiction, fiction. **Considers general nonfiction areas. Considers these fiction areas:** action/adventure; contemporary issues; detective/police/crime; erotica; experimental; historical; humor/satire; literary; mainstream; mystery/suspense; thriller/espionage; young adult.
How to Contact: Query with SASE. Accepts queries by fax. Considers simultaneous queries and submissions. Responds in 1 month. Returns materials only with SASE. Obtains most new clients through recommendations and queries from WGA agency list.
Recent Sales: Sold 8 book titles in the last year. *Biology of Love*, by Art Janov (Prometheus); *Be the Star You Are*, by Cynthia Brian (Ten Speed); *How to Read*, by Maya Hieroglyphs and John Montgomery (Hippocrene); *My Journey to Wellness*, by Celeste Pepe (Hampton Roads).
Terms: Agent receives 10% commission on script sales; 15% on novels; 20% on foreign sales. Offers written contract with 30-day cancellation clause.

🆔 🖉 **STEIN AGENCY,** 5125 Oakdale Ave., Woodland Hills CA 91364. (818)594-8990. Fax: (818)594-8998. E-mail: mail@thesteinagency.com. **Contact:** Mitchel Stein. Estab. 2000. Signatory of WGA. Represents 30 clients. Currently handles: 20% movie scripts; 80% TV scripts.
Member Agents: Mitchel Stein (TV/motion picture); Jim Ford (TV/motion picture).
Represents: Episodic drama, movie scripts, TV scripts, sitcom. **Considers these script subject areas:** action/adventure; detective/police/crime; family saga; fantasy; mainstream; mystery/suspense; psychic/supernatural; romantic comedy; romantic drama; science fiction; teen; thriller/espionage.
How to Contact: Query with SASE. Accepts queries by e-mail and fax. Considers simultaneous queries. Responds in 1 week to queries. Returns materials only with SASE. Discards material without SASE. Obtains most new clients through recommendations from others.
Recent Sales: Sold 10 script projects in the last year. This agency prefers not to share information on specific sales.
Terms: Agent receives 10% commission on domestic sales; 10% on foreign sales. Offers written contract.

🖉 **STONE MANNERS AGENCY,** 8436 W. Third St., Suite 740, Los Angeles CA 90048. (323)655-1313. **Contact:** Tim Stone. Estab. 1982. Signatory of WGA. Represents 25 clients.
Represents: Movie scripts, TV scripts. **Considers all script subject areas.**
How to Contact: *Not considering scripts at this time.*
Recent Sales: This agency prefers not to share information on specific sales.
Terms: Agent receives 10% commission on domestic sales; 10% commission on foreign sales.

🖉 **SUITE A MANAGEMENT,** 1101 S. Robertson Blvd., Suite 210, Los Angeles CA 90035. (310)278-0801. Fax: (310)278-0807. E-mail: suite-A@juno.com. Website: www.suite-a-management.com. **Contact:** Lloyd D. Robinson. Estab. 1996. Represents 50 clients. 15% of clients are new/previously unpublished writers. Currently handles: 40% movie scripts; 20% novels; 10% animation; 15% TV scripts; 10% stage plays; 5% multimedia.
- Prior to becoming an agent, Mr. Robinson owned Lenhoff/Robinson Talent & Literary Agency, Inc. for over 5 years.
Represents: Feature film, theatrical stage play, TV MOW, animation. **Considers "all areas within the current mainstream for film and television."** Also handles Internet interactive segmented movies.
   O➤ This agency represents writers, producers and directors of Movies of the Week for Network and Cable, features with budgets under 10 milllion and pilots/series. Included among clients are a large percentage of novelists whose work is available for adaptation to screen and television. Actively seeking "writers with produced credits."
How to Contact: Fax one page bio (educational/credits), including title, WGA registration number, 2 sentence log line and 1 paragraph synopsis. Accepts queries by fax or e-mail. Consider simultaneous queries. Responds in 10 days to fax queries. Returns unwanted queries and mss. Obtains most new clients through recommendations from existing client base as well as new writers from various conferences.
Recent Sales: Sold 1 book title and 2 script projects in the last year. Books: *Nobody Drowns in Mincral Lake*, by Michael Druxman (Center Press); *Movie TV/MOW scripts optioned sold: Bridge of Dragons*, starring Dolph Lundgreen; *Cold Harvest*, starring Gary Daniels.

Terms: Agent receives 10% commission on domestic sales; 10% on foreign sales. Offers written contract, binding for 1 year. 3 month notice will be given to terminate contract. Charges for overnight mail, printing and duplication charges. All charges require "prior approval" by writer.
Writers' Conferences: Sherwood Oaks College (Hollywood); Infotainment Annual (Black Talent News) (Los Angeles, April); Writers Connection (Los Angeles, August).

◖ SYDRA TECHNIQUES CORP., 481 Eighth Ave. E 24, New York NY 10001. (212)631-0009. Fax: (212)631-0715. E-mail: sbuck@virtualnews.com. **Contact:** Sid Buck. Estab. 1988. Signatory of WGA. Represents 30 clients. 80% of clients are new/previously unpublished writers. Currently handles: 30% movie scripts; 10% novels; 30% TV scripts; 10% nonfiction books; 10% stage plays; 10% multimedia.
  • Prior to opening his agency, Mr. Buck was an artist's agent.
Represents: Feature film, TV MOW, sitcom, animation. **Considers these script subject areas:** action/adventure; biography/autobiography; cartoon/animation; comedy; contemporary issues; detective/police/crime; family saga; mainstream; mystery/suspense; science fiction; sports. "We are open."
How to Contact: Send outline/proposal with SASE. Responds in 1 month. Obtains most new clients through recommendations.
Recent Sales: This agency prefers not to share information on specific sales.
Terms: Agent receives 10% commission on domestic sales; 15% on foreign sales. Offers written contract, binding for 2 years. 120-day notice must be given to terminate contract.

⬛ ⬛ ◯ TAHOE SIERRAS AGENCY, P.O. Box 2179, Dayton NV 89403. (775)241-0881. Fax: (775)241-0413. E-mail: tahoesierras@aol.com. Website: www.cuebon.com/tahoesierras. **Contact:** Ed Oversen. Estab. 1999. 80% of clients are new/previously unpublished writers. Currently handles: 50% novels; 40% movie scripts; 10% TV scripts.
  • See the expanded listing for this agency in the Literary Agents: Fee-charging section.

◖ TALENT SOURCE, 107 E. Hall St., P.O. Box 14120, Savannah GA 31416-1120. (912)232-9390. Fax: (912)232-8213. E-mail: mshortt@ix.netcom.com. Website: www.talentsource.com. **Contact:** Michael L. Shortt. Estab. 1991. Signatory of WGA. 35% of clients are new/previously unpublished writers. Currently handles: 75% movie scripts; 25% TV scripts.
  • Prior to becoming an agent, Mr. Shortt was a television program producer.
Represents: Feature film, episodic drama, TV MOW, sitcom. **Considers these script areas:** comedy; contemporary issues; detective/police/crime; erotica; family saga; horror; juvenile; mainstream; mystery/ suspense; romance (comedy, drama); teen. Also handles CD-Roms, direct videos.
  ०┑ Actively seeking "character-driven stories (e.g., *Sling Blade, Sex Lies & Videotape*)." Does not want to receive "big budget special effects science fiction."
How to Contact: Send outline with character breakdown. Responds in 10 weeks to queries. Obtains most new clients through word of mouth.
Recent Sales: This agency prefers not to share information on specific sales.
Terms: Agent receives 10% commission on domestic sales; 15% on foreign sales. Offers written contract.

⬛ ◖ JEANNE TOOMEY ASSOCIATES, 95 Belden St., Falls Village CT 06031-1113. (860)824-0831/5460. Fax: (860)824-5460. President: Jeanne Toomey. Assistant: Peter Terranova. Estab. 1985. 50% of clients are new/previously unpublished writers. Currently handles: 45% nonfiction books; 20% novels; 35% movie scripts.
  • See the expanded listing for this agency in Literary Agents: Fee-charging.

⬛ ◖ ANNETTE VAN DUREN AGENCY, 11684 Ventura Blvd., #235, Studio City CA 91604. (818)752-6000. Fax: (818)752-6985. **Contact:** Annette Van Duren or Teena Portier. Estab. 1985. Signatory of WGA. Represents 12 clients. No clients are new/previously unpublished writers. Currently handles: 10% novels; 50% movie scripts; 40% TV scripts.
Represents: Feature film, animation, TV MOW, sitcom, drama.
Needs: *Not accepting new clients*. Obtains most new clients only through recommendations from "clients or other close business associates."
Recent Sales: This agency prefers not to share information on specific sales.
Terms: Agent receives 10% commission on domestic sales. Offers written contract, binding for 2 years.

☑ ◖ WARDLOW AND ASSOCIATES, 1501 Main St., Suite 204, Venice CA 90291. (310)452-1292. Fax: (310)452-9002. E-mail: wardlowaso@aol.com. **Contact:** Jeff Ordway. Estab. 1980. Signatory of WGA. Represents 30 clients. 5% of clients are new/previously unpublished writers. Currently handles: 50% movie scripts; 50% TV scripts.
Member Agents: David Wardlow (literary, packaging); Jeff Ordway (literary).
Represents: Feature film, TV MOW, miniseries, episodic drama, sitcom. **Considers all script subject areas**, particularly: action/adventure; comedy; contemporary issues; detective/police/crime; family saga; fantasy; gay; horror; mainstream; mystery/suspense; romance; science fiction; thriller; western/frontier.
  ०┑ Does not want to receive "new sitcom/drama series ideas from beginning writers."

How to Contact: Query with SASE. Accepts queries by fax or e-mail. Considers simultaneous queries. Replies only to queries which they are interested in unless accompanied by SASE. Will not read unsolicited screenplays/manuscripts. Returns unwanted materials only with SASE. Obtains most new clients through recommendations from others and solicitation.

Recent Sales: This agency prefers not to share information on specific sales.

Terms: Agent receives 10% commission on domestic sales; 10% on foreign sales. Offers written contract, binding for 1 year.

☑ ◐ DONNA WAUHOB AGENCY, 3135 Industrial Rd., #204, Las Vegas NV 89109-1122. (702)733-1017. Fax: (702)733-1215. E-mail: dwauhob@aol.com. **Contact:** Donna Wauhob. Represents 7 clients. Currently handles: 10 juvenile books; 60% movie scripts; 40% TV scripts.

• Prior to opening her agency, Ms. Wauhob was a model, secretary, and an AF of M agent since 1968.

Represents: Movie scripts, feature film, episodic drama, soap opera, TV scripts, TV movie of the week, sitcom, theatrical stage play, variety show, poetry books, short story collections, miniseries, animation. **Considers these script subject areas:** action/adventure; cartoon/animation; comedy; detective/police/crime; family saga; juvenile; romantic comedy; romantic drama; teen; thriller/espionage; western/frontier.

○┓ Actively seeking film and TV scripts, juvenile, teen action, cartoon, comedy, family.

Also Handles: Nonfiction books, juvenile books, novels. **Considers these nonfiction areas:** animals; child guidance/parenting; cooking/food/nutrition.

How to Contact: Accepts queries by mail and fax. Considers simultaneous queries and submissions. Responds in 2 months.

Recent Sales: This is a new agency with no recorded sales.

Terms: Agent receives 10% commission on domestic and foreign sales. Offers written contract. 6-month notice must be given to terminate contract.

☑ ◐ PEREGRINE WHITTLESEY AGENCY, 345 E. 80 St., New York NY 10021. (212)737-0153. Fax: (212)734-5176. E-mail: pwag4@aol.com. **Contact:** Peregrine Whittlesey. Estab. 1986. Signatory of WGA. Represents 30 clients. 50% of clients are new/previously unpublished writers. Currently handles: 20% movie scripts, 80% stage plays.

Represents: Feature film, stage plays.

○┓ This agency specializes in playwrights who also write for screen and TV.

How to Contact: Query with SASE. Accepts queries by e-mail. Prefers to read materials exclusively. Responds in 1 week to queries; 1 month to mss. Obtains most new clients through recommendations from others.

Recent Sales: Sold over 20 script objects in the last year. *The Stick Wife* and *0 Pioneers!*, by Darrah Cloud (Dramatic Publishing); *Alabama Rain*, by Heather McCutchen (Dramatic Publishing).

Terms: Agent receives 10% commission on domestic sales; 15% on foreign sales. Offers written contract, binding for 2 years.

⟨$⟩ ◉ WINDFALL MANAGEMENT, 4084 Mandeville Canyon Rd., Los Angeles CA 90049-1032. (310)471-6317. Fax: (310)471-4577. E-mail: windfall@deltanet.com. **Contact:** Jeanne Field. Represents 20 clients. Currently handles: 20% novels; 50% movie scripts; 25% TV scripts; 5% stage plays.

• Prior to becoming a manager, Ms. Field was a producer in the film and television business.

Represents: Movie scripts, TV scripts, TV MOW, theatrical stage plays, documentary, miniseries, books to the film industry. **Considers these script subject areas:** action/adventure; biography/autobiography; comedy; contemporary issues; detective/police/crime; experimental; family saga; fantasy; feminist; gay/lesbian; historical; juvenile; mainstream; multimedia; mystery/suspense; romantic comedy; romantic drama; science fiction; sports; teen; thriller/espionage; western/frontier.

○┓ Windfall is a management company representing writers and books to the film and television industry. "We are especially interested in mainstream and independent film writers or playwrights." Actively seeking "well-written material that can be attractive to the entertainment industry."

How to Contact: Query with SASE. Accepts queries by e-mail. Considers simultaneous queries. Responds in 2 weeks to queries. Discards unwanted queries and mss. Obtains most new clients through recommendations and referrals.

Recent Sales: Sold 5 book titles and 10 script projects in the last year. *The Animal Factory*, by Edward Bunker (No Exit Press); *Cold Caller*, by Jason Starr (Norton); *Nothing Personal*, by Jason Starr (No Exit Press); *Little Boy Blue*, by Edward Bunker (St. Martin's Press). **Movie/TV MOW scripts optioned:** *The Devil In Me*, by Beaty Reynolds (Daly-Harris Productions); *Just Another Dead Man*, by John Binder (Pressman Co.). Other clients include Joshua Binder, Randall Sullivan, Leon Martell, Stephanie Waxman, Nell Cox, Dani Minnick, Benjie Aeronson, Jon Klein, Charles Oyamo Gordon.

Terms: Agent receives 10% commission on domestic sales. Offers written contract, binding for 1 year. 60-day notice must be given to terminate contract.

Fees: Charges a maximum of $150/year on copying, postage, for new clients who are unproved only.

Tips: "Live in either New York of Los Angeles. A writer must be available for meetings."

☑ ◩ **THE WRIGHT CONCEPT**, 1612 W. Olive Ave., Suite 205, Burbank CA 91506. (818)954-8943. Fax: (818)954-9370. E-mail: mrwright@www.wrightconcept.com. Website: www.wrightconcept.com. **Contact:** Marcie Wright, Janette Reid, Steven Dowd. Estab. 1985. Signatory of WGA, DGA. Currently handles: 50% movie scripts; 50% TV scripts.
Member Agents: Marcie Wright (TV/movie).
Represents: Feature film, TV MOW, episodic drama, sitcom, variety show, animation, syndicated material. **Considers these script subject areas:** action/adventure, teen; thriller. Also handles CD-Rom games.
   O➡ This agency specializes in TV comedy writers and feature comedy writers.
How to Contact: Query with SASE. Responds in 2 weeks. Obtains most new clients through recommendations and queries.
Recent Sales: *Movie/TV MOW script(s) optioned/sold:* Mickey Blue Eyes (Castlerock); *The Pentagon Wars* (HBO); *Shot Through the Heart* (HBO); *Who Wants To Be A Millionaire* (ABC); *Kiss Me Guido* (CBS); *Los Beltrans* (Telemundo).
Terms: Agent receives 10% commission on sales. Offers written contract, binding for 1 year, with 90-day cancellation clause.
Writers' Conferences: Speaks at UCLA 3-4 times a year; Southwest Writers Workshop (Albuquerque, August); *Fade-In Magazine* Oscar Conference (Los Angeles, May); *Fade-In Magazine* Top 100 People in Hollywood (Los Angeles, August); University of Georgia's Harriett Austin Writers Conference; Houston Film Festival.

◩ **ANN WRIGHT REPRESENTATIVES**, 165 W. 46th St., Suite 1105, New York NY 10036-2501. (212)764-6770. Fax: (212)764-5125. **Contact:** Dan Wright. Estab. 1961. Signatory of WGA. Represents 23 clients. 30% of clients are new/previously unpublished writers. Currently handles: 50% novels; 40% movie scripts; 10% TV scripts.
   ● Prior to becoming an agent, Mr. Wright was a writer, producer and production manager for film and television (alumni of CBS Television).
Represents: Feature film, TV MOW, episodic drama, sitcom. **Considers these script subject areas:** action/adventure; comedy; detective/police/crime; gay; historical; horror; lesbian; mainstream; mystery/suspense; psychic/supernatural; romantic comedy and drama; sports; thriller; westerns/frontier.
   O➡ This agency specializes in "books or screenplays with strong motion picture potential." Prefers to work with published/established authors; works with a small number of new/previously unpublished authors. "Eager to work with any author with material that we can effectively market in the motion picture business worldwide." Actively seeking "strong competitive novelists and screen writers." Does not want to receive "fantasy or science fiction projects at this time."
Also Handles: Novels. **Considers these fiction areas:** action/adventure; detective/police/crime; feminist; gay/lesbian; humor/satire; literary; mainstream; mystery/suspense; romance (contemporary, historical, regency); sports; thriller/espionage; westerns/frontier.
How to Contact: Query with outline and SASE. Does not read unsolicited mss. Responds in 3 weeks to queries; 4 months to mss. "All work must be sent with a SASE to ensure its return."
Recent Sales: Sold 7 projects in the last year. Prefers not to share information on specific sales.
Terms: Agent receives 10% commission on domestic sales; 10% on dramatic sales; 15-20% on foreign sales; 20% on packaging. Offers written contract, binding for 2 years. Critiques only works of signed clients. Charges clients for photocopying expenses.
Tips: "Send a letter with SASE. Something about the work, something about the writer."

Ⓝ ◩ **WRITER STORE**, 2004 Rockledge Rd., Atlanta GA 30324 (404)874-6260. Fax: (404)874-6330. E-mail: writerstore@mindspring.com. **Contact:** Rebecca Shrager or Brenda Eanes. Signatory of WGA. Represents 16 clients. 80% of clients are new/previously unpublished writers. Currently handles: 10% novels, 90% movie scripts.
Member Agents: Rebecca Shrager; Brenda Eanes.
Represents: Movie scripts, TV scripts, feature film, TV movie of the week, animation, miniseries. **Considers these script subject areas:** action/adventure; biography/autobiography; cartoon/animation; comedy; contemporary issues; detective/police/crime; ethnic; family saga; fantasy; glitz; historical; mainstream; multicultural; mystery/suspense; psychic/supernatural; regional; romantic comedy; romantic drama; science fiction; sports; teen; thriller.
   O➡ This agency makes frequent trips to Los Angeles to meet with producers and development directors. "We make it a priority to know what the buyers are looking for. People Store, the sister company of Writer Store, has been in business since 1983 and is one of the oldest, largest, and most well respected SAG talent agencies in the southeast. Writer Store reaps the benefits of a wide variety of contacts in the industry developed over a number of years by People Store." Actively seeking action-adventure, urban (dramas and comedies), thrillers, GOOD comedies of all types, GOOD science fiction, Native American, MOWs, sports, music related, based on a true story pieces, big budget. Does not want to receive disgusting horror, toilet humor, short stories (unless it's an anthology), children's books.

VISIT WWW.WRITERSMARKET.COM to obtain a searchable database of agents and publishers, and to receive updates on your specific interests on your computer.

Also Handles: Novels. **Considers these fiction areas:** action/adventure; cartoon/comic; contemporary issues; detective/police/crime; ethnic; family saga; fantasy; glitz; historical; humor/satire; literary; mainstream; multicultural; mystery/suspense; New Age/metaphysical; psychic/supernatural; regional; romance; science fiction; sports; thriller/espionage; young adult.

How to Contact: Query with synopsis and SASE. Accepts queries by snail mail, e-mail and fax. Considers simultaneous queries. Responds in a few days to queries; 2 months to mss. Returns materials only with SASE. Obtains most new clients through queries/solicitations.

Recent Sales: This agency prefers not to share information on specific sales.

Terms: Agent receives 10-15% commission on domestic sales; 15-20% on foreign sales. Offers written contract, binding generally for 2 years.

Writers' Conferences: Words Into Pictures (Los Angeles, June).

Tips: "Do not send unsolicited manuscripts. They will not be read. Send brief, concise query letter and synopses. No pictures please. Be sure you understand the craft of screenwriting and are using the proper format.

☑ ◐ **WRITERS & ARTISTS AGENCY**, 19 W. 44th St., Suite 1000, New York NY 10036. (212)391-1112. Fax: (212)575-6397. **Contact:** William Craver, Nicole Graham, Jeff Berger, Michael Smith, Joan Scott. Estab. 1970. Member of AAR, signatory of WGA. Represents 100 clients. West Coast location: 8383 Wilshire Blvd., Suite 550, Beverly Hills CA 90211. (323)866-0900. Fax: (323)659-1985.

Represents: Movie scripts, feature film, TV scripts, TV MOW, miniseries, episodic drama, stage plays. **Considers all script subject areas.**

How to Contact: Query with brief description of project, bio and SASE. Responds in 1 month to queries only when accompanied by SASE. No unsolicited mss accepted. Professional recommendation preferred.

Recent Sales: This agency prefers not to share specific information on specific sales.

Additional Script Agents

The following agencies have indicated they are *primarily* interested in handling book manuscripts but also handle less than 10 to 15 percent scripts. After reading the listing (you can find the page number in the Listings Index), send a query to obtain more information on their needs and manuscript submissions policies.

Alp Arts Co.
AMG/Renaissance
Appleseeds Management
Author's Agency, The
Browne Ltd., Pema
Flannery Literary
Fleury Agency, B.R.
Fort Ross Inc. Russian-American Publishing Projects
Frenkel & Associates, James

Gusay Literary Agency, The Charlotte
Lazear Agency Incorporated
Literary and Creative Artists, Inc.
Menza Literary Agency, Claudia
Morrison, Inc., Henry
Multimedia Product Development, Inc.
National Writers Literary Agency
Norma-Lewis Agency, The

Raintree Literary Agency, Diane
Rose & Associates Literary Agency
Schiavone Literary Agency, Inc.
Sedgeband Literary Associates
Serendipity Literary Agency, LLC
Strong Literary Agency, Marianne
Toad Hall, Inc.
Watt & Associates, Sandra
Wolcott Literary Agency

Canadian/International Script Agents

For the first time, we've included the following section of Canadian/International script agents. These are agents who sell and option movies not only in the U.S. but also in their own and other foreign countries. Several of the agents listed here already have clients who live in the U.S. For many writers, having an agent in another country can be a wonderful opportunity, especially if the material you write appeals to a different sensibility than that held by most U.S. readers. Or, perhaps you even live outside the U.S. In that case, you may want to work with an agent in this section who is closer to home.

In a sense, working with a Canadian or International agent is similar to having an agent outside of Los Angeles. They may not be able to meet with producers every day, but when they do go to Los Angeles, or even London, producers give them priority over local agents. And, of course, with e-mail, the Internet, and fax machines, communicating in the global community is just as easy as meeting your colleague next door for lunch.

Keep in mind, however, that there are a few downsides to working with a Canadian or International agent. For starters, the majority of the agent's contacts will be in his own country, and he may not be as well known by U.S. producers as those abroad. While this fact can be good in terms of reaching foreign markets, it may mean your script will not be sold in the U.S. market. Meeting your agent may prove more difficult than if he lived in the U.S. And even though new technology makes communication easier, if you need to talk with your London agent, you'll have to pay close attention to the difference in time zones to avoid calling him in the middle of the night.

Similar to listings in the Script Agents section, this section includes both nonfee-and fee-charging Canadian and International script agents. Be sure you have a firm understanding of any reading or critique fee before you pay anyone. Some agents in this section may charge office fees to their clients. Researching the agents in this section is just as important as researching any agent: you want to target your submission to ensure you reach a receptive agent, and you want to know the agent is well respected in the entertainment industry and actively making sales.

When you send a Canadian or International agent a query, be sure to include an International Reply Coupon (IRC) with your self-addressed envelope. Regular U.S. postage is not valid in any country outside the U.S., and an agent outside the U.S. is unlikely to respond to your query without an IRC. Contact your local post office for more information about IRCs.

For a more detailed explanation of the information in the following listings, see the introduction to Script Agents on page 267 and "Quick Start Guide to Using Your *Guide to Literary Agents*" at the front of the book.

N ⊕ $ ⊘ FRENCH'S, 9 Elgin Mews South, London W91JZ England. **Contact:** Mark Taylor. Represents 40 clients. 15% of clients are new/previously unpublished writers. Currently handles: 20% nonfiction books; 50% novels; 20% movie scripts; 20% TV scripts.
 • See the expanded listing for this agency in Literary Agents: Fee-charging.

⬟ ⊘ CHARLENE KAY AGENCY, 901 Beaudry St., Suite 6, St. Jean/Richelieu, Quebec J3A 1C6 Canada. (450)348-5296. **Contact:** Louise Meyers, director of development. Estab. 1992. Signatory of WGA; member of BMI. 100% of clients are new/previously unpublished writers. Currently handles: 25% TV scripts; 25% TV spec scripts; 50% movie scripts.
 • Prior to opening her agency, Ms. Kay was a screenwriter.

Represents: Feature film, animation, TV MOW, episodic drama, sitcom, and spec scripts for existing TV series. **Considers these script subject areas:** action/adventure; biography/autobiography; family saga; fantasy; psychic/supernatural; romantic comedy; romantic drama; science fiction.

O—⚓ This agency specializes in teleplays and screenplays. "We seek stories that are out of the ordinary, something we don't see too often. A *well-written* and *well-constructed* script is important." Does not want to receive "thrillers or barbaric and erotic films, novels, books or manuscripts."

How to Contact: Query with outline/proposal by mail only. Include SASE (or SAE with IRC outside Canada). "No reply without SASE." Responds in 1 month to queries; 10 weeks to mss. Returns materials only with SASE with IRC.

Recent Sales: This agency prefers not to share information on specific sales.

Terms: Agent receives 10% commission on domestic sales; 10% on foreign sales. Offers written contract, binding for 1 year.

Tips: "This agency is listed on the WGA lists and query letters arrive by the dozens every week. As our present clients understand, success comes with patience. A sale rarely happens overnight, especially when you are dealing with totally unknown writers. We are not impressed by the credentials of a writer, amateur or professional or by his or her pitching techniques, but by his or her story ideas and ability to build a well-crafted script."

[N] ❧ ◎ LIVINGSTON COOKE/CURTIS BROWN CANADA, 457A Danforth Ave., Suite 201, Toronto, Ontario M4K 1P1 Canada. (416)406-3390. Fax: (416)406-3389. E-mail: livcooke@idirect.ca. **Contact:** Suzanne Brandereth. Estab. 1992. Represents 200 clients. 30% of clients are new/previously unpublished writers. Currently handles: 50% nonfiction books; 30% novels; 10% movie scripts; 10% TV scripts.

• See the expanded listing for this agency in Literary Agents: Nonfee-charging.

ALWAYS INCLUDE an International Reply Coupon (IRC) for reply or return of your material when sending query letters to non-U.S. countries.

Agents Specialties Index: Script

This subject index is divided into script subject categories. Also included are all **Canadian/International** script agencies. To find an agent interested in the type of screenplay you've written, see the appropriate sections under subject headings that best describe your work. Check the Listings Index for the page number of the agent's listing or refer to the section of Script Agents preceding this index. Agents who are open to most script subject areas appear under the "Open to all Script Categories" heading.

Action/Adventure: AEI/Atchity Editorial/Entertainment International; Agency West Entertainment; AMG/Renaissance Literary Agency; Baskow Agency; Brown Ltd., Curtis; Bulger and Associates, Kelvin C.; Cameron Agency, The Marshall; Cedar Grove Agency Entertainment; Client First—A/K/A Leo P. Haffey Agency; Communications Management Associates; CS International Literary Agency; Douroux & Co.; Epstein-Wyckoff and Associates; Esq. Management; Feigen/Parrent Literary Management; Film Artists Associates; Filmwriters Literary Agency; First Look Talent and Literary Agency; FitzGerald Literary Management; Fleury Agency, B.R.; Fran Literary Agency; Freed Co., The Barry; French's; Geddes Agency; Greene, Arthur B.; H.W.A. Talent Representative; Hodges Agency, Carolyn; Hudson Agency; International Leonards Corp.; Jaret Entertainment; Johnson Warren Literary Agency; Kay Agency, Charlene; Ketay Agency, The Joyce; Kick Entertainment; Kohner, Inc., Paul; Kritzer Productions, Eddie; Larchmont Literary Agency; Levine Literary Agency, Paul S.; Luedtke Agency, The; Miller Co., The Stuart M.; Momentum Marketing; Monteiro Rose Agency; Mura Enterprises, Inc., Dee; Niad Management; Omniquest Entertainment; Palmer, Dorothy; Panda Talent; Partos Company, The; Perelman Agency, Barry; Pinkham Literary Agency; PMA Literary and Film Management, Inc.; Redler Entertainment, Dan; Robinson Talent and Literary Management; Scagnetti Talent & Literary Agency, Jack; Shapiro-Lichtman; Silver Screen Placements; Sister Mania Productions, Inc.; Sorice Agency, Camille; Stanton & Associates Literary Agency; Stars, the Agency; Stein Agency; Sydra Techniques Corp.; Wardlow and Associates; Wauhob Agency, Donna; Windfall Management; Wright Concept, The; Wright Representatives, Ann; Writer Store

Biography/Autobiography: Agency West Entertainment; Baskow Agency; Cedar Grove Agency Entertainment; Communications Management Associates; Esq. Management; Film Artists Associates; FitzGerald Literary Management; French's; H.W.A. Talent Representative; Hart Literary Management; Hayes & Assoc., Gil; Jaret Entertainment; Kay Agency, Charlene; Kritzer Productions, Eddie; Larchmont Literary Agency; Levine Literary Agency, Paul S.; Luedtke Agency, The; Miller Co., The Stuart M.; Momentum Marketing; Niad Management; Omniquest Entertainment; Perelman Agency, Barry; Redler Entertainment, Dan; Sydra Techniques Corp.; Windfall Management; Writer Store

Cartoon/Animation: Agency West Entertainment; AMG/Renaissance Literary Agency; Bulger and Associates, Kelvin C.; Client First—A/K/A Leo P. Haffey Agency; Communications Management Associates; CS International Literary Agency; Esq. Management; First Look Talent and Literary Agency; Fran Literary Agency; H.W.A. Talent Representative; Hudson Agency; International Leonards Corp.; Jaret Entertainment; Kritzer Productions, Eddie; Larchmont Literary Agency; Levine Literary Agency, Paul S.; Luedtke Agency, The; Miller Co., The Stuart M.; Momentum Marketing; Monteiro Rose Agency; Mura Enterprises, Inc., Dee; Robinson Talent and Literary Management; Shapiro-Lichtman; Sydra Techniques Corp.; Wauhob Agency, Donna; Writer Store

Comedy: Abrams Artists Agency; AEI/Atchity Editorial/Entertainment International; Agency West Entertainment; Renaissance Literary Agency; Amsterdam Agency, Marcia; Baskow Agency; BAWN Publishers Inc.—Literary Agency; Bennett Agency, The; Brown Ltd., Curtis; Bulger and Associates, Kelvin C.; Cameron Agency, The Marshall; Cedar Grove Agency Entertainment; Client First—A/K/A Leo P. Haffey Agency; Communications Management Associates; International Literary Agency; Douroux & Co.; Epstein-Wyckoff and Associates; Esq. Management; Feigen/Parrent Literary Management; Film Artists Associates; Filmwriters Literary Agency; First Look Talent and Literary Agency; FitzGerald Literary Management; Fleury Agency, B.R.; Fran Literary Agency; Freed, Inc., Samuel; Geddes Agency; Gurman Agency, The Susan; H.W.A. Talent Representative; Hayes & Assoc., Gil; Hodges Agency, Carolyn; Hudson Agency; International Leonards Corp.; Jaret Entertainment; Ketay Agency, The Joyce; Kick Entertainment; Kohner, Inc., Paul; Larchmont Literary Agency; Legacies; Levine Literary Agency, Paul S.; Luedtke Agency, The; Miller Co., The Stuart M.; Momentum Marketing; Monteiro Rose Agency;

Mura Enterprises, Inc., Dee; Niad Management; Omniquest Entertainment; Palmer, Dorothy; Panda Talent; Partos Company, The; Pevner, Inc., Stephen; Pinkham Literary Agency; PMA Literary and Film Management, Inc.; Redler Entertainment, Dan; Redwood Empire Agency; Robinson Talent and Literary Management; Scagnetti Talent & Literary Agency, Jack; Shapiro-Lichtman; Silver Screen Placements; Sister Mania Productions, Inc.; Sorice Agency, Camille; Stanton & Associates Literary Agency; Stars, the Agency; Sydra Techniques Corp.; Talent Source; Wardlow and Associates; Wauhob Agency, Donna; Windfall Management; Wright Representatives, Ann; Writer Store

Contemporary Issues: Abrams Artists Agency; AEI/Atchity Editorial/Entertainment International; AMG/Renaissance Literary Agency; Baskow Agency; Client First—A/K/A Leo P. Haffey Agency; Communications Management Associates; CS International Literary Agency; Epstein-Wyckoff and Associates; Esq. Management; Feigen/Parrent Literary Management; Filmwriters Literary Agency; First Look Talent and Literary Agency; FitzGerald Literary Management; Fran Literary Agency; Freed Co., The Barry; French, Inc., Samuel; French's; Geddes Agency; H.W.A. Talent Representative; Hodges Agency, Carolyn; Hudson Agency; International Leonards Corp.; Johnson Warren Literary Agency; Kritzer Productions, Eddie; Larchmont Literary Agency; Legacies; Levine Literary Agency, Paul S.; Luedtke Agency, The; Miller Co., The Stuart M.; Momentum Marketing; Monteiro Rose Agency; Mura Enterprises, Inc., Dee; Niad Management; Omniquest Entertainment; Palmer, Dorothy; Perelman Agency, Barry; PMA Literary and Film Management, Inc.; Redler Entertainment, Dan; Redwood Empire Agency; Robinson Talent and Literary Management; Scagnetti Talent & Literary Agency, Jack; Shapiro-Lichtman; Silver Screen Placements; Stars, the Agency; Sydra Techniques Corp.; Talent Source; Wardlow and Associates; Windfall Management; Writer Store

Detective/Police/Crime: AEI/Atchity Editorial/Entertainment International; AMG/Renaissance Literary Agency; BAWN Publishers Inc.—Literary Agency; Brown Ltd., Curtis; Cameron Agency, The Marshall; Cedar Grove Agency Entertainment; Client First—A/K/A Leo P. Haffey Agency; Communications Management Associates; CS International Literary Agency; Douroux & Co.; Epstein-Wyckoff and Associates; Esq. Management; Filmwriters Literary Agency; FitzGerald Literary Management; Fleury Agency, B.R.; Fran Literary Agency; Freed Co., The Barry; French, Inc., Samuel; French's; Geddes Agency; Greene, Arthur B.; Gurman Agency, The Susan; H.W.A. Talent Representative; Hudson Agency; International Leonards Corp.; Johnson Warren Literary Agency; Ketay Agency, The Joyce; Kick Entertainment; Kohner, Inc., Paul; Kritzer Productions, Eddie; Larchmont Literary Agency; Levine Literary Agency, Paul S.; Luedtke Agency, The; Major Clients Agency; Miller Co., The Stuart M.; Momentum Marketing; Monteiro Rose Agency; Mura Enterprises, Inc., Dee; Niad Management; Omniquest Entertainment; Palmer, Dorothy; Panda Talent; Partos Company, The; Perelman Agency, Barry; Pevner, Inc., Stephen; Pinkham Literary Agency; PMA Literary and Film Management, Inc.; Redler Entertainment, Dan; Robinson Talent and Literary Management; Scagnetti Talent & Literary Agency, Jack; Shapiro-Lichtman; Silver Screen Placements; Sister Mania Productions, Inc.; Sorice Agency, Camille; Stars, the Agency; Stein Agency; Sydra Techniques Corp.; Talent Source; Wardlow and Associates; Wauhob Agency, Donna; Windfall Management; Wright Representatives, Ann; Writer Store

Erotica: AEI/Atchity Editorial/Entertainment International; AMG/Renaissance Literary Agency; BAWN Publishers Inc.—Literary Agency; Communications Management Associates; Epstein-Wyckoff and Associates; Esq. Management; FitzGerald Literary Management; French's; Levine Literary Agency, Paul S.; Major Clients Agency; Redwood Empire Agency; Robinson Talent and Literary Management; Stars, the Agency; Talent Source

Ethnic: Agency West Entertainment; AMG/Renaissance Literary Agency; BAWN Publishers Inc.—Literary Agency; Brown Ltd., Curtis; Bulger and Associates, Kelvin C.; Camejo & Assoc., Suzanna; CS International Literary Agency; Esq. Management; FitzGerald Literary Management; Fran Literary Agency; Freed Co., The Barry; French, Inc., Samuel; Geddes Agency; H.W.A. Talent Representative; Ketay Agency, The Joyce; Levine Literary Agency, Paul S.; Luedtke Agency, The; Momentum Marketing; Monteiro Rose Agency; Niad Management; Panda Talent; Partos Company, The; Redler Entertainment, Dan; Robinson Talent and Literary Management; Shapiro-Lichtman; Stars, the Agency; Writer Store

Experimental: AMG/Renaissance Literary Agency; French, Inc., Samuel; Geddes Agency; Ketay Agency, The Joyce; Levine Literary Agency, Paul S.; Momentum Marketing; Omniquest Entertainment; Partos Company, The; Robinson Talent and Literary Management; Sister Mania Productions, Inc.; Stars, the Agency; Windfall Management

Family Saga: Agency West Entertainment; AMG/Renaissance Literary Agency; Baskow Agency; BAWN Publishers Inc.—Literary Agency; Bennett Agency, The; Bulger and Associates, Kelvin C.; Camejo & Assoc., Suzanna; Cedar Grove Agency Entertainment; Client First—A/K/A Leo P. Haffey Agency; CS International Literary Agency; Douroux & Co.; Epstein-Wyckoff and Associates; Feigen/Parrent Literary

Management; First Look Talent and Literary Agency; FitzGerald Literary Management; Fleury Agency, B.R.; Fran Literary Agency; Freed Co., The Barry; French's; Geddes Agency; Gurman Agency, The Susan; H.W.A. Talent Representative; Hart Literary Management; Hayes & Assoc., Gil; Hudson Agency; Kay Agency, Charlene; Ketay Agency, The Joyce; Kohner, Inc., Paul; Kritzer Productions, Eddie; Legacies; Levine Literary Agency, Paul S.; Luedtke Agency, The; Major Clients Agency; Miller Co., The Stuart M.; Momentum Marketing; Monteiro Rose Agency; Mura Enterprises, Inc., Dee; Niad Management; Omniquest Entertainment; Palmer, Dorothy; Panda Talent; Partos Company, The; PMA Literary and Film Management, Inc.; Redler Entertainment, Dan; Redwood Empire Agency; Robinson Talent and Literary Management; Scagnetti Talent & Literary Agency, Jack; Shapiro-Lichtman; Silver Screen Placements; Sister Mania Productions, Inc.; Sorice Agency, Camille; Stars, the Agency; Stein Agency; Sydra Techniques Corp.; Talent Source; Wardlow and Associates; Wauhob Agency, Donna; Windfall Management; Writer Store

Fantasy: Agency West Entertainment; AMG/Renaissance Literary Agency; BAWN Publishers Inc.—Literary Agency; Communications Management Associates; CS International Literary Agency; Douroux & Co.; Esq. Management; First Look Talent and Literary Agency; FitzGerald Literary Management; Fran Literary Agency; French, Inc., Samuel; French's; Geddes Agency; H.W.A. Talent Representative; Hudson Agency; Kay Agency, Charlene; Ketay Agency, The Joyce; Kick Entertainment; Kritzer Productions, Eddie; Larchmont Literary Agency; Levine Literary Agency, Paul S.; Luedtke Agency, The; Momentum Marketing; Mura Enterprises, Inc., Dee; Omniquest Entertainment; Partos Company, The; Redler Entertainment, Dan; Robinson Talent and Literary Management; Silver Screen Placements; Stein Agency; Wardlow and Associates; Windfall Management; Writer Store

Feminist: AMG/Renaissance Literary Agency; Brown Ltd., Curtis; Camejo & Assoc., Suzanna; CS International Literary Agency; Epstein-Wyckoff and Associates; Esq. Management; Feigen/Parent Literary Management; H.W.A. Talent Representative; Ketay Agency, The Joyce; Legacies; Levine Literary Agency, Paul S.; Luedtke Agency, The; Momentum Marketing; Mura Enterprises, Inc., Dee; Palmer, Dorothy; Partos Company, The; Redler Entertainment, Dan; Redwood Empire Agency; Windfall Management

Gay/Lesbian: AMG/Renaissance Literary Agency; Brown Ltd., Curtis; Epstein-Wyckoff and Associates; Esq. Management; H.W.A. Talent Representative; Ketay Agency, The Joyce; Levine Literary Agency, Paul S.; Luedtke Agency, The; Momentum Marketing; Mura Enterprises, Inc., Dee; Partos Company, The; Pevner, Inc., Stephen; Redwood Empire Agency; Wardlow and Associates; Windfall Management; Wright Representatives, Ann

Glitz: Baskow Agency; Ketay Agency, The Joyce; Levine Literary Agency, Paul S.; Mura Enterprises, Inc., Dee; Pevner, Inc., Stephen; Writer Store

Historical: AMG/Renaissance Literary Agency; Brown Ltd., Curtis; Camejo & Assoc., Suzanna; Client First—A/K/A Leo P. Haffey Agency; Communications Management Associates; CS International Literary Agency; Douroux & Co.; Epstein-Wyckoff and Associates; Esq. Management; Film Artists Associates; Filmwriters Literary Agency; First Look Talent and Literary Agency; FitzGerald Literary Management; Fleury Agency, B.R.; Fran Literary Agency; Ketay Agency, The Joyce; Kohner, Inc., Paul; Larchmont Literary Agency; Legacies; Levine Literary Agency, Paul S.; Luedtke Agency, The; Miller Co., The Stuart M.; Momentum Marketing; Monteiro Rose Agency; Mura Enterprises, Inc., Dee; Niad Management; Omniquest Entertainment; Perelman Agency, Barry; Pinkham Literary Agency; PMA Literary and Film Management, Inc.; Redler Entertainment, Dan; Scagnetti Talent & Literary Agency, Jack; Shapiro-Lichtman; Silver Screen Placements; Sorice Agency, Camille; Windfall Management; Wright Representatives, Ann; Writer Store

Horror: AEI/Atchity Editorial/Entertainment International; AMG/Renaissance Literary Agency; BAWN Publishers Inc.—Literary Agency; Brown Ltd., Curtis; Communications Management Associates; Esq. Management; Film Artists Associates; First Look Talent and Literary Agency; FitzGerald Literary Management; Fleury Agency, B.R.; Fran Literary Agency; Freed Co., The Barry; French, Inc., Samuel; French's; Geddes Agency; Greene, Arthur B.; Gurman Agency, The Susan; H.W.A. Talent Representative; Hart Literary Management; Hodges Agency, Carolyn; International Leonards Corp.; Kick Entertainment; Kritzer Productions, Eddie; Larchmont Literary Agency; Levine Literary Agency, Paul S.; Luedtke Agency, The; Major Clients Agency; Momentum Marketing; Mura Enterprises, Inc., Dee; Niad Management; Partos Company, The; Perelman Agency, Barry; Pevner, Inc., Stephen; Redler Entertainment, Dan; Scagnetti Talent & Literary Agency, Jack; Shapiro-Lichtman; Sister Mania Productions, Inc.; Talent Source; Wardlow and Associates; Wright Representatives, Ann

Juvenile: Agency West Entertainment; AMG/Renaissance Literary Agency; Cedar Grove Agency Entertainment; Communications Management Associates; CS International Literary Agency; Epstein-Wyckoff and Associates; Esq. Management; First Look Talent and Literary Agency; FitzGerald Literary Management; Fran Literary Agency; Hart Literary Management; Hudson Agency; Ketay Agency, The Joyce; Levine Literary Agency, Paul S.; Luedtke Agency, The; Momentum Marketing; Monteiro Rose Agency; Mura Enterprises, Inc., Dee; Partos Company, The; Redler Entertainment, Dan; Silver Screen Placements; Talent Source; Wauhob Agency, Donna; Windfall Management

Mainstream: Abrams Artists Agency; AEI/Atchity Editorial/Entertainment International; Agency West Entertainment; AMG/Renaissance Literary Agency; Amsterdam Agency, Marcia; Bennett Agency, The; Brown Ltd., Curtis; Cameron Agency, The Marshall; Communications Management Associates; CS International Literary Agency; Douroux & Co.; Epstein-Wyckoff and Associates; Film Artists Associates; First Look Talent and Literary Agency; FitzGerald Literary Management; Fran Literary Agency; Freed Co., The Barry; French's; Geddes Agency; Gurman Agency, The Susan; Hart Literary Management; Hayes & Assoc., Gil; Hodges Agency, Carolyn; Johnson Warren Literary Agency; Ketay Agency, The Joyce; Kick Entertainment; Kohner, Inc., Paul; Larchmont Literary Agency; Levine Literary Agency, Paul S.; Luedtke Agency, The; Major Clients Agency; Miller Co., The Stuart M.; Momentum Marketing; Monteiro Rose Agency; Mura Enterprises, Inc., Dee; Niad Management; Omniquest Entertainment; Palmer, Dorothy; Partos Company, The; Pevner, Inc., Stephen; PMA Literary and Film Management, Inc.; Redler Entertainment, Dan; Redwood Empire Agency; Robinson Talent and Literary Management; Scagnetti Talent & Literary Agency, Jack; Shapiro-Lichtman; Silver Screen Placements; Stars, the Agency; Stein Agency; Sydra Techniques Corp.; Talent Source; Wardlow and Associates; Windfall Management; Wright Representatives, Ann; Writer Store

Multicultural: Abrams Artists Agency; AEI/Atchity Editorial/Entertainment International; Agency West Entertainment; AMG/Renaissance Literary Agency; Amsterdam Agency, Marcia; Baskow Agency; BAWN Publishers Inc.—Literary Agency; Bennett Agency, The; Brown Ltd., Curtis; Bulger and Associates, Kelvin C.; Cameron Agency, The Marshall; Cedar Grove Agency Entertainment; Client First—A/K/A Leo P. Haffey Agency; Communications Management Associates; CS International Literary Agency; Douroux & Co.; Epstein-Wyckoff and Associates; Esq. Management; Feigen/Parrent Literary Management; Film Artists Associates; Filmwriters Literary Agency; First Look Talent and Literary Agency; FitzGerald Literary Management; Fleury Agency, B.R.; Fran Literary Agency; Freed Co., The Barry; French, Inc., Samuel; French's; Geddes Agency; Gurman Agency, The Susan; H.W.A. Talent Representative; Hayes & Assoc., Gil; Hodges Agency, Carolyn; Hudson Agency; International Leonards Corp.; Jaret Entertainment; Johnson Warren Literary Agency; Ketay Agency, The Joyce; Kick Entertainment; Kohner, Inc., Paul; Larchmont Literary Agency; Legacies; Levine Literary Agency, Paul S.; Luedtke Agency, The; Miller Co., The Stuart M.; Momentum Marketing; Monteiro Rose Agency; Mura Enterprises, Inc., Dee; Niad Management; Omniquest Entertainment; Palmer, Dorothy; Panda Talent; Partos Company, The; Pevner, Inc., Stephen; Pinkham Literary Agency; PMA Literary and Film Management, Inc.; Redler Entertainment, Dan; Redwood Empire Agency; Robinson Talent and Literary Management; Scagnetti Talent & Literary Agency, Jack; Shapiro-Lichtman; Silver Screen Placements; Sister Mania Productions, Inc.; Sorice Agency, Camille; Stanton & Associates Literary Agency; Stars, the Agency; Sydra Techniques Corp.; Talent Source; Wardlow and Associates; Wauhob Agency, Donna; Windfall Management; Wright Representatives, Ann; Writer Store

Multimedia: Acme Talent & Literary; Film Artists Associates; Levine Literary Agency, Paul S.; Luedtke Agency, The; Miller Co., The Stuart M.; Omniquest Entertainment; Suite A Management; Sydra Techniques Corp.; Talent Source; Windfall Management

Mystery/Suspense: Abrams Artists Agency; AEI/Atchity Editorial/Entertainment International; AMG/Renaissance Literary Agency; Amsterdam Agency, Marcia; Baskow Agency; BAWN Publishers Inc.—Literary Agency; Brown Ltd., Curtis; Cedar Grove Agency Entertainment; Client First—A/K/A Leo P. Haffey Agency; CS International Literary Agency; Douroux & Co.; Epstein-Wyckoff and Associates; Esq. Management; Film Artists Associates; Filmwriters Literary Agency; First Look Talent and Literary Agency; FitzGerald Literary Management; Fleury Agency, B.R.; Fran Literary Agency; Freed Co., The Barry; French, Inc., Samuel; Geddes Agency; Greene, Arthur B.; Gurman Agency, The Susan; H.W.A. Talent Representative; Hayes & Assoc., Gil; Hodges Agency, Carolyn; Hudson Agency; International Leonards Corp.; Jaret Entertainment; Johnson Warren Literary Agency; Kerwin Agency, William; Ketay Agency, The Joyce; Kick Entertainment; Kohner, Inc., Paul; Larchmont Literary Agency; Levine Literary Agency, Paul S.; Luedtke Agency, The; Major Clients Agency; Miller Co., The Stuart M.; Momentum Marketing; Monteiro Rose Agency; Mura Enterprises, Inc., Dee; Niad Management; Omniquest Entertainment; Palmer, Dorothy; Panda Talent; Partos Company, The; Perelman Agency, Barry; Pinkham Literary Agency; PMA Literary and Film Management, Inc.; Redler Entertainment, Dan; Redwood Empire Agency; Robinson Talent and Literary Management; Scagnetti Talent & Literary Agency, Jack; Shapiro-Lichtman; Silver Screen Placements; Sorice Agency, Camille; Stars, the Agency; Stein Agency; Sydra Techniques Corp.; Talent Source; Wardlow and Associates; Windfall Management; Wright Representatives, Ann; Writer Store

Open to all Script Categories: Acme Talent & Literary; Allred and Allred, Literary Agents; Alpern Group, The; Bohrman Agency, The; Chadwick & Gros Literary Agency; Circle of Confusion Ltd.; Gage Group, The; Kerin-Goldberg Associates; Lake Agency, The Candace; Madsen Agency, Robert; Picture of You, A; Robins & Associates, Michael D.; Sherman & Associates, Ken; Stone Manners Agency; Suite A Management; Wardlow and Associates; Writers & Artists Agency

Psychic/Supernatural: AEI/Atchity Editorial/Entertainment International; AMG/Renaissance Literary Agency; Brown Ltd., Curtis; Communications Management Associates; CS International Literary Agency; Esq. Management; Filmwriters Literary Agency; First Look Talent and Literary Agency; FitzGerald Literary Management; French's; Geddes Agency; H.W.A. Talent Representative; Hodges Agency, Carolyn; Jaret Entertainment; Kay Agency, Charlene; Ketay Agency, The Joyce; Kick Entertainment; Larchmont Literary Agency; Levine Literary Agency, Paul S.; Luedtke Agency, The; Momentum Marketing; Monteiro Rose Agency; Mura Enterprises, Inc., Dee; Niad Management; Omniquest Entertainment; Partos Company, The; Pinkham Literary Agency; PMA Literary and Film Management, Inc.; Redler Entertainment, Dan; Robinson Talent and Literary Management; Stein Agency; Wright Representatives, Ann; Writer Store

Regional: Bulger and Associates, Kelvin C.; Esq. Management; Luedtke Agency, The; Momentum Marketing; Writer Store

Religious/Inspirational: Agency West Entertainment; AMG/Renaissance Literary Agency; Baskow Agency; Communications Management Associates; CS International Literary Agency; Esq. Management; Fran Literary Agency; French, Inc., Samuel; Levine Literary Agency, Paul S.; Luedtke Agency, The; Momentum Marketing; Mura Enterprises, Inc., Dee; Robinson Talent and Literary Management

Romantic Comedy: Abrams Artists Agency; AEI/Atchity Editorial/Entertainment International; Agency West Entertainment; AMG/Renaissance Literary Agency; Amsterdam Agency, Marcia; Baskow Agency; BAWN Publishers Inc.—Literary Agency; Brown Ltd., Curtis; Camejo & Assoc., Suzanna; Cedar Grove Agency Entertainment; Client First—A/K/A Leo P. Haffey Agency; Communications Management Associates; CS International Literary Agency; Douroux & Co.; Epstein-Wyckoff and Associates; Esq. Management; Film Artists Associates; Filmwriters Literary Agency; First Look Talent and Literary Agency; FitzGerald Literary Management; Fleury Agency, B.R.; Fran Literary Agency; Geddes Agency; Gurman Agency, The Susan; H.W.A. Talent Representative; Hodges Agency, Carolyn; Hudson Agency; International Leonards Corp.; Jaret Entertainment; Johnson Warren Literary Agency; Kay Agency, Charlene; Kerwin Agency, William; Ketay Agency, The Joyce; Kohner, Inc., Paul; Kritzer Productions, Eddie; Larchmont Literary Agency; Levine Literary Agency, Paul S.; Luedtke Agency, The; Miller Co., The Stuart M.; Momentum Marketing; Monteiro Rose Agency; Mura Enterprises, Inc., Dee; Niad Management; Omniquest Entertainment; Palmer, Dorothy; Panda Talent; Partos Company, The; Perelman Agency, Barry; Pevner, Inc., Stephen; PMA Literary and Film Management, Inc.; Redler Entertainment, Dan; Redwood Empire Agency; Robinson Talent and Literary Management; Scagnetti Talent & Literary Agency, Jack; Shapiro-Lichtman; Sister Mania Productions, Inc.; Sorice Agency, Camille; Stanton & Associates Literary Agency; Stars, the Agency; Stein Agency; Talent Source; Wardlow and Associates; Wauhob Agency, Donna; Windfall Management; Wright Representatives, Ann; Writer Store

Romantic Drama: Abrams Artists Agency; AEI/Atchity Editorial/Entertainment International; Agency West Entertainment; AMG/Renaissance Literary Agency; Amsterdam Agency, Marcia; Baskow Agency; BAWN Publishers Inc.—Literary Agency; Brown Ltd., Curtis; Camejo & Assoc., Suzanna; Client First—A/K/A Leo P. Haffey Agency; Communications Management Associates; CS International Literary Agency; Douroux & Co.; Epstein-Wyckoff and Associates; Esq. Management; Filmwriters Literary Agency; First Look Talent and Literary Agency; FitzGerald Literary Management; Fleury Agency, B.R.; Fran Literary Agency; Geddes Agency; Gurman Agency, The Susan; H.W.A. Talent Representative; Hodges Agency, Carolyn; Hudson Agency; Jaret Entertainment; Johnson Warren Literary Agency; Kay Agency, Charlene; Kerwin Agency, William; Ketay Agency, The Joyce; Kick Entertainment; Kohner, Inc., Paul; Larchmont Literary Agency; Levine Literary Agency, Paul S.; Luedtke Agency, The; Miller Co., The Stuart M.; Momentum Marketing; Monteiro Rose Agency; Mura Enterprises, Inc., Dee; Niad Management; Omniquest Entertainment; Palmer, Dorothy; Panda Talent; Partos Company, The; Perelman Agency, Barry; Pevner, Inc., Stephen; PMA Literary and Film Management, Inc.; Redler Entertainment, Dan; Redwood Empire Agency; Robinson Talent and Literary Management; Scagnetti Talent & Literary Agency, Jack; Shapiro-Lichtman; Sister Mania Productions, Inc.; Sorice Agency, Camille; Stanton & Associates Literary Agency; Stars, the Agency; Stein Agency; Talent Source; Wardlow and Associates; Wauhob Agency, Donna; Windfall Management; Wright Representatives, Ann; Writer Store

Science Fiction: AEI/Atchity Editorial/Entertainment International; Agency West Entertainment; AMG/ Renaissance Literary Agency; Baskow Agency; BAWN Publishers Inc.—Literary Agency; Camejo & Assoc., Suzanna; Cedar Grove Agency Entertainment; Client First—A/K/A Leo P. Haffey Agency; Communications Management Associates; CS International Literary Agency; Douroux & Co.; Esq. Management; Film Artists Associates; First Look Talent and Literary Agency; FitzGerald Literary Management; Fran Literary Agency; French's; Geddes Agency; H.W.A. Talent Representative; Hart Literary Management; International Leonards Corp.; Jaret Entertainment; Kay Agency, Charlene; Kerwin Agency, William; Kick Entertainment; Larchmont Literary Agency; Levine Literary Agency, Paul S.; Luedtke Agency, The; Miller Co., The Stuart M.; Momentum Marketing; Monteiro Rose Agency; Mura Enterprises, Inc., Dee; Omniquest Entertainment; Panda Talent; Partos Company, The; Perelman Agency, Barry; PMA Literary and Film Management, Inc.; Redler Entertainment, Dan; Robinson Talent and Literary Management; Shapiro-Lichtman; Silver Screen Placements; Stein Agency; Sydra Techniques Corp.; Wardlow and Associates; Windfall Management; Writer Store

Sports: Agency West Entertainment; AMG/Renaissance Literary Agency; Cedar Grove Agency Entertainment; Client First—A/K/A Leo P. Haffey Agency; CS International Literary Agency; First Look Talent and Literary Agency; Fran Literary Agency; H.W.A. Talent Representative; International Leonards Corp.; Jaret Entertainment; Larchmont Literary Agency; Levine Literary Agency, Paul S.; Luedtke Agency, The; Major Clients Agency; Miller Co., The Stuart M.; Momentum Marketing; Mura Enterprises, Inc., Dee; Niad Management; Redler Entertainment, Dan; Robinson Talent and Literary Management; Scagnetti Talent & Literary Agency, Jack; Stars, the Agency; Sydra Techniques Corp.; Windfall Management; Wright Representatives, Ann; Writer Store

Teen: AEI/Atchity Editorial/Entertainment International; Agency West Entertainment; AMG/Renaissance Literary Agency; Communications Management Associates; CS International Literary Agency; Epstein-Wyckoff and Associates; Esq. Management; Filmwriters Literary Agency; First Look Talent and Literary Agency; FitzGerald Literary Management; Fran Literary Agency; Geddes Agency; Hart Literary Management; Hudson Agency; Levine Literary Agency, Paul S.; Luedtke Agency, The; Miller Co., The Stuart M.; Momentum Marketing; Monteiro Rose Agency; Mura Enterprises, Inc., Dee; Niad Management; Partos Company, The; Pevner, Inc., Stephen; Redler Entertainment, Dan; Robinson Talent and Literary Management; Shapiro-Lichtman; Stein Agency; Talent Source; Wauhob Agency, Donna; Windfall Management; Wright Concept, The; Writer Store

Thriller/Espionage: AEI/Atchity Editorial/Entertainment International; Agency West Entertainment; AMG/Renaissance Literary Agency; Baskow Agency; BAWN Publishers Inc.—Literary Agency; Brown Ltd., Curtis; Camejo & Assoc., Suzanna; Cameron Agency, The Marshall; Cedar Grove Agency Entertainment; Client First—A/K/A Leo P. Haffey Agency; Communications Management Associates; CS International Literary Agency; Douroux & Co.; Epstein-Wyckoff and Associates; Esq. Management; Feigen/Parrent Literary Management; Filmwriters Literary Agency; First Look Talent and Literary Agency; FitzGerald Literary Management; Fleury Agency, B.R.; Fran Literary Agency; French, Inc., Samuel; French's; Geddes Agency; Gurman Agency, The Susan; H.W.A. Talent Representative; International Leonards Corp.; Jaret Entertainment; Johnson Warren Literary Agency; Kerwin Agency, William; Ketay Agency, The Joyce; Kick Entertainment; Larchmont Literary Agency; Levine Literary Agency, Paul S.; Luedtke Agency, The; Major Clients Agency; Miller Co., The Stuart M.; Momentum Marketing; Monteiro Rose Agency; Mura Enterprises, Inc., Dee; Niad Management; Omniquest Entertainment; Palmer, Dorothy; Partos Company, The; Perelman Agency, Barry; Pevner, Inc., Stephen; Pinkham Literary Agency; PMA Literary and Film Management, Inc.; Redler Entertainment, Dan; Redwood Empire Agency; Robinson Talent and Literary Management; Scagnetti Talent & Literary Agency, Jack; Shapiro-Lichtman; Silver Screen Placements; Sister Mania Productions, Inc.; Stanton & Associates Literary Agency; Stars, the Agency; Stein Agency; Wardlow and Associates; Wauhob Agency, Donna; Windfall Management; Wright Concept, The; Wright Representatives, Ann; Writer Store

Westerns/Frontier: AMG/Renaissance Literary Agency; Brown Ltd., Curtis; Cedar Grove Agency Entertainment; Client First—A/K/A Leo P. Haffey Agency; Communications Management Associates; CS International Literary Agency; Douroux & Co.; Esq. Management; First Look Talent and Literary Agency; FitzGerald Literary Management; Fran Literary Agency; Hudson Agency; Ketay Agency, The Joyce; Levine Literary Agency, Paul S.; Luedtke Agency, The; Momentum Marketing; Mura Enterprises, Inc., Dee; Panda Talent; PMA Literary and Film Management, Inc.; Robinson Talent and Literary Management; Shapiro-Lichtman; Sorice Agency, Camille; Wardlow and Associates; Wauhob Agency, Donna; Windfall Management; Wright Representatives, Ann

Script Agents/Format Index:

This index will help you determine agencies interested in handling scripts for particular types of movies or tV programs. These formats are delineated into ten categories; animation, documentary; episodic drama; feature film; miniseries; movie of the week (MOW); sitcom; soap opera; stage play; variety show. Once you find the agency you're interested in refer to the Listing Index for the page number.

Animation: Above the Line Agency; Abrams Artists Agency; Allred and Allred, Literary Agents; Chadwick & Gros Literary Agency; Client First—A/K/A Leo P. Haffey Agency; Communications Management Associates; CS International Literary Agency; Douroux & Co.; Epstein-Wyckoff and Associates, Esq. Management; Fran Literary Agency; Hudson Agency; International Leonards Corp.; Jaret Entertainment; Kay Agency, Charlene; Kohner, Inc., Paul; Levine Literary Agency, Paul S.; Monteiro Rose Agency; Mura Enterprises, Inc., Dee; Panda Talent; Pevner, Inc., Stephen; Picture of You, A; Quillco Agency, The; Redwood Empire Agency; Robins & Associates, Michael D.; Robinson Talent and Literary Management; Scagnetti Talent & Literary Agency, Jack; Shapiro-Lichtman; Suite A Management; Sydra Techniques Corp.; Van Duren Agency, Annette; Wauhob Agency, Donna; Wright Concept, The; Writer Store

Documentary: Allred and Allred, Literary Agents; Baskow Agency; Buchwald and Associates, Inc. Don; Bulger and Associates, Kelvin C.; Chadwick & Gros Literary Agency; Charisma Communications, Ltd.; Communications Management Associates; CS International Literary Agency; Fran Literary Agency; Hudson Agency; Kohner, Inc., Paul; Kritzer Productions, Eddie; Levine Literary Agency, Paul S.; Mura Enterprises, Inc., Dee; Pevner, Inc., Stephen; Picture of You, A; Quillco Agency, The; Robinson Talent and Literary Management; Windfall Management

Episodic Drama: Abrams Artists Agency; Allred and Allred, Literary Agents; Alpern Group, The; Baskow Agency; BAWN Publishers Inc.—Literary Agency; Buchwald and Associates, Inc. Don; Chadwick & Gros Literary Agency; Douroux & Co.; Epstein-Wyckoff and Associates; Fran Literary Agency; Geddes Agency; Kay Agency, Charlene; Kerin-Goldberg Associates; Ketay Agency, The Joyce; Kohner, Inc., Paul; Lake Agency, The Candace; Levine Literary Agency, Paul S.; Management Company, The; Momentum Marketing; Monteiro Rose Agency; Mura Enterprises, Inc., Dee; Omniquest Entertainment; Palmer, Dorothy; Panda Talent; Pevner, Inc., Stephen; Picture of You, A; Preminger Agency, Jim; Robins & Associates, Michael D.; Robinson Talent and Literary Management; Scagnetti Talent & Literary Agency, Jack; Shapiro-Lichtman; Stein Agency; Talent Source; Wardlow and Associates; Wauhob Agency, Donna; Wright Concept, The; Wright Representatives, Ann; Writers & Artists Agency

Feature Film: Above the Line Agency; Abrams Artists Agency; Acme Talent & Literary; AEI/Atchity Editorial/Entertainment International; Allred and Allred, Literary Agents; Alpern Group, The; AMG/Renaissance Literary Agency; Amsterdam Agency, Marcia; Baskow Agency; BAWN Publishers Inc.—Literary Agency; Bennett Agency, The; Berman Boals and Flynn Inc.; Bohrman Agency, The; Brown Ltd., Curtis; Buchwald and Associates, Inc. Don; Bulger and Associates, Kelvin C.; Camejo & Assoc., Suzanna; Cameron Agency, The Marshall; Cedar Grove Agency Entertainment; Chadwick & Gros Literary Agency; Charisma Communications, Ltd.; Circle of Confusion Ltd.; Client First—A/K/A Leo P. Haffey Agency; Communications Management Associates; CS International Literary Agency; Douroux & Co.; Epstein-Wyckoff and Associates; Esq. Management; Feigen/Parrent Literary Management; Film Artists Associates; Filmwriters Literary Agency; First Look Talent and Literary Agency; Fishbein Ltd., Frieda; Fitzgerald Literary Management; Fleury Agency, B.R.; Fran Literary Agency; Freed Co., The Barry; Gage Group, The; Geddes Agency; Gelff Agency, The Laya; Graham Agency; Greene, Arthur B.; Gurman Agency, The Susan; Hart Literary Management; Hayes & Assoc., Gil; Hodges Agency, Carolyn; Hogenson Agency, Barbara; Hudson Agency; International Leonards Corp.; Johnson Warren Literary Agency; Kallen Agency, Leslie; Kay Agency, Charlene; Kerin-Goldberg Associates; Ketay Agency, The Joyce; Kick Entertainment; Kohner, Inc., Paul; Kritzer Productions, Eddie; Lake Agency, The Candace; Larchmont Literary Agency; Legacies; Levine Literary Agency, Paul S.; Luedtke Agency, The; Madsen Agency, Robert; Major Clients Agency; Management Company, The; Momentum Marketing; Monteiro Rose Agency; Mura Enterprises, Inc., Dee; Niad Management; Omniquest Entertainment; Oscard Agency Inc., Fifi; Palmer, Dorothy; Panda

Talent; Partos Company, The; Pevner, Inc., Stephen; Picture of You, A; Pinkham Literary Agency; PMA Literary and Film Management, Inc.; Preminger Agency, Jim; Quillco Agency, The; Redwood Empire Agency; Robins & Associates, Michael D.; Robinson Talent and Literary Management; Scagnetti Talent & Literary Agency, Jack; Shapiro-Lichtman; Silver Screen Placements; Sister Mania Productions, Inc.; Sorice Agency, Camille; Stanton & Associates Literary Agency; Stars, the Agency; Suite A Management; Sydra Techniques Corp.; Talent Source; Van Duren Agency, Annette; Wardlow and Associates; Wauhob Agency, Donna; Whittlesey Agency, Peregrine; Wright Concept, The; Wright Representatives, Ann; Writer Store; Writers & Artists Agency

Miniseries: Alpern Group, The; Baskow Agency; Buchwald and Associates, Inc. Don; Chadwick & Gros Literary Agency; Charisma Communications, Ltd.; Communications Management Associates; Epstein-Wyckoff and Associates; Esq. Management; Filmwriters Literary Agency; Fran Literary Agency; Geddes Agency; Hudson Agency; Kerin-Goldberg Associates; Kohner, Inc., Paul; Levine Literary Agency, Paul S.; Luedtke Agency, The; Management Company, The; Mura Enterprises, Inc., Dee; Niad Management; Omniquest Entertainment; Palmer, Dorothy; Pevner, Inc., Stephen; Picture of You, A; PMA Literary and Film Management, Inc.; Robins & Associates, Michael D.; Robinson Talent and Literary Management; Scagnetti Talent & Literary Agency, Jack; Shapiro-Lichtman; Wardlow and Associates; Wauhob Agency, Donna; Windfall Management; Writer Store; Writers & Artists Agency

Sitcom: Abrams Artists Agency; Allred and Allred, Literary Agents; Amsterdam Agency, Marcia; Baskow Agency; Bennett Agency, The; Buchwald and Associates, Inc. Don; Cedar Grove Agency Entertainment; Chadwick & Gros Literary Agency; CS International Literary Agency; Douroux & Co.; Epstein-Wyckoff and Associates; Esq. Management; Fran Literary Agency; Geddes Agency; Hogenson Agency, Barbara; Hudson Agency; International Leonards Corp.; Kay Agency, Charlene; Kerin-Goldberg Associates; Ketay Agency, The Joyce; Kohner, Inc., Paul; Kritzer Productions, Eddie; Lake Agency, The Candace; Levine Literary Agency, Paul S.; Luedtke Agency, The; Major Clients Agency; Management Company, The; Momentum Marketing; Mura Enterprises, Inc., Dee; Omniquest Entertainment; Palmer, Dorothy; Panda Talent; Picture of You, A; Preminger Agency, Jim; Scagnetti Talent & Literary Agency, Jack; Shapiro-Lichtman; Stein Agency; Sydra Techniques Corp.; Talent Source; Van Duren Agency, Annette; Wardlow and Associates; Wauhob Agency, Donna; Wright Concept, The; Wright Representatives, Ann

Soap Opera: Abrams Artists Agency; Allred and Allred, Literary Agents; Chadwick & Gros Literary Agency; Epstein-Wyckoff and Associates; Hogenson Agency, Barbara; Kohner, Inc., Paul; Luedtke Agency, The; Shapiro-Lichtman; Wauhob Agency, Donna

Theatrical Stage Play: Abrams Artists Agency; Allred and Allred, Literary Agents; Berman Boals and Flynn Inc.; Bohrman Agency, The; Brown Ltd., Curtis; Buchwald and Associates, Inc. Don; Dramatic Publishing; Epstein-Wyckoff and Associates; Film Artists Associates; First Look Talent and Literary Agency; Fishbein Ltd., Frieda; Freedman Dramatic Agency, Inc., Robert A.; French, Inc., Samuel; Graham Agency; Greene, Arthur B.; Gurman Agency, The Susan; Hogenson Agency, Barbara; Kerin-Goldberg Associates; Ketay Agency, The Joyce; Kohner, Inc., Paul; Luedtke Agency, The; Madsen Agency, Robert; Niad Management; Omniquest Entertainment; Oscard Agency Inc., Fifi; Pevner, Inc., Stephen; Robinson Talent and Literary Management; Shapiro-Lichtman; Suite A Management; Wauhob Agency, Donna; Whittlesey Agency, Peregrine; Windfall Management; Writers & Artists Agency

TV Movie of the Week (TV MOW): Above the Line Agency; AEI/Atchity Editorial/Entertainment International; Allred and Allred, Literary Agents; Alpern Group, The; Amsterdam Agency, Marcia; Baskow Agency; BAWN Publishers Inc.—Literary Agency; Brown Ltd., Curtis; Buchwald and Associates, Inc. Don; Bulger and Associates, Kelvin C.; Cedar Grove Agency Entertainment; Chadwick & Gros Literary Agency; Charisma Communications, Ltd.; Communications Management Associates; CS International Literary Agency; Douroux & Co.; Epstein-Wyckoff and Associates; Esq. Management; Feigen/Parrent Literary Management; Filmwriters Literary Agency; First Look Talent and Literary Agency; Fishbein Ltd., Frieda; FitzGerald Literary Management; Fleury Agency, B.R.; Fran Literary Agency; Freed Co., The Barry; Geddes Agency; Greene, Arthur B.; Gurman Agency, The Susan; Hart Literary Management; Hodges Agency, Carolyn; Hogenson Agency, Barbara; Hudson Agency; International Leonards Corp.; Jaret Entertainment; Johnson Warren Literary Agency; Kallen Agency, Leslie; Kay Agency, Charlene; Kerin-Goldberg Associates; Ketay Agency, The Joyce; Kohner, Inc., Paul; Kritzer Productions, Eddie; Lake Agency, The Candace; Levine Literary Agency, Paul S.; Luedtke Agency, The; Major Clients Agency; Momentum Marketing; Monteiro Rose Agency; Mura Enterprises, Inc., Dee; Niad Management; Omniquest Entertainment; Palmer, Dorothy; Panda Talent; Partos Company, The; Pevner, Inc., Stephen; Picture of You, A; Pinkham Literary Agency; PMA Literary and Film Management, Inc.; Preminger Agency, Jim; Quillco Agency, The; Redwood Empire Agency; Robins & Associates, Michael D.; Robinson Talent and Literary Management; Scagnetti Talent & Literary Agency, Jack; Shapiro-Lichtman; Stanton & Associates Literary Agency; Stars, the Agency; Suite A Management; Sydra Techniques Corp.; Talent Source; Van

Duren Agency, Annette; Wardlow and Associates; Wauhob Agency, Donna; Windfall Management; Wright Concept, The; Wright Representatives, Ann; Writer Store; Writers & Artists Agency

Variety Show: Allred and Allred, Literary Agents; Baskow Agency; Chadwick & Gros Literary Agency; French, Inc., Samuel; Geddes Agency; International Leonards Corp.; Kerin-Goldberg Associates; Kohner, Inc., Paul; Mura Enterprises, Inc., Dee; Robinson Talent and Literary Management; Shapiro-Lichtman; Wauhob Agency, Donna; Wright Concept, The;

Publicize or Perish

BY DICK LEHT

Their new book was due out shortly, a critical study of speech and conduct codes at U.S. college campuses today, and with that co-authors Harvey Silverglate and Alan Kors eagerly anticipated word from their publisher about its plans to promote *The Shadow University.*

But quickly their hearts sank when they learned the publisher had little promotion in mind for a work that had taken its authors, one a Boston lawyer, the other a college professor, years to research and write. Basically, says Silverglate, the publisher planned to send out a batch of review copies to the media, take out a couple of small, print advertisements, and had lined up a three-city book tour.

Three-city? Silverglate worked in one of the cities, Boston, Kors in the other, Philadelphia. The simple math and simple reality of the so-called book tour their publisher had put together amounted to a single appearance in Washington, D.C.

"That was it," says Silverglate, recalling recently the dismay he and Kors felt once they realized their book was not slated as one of The Free Press's big books for the fall season just ended. Making matters worse, Silverglate tracked the mailing of review copies to potential reviewers at newspapers and other media and discovered that, for a variety of reasons, "Twenty percent of the people never even got it."

"We realized the book would sink like a rock," he says.

But the tide has since turned.

Like an increasing number of authors today, Silverglate and Kors combined the hiring of a private publicist with their own on-the-run public relations scramble. Mostly, critics embraced the work, but the authors did not know if the book-buying public would; now, three months after its release, the two have traveled to more than thirty cities to push their book at lectures, talks, and book signings. The authors created a website. They've done more than forty print interviews. The private publicist they hired targeted radio, and, says Silverglate, "We've easily done more than 250 shows."

"I'll tell you what we've done," Silverglate says about all the hustle. "We've sold out the first printing (13,000 books), and the publisher clearly wasn't expecting that."

Selling their story

In the U.S. alone, about fifty thousand books are published each year, according to industry observers. That's a lot of noise, with a lot of authors competing to have their works noticed by the book-buying public. Likewise, these observers note, unless you're a celebrity author or have written one of the firm's big books, there's been a falloff in the promotional efforts publishers give to the rest of the list.

"It's very much a common practice for New York publishers to do very little publicity for other than their 'A-list' titles, which means, essentially they throw books out there and see what happens," says John Kremer, a guru of sorts in the world of book promotion. Kremer, who is based in Iowa, is a one-man clearinghouse of information. He manages a Website, puts out a monthly newsletter, and is the author of *1001 Ways to Market Your Books* (Open Horizons).

Kremer says when he wrote his guide in 1986, it sold mostly to public relations professionals, but now, "I would say, the majority of sales are to authors.

"If you want your book to do well in today's market you have to be actively involved in the marketing of the book." That's become a publishing fact of life, Kremer says, matters of case-loads and manpower. "The major publishers in New York put out between 300 and 1,000 books a year, and their publicity staffs range from 3 to 20. There's no way they can publicize all those books adequately."

Freelance solution

Virtually unheard of a decade ago, a growing number of authors are now dipping into their back pockets to hire freelance publicists. It's a trend with enough vigor to fuel the emergence of a new subset of publicists in the field of public relations—those who work exclusively on author promotion. In Boston, for example, there is a handful of publicists who specialize in promoting authors and their books, and all of them set up shop in the 1990s.

The best known locally, and probably the most expensive, is Sandra Goroff-Mailly, who worked for years in publicity at Houghton-Mifflin before setting out on her own in 1994. Goroff-Mailly is hired directly by authors as well as by publishing houses, and she's handled the publicity for a range of local and nationally known writers, such as Tracy Kidder, James Carroll, Clive Cussler, Elvis biographer Peter Guralnick, and William M. Bulger, currently the president of the University of Massachusetts, who wrote a memoir.

There's also Gail Leondar-Wright, who dropped out of her Ph.D. program in the early 1990s after helping a friend promote her book and found the work "enormously empowering, satisfying, and fun." Based in Arlington, Leondar-Wright has carved out her own niche. "I mostly just promote progressive books, something with a left-of-center agenda." In Newton, there's Victor Gulotta, who also worked in publicity at various publishing houses before forming his own firm in 1993. His client list tilts heavily in favor of authors of self-help books. There are others, including ultra-specialists like Lisa Ekus of Hatfield, who is known nationally as the go-to publicist for food writers launching a cookbook.

In hands-on fashion, the personal publicist works with authors to devise campaigns either to complement the promotional effort their publisher has in mind or to pick up after the publisher's "launch campaign" has ended. They look to set up book tours that, at best, include book signings, lectures, radio, TV, and print interviews.

The fees range widely. The publicists interviewed locally all said they prefer a minimum of three months of work, with the cost ranging from $1,000 to $10,000 a month depending on the proposed campaign. In New York, the fees run even higher. "It's a real investment," says Kremer.

Indeed, many cash-strapped authors face spending more for a private publicist than what they got paid to write their book. But each of the Boston-area publicists all talked about a certain kind of flexibility. "I don't want any author to be bankrupt because they are paying for my services," says Leondar-Wright about her sliding scale.

Poet Alicia Ostriker is one beneficiary of Leondar-Wright's approach. Twice Ostriker turned to Leondar-Wright to help promote her poetry. Rutgers University Press, she says, had "really nothing" planned in 1994 for promoting the publication of her book of poems, *Nakedness of the Fathers*.

Leondar-Wright, she says, set up interviews for her in the cities she was already traveling to for other work-related reasons, such as Los Angeles and the San Francisco Bay area. There was no time limit to their deal, just a modest fee whenever Leondar-Wright pitched in. "I didn't have the contacts, and Gail got my name out there in places it wouldn't have gotten otherwise," says the poet, who lives in Princeton, N.J. "It's nice for any author who works on something serious to have a publicist who understands what you are doing."

Supplemental publicity

What do the publicists at the major publishing houses make of all this? "I almost always think it's a good idea," says Barb Burg, the director of publicity and a vice president at Bantam Books, which publishes more than 300 titles a year. "Think about it. We live in a world now where it seems everyone has a publicist, and publicity is an infinite world. It's never done. There's always another phone call you can make, another radio show you can do.

"The reality of our jobs is that we only have a certain amount of time we can devote to each project." Burg has eight publicists working inhouse for her. Upon publication, she says, they oversee three months of launch publicity, "and after that, we have to move on to the next books."

That's when Burg says it makes the most sense for an author to hire their own publicist, "if an author wants to keep things going." There are times during the launch, she concedes, when authors might want to hire private publicists to supplement the house's efforts, "when the author doesn't think the book is getting enough attention initially." But she also cautions against authors' rushing out and hiring a publicist from the get-go. "I hate to see authors waste their money. Some books just are not publicize-able."

Burg also rebuts the widely held notion that only a house's big books get the backing of the publicity department. "That's a great misconception by authors. We bought the book. We care. We want to publicize our books."

Try convincing biographer Susan Quinn of that.

"I was essentially orphaned," she recalls about the publication four years ago of her biography, *Marie Curie*. "I had a wonderful editor, and then he got fired, and I got passed on to someone who had very little interest in my book, who's main claim to fame was that he'd edited a Princess Di book that had done very well. It was very clear from the first lunch with him that he didn't have any kind of plan to market my book."

Then came a meeting with the sales staff at which she learned the publisher was not going to take out spots on National Public Radio to promote the book. "That was the turning point for me. It showed me they had no commitment at all to doing anything for the book." Quinn, who lives in Brookline and is president of the writers' group PEN/New England, began asking around, and was referred to Goroff-Mailly. The book was reviewed favorably and widely, and even though her publisher, she says, had no book tour scheduled for her, Goroff-Mailly "arranged for a huge number of public radio interviews all over the country." She says she paid $3,000 for the extra help.

"Did I sell enough books to cover the cost of hiring Sandy? There is no way of knowing. But I do know it helped sell more books, and I'd spent seven years working on it, and I thought, after putting so much effort into this, I'd blame myself if I didn't give it my best shot marketing the book. If I hadn't done that, I'd live with that regret, because really good books do get lost. I knew that."

Giving Yourself a Promotion

BY MICHAEL LARSEN, JAY CONRAD LEVINSON, AND RICK FRISHMAN

Writing a book without a promotion plan is like driving a car with the windows painted over and no brakes. It will only get you as far as the nearest stationary object. But new authors are sometimes intimidated by the prospect of promoting their first book. It may seem impossible to
- know all you need to know about promotion
- build your nationwide publishing and field networks
- develop a promotion plan
- promote your book from coast to coast

And you must still find the time and energy to write books! But thousands of writers who aren't as smart, creative, and determined as you are do it every year. Believe us when we assure you: if they can, you can.

Start with a promotion plan

Marketing people are territorial. Your promotion plan will cover everything you will do to market your books. But marketing people don't like writers infringing on their territory, which includes marketing to the book trade as well as the consumer marketing that you will be doing. Since you will need the support of your publisher's marketing department, we recommend calling it a promotion plan.

Although your promotion plan will be flexible enough to change as you learn what works best for you and respond to new opportunities, your plan is the foundation of the campaign you will wage for your book's success.

It will be the blueprint of your plan to transform yourself from an unknown writer into one of the top players in your field with an unbroken string of successful books, all of which sell each other. Your plan will also be the model for the plans you create for future books.

Gather your team

Promotion is tooting your own horn. But rather than thinking about yourself as a horn player, think of yourself as a conductor leading a symphony orchestra or a general leading an army of volunteers.

Your army consists of your personal and professional direct and indirect publishing and field networks. You will continue to swell its ranks with every new relationship you create as long as you continue to write, speak, and travel.

You want your army to help you recruit everyone in the world who will enjoy and benefit from reading your books. Your army faces a lifelong campaign in which every book you write is another victory in the battle for the hearts and minds of your readers.

JAY CONRAD LEVINSON, *the father of guerrilla marketing, has sold more than one million guerrilla marketing books since 1984. These books have been translated into thirteen languages.* **RICK FRISHMAN** *is the president of Planned Television Arts, one of the top publicity firms in the book publishing industry.* **MICHAEL LARSEN** *is a successful literary agent and the author of* How to Write a Book Proposal *(Writer's Digest Books). This article is excerpted from* Guerrilla Marketing for Writers *copyright © 2000 by Jay Conrad Levinson, Rick Frishman, and Michael Larsen. Used with permission of Writer's Digest Books. To obtain your copy, visit your local book seller or call (800)289-0963.*

How successful you are at building and maintaining your army depends on how its members feel about themselves and about you. You are the heart and soul of the identity you create through everything you do. So no matter what you write, make sure your books have a lasting impact on your readers—make them eager to recommend them and eager to read your future work. Mystery writer Mickey Spillane once said, "The first page sells the book." To which he added, "The last page sells the next book."

Whether you write your books primarily to enlighten or entertain your readers, always strive to do both. This is the surest way for your books to benefit from the gift that keeps on giving: word of mouth.

Power beyond measure

There's a poster showing a caterpillar on a branch and a butterfly hovering in the air above it saying, "You can fly, but that cocoon has to go."

You should be perpetually breathless from the opportunities for writing, promoting, and profiting from your books. So starting from the moment you finish reading these words, stop thinking of yourself as a writer with something to say. Start thinking of yourself as an author with a lifetime's worth of books to sell to the millions of people around the world who want to read your work.

If you believe you can become a successful author—however you define the word successful-you can. The right ideas pursued with relentless determination will enable you to become a one-person Bertalsmann—a multimedia, multinational conglomerate all by yourself.

This is not a challenge for the faint-hearted. Only a total commitment to your literary and financial objectives will motivate you to hit the keys and the streets and enable you to overcome the challenges you will encounter.

At his inauguration as president of South Africa, Nelson Mandela immortalized the words of Marianne Williamson in her bestseller, *A Return to Love*:

> 'Our deepest fear is not that we are inadequate. Our deepest fear is that we are powerful beyond measure. It is our light, not our darkness, that most frightens us.' We ask ourselves, Who am I to be brilliant, gorgeous, talented, fabulous? Actually, who are you not to be? . . . Your playing small doesn't serve the world. There's nothing enlightened about shrinking so that other people won't feel insecure around you. We are all meant to shine, as children do. . . . And as we let our own light shine, we unconsciously give other people permission to do the same. As we're liberated from our own fear, our presence automatically liberates others.

You are needed. Millions of readers around the world hunger for the entertainment novels provide and the empowering information and inspiration in nonfiction books. They want to be moved and enlightened by ideas that transcend time and space. They need only learn about your books. In promoting your work, you are doing them a service as well as yourself.

Ten Tips for Working with a Publicist

BY TAMI DEPALMA

To get the biggest and best in media coverage, many authors and publishers find that hiring a publicist produces the best results. But how do you know what to look for in a publicist? How do you work together to get maximum exposure?

Expect to work with a publicist for at least six to nine months if you want coverage in magazines. This gives the publicist time to become intimately familiar with your goals, produce a strong media release, design a catchy media kit, follow-up until they get to "yes" . . . then wait four to six months for the issues to finally hit the stands.

The following tips will help you select the best publicist and develop a strong, productive working relationship:

1) Find a publicist who believes in you. If media follow-up is part of why you are working with a publicist, only hire one who is passionate about your project. Follow-up calls are *hard*. A publicist must believe in your project, sell your story, and keep motivated to get you exposure.

2) Discuss your expectations. Your publicist must know what results you expect her to achieve within the confines of your budget. As much as publishers hate it, a publicist should be prepared to strive for all possibilities but shouldn't promise anything. No matter how good your publicist is, one single, significant world event can wipe out any given media appearance.

3) Start with a plan. This may seem like a waste of precious moments, especially when there is so much to do in so little time. You and your publicist must know and agree who you are targeting, how you will reach them repetitively, how you will capture their attention, and why they will buy your book. Skipping this step in the beginning will lead both you and your publicist to frustration.

4) Communicate with your publicist. If you don't like an angle, explain to your publicist and listen to her answer. You have the inside scoop on what's hot in the industry and what might be the next emerging trend. But your publicist knows how to sell it to the media and your other targeted markets. You should always have final approval of all materials, but trust your publicist to know which story angles the media will "buy."

5) Revisit your plan often and decide to stay on track and/or follow new opportunities.

6) If on a strict budget, ask your publicist what items you can do to save money, without compromising the effectiveness of the campaign. Internet marketing implementation is something the author can often do even better than a publicist. (You are the expert in your field, not us!) Preparation and mailing of your materials is an expense the publisher can eliminate. Have your publicist send originals and a complete sample media kit. Then stuff, seal, and label the envelopes yourself. If your marketing materials are strong enough to

TAMI DEPALMA *is a publicist at MarketAbility which has helped authors and publishers in thirty-eight states get millions of dollars of free publicity through creative, connected, unbeatable publicity and promotion "with a twist." In Denver, Colorado since 1989, partners Tami DePalma and Kim Dushinski created* MAXIMUM EXPOSURE *Marketing System for publishers who expect (and deserve) unlimited results on limited budgets.*

stimulate response from the media, consider eliminating the media kit folder. This will not only cut the expense of the folder but will dramatically reduce your postage.

7) Before you call your publicist, list questions or concerns you have about your campaign plan. We often ask that our clients e-mail or fax us with questions. The publisher asks better thought-out questions and receives more complete answers in writing. It is also the quickest way to communicate—allowing the maximum time for follow up! Ask your publicist when she does the majority of her follow-up calls to the media, and avoid calling at those times.

8) Encourage your publicist! As they make your media calls, publicists hear "no" more than a salesperson and a two-year-old combined. You'd be surprised what a kind word can do for morale. Ask your publicist what common rejections she is receiving so you can offer new ideas. Together you can reformulate the pitches.

9) Discuss report times. Publicists are creative people. Good publicists have discovered how to become detail oriented, as well. During the planning stages, ask the publicist how she will let you know what is happening throughout your campaign. There is a lot of "behind the scenes" work, and it takes several contacts to get the media to say "yes." Let your publicist know your expectations. Do you want weekly reports? Reports as possibilities arise? Reports when results happen?

10) Get involved! Attend meetings of publishing associations and organizations, universities, private seminars, trade shows, conventions. You can't place a value on the contacts you can make and the things you will learn.

Don't Let Your Publicist Disappoint You

BY STACY MILLER

When authors place sole responsibility for their books' PR success into a publicist's lap and leave it there, the results are often disappointing. Despite their best intentions, publicists may fail to generate important reviews. Interview opportunities may slip through the cracks. Worse still, highly promotable books may languish without visibility in a highly competitive marketplace.

Does that mean you should give up on publicists and wait for Oprah to call you? Or that you should give up on publicity altogether? There is another option. You can work in partnership with your publicist and take the following steps to maximize your chances of success:

☑ Be clear about your expectations from the outset, and make sure there is a meeting of the minds. If landing on the front page of *The Wall Street Journal* would be the ideal coup for your book, make sure your publicist focuses on accomplishing that instead of pitching you to every producer at National Public Radio. Give your publicist your wish list, and offer to prioritize your publicist's to-do list; you'll both be happier in the long run.

☑ Suggest news angles for promoting your book, and provide your publicist with a list of buzz words and phrases. Your publicist most likely isn't an expert in your field and will welcome your help, even if she doesn't specifically ask for it.

☑ Tout your credentials and sing the praises of your book to your publicist at every opportunity. Don't worry about sounding pompous or immodest; your publicist will appreciate your self-confidence and be even more enthusiastic in pitching you to the media.

☑ Keep an eye on the media, and inform your publicist about developing news stories and current events that might tie into your book. Ask your publicist what else you can do to complement her efforts. Are there professional associations or mailing lists you can steer her toward? Have you compiled contact information for your alumni, professional, and hometown publications?

☑ Ask your publicist for what you need, whether it's a redirection of energies, an accommodation to your schedule, or a weekly progress report. You'll come out a winner if you ask your publicist to communicate with you and commit yourself to doing the same. And you won't be disappointed with the results.

STACY MILLER's *publicity firm, SJ Miller Communications, is located at 10 Turning Mill Lane, Randolph MA 02368. Reprinted with permission from Stacy Miller.*

Independent Publicists

You spent years writing your book, then several more months sending queries to agents. You finally find an agent who loves your work, but then you have to wait even more time as she submits your manuscript to editors. After a few months, your agent closes a great deal for your work with a publishing house you really admire. Now you can sit back and wait for the money to start rolling in, right?

If you've learned anything about publishing so far, you've learned that getting a book published takes a lot of work. And once you find a publisher, your work doesn't stop. You have to focus now on selling your book to make money and to ensure that publishing companies will work with you again. Industry experts estimate that 50,000 books are published each year in the U.S. This number is only going to increase with the ease of Internet publishing. What can you do to ensure that your book succeeds with this amount of competition?

While most publishing houses do have in-house publicists, their time is often limited and priority is usually given to big-name authors who have already proved they will make money for the publisher. Often writers feel their books aren't getting the amount of publicity they had hoped for. Because of this, many authors have decided to work with an independent publicist.

For the first time, we've included a section of independent publicists, or speakers' agents, in this book. Like agents, publicists view publishing as a business. And their business goal is to see that your book succeeds. And usually publicists are more than happy to work in conjunction with your editor, your publisher, and your agent. Together they can form a strong team that will help make you a publishing sensation.

What to look for in a publicist

When choosing an independent publicist, you'll want someone who has business savvy and experience in sales. And, of course, you'll want someone who is enthusiastic about you and your writing. When looking through the listings in this section, look at each person's experience both prior to and after becoming a publicist. The radio and television shows on which their clients have appeared can indicate the caliber of their contacts, and the recent promotions they have done for their clients' books can reveal their level of creativity.

You'll also want to look for a publicist who is interested in your subject area. Like agents and publishing houses, most independent publicists specialize. By focusing on specific areas, publicists can actually do more for their clients. For example, if a publicist is interested in cookbooks, she can send her clients to contacts she has on Cooking Network shows, editors at gourmet cooking magazines, bookstores which have cafés, and culinary conferences. The more knowledge a publicist has about your subject, the more opportunities she will find to publicize your work.

How to make the initial contact

Contacting independent publicists should be much less stressful than the query process you've gone through to find an agent. Most publicists are open to a phone call, though some still prefer to receive a letter or an e-mail as the initial contact. Often you can receive a referral to a publicist through an agent, an editor, or even another writer. Because publicists do cost more out-of-pocket money than an agent, there isn't the same competition for their time. Of course, not every publicist you call will be the best fit for you. Be prepared to hear that the publicist already has a full client load, or even that she doesn't have the level of interest in your work that you want a publicist to have.

How much money should I spend?

As you read over the listings of independent publicists, you'll quickly notice that many charge a substantial amount of money for their services. The cost of a publicist can be quite daunting, especially to a new writer. *You should only pay what you feel comfortable paying and what you can reasonably afford.* Keep in mind, however, that any money you spend on publicity will come back to you in the form of more sold books. A general rule of thumb is to budget one dollar for every copy of your book that is printed. For a print run of 10,000, you should expect to spend $10,000. There are ways you can make working with a publicist less of a strain on your purse strings. If you received an advance for your book, you can use part of it to help with your marketing expenses. Some publishers will agree to match the amount of money an author pays for outside publicity. If your publicist's bill is $2,000, you would pay half and your publisher would pay the other half. Be sure to ask your publishing house if this option is available to you. And most publicists are very willing to work with their clients on a marketing budget.

When reading through the listings of independent publicists, use the following key to help you fully understand the information provided:

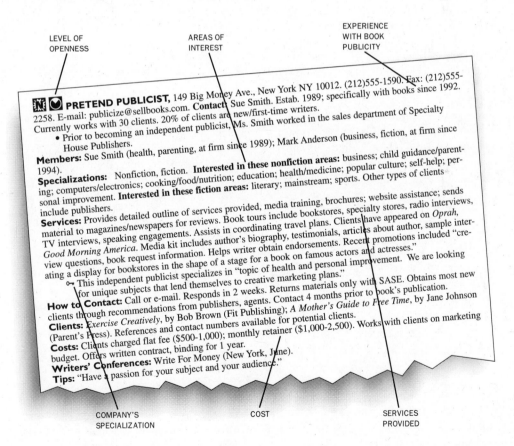

LEVEL OF OPENNESS

AREAS OF INTEREST

EXPERIENCE WITH BOOK PUBLICITY

PRETEND PUBLICIST, 149 Big Money Ave., New York NY 10012. (212)555-1590. Fax: (212)555-2258. E-mail: publicize@sellbooks.com. **Contact** Sue Smith. Estab. 1989; specifically with books since 1992. Currently works with 30 clients. 20% of clients are new/first-time writers.
• Prior to becoming an independent publicist, Ms. Smith worked in the sales department of Specialty House Publishers.
Members: Sue Smith (health, parenting, at firm since 1989); Mark Anderson (business, fiction, at firm since 1994).
Specializations: Nonfiction, fiction. **Interested in these nonfiction areas:** business; child guidance/parenting; computers/electronics; cooking/food/nutrition; education; health/medicine; popular culture; self-help; personal improvement. **Interested in these fiction areas:** literary; mainstream; sports. Other types of clients include publishers.
Services: Provides detailed outline of services provided, media training, brochures; website assistance; sends material to magazines/newspapers for reviews. Book tours include bookstores, specialty stores, radio interviews, TV interviews, speaking engagements. Assists in coordinating travel plans. Clients have appeared on *Oprah*, *Good Morning America.* Media kit includes author's biography, testimonials, articles about author, sample interview questions, book request information. Helps writer obtain endorsements. Recent promotions included "creating a display for bookstores in the shape of a stage for a book on famous actors and actresses."
  ☞ This independent publicist specializes in "topic of health and personal improvement. We are looking for unique subjects that lend themselves to creative marketing plans."
How to Contact: Call or e-mail. Responds in 2 weeks. Returns materials only with SASE. Obtains most new clients through recommendations from publishers, agents. Contact 4 months prior to book's publication.
Clients: *Exercise Creatively*, by Bob Brown (Fit Publishing); *A Mother's Guide to Free Time*, by Jane Johnson (Parent's Press). References and contact numbers available for potential clients. Works with clients on marketing
Costs: Clients charged flat fee ($500-1,000); monthly retainer ($1,000-2,500). Works with clients on marketing budget. Offers written contract, binding for 1 year.
Writers' Conferences: Write For Money (New York, June).
Tips: "Have a passion for your subject and your audience."

COMPANY'S SPECIALIZATION

COST

SERVICES PROVIDED

Quick Reference Icons

N Independent publicist new to this edition.
◻ New independent publicist actively seeking clients.
◑ Independent publicist interested in working with both new and established writers.
◉ Independent publicist open only to established writers.
◎ Independent publicist who specializes in specific types of work.
⊘ Independent publicist not currently open to new clients.

SUBHEADS FOR QUICK ACCESS TO INFORMATION

Each listing is broken down into subheads to make locating specific information easier. In this first paragraph, you'll find contact information for each independent publicist. Further information is provided which indicates the company's size and experience in the publishing industry.

Members: To help you find a publicist with a firm understanding of your book's subject and audience, we include the names of all publicists and their specialties. The year the member joined the company is also provided, indicating an individual's familiarity with book publicity.

Specializations: Similar to the agents listed in this book, most publicists have specific areas of interest. A publicist with a knowledge of your book's subject will have contacts in your field and a solid sense of your audience.

Services: This subhead provides important details about what the publicist can do for you, including a list of services available for clients, book tour information, television shows on which clients have appeared, contents of media kits, and examples of recent promotions done by the publicist.

☞ Look for the key icon to quickly learn the publicist's areas of specialization and specific marketing strengths.

How to Contact: Unlike literary agents, most independent publicists are open to phone calls, letters, and e-mail. Check this subhead to see the individual publicist's preference. Also pay close attention to the time frame the publicist needs between your initial contact and your book's publication date.

Clients: To give a better sense of their areas of interest, independent publicists list authors they have helped to promote. Publicists also indicate here if they are willing to provide potential clients with references.

Costs: Specific details are provided on how publicists charge their clients. Although the costs seem high, the payback in terms of books sold is usually worth the additional expense. Publicists indicate if they work with clients on a marketing budget and if they offer a written contract.

Writers' Conferences: A great way to meet and learn more about publicists is at writers' conferences. Here publicists list the ones they attend. For more information about a specific conference, check the **Writers' Conferences** section starting on page 333.

Tips: Advice and additional instructions are given for writers interested in working with an independent publicist.

SPECIAL INDEXES TO HELP YOUR SEARCH

Independent Publicists Indexed by Openness to Submissions: This index lists publicists according to their receptivity to new clients.

Geographic Index: For writers looking for a publicist close to home, this index lists independent publicists state-by-state.

Listing Index: This index lists all agencies, independent publicists, and writers' conferences listed in the book.

INDEPENDENT PUBLICISTS

N **Ⓓ** **THE FORD GROUP**, 1250 Prospect St., Suite Ocean-5, La Jolla CA 92037. (858)454-3314. Fax: (858)454-3319. E-mail: fordgroup@aol.com. Website: www.fordsisters.com. **Contact:** Arielle Ford. Estab. 1987; specifically with books since 1990. Currently works with 10 clients. 50% of clients are new/first-time writers.

• Ms. Ford has been a publicist since 1976.

Members: Laura Clark (how-to, health, self-help, at firm since 1996); Katherine Kellmeyer (spirituality, relationships, at firm since 1997).

Specializations: Nonfiction. **Interested in these nonfiction areas:** health/medicine; how-to; New Age/metaphysics; psychology; religious/inspirational; self-help/personal improvement.

Services: Provides detailed outline of services provided, audio/video tapes, media training, fax news releases, electronic news release, material to magazines/newspapers for reviews. Book tours include bookstores, radio interviews, TV interviews, newspaper interviews, magazine interviews, speaking engagements (limited amount). Clients have appeared on *Oprah, Larry King Live, Good Morning America, AP Radio, The Today Show, CNN, Fox News, Art Bell Show.* Media kit includes author's biography, testimonials, articles about author, basic information on book, professional photos, sample interview questions. Helps writer obtain endorsements. "We created the 'World's Largest Pot of Chicken Soup' to serve 7,000 homeless on Thanksgiving 5 years ago to launch one of the *Chicken Soup for the Soul* books. We ended up on NBC-TV network news and a photo in *USA Today.*"

    O━ "We live and breathe our niche: self-help, alternative medicine and spirituality—we completely understand the category and love promoting it."

How to Contact: Call, e-mail or fax. Responds within 3 days. Returns unwanted material. Obtains most new clients through recommendations from others. Contact 6 months prior to book's publication.

Clients: *How to Know God*, by Depak Chopra (Harmony); *The Isaiah Effect*, by Gregg Braden (Harmony); *Radical Honesty*, by Brad Blanton (Dell); *Nature's Virus Killers*, by Mark Stengler (M. Evans). Other clients include Gary Zukav, Marianne Williamson, Rachael Kessler, Rabbi Irwin Katsof, George Pratt and Peter Lambrou.

Costs: Charges clients flat fee ($6,000-26,000); monthly retainer ($4,000-7,000). Works with clients on marketing budget. Offers written contract, binding on a book-by-book basis. 30-day notice must be given to terminate contract.

Tips: "Make sure your publicist (the person who actually will be making the calls on your behalf) is passionate about your book and is experienced in pitching your subject matter."

N **Ⓓ** **GARIS AGENCY—NATIONAL PUBLICISTS**, 6965 El Camino Real, #105-110, La Costa CA 92009-4195. (760)471-4807. Fax: (253)390-4262. E-mail: publicists@aol.com. Website: www.fastlink.to/publicity. **Contact:** R.J. Garis. Estab. 1989; specifically with books since 1989. Currently works with 50 clients. 20% of clients are new/first-time writers.

• Prior to becoming an independent publicist, Mr. Garis was a promoter and producer.

Members: Taryn Roberts (associate national publicist, at firm since 1997); R.J. Garis.

Specializations: Nonfiction, fiction, script. **Interested in these nonfiction areas:** animals; biography/autobiography; business; child guidance/parenting; current affairs; gay/lesbian issues; government/politics/law; health/medicine; how-to; humor; interior design/decorating; juvenile nonfiction; memoirs; military/war; money/finance/economics; multicultural; music/dance/theater/film; nature/environment; New Age/metaphysics; photography; popular culture; psychology; science/technology; self-help/personal improvement; sociology; sports; travel; true crime/investigative; women's issues/women's studies; young adult. **Interested in these fiction areas:** action/adventure; cartoon/comic; contemporary issues; detective/police/crime; erotica; ethnic; family saga; fantasy; feminist; gay/lesbian; glitz; horror; humor/satire; juvenile; literary; mainstream; multicultural; mystery/suspense; New Age/metaphysical; picture book; psychic/supernatural; romance; science fiction; sports; thriller/espionage; westerns/frontier; young adult.

Services: Provides media training, international publicity, if applicable, fax news releases, electronic news release, material to magazines/newspapers for reviews, website assistance, website publicity. Book tours include bookstores, specialty stores, radio interviews, TV interviews, newspaper interviews, magazine interviews, speaking engagements, conferences. Assists in coordinating travel plans. Clients have appeared on *Oprah, Dateline, Leeza, CNN, Sally, Extra, 48 Hours, Good Morning America, Montel, Inside Edition, 20/20, Today.* Media kits include résumé, author's biography, testimonials, articles about author, basic infomation on book, professional photos, sample interview questions, book request information. Helps writer obtain endorsements. "We designed media information for author Missy Cummings (*Hornet's Nest*)—which resulted in TV interviews on *Extra, Inside Edition* and a print feature in *The Star.*"

    O━ This company specializes in "quality media that works! Morning radio, national TV, regional TV, major newspapers and national magazines. We currently book over 2,000 media interviews a year."

How to Contact: Call or e-mail. Responds in 2 weeks. Discards unwanted materials. Obtains most new clients through recommendations from others. Contact 4-6 months prior to book's publication.

Clients: *Hornet's Nest*, by Missy Cummings (iUniverse); *Little Kids Big Questions*, by Dr. Judi Craig (Hearst Books); *There Are No Accidents*, by Robert Hopcke (Penguin Putnam); *Anger Work*, by Dr. Robert Puff (Vantage Press). References and contact numbers available for potential clients.

Costs: Charges clients flat fee ($1,500-5,000); monthly retainer ($1,000-3,000). Works with clients on marketing budget. Offers written contract, binding for a minimum of 6 months. 30-day notice must be given to terminate contract.

Tips: "Check references. Look for a publicist based in California or New York (that is where the media is)."

N ○ CAMERON GRAY COMMUNICATIONS, 12101 Greenway Ct., Suite 101, Fairfax VA 22033. (703)725-9300. Fax: (703)832-0711. E-mail: cameron@camerongray.com. **Contact:** Cameron Gray. Estab. 2000; specifically with books since 2000.

● Prior to becoming an independent publicist, Ms. Gray was an assistant producer and guest coordinator with the *G. Gordon Liddy Show* for eight years.

Members: Cameron Gray (nonfiction, lifestyle, pop culture, political works).

Specializations: Nonfiction. **Interested in these nonfiction areas:** biography/autobiography; business; child guidance/parenting; computers/electronics; current affairs; education; government/politics/law; health/medicine; military/war; money/finance/economics; popular culture; psychology; science/technology; self-help/personal improvement; sociology; sports; true crime/investigative; women's issues/women's studies. Other types of clients include "anyone looking for affordable, broad radio exposure."

Services: Provides international publicity, if applicable, fax news releases, electronic news releases. Book tours include radio interviews, selected chat room events. Clients have appeared on *The G. Gordon Liddy Show, The Roger Hedgecock Show, Daybreak USA, Online Tonight,* and countless other radio shows. Media kit includes author's biography, testimonials, articles about author, basic information on book, sample interview questions.

○⚞ Cameron Gray Communications is "one of the nation's only publicity firms that specifically targets radio outlets, and radio sells the most books of any media."

How to Contact: Call, e-mail, or fax, or send letter with entire ms, outline/proposal. Responds in 1 week. Discards unwanted material. Obtains most new clients through recommendations from others. Contact after book's publication.

Clients: *Avoiding Mr. Wrong,* by Stephen Arterburn (Thomas Nelson Publishers); *Get Anyone To Do Anything,* by David Lieberman (St. Martin's Press). References and contact numbers available for potential clients.

Costs: Client charged monthly retainer ($2,000-4,000). Offers written contract.

N ◑ ◎ KSB PROMOTIONS, (Specializes: general lifestyle books), 55 Honey Creek NE, Ada MI 49301-9768. (616)676-0758. Fax: (616)676-0759. E-mail: ksbpromo@aol.com. **Contact:** Kate Bandos. Estab. 1988; specifically with books since 1988. Currently works with 20-40 clients; 25% of clients are new/first-time writers.

● Prior to becoming an independent publicist, Ms. Bandos was a PR director for several publishers.

Members: Kate Bandos (travel, cookbooks, at firm since 1988); Doug Bandos (radio/TV, at firm since 1989).

Specializations: Nonfiction, children's books. **Interested in these nonfiction areas:** child guidance/parenting; cooking/food/nutrition; health/medicine; travel; gardening; general lifestyle.

Services: Provides detailed outline of services provided, sends material to magazines/newspapers for reviews. Book tours include radio interviews, TV interviews, newspaper interviews, magazine interviews. Clients have appeared on *Good Morning America, CNN, Business News Network, Parent's Journal, New Attitudes* and others. Media kit includes author's biography, testimonials, articles about author, basic information on book, sample interview questions, book request information, recipes for cookbooks, other excerpts as appropriate. Helps writers obtain endorsements. Recent promotions included feathers sent in press kits and review copies of *Create a Life That Tickles Your Soul* (which featured a feather in the cover art); a loaf of dandelion bread was sent with *Dandelion Celebration: A Guide to Unexpected Cuisine* helped get a client on *Good Morning AM.*

○⚞ This company specializes in cookbooks, travel guides, parenting books, and other general lifestyle books. "Our specialty has allowed us to build relationships with key media in these areas. We limit ourselves to those clients we can personally help."

How to Contact: Call or e-mail. Responds in 2 weeks. Returns unwanted material only with SASE. Obtains most new clients through recommendations from others, conferences, listings in books on publishing. Contact 6-8 months prior to book's publication. Can do limited PR after book's publication.

Clients: *Quick & Healthy Recipes & Ideas,* by Brenda Ponichtera (ScaleDown Publications); *Along Interstate 75,* by Dave Hunter (Mile Oak Publishing). Other clients include Willow Creek Press, PassPorter, World Leisure Corp. References and contact numbers available for potential clients.

Costs: Client charged per service fee ($500 minimum). Works with clients on marketing budget. "Total of contracted services is divided into monthly payments." Offers written contract. 30-day notice must be given to terminate contract.

Writers' Conferences: PMA University (Chicago, May 29-31); BookExpo America (Chicago, June 1-3).

Tips: "Find a publicist who has done a lot with books in the same area of interest since they know the key media, etc."

N ◑ MARKETABILITY, INC., 813A 14th St., Golden CO 80401. (303)279-4349. Fax: (303)279-7950. E-mail: twist@marketability.com. Website: www.marketability.com. **Contact:** Kim Dushinski; Tami DePalma. Estab. 1989; specifically with books since 1995. Currently works with 20 clients. 50% of clients are new/first-time authors.

MARKET UPDATE FROM *WRITER'S MARKET* Looking for advice for getting published, pubishing trends, information about the shifting writing marketplace? All are available free by subscribing to *Market Update From Writer's Market.* Our e-mail newsletter will deliver this invaluable information straight to your e-mailbox every two weeks absolutely free. Sign up at www.WritersMarket.com.

• Prior to becoming independent publicists, Ms. Dushinski and Ms. DePalma were in marketing/public relations for all types of companies.

Members: Tami DePalma, partner (creative PR, at firm since 1993); Kim Dushinski, partner (strategic PR, at firm since 1989); Bradley James (lifestyle, gay/lesbian, at firm since 1998); Malea Melis (women, history, at firm since 1999).

Specializations: Nonfiction. **Interested in these nonfiction areas:** business; child guidance/parenting; cooking/food/nutrition; crafts/hobbies; gay/lesbian issues; health/medicine; history; how-to; interior design/decorating; money/finance/economics; self-help/personal improvement; travel; women's issues/women's studies. Other types of clients include publishers.

Services: Provides detailed outline of services provided, fax news releases, electronic news release, material to magazines/newspapers for reviews. Book tours include radio interviews, TV interviews, newspaper interviews, magazine interviews. Media kit includes author's biography, basic information on book, professional photos, sample interview questions, book request information, other items as needed such as creative packaging/gimmicks. Helps writer obtain endorsements.

> **O—** "Not only can we be hired to do publicity, we also offer MAXIMUM EXPOSURE Marketing System—a book marketing training program for publishers and authors."

How to Contact: Call, e-mail or fax. Responds in 3 weeks. Returns materials only with SASE. Obtains most new clients through recommendations from others. Contact 6 months prior to book's publication or anytime after book's publication.

Clients: References and contact numbers available for potential clients.

Costs: Charges clients per service fee ($2,000-3,000/monthly payment for 9-12 campaigns). "We have prices for each service we do and then we divide the total into monthly payments." Works with clients on marketing budget. Offers written contract. "We work on 9-12 month contracts typically." 30-day or for cause notice must be given to terminate contract.

Tips: "Keep in mind that whether you are published by a publisher or independently publish your work, you will have to do marketing if you want your work to sell. We can help you do this marketing."

N ☉ MEDIA MASTERS PUBLICITY, 1957 Trafalger Dr., Romeoville IL 60446. (815)254-7383. Fax: (815)254-7357. E-mail: tracey@mmpublicity.com. Website: www.mmpublicity.com. **Contact:** Tracey Daniels. Estab. 1998. Currently works with 10 clients. 10% of clients are new/first-time writers.

• Prior to becoming an independent publicist, Ms. Daniels worked in English Education—middle school and high school.

Members: Tracy Defina (new authors, education, at firm since 1999).

Specializations: Children's books, nonfiction. **Interested in these nonfiction areas:** biography/autobiography; child guidance/parenting; cooking/food/nutrition; education; how-to; juvenile nonfiction; self-help/personal improvement; young adult. **Interested in these fiction areas:** juvenile; picture book; young adult. Other types of clients include publishers.

Services: Provides detailed outline of services provided, fax news releases, electronic news release, material to magazines/newspapers for reviews, brochures, website assistance, website publicity. Book tours include bookstores, specialty stores, radio interviews, TV interviews, newspaper interviews, magazine interviews, schools. Clients have appeared on *CNN, Talk America*, CBS, ABC, VOA, *USA Radio Network*, *AP Radio Network*, *20/20*. "Each media kit varies depending on focus, client needs and budget." Helps writer obtain endorsements. "For a picture book called *Bee Keepers*, we promoted a Pennsylvania author and Pennsylvania publisher to Pennsylvania bookstores (as well as national outlets) by sending 'Made-in-Pennsylvania' honey along with the book."

> **O—** "I have over eight years of book publicity experience. My company delivers 'publicity with personality'—we go beyond just covering the basics."

How to Contact: E-mail or send letter with outline/proposal and sample chapters. Responds in 2 weeks. Returns materials only with SASE. Obtains most new clients through recommendations from others. Contact 3 months prior to book's publication.

Clients: Clients include Fitzhenry & Whiteside Children's Books, HarperCollins Children's Books, Choutte, Chicago Review Press, Boyds Mills Press, Element Books plus individual authors. Reference and contact numbers available for potential clients.

Costs: Charges for services depend on client's needs and budget. Offers written contract. 30-day notice must be given to terminate contract.

Writers' Conferences: BEA, ALA.

N ☉ PHENIX & PHENIX LITERARY PUBLICISTS, INC., 4412 Spicewood Springs, Suite 102, Austin TX 78759. (512)478-2028. Fax: (512)478-2117. E-mail: info@bookpros.com. Website: www.bookpros.com. **Contact:** Marika Flatt. Estab. 1994; specifically with books since 1994. Currently works with 15 clients. 50% of clients are new/first-time writers.

Members: Marika Flatt (director of media relations, at firm since 1997); Andrew Berzanskis (tour media, at firm since 1999); Leann Phenix (CEO/marketing, at firm since 1994); Jill Burpo (senior publicist); Elaine Froelich (tour coordinator).

Specializations: Nonfiction, fiction, children's books, academic, coffee table books, biographies. **Interested in these nonfiction areas:** animals; biography/autobiography; business; child guidance/parenting; computers/electronics; current affairs; health/medicine; money/finance/economics; multicultural; religious/inspirational; self-help/personal improvement; sports; travel; true crime/investigative; women's issues/women's studies; young adult. **Interested in these fiction areas:** action/adventure; confessional; contemporary issues; detective/police/crime; family saga; historical; humor/satire; multicultural; mystery/suspense; regional; religious/inspirational; sports; young adult. Other types of clients include publishers.

Services: Provides detailed outline of services provided, media training, fax news releases, electronic news release, material to magazines/newspapers for reviews, brochures, website publicity. Book tours include bookstores, specialty stores, radio interviews, TV interviews, newspaper interviews, magazine interviews. Clients have appeared on *Oprah*, CNN, CNBC, *Fox News Network, Leeza, Montel, Good Morning America, Talk America Radio Network, Business News Network, Westwood One Radio Network, UPI Radio Network*. Media kit includes author's biography, testimonials, articles about author, basic information on book, professional photos, sample interview questions, book request information, press releases, excerpts. Recent promotions included video press releases, mystery contest, online publicity campaigns, creative angles for fiction positioning.

○─ This company has a first 30-day strategy (develop strategy, positioning, press materials), guaranteed media exposure rates, and created 4 bestsellers in 1999.

How to Contact: Call, e-mail, fax or send letter with entire ms. Responds in 5 days. Discards unwanted material. Obtains most new clients through recommendations from others, conferences, website. Contact 2-4 months prior to book's publication or after book's publication.

Clients: *Kiss of God*, by Marshall Ball (Health Communications); *True Women/Hill Country*, by Janice Woods Windle (Longstreet Press); *Wizard of Ads*, by Roy Williams (Bard Press); *Faith on Trial*, by Pamela Ewen (Broadman & Holman). Other clients include Dr. Ivan Misner, Lisa Shaw-Brawley, Michele O'Donnell, Patrick Seaman (Timberwolf Press), Continuum Press. References and contact number available for potential clients.

Costs: Charges clients per placement basis ($100-5,000); per service fee ($500-3,000); monthly retainer ($2,500-6,500). Works with clients on a marketing budget. Offers written contract binding for 4-6 months.

Writers' Conferences: Craft of Writing (Denton, TX).

Tips: "Find a publicist that will offer a guarantee. Educate yourself on the book/publicity process."

N ◎ RAAB ASSOCIATES, (Specialized: children's books, parenting), 345 Millwood Rd., Chappaqua NY 10514. (914)241-2117. Fax: (914)241-0050. E-mail: info@raabassociates.com. Website: www.raabassociates.com. **Contact:** Susan Salzman Raab. Estab. 1986; specifically with books since 1986. Currently works with 10 clients. 1% of clients are new/first-time writers.

● Prior to becoming an independent publicist, Ms. Salzman Raab worked on staff at major publishing houses in the children's book industry.

Members: Chip Edmonston (publicist, at firm since 2000); Susanna Reich (associate, at firm since 2000); Susan Salzman Raab (publisher, at firm since 1986).

Specializations: Children's books, parenting books. **Interested in these nonfiction areas:** juvenile nonfiction, young adult, parenting. **Interested in these fiction areas:** juvenile, picture book, young adult, parenting. Other types of clients include publishers, toy companies, audio companies.

Services: Provides detailed outline of services provided; market research; material to magazines/newspapers for review; website assistance; website development and extensive online publicity. Book tours include bookstores, specialty stores, radio interviews, TV interviews, newspaper interviews, magazine interviews, schools, libraries. Can also assist in coordinating travel plans. Clients have appeared on NPR, CNN, C-Span, Radio-Disney, PRI. Media kit includes author's biography, testimonials, articles about author, basic information on book, sample interview questions, book request information. Helps writer obtain endorsements.

○─ "We are the only PR agency to specialize in children's and parenting books."

How to Contact: Call or e-mail. Responds in 2 weeks. Returns materials only with SASE. Obtains most new clients through recommendations from others, conferences. Contact 4 months prior to book's publication.

Clients: Sometimes references and contact numbers available to potential clients (most often to publishers, rather than authors).

Costs: Clients charged per service fee. Offers written contract. 90-day notice must be given to terminate contract.

Writers' Conferences: Society of Children's Book Writers & Illustrators (New York National); Society of Children's Book Writers & Illustrators (Regional Meeting); Book Expo America (Chicago, May/June); American Library Association (Chicago, July); Bologna Bookfair (April).

N ◎ ROCKS-DEHART PUBLIC RELATIONS (BOOK PUBLICITY), 1015 2nd St., NE, Suite 211, Hickory NC 28601. (828)322-3111. Fax: (828)322-1839. E-mail: celiarocks@aol.com. Website: www.Rocks-DeHartPublicRelations.com. **Contact:** Celia Rocks. Estab. 1993; specifically with books since 1993. Currently works with 10 clients; 20% of clients are new/first-time writers.

TO LEARN MORE ABOUT THE PUBLISHING INDUSTRY, look for the helpful resources in **Books of Interest** and **Websites of Interest** listed in the back of this book.

• Prior to becoming a publicist, Ms. Rocks was a publicity specialist at Burson Marsteller.

Members: Dottie DeHart (principal, at firm since 1993); Leslie Ogle (copywriter, at firm since 1996); Megan Johnson (account executive, at firm since 1999).

Specializations: Nonfiction, children's books, business, lifestyle. **Interested in these nonfiction areas:** biography/autobiography; business; cooking/food/nutrition; current affairs; health/medicine; how-to; humor; popular culture; psychology; religious/inspirational; self-help/personal improvement; sociology; travel; women's issues/women's studies. Other types of clients include major publishing houses.

Services: Provides detailed outline of services provided. Book tours include bookstores, specialty stores, radio interviews, TV interviews, newspaper interviews, magazine interviews, speaking engagements, conferences, libraries, schools, universities. Clients have appeared on *ABC World News, Oprah* and others. Media kit includes author's biography, testimonials, articles about author, basic information on book, professional photos, sample interview questions, book request information, breakthrough plan materials, and "any other pieces that are helpful." Helps writers obtain endorsements. Recent promotions included "taking a book like *Fishing for Dummies* and sending gummy worms with packages."

☛ This company specializes in IDG "Dummies" Books, business, management, and lifestyle titles. "We are a highly creative firm that understands the best way to obtain maximum publicity."

How to Contact: Call or e-mail. Responds in 1 week. Obtains most new clients through recommendations from others. Contact 4-6 months prior to book's publication.

Clients: Clients include Prima Press, IDG, Dearborn, Incredible Internet Guides.

Costs: Client charged monthly retainer ($ 3,000-5,000). Works with clients on marketing budget. Offers written contract. 30-day notice must be given to terminate contract.

Tips: "We have a solid reputation for excellence and results."

ℕ ◑ ROYCE CARLTON, INC., 866 United Nations Plaza, Suite 587, New York, NY 10017. (212)335-7700. Fax: (212)888-8659. E-mail: info@roycecarlton.com. Website: www.roycecarlton.com. **Contact:** Carlton Sedgeley. Estab. 1968. Currently works with 50 clients.

• Royce Carlton, Inc. is a lecture agency and management firm that helps find events and conferences for their clients to attend as speakers.

Members: Carlton S. Sedgeley, president (at firm since 1968); Lucy Lepage, executive vice president (at firm since 1968); Helen Churko, vice president (at firm since 1984).

Specializations: Royce Carlton works with many different types of writers. Other clients include celebrities, editors.

Services: Provides "full service for all our clients to lecture."

☛ "We are the only lecture agency representing all our clients exclusively."

How to Contact: Call, e-mail, or fax. Discards unwanted material. Obtains most new clients through recommendations from others, or initial contact on our part.

Clients: *Tuesday with Morrie*, by Mitch Albom; *House Made of Dawn*, by N. Scott Momaday. Other clients include Joan Rivers, Elaine Pagels, Walter Mosley. References and contact numbers available for potential clients.

Costs: Client charged per placement basis; commission. Offers written contract. 30-day notice must be given to terminate contract.

ℕ ◑ WORLD CLASS SPEAKERS & ENTERTAINERS, 28025 Dorothy Dr., Suite 202, Aqoura Hills CA 91301. (818)991-5400. Fax: (818)991-2226. E-mail: info@speak.com. Website: www.speak.com. **Contact:** Joseph I. Kessler. Estab. 1965.

Specializations: Nonfiction, academic. **Interested in these nonfiction areas:** business; humor; money/finance/economics; psychology; science/technology; self-help/personal improvement; sociology; sports; women's issues/women's studies; high profile/famous writers. Other types of clients include experts in all fields.

Services: Provides market research, send material to magazines/newspapers for reviews, brochures, website publicity. Book tours include radio interviews, TV interviews, newspaper interviews, magazine interviews, speaking engagements, conferences, universities. Assists in coordinating travel plans. Media kits include author's biography, testimonials, articles about author, professional photos. Helps writer obtain endorsements.

How to Contact: Call, e-mail or fax. Responds in 1 week. Discards unwanted materials. Obtains most new clients through recommendations from others. Contact prior to book's publication.

Costs: Charges clients per placement basis ($1,500 minimum); 30% commission. Works with clients on marketing budget. Offers written contract. 60-90 day notice must be given to terminate contract.

Power Consultations: Ten Minutes to Representation

BY JILLIAN MANUS

You've plunked down a few hundred dollars, traveled more than a few hundred miles, and now you're at the writers' conference you've been looking forward to for months. And—as is the case at most conferences—part of your experience will be a personal consultation with an agent. The ultimate goal, of course, is to get an agent to offer you representation. If you're not ready for an agent yet, you'll still be looking for advice on how to shape your material into something that will be ready to sell.

Usually consultations with agents are fairly brief: often only ten minutes, rarely more than fifteen. Obviously, you don't want to go in and spend the first half of those precious minutes shuffling through your papers and collecting your thoughts. At dozens of conferences, I have talked to literally hundreds of writers and I have a pretty good idea of what works from the agent's point of view. It might be presumptuous to say I've seen it all, but I've seen my share: Not long ago a woman who came in for a consultation with me was so anxious, she actually fainted onto the floor!

There's no need to be that scared of a close encounter with an agent. Instead, armed with the following tips, you can make the most of the opportunities the meeting provides and even come away with an agency contract. It happens! So, how do you make the most of your time?

Come prepared with a pitch

Your pitch is the heart of your agent consultation. It is three to five sentences that distill the concept of your book into a concise and compelling form. Its purpose is to inform and to intrigue the agent. After the briefest introduction, launch your consultation with your pitch. If you're a little nervous, you can read it aloud from an index card. If you're extremely nervous, you can hand the (legibly printed) index card to the agents to read themselves.

Whether your project is fiction or nonfiction, take as much time as you need to get your pitch perfect. Ask for help from colleagues in your writing group; practice with them. If, after some effort, you really can't come up with a pithy pitch, then consider that your concept (for nonfiction) or your plot (for fiction) might need work. Not only will the perfect pitch ease your way into selling your project to an agent (either on a cover letter or in a consultation), but the agent can then turn around and use your pitch to sell your book to an editor, who will use it to sell the book to her marketing and subsidiary rights departments. A modified form might even end up on the book jacket to sell the book to readers. Talk about a good investment of your time!

The nonfiction pitch

The art and craft of writing a pitch could take up a whole chapter in a book, but the basics are fairly simple. For nonfiction, your pitch should contain four elements: the audience for your

JILLIAN WILKENS MANUS *is President of Manus & Associates Literary Agency and Director of the West Coast offices. Manus & Associates is a national firm representing independent authors for over fifteen years from offices in both New York and in the San Francisco Bay area. Manus is a frequent lecturer and author on writing and the media industry. The tremendous scope of her background provides her with the expertise to both edit and properly assess many types of material.*

Get the 2002 EDITION

at this year's price!

You already know an agent can be the key to selling your work. But, how do you know when you're ready to sign on with one? And, how do you select an agent that's right for you? To make such crucial decisions you need the most up-to-date information on the agents out there and what they can offer you. That's exactly what you'll find in *Guide to Literary Agents*.

Through this special offer, you can get a jump on next year today! If you order now, you'll get the *2002 Guide to Literary Agents* at the 2001 price—just $21.99—no matter how much the regular price may increase!

2002 Guide to Literary Agents will be published and ready for shipment in January 2002.

More books to help you write & sell your work

☐ **Yes!** I want the most current edition of *Guide to Literary Agents*. Please send me the 2002 edition at the 2001 price—$21.99. (NOTE: *2002 Guide to Literary Agents* will be ready for shipment in January 2002.) #10758

Additional books from the back of this card:

Book	Price
#	$
#	$
#	$
#	$
Subtotal	$

*Add $3.95 postage and handling for one book; $1.95 for each additional book.

Postage & Handling	$

Payment must accompany order. Ohioans add 6% sales tax. Canadians add 7% GST.

Total	$

VISA/MasterCard orders call TOLL FREE 1-800-289-0963 or FAX 1-888-590-4082

☐ Payment enclosed $_____ (or)

Charge my: ☐ Visa ☐ MasterCard Exp._____

Account #_____

Signature_____

Name_____

Address_____

City_____

State/Prov._____ Zip/PC _____

30-Day Money Back Guarantee on every book you buy!

6637

Mail to: Writer's Digest Books • 1507 Dana Avenue • Cincinnati, OH 45207
www.writersdigest.com

Write Better & Sell More
with help from these Writer's Digest Books!

Fiction Writer's Brainstormer
Make your writing richer, livelier and more imaginative with this liberating guide. It supplies clear instruction and provocative brain-teasers that help get your brain going, stimulate the creative flow, and find new and unusual ways of creating professional, salable works.
#10691/#18.99/256p/hc

The Writer's Digest Flip Dictionary
You know what you want to say but can't think of the word. You can describe what you're thinking but you don't know the name for it. If you have a general word in mind but need a more specific term, then *The Writer's Digest Flip Dictionary* is your remedy!
#10690/$24.99/720p/hc

Writer's Online Marketplace
Get essential information for online queries, rights and markets. This guide features more than 250 paying markets, plus techniques for succeeding in the online writing world.
#10697/$17.99/240p/pb

Guerrilla Marketing for Writers
Packed with more than 100 low-cost weapons to help you sell your work, this guide will show you how to network, promote and plug your way to publishing success.
#10667/$14.99/224p/pb

The Insider's Guide to Getting an Agent
Getting an agent is sometimes crucial to getting published. But, how do you locate the one that's right for you? This New York literary agent offers advice, sample queries and proposals that provide the guidance you need to find an agent that suits your needs.
#10630/$16.99/240p/pb

Formatting & Submitting Your Manuscript
Learn how to prepare and present your novels, personal essays, articles and proposals, screenplays and scripts, short stories, poetry, children's books, greeting cards, and more. Successful agents and editors share their formatting do's and don'ts using dozens of visual samples.
#10618/$18.99/208p/pb

Books are available at your local bookstore, or directly from the publisher using the order card on the reverse.

book, their need for your book, your authority to write it, and what distinguishes it from other books on the market. These four elements should be summarized in one sentence each.

Here is the pitch for Stephen R. Covey's *The Seven Habits of Highly Effective People*: "All the people you know have calendars because they want to be organized and in control of their lives." That's the audience for the book: everyone who has a calendar, which is a large segment of the population. "So all those people need to read Covey's book about how to identify their priorities and accomplish their goals, both short and long-term, by keeping them in sight every day." That is the audience's need for the book: to accomplish its personal goals. "Covey has distilled years of seminars and personal experiences into seven easy-to-follow steps that can radically change your life into one that is calmer, and more fulfilling." This final sentence both establishes the author's authority to write the book and sets it apart from others already written.

The platform

If you are pitching nonfiction, you should also come prepared to tell the agent about your "platform." Platform is the existing audience for your proposed book that comes from your visibility or access to readers. If you are writing a cookbook, you have a natural platform if you are a chef in a restaurant. If you are writing a book about relationships, one possible platform would be if you were a psychologist who runs workshops for couples.

The author's platform is an increasingly large part—at least 50 percent—of the agent's sell to the publisher. Don't panic; you don't have to be famous to sell a nonfiction book proposal. What you **do** need to do is to demonstrate that you are savvy about the marketplace and willing to work to promote your book. Do **not** tell the agent, "Well, the publisher should put me on *Oprah* to get the ball rolling." (You'd be amazed how often we hear that phrase.) Instead, talk about mailing lists you have access to, magazine articles you've published on your topic, universities with which you are affiliated, and connections you have with well-known people who can give you endorsements for your book. If you do all this legwork, you won't need *Oprah*.

The fiction pitch

For fiction, your platform is less crucial, although any marketing ideas you have will only be to your advantage. The fiction pitch is also structured differently, but its pithiness is no less important. When you go to a conference, go with the mind-set not of a suffering artist but of a professional with a product to sell. You are not going to discuss the motives of your characters in great detail—nor will you discuss your motives in writing the book. Save that for your mom and your shrink.

The fiction pitch has three elements: setup, hook, and resolution. "When feisty Rosie Threathaway inherits a shack on a remote tip of Great Barrier Island, she decides it is time to begin a new life." This is the setup.

"Little does she know that her only two neighbors are two misanthropic men." The hook.

"The three of them become entangled in an intricate emotional web that forces all of them eventually to come to terms with themselves and the encroaching world." This is the resolution.

This was the pitch I used to sell *Sole Survivor*, by Derek Hansen, to Michael Korda at Simon & Schuster, and then to the movie industry for $1.2 million.

Pitch one project with passion

You will not impress an agent by beginning, "I'm working on four/five/seventeen projects, which one would you like to hear about?" You will sound like a dilettante. Instead, choose in advance the project you think is the most viable and is the closest to being ready. Pitch it well and passionately. The agent will ask questions and make suggestions, and the discussion will go from there.

Time permitting, you can mention that you have future projects in mind, and pitch them as well. This gentle reframing presents you as a serious writer who is looking ahead.

Listen open-mindedly

Your meetings with agents may be brief, but during that time you have their undivided attention. They are there because they want to help you as a writer, whether or not they plan to offer you representation. So it is to your benefit to listen to what the agents have to say. A common trap writers fall into, instead, is to argue: "You just don't understand what I'm trying to do," or, "If you'd read more of my pages you wouldn't say that."

My favorite example of closed-mindedness comes from a consultation in which a young man pitched his book, *100 Ways to Kill a Cat*. At first I assumed it was a humor book—but it turned out that he was serious. When I ventured that there might not be a big audience for a serious book about killing animals (and breaking the law in the process), he replied coldly, "You obviously don't hate cats as much as most people." This argumentativeness simply wastes everyone's time. If an agent doesn't want to sell your book the way you've written it, you are not going to change her mind. Meanwhile, you may miss an opportunity to hear helpful advice on how to make the project more marketable. You are free to disagree with, ignore, or even (later, in private) make fun of what agents have to say. But during the consultation, give them the benefit of the doubt.

Research your agent

You may not know with whom your consultation will be before the conference begins but, barring last-minute substitutions, you will know in advance which agents are attending the conference. Look each one up in this book or any other source of information on agents. Check out their websites, if they have them. In the process you'll find the names of recent titles they've sold; browse through those books at the library or bookstore. An agent can only be flattered that you're familiar with her client list, but the purpose isn't to butter her up: the purpose is to present your work to your best advantage. For example, if you do have more than one pitchable project, knowing your agent's tastes will help you decide which one to discuss. This research is especially important at a conference where there are a multitude of agents from which to choose. You want to find the one who handles your type of book.

Accentuate the positive; eliminate the negative

Your consultation won't always lead immediately to representation. Perhaps your idea needs fleshing out, or perhaps you don't end up with an agent who is particularly right for you.

Please don't regard this as a failure or even as a setback. Instead, look at it as the next necessary step. If the agent passes on your book, she may also give you the information you need to take it to the next level. Ask the agent if she'd be interested in seeing a later version of your work. If she says yes, then take her up on the offer. If she says no, ask her if she'd like to recommend someone else who would be interested. If she can't, then you can still ask yourself, what can I learn from this to make my work more salable? If the agent hasn't given a specific answer to that question, ask her!

In one case, I met with a writer four times over a period of four years. Nothing he pitched was quite right for me. But I liked his work and I liked him, and I was always happy to see him, just as I'm always happy to see any conference participant return. Finally, we clicked on a project, and then I closed a two-book hardcover deal for him within a month. Behind most overnight successes are those four years of pitches. Over the years, in fact, I've watched many writers keep coming back to the same and to different conferences. Those same writers keep pitching in those consultations. Of the ones who keep coming back, a very high percentage eventually get agents and publish books. You can, too. With these tips in mind, it might happen sooner rather than later. Good luck!

Writers' Conferences

Attending a writers' conference that includes agents gives you the opportunity to listen and learn more about what agents do, as well as the chance to show an agent your work. Ideally, a conference should include a panel or two with a number of agents to give writers a sense of the variety of personalities and tastes of different agents.

Not all agents are alike: some are more personable and sometimes you simply click better with one agent over another. When only one agent attends a conference there is tendency for every writer at that conference to think, "Ah, this is the agent I've been looking for!" When the number of agents attending is larger, you have a wider group from which to choose and you may have less competition for the agent's time.

Besides including panels of agents discussing what representation means and how to go about securing it, many of these gatherings also include time, either scheduled or impromptu, to meet briefly with an agent to discuss your work.

You may interest agents by meeting them in person and discussing your work. If they're impressed, they will invite you to submit a query, a proposal, a few sample chapters, or possibly your entire manuscript. Some conferences even arrange for agents to review manuscripts in advance and schedule one-on-one sessions where you can receive specific feedback or advice on your work. Such meetings often cost a small fee, but the input you receive is usually worth the price. For helpful hints on how to make the most of meetings with agents, see "Power Consultations: Ten Minutes to Representation," by agent Jillian Manus on page 330. Ask writers who attend conferences and they'll tell you that at the very least you'll walk away with more knowledge than you came with. At the very best, you'll receive an invitation to send an agent your material!

FINDING A CONFERENCE

Many writers try to make it to at least one conference a year, but cost and location can count as much as subject matter when determining which conference to attend. There are conferences in almost every state and province that can provide answers to your questions about writing and the publishing industry. Conferences also connect you with a community of other writers. Such connections help you learn about the pros and cons of different agents writers have worked with, and give you a renewed sense of purpose and direction in your own writing.

When reading through this section, keep in mind the following information to help you pick the best conference for your needs:

Quick Reference Icons

At the beginning of some listings, you will find one or more of the following symbols for quick identification of features particular to that listing.

N: Conference new to this edition.

☑ Change in address, contact information, phone number or e-mail address from last year's edition.

⬛ Canadian conference.

REGION   COST   SIZE   FOCUS

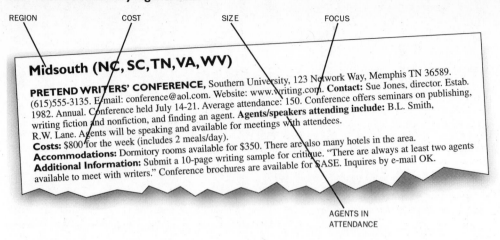

Midsouth (NC, SC, TN, VA, WV)

PRETEND WRITERS' CONFERENCE, Southern University, 123 Network Way, Memphis TN 36589. (615)555-3135. E-mail: conference@aol.com. Website: www.writing.com. **Contact:** Sue Jones, director. Estab. 1982. Annual. Conference held July 14-21. Average attendance: 150. Conference offers seminars on publishing, writing fiction and nonfiction, and finding an agent. **Agents/speakers attending include:** B.L. Smith, R.W. Lane. Agents will be speaking and available for meetings with attendees.
Costs: $800 for the week (includes 2 meals/day).
Accommodations: Dormitory rooms available for $350. There are also many hotels in the area.
Additional Information: Submit a 10-page writing sample for critique. "There are always at least two agents available to meet with writers." Conference brochures are available for SASE. Inquires by e-mail OK.

AGENTS IN
ATTENDANCE

REGIONS

To make it easier for you to find a conference close to home—or to find one in an exotic locale to fit into your vacation plans—we've separated this section into geographical regions. The regions are as follows:

Northeast (pages 335-338): Connecticut, Maine, Massachusetts, New Hampshire, New York, Rhode Island, Vermont.
Midatlantic (pages 338-339): Washington DC, Delaware, Maryland, New Jersey, Pennsylvania.
Midsouth (pages 340-341): North Carolina, South Carolina, Tennessee, Virginia, West Virginia.
Southeast (pages 341-342): Alabama, Arkansas, Florida, Georgia, Louisiana, Mississippi, Puerto Rico.
Midwest (pages 342-344): Illinois, Indiana, Kentucky, Michigan, Ohio.
North Central (pages 344-345): Iowa, Minnesota, Nebraska, North Dakota, South Dakota, Wisconsin.
South Central (pages 345-348): Colorado, Kansas, Missouri, New Mexico, Oklahoma, Texas.
West (pages 349-355): Arizona, California, Hawaii, Nevada, Utah.
Northwest (pages 355-357): Alaska, Idaho, Montana, Oregon, Washington, Wyoming.
Canada (pages 357-358).

SUBHEADS

Each listing is divided into subheads to make locating specific information easier. In the first section, you'll find contact information for each conference. Also given are conference dates, specific focus, and size. If a conference is small, you may receive more individual attention from speakers. If it is large, there may be a greater number and variety of agents in attendance. Finally, names of agents who will be speaking or have spoken in the past are listed along with details about their availability during the conference. Calling a conference director to verify the names of agents in attendance is always a good idea.
Costs: Looking at the price of seminars, plus room and board, may help writers on a tight budget narrow their choices.
Accommodations: Here conferences list overnight accommodation and travel information. Often conferences held in hotels will reserve rooms at a discount price and may provide a shuttle bus to and from the local airport.
Additional Information: A range of features are given here, including information on contests, individual meetings, and the availability of brochures.

WRITERS' CONFERENCES

Northeast (CT, MA, ME, NH, NY, RI, VT)

BREAD LOAF WRITERS' CONFERENCE, Middlebury College, Middlebury VT 05753. (802)443-5286. Fax: (802)443-2087. E-mail: blwc@middlebury.edu. Website: www.middlebury.edu/~blwc. **Contact:** Carol Knauss, administrative coordinator. Estab. 1926. Annual. Conference held in late August. Conference duration: 11 days. Average attendance: 230. For fiction, nonfiction and poetry. Held at the summer campus in Ripton, Vermont (belongs to Middlebury College).
Costs: $1,780 (includes room/board) (2000).
Accommodations: Accommodations are at Ripton.

✅ **FEMINIST WOMEN'S WRITING WORKSHOPS, INC.**, P.O. Box 6583, Ithaca NY 14851. E-mail: FW3@st ny.rr.com. **Contact:** Margo Gumosky, director. Estab. 1975. Workshop held every summer. Workshop duration: 8 days. Average attendance: 30-45 women writers. "Workshops provide a women-centered community for writers of all levels and genres, including fiction, nonfiction, poetry, and playwriting." Workshops are held on the campuses of Hobart/William Smith Colleges in Geneva, NY. **Previous agents/speakers have included:** Deborah Tall; Dorothy Allison, National Book Award Finalist for *Bastard Out of Carolina*; and Ruth Stone, author of *Second-Hand Coat, Who Is The Widow's Muse?* and *Simplicity*.
Costs: $550 for tuition, room, board.
Accommodations: Private room and 3 meals included in fee. Geneva is approximately mid-way between Rochester and Syracuse. College facilities such as pool, tennis courts and library are available.
Additional Information: FWWW invites all interests. "Writers may submit manuscripts up to 10 pages with application." Brochures/guidelines available for SASE.

✅ **HIGHLIGHTS FOUNDATION WRITERS WORKSHOP AT CHAUTAUQUA**, Dept. NM, 814 Court St., Honesdale PA 18431. (570)253-1192. Fax: (570)253-0179. E-mail: lori@highlightsfoundation.org. **Contact:** Kent Brown, executive director. Estab. 1985. Annual. Workshop held July 14-21, 2001. Average attendance: 100. "Writer workshops geared toward those who write for children—beginner, intermediate, advanced levels. Small group workshops, one-to-one interaction between faculty and participants plus panel sessions, lectures and large group meetings. Workshop site is the picturesque community of Chautauqua, New York." Classes offered include "Children's Interests," "Writing Dialogue," "Outline for the Novel," "Conflict and Developing Plot." **Previous agents/speakers have included:** Eve Bunting, James Cross Giblin, Walter Dean Myers, Jane Yolen, Patricia Gauch, Jerry Spinelli, Joy Cowley and Ed Young.
Accommodations: "We coordinate ground transportation to and from airports, trains and bus stations in the Erie, PA and Jamestown/Buffalo, NY area. We also coordinate accommodations for conference attendees."
Additional Information: "We offer the opportunity for attendees to submit a manuscript for review at the conference." Workshop brochures/guidelines are available after January for SASE. Inquiries by fax OK.

✅ **HOFSTRA UNIVERSITY SUMMER WRITERS' CONFERENCE**, 250 Hofstra University, UCCE, Hempstead NY 11549-1090. (516)463-5016. Fax: (516)463-4833. E-mail: uccelibarts@hofstra.edu. Website: www.hofstra.edu (under "Continuing Learner," there are details on dates, faculty, general description, tuition). **Contact:** Kenneth Henwood, director, Liberal Arts Studies. Estab. 1972. Annual (every summer, starting week after July 4). Conference held July 9 to July 20, 2001. Average attendance: 65. Conference offers workshops in short fiction, nonfiction, poetry, juvenile fiction, stage/screenwriting and, on occasion, one other genre such as detective fiction or science fiction. Workshops in prose and poetry for high school student writers are also offered. Site is the university campus, a suburban setting, 25 miles from NYC. **Previous agent/speakers have incuded:** Oscar Hijuelos, Robert Olen Butler, Hilma and Meg Wolitzer, Budd Schulberg and Cynthia Ozick. Agents will be speaking and available for meetings with attendees.
Costs: Non-credit (2 meals, no room): approximately $400 per workshop or $625 for two workshops. Credit: Approximately $1,100/workshop (2 credits) and $2,100/workshop (4 credits), graduate and undergraduate.
Accommodations: Free bus operates between Hempstead Train Station and campus for those commuting from NYC. Dormitory rooms are available for approximately $350 for the 2 week conference. Those who request area hotels will receive a list. Hotels are approximately $75 and above/night.
Additional Information: "All workshops include critiquing. Each participant is given one-on-one time for a half hour with workshop leader. We submit work to the Shaw Guides Contest and other writers' conferences and retreats contests when appropriate."

IWWG MEET THE AUTHORS, AGENTS AND EDITORS: THE BIG APPLE WORKSHOPS, % International Women's Writing Guild, P.O. Box 810, Gracie Station, New York NY 10028-0082. (212)737-7536. Fax: (212)737-9469. E-mail: iwwg@iwwg.com. Website: www.iwwg.com. **Contact:** Hannelore Hahn, executive director. Estab. 1980. Conferences held April 21-22, 2001 and October 14-15, 2000. Average attendance: 200. Workshops to promote creative writing and professional success. Held at the City Athletic Club of New York, mid-town New York City. **Previous agents/speakers have included:** Meredith Bernstein and Rita Rosenkranz. Sunday afternoon openhouse with agents and editors. Agents will be speaking and available for meetings with attendees.

Costs: $110 for members for the weekend; $130 for nonmembers for the weekend.

Accommodations: Information on transportation arrangements and overnight accommodations made available.

Additional Information: Workshop brochures/guidelines are available for SASE. Inquires by fax and e-mail OK. "Many contacts have been made between agents and authors over the years."

IWWG SUMMER CONFERENCE, % International Women's Writing Guild, P.O. Box 810, Gracie Station, New York NY 10028-0082. (212)737-7536. Fax: (212)737-9469. E-mail: dirhahn@aol.com. Website: www.iwwg.com. **Contact:** Hannelore Hahn, executive director. Estab. 1977. 24th Annual. Conference held from August 10-17, 2000. Average attendance: 500, including international attendees. Conference to promote writing in all genres, personal growth and professional success. Conference is held "on the tranquil campus of Skidmore College in Saratoga Springs, NY, where the serene Hudson Valley meets the North Country of the Adirondacks." Seventy-five different workshops are offered every day. Theme: "Writing Towards Personal and Professional Growth."

Costs: $850 for week-long program with room and board. $400 for week-long program for commuters.

Accommodations: Transportation by air to Albany, New York, or Amtrak train available from New York City. Conference attendees stay on campus.

Additional Information: Features "lots of critiquing sessions and networking." Conference brochures/guidelines available for SASE. Inquires by fax and e-mail OK.

MANHATTANVILLE SUMMER WRITERS' WEEK, 2900 Purchase St., Purchase NY 10577-0940. (914)694-3425. Fax: (914)694-3488. E-mail: rdowd@mville.edu. Website: www.mville.edu. **Contact:** Ruth Dowd, RSCJ, dean, graduate and professional studies. Estab. 1983. Annually. Conference held June 25-29, 2001. Conference duration: 5 days. Average attendance: 100. Workshops in fiction, short fiction, creative nonfiction, poetry, children's/young adult literature. Held at suburban college campus 30 miles from New York City. Workshop sessions are held in a 19th century Norman Castle which serves as the college's administration building. **Previous agents/speakers have included:** Michael Carlisle (Carlisle & Company), Tracey Adams and Dorothy Markinko (MacIntosh & Otis). Agents will be speaking and available for meetings with attendees.

Costs: For noncredit: $560 (includes all workshops, readings, special lecture). Program may also be taken for graduate credit. Participants may purchase meals in the college cafeteria or cafe.

Accommodations: A list of hotels in the area is available upon request. Overnight accommodations are available in the college residence halls for $25/night.

Additional Information: Brochures available for SASE or on website by end of February. Inquiries by e-mail and fax OK.

NEW ENGLAND WRITERS CONFERENCE, Box 483, Windsor VT 05089-0483. (802)674-2315. Fax: (802)674-5503. E-mail: newvtpoet@aol.com. Website: www.hometown.aol.com/newvtpoet/myhomepage/profile/html. **Contact:** Dr. Frank and Susan Anthony, co-directors. Estab. 1986. Annually. Conference held July 21, 2001. Conference duration: 1 day. Average attendance: 120. Held at The Grace-Outreach building 1 mile from Dartmouth campus. 2001 theme: "Diversity Defines Direction," and panels on agents, children's publishing, fiction, nonfiction, and poetry. **Previous agents/speakers have included:** John Talbot Agency, Dana Gioia, Wesley McNair, Tim Parrish.

Costs: $10 (includes workshop sessions, open readings, light lunch, writers' panels and door prizes).

Accommodations: "Hotel list can be made available. There are many hotels in the area."

Additional Information: "This, our 13th conference, continues our attempt to have a truly affordable writers conference that has as much as most 3-4 day events." Brochures available for SASE or on website. Inquiries by e-mail and fax OK.

THE PERIPATETIC WRITING WORKSHOP, INC., P.O. Box 299, Mount Tremper NY 12457. (212)924-0781. E-mail: peripateticrodigy.net. Website: http://pages.prodigy.net/peripatetic. Estab. 1991. Annual and ongoing through the year. Summer conference held in June; two ongoing conferences held throughout the year. Summer conference duration: 1-2 weeks. Average attendance: 14. Fiction, nonfiction, short story collections. Conference held often at Byrdcliffe Artist Colony in Woodstock, NY. In 2001, conference held in Ireland. "In 2000, the publishing panel centered

FOR EXPLANATIONS OF THESE SYMBOLS,
SEE THE INSIDE FRONT AND BACK COVERS OF THIS BOOK

on changes in publishing brought about by the Internet." **Previous agents/speakers have included:** Ann Rittenberg (agent, Ann Rittenberg Literary Agency, Inc.); John Baker (editorial director, *Publishers Weekly*). Agents will be speaking and available for meetings with attendees.
Costs: In 2000, $1500 for 2 weeks, live in; $850 for 1 week, live in; $550 for 2 weeks, local; $300 for 1 week, local.
Accommodations: Accommodations are available and include bedroom/study and breakfast and lunch. "We rent a large house either in Woodstock or from the Byrdcliffe Artist Colony."
Additional Information: "In 2000, we offered an 'Internet for Writers' workshop, plus beginning website design. Cost was $120 for 6 hours. We also offer a free 50-page private tutorial with a published writer. We specialize in full-length nonfiction and fiction manuscripts, short story collections, and developing book proposals." Brochures available for SASE or on website. Inquiries by e-mail OK.

☑ **THE PERSPECTIVES IN CHILDREN'S LITERATURE CONFERENCE**, 226 Furcolo Hall, School of Education, U-Mass, Amherst MA 01003-3035. Fax: (413)545-2879. E-mail: childlit@educ.umass.edu. Website: www-unix.oit.umass.edu/~childlit/. **Contact:** Jane Pierce and Jamie Broadhead, coordinators. Estab. 1970. Annual. Conference held March 31, 2001. Conference duration: 1 day. Average attendance: 500. Conference focuses on various aspects of children's writing and illustration, including picture books. Held at the University of Massachusetts School of Management. **Agents/speakers attending include:** Julius Lester, Jane Yolen, Barry Moser, Gail Carson Levine, Jane Dyer, Liza Ketchum, Rich Michaelson. Agents will be speaking and available for meetings with attendees.
Costs: $50-55 (includes light breakfast, lunch, freebies, snacks). For an additional fee, attendees can earn academic credit.
Additional Information: "During lunch, authors, writers, editors are assigned to a table giving participants an opportunity to converse, share experiences." Books available for sale. Inquiries by e-mail and fax OK.

☑ **PUBLISH & PROSPER IN 2001**, ASJA 1501 Broadway, Suite 302, New York NY 10036. (212)997-0947. Fax: (212)768-7414. E-mail: staff@asja.org. Website: www.asja.org. **Contact:** Brett Harvey, executive director. Estab. 1971. Annual. Conference held sometime in late April. Conference duration: 2 days. Average attendance: 500. Nonfiction. Held at a hotel in New York. For 2000, panels included "Freelancing for Magazines," "Techniques For Narrative Nonfiction," "Carving a Niche." **Previous agents/speakers have included:** Dominick Dunne, Michael Gross. Agents will be speaking.
Costs: $195 (includes lunch).
Accommodations: "The hotel holding our conference always blocks out discounted rooms for attendees."
Additional Information: Brochures available in March. Inquiries by e-mail and fax OK.

☑ **SOCIETY OF CHILDREN'S BOOK WRITERS & ILLUSTRATORS CONFERENCE/HOFSTRA CHILDREN'S LITERATURE CONFERENCE**, University College for Continuing Education, 250 Hofstra University, Hempstead NY 11549-1090. (516)463-5016. Fax: (516)463-4833. E-mail: uccelibarts@hofstra.edu. **Contact:** Kenneth Henwood. Estab. 1985. Annual. Conference to be held April 21, 2001. Average attendance: 175. Conference to encourage good writing for children. "The conference brings together writers, illustrators, librarians, agents, publishers, teachers and other professionals who are interested in writing for children. Each year we organize the program around a theme. Last year it was 'Expanding Horizons.' The conference takes place at the Student Center Building of Hofstra University, located in Hempstead, Long Island. "We have two general sessions, five break-out groups." **Previous agents/speakers have included:** Paula Danziger and Ann M. Martin, and a panel of children's book editors who critique randomly selected first-manuscript pages submitted by registrants. Agents will be speaking and available for meetings with attendees.
Costs: $66 (previous year) for SCBWI members; $72 for nonmembers. Continental breakfast and full luncheon included.
Additional Information: Special interest groups are offered in submission procedures, fiction, nonfiction, writing picture books, illustrating picture books, poetry and scriptwriting.

STATE OF MAINE WRITERS' CONFERENCE, 18 Hill Rd., Belmont MA 02478-4303. **Contact:** June A. Knowles, Mary E. Pitts, co-chairs. Estab. 1941. Annual. Conference held in August. Conference duration: 4 days. Average attendance: 50. "We try to present a balanced as well as eclectic conference. In addition to time and attention given to poetry, we also have children's literature, mystery writing, travel, novels/fiction, nonfiction, and other issues of interest to writers. Our speakers are publishers, editors, writers and other professionals. Our concentration is, by intention, a general view of writing to publish. We are located in Ocean Park, a small seashore village 14 miles south of Portland. Ours is a summer assembly center with many buildings from the Victorian Age. The conference meets in Porter Hall, one of the assembly buildings which is listed on the National Register of Historic Places." **Previous agents/speakers have included:** Carolyn Barstow (author/teacher/librarian); Ray Zairfield (author/teacher); Oscar Greene (author); Del Jakeman (author); Lewis Ledaun (author/librarian); Carl Little (author/artist/lecturer); Elizabeth Mouse (researcher/teacher); Wesley McNair (poet, Maine faculty); and others. "We usually have about 10 guest presenters a year." Agents will be speaking, leading workshops and available for meetings with attendees.
Costs: $90 (includes the conference banquet; if registering after August 10, $100). There is a reduced fee, $45, for students ages 21 and under. The fee does not include housing or meals which must be arranged separately by the conferees.
Accommodations: An accommodations list is available. "We are in a summer resort area and motels, guest houses and restaurants abound."

Additional Information: "We have about nine contests on various genres. An announcement is available in the spring. The prizes, all modest, are awarded at the end of the conference and only to those who are registered." Program available in May for SASE.

WESLEYAN WRITERS CONFERENCE, Wesleyan University, Middletown CT 06459. (860)685-3604. Fax: (860)347-3996. E-mail: agreene@wesleyan.edu. Website: www.wesleyan.edu/writing/conferen.html. **Contact:** Anne Greene, director. Estab. 1956. Annual. Conference held the last week in June. Average attendance: 100. Fiction techniques, novel, short story, poetry, screenwriting, nonfiction, literary journalism, memoir. The conference is held on the campus of Wesleyan University, in the hills overlooking the Connecticut River. Features readings of new fiction, guest lectures on a range of topics including publishing and daily seminars. "Both new and experienced writers are welcome." **Agents/speakers attending include:** Edmond Harmsworth (Zachary Schuster Agency); Daniel Mandel (Sanford J. Greenburger Associates); Dorian Karchmar. Agents will be speaking and available for meetings with attendees. **Costs:** In 2000, day rate $690 (includes meals); boarding students' rate $805 (includes meals and room for 5 nights). **Accommodations:** "Participants can fly to Hartford or take Amtrak to Meriden, CT. We are happy to help participants make travel arrangements." Meals and lodging are provided on campus. Overnight participants stay on campus. **Additional Information:** Manuscript critiques are available as part of the program but are not required. Participants may attend seminars in several different genres. Scholarships and teaching fellowships are available, including the Jakobson awards for fiction writers and poets and the Jon Davidoff Scholarships for journalists. Inquiries by e-mail and fax OK.

Midatlantic (DC, DE, MD, NJ, PA)

N. BALTIMORE WRITERS' ALLIANCE CONFERENCE, P.O. Box 410, Riderwood MD 21139. (410)377-5265. Fax: (410)377-4325. E-mail: hdiehl@bcpl.net. Website: www.baltimorewriters.org. **Contact:** Barbara Diehl, coordinator. Estab. 1994. Annual. Conference held November 18, 2000. Conference duration: 1 day. Average attendance: 150-200. Writing and getting published—all areas. Held at Towson University. Previous themes focused on mystery, science fiction, poetry, children's writing, legal issues, grant funding, working with an agent, book and magazine panels. **Previous agents/speakers have included:** Nat Sobel (Sobel/Weber Associates). Agents will be speaking. **Costs:** $75 (includes all-day conference, lunch and snacks). Manuscript critiques for additional fee. **Accommodations:** Hotels close by, if required. **Additional Information:** Brochures available for SASE. Inquiries by e-mail OK.

☑ THE COLLEGE OF NEW JERSEY WRITERS' CONFERENCE, English Dept., The College of New Jersey, P.O. Box 7718, Ewing NJ 08628-0718. (609)771-3254. Fax: (609)637-5112. E-mail: write@tcnj.edu. **Contact:** Jean Hollander, director. Estab. 1980. Annual. Conference held April 18-19, 2001. Conference duration: 9 a.m. to 10 p.m. Average attendance: 600-1,000. "Conference concentrates on fiction (the largest number of participants), poetry, children's literature, play and screenwriting, magazine and newspaper journalism, overcoming writer's block, nonfiction and memoir writing. Conference is held at the student center at the college in two auditoriums and workshop rooms; also Kendall Theatre on campus. We focus on various genres: romance, detective, mystery, TV writing, etc." Topics have included "How to Get Happily Published," "How to Get an Agent" and "Earning a Living as a Writer." The conference usually presents twenty or so authors, editors and agents, plus two featured speakers. **Previous agents/speakers have included:** Arthur Miller, Saul Bellow, Toni Morrison, Joyce Carol Oates, Erica Jong, Alice Walker and John Updike. Last year's evening presentation featured keynote speaker Anne Quinalen. Agents will be speaking and available for meetings with attendees. **Costs:** General registration $45 for entire day, plus $8 for evening presentation. Lower rates for students. **Additional Information:** Brochures/guidelines available.

N. METROPOLITAN WRITERS CONFERENCE, Seton Hall University, South Orange NJ 07079. (973)761-9430. Fax: (973)761-9453. E-mail: rawnkirk@shu.edu. **Contact:** Kirk Rawn. Estab. 1987. Conference to help writers get their fiction and writing for children published. Held on the campus of Seton Hall University. Workshop topics focus on helping writers improve their use of plot, characterization, setting, point of view, etc., as well as a discussion on how to get an agent. **Previous agents/speakers have included:** Belva Plain, Meredith Sue Willis, Stefanie Matteson and Mary Higgins Clark.

MID-ATLANTIC MYSTERY BOOK FAIR & CONVENTION, Detecto Mysterioso Books at Society Hill Playhouse, 507 S. Eighth St., Philadelphia PA 19147-1325. (215)923-0211. Fax: (215)923-1789. E-mail: shp@erols.com. Website: www.erols.com/shp. **Contact:** Deen Kogan, chairperson. Estab. 1991. Annual. Convention held October. Average attendance: 450-500. Focus is on mystery, suspense, thriller, true crime novels, "an examination of the genre from many points of view." **Previous agents/speakers have included:** Lawrence Block, Jeremiah Healy, Neil Albert, Michael Connelly, Paul Levine, Eileen Dreyer, Earl Emerson, Wendy Hornsby. Agents will be speaking and available for informal meetings with attendees. **Costs:** $125 registration fee.

Accommodations: Attendees must make their own transportation arrangements. Special room rate available at convention hotel.

Additional Information: "The Bookroom is a focal point of the convention. Twenty-five specialty dealers are expected to exhibit and collectables range from hot-off-the-press bestsellers to 1930's pulp; from fine editions to reading copies." Conference brochures/guidelines are available for SASE or by telephone. Inquiries by e-mail and fax OK.

NEW JERSEY ROMANCE WRITERS PUT YOUR HEART IN A BOOK CONFERENCE, P.O. Box 513, Plainsboro NJ 08536. (215)348-5948. E-mail: CBMATTERA@aol.com. Website: www.geocities.com/SoHo/Gallery/7019. **Contact:** Christine Bush Mattera, president. Estab. 1984. Annual. Conference held October 5-6, 2001. Average attendance: 500. Conference concentrating on romance fiction. "Workshops offered on various topics for all writers of romance, from beginner to multi-published." Held at the Doubletree Hotel in Somerset NJ. **Agents/speakers attending include:** Kathleen Woodiwiss, Nora Roberts, Kathleen Eagle and Shirley Hailstock (authors); and Linda Hyatt and others (agents). Agents will be speaking and available for meetings with attendees.

Costs: $125 (New Jersey Romance Writers members) and $145 (nonmembers).

Accommodations: Special hotel rate available for conference attendees.

Additional Information: Sponsors Put Your Heart in a Book Contest for unpublished writers and the Golden Leaf Contest for published members of RWA. Conference brochures, guidelines and membership information are available for SASE. "Appointments offered for conference attendees, both published and unpublished, with editors and/or agents in the genre." Massive bookfair open to public with authors signing copies of their books; proceeds donated to literacy charities.

N: PENNWRITERS ANNUAL CONFERENCE, R.R. #2, Box 241, Middlebury Center PA 16935-9776. (717)871-9712. Fax: (717)871-6104. E-mail: Elizwrite8@aol.com. Website: www.pennwriters.org. **Contact:** Elizabeth Darrach, conference co-chair 2001. Estab. 1987. Annually. Conference held May 18-20, 2001. Conference duration: 3 days. Average attendance: 120. "We try to cover as many genres each year as we can." Held at the Holiday Inn Grantville—spacious facility with most workshop rooms on one level. "For 2001 some of our workshops planned include: 'Overcoming Writer's Block,' 'Writing Memoirs,' 'Freelance Writing as a Career,' much more." **Previous agents/speakers have included:** Cherry Weiner, Fran Collin. Agents will be speaking and available for meetings with attendees.

Costs: $125 for members in 2000 (includes all workshops and panels, as well as any editor or agent appointments). There is an additional charge for Friday's keynote dinner and Saturday night's dinner activity.

Accommodations: "We have arranged a special rate with the hotel, and details will be in our brochure. Our rate for conference attendees is $82 plus tax/night. The hotel has a shuttle to and from the airport."

Additional Information: "We are a multi-genre group encompassing the state of PA and beyond." Brochures available February for SASE. Inquiries by e-mail and fax OK.

N: SANDY COVE CHRISTIAN COMMUNICATORS CONFERENCE, Sandy Cove Bible Conference, 60 Sandy Cove Rd., North East MD 21901. (800)287-4843 or (800)234-2683. **Contact:** Jim Watkins, director. Estab. 1991. Annual. Conference begins first Sunday in October. Conference duration: 4 days (Sunday dinner to Thursday breakfast). Average attendance: 200. "There are major, continuing workshops in fiction, article writing, nonfiction books, and beginner's and advanced workshops. Twenty-eight one-hour classes touch many topics. While Sandy Cove has a strong emphasis on available markets in Christian publishing, all writers are more than welcome. Sandy Cove is a full-service conference center located on the Chesapeake Bay. All the facilities are first class with suites, single or double rooms available." **Previous agents/speakers have included:** Francine Rivers (bestselling novelist); Lisa Bergen (Waterbrook Press); Ken Petersen (editor, Tyndale House); Linda Tomblin (editor, *Guideposts*); and Andrew Scheer (*Moody Magazine*).

Costs: Call for rates.

Accommodations: "Accommodations are available at Sandy Cove. Information available upon request." Cost is $250 double occupancy room and board, $325 single occupancy room and board for 4 nights and meals.

Additional Information: Conference brochures/guidelines are available.

N: WASHINGTON INDEPENDENT WRITERS (WIW) SPRING WRITERS CONFERENCE, #220, 733 15th St. NW, Suite 220, Washington DC 20005. (202)347-4973. Fax: (202)628-0298. E-mail: washwriter@aol.com. Website: www.washwriters.org. **Contact:** Isolde Chapin, executive director. Estab. 1975. Annual. Conference held May 11-12. Conference duration: Friday evening and Saturday. Average attendance: 250. "Gives participants a chance to hear from and talk with dozens of experts on book and magazine publishing as well as on the craft, tools and business of writing." **Previous agents/speakers have included:** Erica Jong, Haynes Johnson, Kitty Kelley, Diane Rehm and Lawrence Block.

Costs: $125 members; $175 nonmembers; $210 membership and conference.

Additional Information: Brochures/guidelines available for SASE in mid-March.

Midsouth (NC, SC, TN, VA, WV)

AMERICAN CHRISTIAN WRITERS CONFERENCES, P.O. Box 110390, Nashville TN 37222-0390. (800)21-WRITE. E-mail: regaforder@aol.com. Website: www.ECPA.ORG/ACW (includes schedule of cities). **Contact:** Reg Forder, director. Estab. 1981. Annual. Conference duration: 2 days. Average attendance: 60. Fiction, nonfiction, scriptwriting. To promote all forms of Christian writing. Conferences held throughout the year in 36 US cities.
Costs: Approximately $149 plus meals and accommodation.
Accommodations: Special rates available at host hotel. Usually located at a major hotel chain like Holiday Inn.
Additional Information: Conference brochures/guidelines are available for SASE.

N CAPON SPRINGS WRITERS' WORKSHOP, P.O. Box 11116, Cincinnati OH 45211-0116. (513)481-9884. Fax: (513)481-2666. **Contact:** Wendy Beckman, director. Estab. 2000. Annual. Conference held mid-June or mid-September. Conference duration: 3 days. Fiction, poetry, creative nonfiction. Conference held at Farm Resort, 5,000-acre secluded mountain resort in West Virginia. In 2000, theme was "A Sense of Place." Agents will be speaking and available for meetings with attendees.
Costs: $375, in 2000 (includes seminars, meals, lodging, manuscript critique).
Accommodations: Facility has swimming, hiking, fishing, tennis, badminton, volleyball, basketball, ping pong, campfire sing along. Nine-hole golf course available for additional fee.
Additional Information: Brochures available for SASE. Inquiries by fax and e-mail OK.

HIGHLAND SUMMER CONFERENCE, Box 7014, Radford University, Radford VA 24142-7014. (540)831-5366. Fax: (540)831-5004. E-mail: gedwards@runet.edu or jasbury@runet.edu. Website: www.runet.edu/~arsc. **Contact:** Jo-Ann Asbury. Chair, Appalachian Studies Program: Dr. Grace Toney Edwards. Estab. 1978. Annual. Conference held first 2 weeks of June in 2001. Conference duration: 12 days. Average attendance: 25. "The HSC features one (two weeks) or two (one week each) guest leaders each year. As a rule, our leaders are well-known writers who have connections, either thematic or personal, or both, to the Appalachian region. The genre(s) of emphasis depends upon the workshop leader(s). In the past we have had as our leaders Robert Morgan, poet, essayist, fiction writer, teacher; Richard Hague, poet, essayist, author, teacher; Maggi Vaughn, Poet Laureate of Tennessee; and Betty Smith, author, musician, songsmith, among others. The Highland Summer Conference is held at Radford University, a school of about 9,000 students. Radford is in the Blue Ridge Mountains of southwest Virginia about 45 miles south of Roanoke, VA."
Costs: "The cost is based on current Radford tuition for 3 credit hours plus an additional conference fee. On-campus meals and housing are available at additional cost. In 1999, conference tuition was $433 for in-state undergraduates, $1,075 for out-of-state undergraduates, $475 for in-state graduates, $987 for out-of-state graduates."
Accommodations: "We do not have special rate arrangements with local hotels. We do offer accommodations on the Radford University Campus in a recently refurbished residence hall. (In 1998 cost was $19-28 per night.)"
Additional Information: "Conference leaders typically critique work done during the two-week conference, but do not ask to have any writing submitted prior to the conference beginning." Conference brochures/guidelines are available after February for SASE. Inquiries by e-mail and fax OK.

NORTH CAROLINA WRITERS' NETWORK FALL CONFERENCE, P.O. Box 954, Carrboro NC 27510-0954. (919)967-9540. Fax: (919)929-0535. E-mail: mail@ncwriters.org. Website: www.ncwriters.org (includes "history and information about the NC Writers' Network and our programs. Also has a links page to other writing-related websites"). **Contact:** Linda Hobson, executive director. Estab. 1985. Annual. "2000 Conference will be held in Raleigh, NC, November 10-12, 2000." Average attendance: 450. "The conference is a weekend full of workshops, panels, readings and discussion groups. We try to have a variety of genres represented. In the past we have had fiction writers, poets, journalists, editors, children's writers, young adult writers, storytellers, playwrights, screenwriters, technical writing, web-based writing, etc. We take the conference to a different location in North Carolina each year in order to best serve our entire state. We hold the conference at a conference center with hotel rooms available." **Previous agents/speakers have included:** Christy Fletcher and Neal Bascomb (Carlisle & Co.); Delin Cormeny (PMA Literary & Film Agency); Joe Regal (Viking Press). Agents will be speaking and available for meetings with attendees.
Costs: "Conference cost is approximately $175-200 and includes two meals."
Accommodations: "Special conference hotel rates are available, but the individual makes his/her own reservations."
Additional Information: Conference brochures/guidelines are available for SAE with 2 first-class stamps or on website. Inquiries by fax or e-mail OK.

N POLICE WRITERS CONFERENCE, Police Writers Club, P.O. Box 416, Hayes VA 23072. (804)642-2343. Fax: (804)642-2343. Website: www.policewriter.com. **Contact:** Ginny Harrell. Estab. 1996. Annually. Conference held November 2001. Conference duration: 2 days. Average attendance: 50. Related writing—both fiction and nonfiction. Focuses on police. Held in various hotels in various regions, determined annually. "Each year the conference focuses on helping club members get their work polished and published." **Previous agents/speakers have included:** Paul Bishop (novelist), Ed Dee (novelist), Roger Fulton (editor). Agents will be speaking and available for meetings with attendees.
Costs: $225 in 2000 (includes all classes and seminars, writing contest entries and awards luncheons).
Accommodations: Hotel arrangements, at special conference rates, are available.

Additional Information: "Unpublished police writers are welcome at the conference and as Police Writers Club Members." Brochures available on website. Inquiries by fax OK.

SEWANEE WRITERS' CONFERENCE, 310 St. Luke's Hall, Sewanee TN 37383-1000. (931)598-1141. Fax: (931)598-1145. E-mail: cpeters@sewanee.edu. Website: www.sewanee.edu/writers_conference/home.html. (includes general conference information including schedule of events). **Contact:** Wyatt Prunty, conference director. Conference Coordinator: Cheri B. Peters. Estab. 1990. Annual. Conference held in July. Conference duration: 12 days. Average attendance: 110. "We offer genre-based workshops (in fiction, poetry and playwriting), not theme-based workshops. The Sewanee Writers' Conference uses the facilities of the University of the South. Physically, the University is a collection of ivy-covered Gothic-style buildings, located on the Cumberland Plateau in mid-Tennessee. We allow invited editors, publishers and agents to structure their own presentations, but there is always opportunity for questions from the audience." **Previous agents/speakers have included:** Laura Maria Censabella, Tony Earley, Barry Hannah, Andrew Hudgins, Diane Johnson, Romulus Linney, Alice McDermott, Erin McGraw, Claire Messud, Padgett Powell, Francine Prose, Mary Jo Salter, Dave Smith and Mark Strand.
Costs: Full conference fee was $1,205 in 2000 (includes tuition, board, and basic room).
Accommodations: Complimentary chartered bus service is available, on a limited basis, on the first and last days of the conference. Participants are housed in University dormitory rooms. Motel or B&B housing is available but not abundantly so. Dormitory housing costs are included in the full conference fee.
Additional Information: "We offer each participant (excluding auditors) the opportunity for a private manuscript conference with a member of the faculty. These manuscripts are due one month before the conference begins." Conference brochures/guidelines are available, "but no SASE is necessary. The conference has available a limited number of fellowships and scholarships; these are awarded on a competitive basis."

VIRGINIA ROMANCE WRITERS CONFERENCE: Step Back in Time, Romance, History, and Crime, Virginia Romance Writers, 13 Woodlawn Terrace, Fredericksburg VA 22405-3360. Fax: (540)371-3854. E-mail: spgreen man@aol.com. Website: www.Geocities.com/SoHo/museum/2164 (includes information about Virginia Romance Writers, authors, monthly meetings, workshops, conferences, contests). **Contact:** Sandra Greeman, conference coordinator. Conference held biennially. Next conference held March 23-25, 2001 in Williamsburg VA. Average attendance: 300. Offers workshops in basic and advanced writing, history and criminology. Also offers opportunities to meet with editors and agents, networking, book signing, Holt Medallion Awards Ceremony, special guest speakers, etc. **Previous agents/speakers have included:** Damaris Rowland (Damaris Rowland Agency), Irene Goodman (Irene Goodman Literary Agency), Lynne Whitaker (Graybill & English), Caroline Tolley (Pocket Books/Prentice Hall), Kara Cesare (Bantam) and Martha Zinberg (Harlequin). Agents will be available for meetings with attendees.
Additional Information: Write for additional information.

Southeast (AL, AR, FL, GA, LA, MS, Puerto Rico)

ARKANSAS WRITERS' CONFERENCE, #17 Red Maple Ct., Little Rock AR 72211. (501)312-1747. **Contact:** Barbara Longstreth Mulkey, director. Estab. 1944. Annual. Conference held first weekend in June 2001. Average attendence: 225. Fiction, nonfiction, scriptwriting and poetry. "We have a variety of subjects related to writing—we have some general sessions, some more specific, but try to vary each year's subjects."
Costs: Registration: ($10 one day, $15 for 2), contest entry $5.
Accommodations: "We meet at a Holiday Inn, select in Little Rock." Holiday Inn has a bus to and from airport. Rooms average $65-70.
Additional Information: "We have 36 contest categories. Some are open only to Arkansans, most are open to all writers. Our judges are not announced before conference but are qualified, many from out of state." Conference brochures are available for SASE after February 1. "We have had 226 attending from 12 states—over 3,000 contest entries from 43 states and New Zealand, Mexico and Canada."

FLORIDA FIRST COAST WRITERS' FESTIVAL, 101 W. State St., Room 1166, FCCJ Downtown Campus, Jacksonville FL 32202. (904)633-8243. Fax: (904)633-8435. E-mail: kclower@fccj.org. Website: ww.fccj.org/wf/ (includes festival workshop speakers, contest information). **Contacts:** Kathy Clower and Margo Martin. Estab. 1985. Annual. Conference held May 17-19, 2001. Average attendance: 300. Held at Sea Turtle Inn, Atlantic Beach, FL. All areas: mainstream plus genre. Fiction, nonfiction, scriptwriting, poetry, freelancing, etc. Offers seminars on narrative structure and plotting character development. **Agents/speakers attending include:** Randy Wayne White, Nancy Slonim Aronie, Lorraine Johnson-Coleman, Mark Ryan (agent), Sheree Bykofsky (agent), Elizabeth Lund, David Poyer, Lenoe hart and more to be announced. Agents will be speaking and available for meetings with attendees.
Costs: Maximum of $145 for 2 days, with 2 meals.
Accommodations: Sea Turtle Inn, (904)249-7402, has a special festival rate.
Additional Information: Conference brochures/guidelines are available for SASE. Sponsors a contest for short fiction, poetry and novels. Novel judges are David Poyer and Lenore Hart. Entry fees: $30, novels; $10, short fiction; $5, poetry. Deadline: November 1 in each year. "We offer one-on-one sessions at no additional costs for attendees to speak to selected writers, editors, agents on first-come, first served basis."

☑ **MOONLIGHT AND MAGNOLIAS WRITER'S CONFERENCE**, 1340 Cottonwood Trail, Cumming GA 30041. Fax: (770)967-4319. E-mail: warickent@aol.com. Website: www.georgiaromancewriters.org. Estab. 1982. President, Georgia Romance Writers: Betty Cothran. **Contact:** Cheryl Wilson, 2001 conference chair. Conference held 3rd weekend in September. Average attendance: 300. "Conference focuses on writing women's fiction with emphasis on romance. 1999 conference included agents and editors from major publishing houses. Workshops included: beginning writer track, general interest topics, and professional issues for the published author, plus sessions for writing for alternative markets, young adult, inspirational, multicultural and Regency. Speakers included experts in law enforcement, screenwriting and research. Literacy raffle and advertised speaker and GRW member autographing open to the public. Published authors make up 25-30% of attendees. Send requests with SASE to Cheryl Wilson.
Costs: Hotel $79/day, single, double, triple, quad (1999). Conference: non-GRW members $135 (early registration).
Additional Information: Maggie Awards for excellence are presented to unpublished writers. The Maggie Award for published writers is limited to Region 3 members of Romance Writers of America. Proposals per guidelines must be submitted in early June. Please check with conference chair for new dates. Published authors judge first round, category editors judge finals. Guidelines available for SASE in February or on website.

☑ **SOUTHEASTERN WRITERS CONFERENCE**, 1399 Vista Leaf Dr., Decatur GA 30033-2028. (404)636-1316. E-mail: g&dworth@gsu.edu. **Contact:** Dorothy Williamson Worth, president. Estab. 1975. Annual. Conference held June 17-23, 2001. Conference duration: 1 week. Average attendence: 100 (limited to 100 participants). Concentration is on fiction, poetry, juvenile, nonfiction, playwriting, storytelling and genre. Site is St. Simons Island, GA. Conference held at Epworth-by-the-Sea Conference Center—tropical setting, beaches. "Each year we offer market advice, agent updates. All our instructors are professional writers presently selling in New York." **Agents/speakers attending include:** Nancy Love (Nancy Love Agency), Andrea Schneeman (North-South Books), Deidre Knight, Alice Orr and Meg Ruley. Agents will be speaking and available for meetings with attendees.
Costs: $245 for early bird registration before April 15, 2001. $285 regular tuition. Meals and lodging are separate.
Accommodations: Information on overnight accommodations is made available. "On-site facilities at a remarkably low cost. Facilities are motel style of excellent quality. Other hotels are available on the island."
Additional Information: "Three manuscripts of one chapter each are allowed in three different categories." Sponsors several contests, MANY cash prizes. Brochures are available March for SASE.

WORDS & MUSIC: A LITERARY FEAST IN NEW ORLEANS, (formerly New Orleans Writers' Conference), 632 Pirates Alley, New Orleans LA 70116. (504)586-1609. Fax: (504)522-9725. E-mail: faulkhouse@aol.com. Website: www.Wordsandmusic.org or members.aol.com/faulkhouse. Conference Director: Rosemary James DeSalvo. Estab. 1997. Annual. Conference held September. Conference duration: 5 days. Average attendance: 350-400. Presenters include authors, agents, editors and publishers. **Previous agents/speakers have included:** Deborah Grosvenor (Deborah Grosvenor Literary Agency); Vicky Bijur (Vicky Bijur Agency); and Mitch Douglas (International Creative Management). Agents will be speaking and available for meetings with attendees.
Additional Information: Write for additional information.

WRITING TODAY—BIRMINGHAM-SOUTHERN COLLEGE, Box 549003, Birmingham AL 35254. (205)226-4921. Fax: (205)226-3072. E-mail: dcwilson@bsc.edu. Website: www.bsc.edu. **Contact:** Martha Ross, director of special events. Estab. 1978. Annual. Conference held March 16-17, 2001. Average attendance: 400-500. "This is a two-day conference with approximately 18 workshops, lectures and readings. We try to offer workshops in short fiction, novels, poetry, children's literature, magazine writing, and general information of concern to aspiring writers such as publishing, agents, markets and research. The conference is sponsored by Birmingham-Southern College and is held on the campus in classrooms and lecture halls." **Previous agents/speakers included:** Ernest Gaines, Claudia Johnson, Ishmael Reed, Sena Jeeter Naslund.
Costs: $120 for both days (includes lunches, reception, and morning coffee and rolls).
Accommodations: Attendees must arrange own transporation. Local hotels and motels offer special rates, but participants must make their own reservations.
Additional Information: "We usually offer a critique for interested writers. We have had poetry and short story critiques. There is an additional charge for these critiques." Sponsors the Hackney Literary Competition Awards for poetry, short story and novels. Brochures available for SASE.

Midwest (IL, IN, KY, MI, OH)

🆕 **CLEVELAND HEIGHTS/UNIVERSITY HEIGHTS WRITER MINI CONFERENCE**, 34200 Ridge Rd., #201, Willoughby OH 44094. (216)943-3047 or (800)653-4261. E-mail: lealoldham@aol.com. **Contact:** Lea Leever Oldham, coordinator. Estab. 1991. Annual. Conference held the third Saturday in October. Conference duration: 1 day. Average attendance: 100. Fiction, nonfiction, children's, artistic, self-publishing, poetry, science fiction and other topics. Conference held at Taylor Academy in Cleveland Heights.
Costs: $39 (includes lunch).
Additional Information: Conference brochures/guidelines available for SASE.

THE COLUMBUS WRITERS CONFERENCE, P.O. Box 20548, Columbus OH 43220. (614)451-3075. Fax: (614)451-0174. E-mail: AngelaPL28@aol.com. Director: Angela Palazzolo. Estab. 1993. Annual. Conference held in September. Average attendance: 200. "The conference covers a wide variety of fiction and nonfiction topics presented by writers, editors and agents. Writing topics have included novel, short story, children's, young adult, science fiction, fantasy, humor, mystery, playwriting, screenwriting, personal essay, travel, humor, cookbook, technical, query letter, corporate, educational and greeting cards. Other topics for writers: finding and working with an agent, targeting markets, research, time management, obtaining grants and writers' colonies." **Previous agents/speakers have included:** Lee K. Abbott, Lore Segal, Jeff Herman, Doris S. Michaels, Sheree Bykofsky, Mike Harden, Oscar Collier, Maureen F. McHugh, Ralph Keyes, Stephanie S. Tolan, Bonnie Pryor, Dennis L. McKiernan, Karen Harper, Melvin Helitzer, Susan Porter, Les Roberts, Tracey E. Dils, J. Patrick Lewis and many other professionals in the writing field.
Costs: Early registration fee is $149 for full conference (includes Friday and Saturday sessions, Friday dinner program, and Saturday continental breakfast, lunch, and afternoon refreshments); otherwise, fee is $169. Early registration fee for Saturday only is $119; otherwise, fee is $139. Friday dinner program is $30.
Additional Information: Call, write, e-mail or send fax to obtain a conference brochure, available mid-summer.

N: HUDSON WRITERS MINI CONFERENCE, 34200 Ridge Rd., #201, Willoughby OH 44094. (216)943-3047 or (800)653-4261. E-mail: lealoldham@aol.com. **Contact:** Lea Leever Oldham, coordinator. Estab. 1999. Annual. Conference held first Saturday in May. Conference duration: 1 day. Average attendance: 100. Fiction, nonfiction, inspirational, children's, poetry, science fiction, copyright and tax information, etc. Held at Hudson High School in Hudson, OH. Panels include "no themes, simply published authors and other experts sharing their secrets."
Costs: $39.
Accommodations: "Classrooms wheelchair accessible. Accessible from I-90, east of Cleveland."
Additional Information: Conference brochures/guidelines available for SASE.

N: KENTUCKY WOMEN WRITERS CONFERENCE, The Carnegie Center for Literacy and Learning, 251 W. Second St., Lexington KY 40507. (859)254-4175. Fax: (606)281-1151. E-mail: kywwc@hotmail.com. **Contact:** Jan Isenhour/Crystal Wilkinson, advisory board members. Annual. Conference held spring 2001. "Gathering of women writers and scholars—novelists, poets, playwrights, essayists, biographers, journalists—and readers and students of literature. For the past twenty years, several days of reading, lectures, workshops, musical and theater performances and panel discussions about women writers and women's writing have been held both on campus and out in the community." Future sites will be in various venues in the community. Also traditional activities will involve creative writing of all kinds. **Previous agents/speakers have included:** Alice Walker, Barabar Kingsolver, Margaret Atwood, Sena Jeter Naslund, Judith Ortiz Cofer.
Costs: To be announced for 2001.
Accommodations: A list of area hotels will be provided by the Lexington Convention & Tourist Bureau upon request. Call (859)233-1221.
Additional Information: "Manuscript critiques of pre-submitted fiction, poetry, playwriting and nonfiction by registered conference participants will be provided by regional writers. Feedback will be given in 15-minute private sessions. The fee is $25. Check for deadline for the receipt of manuscripts. Submit two copies of your double-spaced manuscript, 15 pages maximum in all categories except poetry, where the maximum is six pages." Scholarships are available for those who would otherwise be unable to attend. Attach a brief letter of explanation to the registration form detailing why the conference is important to you.

N: THE MID AMERICA MYSTERY CONFERENCE, Magna cum Murder, The E.B. Ball Center, Ball State University, Muncie IN 47306. (765)285-8975. Fax: (765)747-9566. E-mail: kennisonk@aol.com. **Contact:** Kathryn Kennison. Estab. 1994. Annual. Conference held from October 27-29. Average attendance: 400. Held in the Horizon Convention Center and Historic Radisson Hotel Roberts. Conference for crime and detective fiction. **Previous agents/speakers have included:** Mickey Spillane, Carolyn G. Hart, Barb D'Amato, Robert Greer, Luci ("The Poison Lady") Zahray and more.
Costs: For 2000 cost was $165 (includes continental breakfasts, boxed lunches, a reception and a banquet).
Additional Information: Sponsors a radio mystery script contest. Send SASE for brochure/guidelines or request via fax or e-mail.

✓ MIDLAND WRITERS CONFERENCE, Grace A. Dow Memorial Library, 1710 W. St. Andrews, Midland MI 48640-2698. (517)837-3430. Fax: (517)837-3468. E-mail: ajarvis@midland-mi.org. Website: www.gracedowlibrary.org. Conference Chair: Katherine Redwine. **Contact:** Ann Jarvis, librarian. Estab. 1980. Annual. Conference held June 9, 2001. Average attendance: 100. Fiction, nonfiction, children's and poetry. "The Conference is composed of a well-known keynote speaker and six workshops on a variety of subjects including poetry, children's writing, nonfiction, freelancing, agents, etc. The attendees are both published and unpublished authors. The Conference is held at the Grace A. Dow Memorial Library in the auditorium and conference rooms." **Previous speakers/agents have included:** Arthur Golden (fiction writer), Russell Thorburn (poet), Pete Hautman (young adult fiction), Sue Robishaw (creativity), Dave Barry, Pat Conroy, Kurt Vonnegut, Roger Ebert and Peggy Noonan. Agents will be speaking.
Costs: Adult - $60; students, senior citizens and handicapped - $50. A box lunch is available. Costs are approximate until plans for upcoming conference are finalized.
Accommodations: A list of area hotels is available.

Additional Information: Conference brochures/guidelines are mailed mid-April. Call or write to be put on mailing list. Inquiries by e-mail and fax OK.

OAKLAND UNIVERSITY WRITERS' CONFERENCE, 231 Varner Hall, Rochester MI 48309-4401. (248)370-3125. Fax: (248)370-4280. E-mail: gjboddy@oakland.edu. Website: www.oakland.edu/contin-ed/writersconf/. **Contact:** Gloria J. Boddy, program director. Estab. 1961. Annual. Conference held in October 20-21, 2000. Average attendance: 400. Held at Oakland University: Oakland Center. Conference covers all aspects and types of writing in 36 concurrent workshops on Saturday. "It is a conference for beginning and established writers. It provides an opportunity to exchange ideas and perfect writing skills by meeting with agents, editors and successful writers." Major writers from various genres are speakers for the Saturday conference and luncheon program. Individual critiques and hands-on writing workshops are conducted Friday. Areas: nonfiction, young adult fiction, poetry, short fiction, chapbooks, magazine fiction, essay, script writing. **Previous agents/speakers have included:** Faye Bender, agent; Lyn Cryderman and Peter Blocksom, editors. Agents will be speaking and available for meetings with attendees.
Costs: 2000: Conference registration: $85; lunch, $15; individual ms, $58; writing workshop, $48.
Accommodations: Hotel list is available.
Additional Information: Conference brochure/guidelines available after August 2000 for SASE. Inquiries by e-mail and fax OK.

OF DARK & STORMY NIGHTS, Mystery Writers of America—Midwest Chapter, P.O. Box 1944, Muncie IN 47308-1944. (765)288-7402. E-mail: spurgeonmwa@juno.com. **Contact:** W.W. Spurgeon, workshop director. Estab. 1982. Annual. Workshop held June 9, 2001. Workshop duration: 1 day. Average attendance: 200. Fiction, nonfiction, scriptwriting, children, young adult. Dedicated to "writing *mystery* fiction and crime-related nonfiction. Workshops and panels presented on plotting, dialogue, promotion, writers' groups, dealing with agents, synopsis and manuscript presentation, plus various technical aspects of crime and mystery." Held at the Holiday Inn, Rolling Meadows IL (suburban Chicago). **Previous agents/speakers have included:** Kimberley Cameron (Reese Halsey North), Javan Kienzle, Victoria Houston, William X. Kienzele, Jay Bonansinga, Michael Raleigh, James Brewer, Jeremiah Healy. "Our agents speak, do critiques and schmooze with those attending." Agents will be speaking and available for meetings with attendees.
Costs: $125 for MWA members; $150 for nonmembers; $50 extra for ms critique.
Accommodations: Easily accessible by car or train (from Chicago) Holiday Inn, Rolling Meadows $96/night plus tax; free airport bus (Chicago O'Hare) and previously arranged rides from train.
Additional Information: "We accept manuscripts for critique (first 30 pages maximum); $50 cost. Writers meet with critics during workshop for one-on-one discussions." Brochures available for SASE after January 1.

WRITERS' RETREAT WORKSHOP, Write It/Sell It, 2507 S. Boston Place, Tulsa OK 74114. Phone/fax: (918)583-1471. E-mail: wrwwisi@aol.com. Website: www.channel1.com/wisi. **Contact:** Gail Provost Stockwell, director. Estab. 1987. Annual. Conference held May 25-June 3. Conference duration: 10 days. Average attendance: 30. Novels-in-progress, all genres, narrative nonfiction. Held at Marydale Retreat Center in northern KY. "Teaches a proven step-by-step process for developing and completing a novel for publication, developed originally by the late Gary Provost. The practical application of lessons learned in classes, combined with continual private consultations with staff members, guarantees dramatic improvement in craft, writing technique and self-editing skills." **Previous agents/speakers have included:** Simon Lipsker (Writers House Agency); Steven Schragis (Publisher/Entertainment Lawyer); Elizabeth Lyon (editor/author); T.J. MacGregor (author). "Varying agents/agencies have been represented over the years." Agents will be speaking and available for meetings with attendees.
Costs: $1,635, new students; $1,475 returning students (includes lodging, meals, consultations and course materials.)
Accommodations: Marydale Retreat Center provides complimentary shuttle services between Cincinnati airport and the center.

North Central (IA, MN, NE, ND, SD, WI)

N: IOWA SUMMER WRITING FESTIVAL, 116 International Center, University of Iowa, Iowa City IA 52242-1802. (319)335-2534. E-mail: peggy-houston@uiowa.edu or amy-margolis@uiowa.edu. Website: www.edu/~iswfest. **Contact:** Peggy Houston, director. Assistant Director: Amy Margolis. Estab. 1987. Annual. Festival held in June and July. Workshops are one week or a weekend. Average attendance: limited to 12/class—over 1,500 participants throughout the summer. Held at University of Iowa campus. "We offer courses in most areas of writing: novel, short story, essay, poetry, playwriting, screenwriting, humor, travel, writing for children, memoir, women's writing, romance and mystery." **Previous agents/speakers have included:** Lee K. Abbott, Susan Power, Joy Harjo, Gish Jen, Abraham Verghese, Robert Olen Butler, Ethan Canin, Clark Blaise, Gerald Stern, Donald Justice, Michael Dennis Browne, Marvin Bell, Hope Edelman. Guest speakers are undetermined at this time.
Costs: $400/week; $150, weekend workshop (1998 rates). Discounts available for early registration. Housing and meals are separate.
Accommodations: "We offer participants a choice of accommodations: dormitory, $30/night; Iowa House, $60/night; Holiday Inn, $60/night (rates subject to changes)."

Additional Information: Brochure/guidelines are available in February. Inquiries by fax and e-mail OK.

SINIPEE WRITERS' WORKSHOP, Loras College, 1450 Alta Vista, Dubuque IA 52004-0178. (319)588-7139. Fax: (319)588-7964. E-mail: lcrosset@loras.edu. Website: www.loras.edu. **Contact:** Linda Crossett, director of continuing education. Director Emeritus: John Tigges. Estab. 1985. Annual. Conference held April 28, 2001. Average attendance: 50-75. To promote "primarily fiction although we do include poetry, nonfiction, and scriptwriting each program. The mentioned areas are treated in such a way that fiction writers can learn new ways to expand their abilities and writing techniques." The workshop is held on the campus of Loras College in Dubuque. "This campus holds a unique atmosphere and everyone seems to love the relaxed and restful mood it inspires. This in turn carries over to the workshop, and friendships are made that last in addition to learning and experiencing what other writers have gone through to attain success in their chosen field." **Previous agents/speakers have included:** Christine DeSmet (screenwriter); Paul Polansky (nonfiction writer); Carrie Radabaugh (editor).
Costs: $60 early registration; $65 at the door (includes all handouts, necessary materials for the workshop, coffee/snack break, lunch, drinks and snacks at autograph party following workshop).
Accommodations: Information is available for out-of-town participants, concerning motels, etc., even though the workshop is 1-day long.
Additional Information: Offers The John Tigges Writing Prize for Short Fiction, Nonfiction and Poetry. Limit 1,500 words (fiction and nonfiction), 40 lines (poetry). 1st prize in all 3 categories: $100 plus publication in an area newspaper or magazine; 2nd prize in both categories: $50; 3rd prize in both categories: $25. Written critique service available for contest entries, $15 extra. Conference brochures/guidelines are available February for SASE.

UNIVERSITY OF WISCONSIN AT MADISON WRITERS INSTITUTE, 610 Langdon St., Madison WI 53703. (608)262-3447. Fax: (608)265-2475. Website: www.dcs.wisc.edu/lsa. **Contact:** Christine DeSmet, director. Estab. 1990. Annual. Conference held July 12-13, 2001. Average attendance: 175. Conference held at University of Wisconsin at Madison. Themes: fiction and nonfiction. Guest speakers are published authors, editors and agents.
Costs: Approximately $195 for 2 days; critique fees additional.
Accommodations: Info on accommodations sent with registration confirmation. Critiques available. Conference brochures/guidelines are available for SASE.

WISCONSIN REGIONAL WRITERS' ASSOCIATION INC. CONFERENCES, Wisconsin Regional Writers' Assn., 510 W. Sunset Ave., Appleton WI 54911-1139. (920)734-3724. E-mail: wrwa@lakefield.net. Website: www.inkwells.net/wrwa. **Contact:** Patricia Dunson Boverhuis, president. Estab. 1948. Conferences held in May and September. Conference duration: 1-2 days. Provides workshops for fiction, nonfiction, scriptwriting, poetry. Presenters include authors, agents, editors and publishers. **Previous agents/speakers have included:** Marcia Preston (editory *Byline Magazine*). Agents will be speaking.
Additional Information: Brochure available for SASE or on website. Inquiries by e-mail and fax OK.

South Central (CO, KS, MO, NM, OK, TX)

ASPEN SUMMER WORDS, Aspen Writers' Foundation, Box 7726, Aspen CO 81612. (800)925-2526. Fax (970)920-5700. E-mail: aspenwrite@aol.com. Website: www.aspenwriters.org. **Contact:** Julie Comins, executive director. Estab. 1975. Annual. Conference held June 2001. Conference duration: 1 week. Average attendance: 75. Retreat for fiction, poetry, nonfiction and children's literature. Festival includes readings, networking opportunities, talks with agents, editors and publishers. **Previous agents/speakers have included:** Pam Houston (fiction writer); Christopher Merrill (poet); Fenton Johnson (memoir writer); Kent Haruf (fiction writer); Adrianne Miller (*Esquire* fiction editor); Elizabeth Hightower (*Outside Magazine* senior editor); Ken Sherman (editor) and many more.
Costs: $475/full tuition; $150/festival pass (2000).
Accommodations Free shuttle to/from airport and around town. Information on overnight accommodations available. Call (800) number for reservations. Rates for 2000: $60/night double; $110/night suggested off-campus housing.
Additional Information: Manuscripts to be submitted for review by faculty prior to conference. Conference brochures are available for SASE or on website.

N AUSTIN FILM FESTIVAL & HEART OF FILM SCREENWRITERS CONFERENCE, 1604 Nueces St., Austin TX 78701. (800)310-3378 or (512)478-4795. Fax:(512)478-6205. E-mail: austinfilm@aol.com. Website: www.austinfilmfestival.com. **Contact:** Barbara Morgan, director. Estab. 1994. Annual. Conference held October 4-7, 2001. Conference duration: 4 days. Average attendance: 1,500. The Austin Film Festival & Heart of Film Screenwriters Conference is a nonprofit organization committed to furthering the art, craft and business of screenwriters, and recognizing their contribution to the filmmaking industry. The 4-day Screenwriters Conference presents over 60 panels, roundtables, and workshops that address various aspects of screenwriting and filmmaking. Held at the Omni and Driskill Hotels, located in downtown Austin. Agents will be speaking and available for meetings with attendees.
Costs: $325 before May 15. Includes entrance to all panels, workshops and roundtables during the 4-day conference, as well as all films during the 8-night Film Exhibition, the Opening Night Party, and Closing Night Party.

Accommodations: Discounted rates on hotel accommodations are available to conference attendees if the reservations are made through the Austin Film Festival office. Contact Austin Film Festival for holds and rates. Continental Airlines offers discounted fares to conference attendees. Contact Austin Film Festival for more information.

Additional Information: "The Austin Film Festival is considered one of the most accessible festivals, and Austin is the premiere town for networking because when industry people are here, they are relaxed and friendly." Brochures available January 1 for SASE or on website. Inquiries by e-mail and fax OK.

AUSTIN WRITERS' LEAGUE WORKSHOPS/CONFERENCES/CLASSES, 1501 W. Fifth St., Suite E-2, Austin TX 78703. (512)499-8914. Fax: (512)499-0441. E-mail: awl@writersleague.org. Website: www.writersleague.org. **Contact:** Jim Bob McMillan, executive director. Estab. 1982. Conference held July 27-28, 2001 and are ongoing through the year. Conference duration: varies according to program. Average attendance from 15 to 200. To promote "all genres, fiction and nonfiction, poetry, writing for children, screenwriting, playwriting, legal and tax information for writers, also writing workshops for children and youth." Programs held at AWL Resource Center/Library, other sites in Austin and Texas. Topics include: finding and working with agents and publishers; writing and marketing short fiction; dialogue; characterization; voice; research; basic and advanced fiction writing/focus on the novel; business of writing; also workshops for genres. **Previous agents/speakers have included:** Carol Abel, Jane Dystel, Marianne Merola, John A. Ware, Andrea Brown, Jandy Nelson, Marlene Connor Lynch, Irene Kraas, Jim Donovan and Jim Hornfischer. Agents will be speaking and available for meetings with attendees. In July the League holds its annual Agents! Agents! Agents! Conference which provides writers with the opportunity to meet top agents from New York and the West Coast.

Costs: Varies from $45-185, depending on program. Most classes, $20-50; workshops $35-75; conferences: $125-185.

Accommodations: Special rates given at some hotels for program participants.

Additional Information: Critique sessions offered at some programs. Individual presenters determine critique requirements. Those requirements are then made available through Austin Writers' League office and in workshop promotion. Contests and awards programs are offered separately. Brochures/guidelines are available on request.

N: THE BAY AREA WRITERS LEAGUE ANNUAL CONFERENCE, P.O. Box 728, Seabrook TX 77586. (281)268-7500. Fax: (409)762-4787. E-mail: seamus@compuserve.com. Website: www.angelfire.com/tx2/bawl. **Contact:** Jim Casey, webmaster. Estab. 1988. Annual. Conference held May 13-14, 2001. Conference duration: 2 days. Average attendance: 100. "We present a comprehensive range of topics." Conference held at the University of Houston-Clear Lake. **Previous agents/speakers have included:** Michelle Brummer (Donald Maass Agency), Angela Adair-Hoy. Agents will be speaking and available for meetings with attendees.

Costs: $85, plus $15 for annual membership (includes all sessions, lunch on both days, Friday evening reception). One-day price is $50.

Accommodations: Information is available. "We attempt to assist out-of-town attendees individually."

Additional Information: "We have a contest for novice writers in conjunction with the conference." Brochures available March for SASE or on website. Inquiries by fax or e-mail OK.

N: CRAFT OF WRITING ANNUAL CONFERENCE, UNT, P.O. Box 310560, Denton TX 76203-0560. (940)565-3481. Fax: (940)565-3801. E-mail: gthompso@scs.cmm.unt.edu. Website: www.orgs.unt.edu/writingcraft/. **Contact:** Gina Thompson, program manager. Estab. 1982. Annual. Conference held October 27-28, 2000. Conference duration: 2 days. Average attendance: 110. Held at the University Union at the University of North Texas, Denton, Texas. Conference purpose: to help new and experienced writers explore the creative, technical, and business aspects of writing. Areas of concentration: novel (mainstream); contemporary and historical romance; science fiction/fantasy/horror; short story; western/action/adventure; poetry; children/young adult; nonfiction; screenplay; short nonfiction articles. Themes: Changes taking place within the publishing industry, especially e-books. "The goal is to help writers improve their craft, provide marketing strategies, and offer tips on how to make it in this competitive business." **Agents/speakers attending include:** Michael Rosenberg; Paul Levine (Paul S. Levine Literary Agency); Jandy Nelson (Manus & Associates Literary). Agents will be speaking and available for meetings with attendees.

Costs: $199 (includes 2-day registration, lunch both days, campus parking, 2 ms contest entries; meet the speaker book signings, "Letters Live," performance of vignettes by professional actors).

Accommodations: Rooms are blocked at local hotels at special rates. Special rates for shuttles available.

Additional Information: "Roundtables allow participants one-on-one access to agents and editors; 30 workshops give participants wide choices; manuscript critique sessions allow participants to have works read and critiqued by experienced writers." Conference sponsored by Greater Dallas Writers' Association. Brochures available in June for SASE. Inquiries by e-mail and fax OK.

FRONTIERS IN WRITING, P.O. Box 19303, Amarillo TX 79114. (806)354-2305. Fax: (806)354-2536. E-mail: cliff@nts-online.net. Website: www.users.arn.net/~ppw/. Estab. 1980. Annual. Conference held June 2001. Duration:

CONTACT THE EDITOR of *Guide to Literary Agents* by e-mail at literaryagents @fwpubs.com with your questions and comments.

1½ days. Average attendance: 100. Nonfiction, poetry, scriptwriting and fiction (including mystery, romance, mainstream, science fiction and fantasy). **Previous agents/speakers have included:** Ann Crispin (science fiction), Don Maass (agent), Cherise Grant (Simon & Schuster editor), Melanie Rigney (*Writer's Digest* editor).
Costs: 1999 conference: $80 Members; $115 Non-members ($20 for membership). (Includes Friday night dinner, Saturday breakfast, lunch and beverages—lodging and transportation separate.)
Accommodations: Special conference room rate.
Additional information: Sponsors a contest. Deadline: April 1, 2001. Guidelines available for SASE or on website. Writers may request information via fax. Brochures and guidelines available December 2000 for SASE or on website.

N: GLORIETA CHRISTIAN WRITERS' CONFERENCE, P.O. Box 8, Glorieta NM 87535-0008. (800)797-4222. Fax: (505)757-6149. E-mail: monadsedena.net. Website: www.desertcritters.com. **Contact:** Mona Hodgson, director. Estab. 1997. Annual. Conference held October 16-20, 2001. Conference duration: Tuesday afternoon through Saturday lunch. Average attendance: 350. Include programs for all types of writing. Conference held in the Glorieta, a Lifeway Conference Center. **Agents/speakers attending include:** Bill Watkins (William Pens Agency), Janet Kobobel Grant (Books & Such Agency). Agents will be speaking and available for meetings with attendees.
Costs: $510, for private rooms, $460, for double-occupancy rooms (includes seminars, meals, lodging). Critiques are available for an additional $35; writing contest held, $5/entry.
Accommodations: Hotel rooms are available at the Glorieta, A Lifeway Conference Center. Sante Fe Shuttle offers service from the Albuquerque or Sante Fe airports to the conference center.
Additional Information: Brochures available April 1 for SASE or on website. Inquiries by fax or e-mail OK.

NATIONAL WRITERS ASSOCIATION FOUNDATION CONFERENCE, 3140 S. Peoria, #295, Aurora CO 80014. (303)841-0246. Fax: (303)751-8593. E-mail address: sandywriter@aol.com. Website: www.nationalwriters.com. **Contact:** Sandy Whelchel, executive director. Estab. 1926. Annual. Conference held in June. Conference held in Denver, CO. Conference duration: 3 days. Average attendance: 200-300. General writing and marketing.
Costs: $200 (approx.).
Additional Information: Awards for previous contests will be presented at the conference. Conference brochures/guidelines are available for SASE.

N: NORTHEAST TEXAS COMMUNITY COLLEGE & NETWO ANNUAL CONFERENCE, Continuing Education, Northeast Texas Community College, P.O. Box 1307, Mount Pleasant TX 75456-9991. (903)572-1911, ext. 241. Fax: (903)572-6712. Website: www.ntcc.cc.tx.us/instruction/conted.html. **Contact:** Charlotte Biggerstaff, dean of continuing education. Estab. 1987. Annual. Conference held April 7, 2001. Conference duration: 1 day. Presenters include agents, writers, editors and publishers.
Additional Information: Write for additional information. Conference is co-sponsored by the Northeast Texas Writers Organization (NETWO).

✓ PIKES PEAK WRITERS CONFERENCE, 5550 North Union Blvd., Colorado Springs CO 80918. Fax: (719)597-8891. E-mail: ppwc@poboxes.com. Website: www.ppwc.net. Estab. 1994. Annual. Conference held April 27-29, 2001. Conference duration: Friday 11:30 am to Sunday 2 pm. Average attendance: 350-400. Commercial fiction. Held at the Wyndham Hotel. "Workshops, presentations and panels focus on writing and publishing genre fiction—romance, scifi and fantasy, suspense thrillers, action adventure, mysteries. **Agents/speakers attending include:** Marc Resnick (St. Martin's Press); Scott Moyers (Random House); Steve Saffel (Del Rey); Robert Crais; Jerry Jenkins; Robert Vaughan; Debra Dixon; Jo Beverly. Faculty added to website as confirmed. Agents will be speaking and available for meetings with attendees.
Costs: $230 (includes all meals).
Accommodations: Marriott Colorado Springs holds a block of rooms for conference attendees until March 30 at a special $73 rate (1-800-962-6982).
Additional Information: Readings with critique are available or Friday afternoon. One-on-one meetings with editors and agents available Saturday and Sunday. Brochures available in October. Inquiries by e-mail OK. Registration form available on website.

✓ ROCKY MOUNTAIN BOOK FESTIVAL, 2123 Downing St., Denver CO 80211-5210. (303)839-8320. Fax: (303)839-8319. E-mail: ccftb@compuserve.com. Website: www.coloradobook.org. **Contact:** Christiane Citron, executive director. Estab. 1991. Annual. Festival held March 3-4, 2001. Festival duration: 2 days. Average attendance: 10,000. Festival promotes work published from all genres. Held at Denver Merchandise Mart in Denver. Offers a wide variety of panels. Approximately 200 authors are scheduled to speak each year. **Previous speakers have included:** Sherman Alexie, Dixie Carter, Dave Barry, Alice Walker, Dr. Andrew Weil, Jill Kerr Conway, Bill Moyers and Dava Sobel.
Costs: $4 adult; $2 child.
Additional Information: Please submit bio and publicity material for consideration.

✓ ROCKY MOUNTAIN CHILDREN'S BOOK FESTIVAL, 2123 Downing St., Denver CO 80205-5210. (303)839-8320. Fax: (303)839-8319. E-mail: ccftb@compuserve.com. Website: www.coloradobook.org. **Contact:** Christiane Citron, executive director. Estab. 1996. Annual festival held March 3-4, 2001. Festival duration: 2 days. Average attendance: 10,000. Fiction, nonfiction, screenwriting. Festival promotes published work for and about children/

families. Held at Denver Merchandise Mart. Approximately 100 authors speak annually. **Previous speakers have included:** Ann M. Martin, Sharon Creech, Laura Numeroff, Jean Craighead George, the Kratt Brothers, Bruce Lansky and Jane Yolen.

Costs: None.

Additional Information: "For published authors of children's/family works only." Brochure/guidelines available for SASE.

N: SANTA FE SCREENWRITING CONFERENCE, P.O. Box 28423. Sante Fe NM 87592-8423. (505)424-1501. Fax: (505)471-7126. E-mail: writeit@sfesc.com. Website: www.sfesc.com. **Contact:** Rick Reichman or Larry N. Stouffer, co-executive directors. Estab. 1999. Annual. Conference held May 25-28, 2001. Conference duration: 4 days. Average attendance: 200. The Santa Fe Screenwriting Conference is designed to teach the art and craft of screenwriting. Held at the scenic campus of St. John's College in Santa Fe, New Mexico. **Previous agents/speakers have included:** Jeff Aghassi (The Alpern Group); Nicole Graham (Writers & Artists Agency). Agents will be speaking and available for meetings with attendees.

Costs: $465 before February 15 or $565 at the door (includes 9 hours of in-depth classroom instruction, 24 one and one-half hour workshops, a panel discussion, live scene readings, Fade In breakfast, Fade Out Luncheon, door prizes, and the outrageous "J.W. Eaves Movie Ranch Barbeque Blowout and Wild West Fiesta" party on Sunday night).

Accommodations: Accommodations are available at both the dorms at St. John's College and through Santa Fe Accommodations which represent hotels, motels, B&B's and condos with a variety of price ranges. Santa Fe Accommodations room prices range from $115 (including breakfast) and up. St. John's dorm prices range from $75-98 (including breakfast and lunch). Shuttle services to and from Albuquerque Airport cost $21 each way (it is a 65 mile drive to Santa Fe). Shuttle service to downtown Santa Fe and to the J.W. Eaves Movie Ranch are provided by the Conference at no cost to the attendees. The Conference has an arrangement with Southwest Airlines to give conference attendees a 10% discount.

Additional Information: "Unique to any other screenwriting conference in the world, the Santa Fe Screenwriting Conference is devoted almost exclusively toward teaching the art and craft of writing screenplays. The Conference is suitable for beginning, intermediate and advanced screenwriters. What separates this from other conferences is the nine hours of in-depth instruction from one Mentor. Classrooms will have no more than 40 students which encourages interactive participation. There will be a minimum of eight classes. Each class will have no more than 40 students and be led by a recognized Mentor in the field of screenwriting. Last year's Mentors were Chris DeVore (*Elephant Man*), William C. Martell (17 produced screenplays), Aaron Mendelsohn (*Air Bud*), Rick Reichman (author of *Formatting Your Screenplay*), Danny Rubin (*Groundhog Day*), Linda Seger (author of *Making A Good Script Great*), Joan Tewkesbury (*Nashville*), and Cynthia Whitcomb (*Buffalo Gals* plus 25 produced screenplays). Most of these will return for the 2001 Conference."

N: SHORT COURSE ON PROFESSIONAL WRITING, University of Oklahoma, 860 Van Vleet Oval, Room 101, Norman OK 73071-0270. (405)325-2721. Fax: (405)325-7565. E-mail: jmadisondavis@ou.edu. Website: http://jmc.ou.edu/conference. **Contact:** J. Madison Davis, professor of professional writing. Estab. 1938. Annual. Conference held June 2001. Conference duration: 3 days. Average attendance: 100-200. All areas of writing for publication, excluding poetry. Held at the Holiday Inn, Norman. **Agents/speakers attending include:** Alison Bond, Lois de la Haba, Peter Rubie. Agents will be speaking and available for meetings with attendees.

Costs: $195 (includes banquet, all sessions) In addition: Private ms consultations for $45. Academic credit available for additional cost.

Accommodations: Special rates at Holiday Inn available: $64/single or double (conference rate).

Additional Information: "A warm, friendly and supportive conference." Brochures available April for SASE. Inquiries by e-mail and fax OK.

WRITERS WORKSHOP IN SCIENCE FICTION, English Department/University of Kansas, Lawrence KS 66045-2115. (785)864-3380. Fax: (785)864-4298. E-mail: jgunn@falcon.cc.ukans.edu. Website: http://falcon.cc.ukans.edu/~sfcenter/. **Contact:** James Gunn, professor. Estab. 1985. Annual. Conference held June 25-July 6, 2001. Average attendance: 15. Conference for writing and marketing science fiction. "Classes meet in university housing on the University of Kansas campus. Workshop sessions operate informally in a lounge." **Previous agents/speakers have included:** Frederick Pohl, Kij Johnson, Chris McKitterich.

Costs: Tuition: $400. Housing and meals are additional.

Accommodations: Housing information available. Several airport shuttle services offer reasonable transportation from the Kansas City International Airport to Lawrence. During past conferences, students were housed in a student dormitory at $12.50/day double, $23.50/day single.

Additional Information: "Admission to the workshop is by submission of an acceptable story. Two additional stories should be submitted by the middle of June. These three stories are copied and distributed to other participants for critiquing and are the basis for the first week of the workshop; one story is rewritten for the second week." Brochures/guidelines are available for SASE. "The Writers Workshop in Science Fiction is intended for writers who have just started to sell their work or need that extra bit of understanding or skill to become a published writer."

West (AZ, CA, HI, NV, UT)

⚅ AMERICAN FOOD MEDIA CONFERENCE, 2555 Main St., St. Helena CA 94574. (707)967-0600. Fax: (707)967-2410. E-mail: s_cussen@culinary.edu. Website: www.ciachef.edu. **Contact:** Sue Cussen, director of marketing. Estab. 1994. Annual. Conference held November 6-9. Conference duration: 4 days. Average attendance: 125. Conference works to define the ever-evolving profession of communicating about food. Held at The Culinary Institute of America's Greystone campus. "The Art & Craft of Food Writing," "Publishing & Marketing." **Agents/speakers attending include:** Doe Cover (The Doe Cover Agency). Agents will be speaking.
Costs: $750 (includes conference, seminary, lunches and breakfasts).
Accommodations: Limited on-site accommodations available. Single: $495. Rental car is needed for transportation to airport.
Additional Information: Brochures available in August for SASE or on website.

⚅ CALIFORNIA WRITER'S CLUB CONFERENCE AT ASILOMAR, 3975 Kim Ct., Sebastopol CA 95472-5736. (800)467-8128. E-mail: gpmansergh@aol.com. **Contact:** Gil Mansergh, director. Estab. 1941. Annual. Conference held June 29-July 1, 2001. Conference duration: 3 days, Friday afternoon through Sunday lunch. Average attendance: 350. Conference offers opportunity to learn from and network with successful writers, agents and editors in Asilomar's beautiful and historic beach side setting on the shores of Monterey Bay. Presentations, panels, hands-on workshops and agent/editor appointments focus on writing and marketing short stories, novels, articles, nonfiction books, poetry and screenplays for children and adults. Skilled writer/teacher provide sessions for novice and professional writers of all genres.
Costs: $450 includes all conference privileges, shared lodging and 6 meals. There is a $90 surcharge for a single room.
Accommodations: Part of the California State Park system, Asilomar is rustic and beautiful. Julia Morgan designed redwood and stone buildings share 105 acres of dunes and pine forests with modern AIA and National Academy of Design winning lodges. Monterey airport is a 15 minute taxi drive away.
Additional Information: First prize winners in all 7 categories of the *California Writers' Club Writing Contest* receive free registration to the Conference. $10 entry fee. Contest deadline is May 7, 2001. Brochure and contest submission rules will be available in late February.

IWWG EARLY SPRING IN CALIFORNIA CONFERENCE, International Women's Writing Guild, P.O. Box 810, Gracie Station, New York NY 10028-0082. (212)737-7536. Fax: (212)737-9469. E-mail: iwwg@iwwg.com. Website: www.IWWG.com. **Contact:** Hannelore Hahn, executive director. Estab. 1982. Annual. Conference held March 16-18, 2001. Average attendance: 80. Conference to promote "creative writing, personal growth and empowerment." Site is a redwood forest mountain retreat in Santa Cruz, California.
Costs: $325 for weekend program with room and board, $150 for weekend program without room and board.
Accommodations: Accommodations are all at conference site.
Additional Information: Conference brochures/guidelines are available for SASE. Inquiries by e-mail and fax OK.

MAUI WRITERS CONFERENCE, P.O. Box 1118, Kihei HI 96753. (808)879-0061. Fax: (808)879-6233. E-mail: writers@maui.net. Website: www.mauiwriters.com (includes information covering all programs offered, writing competitions, presenters past and present, writers forum bulletin board, published attendees books, dates, price, hotel and travel information). **Contact:** Shannon and John Tullius. Estab. 1993. Annual. Conference held the end of August (Labor Day weekend). Conference duration: 4 days. Conference held at Grand Wailea Resort. Average attendance: 800. For fiction, nonfiction, poetry, children's, young adult, horror, mystery, romance, science fiction, journalism, screenwriting. **Previous agents/speakers have included:** Linda Allen (Linda Allen Agency); Andrea Brown (Andrea Brown Literary Agency); Kimberley Cameron (The Reece Halsey Agency); Susan Crawford (Crawford Literary Agency); Laurie Horwitz (Creative Artists Agency); Amy Kossow (Linda Allen Literary Agency); Owen Laster (William Morris); Jillian Manus (Manus & Associates Literary Agency); Craig Nelson (The Craig Nelson Co.); Elizabeth Pomada (Larsen/Pomada Literary Agency); Susan Travis (Susan Travis Literary Agency). Agents will be speaking and available for meetings with attendees.
Additional Information: "We offer a comprehensive view of the business of publishing, with over 2,500 consultation slots with industry agents, editors and screenwriting professionals as well as workshops and sessions covering writing instruction." Write or call for additional information.

MOUNT HERMON CHRISTIAN WRITERS CONFERENCE, P.O. Box 413, Mount Hermon CA 95041-0413. (831)335-4466. Fax: (831)335-9218. E-mail: slist@mhcamps.org. Website: www.mounthermon.org. **Contact:** David R. Talbott, director of specialized programs. Estab. 1970. Annual. Conference held Friday-Tuesday over Palm Sunday weekend, April 6-10, 2001. Average attendance: 350. "We are a broad-ranging conference for all areas of Christian writing, including fiction, children's, poetry, nonfiction, magazines, inspirational and devotional writing, books, educational curriculum, and radio and TV scriptwriting. This is a working, how-to conference, with many workshops within the conference involving on-site writing assignments. The conference is sponsored by and held at the 440-acre Mount Hermon Christian Conference Center near San Jose, California, in the heart of the coastal redwoods. The faculty/student

insider report

Learn about agents in a tropical paradise

Breathing the air of the Hawaiian islands has done Corson Hirschfeld some serious good, in more ways than one. Outside of the sheer tropical pleasure it's offered the sightseer in Hirschfeld, Hawaii has motivated him to expand his twenty-five-year career as a professional photographer. Seduced by Hawaii's prodigious forests and natural wildness, his visits throughout the 1990s provided Hirschfeld a world of photographic possibilities.

Corson Hirschfeld

Those visits also unleashed his newest creative undertaking: Hirschfeld the mystery novelist. As he does in his photography, Hirschfeld captures another wild Hawaiian world in his first novel, *Aloha, Mr. Lucky* (Forge). The novel follows the exploits of a jaded, slap-happy journalist, Star Holly, as well as a group of degenerate thieves. Several murders intertwine Holly and those characters, and affect Holly's quest to grudgingly make something of himself.

"I wanted to tap into a broad range of fictional characters, some of whom were very unfamiliar with Hawaii, and put them against locales that are definitely 'wild Hawaii' and many of them off-the-beaten-path," Hirchfeld says. "It took a lot of soul-searching, drafting, and workshop feedback to know I had the novel down pat."

He was determined, he says, to see his dream of writing a first novel through and to find out "all the peculiarities of the agenting and publishing worlds." When someone suggested he attend the Maui Writers Conference, he promptly made plans to go and started to prepare himself several months beforehand. He planned to be very conscientious, "not to badger and pester to death agents or editors with the papers, synopsis, bio, and the first few chapters I took along."

A mild-mannered yet determined man, Hirschfeld contends he went to Maui "with an intense purpose of finding out about the publishing game," yet without any strategy to "pick the brains" of every agent or editor he met. For writers visiting conferences, he advises the low-key approach: "Be prepared with business cards, a synopsis, bio, first several chapters, or query. In case someone asks, 'Do you have anything with you?' your answer should be in your briefcase. But you shouldn't flaunt those things in agents' faces, as in 'Hey, I've got 250 manuscript pages for you right here . . . take 'em with you.' Use common sense. They don't want to tote around your bundle."

For writers who worry that agents won't be able to get a true sense of their work from short samples, Hirshfeld says you can rest assured. His experience at the Maui conference showed him agents can get interested in your writing by glancing at the synopsis or first manuscript page. "They'll want to feel the urge to turn the page." In the event an agent does take an interest, Hirschfeld suggests that a writer have his work completely polished before making any big conference contacts.

Although he sparked agent interest at the conference, no deal materialized. A few weeks later, however, a friend urged Hirschfeld to contact agent Eleanor Wood from the Spectrum Literary Agency. Following the advice he heard at the conference, he sent a query letter to Wood. When she responded positively, he sent the manuscript of *Aloha, Mr. Lucky* to her on a Thursday. She called him the next Tuesday to confirm her interest in representing him.

From that point, Hirschfeld says he became wiser about the author/agent relationship: about why tactfulness plays a huge role in that relationship and about trusting an agent's know-how of the publishing world. "Most agents are savvy and knowledgeable, and they know the whims of editors and publishers. These agents and editors interact all the time—they have an 'inside' view into what's really going on in publishing and what these houses are looking for."

This trust played an important role when Wood decided to take an uncommon approach to selling the manuscript. Instead of settling for a typical two-book contract, Wood negotiated a one-book deal, based primarily on the faith and hope that *Aloha, Mr. Lucky* would attract wide attention as a strong first novel and, therefore, merit a more lucrative second book deal. It was a risk, of course, but Hirschfeld trusted Wood's confidence in the manuscript. They never second-guessed themselves.

There was an emotional side to the decision as well. "Without another book under contract, I felt a surge of freedom carrying me into that second novel," Hirschfeld says. "I was uncertain about whether I could even produce another novel on such demand. The one-book deal paid off in the interests of my creativity and my approach to what I wanted the book to do. I felt a lot of relief that many writers might not feel under the pressure of a two- or three-book deal."

Because his first novel, *Aloha, Mr. Lucky*, is set in Hawaii, author Corson Hirschfeld decided that attending the Maui Writers Conference would be the perfect way to learn about agents. The knowledge he gained at the conference helped him attract the attention of agent Eleanor Wood.

Reprinted with permission from Forge

Plus, starting the second novel without an absolute deadline was reliving the thrill of doing it from scratch again." Ultimately, that negotiating position paid off. Wood and Hirschfeld sold the second novel, *Too High*, again to Forge who have scheduled it to come out in spring 2001.

Another word of advice from Hirschfeld is to, if possible, "meet your agent after she agrees to represent your work, after the correspondence has taken place. The personal relationship is extremely important, if not most important," he says. "It's kind of like a marriage; there's the paper contract, of course, but the reality is you must get along if it's going to work."

How does he know the book has made it successfully into the world? Hirschfeld mentions a phone call from a friend who lives near the active Kilauea volcano. The acquaintance, he says, is a coy, longtime island resident, and not given to easy praise. "I immediately knew that voice on the other end," Hirschfeld says. "All he said was, 'Cool. Yeah, it works.' That was all I needed to know. That was a great endorsement of the novel to me."

—*Jeffrey Hillard*

---

ratio is about 1:6 or 7. The bulk of our faculty are editors and publisher representatives from major Christian publishing houses nationwide." **Agents/speakers attending include:** Jerry B. Jenkins, Sally E. Stuart, Elaine W. Colvin. Agents speaking and available for meetings with attendees.

Costs: Registration fees include tuition, conference sessions, resource notebook, refreshment breaks, room and board and vary from $545 (economy) to $770 (deluxe), double occupancy (2000 fees).

Accommodations: Registrants stay in hotel-style accommodations, and full board is provided as part of conference fees. Meals are taken family style, with faculty joining registrants. Airport shuttles are available from the San Jose International Airport. Housing is not required of registrants, but about 95% of our registrants use Mount Hermon's own housing facilities (hotel style double-occupancy rooms). Meals with the conference are required and are included in all fees.

Additional Information: "The residential nature of our conference makes this a unique setting for one-on-one interaction with faculty/staff. There is also a decided inspirational flavor to the conference, and general sessions with well-known speakers are a highlight." Registrants may submit 1 work for critique in advance of the conference, then have personal interviews with critiquers during the conference. No advance work is required however. Conference brochures/guidelines are available for SASE. Inquiries by e-mail and fax OK.

PASADENA WRITERS' FORUM, P.C.C. Extended Learning Center, 1570 E. Colorado Blvd., Pasadena CA 91106-2003. (626)585-7608. Fax: (626)796-5204. E-mail: pcclearn@webcom.com. **Contact:** Meredith Brucker, coordinator. Estab. 1954. Annual. Conference held March 17, 2001. Average attendance: 225. "For the novice as well as the professional writer in any field of interest: fiction or nonfiction, including scripts, children's, humor and poetry." Held on the campus of Pasadena City College. A panel discussion by agents, editors or authors is usually featured at the end of the day.

Costs: $100 (includes box lunch and coffee hour).

Additional Information: Brochure upon request, no SASE necessary. "Pasadena City College also periodically offers an eight-week class 'Writing for Publication.' "

N PIMA WRITERS' WORKSHOP, Pima College, 2202 W. Anklam Rd., Tucson AZ 85709. (520)206-6974. Fax: (520)206-6020. E-mail: mfiles@pimacc.pima.edu. **Contact:** Meg Files, director. Estab. 1988. Annual. Conference held May 25-27, 2001. Conference duration 3 days. Average attendance 250. "For anyone interested in writing—beginning or experienced writer. The workshop offers sessions on writing short stories, novels, nonfiction articles and books, children's and juvenile stories, poetry and screenplays." Sessions are held in the Center for the Arts on Pima Community College's West Campus. **Previous agents/speakers have included:** Faye Bender and Sandra Zane (agents), Steve Kaire (screenwriter), Michael Blake, Ron Carlson, Gregg Levoy, Nancy Mairs, Linda McCarriston, Larry McMurty, Barbara Kingsolver, Jerome Stern, Connie Willis. Agents will be speaking and available for meetings with attendees.

Costs: $65 (can include ms critique). Participants may attend for college credit, in which case fees are $83 for Arizona residents and $310 for out-of-state residents. Meals and accommodations not included.

Accommodations: Information on local accommodations is made available, and special workshop rates are available at a specified motel close to the workshop site (about $60/night).

Additional Information: "The workshop atmosphere is casual, friendly, and supportive, and guest authors are very accessible. Readings, films and panel discussions are offered as well as talks and manuscript sessions." Participants may have up to 20 pages critiqued by the author of their choice. Mss must be submitted 3 weeks before the workshop. Conference brochure/guidelines available for SASE. Inquiries by e-mail OK.

N **SAN DIEGO STATE UNIVERSITY WRITERS' CONFERENCE**, SDSU College of Extended Studies, San Diego CA 92182-1920. (619)594-2517. Fax: (619)594-7080. E-mail address: xtension@mail.sdsu.edu. Website: www.ces.sdsu.edu. **Contact:** Paula Pierce, assistant to director of extension and conference facilitator. Estab. 1984. Annual. Conference held the third weekend in January. Conference duration: 2 days. Average attendance: approximately 350. Fiction, nonfiction, scriptwriting, e-books. Held at the Town & Country Hotel, Mission Valley. "Each year the SDSU Writers Conference offers a variety of workshops for the beginner and the advanced writer. This conference allows the individual writer to choose which workshop best suits his/her needs. In addition to the workshops, editor/agent appointments and office hours are provided so attendees may meet with speakers, editors and agents in small, personal groups to discuss specific questions. A reception is offered Saturday immediately following the workshops where attendees may socialize with the faculty in a relaxed atmosphere. Keynote speaker is to be determined." **Agents/speakers attending include:** Loretta Barrett, Jillian Manus, Peter Gethers, Rick Horgan, Richard Walter, Paula Eykelfof, Michael Larsen, Stacy Gremer, Tracy Sherrod. Agents will be speaking and available for meetings with attendees.
Costs: Approximately $230 (includes all conference workshops and office hours, coffee and pastries in the morning, lunch and reception Saturday evening).
Accommodations: Town & Country Hotel (800)772-8527. Attendees must make their own travel arrangements.
Additional Information: Editor/agent appointments are private, one-on-one opportunities to meet with editors and agents to discuss your submission. To receive a brochure, e-mail, call or send a postcard with address to: SDSU Writers Conference, College of Extended Studies, 5250 Campanile Drive, San Diego State University, San Diego CA 92182-1920. No SASE required.

N **SANTA BARBARA WRITERS' CONFERENCE**, P.O. Box 304, Carpinteria CA 93014. (805)684-2250. Fax: (805)684-7003. **Contact:** Mary Conrad, conference co-director. Estab. 1973. Annual. Conference held June 22-29, 2001, at Westmont College in Montecito. Average attendance: 350. For poetry, fiction, nonfiction, journalism, playwriting, screenplays, travel writing, children's literature. **Previous agents/speakers have included:** Phillip Levine, Sol Stein, Dorothy Wall, Robert Fulghum, Gore Vidal and William Styron.
Accommodations: Onsite accommodations available. Additional accommodations available at area hotels.
Additional Information: Individual critiques are also available. Submit 1 ms of no more than 3,000 words in advance with SASE. Competitions with awards sponsored as part of the conference. Send SASE for brochure and registration forms.

N **THE WILLIAM SAROYAN WRITERS' CONFERENCE**, P.O. Box 5331, Fresno CA 93755-5331. Phone/fax: (209)224-2516. E-mail: law@pacbell.net. **Contact:** Linda West. Estab. 1992. Annual. Conference held March 30-April 1, 2001. Conference duration: 3 days. Average attendance: 250-280. "This conference is designed to provide insights that could lift you out of the pack and into publication. You will learn from masters of the writing craft, you will discover current and future market trends, and you will meet and network with editors and agents who can sell, buy, or publish your manuscript." Fiction, nonfiction, scriptwriting. Held at the Piccadilly Inn Hotel across from the Fresno Airport. **Previous agents/speakers have included:** Linda Mead (literary agent); John Baker (editorial director *Publishers Weekly*); John Kremer (marketing guru); Barbara Kuroff (editor, Writer's Digest Books); Andrea Brown (literary agent).
Costs: $225 for 3 days (includes some meals). Single day fees: $85 for Friday, $165 for Saturday, $50 for Sunday.
Accommodations: Special lodging rate at the Piccadilly Inn Hotel: $68 single, $78 double plus room tax. "Be sure to mention the William Saroyan Writers' Conference to obtain this special rate. Reservations must be made two weeks in advance to assure availability of room at the conference site."
Additional Information: Offers "Persie" writing contest in connection with conference. Also offers a pre-conference ms critique service for fiction and nonfiction mss. Fees: $35/book chapter or short story, maximum length 20 pgs., double-spaced. Send SASE for brochure and guidelines. Fax and e-mail inquiries OK.

✓ **SELLING TO HOLLYWOOD**, (formerly Writers Connection Selling to Hollywood), P.O. Box 12860, Cincinnati OH 45212. (513)731-9212. E-mail: sth@sellingtohollywood.com. Website: www.sellingtohollywood.com. **Contact:** Sean Coffman, director. Estab. 1988. Annual. Conference held in August in LA area. Conference duration: 3 days. Average attendance: 275. "Conference targets scriptwriters and fiction writers, whose short stories, books, or scripts have strong cinematic potential, and who want to make valuable contacts in the film industry. Full conference registrants receive a private consultation with the film industry producer or professional of his/her choice who make up the faculty. Panels, workshops, 'Ask a Pro' discussion groups and networking sessions include over 50 agents, professional film and TV scriptwriters, and independent as well as studio and TV and feature film producers."
Costs: In 2000: full conference by July 15, $500; after July 15: $525. Includes some meals.
Accommodations: $100/night (in LA) for private room; $50/shared room. Discount with designated conference airline.
Additional Information: "This is the premier screenwriting conference of its kind in the country, unique in its offering of an industry-wide perspective from pros working in all echelons of the film industry. Great for making contacts." Conference brochure/guidelines available March; phone, e-mail, fax or send written request.

SOCIETY OF CHILDREN'S BOOK WRITERS AND ILLUSTRATORS/NATIONAL CONFERENCE ON WRITING & ILLUSTRATING FOR CHILDREN, 8271 Beverly Blvd., Los Angeles CA 90048-4515. (323)782-1010. Fax: (323)782-1892. E-mail: scbwi@juno.com. Website: www.scbwi.org. **Contact:** Stephen Mooser, president.

Estab. 1972. Annual. Conference held in August. Conference duration: 4 days. Average attendance: 500. Writing and illustrating for children. Held at the Century Plaza Hotel in Los Angeles. **Previous agents/speakers have included:** Andrea Brown, Steven Malk, Scott Treimel (agents), Ashley Bryan, Bruce Coville, Karen Hesse, Harry Mazer, Lucia Monfried and Russell Freedman. Agents will be speaking and available for meetings with attendees.
Costs: $320 (members); $350 (late registration, members); $375 (nonmembers). Cost does not include hotel room.
Accommodations: Information on overnight accommodations available. Conference rates at the hotel average $135/night.
Additional Information: Ms and illustration critiques are available. Conference brochures/guidelines are available June with SASE.

N: SOCIETY OF SOUTHWESTERN AUTHORS WRITERS' CONFERENCE—WRANGLING WITH WRITING, P.O. Box 30355, Tucson AZ 85751-0355. (520)296-5299. Fax: (520)296-0409. E-mail: wporter202@aol.com. Website: www.azstarnet.com/nonprofit/ssa. **Contact:** Penny Porter, conference chair. Estab. 1972. Annual. Two-day conference held January 19-20, 2001. Maximum attendance: 300. Fiction, nonfiction, screenwriting, poetry. Conference offers 36 workshops covering all genres of writing; pre-scheduled one-on-one interviews with agents, editors and publishers. **Agents/speakers attending include:** Editors: Bob Early, John Kremer, Bob Bose, Brad Melton and Harvey Starbrough. Agents: Irene Kraas, Rosenberg Group, Mark Ryan, Andrea Brown and Michelle Frey. Keynote speakers for 2001: Ray Bradbury (author); Jack Heffron (Writer's Digest Book Division editor-in-chief). Agents will be speaking and available for meetings with attendees.
Costs: $175.
Additional Information: Conference brochures/guidelines are available for SASE.

N: SOUTHERN CALIFORNIA WRITERS' CONFERENCE, 4555 Rhode Island, San Diego CA 92116-1055. (619)291-6805. Fax: (253)390-8577. E-mail: wewrite@writersconference.com. Website: www.writersconference.com. **Contact:** Michael Steven Gregory, executive director. Estab. 1986. Annually. Conference held Februrary 16-19, 2001. Conference duration: 3 days. Average attendance: 250. Fiction and nonfiction, with particular emphasis on reading and critiquing. Held at Holiday Inn Hotel and Suites located in Old Town, San Diego. "Extensive reading and critiquing workshops by working writers. Over 3 dozen 2-hour workshops and no time limit late-night sessions." Agents will be speaking and available for meetings with attendees.
Costs: $250 (includes all workshops and events, as well as Saturday evening banquet).
Accommodations: Discounted rates available at Holiday Inn. Complimentary shuttle service provided from airport and Amtrak.
Additional Information: Late-night read and critique workshops run until 3 or 4 a.m. Brochures available for SASE or on website. Inquiries by e-mail and fax OK.

N: SQUAW VALLEY COMMUNITY OF WRITERS FICTION WORKSHOP, P.O. Box 2352. Olympic Valley CA 96146-2352. (530)274-8551. E-mail: svcw@oro.net. Website: www.squawvalleywriters.org. **Contact:** Ms. Brett Hall Jones, executive director. Estab. 1969. Annual. Conference held August. Conference duration: 1 week. Average attendance: 125. Fiction. Held in Squaw Valley, California—the site of the 1960 Winter Olympics. The workshops are held in a ski lodge at the foot of this spectacular ski area. **Previous agents/speakers have included:** Betsy Amster, Michael Carlisle, Elyse Cheney, Kristy Fletcher, B.J. Robbins. Agents will be speaking and available for meetings with attendees.
Costs: $590 (includes tuition, dinners). Housing is extra.
Accommodations: Rooms available. Single: $385/week. Double: $275/week per person. Multiple room: $175/week per person. Shuttle available for additional cost. Contact conference for more information.
Additional Information: Brochures available March for SASE or on website. Inquiries by e-mail OK.

✓ TELEVISION WRITERS WORKSHOP, AFI, 2021 N. Western Ave., Los Angeles CA 90027. (323)856-7721. Fax: (323)856-7778. E-mail: jpetricca@afionline.org. Website: www.afionline.org. **Contact:** Joe Petriccia, associate dean, education and training. Estab. 1986. Annual. Conference duration: 3 weeks. Average attendance: Up to 12 participants. Television writing, with an annual focus that changes each year (e.g. sitcom, MOW). Held at the American Film Institute Campus in Los Angeles. Past workshops were "Writing the Television Movie," "AFI/Sloan TV Writing Workshop—Writing One-Hour Dramas." Agents will be speaking.
Costs: $695 (includes staged readings, seminars with working writers/producers/directors, lunch and breakfast each day).
Additional Information: Brochures available for SASE. Inquiries by e-mail OK.

N: UCLA EXTENSION WRITERS' PROGRAM, 10995 Le Conte Ave., #440, Los Angeles CA 90024. (310)825-9415 or (800)388-UCLA. Fax: (310)206-7382. E-mail: writers@unex.ucla.edu. Website: www.unex.ucla.edu/writers. Estab. 1891. Courses held year-round with one-day or intensive weekend workshops to 12-week courses. "The diverse offerings span introductory seminars to professional novel and script completion workshops. The annual Los Angeles Writers Conference and a number of 1, 2 and 4-day intensive workshops are popular with out-of-town students due to their specific focus and the chance to work with industry professionals. The most comprehensive and diverse continuing education writing program in the country, offering over 400 courses a year including: screenwriting, fiction, writing for young people, poetry, nonfiction, playwriting, publishing and writing for interactive multimedia. Courses are offered in

Los Angeles on the UCLA campus and Universal City as well as online over the Internet. Adult learners in the UCLA Extension Writers' Program study with professional screenwriters, fiction writers, playwrights, poets, nonfiction writers, and interactive multimedia writers, who bring practical experience, theoretical knowledge, and a wide variety of teaching styles and philosophies to their classes." Online courses are also available. Call for details.
Costs: Vary from $75-425.
Accommodations: Students make own arrangements. The program can provide assistance in locating local accommodations.
Additional Information: "Some advanced-level classes have manuscript submittal requirements; instructions are always detailed in the quarterly UCLA Extension course catalog." Screenwriting prize, the Diane Thomas Award, is given annually. Contact program for details. Conference brochures/guidelines are available in the Fall. Inquiries by e-mail and fax OK.

WATERSIDE PUBLISHING CONFERENCE, 2191 San Elijo Ave., Cardiff CA 92007. (760)632-9190. Fax: (760)632-9295. E-mail: admin@waterside.com. Website: www.waterside.com. **Contact:** Nancy Azevedo, controller. Estab. 1990 Annually. Conference held April 5, 6, 7, 2001. Conference duration: 3 days. Average attendance: 200. Focused on computer and technology, books and their writers and publishers. Issues in the industry that affect the genre. Held at Hilton Beach and Tennis Resort, San Diego, CA. A bayside hotel with full amenities and beautiful view. Past themes: Digital Delivery; Ask the Buyer; Author Taxes, Branding, Contracts. **Previous agents/speakers have included:** Maggie Canon (MightyWords.com); Bob Deely (HP Press); Paul Hilts (*Publishers Weekly*); Carla Bayha (Borders Books); Bob Ipsen (John Wiley & Sons); Microsoft. Agents will be speaking and available for meetings with attendees.
Costs: In 2000: $500 general; $250 for authors (includes all sessions and parties, meals, coffee breaks). Conference attendees get a discounted room rate at the Hilton.
Accommodations: Other hotels are in the area if conference hotel is booked or too expensive. Shuttle service available direct from airport for discounted fee.
Additional Information: Brochures available for SASE or on website. Inquiries by e-mail and fax OK.

Northwest (AK, ID, MT, OR, WA, WY)

CLARION WEST WRITERS' WORKSHOP, 340 15th Ave. E., Suite 350, Seattle WA 98112-5156. (206)322-9083. E-mail: kfishler@fishler.com. Website: www.sff.net.clarionwest/ (includes critiquing, workshopping, names, dates). **Contact:** Leslie Howle, administrator. Workshop held June 18-July 28, 2000. Workshop duration 6 weeks. Average attendance: 20. "Conference to prepare students for professional careers in science fiction and fantasy writing." Held at Seattle Central Community College on Seattle's Capitol Hill, an urban site close to restaurants and cafes, not too far from downtown. Deadline for applications: April 1. Agents will be speaking and available for meetings with attendees.
Costs: Workshop: $1,400 ($100 discount if application received by March 1). Dormitory housing: $800, meals not included.
Accommodations: Students are strongly encouraged to stay on-site, in dormitory housing at Seattle University. Cost: $800, meals not included, for 6-week stay. Dormitory and classrooms are handicapped accessible.
Additional Information: "This is a critique-based workshop. Students are encouraged to write a story a week; the critique of student material produced at the workshop forms the principal activity of the workshop. Students and instructors critique manuscripts as a group." Limited scholarships are available, based on financial need. Students must submit 20-30 pages of ms to qualify for admission. Conference guidelines and brochure available for SASE.

FLATHEAD RIVER WRITERS CONFERENCE, P.O. Box 7711, Whitefish MT 59904-7711. (406)755-7272. Fax: (406)862-4839. E-mail: thehows@digisys.net. **Contact:** Jake How, chairman. Estab. 1990. Annual. Conference held October 5-7, 2001. Conference duration: 3 days. Average attendance: 90. "We provide a wide variety of subjects every year, including fiction, nonfiction, screenwriting, and working with editors and agents." Held at Grouse Mountain Lodge. Workshops, panel discussions and speakers focus on novels, nonfiction, screenwriting, short stories, magazine articles, and the writing industry. **Previous agents/speakers have included:** Julie McCarron (Sandra Dijkstra Literary Agency); Esmond Harmsworth (Zachary Shuster Agency); Elizabeth Wales (Wales Literary Agency). Agents will be speaking and available for meetings with attendees.
Costs: $135 (includes breakfast and lunch).
Accommodations: Rooms available at discounted rates: $75/night. Whitefish is a resort town, and less expensive lodging can be arranged.
Additional Information: "By limiting attendance, we assure a quality experience and informal, easy access to the presentors and other attendees." Brochures available June. Inquiries by e-mail OK.

NORWESCON 23, P.O. Box 68547, Seattle WA 98168-9986. (206)270-7850. Fax: (520)244-0142. E-mail: info@norwescon.org. Website: www.norwescon.org. **Contact:** Robert J. Grieve, programming director. Estab. 1978. Annual. Conference held April 20-23. Conference duration: Thursday-Sunday. Average attendance: 2,800. General multitrack programming convention focusing on science fiction and fantasy literature with wide spectrum coverage of other media. Held at Seatac Doubletree Hotel. Previous themes: Ad Astra: To the Stars, Colonizing the Universe with

Full Tracks of Science, Socio-Cultural, Literary, Publishing, Editing, Writing, Art, and other media of a science fiction/fantasy orientation. **Agents/speakers attending include:** Agents will be speaking and available for meetings with attendees.

Costs: $50 until March 17, $60 at the door (includes membership with Norwescon 23, program book, membership privileges.

Accommodations: Accommodations available, see website for details. On-site special convention room rate of $94/night.

Additional Information: "Please write ahead or make contact with programming director." Brochures available for SASE or on website. Inquiries by e-mail and fax OK.

N: PACIFIC NORTHWEST WRITERS ASSOCIATION, 2608 Third Ave., Suite B, Seattle WA 98121-1214. (206)443-3807. E-mail: jmaread@aol.com. Website: www.pnwa.org. **Contact:** Scott McDonald. Estab. 1955. Annual. Conference held in July. Average attendance: 400. Conference focuses on "fiction, nonfiction, poetry, film, drama, self-publishing, the creative process, critiques, core groups, advice from pros and networking." Site is Sheraton Hotel in Tacoma WA. "Editors and agents come from both coasts. They bring lore from the world of publishing. The PNWA provides opportunities for writers to get to know editors and agents. The literary contest provides feedback from professionals and possible fame for the winners." **Previous speakers have included:** Charles Johnson, author of *Dreamer*; Tobias Wolff, author of *This Boy's Life*.

Costs: For 2000: $300 (members) and $350 (nonmembers). Meals and lodging are available at hotel.

Additional Information: On-site critiques are available in small groups. Literary contest in these categories: Stella Cameron Romance, adult article/essay, adult genre novel, adult mainstream novel, adult short story, juvenile/young adult, screenwriting, nonfiction book, playwriting and poetry. Deadline: February 13. Over $9,000 awarded in prizes. Guidelines available for SASE in May 2001.

N: SWA WINTER WORKSHOP, Seattle Writers Association, P.O. Box 33265, Seattle WA 98133. (206)524-0441. E-mail: gibbons99@earthlink.net. **Contact:** Richard Gibbons, president. Estab. 1986. Annual. Conference held February. Workshop 1 day, 9 a.m. to 4 p.m. Average attendance: 50. Guest speakers and panelists are regional publishing representatives (editors), radio representatives and booksellers.

Costs: $20; snacks provided, bring lunch (1998).

Additional Information: SWA sponsors "Writers in Performance," a jury selected public presentation of Seattle's best writing. Judges are writers, editors and consultants. Guidelines for SASE.

✓ WILLAMETTE WRITERS CONFERENCE, 9045 SW Barbur, Suite 5-A, Portland OR 97219. (503)452-1592. Fax: (503)452-0372. E-mail: wilwrite@willamettewriters.com. Website: www.willamettewriters.com. (includes meeting news; conference news; links to other sites). **Contact:** Bill Johnson. Estab. 1968. Annual. Conference held August 12-13. Average attendance: 320. "Willamette Writers is open to all writers, and we plan our conference accordingly. We offer workshops on all aspects of fiction, nonfiction, marketing, scriptwriting, the creative process, etc. Also we invite top notch inspirational speakers for key note addresses. Recent theme was 'Writing Your Future.' We always include at least one agent or editor panel and offer a variety of topics of interest to both fiction, screenwriters and nonfiction writers." **Previous agents/editors have included:** Donald Maass, Jeff Herman, Marcie Wright, agents; Scott Moyers, Martha Bushko, Mark Waldman, editors; Alex Rose, Dan Paulson, Scott Anderson, producers. Agents will be speaking and available for meetings with attendees.

Costs: Cost for full conference including meals is $210 members; $250 nonmembers.

Accomodations: If necessary, these can be made on an individual basis. Some years special rates are available.

Additional Information: Conference brochures/guidelines are available for catalog-size SASE.

✓ YELLOW BAY WRITERS' WORKSHOP, Center for Continuing Education, University of Montana, Missoula MT 59812-1990. (406)243-2094. Fax: (406)243-2047. E-mail: kboilek@selway.umt.edu. **Contact:** Administrative Support. Estab. 1988. Annual. Conference held mid August. Average attendance: 50-60. Includes four workshops: 2 fiction; 1 poetry; 1 creative nonfiction/personal essay. Conference "held at the University of Montana's Flathead Lake Biological Station, a research station with informal educational facilities and rustic cabin living. Located in northwestern Montana on Flathead Lake, the largest natural freshwater lake west of the Mississippi River. All faculty are requested to present a craft lecture—usually also have an editor leading a panel discussion." **Previous agents/speakers have included:** Pam Houston, Denis Johnson, Jane Miller and Fred Haefele.

CAN'T FIND A CONFERENCE? Conferences are listed by region. Check the introduction to this section for a list of regional categories.

Canada

N̲ ☑ BLOODY WORDS, 12 Roundwood Court, Toronto, Ontario M1W 1Z2 Canada. Phone/fax: (416)497-5293. E-mail: carosoles@home.com. Website: www.bloodywords.com. **Contact:** Caro Soles, chair. Estab. 1999. Annual. Conference held June 8-9, 2001. Conference duration: 2 days. Average attendance: 200. Focus on mystery fiction—to provide a showcase for Canadian fiction writers and others, and to provide writing information to aspiring writers. Held at the Delta Chelsea Hotel in downtown Toronto. "We will present a true crime/factual and procedural track of programming as well as a track for readers/writers of mysteries and a writers workshop. There will also be a reading cafe." **Agents/speakers attending include:** Agents will be speaking and available for meetings with attendees.
Costs: $110-135 (Canadian). Price depends on when attendee registers.
Accommodations: Special conference rate available at the Hotel Delta Chelsea.
Additional Information: Brochures available on website. Inquiries by e-mail and fax OK.

☑ THE FESTIVAL OF THE WRITTEN ARTS, Box 2299, Sechelt, British Columbia V0N 3A0 Canada. (800)565-9631 or (604)885-9631. Fax: (604)885-3967. E-mail: written_arts@sunshine.net. Website: www.sunshine.net/rockwood. **Contact:** Gail Bull, festival producer. Estab. 1983. Annual. Festival held August 9-12, 2001. Average attendance: 3,500. To promote "all writing genres." Festival held at the Rockwood Centre. "The Centre overlooks the town of Sechelt on the Sunshine Coast. The lodge around which the Centre was organized was built in 1937 as a destination for holidayers arriving on the old Union Steamship Line; it has been preserved very much as it was in its heyday. A new twelve-bedroom annex was added in 1982, and in 1989 the Festival of the Written Arts constructed a 500-seat Pavilion for outdoor performances next to the annex. The festival does not have a theme. Instead, it showcases 20 or more Canadian writers in a wide variety of genres each year." **Previous agents/speakers have included:** Michael Ondaatje, Shelagh Rogers, Paddy Wales, Katherine Govier, Diane Schoemperlen, Linda Spalding, Robert Bringhurst, Stevie Cameron, Paul Quarrington, L.R. Wright, Gail Bowen, Karen Irving, Mark Winston, Janet Lunn, Sharon Butala, Rosemary Sullivan, Tomson Highway, Caroline Adderson, Kerri Sakamoto, Audrey Thomas, John Ralston Saul, Margaret Horsfield, Keith Maillard, Joan Skogan, Denise Chong, Bonnie Burnard, Robert J. Sawyer. Agents will be speaking.
Costs: $12 per event or $150 for a four-day pass (Canadian).
Accommodations: Lists of hotels and bed/breakfast available.
Additional Information: The festival runs contests during the 3½ days of the event. Prizes are books donated by publishers. Brochures/guidelines are available.

☑ FESTIVAL OF WORDS, 88 Saskatchewan St. E., Moose Jaw, Saskatchewan S6H 0V4 Canada. (306)691-0557. Fax: (306)693-2994. E-mail: word.festival@sk.sympatico.ca. Website: www.3.sk.sympatico.ca/praifes. **Contact:** Gary Hyland, coordinator; or Lori Dean, operations manager. Estab. 1997. Annual. Festival held July 26-30, 2001. Festival duration: 4 days. The festival celebrates the imaginative uses of language, and features fiction and nonfiction writers, screenwriters, poets, children's authors, songwriters, dramatists and film makers. Held at the Moose Jaw Public Library/Art Museum complex and in Crescent Park. **Previous agents/speakers have included:** Jane Urquhart, Susan Musgrave, M.T. Kelly, Terry Jordan, Sharon Butala, Maryann Kovalski, Allan Fotheringham, Pamela Wallin, Bonnie Burnard, Erika Ritter, Wayson Choy, Koozma Tarasoff, Lorna Crozier, Sheree Fitch, Nino Ricci.
Costs: $100 for 2000 (includes 2 meals).
Accommodations: Motels, hotels, campgrounds, bed and breakfasts.
Additional Information: "Our festival is an ideal meeting ground for people who love words to meet and mingle, promote their books and meet their fans." Brochures available for SASE. Inquiries by e-mail and fax OK.

N̲ ☑ MARITIME WRITERS' WORKSHOP, Extension & Summer Session, UNB Box 4400, Fredericton, New Brunswick E3B 5A3 Canada. Phone/fax: (506)474-1144. E-mail: k4jc@unb.ca. Website: www.unb.ca/coned/writers/marritrs.html. **Contact:** Glenda Turner, coordinator. Estab. 1976. Annual. Conference held July 1999. Average attendance: 50. "Workshops in four areas: fiction, poetry, nonfiction, writing for children." Site is University of New Brunswick, Fredericton campus.
Costs: In 2000: $350, tuition; $135 meals; $125/double room; $145/single room (Canadian).
Accommodations: On-campus accommodations and meals.
Additional Information: "Participants must submit 10-20 manuscript pages which form a focus for workshop discussions." Must be at least 18 years old. Brochures are available after March. No SASE necessary. Inquiries by e-mail and fax OK.

☑ THE VANCOUVER INTERNATIONAL WRITERS FESTIVAL, 1398 Cartwright St., Vancouver, British Columbia V6H 3R8 Canada. (604)681-6330. Fax: (604)681-8400. E-mail: viwf@writersfest.bc.ca. Website: www.writersfest.bc.ca (includes information on festival). **Contact:** Dawn Brennan, general manager. Estab. 1988. Annual. Held October 18-22, 2000. Average attendance: 11,000. "This is a festival for readers and writers. The program of events is diverse and includes readings, panel discussions, seminars. Lots of opportunities to interact with the writers who attend." Held on Granville Island—in the heart of Vancouver. Two professional theaters are used as well as Performance Works (an open space). "We try to avoid specific themes. Programming takes place between February and June each year and is by invitation." **Previous agents/speakers have included:** Margaret Atwood, Maeve Binchy, J.K. Rowling.
Costs: Tickets are $6-20 (Canadian).

Accommodations: Local tourist info can be provided when necessary and requested.

Additional Information: Brochures/guidelines are available for SASE after August. Inquiries by e-mail and fax OK. "A reminder—this is a festival, a celebration, not a conference or workshop."

N **☑** **WINNIPEG INTERNATIONAL WRITERS FESTIVAL**, 209-100 Arthur St., Winnipeg, Manitoba R3B 1H3 Canada. (204)956-7323. Fax: (204)942-5754. E-mail: info@winnipegwords.com. Website: www.winnipegwords.com. **Contact:** Kathleen Darby, general manager. Estab. 1997. Annual. Conference held October 12-17. Conference duration: 5 days. Average attendance: 4,300. All areas of written/spoken word. Previous themes: Words of Wisdom. Agents will be speaking.

Costs: $60 (includes entry to events).

Accommodations: Hotel information on festival website.

Additional Information: Brochures available on website. Inquiries by e-mail or fax OK.

Resources

Professional Organizations

ORGANIZATIONS FOR AGENTS

Association of Authors' Representatives (AAR), P.O. Box 237201, Ansonia Station, New York NY 10023. Website: www.aar-online.org. A list of member agents is available for $7 and SAE with 99¢ postage.

Association of Authors' Agents, 62 Grafton Way, London W1P 5LD, England. (011) 44 7387 2076.

ORGANIZATIONS FOR WRITERS

The following professional organizations publish newsletters and hold conferences and meetings at which they often share information on agents. Organizations with an asterisk (*) have members who are liaisons to the AAR

Academy of American Poets, 584 Broadway, Suite 1208, New York NY 10012-3250. (212)274-0343. Website: www.poets.org/index.cfm.

American Medical Writers Association, 40 W. Gude Dr., Suite 101, Rockville MD 20850-1192. (301)294-5303. Website: www.amwa.org.

*American Society of Journalists & Authors, 1501 Broadway, Suite 302, New York NY 10036. (212)997-0947. Website: www.asja.org.

American Translators Association, 225 Reinekers Lane, Suite 590, Alexandria VA 22314. (703)683-6100. Website: www.atanet.org.

Asian American Writers' Workshop, 16 W. 32nd St., Suite 10A, New York NY 10001. (212)494-0061. Website: www.aaww.org

*Associated Writing Programs, The Tallwood House, Mail stop 1E3, George Mason University, Fairfax VA 22030. (703)993-4301. Website: www.awpwriter.org.

*The Authors Guild Inc., 330 W. 42nd St., 29th Floor, New York NY 10036. (212)563-5904. Website: www.authorsguild.org.

The Authors League of America, Inc., 330 W. 42nd St., New York NY 10036. (212)564-8350.

Council of Writers Organizations, 12724 Sagamore Rd., Leawood KS 66209. (913)451-9023. Website: www.councilofwriters.com.

*The Dramatists Guild, 1501 Broadway, Suite 701, New York NY 10036. (212)398-9366.

Education Writers Association, 1331 H. St. NW, Suite 307, Washington DC 20005. (202)637-9700. Website: www.ewa.org.

*Horror Writers Association, S.P. Somtow, President, P.O. Box 50577, Palo Alto CA 94303. Website: www.horror.org.

International Association of Crime Writers Inc., North American Branch, P.O. Box 8674, New York NY 10016. (212)243-8966.

International Television Association, 9202 N. Meridian St., Suite 200, Indianapolis IN 46260. (317)816-6269. Website: www.itva.org.

The International Women's Writing Guild, P.O. Box 810, Gracie Station, New York NY 10028-0082. (212)737-7536. Website: www.iwwg.com. Provides a literary agent list to members and holds "Meet the Agents and Editors" in April and October.

*Mystery Writers of America (MWA), 17 E. 47th St., 6th Floor, New York NY 10017. (212)888-8171. Website: www.mysterynet.com/mwa/.

National Association of Science Writers, Box 294, Greenlawn NY 11740. (631)757-5664. Website: www.nasw.org.

National League of American Pen Women, 1300 17th St. NW, Washington DC 20036-1973. (202)785-1997. Website: http://members.aol.com/penwomen/pen.htm.

National Writers Association, 3140 S. Peoria, Suite 295, Aurora CO 80014. (303)841-0246. Website: www.nationalwriters.com. In addition to agent referrals, also operates an agency for members.

*National Writers Union, 113 University Place, 6th Floor, New York NY 10003-4527. (212)254-0279. Website: www.nwu.org. A trade union, this organization has an agent database available to members.

*PEN American Center, 568 Broadway, New York NY 10012-3225. (212)334-1660. Website: www.pen.org.

*Poets & Writers, 72 Spring St., Suite 301, New York NY 10012. (212)226-3586. Website: www.pw.org. Operates an information line, taking calls from 11-3 EST Monday through Friday.

Poetry Society of America, 15 Gramercy Park, New York NY 10003. (212)254-9628. Website: www.poetryso ciety.org.

*Romance Writers of America, 3707 F.M. 1960 West, Suite 555, Houston TX 77068. (281)440-6885. Website: www.rwanational.com. Publishes an annual agent list for members for $10.

*Science Fiction and Fantasy Writers of America, P.O. Box 171, Unity ME 04988-0171. Website: www.sf-wa.org.

Society of American Business Editors & Writers, University of Missouri, School of Journalism, 76 Gannett Hall, Columbia MO 65211. (573)882-7862. Website: www.sabew.org.

Society of American Travel Writers, 4101 Lake Boone Trail, Suite 201, Raleigh NC 27607. (919)787-5181. Website: www.satw.org.

*Society of Children's Book Writers & Illustrators, 8271 Beverly Blvd., Los Angeles CA 90048. (323)782-1010. Website: www.scbwi.org.

Volunteer Lawyers for the Arts, One E. 53rd St., 6th Floor, New York NY 10022. (212)319-2787. Website: www.vlany.org.

Washington Independent Writers, 220 Woodward Bldg., 733 15th St. NW, Washington DC 20005. (202)347-4973. Website: www.washwriter.org/.

Western Writers of America, 1012 Fair St., Franklin TN 37064. (615)791-1444. Website: www.imt.net/~gedison.

Writers Guild of Alberta, Main Floor, Percy Page Centre, 11759 Groat Rd., Edmonton, Alberta T5M 3K6 Canada. (780)422-8174. Website: http://writersguild.ab.ca.

*Writers Guild of America-East, 555 W. 57th St., New York NY 10019. (212)767-7800. Website: www.w-gaeast.org/. Provides list of WGA signatory agents for $1.29.

Writers Guild of America-West, 7000 W. Third St., Los Angeles CA 90048. (323)951-4000. Website: www.wga.org. Provides a list of WGA signatory agents for $2.50 and SASE sent to Agency Department.

Books & Publications of Interest

BOOKS
Information on agents and publishing

Be Your Own Literary Agent, by Martin Levin, published by Ten Speed Press, P.O. Box 7123, Berkeley CA 94707. (800)841-BOOK.

Business & Legal Forms for Authors and Self-Publishers, by Tad Crawford, published by Allworth Press, c/o Writer's Digest Books, 1507 Dana Ave., Cincinnati OH 45207. (800)289-0963. Website: www.writersdigest.-com.

The Career Novelist, by Donald Maass, published by Heinemann, 361 Hanover St., Portsmouth NH 03801-3912. (800)541-2086.

Children's Writer's & Illustrator's Market, edited by Alice Pope, published by Writer's Digest Books, 1507 Dana Ave., Cincinnati OH 45207. (800)289-0963. Website: www.writersdigest.com.

The Complete Idiot's Guide to Getting Published, by Sheree Bykofsky and Jennifer Basye Sander, published by Alpha Books, Macmillan General Reference, Simon & Schuster, 1633 Broadway, New York NY 10019-6785.

The Copyright Handbook: How to Protect and Use Written Works, fifth edition, by Stephen Fishman, published by Nolo.com, 950 Parker St., Berkeley CA 94710. (800)992-6656. Website: www.nolo.com.

Editors On Editing: What Writers Should Know About What Editors Do, edited by Gerald Gross, published by Grove-Atlantic, 841 Broadway, New York NY 10003-4793. (800)521-0178.

The First Five Pages: A Writer's Guide to Staying Out of the Rejection Pile, by Noah Lukeman, published by Fireside, Simon & Schuster, 1230 Ave. of the Americas, New York NY 10020. Website: www.simons ays.com.

The Forest for the Trees: An Editor's Advice to Writers, by Betsy Lerner, published by Riverhead Books, Penguin Putnam, Inc., 375 Hudson St., New York NY 10014. Website: www.pentuinputnam.com.

Formatting & Submitting Your Manuscript, by Jack and Glenda Neff, Don Prues, and the editors of *Writer's Market*, published by Writer's Digest Books, 1507 Dana Ave., Cincinnati OH 45207. (800)289-0963. Website: www.writersdigest.com.

How to Be Your Own Literary Agent, expanded revised edition, by Richard Curtis, published by Houghton Mifflin Company, 215 Park Ave. S., New York NY 10003. (800)225-3362. Website: www.hmco.com.

How to Find and Work with a Literary Agent, audiotape, by Anita Diamant, published by Writer's Audio-Shop, 204 E. 35th St., Austin TX 78705.

How to Write Attention-Grabbing Query & Cover Letters, by John Wood, published by Writer's Digest Books, 1507 Dana Ave., Cincinnati OH 45207. (800)289-0963. Website: www.writersdigest.com.

How to Write Irresistible Query Letters, by Lisa Collier Cool, published by Writer's Digest Books, 1507 Dana Ave., Cincinnati OH 45207. (800)289-0963. Website: www.writersdigest.com.

The Insider's Guide to Getting an Agent, by Lori Perkins, published by Writers Digest Books, 1507 Dana Ave., Cincinnati OH 45207. (800)289-0963. Website: www.writersdigest.com.

Insider's Guide to Getting Published: Why They Always Reject Your Manuscript and What You Can Do About It, by John Boswell, published by Bantam Doubleday Dell, 1540 Broadway, New York NY 10036-4094.

Kirsch's Handbook of Publishing Law: For Authors, Publishers, Editors and Agents, by Jonathan Kirsch, published by Acrobat Books, P.O. Box 870, Venice CA 90294. (310)578-1055.

Literary Agents: A Writer's Introduction, by John F. Baker, published by Macmillan, 1633 Broadway, New York NY 10019-6785.

Literary Agents: What They Do, How They Do It, How to Find & Work with The Right One For You, by Michael Larsen, published by John Wiley & Sons, 605 Third Ave., New York NY 10158-0012. (212)850-6000. Website: www.wiley.com.

Mastering the Business of Writing: A Leading Literary Agent Reveals the Secrets of Success, by Richard Curtis, published by Allworth Press, 10 E. 23rd St., Suite 510, New York NY 10010. (800)491-2808. Website: www.allworth.com.

Novel & Short Story Writer's Market, edited by Anne Bowling, published by Writer's Digest Books, 1507 Dana Ave., Cincinnati OH 45207. (800)289-0963. Website: www.writersdigest.com.

The Writer's Digest Guide to Manuscript Formats, by Dian Dincin Buchman and Seli Groves, published by Writer's Digest Books, 1507 Dana Ave., Cincinnati OH 45207. (800)289-0963. Website: www.writersdigest.com.

Writer's Essential Desk Reference, Second Edition, published by Writer's Digest Books, 1507 Dana Ave., Cincinnati OH 45207. (800)289-0963. Website: www.writersdigest.com.

The Writer's Legal Companion, Third Edition, by Brad Bunnin and Peter Beren, published by Perseus Book Group, Addison Wesley, One Jacob Way, Reading MA 01867. (718)944-3700.

Writer's Market, edited by Kirsten Holm, published by Writer's Digest Books, 1507 Dana Ave., Cincinnati OH 45207. (800)289-0963. Website: www.writersmarket.com.

The Writer's Market Companion, by Joe Feiertag and Mary Carmen Cupito, published by Writer's Digest Books, 1507 Dana Ave., Cincinnati OH 45207. (800)289-0963. Website: www.writersmarket.com.

Writing from the Inside Out, by Dennis Palumbo, published by John Wiley & Sons, Inc., 605 Third Ave., New York NY 10158-0012. Website: www.wiley.com.

Script agents and screenwriting

Adventures in the Screen Trade: A Personal View of Hollywood & Screenwriting, by William Goldman, published by Warner Books, 1271 Avenue of the Americas, New York NY 10020. (212)522-7200.

The Art of Dramatic Writing, by Lajos Egri, published by Simon & Schuster, 1230 Avenue of the Americas, New York NY 10020. (800)233-2348.

The Complete Book of Scriptwriting, revised edition, by J. Michael Straczynski, published by Writer's Digest Books, 1507 Dana Ave., Cincinnati OH 45207. (800)289-0963. Website: www.writersdigest.com.

The Complete Guide to Standard Script Formats: The Screenplay, by Hillis R. Cole and Judith H. Haag, published by CMC Publishing, 11642 Otsego St., N. Hollywood CA 91601. (818)980-9759.

Dramatists Sourcebook, edited by Kathy Sova and Samantha Rachel Rabetz, published by Theatre Communications Group, Inc., Consortium Book Sales & Distribution, 355 Lexington Ave., New York NY 10017-0217. (212)697-9387. Website: www.tcg.org.

Elements of Style for Screenwriters: The Essential Manual for Writers of Screenplays, by Paul Argentini, published by Lone Eagle Publishing Company, 1024 N. Orange Ave., Hollywood CA 90038. (800)345-6257. Website: www.loneeagle.com.

Four Screenplays: Studies in the American Screenplay, by Syd Field, published by Dell Publishing, 1540 Broadway, New York NY 10036-4094. (800)223-6834. Website: www.bdd.com.

From Script to Screen: Collaborative Art of Filmmaking, by Linda Seger and Edward Jay Whetmore, published by Owl Books, Henry Holt & Co., Inc., 115 W. 18th St., New York NY 10011. (800)488-5233.

Getting Your Script Through the Hollywood Maze: An Insider's Guide, by Linda Stuart, published by Acrobat Books, P.O. Box 870, Venice CA 90294. (310)578-1055.

How to Sell Your Screenplay: The Real Rules of Film & Television, by Carl Sautter, published by New Chapter Press, P.O. Box 383, Pound Ridge NY 10576. (914)742-9974.

How to Write a Selling Screenplay, by Christopher Keane, published by Bantam Doubleday Dell, 1540 Broadway, New York NY 10036. (800)223-6834.

How to Write It, How to Sell It: Everything a Screenwriter Needs to Know About Hollywood, by Linda Palmer, published by Griffin Trade Paperback, St. Martin's Press, 175 Fifth Ave., New York NY 10010. (212)982-3900.

The Insider's Guide to Writing for Screen and Television, by Ronald B. Tobias, published by Writer's Digest Books, 1507 Dana Ave., Cincinnati OH 45207. (800)289-0963. Website: www.writersdigest.com.

Making a Good Script Great, second edition, by Dr. Linda Seger, published by Samuel French Trade, 7623 Sunset Blvd., Hollywood CA 90046. (212)206-8990.

The New Screenwriter Looks at the New Screenwriter, by William Froug, published by Silman-James Press, 1181 Angelo Dr., Beverly Hills CA 90210.

Opening the Doors to Hollywood: How to Sell Your Idea, Story Book, Screenplay, by Carlos de Abreu & Howard J. Smith, published by Random House, 201 E. 50th St., New York NY 10012 (212)751-2600. Website: www.randomhouse.com.

The Screenwriter's Bible: A Complete Guide to Writing, Formatting & Selling Your Script, by David Trottier, published by Silman-James Press, 3624 Shannon Rd., Los Angeles CA 90027. (323)661-9922.

Screenwriters on Screenwriting: The Best in the Business Discuss Their Craft, by Joel Engel, published by Hyperion, 114 Fifth Ave., New York NY 10011. (800)343-9204.

Screenwriting Tricks of the Trade, by William Froug, published by Silman-James Press, 3624 Shannon Rd. Los Angeles CA 90027. (323)661-9922.

Successful Scriptwriting, by Jurgen Wolff and Kerry Cox, published by Writer's Digest Books, 1507 Dana Ave., Cincinnati OH 45207. (800)289-0963. Website: www.writersdigest.com.

Television & Screen Writing: From Concept to Contract, by Richard A. Blum, published by Butterworth-Heinemann, 225 Wildwood Ave., Woburn MA 01801. (800)366-2665.

This Business of Screenwriting, by Ron Suppa, Esq., published by Lone Eagle Publishing Company, 1024 N. Orange Ave., Hollywood CA 90038. (800)345-6257. Website: www.loneeagle.com.

The Whole Picture: Strategies for Screenwriting Success in the New Hollywood, by Richard Walter, published by Plume, an imprint of Penguin Putnam, 375 Hudson St., New York NY 10014-3657. (212)366-2000. Website: www.penguinputnam.com.

Directories of literary and script agents

Agents & Managers, published by Hollywood Creative Directory, 3000 Olympic Blvd., Santa Monica CA 90404. (800)815-0503. Website: www.hcdonline.com.

Film Producers, Studios, Agents, and Casting Directors Guide, edited by Lone Eagle Publishing, 1024 N. Orange Ave., Hollywood CA 90038. (800)345-6257. Website: www.loneeagle.com.

Literary Market Place (LMP), R.R. Bowker Company, 121 Chanlon Road, New Providence NJ 07974. (908)464-6800. Website: www.bowker.com.

Writer's Guide to Book Editors, Publishers and Literary Agents, by Jeff Herman, published by Prima Publishing, Box 1260, Rocklin CA 95677. (916)632-4400. Website: www.primapublishing.com.

The Writer's Guide to Hollywood Producers, Directors, & Screenwriter's Agents, by Skip Press, published by Prima Publishing, P.O. Box 1260, Rocklin CA 95677. (916)632-4400. Website: www.primapublishing.com.

Publicists and marketing

The Author's Guide to Marketing Your Book: From Start to Success, for Writers and Publishers, by Don Best and Peter Goodman, published by Stone Bridge Press, P.O. Box 8208, Berkley CA 94707. (510)524-8732. Website: www.stonebridge.com.

Complete Guide to Book Marketing, by David Cole, published by Allworth Press, 10 E. 23rd St., Suite 510, New York NY 10010-4402. Website: www.allworth.com.

Guerrilla Marketing for Writers, by Jay Conrad Levinson, Rich Frishman, and Michael Larsen, published by Writer's Digest Books, 1507 Dana Ave., Cincinnati OH 45207. (800)289-0963. Website: writersdigest.com.

1001 Ways to Market Your Book, by John Kremer, published by Open Horizons, P.O. Box 205, Fairfield IA 52556. (515)472-6130. Website: www.bookmarket.com.

BOOKSTORES AND CATALOGS

Book City, 308 N. San Fernando Blvd., Burbank CA 91502, (818)848-4417, and 6627 Hollywood Blvd., Hollywood CA 90028. (323)466-2525. Website: www.hollywoodbookcity.com.

Samuel French Theatre & Film Bookshops, 7623 Sunset Blvd., Hollywood CA 90046. (323)876-0570 and 45 W. 25th St., Dept. W., New York NY 10010. (212)206-8990. Website: www.samuelfrench.com.

Script City, 8033 Sunset Blvd., Suite 1500, Hollywood CA 90046. (800)676-2522. Website: www.scriptcity.net.

PUBLICATIONS

Book: The Magazine for the Reading Life, 4645 N. Rockwell St., Chicago IL 60625. (800)317-BOOK. Website: www.bookmagazine.com.

Daily Variety, Daily Variety Ltd./Cahners Publishing Co., 5700 Wilshire Blvd., Suite 120, Los Angeles CA 90036. (323)857-6600.

Editor & Publisher, The Editor & Publisher Co., Inc., 770 Broadway, New York NY 10003-9595. (646)654-5270. Website: www.mediainfo.com.

Fade in Magazine, 289 S. Robertson Blvd., Suite 465, Beverly Hills CA 90211. (800)646-3896.

Hollywood Agents & Managers Directory, published by Hollywood Creative Directory, 1024 N. Orange Dr., Hollywood CA 90038. (800)815-0503. Website: www.hcdonline.com.

Hollywood Creative Directory, published by Hollywood Creative Directory, 1024 N. Orange Dr., Hollywood CA 90038. (800)815-0503. Website: www.hcdonline.com.

Hollywood Reporter, 5055 Wilshire Blvd., Los Angeles CA 90036-4396. (323)525-2000. Website: www.hollywoodreporter.com.

Hollywood Scriptwriter, P.O. Box 10277, Burbank CA 91510. (818)845-5525. Website: www.hollywoodscriptwriter.com.

New York Screenwriter, published by the New York Screenwriter Monthly, 655 Fulton St., #276, Brooklyn NY 11217. Website: www.nyscreenwriter.com.

Poets & Writers, 72 Spring St., 3rd Floor, New York NY 10012. (212)226-3586. Website: www.pw.org.

Premiere Magazine, published by Hachette Filipacchi Magazines, 1633 Broadway, New York NY 10019. (800)289-2489. Website: premieremag.com.

Publishers Weekly, Bowker Magazine Group, 245 W. 17th St., New York NY 10011. (212)463-6758. Website: www.publishersweekly.com.

The Writer, Kalmbach Publishing Company, P.O. Box 1612, Waukesha, WI 53187-1612. (617)423-3157.

Writer's Digest, 1507 Dana Ave., Cincinnati OH 45207. (800)888-6888. Website: www.writersdigest.com.

Written By, The Journal of the Writers Guild of America, 7000 W. Third St., Los Angeles CA 90048. (888)WRITNBY. 974-8629. Website: www.wga.org/WrittenBY.

Websites of Interest

WRITING

Delphi Forums (www.delphi.com)
This site hosts forums on many topics including writing and publishing. Just type "writing" in the search bar, and you'll find pages where you can talk about your craft.

Zuzu's Petals Literary Resource (www.zuzu.com)
Contains 7,000 organized links to helpful resources for writers, artists, performers, and researchers. Zuzu's Petals also publishes an electronic quarterly.

Writer's Exchange (http://writerexchange.about.com)
This site, hosted by writer Susan Molthrop, is a constantly updated resource devoted to the business of writing. Molthrop's goal is to include "everything I can discover to make your writing better, easier, and more fun."

Inkspot (www.inkspot.com)
This site by the publishers of *Inklings*, a free biweekly newsletter for writers, includes market information, writing tips, interviews, and networking opportunities.

AGENTS

WritersNet (www.writers.net)
This site includes a bulletin board where writers can discuss their experiences with agents.

Agent Research and Evaluation (www.agentresearch.com)
This is the website of AR&E, a company that specializes in keeping tabs on literary agents. For a fee you can order their varied services to learn more about a specific agent.

The Query Guild (www.queryguild.com)
A working tool where writers can post queries for samples or receive feedback from other authors.

Writer Beware (www.sfwa.org/beware)
The Science Fiction Writers of America's page of warnings about agents and subsidy publishers.

Writer's Market (www.writersmarket.com)
This giant, searchable database includes agents and publishers, and offers daily updates tailored to your individual needs.

SCREENWRITING

The Hollywood Reporter (www.hollywoodreporter.com)
Online version of print magazine for screenwriters. Get the buzz on the movie biz.

Hollywood Creative Directory (www.hcdonline.com)
By joining this website, you'll have access to listings of legitimate players in the film, television, and new media industry.

MovieBytes (www.moviebytes.com)
Subscribe to **MovieBytes'** Who's Buying What to learn which agencies and managers have sold which screenplays to which studios and production companies.

Daily Variety (http://nt.excite.com/142/variety)
This site archives the top stories from Daily Variety. Check here for the latest scoop on the movie and TV biz.

Samuel French, Inc. (www.samuelfrench.com/index.html)
This is the website of play publisher Samuel French that includes an index of authors and titles.

Screenwriter's Heaven (www.impactpc.freeserve.co.uk)
This is a page of links to many resources for screenwriters from workshops and competitions to scripts and software.

Done Deal (www.scriptsales.com)
The most useful features of this screenwriting site include descriptions of recently sold scripts, a list of script agents, and a list of production companies.

MARKETING AND PUBLICISTS

BookTalk (www.booktalk.com)
This site "offers authors an opportunity to announce and market new releases to millions of viewers across the globe."

Book Marketing Update (http://bookmarket.com)
This website by John Kremer, author of *1001 Ways to Market Your Book*, offers helpful tips for marketing books and many useful links to publishing websites. Also offers an e-newsletter so writers may share their marketing success stories.

Guerrilla Marketing (www.gmarketing.com)
The writers of *Guerrilla Marketing for Writers* provide many helpful resources to help you successfully market your book.

About Publishing (http://publishing.about.com)
This website provides a wide range of information about publishing, including several articles on independent publicists.

Authorlink (www.authorlink.com)
"The news, information and marketing community for editors, literary agents and writers." Showcases manuscripts of experienced and beginning writers.

BookWire (www.bookwire.com)
BookWire bills itself as the book industry's most comprehensive online information source. The site includes industry news, features, reviews, fiction, events, interviews, and links to other book sites.

Writer's Digest (www.writersdigest.com)
This site includes information about writing books and magazines from Writer's Digest. It also has a huge, searchable database of writer's guidelines from thousands of publishers.

ORGANIZATIONS

The Association of Authors' Representatives (www.bookwire.com/aar/)
This association page includes a list of member agents, their newsletter and their canon of ethics.

National Writer's Union (www.nwu.org/)
Site of the National Writer's Union—the trade union for freelance writers of all genres publishing in the U.S.

PEN American Center (www.pen.org)

Site of the organization of writers and editors that seek to defend the freedom of expression and promote contemporary literature.

Writer's Guild of America (www.wga.org)
The WGA site includes advice and information on the art and craft of professional screenwriting for film, television, and interactive projects. This site offers script registration and a list of WGA signatory agencies.

TABLE OF ACRONYMS

The organizations and their acronyms listed below are frequently referred to in the listings and are widely used in the industries of agenting and writing.

AAA	Association of Authors' Agents	NLAPW	National League of American Pen Women
AAP	American Association of Publishers	NWA	National Writers Association
AAR	Association of Authors' Representatives	OWAA	Outdoor Writers Association of America, Inc.
ABA	American Booksellers Association	RWA	Romance Writers of America
ABWA	Associated Business Writers of America	SAG	Screen Actor's Guild
		SATW	Society of American Travel Writers
AEB	Association of Editorial Businesses		
AFTRA	American Federation of TV and Radio Artists	SCBWI	Society of Children's Book Writers & Illustrators
AGVA	American Guild of Variety Artists	SFRA	Science Fiction Research Association
AMWA	American Medical Writer's Association	SFWA	Science Fiction and Fantasy Writers of America
ASJA	American Society of Journalists and Authors	SPWA	South Plains Writing Association
ATA	Association of Talent Agents	WGA	Writers Guild of America
AWA	Aviation/Space Writers Association	WIA	Women in the Arts Foundation, Inc.
CAA	Canadian Authors Association	WIF	Women in Film
DGA	Director's Guild of America	WICI	Women in Communications, Inc.
GWAA	Garden Writers Association of America	WIW	Washington Independent Writers
		WMG	Women's Media Group
HWA	Horror Writers of America	WNBA	Women's National Book Association
IACP	International Association of Culinary Professionals		
		WRW	Washington Romance Writers (chapter of RWA)
MOW	Movie of the Week		
MWA	Mystery Writers of America, Inc.	WWA	Western Writers of America
NASW	National Association of Science Writers		

Glossary

Above the line. A budgetary term for movies and TV. The line refers to money budgeted for creative talent, such as actors, writers, directors, and producers.

Advance. Money a publisher pays a writer prior to book publication, usually paid in installments, such as one-half upon signing the contract; one-half upon delivery of the complete, satisfactory manuscript. An advance is paid against the royalty money to be earned by the book. Agents take their percentage off the top of the advance as well as from the royalties earned.

Auction. Publishers sometimes bid for the acquisition of a book manuscript with excellent sales prospects. The bids are for the amount of the author's advance, guaranteed dollar amounts, advertising and promotional expenses, royalty percentage, etc.

Backlist. Those books still in print from previous years' publication.

Backstory. The history of what has happened before the action in your script takes place, affecting a character's current behavior.

Beat. Major plot points of a story.

Below the line. A budgetary term for movies and TV, referring to production costs, including production manager, cinematographer, editor and crew members such as gaffers, grips, set designers, make-up, etc.

Bible. The collected background information on all characters and storylines of all existing episodes, as well as projections of future plots.

Bio. Brief (usually one page) background information about an artist, writer, or photographer. Includes work and educational experience.

Boilerplate. A standardized publishing contract. Most authors and agents make many changes on the boilerplate before accepting the contract.

Book club rights. Rights to sell a book through a book club.

Book packager. Draws elements of a book together, from the initial concept to writing and marketing strategies, then sells the book package to a book publisher and/or movie producer. Also known as book producer or book developer.

Business-size envelope. Also known as a #10 envelope.

Castable. A script with attractive roles for known actors.

Category fiction. A term used to include all various types of fiction. See *genre*.

Client. When referring to a literary or script agent, "client" is used to mean the writer whose work the agent is handling.

Clips. Writing samples, usually from newspapers or magazines, of your published work.

Commercial novels. Novels designed to appeal to a broad audience. These are often broken down into categories such as western, mystery, and romance. See also *genre*.

Concept. A statement that summarizes a screenplay or teleplay—before the outline or treatment is written.

Contributor's copies. Copies of the author's book sent to the author. The number of contributor's copies is often negotiated in the publishing contract.

Co-agent. See *subagent*.

Co-publishing. Arrangement where author and publisher share publication costs and profits of a book. Also known as cooperative publishing.

Copyediting. Editing of a manuscript for writing style, grammar, punctuation, and factual accuracy.

Copyright. A means to protect an author's work.

Cover letter. A brief descriptive letter sent with a manuscript submitted to an agent or publisher.

Coverage. A brief synopsis and analysis of a script, provided by a reader to a buyer considering purchasing the work.

Critiquing service. A service offered by some agents in which writers pay a fee for comments on the saleability or other qualities of their manuscript. Sometimes the critique includes suggestions on how to improve the work. Fees vary, as do the quality of the critiques. See also *editing service*.

Curriculum vitae. Short account of one's career or qualifications (i.e., résumé).

D person. Development person. Includes readers and story editors through creative executives who work in development and acquisition of properties for TV and movies.

Deal memo. The memorandum of agreement between a publisher and author that precedes the actual contract and includes important issues such as royalty, advance, rights, distribution, and option clauses.

Development. The process where writers present ideas to producers overseeing the developing script through various stages to finished product.

Division. An unincorporated branch of a company.

Docudrama. A fictional film rendition of recent newsmaking events or people.

Editing service. A service offered by some agents in which writers pay a fee—either lump sum or per-page—to have their manuscript edited. The quality and extent of the editing varies from agency to agency. See also *critiquing service*.

Electronic rights. Secondary or subsidiary rights dealing with electronic/multimedia formats (e.g., the Internet, CD-ROMs, electronic magazines).

Elements. Actors, directors, and producers attached to a project to make an attractive package.

El-hi. Elementary to high school. A term used to indicate reading or interest level.

Episodic drama. Hour-long continuing TV show, often shown at 10 p.m.

Evaluation fees. Fees an agent may charge to evaluate material. The extent and quality of this evaluation varies, but comments usually concern the saleability of the manuscript.

Exclusive. Offering a manuscript, usually for a set period of time, to just one agent and guaranteeing that agent is the only one looking at the manuscript.

Film rights. May be sold or optioned by author to a person in the film industry, enabling the book to be made into a movie.

Flap copy. The text which appears on the inside covers of a published book which briefly tell the book's premise. Also called jacket copy.

Floor bid. If a publisher is very interested in a manuscript he may offer to enter a floor bid when the book goes to auction. The publisher sits out of the auction, but agrees to take the book by topping the highest bid by an agreed-upon percentage (usually 10 percent).

Foreign rights. Translation or reprint rights to be sold abroad.

Foreign rights agent. An agent who handles selling the rights to a country other than that of the first book agent. Usually an additional percentage (about 5 percent) will be added on to the first book agent's commission to cover the foreign rights agent.

Genre. Refers to either a general classification of writing such as a novel, poem, or short story or to the categories within those classifications, such as problem novels or sonnets. Genre fiction is a term that covers various types of commercial novels such as mystery, romance, western, science fiction, or horror.

Ghosting/ghostwriting. A writer puts into literary form the words, ideas, or knowledge of another person under that person's name. Some agents offer this service; others pair ghostwriters with celebrities or experts.

Green light. To give the go-ahead to a movie or TV project.

Half-hour. A 30-minute TV show, also known as a *sitcom.*

High concept. A story idea easily expressed in a quick, one-line description.

Hook. Aspect of the work that sets it apart from others.

Imprint. The name applied to a publisher's specific line of books.

IRC. International Reply Coupon. Buy at a post office to enclose with material sent outside your country to cover the cost of return postage. The recipient turns them in for stamps in their own country.

Log line. A one-line description of a plot as it might appear in *TV Guide.*

Long-form TV. Movies of the week (MOW) or *miniseries.*

Mainstream fiction. Fiction on subjects or trends that transcend popular novel categories such as mystery or romance. Using conventional methods, this kind of fiction tells stories about people and their conflicts.

Marketing fee. Fee charged by some agents to cover marketing expenses. It may be used to cover postage, telephone calls, faxes, photocopying or any other expense incurred in marketing a manuscript.

Mass market paperbacks. Softcover book, usually around 4×7, on a popular subject directed at a general audience and sold in groceries and drugstores as well as bookstores.

MFTS. Made for TV series. A series developed for television. See also episodics.

Middle reader. The general classification of books written for readers 9-11 years old.

Midlist. Those titles on a publisher's list expected to have limited sales. Midlist books are mainstream, not literary, scholarly, or genre, and are usually written by new or relatively unknown writers.

Miniseries. A limited dramatic series written for television, often based on a popular novel.

MOW. Movie of the week. A movie script written especially for television, usually seven acts with time for commercial breaks. Topics are often contemporary, sometimes controversial, fictional accounts. Also known as a made-for-TV-movie.

Multiple contract. Book contract with an agreement for a future book(s).

Net receipts. One method of royalty payment based on the amount of money a book publisher receives on the sale of the book after the booksellers' discounts, special sales discounts and returned copies.

Novelization. A novel created from the script of a popular movie, usually called a movie "tie-in" and published in paperback.

Novella. A short novel or long short story, usually 7,000 to 15,000 words. Also called a novelette.

One-time rights. This right allows a short story or portions of a fiction or nonfiction book to be published. The work can be printed again without violating the contract.

Option. Also known as a script option. Instead of buying a movie script outright, a producer buys the right to a script for a short period of time (usually six months to one year) for a small down payment. At the end of the agreed time period, if the movie has not begun production and the producer does not wish to purchase the script, the rights revert back to the scriptwriter.

Option clause. A contract clause giving a publisher the right to publish an author's next book.

Outline. A summary of a book's contents in 5 to 15 double-spaced pages; often in the form of chapter headings with a descriptive sentence or two under each one to show the scope of the book. A script's outline is a scene-by-scene narrative description of the story (10-15 pages for a ½-hour teleplay; 15-25 pages for 1-hour; 25-40 pages for 90 minutes; and 40-60 pages for a 2-hour feature film or teleplay).

Over-the-transom. Slang for the path of an unsolicited manuscript into the slush pile.

Packaging. The process of putting elements together, increasing the chances of a project being made. See also *book packager.*

Platform. A writer's speaking experience, interview skills, website, and other abilities which helps form a following of potential buyers for that author's book.

Picture book. A type of book aimed at the preschool to 8-year-old that tells the story primarily or entirely with artwork. Agents and reps interested in selling to publishers of these books often handle both artists and writers.

Pitch. The process where a writer meets with a producer and briefly outlines ideas that could be developed if the writer is hired to write a script for the project.

Proofreading. Close reading and correction of a manuscript's typographical errors.

Property. Books or scripts forming the basis for a movie or TV project.

Proposal. An offer to an editor or publisher to write a specific work, usually a package consisting of an outline and sample chapters.

Prospectus. A preliminary, written description of a book, usually one page in length.

Query. A letter written to an agent or a potential market, to elicit interest in a writer's work.

Reader. A person employed by an agent or buyer to go through the slush pile of manuscripts and scripts and select those worth considering.

Release. A statement that your idea is original, has never been sold to anyone else, and that you are selling negotiated rights to the idea upon payment.

Remainders. Leftover copies of an out-of-print or slow-selling book purchased from the publisher at a reduced rate. Depending on the contract, a reduced royalty or no royalty is paid on remaindered books.

Reporting time. The time it takes the agent to get back to you on your query or submission.

Reprint rights. The rights to republish your book after its initial printing.

Royalties. A percentage of the retail price paid to the author for each copy of the book that is sold. Agents take their percentage from the royalties earned as well as from the advance.

SASE. Self-addressed, stamped envelope; should be included with all correspondence.

Scholarly books. Books written for an academic or research audience. These are usually heavily researched, technical, and often contain terms used only within a specific field.

Screenplay. Script for a film intended to be shown in theaters.

Script. Broad term covering teleplay, screenplay, or stage play. Sometimes used as a shortened version of the word "manuscript" when referring to books.

Serial rights. The right for a newspaper or magazine to publish sections of a manuscript.

Simultaneous submission. Sending a manuscript to several agents or publishers at the same time. Simultaneous queries are common; simultaneous submissions are unacceptable to many agents or publishers.

Sitcom. Situation comedy. Episodic comedy script for a television series. Term comes from the characters dealing with various situations with humorous results.

Slush pile. A stack of unsolicited submissions in the office of an editor, agent or publisher.

Spec script. A script written on speculation without confirmation of a sale.

Standard commission. The commission an agent earns on the sales of a manuscript or script. For literary agents, this commission percentage (usually between 10 and 20 percent) is taken from the advance and royalties paid to the writer. For script agents, the commission is taken from script sales; if handling plays, agents take a percentage from the box office proceeds.

Story analyst. See *reader*.

Storyboards. Series of panels which illustrates a progressive sequence or graphics and story copy for a TV commercial, film, or filmstrip.

Subagent. An agent handling certain subsidiary rights, usually working in conjunction with the agent who handled the book rights. The percentage paid the book agent is increased to pay the subagent.

Subsidiary. An incorporated branch of a company or conglomerate (e.g., Alfred Knopf, Inc. is a subsidiary of Random House, Inc.).

Subsidiary rights. All rights other than book publishing rights included in a book publishing contract, such as paperback rights, bookclub rights, movie rights. Part of an agent's job is to negotiate those rights and advise you on which to sell and which to keep.

Syndication rights. The right which allows a television station to rerun a sit-com or drama, even if the show appeared originally on a different network.

Synopsis. A brief summary of a story, novel. or play. As a part of a book proposal, it is a comprehensive summary condensed in a page or page and a half, single-spaced. See also *outline*.

Tearsheet. Published samples of your work, usually pages torn from a magazine.

Teleplay. Script for television.

Terms. Financial provisions agreed upon in a contract.

Textbook. Book used in a classroom on the elementary, high school, or college level.

Trade book. Either a hard cover or soft cover book; subject matter frequently concerns a special interest for a general audience; sold mainly in bookstores.

Trade paperback. A softbound volume, usually around 5×8, published and designed for the general public, available mainly in bookstores.

Translation rights. Sold to a foreign agent or foreign publisher.

Treatment. Synopsis of a television or film script (40-60 pages for a 2-hour feature film or teleplay).

Turnaround. When a script has been in development but not made in the time allotted, it can be put back on the market.

Unsolicited manuscript. An unrequested manuscript sent to an editor, agent, or publisher.

Young adult. The general classification of books written for readers age 12-18.

Young reader. Books written for readers 5-8 years old, where artwork only supports the text.

Agencies Indexed by Openness to Submissions

We've ranked the agencies and independent publicists according to their openness to submissions. Check this index to find an agent or independent publicist who is appropriate for your level of experience. Some companies are listed under more than one category.

☐ NEWER AGENCIES ACTIVELY SEEKING CLIENTS

Nonfee-charging agents
Barbara's Literary Agency
Elite Online
Grace Literary Agency, Carroll
Grosjean Literary Agency, Jill
Larken, Sabra Elliott
Rose & Associates Literary Agency
Scherf, Inc. Literary Management
Serendipity Literary Agency, LLC
Turner Agency, Paige
United Tribes
Wray Literary Agency, Pamela D.

Fee-charging agents
Amber Literary
Creative Literary Agency
Renaud, Literary Agent, Janis
Tahoe Sierras Agency
Wolcott Literary Agency

Script
Chadwick & Gros Literary Agency
Larchmont Literary Agency
Tahoe Sierras Agency

Publicists
Gray Communications, Cameron

☑ AGENCIES SEEKING BOTH NEW AND ESTABLISHED WRITERS

Nonfee-charging agents
Acacia House Publishing Services Ltd.
Agency West Entertainment
Agents Inc. for Medical and Mental Health Professionals
Alive Communications, Inc.
Allen Literary Agency, Linda
Allred and Allred Literary Agents
Altair Literary Agency
Altshuler Literary Agency, Miriam
Amster Literary Enterprises, Betsy
Amsterdam Agency, Marcia
Andrews & Associates Inc., Bart

Anubis Literary Agency
Appleseeds Management
Baldi Literary Agency, Malaga
Balkin Agency, Inc.
Barrett Books Inc., Loretta
Bedford Book Works, Inc., The
Bernstein Literary Agency, Meredith
Bial Agency, Daniel
BigScore Productions Inc.
Bleecker Street Associates, Inc.
Book Deals, Inc.
Brandt Agency, The Joan
Brandt & Brandt Literary Agents Inc.
Briggs, M. Courtney
Brown Literary Agency, Inc., Andrea
Brown Ltd., Curtis
Browne Ltd., Pema
Bykofsky Associates, Inc., Sheree
Carvainis Agency, Inc., Maria
Castiglia Literary Agency
Charlton Associates, James
Circle of Confusion Ltd.
Clausen, Mays & Tahan, LLC
Client First—A/K/A Leo P. Haffey Agency
Connor Literary Agency
Coover Agency, The Doe
Crawford Literary Agency
Cypher, The Cypher Agency, James R.
Daves Agency, Joan
Dawson Associates, Liza
DeFiore and Company
DHS Literary, Inc.
Dickens Group, The
Dolger Agency, The Jonathan
Donovan Literary, Jim
Ducas, Robert
Dupree/Miller and Associates Inc. Literary
Dystel Literary Management, Jane
Educational Design Services, Inc.
Elek Associates, Peter
Ellenberg Literary Agency, Ethan
Ellison Inc., Nicholas
Eth Literary Representation, Felicia
Feigen/Parrent Literary

Management
Fernandez Agent/Attorney, Justin E.
First Books
FitzGerald Literary Management
Flaherty, Literary Agent, Joyce A.
Flaming Star Literary Enterprises
Flannery Literary
Fleury Agency, B.R.
ForthWrite Literary Agency
Franklin Associates, Ltd., Lynn C.
Fredericks Literary Agency, Inc., Jeanne
Frenkel & Associates, James
Fullerton Associates, Sheryl B.
Greenburger Associates, Inc., Sanford J.
Gregory and Radice Authors' Agents
H.W.A. Talent Representative
Halsey Agency, Reece
Halsey North, Reece
Hamilburg Agency, The Mitchell J.
Harris Literary Agency
Heacock Literary Agency, Inc.
Henshaw Group, Richard
Herman Agency LLC, The Jeff
Herner Rights Agency, Susan
Hill Associates, Frederick
Hopkins Literary Associates
Jabberwocky Literary Agency
James Peter Associates, Inc.
JCA Literary Agency, Inc.
Jellinek & Murray Literary Agency
Jenks Agency, Carolyn
Kern Literary Agency, Natasha
Ketz Agency, Louise B.
Kidde, Hoyt & Picard
Kirchoff/Wohlberg, Inc., Authors' Representation Division
Kleinman, Esq., of Graybill & English L.L.C., Jeffrey M.
Knight Agency, The
Konner Literary Agency, Linda
Kraas Agency, Irene
Kritzer Productions, Eddie
Kroll Literary Agency Inc., Edite
Lake Agency, The Candace
Larsen/Elizabeth Pomada Literary Agents, Michael
Lasher Agency, The Maureen

Oscard Agency Inc., Fifi
Panda Talent
Perelman Agency, Barry
Pevner, Inc., Stephen
Picture of You, A
Pinkham Literary Agency
PMA Literary and Film
    Management, Inc.
Preminger Agency, Jim
Puddingstone Literary Agency
QCorp Literary Agency
Redwood Empire Agency
Silver Screen Placements
Sorice Agency, Camille
Stanton & Associates Literary
    Agency
Stars, the Agency
Suite A Management
Sydra Techniques Corp.
Talent Source
Wardlow and Associates
Wauhob Agency, Donna
Whittlesey Agency, Peregrine
Wright Concept, The
Wright Representatives, Ann
Writer Store

Publicists
Ford Group, The
Garis Agency—National Publicists
KSB Promotions
MarketAbility, Inc.
Media Masters Publicity
Phenix & Phenix Literary
    Publicists, Inc.
Rocks-Dehart Public Relations
    (Book Publicity)
World Class Speakers &
    Entertainers

☻ AGENCIES PREFER-RING TO WORK WITH ESTABLISHED WRIT-ERS, MOSTLY OBTAIN NEW CLIENTS THROUGH REFERRALS

Nonfee-charging agents
Ajlouny Literary Agency, Joseph
Allen, Literary Agent, James
AMG/Renaissance
Authentic Creations Literary Agency
Authors Alliance Inc.
Axelrod Agency, The
Black Literary Agency, David
Boates Literary Agency, Reid
Books & Such
Borchardt Inc., Georges
Boston Literary Group, The
Bova Literary Agency, The Barbara
Casselman Literary Agency, Martha
Charisma Communications, Ltd.
Clark Associates, Wm
Collin Literary Agent, Frances
Communications and Entertain-
    ment, Inc.
Congdon Associates Inc., Don
Contemporary Management

Curtis Associates, Inc., Richard
DH Literary, Inc.
Dijkstra Literary Agency, Sandra
Donnaud & Associates, Inc.,
    Janis A.
Doyen Literary Services, Inc.
Elmo Agency Inc., Ann
Evans Inc., Mary
Farber Literary Agency Inc.
Fogelman Literary Agency, The
Fort Ross Inc. Russian-American
    Publishing Projects
Gartenberg, Literary Agent, Max
Gelfman Schneider Literary
    Agents, Inc.
Goldfarb & Associates
Goodman Associates
Greene, Arthur B.
Gregory, Inc. Blanche C.
Grosvenor Literary Agency, The
Halsey Agency, Reece
Harris Literary Agency, Inc.,
    The Joy
Hawkins & Associates, Inc., John
Henshaw Group, Richard
Hochmann Books, John L.
Hoffman Literary Agency, Beren-
    ice
Hogenson Agency, Barbara
International Creative Manage-
    ment
J de S Associates Inc.
Kellock Company, Inc., The
Kidd Agency, Inc., Virginia
Klinger, Inc., Harvey
Koster Literary Agency, LLC,
    Elaine
Kouts, Literary Agent, Barbara S.
Lampack Agency, Inc., Peter
Lasher Agency, The Maureen
Lawyer's Literary Agency, Inc.
Lescher & Lescher Ltd.
Levine Communications, Inc.,
    James
Levine Literary Agency, Inc., Ellen
Lieberman Associates, Robert
Limelight Management
Lincoln Literary Agency, Ray
Lipkind Agency, Wendy
Literary and Creative Artists, Inc.
Lord Literistic, Inc., Sterling
Lowenstein Associates, Inc.
Maccoby Literary Agency, Gina
Mann Agency, Carol
March Tenth, Inc.
Markson Literary Agency, Elaine
Michaels Literary Agency, Inc.,
    Doris S.
Miller Agency, The
Moran Agency, Maureen
Morris Agency, Inc., William
Morrison, Inc., Henry
Multimedia Product Development,
    Inc.
Ober Associates, Harold
Oscard Agency, Inc., Fifi
Palmer & Dodge Agency, The
Paraview, Inc.
Parks Agency, The Richard

Pelter, Rodney
Perkins Associates, L.
Protter Literary Agent, Susan Ann
Raymond, Literary Agent, Char-
    lotte Cecil
Rein Books, Inc., Jody
Rittenberg Literary Agency, Inc.,
    Ann
Riverside Literary Agency
Robbins Office, Inc., The
Robinson Talent and Literary Man-
    agement
Ross Literary Agency, The Gail
Scovil Chichak Galen Literary
    Agency
Shukat Company Ltd., The
Siegel, International Literary
    Agency, Inc., Rosalie
Singer Literary Agency Inc., Evelyn
Slopen Literary Agency, Beverley
Stauffer Associates, Nancy
Straus Agency, Inc., Robin
Swayne Agency Literary Manage-
    ment & Consulting, Inc., The
Talbot Agency, The John
Teal Literary Agency, Patricia
Tiersten Literary Agency, Irene
Wallace Literary Agency, Inc.
Weiner Literary Agency, Cherry
Weingel-Fidel Agency, The
Weyr Agency, Rhoda
Wieser & Wieser, Inc.
Writers House (CA)
Writers House (NY)
Writers' Representatives, Inc.
Wylie-Merrick Literary Agency

Fee-charging agents
Collier Associates
Hartline Literary Agency
Howard Agency, The Eddy
Litopia Corporation Ltd.
Mews Books Ltd.
Scagnetti Talent & Literary
    Agency, Jack
Steinberg Literary Agency,
    Michael
Strong Literary Agency, Marianne
Toomey Associates, Jeanne
Windfall Management
Zahler Literary Agency, Karen
    Gantz

Script
Above the Line Agency
Acme Talent & Literary
AMG/Renaissance Literary
    Agency
Authors Alliance Inc.
Baskow Agency
Bennett Agency, The
Berman Boals and Flynn Inc.
Bohrman Agency, The
Buchwald and Associates, Inc. Don
Cameron Agency, The Marshall
Cedar Grove Agency
    Entertainment
Communications and

AGENCIES HANDLING ONLY CERTAIN TYPES OF WORK OR WORK BY WRITERS UNDER CERTAIN CIRCUMSTANCES

Nonfee-charging agents

Fee-charging agents

Script

Publicists

AGENCIES NOT CURRENTLY SEEKING NEW CLIENTS

Nonfee-charging agents

Fee-charging agents

Script

Geographic Index

Some writers prefer to work with an agent or independent publicist in their vicinity. If you're such a writer, this index offers you the opportunity to easily select agents closest to home. Agencies and independent publicists are separated by state. We've also arranged them according to the sections in which they appear in the book (Nonfee-charging, Fee-charging, Script or Publicist). Once you find the agency you're interested in, refer to the Listing Index for the page number.

Manus & Associates Literary
 Agency, Inc.
Miller Co., The Stuart M.
Monteiro Rose Agency
Nelson Literary Agency & Lecture
 Bureau, BK
Niad Management
Omniquest Entertainment
Panda Talent
Partos Company, The
Perelman Agency, Barry
Pevner, Inc., Stephen
Preminger Agency, Jim
Quillco Agency, The
Redler Entertainment, Dan
Redwood Empire Agency
Robins & Associates, Michael D.
Robinson Talent and Literary
 Management
Scagnetti Talent & Literary
 Agency, Jack
Shapiro-Lichtman
Sherman & Associates, Ken
Sorice Agency, Camille
Stars, the Agency
Stein Agency
Stone Manners Agency
Suite A Management
Van Duren Agency, Annette
Wardlow and Associates
Windfall Management
Wright Concept, The

Publicists
Ford Group, The
Garis Agency—National Publicists
World Class Speakers &
 Entertainers

COLORADO
Nonfee-charging
Alive Communications, Inc.
Toomey Associates, Jeanne
Core Creations, Inc.
National Writers Literary Agency
Rein Books, Inc., Jody
Rose & Associates Literary Agency

Fee-charging
Alp Arts Co.
Pelham Literary Agency

Script
Hodges Agency, Carolyn

Publicists
MarketAbility, Inc.

CONNECTICUT
Nonfee-charging
Evans Inc., Mary
Brann Agency, Inc., The Helen
Fredericks Literary Agency, Inc.,
 Jeanne
J de S Associates Inc.
New England Publishing
 Associates, Inc.

Writers' Productions

Fee-charging
Independent Publishing Agency: A
 Literary and Entertainment
 Agency
Mews Books Ltd.
Toomey Associates, Jeanne

Script
Toomey Associates, Jeanne

DISTRICT OF COLUMBIA
Nonfee-charging
Goldfarb & Associates
Kleinman, Esq., of Graybill &
 English L.L.C., Jeffrey M.
Literary and Creative Artists, Inc.
Ross Literary Agency, The Gail
Tobias—A Literary Agency for
 Children's Books, Ann
Wolf Literary Agency, Audrey A.

FLORIDA
Nonfee-charging
Bova Literary Agency, The Barbara
Fleury Agency, B.R.
Grace Literary Agency, Carroll
Kellock Company, Inc., The
Schiavone Literary Agency, Inc.

Fee-charging
Collier Associates
Taylor Literary Agency, Dawson

Script
Fleury Agency, B.R.
Cameron Agency, The Marshall
Legacies

GEORGIA
Nonfee-charging
Pelter, Rodney
Authentic Creations Literary
 Agency
Brandt Agency, The Joan
Knight Agency, The
Taylor, Literary Agent, Rebecca

Script
Talent Source
Writer Store

HAWAII
Nonfee-charging
Fogelman Literary Agency, The
Jellinek & Murray Literary Agency

IDAHO
Nonfee-charging
McHugh Literary Agency

Fee-charging
Author's Agency, The

ILLINOIS
Nonfee-charging
Book Deals, Inc.
First Books
Flannery Literary
Joy Literary Agency
Multimedia Product Development,
 Inc.

Fee-charging
SLC Enterprises
Steinberg Literary Agency,
 Michael

Script
Bulger and Associates, Kelvin C.
Communications Management
 Associates
Dramatic Publishing
Silver Screen Placements

Publicists
Media Masters Publicity

INDIANA
Nonfee-charging
Wylie-Merrick Literary Agency

Script
International Leonards Corp.

IOWA
Nonfee-charging
Doyen Literary Services, Inc.

KANSAS
Fee-charging
Baranski Literary Agency, Joseph A.
Wolcott Literary Agency

Script
Baranski Literary Agency, Joseph A.

KENTUCKY
Nonfee-charging
Dickens Group, The

LOUISIANA
Fee-charging
Ahearn Agency, Inc., The

Script
Chadwick & Gros Literary Agency

MAINE
Nonfee-charging
Kroll Literary Agency Inc., Edite

MARYLAND
Nonfee-charging
Grosvenor Literary Agency, The
Sagalyn Agency, The

Fee-charging
Devereux Company, The Wilson

MASSACHUSETTS
Nonfee-charging
Balkin Agency, Inc.
Boston Literary Group, The
Coover Agency, The Doe
Jenks Agency, Carolyn
McClellan Associates, Anita D.
Palmer & Dodge Agency, The
Raymond, Literary Agent,
    Charlotte Cecil
Rees Literary Agency, Helen
Riverside Literary Agency
Roghaar Literary Agency, Inc.,
    Linda
Snell Literary Agency, Michael
Stauffer Associates, Nancy
Zachary Shuster Harmsworth

Fee-charging
Janus Literary Agency
Pinkham Literary Agency
Tornetta Agency, Phyllis

Script
Pinkham Literary Agency

MICHIGAN
Fee-charging
Creative Literary Agency

Script
Ajlouny Literary Agency, Joseph

Publicists
KSB Promotions

MINNESOTA
Nonfee-charging
Book Peddlers, The
Gislason Agency, The
Hanson Literary Agency, Jeanne K.
Lazear Agency Incorporated
Sebastian Literary Agency

MISSOURI
Nonfee-charging
Flaherty, Literary Agent, Joyce A.

NEVADA
Nonfee-charging
Scherf, Inc. Literary Management

Fee-charging
Tahoe Sierras Agency

Script
Baskow Agency
Tahoe Sierras Agency
Wauhob Agency, Donna

NEW HAMPSHIRE
Nonfee-charging
Crawford Literary Agency
Dwyer & O'Grady, Inc.

NEW JERSEY
Nonfee-charging
Boates Literary Agency, Reid
Dawson Associates, Liza
Ghosts & Collaborators
    International
James Peter Associates, Inc.
March Tenth, Inc.
Marshall Agency, The Evan
Millard Literary Agency, Martha
Seligman, Literary Agent, Lynn
Siegel, International Literary
    Agency, Inc., Rosalie
Smith-Skolnik Literary
Tiersten Literary Agency, Irene
Weiner Literary Agency, Cherry

Fee-charging
Howard Agency, The Eddy
Puddingstone Literary Agency
Simenauer Literary Agency,
    Jacqueline

Script
Puddingstone Literary Agency

NEW MEXICO
Nonfee-charging
FitzGerald Literary Management
Kraas Agency, Irene

Script
FitzGerald Literary Management

NEW YORK
Nonfee-charging
Abel Literary Agent, Carole
Altair Literary Agency
Altshuler Literary Agency, Miriam
Amsterdam Agency, Marcia
Authors Alliance Inc.
Axelrod Agency, The
Bach Literary Agency, Julian
Baldi Literary Agency, Malaga
Barrett Books Inc., Loretta
Bedford Book Works, Inc., The
Bernstein & Associates, Inc., Pam
Bernstein Literary Agency,
    Meredith
Bial Agency, Daniel
Bijur, Vicky
Black Literary Agency, David
Bleecker Street Associates, Inc.
Borchardt Inc., Georges
Brandt & Brandt Literary
    Agents Inc.
Broadway Play Publishing
Brown Associates Inc., Marie
Brown Ltd., Curtis
Browne Ltd., Pema
Burger Associates, Ltd., Knox

Bykofsky Associates, Inc., Sheree
Carlisle & Company
Carvainis Agency, Inc., Maria
Charisma Communications, Ltd.
Charlton Associates, James
Chelius Literary Agency, Jane
Childs Literary Agency, Inc., Faith
Circle of Confusion Ltd.
Clark Associates, Wm
Clausen, Mays & Tahan, LLC
Cohen Agency, The
Cole, Literary Agent, Joanna Lewis
Columbia Literary Associates, Inc.
Congdon Associates Inc., Don
Connor Literary Agency
Cornfield Literary Agency, Robert
Curtis Associates, Inc., Richard
Cypher, The Cypher Agency,
    James R.
Darhansoff & Verrill Literary
    Agents
Daves Agency, Joan
DeFiore and Company
DH Literary, Inc.
Dolger Agency, The Jonathan
Donadio and Olson, Inc.
Donnaud & Associates, Inc., Janis A.
Ducas, Robert
Dunow Literary Agency, Henry
Dystel Literary Management, Jane
Edelstein Literary Agency, Anne
Educational Design Services, Inc.
Elek Associates, Peter
Ellenberg Literary Agency, Ethan
Ellison Inc., Nicholas
Elmo Agency Inc., Ann
Evans Inc., Mary
Fallon Literary Agency
Farber Literary Agency Inc.
Flaming Star Literary Enterprises
Fogelman Literary Agency, The
Foley Literary Agency, The
Fort Ross Inc. Russian-American
    Publishing Projects
Franklin Associates, Ltd., Lynn C.
Gartenberg, Literary Agent, Max
Gelfman Schneider Literary
    Agents, Inc.
Goldin, Frances
Goodman Associates
Greenburger Associates, Inc.,
    Sanford J.
Greene, Arthur B.
Gregory, Inc. Blanche C.
Groffsky Literary Agency, Maxine
Grosjean Literary Agency, Jill
Harden Curtis Associates
Harris Literary Agency, Inc., The
    Joy
Hawkins & Associates, Inc., John
Henshaw Group, Richard
Herman Agency LLC, The Jeff
Herner Rights Agency, Susan
Hochmann Books, John L.
Hoffman Literary Agency,
    Berenice
Hogenson Agency, Barbara
Hopkins Literary Associates
International Creative

Fee-charging

Script

Publicists

NORTH CAROLINA

Fee-charging

Publicists

OHIO

Nonfee-charging

Fee-charging
BAWN Publishers Inc.—Literary Agency

Script
BAWN Publishers Inc.—Literary Agency
Kick Entertainment
Picture of You, A

OKLAHOMA

Nonfee-charging
Briggs, M. Courtney

OREGON

Nonfee-charging
Kern Literary Agency, Natasha

Fee-charging
ABS Literary Agency
QCorp Literary Agency
Tolls Literary Agency, Lynda

Script
QCorp Literary Agency

PENNSYLVANIA

Nonfee-charging
Allen, Literary Agent, James
BigScore Productions Inc.
Collin Literary Agent, Frances
Elite Online
Fox Chase Agency, Inc.
Kidd Agency, Inc., Virginia
Lincoln Literary Agency, Ray
Toad Hall, Inc.

Fee-charging
Amber Literary
Hartline Literary Agency

Script
Sister Mania Productions, Inc.

SOUTH CAROLINA

Script
Pevner, Inc., Stephen
Hayes & Assoc., Gil

TENNESSEE

Script
Client First—A/K/A Leo P. Haffey Agency
Hayes & Assoc., Gil

TEXAS

Nonfee-charging
DHS Literary, Inc.
Donovan Literary, Jim
Dupree/Miller and Associates Inc. Literary
Lewis & Company, Karen
New Century Literary Agency
Sedgeband Literary Associates

Fee-charging
Fran Literary Agency

Script
Fran Literary Agency
Stanton & Associates Literary Agency

Publicists
Phenix & Phenix Literary Publicists, Inc.

VERMONT

Nonfee-charging
Rowland Agency, The Damaris

VIRGINIA

Nonfee-charging
Communications and Entertainment, Inc.

Script
Communications and Entertainment, Inc.
Filmwriters Literary Agency

Publicists
Gray Communications, Cameron

WASHINGTON

Nonfee-charging
Wales, Literary Agency, Inc.

Fee-charging
Catalog Literary Agency, The

Script
Cedar Grove Agency Entertainment

WISCONSIN

Nonfee-charging
Frenkel & Associates, James
Sternig & Byrne Literary Agency

CANADA

Nonfee-charging
Acacia House Publishing Services Ltd.
Contemporary Management
Livingston Cooke/Curtis Brown Canada
Slopen Literary Agency, Beverley
Swayze Literary Agency, Carolyn

Fee-charging
Author Author Literary Agency Ltd.
Authors Marketing Services Ltd.
Renaud, Literary Agent, Janis

Script
Kay Agency, Charlene
Livingston Cooke/Curtis Brown Canada

INTERNATIONAL

Nonfee-charging
Anubis Literary Agency
Dorian Literary Agency
Gregory and Radice Authors' Agents
Limelight Management
Lownie Literary Agency Ltd., Andrew
Simmons Literary Agency, Jeffrey
Smith Literary Agency, Robert
Susijn Agency, The

Fee-charging
French's
Litopia Corporation Ltd.

Script
French's

Agents Index

This index of agent names can help you locate agents you may have read or heard about even when you do not know which agency for which they work. Agent names are listed with their agencies' names.

Listing Index

Agencies that appeared in the 2000 *Guide to Literary Agents* but are not included this year are identified by a two-letter code explaining why the agency is not listed: **ED**)—Editorial Decision, (**NS**)—Not Accepting Submissions/Too Many Queries, (**NR**)—No (or Late) Response to Listing Request, (**OB**)—Out of Business, (**RR**)—Removed by Agency's Request, (**UF**)—Uncertain Future, (**UC**)—Unable to Contact, (**RP**)—Business Restructured or Sold.

LISTING INDEX